Development Co-operation Report 2017

DATA FOR DEVELOPMENT

OECD
BETTER POLICIES FOR BETTER LIVES

Please cite this publication as:
OECD (2017), *Development Co-operation Report 2017: Data for Development*, OECD Publishing, Paris.
http://dx.doi.org/10.1787/dcr-2017-en

ISBN 978-92-64-27446-4 (print)
ISBN 978-92-64-27450-1 (PDF)
ISBN 978-92-64-27609-3 (HTML)
ISBN 978-92-64-27608-6 (epub)

Series: Development Co-operation Report
ISSN 2074-773X (print)
ISSN 2074-7721 (on line)

Foreword

Data and statistics are part of the OECD's DNA. They underpin, shape and inform our policy advice to promote better policies for better lives in all the countries we work with, numbering over 100, across all regions and levels of development.

In an era of fake news and alternative facts, good data are even more vital. All citizens have the right to true, reliable and accessible information. This is particularly important in the development field, since world leaders adopted the transformative 2030 Agenda for Sustainable Development in September 2015. Achieving the Sustainable Development Goals (SDGs) will require informed choices about priorities and strategies, and for this we will need a better evidence base than we have today.

The continued lack of basic data along with weak statistical systems remain major stumbling blocks to achieving the SDGs. For example, there are no data for about two-thirds of the 232 SDG indicators, and 88 indicators have neither an agreed methodology nor data for measuring them. Even when data are available, they are often insufficiently disaggregated, making it difficult for policy makers to track or compare the situations of different population groups or communities.

A key reason for this poor capacity is that official statistics in developing countries do not get the resources they need. Aid for building statistical systems was about 0.30% of total official development assistance over the past three years, equivalent to USD 600 million per year.

This is why the OECD decided to focus its annual Development Co-operation Report *on data for development. The good news is that conditions have never been riper for developing countries to harness the data revolution. The global push for evidence-based policy making and the centrality of data to deliver the SDGs, combined with new technology, make it easier, faster and cheaper to produce and use the data we need.*

This report not only provides a comprehensive and in-depth analysis of the political and structural constraints faced by countries; it also formulates concrete options for policy makers to build on the new opportunities and make data work for sustainable development. It shows how governments, national statistical offices, citizens, and public and private development partners can work together to fill data gaps, generating and using better data, for better development policies for better lives.

Angel Gurría,
OECD Secretary-General

Acknowledgements

The 2017 edition of the OECD *Development Co-operation Report* was prepared under the direction of Jorge Moreira da Silva, Director of the OECD Development Co-operation Directorate (DCD). The report was managed and edited by Ida Mc Donnell, Senior Policy Analyst and Team Lead for the *Development Co-operation Report*, in close collaboration with Johannes Jütting, Secretariat Manager of PARIS21 – the Partnership in Statistics for Development in the 21st Century – under the strategic guidance and oversight of Karen Jorgensen, Head of the Review, Evaluation and Engagement Division, DCD.

The Chair of the OECD Development Assistance Committee (DAC), Charlotte Petri-Gornitzka, provided direction and advice. Martine Durand, OECD Chief Statistician and Director of the OECD Statistics Directorate (STD), provided advice, guidance and support throughout the process while also contributing content for the report. Thanks go to Paul Schreyer (Deputy Director, STD), Simon Scott (Counsellor, STD) and Brenda Killen (Deputy Director, DCD) for their inputs. Thanks also go to Mario Pezzini, Director of the OECD Development Centre and Special Advisor to the OECD Secretary-General on Development, for his guidance on the inception of the report in 2016 when he was Acting Director of DCD.

The report was supported by a core team: Valentina Sanna, Stacey Bradbury, Thilo Klein, Ragini Malik, Henri-Bernard Solignac-Lecomte, El Iza Mohamedou, Peter Carlson and Talisa Zur Hausen along with Shaida Badiee and her colleagues Deirdre Appel and Eric Swanson at Open Data Watch. Christine Graves gave editorial advice and copy-edited the report, with proof reading by Jennifer Allain, and cover design and infographics by Stephanie Coic. The French version of the report was translated by the OECD Translation Division, under the supervision of Florence Burloux-Mader and proofread by Sophie Alibert. The OECD Public Affairs and Communication Directorate produced the publication – special thanks to Anne-Lise Prigent, Cicely Dupont-Nivore, Damian Garnys, Audrey Garrigoux, Florence Guérinot, Ghani Kadem and Maria Petit-Breuilh David. Thanks also to Hilary Balbuena and Beth Del Bourgo for helping us get started and to Joachim Beijmo, Catherine Bremer, Scarlette Elizée, Claudia Gemmel and Erin Renner Cordell for communication, editorial and media relations support; and Heidi Johnson, Hannah Murray Kelly, Ola Kasneci, Anne Keller and Angela Stuart for administrative support.

Special thanks go to all of the authors, who are named by chapter, and to all staff from across the Development Co-operation Directorate, including the Joint Support Team of the Global Partnership for Effective Development Co-operation and DCD's statisticians, who provided input and support in a variety of ways. Chapters were reviewed by Samantha Custer (AidData), Neil Jackson (DFID), Vinisha Bhatia-Murdach, Paige Kirby and Joshua Powell (Development Gateway), Frans Lammersen (OECD), Rahul Malhotra (OECD), Estelle Raimondo (Independent Evaluation Group of the World Bank) and Jan Rielander (OECD). "In my view" pieces were authored by Lisa Grace Bersales (the Philippine Statistics Authority); Martine Durand (OECD); Sarah Hendriks (Bill & Melinda Gates Foundation); Morten Jerven (Norwegian University of Life Sciences); Ellen Cathrine Kiøsterud (Statistics Norway); and Stefan Schweinfest (United Nations Statistics Division). Thanks also to the individuals and organisations that contributed case studies on data for development.

Many people were consulted to define the scope and content of this report, including through an experts workshop on data for development which took place in April 2017. The team would like to thank, hoping not to miss anyone, the many great experts, and the members of the DCD Publications Review Board, for their valuable advice, insights and suggestions: Yasmin Ahmad, Angel Alonso Arroba, Eric Bensel, Thomas Boehler, Federico Bonaglia, Kim Bradford-Smith, Soniya Carvalho, Oliver Chinganya, Rory Clarke, Catalina Covacevich, Nicolas De Cordes, Juan de Laiglesia, Poul Engberg-Pedersen, Emily Esplen, Anais Fahd, Gaëlle Ferrant, Mags Gaynor, Nadine Gbossa, Susan Greene, Alejandro Guerrero-Ruiz, Michelle Harding, Barbro Hexeberg, Erin Hohlfelder, Thomas Hos, Neil Jackson, Hanna-Mari Kilpeläinen, James Kim, Hetty Kovach, Michael Laird, Yohanna Loucheur, Patrick Love, Hans Lundgren, Claire Melamed, Suneeta Millington, Bathylle Missika, El Iza Mohamedou, Keiko Nowacka, David O'Connor, Ewelina Oblacewicz, Valentina Orrù, Nicolas Pinaud, Beatriz Pont, Leslie Rae, Judith Randel, Jorge Rivera, Haje Schütte, Rachel Scott, Linda Smiroldo Herda, Joe Stead, Suzanne Steensen, Cushla Thomson, Yu Tian, Piera Tortora, Irene Tuveng, Koen Van Acoleyen, Michael Ward, Cara Williams and Felix Zimmermann.

The OECD would like to thank all DAC members and the providers of development co-operation beyond the DAC membership for fact-checking the "Profiles of providers of development co-operation" section, and for responding to the survey on DAC members' policies and practices to "Make data work for sustainable development".

Table of contents

Part II

Profiles of development co-operation providers

Tables

Figures

Abbreviations and acronyms

ADAPT	Advanced Data Planning Tool
CAPI	Computer assisted personal interview
CPI	Climate Policy Initiative
CRS	Creditor Reporting System
CRVS	Civil registration and vital statistics
CSO	Civil society organisation
DAC	Development Assistance Committee
DFID	Department for International Development (United Kingdom)
EU	European Union
GDP	Gross domestic product
GNI	Gross national income
GPEDC	Global Partnership for Effective Development Co-operation
GPSDD	Global Partnership for Sustainable Development Data
IAEG-SDGs	Inter-Agency and Expert Group on Sustainable Development Goal Indicators
IATI	International Aid Transparency Initiative
ICT	Information and communication technology
IDA	International Development Association
IMF	International Monetary Fund
LDC	Least developed country
LIC	Low-income country
LMIC	Lower middle-income country
MAPS	Marrakech Action Plan for Statistics
MDG	Millennium Development Goal
NGO	Non-governmental organisation
ODA	Official development assistance
ODC	Open Data Charter
ODI	Overseas Development Institute
ODIN	Open Data Inventory
OECD	Organisation for Economic Co-operation and Development
OPAL	Open Algorithms Project
PARIS21	Partnership in Statistics for Development in the 21st Century
PRESS	Partner Report on Support to Statistics
RCT	Randomised control trial
SDG	Sustainable Development Goal
SDSN	Sustainable Development Solutions Network
TOSSD	Total official support for sustainable development
UMIC	Upper middle-income country
UN	United Nations
UNDP	United Nations Development Programme
UNFCCC	United Nations Framework Convention on Climate Change
UNSC	United Nations Statistical Commission
UNSD	United Nations Statistical Division

Editorial: With great data comes great responsibility

by
Charlotte Petri Gornitzka, Chair, Development Assistance Committee
and Jorge Moreira da Silva, Director, Development Co-operation Directorate, OECD

If USD 142.6 billion falls in the forest of development and no one hears it, does it matter?

That depends on who you are. While mothers in Afghanistan or South Sudan can tell you how their families' lives have been transformed by effective development programmes every single day, strong data are needed to communicate how these billions of dollars improve the human condition and create more stable societies for all.

In 2016 official development assistance (ODA) to support development goals represented 0.32% of gross national income, an all-time high. However, aid to those who need it most, including least developed countries (LDCs), is declining. The June 2017 report card on the 2030 Development Agenda – the world's roadmap to end poverty, inequality and injustice for all by 2030 through a set of 17 goals and 232 indicators – tells us progress is slow and data are incomplete.

Now, more than ever, we need to tell the 360-degree story of how development investment touches lives and supports a more secure, stable and prosperous world. Data on development have the ability to amplify human stories beyond the borders of fragile and least developed states. The future of development co-operation depends on hard evidence about the impact that ODA has – and can have – with increased and well-targeted investments. We can't afford not to get a clear picture and turn up the volume.

Fortunately, we have better tools than ever to get the data on development results right. Big data are now being used to tell us how to respond to an e-mail and what news we should read. We know that big data are being used by corporations to predict customers' behaviour, suppliers' performance, equipment failures and planning preventive maintenance. But big data also offer significant impact on energy, environment and healthcare. The combination of big data with genomics has the potential to uncover diseases that prevail in localised geographical areas. The data revolution has tremendous potential to inform innovative development policies and open new doors for individuals in developing countries. However, a dangerous data gap is leaving some of the most vulnerable groups of people invisible while others are propelled forward.

Let us take a look at the data on the development data gap. Just over half of all countries fully register when babies are born and when people die. Only 37 countries have statistical laws that meet UN standards. Not surprising, then, that no data whatsoever exist for two-thirds of the Sustainable Development Goal (SDG) indicators.

The development co-operation community has a responsibility to translate the ever-accelerating developments in data to on-the-ground development results by supporting sophisticated country-led systems, especially in LDCs. Strong systems require human brainpower and heart if they are to collect quality, timely and disaggregated data, especially for those most at risk of being left behind. The *2017 Development Co-operation Report* highlights six immediate recommendations for existing and future investments in development.

What will these actions take? Simply increasing the quantity of aid will not guarantee success. The quality of financing for statistics needs to improve to reduce duplication and better target and co-ordinate investments where the impact is greatest. It requires political will to make data a strategic cross-cutting priority in development co-operation policies. If current levels of ODA spent on statistics increased by USD 200 million annually it would fill the funding gap for producing data for the SDGs in developing countries. Talk about bang-for-buck: less than 1% of total assistance to maintain the credibility of the other 99% and its delivery to those who need it most. That's the development win-win: investing in data for development gives voice to those who feel its impact, helps target aid to where it is needed most, while presenting a higher definition picture of results to taxpayers in countries that provide development co-operation.

Executive summary

Data are a prerequisite for delivering the United Nations (UN) 2030 Agenda for Sustainable Development and ensuring that no one is left behind. The *Development Co-operation Report 2017* focuses on data for development because quality, timely and disaggregated data are crucial for achieving the ultimate goal of development: improving the welfare of people and fighting poverty. There is, however, a major risk that the continued scarcity of basic data in developing countries about people and the planet, and weak incentives and capacity to fill these gaps, will hold back success.

The Sustainable Development Goals (SDGs) are putting high demands on national statistical systems the world over. Most countries, including many OECD countries, have not yet started collecting data for many indicators in the UN global SDG indicators framework. The challenges are even more critical for many developing countries with low statistical capabilities. For example, 77 developing countries have inadequate poverty data. Only 56% of countries worldwide have birth registration data that are 90% complete, with just 15% of countries in sub-Saharan Africa having these data, 33% in Southern Asia and 36% in Southeast Asia. Only 37 countries have national statistical legislation that complies with the UN's Fundamental Principles of Official Statistics. Serious methodological and strategic challenges still need to be met, including the need to strike a balance between producing the data for global monitoring, on the one hand, and for national policy making on the other.

This report analyses how developing countries and their development co-operation partners can bridge the data divide by seizing the unprecedented opportunity – and mitigate the risks – presented by the convergence of the power of technology with the most ambitious development plan to date: the 2030 Agenda. New technology and the so-called data revolution make it easier, faster and cheaper to produce data that decision makers need to make informed choices on policies and priorities. However, simply producing more data is not enough: data must be transformed, analysed and used to be useful for policy making, monitoring and accountability.

The data revolution offers governments and national statistical offices a welcome opportunity to produce more useful data by generating data from new sources, which can complement and strengthen, though not replace, official statistics. Some developing countries are already embarking on the data revolution with positive results. Ethiopia, South Africa, Sri Lanka and Uganda have improved the efficiency and accuracy of census and survey data collection by using computer-assisted personal interview devices, such as computer tablets or other handheld devices. Geospatial data are helping national statistical systems monitor socio-economic and environmental conditions, enabling geographic disaggregation and making geo-located data more dynamic.

This report identifies ways to bridge the data divide for sustainable development. There is a need for strong political leadership in developing countries to ensure that data enable development. This involves promoting the cause of data for development while making certain that data are produced to high-quality standards, protecting privacy and confidentiality.

The *Development Co-operation Report 2017* recommends six concrete actions to make the most of the power of data for sustainable development.

Data action 1. *Make statistical laws, regulations and standards fit for evolving data needs.*

To build inclusive data ecosystems that benefit global development and individual citizens, institutional and legal frameworks need to be fit for purpose. The growing number of public, private, and civil society actors and institutions involved in the production and use of data make the need for clear legal, ethical, and quality standards and protocols even more urgent. These should regulate the use of traditional and new sources of data, fostering the trust that is needed to inform good policies and development results.

Data action 2. *Improve the quantity and quality of financing for data.*

Investing in statistical systems must become a strategic priority for developing countries and their development co-operation partners alike. Budgets need to grow if national statistical systems are to respond to the growing demand for more and better data. By making data a cross-cutting priority for development co-operation, providers can start to recognise it as part of the essential infrastructure for delivering on national, regional and global development commitments.

Data action 3. *Boost statistical capacity and data literacy through new approaches.*

New, more comprehensive approaches to statistical capacity development need to be developed and piloted that go beyond building capacity to collect data, to building the capacity of national statistical offices to play an evolving and multifunctional role in the data ecosystem, and to improve the institutional and enabling environment for data and statistics.

Data action 4. *Increase efficiency and impact through "data compacts" or other co-ordinated, country-led approaches.*

Developing countries should better align incentives for producing data for national policy making and global monitoring through mutually accountable inclusive partnerships among data producers and users. The establishment of data compacts for co-ordinating and harmonising investment in data and support for statistical systems is a promising approach; it should be tested further to ensure that it meets the needs of all actors and fosters mutual accountability for delivering on joint, performance-based action plans.

Data action 5. *Invest in and use country-led results data to monitor progress towards the Sustainable Development Goals.*

International development actors must break with the business-as-usual approach; rather than collecting and using data to meet their own reporting and accountability pressures, they need to support country-led strategies and data ecosystems. This requires clear vision and pragmatism in dealing with the pressure to attribute results to every aid dollar. It also means ensuring that results from any independent data collection efforts are accessible to all development actors and co-ordinated with the statistical objectives of developing country governments.

Data action 6. *Produce and use better data to help understand the overall state of SDG financing.*

Data on development finance also need to improve. This means producing a comprehensive financing picture by increasing the availability and transparency of quality development finance data and improving methodologies and standards with the objective of equipping developing countries to plan and budget their national development strategies and priorities.

Bridging the data divide for development

Why it matters

WHAT WE KNOW
Better policies demand better data

THE GLOBAL CHALLENGE
To achieve the Sustainable Development Goals, we need to know more about people's lives

WHAT'S NEW
New technology makes it easier, faster and cheaper to produce better data for policy making

Good data for development are lacking

44% of countries worldwide do not have comprehensive birth and death registration data

13% of countries worldwide have a dedicated budget for gender statistics

37 countries have statistical laws that meet UN standards

No data exist for two thirds of Sustainable Development Goal indicators

Together, development partners can help bridge the data divide

SIX DATA ACTIONS

- Make **statistical laws, regulations and standards** fit for evolving data needs
- Improve the quantity and quality of **financing for data**
- Boost **data literacy** and modernise **statistical capacity building**
- Increase efficiency and impact of **investment in data** and **capacity building** through co-ordinated, **country-led** approaches
- Invest in and use **country-led results data** to monitor progress made towards the Sustainable Development Goals
- Make **data on development finance** more comprehensive and transparent

Source: OECD (2017), *Development Co-operation Report 2017: Data for Development*, OECD Publishing, Paris, *http://dx.doi.org/10.1787/dcr-2017-en*.

Chapter 1

Overview: What will it take for data to enable development?

by
Johannes Jütting, Partnership in Statistics for Development in the 21st Century (PARIS21)
and Ida Mc Donnell, OECD Development Co-operation Directorate

Data are a prerequisite for delivering the 2030 Agenda for Sustainable Development, ensuring that no one is left behind. However, simply producing more data is not enough: data must be transformed, analysed and used to be useful for policy making, monitoring and accountability. The Development Co-operation Report 2017 *focuses on data for development because the quality, timely and disaggregated data that are crucial for achieving the ultimate goals of development – improving the welfare of people and fighting poverty – are missing. Investing in statistical systems needs to become a strategic priority for developing countries and providers of development co-operation alike. Strong political leadership in developing countries is needed to promote the cause of data for development and ensure data are produced with high-quality standards, protecting privacy and confidentiality. Development co-operation can help developing countries produce and use more and better data in a responsible and transparent way for good policy outcomes.*

Key messages

- Achieving the Sustainable Development Goals (SDGs) requires informed choices about priorities and strategies that are based on better evidence than is available today.
- Improving sustainable development data is a task for all. Political leadership, combined with the right institutional framework; financial, technical and human resources; and partnerships among public and private data producers and users are crucial for data to enable development.
- The total cost for 144 developing countries to produce data for the SDG indicators (Tiers 1 and 2) is estimated at USD 2.8-3.0 billion per year up to 2030 (GPSDD, 2016).
- With relatively little additional financial effort, development co-operation providers can fill the estimated annual funding gap of USD 685 million for SDG data in developing countries. To achieve this, aid for statistics needs to increase by about USD 200 million per year, beyond the 2015 level of USD 541 million (in current prices), and these volumes need to be sustained up to 2030.
- Increasing the quantity of aid alone will not guarantee success. The quality of financing for statistics must be improved by reducing duplication, targeting investments where needs are greatest, ensuring everyone's needs are counted, aligning to country priorities for data, and providing more relevant and sustainable statistical capacity building.
- To capture the full picture of resource flows for implementing the SDGs, a more comprehensive system and database are needed – such as the total official support for sustainable development (TOSSD) measure, which systematically captures all international development finance flows to developing countries and brings more actors on board for greater transparency.

Six concrete actions can bridge the data divide for sustainable development

- **Data action 1.** *Make statistical laws, regulations and standards fit for evolving data needs.*
- **Data action 2.** *Improve the quantity and quality of financing for data.*
- **Data action 3.** *Boost statistical capacity and data literacy through new approaches.*
- **Data action 4.** *Increase efficiency and impact through "data compacts" or other co-ordinated, country-led approaches.*
- **Data action 5.** *Invest in and use country-led results data to monitor progress towards the Sustainable Development Goals.*
- **Data action 6.** *Produce and use better data to help understand the overall state of SDG financing.*

The *Development Co-operation Report 2017* provides a holistic view of data-driven development and identifies concrete actions to advance the job of improving the quality of data and statistics, which are so important for driving development. But for data to be really effective, strong political backing is essential to forge a new mind-set that recognises and values the key role of data in delivering inclusive growth, prosperity and well-being. This, in turn, will improve the availability of independent, relevant and high-quality data, and their use in policy making, monitoring and accountability.

This report shows how international development partners, civil society and the private sector can work together to support the priorities and efforts of partner governments and national statistical systems so that they are capable of producing and using the right development data in a sustainable and responsible way (Box 1.1).

Box 1.1. **What are development data?**

"Development data" are important for setting development targets, measuring progress towards them and implementing development goals. Sources of development data include, but are not limited to, censuses, sectoral surveys, economic statistics, administrative data, civil registration and vital statistics, citizen-generated data, environmental data, and remote sensing and geospatial data. Development data are also compiled by international organisations and financial institutions to monitor the pace of economic and social development, as well as the status of the environment. There is strong complementarity and interdependence among diverse development data, which makes it important to take a systematic and comprehensive approach to producing data and strengthening statistical systems.

Source: SDSN (2015), "Data for development: A needs assessment for SDG monitoring and statistical capacity development", *http://unsdsn.org/wp-content/uploads/2015/04/Data-for-Development-Full-Report.pdf.*

Making the most of the power of technology can help to ensure that data serve development

The United Nations (UN) 2030 Agenda for Sustainable Development leaves no doubt that data are central to helping societies make real and meaningful progress. The 2030 Agenda is a data-driven programme of action. The SDGs create incentives for closing global data gaps and collecting new data to help achieve a transformative and universal agenda, improving well-being and leaving no one behind. Moreover, data needs are changing: to address intertwined global challenges ranging from climate change to the spread of infectious diseases and the effects of instability, vulnerability and conflict, policy action must be informed by reliable and high-quality data (SDSN, 2015; OECD, 2016).

Clearly, to be useful, data must come in a form and at a time when people can actually use them. In other words, they need to be accessible, usable and reused, refined and relevant. The data revolution offers governments and national statistical offices a welcome opportunity to produce more useful data by generating data from new sources that can complement and strengthen, though not replace, official statistics.[1]

Yet there is a somewhat paradoxical global data divide. This divide is characterised, on the one hand, by the continued scarcity in developing countries of basic data about people and the planet, and weak incentives and capacity to fill these gaps (Box 1.2). On the other hand, there is a surge in new sources and types of data emerging from digital and other technology. The transformative and at the same time potentially disruptive impact of the data revolution, and big data in particular, on the global economy and society has become a highly topical subject of research and debate.[2] But the so-called data deluge does not just stem from the data revolution. Development co-operation actors also collect and produce data for planning, programming and monitoring, often with limited benefit for developing

Box 1.2. **Key facts on data scarcity**

Lack of data for the Sustainable Development Goals (SDGs): There are no data yet for about two-thirds of the 232 SDG indicators. Eighty-eight indicators have neither an agreed methodology nor data for measuring them; 55 indicators have a methodology but no data (IAEG, 2017).

Seventy-seven countries have inadequate poverty data: About half of the 155 countries for which the World Bank monitors poverty data through the *World Development Indicators* database faced challenges in producing poverty estimates for the 2002-11 period, or in producing them in a timely fashion. If one considers having data for intervals shorter than five years, the picture is even less encouraging (Serajuddin et al., 2015).

Civil registration and vital statistics are missing: Only 56% of all countries worldwide (138 out of 246) have birth registration data that are at least 90% complete; on a regional basis, only 15% have these data in sub-Saharan Africa, 33% in Southern Asia and 36% in Southeast Asia. The number and proportion of countries with death registration data that are at least 75% complete are similar to those for birth registration (UN, 2017).

Lack of disaggregation: Even when data are available, they are often insufficiently disaggregated, making it impossible for policy makers to track or compare the situations of different population groups or communities (IEAG, 2014). For example, many countries worldwide do not have the strategies or skills to ensure robust gender-disaggregated data collection (UN, 2013).

Lack of legal frameworks: Only 37 countries have national statistical legislation that complies with the UN's Fundamental Principles of Official Statistics.[1] This legislation is strikingly absent in the least developed countries, small island developing states and middle-income countries across continents. Some OECD member countries also lack such legislation (UN, 2017).

Lack of financing: Across the globe, 81 national statistical plans are being implemented;[2] only 17 of these are fully funded, of which 11 are in Europe and North America (UN, 2017). Only 13% of countries dedicate a budget to gender statistics and many lack the national strategies and training needed to ensure robust gender-disaggregated data collection (UN, 2013).

1. As outlined in UNSC (2014).
2. Out of a sample of 154 countries.

Source: Authors' compilation.

countries (see Chapter 5). Custer and Sethi (2017) use the term "data graveyards" to refer to data that are collected but not used – or usable – by decision makers because the "data producers are often far removed from the people they hope will use this information to make decisions and advocate reforms". According to Custer and Sethi, "the data revolution could succeed in building a supply of better data, but may falter if there is insufficient demand for its use. [...] A ready supply of development data that lies fallow from disuse is little more than a graveyard, a place where data go to die".

Still, there continues to be a scarcity of key data about people in many developing countries. In her "In my view" piece (see Chapter 4), Sarah Hendriks of the Bill & Melinda Gates Foundation reminds us that "even the most basic information on women and girls is often lacking", stating that closing the gender gap requires closing the data gap. It is impossible to design good policies when basic information about the population – including the number of births and deaths – or data disaggregated by gender and disability are simply missing. But how can high-quality, trusted data be delivered when most developing countries still have a way to go to meet fundamental statistical standards and to finance their national strategies for the development of statistics? Figure 1.1 shows that the majority of developing countries, whether they are considered to have high or low capacity to produce statistics, do not yet have functioning systems for civil registration and vital statistics (see Chapter 3).

Figure 1.1. **Number of countries with capacity to deliver fundamental statistics, 2016**

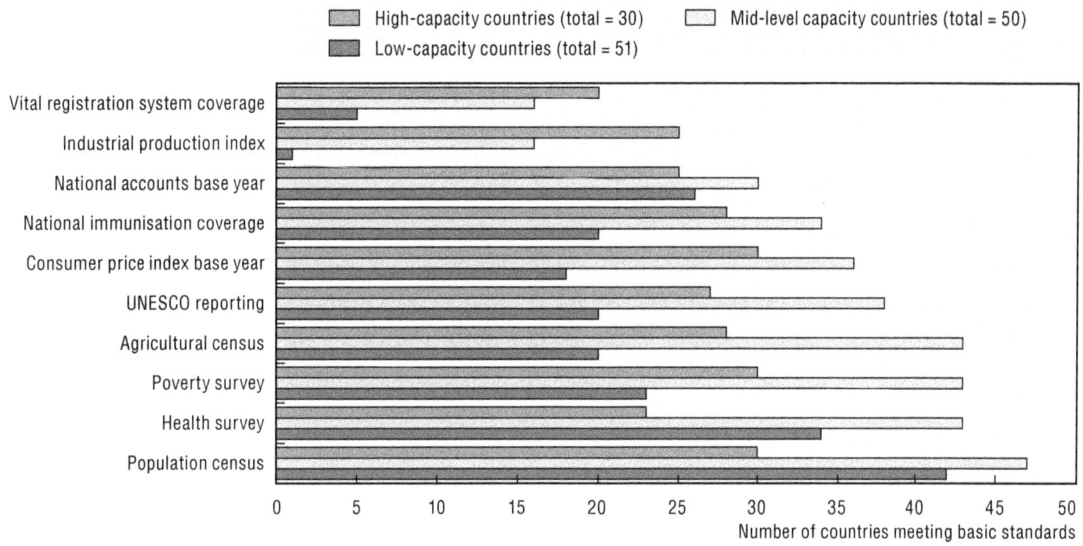

Source: Calculation by authors of Chapter 3 based on World Bank (2017), *Statistical Capacity Indicators* (database), *http://databank.worldbank.org/data/reports.aspx?source=statistical-capacity-indicators#.*

StatLink http://dx.doi.org/10.1787/888933591803

The impact of the lack of data in developing countries ranges from lost business opportunities to costly and ineffective public service interventions by governments and providers of development co-operation, in particular for the poor (World Bank, 2016a). Unless countries improve their capacity, there is a risk that the data divide will get wider and that data limitations will hold back progress on the SDGs. This report analyses how developing countries and their development co-operation partners can bridge the data divide, seize the unprecedented opportunity and mitigate risks to make the most of the convergence of the power of technology with the most ambitious development agenda to date: the 2030 Agenda for Sustainable Development.

Harnessing the data revolution is challenging

The data revolution is often described in terms of a vast increase in the volume of digital data that has resulted in the phenomenon known as "big data", characterised by the four "V's" of volume, velocity, veracity and variety.[3] The size and scope of this revolution can be gauged by the increase in the amount of online digital information; the growth of new occupations such as "data scientist" and "data broker"; and the manifold impacts of digital information on our daily lives. Social media, call detail records, sensors, web scraping and satellite imagery, to name a few, represent new sources of information that provide the opportunity to produce more and better data for development (Coppola et al., 2014; UN Global Pulse, 2012).

Some developing countries are already embarking on the data revolution (see Chapters 2 and 3 and case studies collected for this report[4]). For example, Bangladesh, Haiti, Kenya, Nigeria and the United Republic of Tanzania (hereafter "Tanzania") are using a large, geospatial database to improve their understanding of stunting, literacy and access to contraceptives. Yet many countries, as shown by the report "Informing a data revolution", are not yet prepared or resourced to seize the data revolution in a systematic way; they need people with the relevant skills, investment in the necessary infrastructure, and reforms in their institutional and regulatory context (PARIS21, 2015).

The UN Global Working Group on Big Data for Official Statistics has demonstrated that unconventional data sources can be of great use when combined with more traditional data sources such as censuses or surveys (GWG, 2017a; 2017b; 2017c). National statistical systems in developing countries are starting to make use of new technologies and methods to respond to the growing demand for actionable, empirical information. Geospatial data, for example, can help monitor socio-economic or environmental conditions, enable geographic disaggregation, and make geo-located data more dynamic.

A key challenge is that the data revolution is not yet producing dividends for most developing countries. Having appropriate information and communications technology (ICT) infrastructure is a pre-condition for seizing the opportunities presented by the data revolution. ICT can also increase the speed, accuracy and impact of data collection and dissemination while reducing costs.[5] Yet for this to happen, it is essential to bridge the significant digital divide that underlies the data divide. The Internet needs to be universally accessible and affordable if it is to empower people, and if digital economies are to provide dividends (World Bank, 2016a). According to *Aid for Trade at a Glance 2017* (OECD/WTO, 2017), 3.9 billion people, constituting more than half the world's total population, are still offline. The majority of these people live in the world's most vulnerable countries. In many developing countries – in particular the least developed countries, landlocked developing countries and small island developing states – development challenges hamper the spread of ICTs. These challenges include limited and costly access to national and international connectivity in small and isolated communities, difficulties in the rollout of terrestrial communication infrastructure across large land areas, and lack of, or limited, direct access to the sea.

In all its manifestations, the data revolution has the potential to transform how national statistical systems work in rich and poor countries alike. Policy making can also be improved by exploiting the massive streams of accurate, timely and granular data, as well as the opportunity to engage other data producers from the private sector and civil society. The analysis of big data can allow decision makers to track development progress in real time, improving social protection and the understanding of where existing policies and programmes require adjustment. This presents a tremendous opportunity to gain richer, deeper, timelier insights to complement the data that are being collected through censuses and surveys. As suggested in Chapter 2, a true data revolution would draw on both traditional and new sources of data to fully integrate statistics into decision making, promote open access to and use of data, and ensure increased support for statistical systems.

Developing countries struggle to respond to the increasing demand for data

The SDGs are putting high demands on national statistical systems the world over (see the "In my view" piece by Martine Durand). Most countries, including many OECD countries, have not yet started collecting data for many indicators in the UN global SDG indicators framework. There are serious methodological and strategic challenges to solve as well, including the need to strike a balance between producing the data for global monitoring, on the one hand, and for national policy making on the other. These challenges are even more critical for developing countries with low statistical capabilities.

Moving towards a virtuous data cycle is a challenge with growing complexity

Achieving a virtuous data cycle within a national statistical system is a challenge of growing complexity, with a multitude of actors involved in producing and using these data and a range of data demands and uses (Figure 1.2). Many developing countries are, however, stuck in a vicious cycle of low interest in and demand for quality data for policy making. Low interest and demand result in weak statistical institutions with poor governance; lack of investment in staff, infrastructure and tools; low human capacity; and highly fragmented statistical systems. These shortcomings, in turn, translate into low-quality data, which reinforce the starting point of lack of demand. The international community can compound these problems – notably when external actors produce and collect data through parallel channels with little positive spillover for the national statistical system or relevance for national policy making (see Chapters 2, 4 and 5).

In my view: Improving sustainable development data is a task for all

Martine Durand,
OECD Chief Statistician and Director of the OECD Statistics Directorate

In an era of fake news and alternative facts, statisticians have a special responsibility. As the custodians of the evidence base for policy making, they must stand up for the right of all citizens to true, reliable and accessible information.

This is especially the case in the development field, and even more so since world leaders adopted the extraordinarily ambitious and wide-ranging 2030 Agenda for Sustainable Development in September 2015. At the heart of this global "plan of action for people, planet and prosperity" are 17 Sustainable Development Goals (SDGs) that "are integrated and indivisible and balance the three dimensions of sustainable development: the economic, social and environmental", with the ultimate objective to leave no one behind. Achieving the SDGs will require informed choices about priorities and strategies, and for this we will need a better evidence base than we have today.

But statisticians – and especially statisticians in developing countries – cannot do this job alone. They will need the support of the whole of government and society to develop the data and analysis that will show how to meet agreed national and global objectives efficiently. Finance ministries must guarantee adequate funding over the medium term to develop sound national statistical systems and institutions, with national statistical offices playing a central role. Aid providers must be ready to co-ordinate and support the right technical capacity to help fill data gaps. Central governments must ensure that statisticians can work without political interference. And civil society, including the private sector, must work in partnership with national statistical offices to provide feedback and – where appropriate standards and safeguards are in place – contribute their own data.

When the then United Nations' Secretary-General Ban Ki-moon came to Paris in the run-up to the 2015 leaders' summit, OECD Secretary-General Gurría promised that the OECD would be the UN's "best supporting actor" in the global effort to achieve the SDGs. Since then, the OECD has been active on numerous fronts to help the world rise to the information challenge posed by the 2030 Agenda.

The OECD's first contribution has been to lend direct support to the UN by providing data on the agreed set of global SDG indicators, either straight from its own datasets or in combination with data from other agencies. The OECD has also contributed to both the 2016 and 2017 UN reports on SDG progress, and is working actively to help develop the required new, but yet unavailable, indicators identified by the UN's Inter-Agency and Expert Group on Sustainable Development Goal Indicators.

A substantial share of the OECD's data contribution to tracking SDG progress comes from the Organisation's database on official and private international flows for development. Annual data collection started in 1961 and has been successively extended and elaborated to provide ever more detailed and precise information, reaching down to the level of individual aid activities. In the context of the financing for development agenda endorsed in Addis Ababa in 2015, these data are vital for assessing whether aid is being directed to the areas of greatest need, pinpointing where donors may need to better co-ordinate, or comparing aid inputs with development results.

The universality of the 2030 Agenda also means that OECD countries have broader responsibilities. They should both set an example in implementing the 2030 Agenda themselves and ensure that their actions contribute to its achievement elsewhere. This thinking inspired the approach to the OECD Study on Measuring Distance to the SDG Targets,[1] which responded to demands from several OECD member countries for help in planning their policy and data responses to the SDGs. The study identifies relevant indicators, proposes a method for setting 2030 target levels, and suggests how performance can be compared among targets so as to identify priorities for action. It places special emphasis on transboundary or "spillover" effects. Several OECD countries have used the study to stimulate national dialogue on the SDGs, and OECD committees are finding it useful when considering how to integrate the SDGs into their policy work.

Two decades ago the OECD helped conceive and promote the Millennium Development Goals through its Shaping the 21st Century[2] strategy and its co-ordination of the inter-agency publication calling for *A Better World for All*.[3] The challenge posed today by the SDGs is even greater, especially in the field of data and evidence. The OECD intends to play its full part in the global effort to meet this challenge, and encourages all involved to do the same.

1. *www.oecd.org/std/measuring-distance-to-the-sdgs-targets.htm.*
2. *www.oecd.org/dac/2508761.pdf.*
3. *www.oecd.org/dac/abetterworldforall-reportandwebsite.htm.*

Figure 1.2. **The virtuous data cycle**

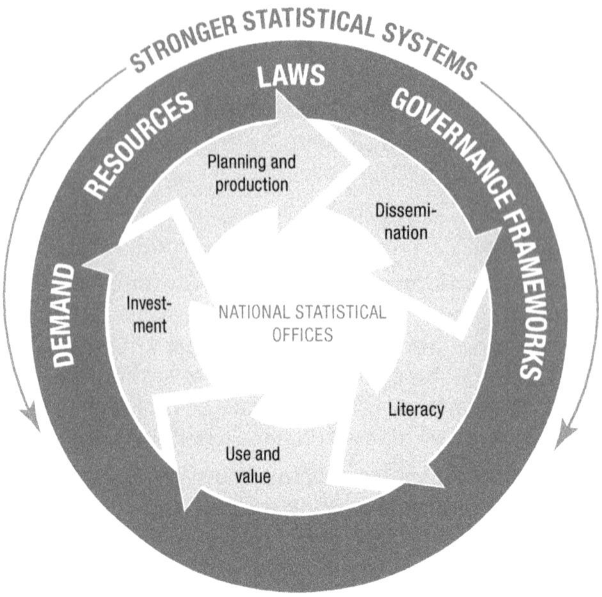

Source: OECD, based on PARIS21 and Open Data Watch.

To create a virtuous data cycle, national contexts and politics matter. The political appetite and demand for solid evidence for policy making varies among countries and governments, while the nature of this demand has a direct impact on data supply and on how the data ecosystem functions and whether it is capable of managing and benefiting from the data revolution. In countries such as Colombia, Grenada, Kenya, the Philippines, Samoa and Senegal, data and statistics are valued explicitly by the political leadership and government as being integral to economic and social development. As a result, the data ecosystems are flourishing in these countries. In the Philippines, for example, there is high demand by the Cabinet for data to inform government policies and decisions; this has translated into resources to strengthen the capacity and scope of the statistics office. Media outlets in the Philippines are also active users of statistics: data visualisations appear in print, on line and on television. In addition, there is a vibrant community of non-official data producers outside the official system, such as the "social weather station", which measures social indicators including poverty, happiness and well-being.[6]

National governments are ultimately responsible for ensuring that the data ecosystem is capable of producing and using quality data to design and implement policy priorities and monitor their outcomes. External partners can support this by, at a minimum, adopting a do-no-harm approach when investing in data and statistics for their specific development programmes and projects (see Chapter 5).

Ways to bridge the data divide for sustainable development

Data and statistics provide essential insights for understanding the practicalities of the development process, the interactions and feedback among different systems, and the factors that should shape decisions. Development is held back when the economic and demographic data that form the basis for decision making are lacking or insufficient to form a complete picture of what is needed. Moreover, as discussed in Chapter 2, the data revolution can enhance the availability of disaggregated, granular data that can enable policy makers to get beyond national averages to build real-time awareness of the status of a population. Real-time feedback on the effectiveness of policy actions should in turn lead to a more agile and adaptive approach to international development and, ultimately, to greater resilience and better outcomes in the spirit of leaving no one behind.

This report identifies several steps that can be taken to make the most of the power of data for development in the doubly promising context of the SDGs and the data revolution. It puts special emphasis on how development co-operation can invest in country-led strategies and data ecosystems, identifying clear, achievable actions for developing countries, bilateral and multilateral actors, and other development partners.

Data action 1. *Make statistical laws, regulations and standards fit for evolving data needs.*

To build inclusive data ecosystems that benefit global development and individual citizens, governments will need to transform their legal and strategic frameworks for data and statistics. Over the past two decades, developing countries have taken steps to reform their national statistical systems. Nonetheless, significant challenges remain, including the absence of legislative frameworks for statistics (Krätke and Byiers, 2014; and Box 1.2). The growing number of public, private, and civil society actors and institutions involved in the production and use of data make the need for clear legal, ethical, and quality standards and protocols even more urgent. These should regulate the use of traditional as well as new and non-traditional sources of data, fostering the trust that is needed for data to inform good policies and development results (Durand, 2017; Robin, Klein and Jütting, 2016).

National statistical offices should be at the centre of reform efforts, with laws and regulations protecting statistical agencies from partisan influence. The UN's Fundamental Principles of Official Statistics state that the "professional independence and accountability of statistical agencies are crucial", and that these "have to be guaranteed by legal and institutional frameworks and respected at all political levels and by all stakeholders in national statistical systems" (UNSC, 2014). National strategies for statistics also play a crucial role in setting priorities and ensuring accountability.

In the context of the data revolution, national statistical offices need to have the authority, legitimacy and capacity to partner with new actors that traditionally have not been part of the statistical system. As Chapter 3 describes, they must have the capacity to co-ordinate the system, manage strategic partnerships and propose solutions that can address hurdles to data sharing while protecting privacy. This includes putting in place the incentives that will encourage the private sector to share the data it owns, while also ensuring that the regulatory environment for the use of private data for commercial purposes is fit for purpose. The World Economic Forum's report "Data-driven development: Pathways for progress" (World Economic Forum, 2015) stresses the reluctance of many private actors to share their data because of regulatory uncertainties and associated risks of incurring liabilities or concerns about data security. Robin, Klein and Jütting (2016) discuss models that can help to overcome some of the obstacles associated with data sharing.

While the data revolution offers great opportunities to respond to a surge in demand for more and better data by all parts of society, there are also associated risks. As Chapters 2 and 3 point out, access to and use of private data raises important questions related to ownership, fraud, privacy and confidentiality. In Andreas Weigend's book *Data for the People* (Weigend, 2017), the former Chief Scientist of Amazon gives several examples of how companies use customers' "social data" without their knowledge or consent. He calls for a better balance of power between data creators and data companies (Weigend, 2017: 11).

In many developing countries, where the already weak regulations and standards for data protection tend not to be enforced, using new sources of data will only accentuate these weaknesses to the detriment of the public. As most countries face similar challenges in understanding and managing the benefits and risks of using new data sources (OECD, 2015), this is an area where international co-operation, including peer learning, can add value. For example, knowledge sharing can contribute to the development of guidelines, standards and best practices for managing and mitigating risks. Moreover, to be effective in stimulating data use and evidence-based decision making, national statistical offices must also improve data accessibility by adopting open data policies.

It is fundamental that international development partners, including South-South providers of development co-operation, support countries in establishing and enforcing their legal and strategic frameworks. Through policy dialogue and technical co-operation, they can advocate and provide support for inclusive data ecosystems with strong and independent institutions, as well as appropriate checks and balances to ensure that development data are reliable, inclusive and freely available.

Making statistical systems fit for purpose, for immediate action:

- Countries should develop or update national statistical laws and regulations, authorising national statistical offices to adopt new modes of data collection, to engage in partnerships with external organisations, and to openly disseminate data from the statistical system. These regulations should be complemented by right-to-information laws and open data policies that guarantee access by citizens to statistics and other forms of government information while protecting privacy and confidentiality.
- Development co-operation providers should support their partners in developing open data policies and using non-traditional data sources and technologies, including through legal and regulatory reform. As many advanced economies are also embarking on these reforms, international knowledge-sharing mechanisms could help interested countries learn from good practices and experiences with developing new regulations.

Data action 2. *Improve the quantity and quality of financing for data.*

Budgets need to grow if national statistical systems are to respond to the growing demand for more and better data. Financing for statistics reflects the level of priority accorded by governments, the state of public finances and the trade-offs that are made when national budgets are constrained. Just 17 of the 81 countries with statistical plans have secured adequate financing to implement them, of which 11 are in America and Europe (see Box 1.2).

Official statistics in the developing world are particularly underfunded, especially in the least developed countries and the small island developing states, where national statistical offices are largely dependent on external resources. Part of the challenge is that the costs of producing data and statistics, and of building and maintaining statistical capacity, are not integrated into national development plans and budgets, limiting the visibility of these needs and, inevitably, the resources allocated to them (PARIS21, 2017). Moreover, national and international financing for statistics very often tends to prioritise the collection of sector-specific data mirroring investments (e.g. in health and education) over civil registration and vital statistics, and administrative data; or over capacity building for the sustainable production and use of key data (see the "In my view" piece by Ellen Cathrine Kiøsterud in Chapter 5).

The demand for more and better data for the SDGs is not yet translating into a corresponding growth in funding. Aid for statistics, as calculated by PARIS21 in its "Partner report on support to statistics" (PARIS21, 2017), averaged 0.30% of total official development assistance (ODA) between 2013 and 2015 (about USD 600 million per year). By way of comparison, aid for capacity building in financial policies and administrative management received about USD 800 million in ODA

Box 1.3. **The successful case of Progresso Social Brasil**

Innovative partnership approaches to data collection and analysis, and use of these data by policy makers, are improving people's lives in the Brazilian Amazon.

In 2014, under the leadership of Fundación Avina and Deloitte Brazil, a cross-sector network comprising Brazilian business and civil society organisations was formed. They launched Progresso Social Brasil, a unique initiative to develop localised, highly contextual social and environmental metrics for the 773 municipalities in the Brazilian Amazon based on the Social Progress Index methodology.[1] The index, which focuses on social and environmental variables to complement traditional economic measures, was chosen as the best tool available to offer a clear lens on the Amazon's social dynamics.

The Brazilian Amazon region is home to nearly one-third of the world's tropical forests, providing upwards of 20% of the Earth's oxygen. It is also home to more than 24 million people, for many of whom social conditions are worse than those of people in other regions of Brazil. Infrequent data updates and the limited geographic scope of official statistics, coupled with a reliance on economics-focused metrics, have until recently limited insight into this highly complex region, its people and the key barriers to improving their social conditions.

Progresso Social Brasil launched IPS Amazônia (Índice de Progresso Social Amazônia) in August 2014. IPS Amazônia published performance scorecards for 772 municipalities (one municipality lacked sufficient data to be included) and an interactive tool with comprehensive datasets for each. This enabled them to reveal the specific needs of these communities and highlight success stories that shed light on what works.

The publication of the IPS Amazônia study has had significant impact, shifting development priorities and prompting government, businesses and civil society to focus their resources on real needs throughout the region. For example, it motivated a USD 20 billion investment plan targeting specific social progress priorities in 95 municipalities in the state of Para in the Brazilian Amazon. IPS Amazônia has inspired similar action by local governments beyond the region, including the city of Rio de Janeiro. Working with Progresso Social Brasil and the Social Progress Imperative[2] – the creators of the Social Progress Index – Rio de Janeiro has developed a municipal-level index to measure the impact of Olympic activity and more general development throughout the city.

The study has also inspired a new form of corporate social investment in the region. For example, since it identified Carauari (state of Amazonas) as one of the most deprived municipalities, Carauari has been the focus of continued engagement by several large corporations. Coca-Cola Brasil and Natura, a Brazilian cosmetics company, partnered with the data collection experts IPSOS to create a community needs survey – IPS Comunidades – based on the Social Progress Index framework. This survey investigates the unique social and environmental concerns of the people in three communities within the Carauari municipality. The findings of IPS Comunidades were released in June 2015 and the study now serves as the foundation for a Participatory Community Management Strategy, which fosters collaboration with local community organisations, businesses, municipal and state governments, and federal agencies.

1. See *www.socialprogressindex.com*.
2. See *www.socialprogressimperative.org*.

Source: Social Progress Imperative case study available at: *www.oecd.org/dac/development-co-operation-report-20747721.htm*.

on average over the same three years. Supporting statistics does not appear to be a high priority for Development Assistance Committee (DAC) members. In 2015, ten DAC members[7] accounted for 96% of bilateral commitments (USD 181 million). Nevertheless, most of the aid for statistics is going to the countries with the lowest capacity, and fragile states receive a relatively high share of the total (see Chapter 4).

Given the changing landscape for development finance (see Chapter 6), fundraising strategies will need to find innovative ways of leveraging new sources of finance, including from the private sector. Filling the estimated SDG data funding gap of approximately USD 685 million per year in developing countries is achievable: an additional USD 200 million annually in ODA (USD 541 million in 2015) would make a huge difference in helping to enable countries to put in place statistical systems capable of supporting the SDGs, as long as the aid focuses on building sustainable statistical systems (UN, 2015; SDSN, 2015).

The quality of investments in data and statistics also needs to improve to have greater impact, as outlined in Chapter 4. Better measurement of international support to statistics would help increase accountability over how it is spent. By treating data as a cross-cutting priority in development co-operation, providers can start to recognise it as part of the core infrastructure for achieving the SDGs. With these objectives in mind, Chapter 4 proposes the creation of a marker for development data in the OECD-DAC Creditor Reporting System (CRS).[8] At the same time, wide participation in efforts to increase the transparency of funding for development data is essential. This includes the participation of philanthropic organisations, which could follow the example of the Bill & Melinda Gates Foundation by reporting data on their funding to statistics (see Chapter 4).

Public-private partnerships for statistics can offer countries more room for innovation and risk-taking than traditional funding modalities (Box 1.3). For example, data philanthropy[9] – donations to the public sector of data held by corporations – is emerging as a movement in corporate citizenship. Through data philanthropy, governments might be better placed to track diseases, avert economic crises, relieve traffic congestion and contribute to development in many other ways.

Improving the quantity and quality of financing for data, for immediate action:

- Increase public and private resources for statistics to meet the SDGs, including through innovative mechanisms, e.g. developing country domestic resources, peer-to-peer capacity building, public-private partnerships and data philanthropy.
- Make data a cross-cutting priority for development co-operation and recognise it as part of the essential infrastructure for delivering on national, regional and global development commitments. International leadership by the OECD DAC, the G20, the UN General Assembly and other fora can build support for improving sustainable development data and enabling accountability through reviews of progress.
- Increase the transparency and accountability of financing for development data and statistics. Developing countries should budget for data and integrate data priorities into national development strategies. Development co-operation providers should agree on a measure for tracking international support to statistics in a systematic and comparable way.
- Development co-operation providers should target aid for statistics where the need is greatest, notably in the countries that rely most on external sources of finance for data and statistics: the least developed countries, small island developing states and fragile states.

Data action 3. *Boost statistical capacity and data literacy through new approaches.*

By itself, the data revolution will not reform national statistical systems, expand capacity, or lead to better use of statistics and greater impact from them. Success in building capable national statistical systems requires long-term political commitment to strengthen and improve the core statistical capacities required to use new technologies. When statistical offices are isolated from the decision-making process or lack control over their own budgets and administrative processes, their ability to promote the effective use of statistics is inhibited (see Chapter 4).

There are large differences in the capabilities of national statistical systems. Despite some progress made, many countries still lack the skills and infrastructure needed to produce high-quality data and respond to growing demand. In his "In my view" piece in Chapter 3, Stefan Schweinfest flags the need not only for more data – covering all countries and relevant areas – but also for more integrated and disaggregated data and the resources and technical capacity to have data that are fit for purpose.

Increasing statistical capacity is a long-term process. It encompasses investments in people and institutions as well as improvements in the environment in which national statistical offices work. Capacity development efforts are often limited to training and workshops, with success measured by numbers of people trained or other quantifiable output indicators. Traditional approaches have largely focused on building technical skills or improving business procedures; on the margins, they may include statistical laws, funding arrangements and co-ordination within the national statistical system. Today's investments in capacity development should use new approaches that are broader in substance and scope, reaching far beyond national statistical offices to include other actors – for example civil society – to produce more and better data, generated by and useful to citizens.

PARIS21 promotes a radically different starting point from traditional approaches to capacity development: "capacity development 4.0".[10] This approach begins by acknowledging that capacity development entails three distinct features – people, organisations and the enabling environment – and that the capacity of all three needs to be fostered. It places emphasis on the development of "soft skills" such as leadership, change management, advocacy and networking capacities. In capacity development 4.0, strengthening the demand side for capacity development – the user perspective – is also essential. What kind of data do citizens want and what skills do they need to be able to make informed decisions? Finally, a new approach to capacity development needs to help national staff, partners and citizens connect the dots within the data ecosystem – for which building partnerships is an essential feature.

Boosting statistical capacity and data literacy, for immediate action:

- Developing countries and their partners should develop and pilot new, more comprehensive approaches to capacity development that go beyond the capacity to collect data and build the capacity of national statistical offices to play an evolving and multifunctional role in the data ecosystem and to improve the institutional and enabling environment for data and statistics. This includes improving data dissemination and promoting data literacy to spur the use of statistics and promote active user communities.
- Countries should continue to build capacity for "core" statistics, including censuses, surveys and administrative records – which are essential in the national statistical system.
- National statistical offices worldwide face similar challenges in harnessing the data revolution; they could benefit from a new mechanism for "knowledge solidarity", allowing data stakeholders across the globe to share knowledge and work together in an effective manner.

Data action 4. *Increase efficiency and impact through "data compacts" or other co-ordinated, country-led approaches.*

Co-ordinating support to statistics is challenging, with a diversity of actors and objectives for investing in statistics, making it difficult to streamline (Box 1.4). As Ellen Cathrine Kiøsterud points out in her "In my view" piece in Chapter 5, there is much discussion about the need for improved co-ordination, yet very little change in behaviour. Stefan Schweinfest (see Chapter 3) calls for "a new global data architecture for sustainable development" while Martine Durand insists that "improving sustainable data is a task for all". Developing country governments struggle to steer providers

Box 1.4. **Dedicated planning tools can help to streamline global and national data needs**

The need to manage, measure and report on progress against the Sustainable Development Goal (SDG) indicators is placing a heavy burden on developing countries' statistical systems. For global monitoring, countries need to collect comparable data over time and adhere to common standards and methods. However, many of the SDG indicators lack clear definitions and may require new data collection instruments that will need to be tested and calibrated. Where standards and methods already exist, baseline measurements need to be coupled with an agreed programme of regular data collection. In addition, national statistical offices need to provide granular, local data related to each country's unique situation and challenges.

The Advanced Data Planning Tool (ADAPT) is being piloted or used by the Plurinational State of Bolivia, Cambodia, Cameroon, the Philippines, Rwanda and Tanzania (PARIS21, n.d.). This tool helps to improve synergies between regional and global indicators by charting them in the context of local realities. It highlights gaps in data, reporting and financing for the specific data that the country has committed to report for global and regional monitoring. In this way, ADAPT helps integrate and co-ordinate international and national statistical processes, estimate costs, raise awareness of needs, and streamline international financial and technical support in the framework of each country's national strategy for the development of statistics.

In Tanzania, for example, the National Bureau of Statistics used ADAPT to assess data gaps for its five-year national development plan (2016/17-2020/21) and to co-ordinate among various data producers. The assessment found that of the 282 indicators in the national development plan, the National Bureau of Statistics produced the data needed for only 39%; the remaining 61% relied on data produced by other government departments or agencies. Regarding the SDG indicators, 180 (64%) do not have corresponding indicators in Tanzania's development plan. The National Bureau of Statistics concluded that to fill the gaps, it needs to strengthen routine data collection within the national statistics system. As part of the ADAPT process, workshops and technical support provided by the Tanzania Data Lab have helped to build awareness and capacity in the National Bureau of Statistics and among Tanzanian data scientists.

The Global Partnership for Sustainable Development Data's SDG Data Roadmaps (n.d.) also promote a tool for SDG monitoring. The roadmaps bring together national data producers and users, as well as international experts, to understand the potential for applying the international development agenda at the national level. They also help to identify how the country can strengthen the relevant development data (GPSDD, 2016).

Source: PARIS21 (n.d.), "Advanced Data Planning Tool (ADAPT)", *www.paris21.org/ADAPT*; Chuwa, A. (2017), "Tanzania case: Advanced Data Planning Tool – ADAPT and linking key indicators in Tanzania".

towards joint action in support of their national priorities. Yet the use of numerous related, but different, indicators leads to overlapping systems and reporting, with limited participation by national statistical offices – and high transaction costs for them. If involved at all, their role may be reduced to that of data collectors, while the processing and analysis takes place elsewhere.

The SDGs can serve as a platform for the shared generation and use of results data, enabling mutual accountability among all stakeholders. They offer an opportunity and incentive that developing countries can use to step-up alignment and harmonisation with their priorities. Indeed, many DAC members have recognised this opportunity, calling for a better division of labour among providers of development co-operation to enhance synergies and impact and to ensure more effective allocation of resources and minimise the burden on constrained national statistical offices. They have also identified the need for cross-government co-ordination in developing countries (Sanna and Mc Donnell, 2017).

To resolve many of the problems with support to statistics – including growing fragmentation, with more actors than ever before – closer co-operation among all stakeholders in the data ecosystem is urgently needed. Creating country-led data compacts can facilitate a mutually accountable multi-stakeholder approach, bringing together national governments, external funders, citizen groups, media and technical agencies (see Chapter 4). Signatories to data compacts engage from an early stage, buying into a joint action plan and a performance agreement based on the national development plan; the accompanying results framework specifies the indicators that will be used to measure progress. The compacts can build in incentives to improve data quality, ensure open data, promote data use and heighten data impact.

Governments in developing countries need to a play strong leadership role in identifying the needs of their national statistical systems and raising adequate resources and support to address them through data compacts, strategic planning or other joined-up approaches. Pooling resources can reduce transaction costs while enabling more harmonised support in line with the differing strengths of individual partners.

Improving co-ordination through country-led approaches, for immediate action:

- Developing countries and development partners should better align incentives for producing data for national policy making and global monitoring. The establishment of data compacts for co-ordinating and harmonising investment in data and support for statistical systems is a promising approach; it should be tested further to ensure that it meets the needs of all actors and fosters mutual accountability for delivering on joint, performance-based action plans.
- International development partners should be accountable for better aligning their data investments and new collection efforts with national strategies for statistics and for focusing on the development outcomes and change monitored and measured by national statistical systems.

Data action 5. *Invest in and use country-led results data to monitor progress towards the Sustainable Development Goals.*

Politicians in provider countries are under pressure to show that aid is being well spent. Taxpayers want to know how their money is being used and the results it is achieving. This leads providers to monitor and report on the immediate outputs of the projects they have funded, for example the number of people trained, facilities built, children educated, mothers reached during pregnancy, and households provided with safe water or reliable electricity (OECD, 2017). To shift the focus from the outputs of development co-operation to what aid is achieving for development in countries, or ultimately to progress towards the SDGs, requires data on outcomes, impact[11] and change – and these data should come from country's national statistical systems.

Chapters 3 and 5 discuss the challenges related to the quality and availability of country-led results data, which often are not sufficient to provide the results data that DAC members want. Many DAC members are unwilling to use countries' indicators, data and monitoring systems, citing the unreliability of national reporting and mismatches between provider and country reporting requirements and indicators (OECD, 2012). This creates a challenging balancing act for providers of development co-operation grappling to:

- maximise their contribution to the SDG results that developing countries have prioritised within their national systems and frameworks
- better understand the linkages between progress towards SDG targets and the allocation and use of development co-operation resources

- use results data to inform decisions about their development co-operation interventions and make course corrections
- safeguard ODA budgets by demonstrating impact to their constituencies.

Faced with these challenges, providers of development co-operation often invest in their own metrics and data to document the impact of development policies and interventions. This approach, however, goes counter to the universal process of delivering on the SDGs, as well as to commitments to use country-led results frameworks and associated systems (OECD, 2006; 2012).[12] In his "In my view" piece in Chapter 2, Morten Jerven points out that investing in monitoring for the sake of monitoring is unsustainable and calls for a rebalancing of the political economy of statistics.

Honouring commitments to invest in and use country-led results data and participate in accountability mechanisms that are relevant to developing countries and their priorities will entail changing providers' mind-sets as well as behaviour. It requires clear vision and pragmatism in dealing with the pressure to attribute results to every aid dollar. And it means ensuring that results from any independent data collection efforts are accessible to all development actors and co-ordinated with the statistical objectives of developing country governments. In this way, international development partners can go a long way in improving the value, use and relevance of data for development.

Investing in and using country-led results data, for immediate action:

- Countries should formulate data policies and strategies that will meet their needs and guide partners. There is scope to be assertive. Partners should respect national priorities for the supply of statistics, investing in statistics that are coherent with those priorities.
- International organisations and providers of development co-operation must work towards the sustainable supply of statistics rather than simply demanding more data for global monitoring and domestic accountability needs. When introducing or updating standard indicators for results reporting, DAC members should demonstrate how they are supporting country systems, linking project results to the SDG targets and indicators prioritised locally and, at a minimum, ensuring that there is no duplication. They should also make efforts to harmonise indicators among providers.
- Bilateral aid providers should be realistic about attributing aid to specific development results. If attribution is essential for domestic accountability, they should keep it to a minimum based on a small number of output indicators and use narratives to explain how results contribute to outcomes and change.

Data action 6. *Produce and use better data to help understand the overall state of SDG financing.*

Over the past two decades, financing for development has undergone fundamental changes in terms of sources, volumes and patterns of flows. Chapter 6 focuses on data related to development finance, setting out the current landscape and looking at how data systems are evolving in the context of the Addis Ababa Action Agenda on financing for development and the 2030 Agenda.

Data on development finance support better decision making for development outcomes by providing evidence on the reality of resource flows for sustainable development. They also help to shed light on how successfully the international community and individual countries mobilise resources to meet their commitments, and how they collectively work together to leave no one behind. In addition, data incentivise official providers of development co-operation and investors to step up efforts to fill financing gaps, leveraging a range of resources to deliver the 2030 Agenda (UN, 2015).

Chapter 6 explains that getting development finance data right means producing a comprehensive picture – from current flows and global gaps to specific needs, shortfalls and opportunities – in order to equip developing countries to plan and resource their national development strategies and priorities.

The fundamental condition for ensuring the quality of development finance data, however, is a sound measurement system with clear definitions and methodologies that make the collected data comparable across providers. The lack of agreed standards and systems for reporting of finance data beyond ODA means that the financing efforts of key development actors – notably providers of South-South co-operation, civil society organisations, philanthropic foundations and the private sector – are largely under-reported internationally. A better understanding of how all financing for the SDGs comes together, at the country level and globally, requires not only modernised measures and new data series, but also a new framework that captures this information in a systematic manner.

In order to track resources invested to achieve the SDGs, the international community is developing a new international statistical standard known as total official support for sustainable development (TOSSD).[13] The new framework will increase recognition and facilitate transparency about the full array of officially supported bilateral, multilateral and South-South support for sustainable development. It responds to new financing imperatives implicit in the 2030 Agenda, including the importance of mobilising SDG-supportive investments by the private sector; of marshalling more resources to provide global public goods; and of encouraging investments and services to promote the enabling conditions for sustainable development and to address global challenges. In addition to yielding a richer picture at the global level, a key plus of the TOSSD framework is the ability to provide enhanced information on development finance at the country level, as found in recent TOSSD pilots in the Philippines and Senegal. Key findings include:

- TOSSD has high potential as an international standard, including by ensuring comparability of data across different sources.
- TOSSD can enhance transparency and help to unpack complex financial packages.
- A framework such as TOSSD is essential to reflect all contributions to sustainable development, including those by emerging economies.
- Better tracking of triangular and South-South co-operation, the activities of non-governmental organisations and subnational co-operation in the TOSSD framework would strengthen TOSSD as a tool that responds to recipient countries' needs.
- It is critical to develop the technical features and boundaries of the TOSSD measure.

Making progress on addressing the challenges of improving data on development finance and coming up with new measures, methods and systems requires political leadership and consensus building through inclusive mechanisms. At the same time, development co-operation providers will need to reinforce or build up their capacity to collect, report and analyse development finance data to allow it to play its transformative role. Knowing that their efforts will be recognised better offers an incentive for providers and other development finance actors to invest in getting the data right. Yet the needs of developing countries for comprehensive, timely and predictable data should drive and shape this work.

Understanding the overall state of SDG financing, for immediate action:

Step up collective efforts to ensure that transparent and accountable financing is in place to deliver on the 2030 Agenda by:

- Increasing the availability and transparency of quality data on development finance, including concessional and non-concessional official flows, private finance mobilised through official interventions, private flows at market terms, South-South and triangular co-operation, and giving by philanthropic foundations and civil society organisations.
- Improving methodologies and standards, including the TOSSD standard, through an inclusive, international process that integrates them into the SDG monitoring framework; measures private sector ODA instruments; and establishes global data standards for social impact investment.
- Improving analysis of financing patterns, modalities and trends for both climate and development goals by exploiting synergies between existing systems for climate-related development finance and country reporting on climate finance to UNFCCC.

Notes

1. The United Nations' Cape Town Global Action Plan for Sustainable Development Data, adopted in March 2017, seeks to support the application of new technologies and new data sources in mainstream statistical activities. It sets out guidelines for the use of new and innovative data – generated outside the official statistical system – in official statistics (UNSC, 2017).
2. According to an article by Yuval Noah Harari (2016), "high-tech gurus and Silicon Valley prophets are creating a new universal narrative that legitimises the authority of algorithms and big data. This novel creed may be called 'Dataism'. [...] Dataists further believe that given enough biometric data and computing power, the global data-processing system could understand humans much better than we understand ourselves".
3. See, for example, IBM's Big Data & Analytics Hub (n.d.).
4. The case studies are available at: *www.oecd.org/dac/development-co-operation-report-20747721.htm*.
5. Researchers belonging to the UN Sustainable Development Solutions Network calculated that the use of mobile phones could bring down the cost of surveys by up to 60% in some East African countries over a ten-year period (SDSN, 2015).
6. More information is available at: *www.sws.org.ph/swsmain/home*.
7. The top ten bilateral providers by size of contributions are Canada, Sweden, United Kingdom, Korea, Australia, Norway, Italy, Switzerland, United States and Japan.
8. The current CRS sector code for statistical capacity building fails, for example, to identify multi-sector projects that comprise only a small statistics component.
9. According to UN Global Pulse, the conversation around data philanthropy has been advancing since its emergence at the World Economic Forum in Davos in 2011 (UN Global Pulse, 2011).
10. Capacity development 4.0 is built on similar principles to "industry 4.0", namely that in an increasingly digitalised world the drivers of supply and demand for capacity development in data and statistics have fundamentally changed. In the new data ecosystems, the diverse actors are all interacting, exchanging and processing data and information. Hence, there is a need to change and adapt training models – and create new ones – for literacy in the age of data.
11. In the context of development results, impact is defined as: positive and negative, primary and secondary long-term effects produced by development interventions, directly or indirectly, intended or unintended (OECD, 2010).
12. By country results data and systems we refer both to the government's national statistical system and the country-led results framework. "A country-led results framework is understood as one that is led or originated by the government of the country itself. [...] This can include any form of government-led planning instrument that defines a country's approach to development, sets out its development priorities and establishes the results expected to be achieved. It also outlines the systems and tools that will be used to monitor and evaluate progress towards these targets, establishes the indicators of progress and determines the baseline against which results will be measured" (OECD/UNDP, 2016).
13. For further information please refer to: *www.oecd.org/dac/financing-sustainable-development/development-finance-standards/TOSSD Flyer crops.pdf*. (accessed 28 July 2017).

References

Chuwa, A. (2017), "Tanzania case: Advanced Data Planning Tool – ADAPT and linking key indicators in Tanzania", Powerpoint presentation at the High-Level Meeting on Data for Development in Africa, June 2017, Nairobi, Kenya, unpublished.

Coppola, A. et al. (2014), "Big data in action for development", The World Bank, Washington, DC, *http://live.worldbank.org/sites/default/files/Big%20Data%20for%20Development%20Report_final%20version.pdf.*

Custer, S. and T. Sethi (eds.) (2017), "Avoiding data graveyards: Insights from data producers and users in three countries", AidData at the College of William & Mary, Williamsburg, Virginia, *http://aiddata.org/sites/default/files/avoiding_data_graveyards_full_report.pdf.*

Durand, M. (2017), "New ways to measure the goals", *Sustainable Development Goals 2017*, pp. 78-79, United Nations Association-UK, *www.sustainablegoals.org.uk/wp-content/uploads/2017/03/078-079-SDG-DURAND.pdf.*

GPSDD (2016), "The state of development data funding 2016", Global Partnership for Sustainable Development Data, *http://opendatawatch.com/wp-content/uploads/2016/09/development-data-funding-2016.pdf.*

GPSDD (n.d.), "Data Roadmaps for Sustainable Development Guidelines", Global Partnership for Sustainable Development Data, *www.data4sdgs.org/toolbox.*

GWG (2017a), "Assessing use of scanner data for compiling the Consumer Price Index", Big Data Project Inventory, United Nations Global Working Group, *https://unstats.un.org/bigdata/inventory/?selectID=201431.*

GWG (2017b), "A big data pilot project: With smart meter data", Big Data Project Inventory, United Nations Global Working Group, *https://unstats.un.org/bigdata/inventory/?selectID=201429.*

GWG (2017c), "How good are CDR-derived measures of income and inequality, and can governments systematically use them?", Big Data Project Inventory, United Nations Global Working Group, *https://unstats.un.org/bigdata/inventory/?selectID=WB3.*

Harari, Y.N. (2016), "Yuval Noah Harari on big data, Google and the end of free will", *The Financial Times*, 26 August, *www.ft.com/content/50bb4830-6a4c-11e6-ae5b-a7cc5dd5a28c.*

IAEG (2017), "Annex III: Revised list of global Sustainable Development Goal indicators", Report of the Inter-Agency and Expert Group on Sustainable Development Goal Indicators, E/CN.3/2017/2, United Nations Statistical Commission, *https://unstats.un.org/sdgs/indicators/Official%20Revised%20List%20of%20global%20SDG%20indicators.pdf.*

IEAG (2014), "A world that counts: Mobilizing the data revolution for sustainable development", Independent Expert Advisory Group on a Data Revolution for Sustainable Development, United Nations, New York, *www.undatarevolution.org/wp-content/uploads/2014/11/A-World-That-Counts.pdf.*

IBM Big Data & Analytics Hub (n.d.), "The four V's of big data", *www.ibmbigdatahub.com/infographic/four-vs-big-data* (accessed 28 July 2017).

Krätke, F. and B. Byiers (2014), "The political economy of official statistics: Implications for the data revolution in sub-Saharan Africa", *PARIS21 Discussion Papers*, No. 5, Partnership in Statistics for Development in the 21st Century, Paris, *http://ecdpm.org/wp-content/uploads/DP-170-Political-Economy-Official-Statistics-Africa-December-2014.pdf.*

OECD (2017), "Strengthening the results chain: Synthesis of case studies of results-based management by providers", OECD, Paris, *http://dx.doi.org/10.1787/544032a1-en.*

OECD (2016), *States of Fragility 2016: Understanding Violence*, OECD Publishing, Paris, *http://dx.doi.org/10.1787/9789264267213-en.*

OECD (2015), *Data-Driven Innovation: Big Data for Growth and Well-Being,* OECD Publishing, Paris, *http://dx.doi.org/10.1787/9789264229358-en.*

OECD (2012), *Aid Effectiveness 2011: Progress in Implementing the Paris Declaration*, OECD Publishing, Paris, *http://dx.doi.org/10.1787/9789264125780-en.*

OECD (2010), "Glossary of key terms in evaluation and results-based management", OECD, Paris, *www.oecd.org/dac/evaluation/publicationsanddocuments.htm.*

OECD (2006), "2006 Survey on Monitoring the Paris Declaration", *OECD Journal on Development*, Vol. 8/2, OECD Publishing, Paris, *http://dx.doi.org/10.1787/journal_dev-v8-2-en.*

OECD/UNDP (2016), *Making Development Co-operation More Effective: 2016 Progress Report*, OECD Publishing, Paris, *http://dx.doi.org/10.1787/9789264266261-en.*

OECD/WTO (2017), *Aid for Trade at a Glance 2017: Promoting Trade, Inclusiveness and Connectivity for Sustainable Development*, World Trade Organization, Geneva/OECD Publishing, Paris, *http://dx.doi.org/10.1787/aid_glance-2017-en.*

PARIS21 (2017), "National Strategy for the Development of Statistics Guidelines", OECD, Paris, *http://nsdsguidelines.paris21.org.*

PARIS21 (2016), "Partner report on support to statistics: PRESS 2016", OECD, Paris, *www.paris21.org/Press2016*.

PARIS21 (2015), "Informing a data revolution", OECD, Paris, *http://datarevolution.paris21.org*.

PARIS21 (n.d.), "Advanced Data Planning Tool (ADAPT)", *www.paris21.org/ADAPT*.

Robin, N., T. Klein and J. Jütting (2016), "Public-private partnerships for statistics: Lessons learned, future steps: A focus on the use of non-official data sources for national statistics and public policy", *OECD Development Co-operation Working Papers*, No. 27, OECD Publishing, Paris, *http://dx.doi.org/10.1787/5jm3nqp1g8wf-en*.

Sanna, V. and I. Mc Donnell (2017), "Data for development: DAC member priorities and challenges", *OECD Development Co-operation Working Papers*, No. 35, OECD Publishing, Paris, *http://4dx.doi.org/10.1787/6e342488-en*.

SDSN (2015), "Data for development: A needs assessment for SDG monitoring and statistical capacity development", United Nations Sustainable Development Solutions Network, *http://unsdsn.org/wp-content/uploads/2015/04/Data-for-Development-Full-Report.pdf*.

Serajuddin, U. et al. (2015), "Data deprivation: Another deprivation to end", *Policy Research Working Paper*, No. 7252, The World Bank, Washington, DC, *http://documents.worldbank.org/curated/en/700611468172787967/pdf/WPS7252.pdf*.

UN (2017), *The Sustainable Development Goals Report 2017*, United Nations Department if Economic and Social Affairs, New York, *https://www.un.org/development/desa/publications/sdg-report-2017.html*.

UN (2015), "Transforming our world: The 2030 Agenda for Sustainable Development", United Nations, New York, *https://sustainabledevelopment.un.org/content/documents/21252030%20Agenda%20for%20Sustainable%20Development%20web.pdf*.

UN (2013), "Report of the UN Secretary-General on gender statistics", United Nations, New York, *https://unstats.un.org/unsd/statcom/doc13/2013-10-GenderStats-E.pdf*.

UNSC (2017), "Cape Town Global Action Plan for Sustainable Development Data", United Nations Statistics Commission, New York, *http://unstats.un.org/sdgs/hlg/Cape-Town-Global-Action-Plan*.

UNSC (2014), "Fundamental Principles of Official Statistics", A/RES/68/261, United Nations Statistics Commission, New York, *https://unstats.un.org/unsd/dnss/gp/fundprinciples.aspx*.

UN Global Pulse (2012), "Big data for development: Challenges and opportunities", United Nations Global Pulse, *www.unglobalpulse.org/sites/default/files/BigDataforDevelopment-UNGlobalPulseJune2012.pdf*.

UN Global Pulse (2011), "Data philanthropy: Public & private sector data sharing for global resilience", United Nations Global Pulse Blog, 16 September, *www.unglobalpulse.org/blog/data-philanthropy-public-private-sector-data-sharing-global-resilience*.

Weigend, A. (2017), *Data for the People: How to Make Our Post-Privacy Economy Work for You*, Basic Books.

World Bank (2017), *Statistical Capacity Indicators* (database), *http://databank.worldbank.org/data/reports.aspx?source=statistical-capacity-indicators*.

World Bank (2016a), *Digital Dividends*, World Development Report 2016, The World Bank, Washington, DC, *http://documents.worldbank.org/curated/en/896971468194972881/pdf/102725-PUB-Replacement-PUBLIC.pdf*.

World Bank (2016b), "Trust fund for statistical capacity building: Annual progress report", The World Bank, Washington, DC, *http://pubdocs.worldbank.org/en/946261466521915545/TFSCB-Annual-Report-FY16-final.pdf*.

World Economic Forum (2015), "Data-driven development: Pathways for progress", World Economic Forum, Geneva, *www3.weforum.org/docs/WEFUSA_DataDrivenDevelopment_Report2015.pdf*.

Further reading

Beguy, D. (2016), "Poor data hurts African countries' ability to make good policy decisions", Quartz Africa, *https://qz.com/762729/poor-data-is-hurting-african-countries-ability-to-make-good-policy-decisions*.

Davies, W. (2017), "How statistics lost the power – and why we should fear what comes next", *The Guardian*, 19 January, *www.theguardian.com/politics/2017/jan/19/crisis-of-statistics-big-data-democracy*.

Gantz, J. and D. Reinsel (2012), "The digital universe in 2020: Big data, bigger digital shadows, and biggest growth in the Far East", IDC Iview, IDC, Framingham, Massachusetts, *www.emc.com/collateral/analyst-reports/idc-the-digital-universe-in-2020.pdf*.

Glassman, A. (2014), "Delivering on the data revolution in sub-Saharan Africa", Views from the Center, Global Health Policy Blog, Center for Global Development, Washington, DC, *www.cgdev.org/publication/delivering-data-revolution-sub-saharan-africa-0*.

Green, M. (2013), "We must end the world's data divide", *The Guardian*, 1 November, *www.theguardian.com/news/datablog/2013/nov/01/we-must-end-the-worlds-data-divide*.

Internet World Stats (2017), "Internet penetration in Africa, March 31, 2017", *www.internetworldstats.com/stats1.htm.*

Isson, J.P. and H.S. Jesse (2016), *People Analytics in the Era of Big Data: Changing the What You Attract, Acquire, Develop, and Retain Talent*, Wiley, *http://eu.wiley.com/WileyCDA/WileyTitle/productCd-1119050782.html.*

Melamed, C. (2014), "Development data: How accurate are the figures?", *The Guardian*, 31 January, *www.theguardian.com/global-development/poverty-matters/2014/jan/31/data-development-reliable-figures-numbers.*

ODW (2016), "The state of development data funding report", Open Data Watch, *http://opendatawatch.com/wp-content/uploads/2016/09/development-data-funding-2016.pdf.*

OECD (2017), OECD Broadband Portal, *www.oecd.org/sti/broadband/oecdbroadbandportal.htm#map.*

PARIS21 (2015), *A Road Map for a Country-led Data Revolution*, OECD, Paris, *http://datarevolution.paris21.org/sites/default/files/Road_map_for_a_Country_led_Data_Revolution_web.pdf.*

Pullinger, J. (2017), "In a post-truth world, statistics could provide an essential public service", *The Guardian*, 31 January, *www.theguardian.com/commentisfree/2017/jan/31/post-truth-statistics-data-facts.*

Round, J.I. (2014), "Assessing the demand and supply of statistics in the developing world: Some critical factors", *PARIS21 Discussion Paper*, No. 4, Partnership in Statistics for Development in the 21st Century, Paris, *www.paris21.org/sites/default/files/PARIS21-DiscussionPaper4-Demand.pdf.*

Social Weather Stations (n.d.), Social Weather Stations website, *www.sws.org.ph/swsmain/home.*

The Economist (2017), "Data is giving rise to a new economy", *The Economist*, 6 May, *www.economist.com/news/briefing/21721634-how-it-shaping-up-data-giving-rise-new-economy.*

The Economist (2017), "The world's most valuable resource is no longer oil, but data", *The Economist*, 6 May, *www.economist.com/news/leaders/21721656-data-economy-demands-new-approach-antitrust-rules-worlds-most-valuable-resource.*

The Economist (2014), "Rich countries are deluged with data; Developing ones are suffering from drought", *The Economist*, 13 November, *www.economist.com/news/international/21632520-rich-countries-are-deluged-data-developing-ones-are-suffering-drought.*

The Lancet (2015), "Towards 2030: Counting and accountability matter", Vol. 386, 3 October, *www.thelancet.com/pdfs/journals/lancet/PIIS0140-6736(15)00396-7.pdf.*

UN (2017), "Progress towards the Sustainable Development Goals, Report of the Secretary-General", E/2017/66, United Nations Economic and Social Council, New York, *https://unstats.un.org/sdgs/files/report/2017/secretary-general-sdg-report-2017–Statistical-Annex.pdf.*

UNECA (2016), "The Africa data revolution report 2016: Highlighting developments in African data ecosystems", United Nations Economic Commission for Africa, *www.africa.undp.org/content/rba/en/home/library/reports/the_africa_data_revolution_report_2016.html.*

UNICEF (2013), "Every child's birth right: Inequities and trends in birth registration", United Nations Children's Fund, New York, *www.unicef.org/publications/files/Birth_Registration_11_Dec_13.pdf.*

UNSC (2017), "Cape Town Global Action Plan for Sustainable Development Data", United Nations Statistics Commission, New York, *http://unstats.un.org/sdgs/hlg/Cape-Town-Global-Action-Plan.*

UN Global Pulse (2013), "Big data for development: A primer", United Nations Global Pulse, *www.unglobalpulse.org/sites/default/files/Primer%202013_FINAL%20FOR%20PRINT.pdf.*

United Nations Sustainable Development Knowledge Platform (2015), "Progress of Goal 17", *https://sustainabledevelopment.un.org/sdg17.*

World Bank/WHO (2014), "Global civil registration and vital statistics: Scaling up investment plan 2015-24", The World Bank, Washington, DC, *http://documents.worldbank.org/curated/en/457271468148160984/Global-civil-registration-and-vital-statistics-scaling-up-investment-plan-2015-24.*

PART I

Making data work for development

Development Co-operation Report 2017
Data for Development

PART I

Chapter 2

The value of data for development

by
William Hynes, New Approaches to Economic Challenges Unit, OECD

This chapter discusses how thinking on development and development co-operation have been informed by the availability and use of data, and what now needs to change to efficiently exploit traditional data sources and take advantage of new ones. It argues that the data revolution is contributing to three shifts in focus: from gross domestic product to multi-dimensional well-being; from aggregate to micro data; and from administrative data to smart data.

Life can only be understood backwards; but it must be lived forwards. (Søren Kierkegaard)

How do you know if an anti-poverty strategy is working if you don't know how many poor people there are? How do you know if a school or a clinic is the better investment if you have no information base with which to estimate or track their impact? Data and statistics provide the essential basis for understanding the practicalities of the development process, the interactions and feedbacks between different systems, and the factors that should shape decisions.

Data are also vital for answering larger questions about the development process. Identifying the factors behind differential rates of growth, development and well-being have been central questions of development economics. Proposed explanations include factors ranging from geography, history, institutions and culture to politics and governance. Another central debate has been over the role and importance of development co-operation in promoting economic growth. While some progress has been made on these deeper questions, neither debate has reached anything like closure, and many of the obstacles to resolving them stem from data limitations.

New and better data sources offer the opportunity to let questions determine the data to be obtained, instead of the data determining the questions that can be asked.

But what data? The quality, availability, timeliness and use of basic economic and demographic data remain deficient in many parts of the developing world. While progress is being made, much more work is needed to improve census and other population data which form the traditional basis for policy making. At the same time, completely new sources of data are emerging through telecommunications, social media and e-commerce. New and better data sources offer the opportunity to let questions determine the data to be obtained, instead of the data determining the questions that can be asked (Duflo, 2006: 2), and new sources are already leading to the emergence of new policy-oriented analytics (Dum and Johnson, 2016: 278).

From relying on gross domestic product to looking at multi-dimensional well-being

Modernisation theory, e.g. Rostow's theory of the five stages of economic growth, suggested that development progress occurred in a linear fashion. Structural transformation would see an evolution from an agricultural economy to a modern industrialised one. Data on returns to capital and structural transformation were key to tracking and guiding this progress. The model led to an almost exclusive focus in aid programmes on financing capital goods and infrastructural investment, which were considered essential in driving developing countries' rise through the stages of development.

Unfortunately, early aid-financed capital projects were sometimes premature in scale or technology and lacked provision for management and maintenance. Though projects gradually became more cost-effective and their successors were built with greater attention to long-term feasibility, the perception grew that infrastructure spending had been relatively ineffective, especially in poor, narrowly based and vulnerable economies that had limited margin for error (OECD, 1985: 16).

Moreover, even by the end of the 1960s, it was realised that high rates of gross domestic product (GDP) growth had not made a real dent in the prevailing social conditions (Emmerij, 2002). The potential for a disconnect between GDP and welfare has long been recognised. Robert Kennedy observed almost 50 years ago that GDP "measures everything, except that which makes life worthwhile". At almost the same time, Gunnar Myrdal's vision that development was "the movement of the whole social system upwards" led to the prioritisation of basic human needs in the 1970s and the improvement of social data on health, education and poverty.

Measurement difficulties in developing countries exacerbate the problems of relying just on GDP to measure and understand progress. Morten Jerven (2013) highlighted the difficulties arising from a pervasive shadow economy, differing standards, errors and guestimates. He also highlighted the impact of rebasing – revising the methods and base data used to calculate GDP. For instance, Ghana rebased in 2010, and the GDP estimate rose by 62%. Nigeria rebased in 2014, the GDP figure rose by 89%, and Kenya saw a 25% rise after rebasing in 2014. The revisions took into account formerly omitted economic activities performed by informal businesses, as well as recent booms in several sectors, such as information and communications technologies, telecommunications, banking, and real estate. This provided a much more precise assessment of the economies' current sizes and of the contributions of different sectors to GDP, but rendered historical data practically unusable (Sy, 2015).

Any measure is, by definition, a quantity that is at best only roughly correlated with quality of life as it is actually experienced by individuals.

By many measures, especially those having to do with material sufficiency, the average person's quality of life has clearly improved over the past 100 years. By others, especially those having to do with the environment, social harmony and individual fulfilment, the quality of life may well have declined. But any measure is, by definition, a quantity that is at best only roughly correlated with quality of life as it is actually experienced by individuals. Similarly, the Pearson Report (1969) argued that economic statistics alone could not give a true comparison between the living standards and satisfaction of a tenant in a high-rise housing development in a packed and polluted megalopolis and those of a village in sunny Ceylon.

Sen (1989) has long criticised the danger of using one number to try to capture the breadth of the development experience. He conceptualised development as having the capabilities to live the kind of life one values, for example in terms of political freedom, economic facilities, social opportunities, transparency guarantees and protective security. In his way of thinking, development is not about what you have, but about what you can do. The UN Human Development Index (HDI), first published in 1990, took this approach forward with its three components of life expectancy, literacy/schooling and GDP per capita. Subsequent UNDP reports tweaked the measure and added further indices such as Inequality adjusted HDI, the Gender Inequality Index and Multidimensional Poverty Index, but the very proliferation of these indexes testifies to the difficulty of capturing overall well-being with any single metric.

More sophisticated measures of welfare, such as the OECD's Better Life Index, now allow users to establish their own priorities among dimensions of well-being, and construct international comparisons accordingly. But data limitations severely constrain such approaches in all but the most advanced developing countries. Even tracking such basic well-being objectives as those contained in the Millennium Development Goals proved a major challenge. According to a report by an independent UN advisory group, the availability of annual data on 55 core indicators for 157 countries never exceeded 70%. The Sustainable Development Goals (SDGs) now pose a much larger data

In my view:
We need to rebalance the political economy of statistics

Morten Jerven,
Professor, Norwegian University of Life Sciences

The Sustainable Development Goals (SDGs) have launched us into a new era of global development measurement and monitoring in a world increasingly focused on gauging progress against quantifiable targets. Yet data remain unavailable or scarce for many SDG indicators. The global demand for data often overshoots the capacity of national governments to supply statistics, putting pressure on their national statistical offices. The resulting stress lessens their survey capacity even further, hampering their efforts to collect, report and disseminate data.

The resulting distortion of our knowledge base on data for development is double-edged: we know less than we need to about poor countries; but our knowledge is even slimmer when it comes to the poor people who live in these countries. These knowledge gaps result from problems at various levels. At the design level, there is a lack of compatibility between statistical categories that were conceived for industrialised societies and the developing contexts they are applied to. At the implementation level, lack of capacity and poor record keeping in national statistical offices, compounded by other challenges, make the transaction costs of recording certain activities much higher than the value of the activities themselves. Numbers and indicators are especially inadequate in the least developed countries.

This has implications for the "political economy of statistics". Different data benefit different actors. The question that needs to be asked is: do the data needed for global monitoring of development constrain or benefit the supply of information for the priorities and policy making of developing countries? It is, of course, perfectly conceivable that the international demand for data may have a direct positive impact on the provision of data for national policy and planning. For instance, if a country agrees to receive financial and technical support for a labour force survey, the survey may yield labour data for the providers of the support that is also useful for the formulation of national industrial or other policy.

Yet in many cases, the data collected for global monitoring may have little or no usefulness for national policy making. Using the example above, the data gathered for global monitoring may be based on a single-occupation approach, making it irrelevant for national policy making in countries where the labour market is predominantly seasonal; or the data may not be available in a timely enough fashion, reducing their impact on policy (e.g. a survey for the year 2011 may only become available in 2014). In countries with scarce national resources, global monitoring may even have a negative impact, diverting funding from national data priorities to fulfil needs for global monitoring.

In my view, it is important to rebalance the political economy of statistics. To begin with, donors must work towards the sustainable supply of statistics – rather than simply demanding more data for current monitoring needs. Second, countries must be assertive in managing the supply of statistics while investing in statistics that are coherent with their own national priorities. Finally, coherence in the formulation of statistical policy is essential. Investment in monitoring for the sake of monitoring is unsustainable.

challenge as they recognise a broader range of well-being dimensions and greatly extend the scope of measurement. Strong statistical systems that can measure and create incentives for progress across the goals will be essential. There are estimates that USD 1 billion a year will be required to enable 77 of the world's lower income countries to catch up and put in place statistical systems capable of supporting and measuring the SDGs (SDSN, 2015).

From the general picture using macro-level aggregates to specific cases using micro data

The "Washington Consensus" which dominated development policy during the 1980s and early 1990s was based on empirical evidence documenting superior economic performance of countries – at least as measured by GDP – that established and maintained outward-oriented market economies subject to macroeconomic discipline. This approach led to structural adjustment programmes for developing countries under which aid and other financial flows were made conditional on applying policies such as trade liberalisation and privatisation.

The overall success or failure of these programmes has been disputed, but it is clear that targeting aggregate outcomes often led to policy mistakes. Simplistic notions of social aggregates as the mere sum of individual data on people, households or organisations are problematic. Such "black-box" data do not take into account all the complex interactions characterising social systems, may downplay rises in inequalities, and may overestimate past trends and underestimate the likelihood of extreme events (Omerod, 2016).

The initial statistical case for the approach has also been questioned, despite early claims that cross-country regression analysis had established "proof [that] may not be quite as conclusive as the proof that the Earth is not flat, [yet]...is sufficiently well established as to give sensible people better things to do with their time than to challenge its veracity" (Williamson, 1993: 1330). Even in the early 1980s, Leamer (1983) suggested that hardly anyone took such data analysis seriously, while Rodrik (2012) has asserted more recently that standard cross-country regressions tell us nothing about the effectiveness of policy.

Even such a basic question as the impact of official development assistance on growth has received no consensual answer from analysis of macro aggregates.

Even such a basic question as the impact of official development assistance on growth has received no consensual answer from analysis of macro aggregates. The number of cross-country empirical studies attempting to measure the contribution of aid to economic growth has proliferated, but they are plagued by conceptual and methodological challenges. Roodman (2007) states that while aid has eradicated diseases, prevented famines and done many other good things, its effects on growth, given the limited and noisy data available, probably cannot be detected.

But while faith in cross-country regression and macro-level analysis has been dented, advances have been made at the micro level – the level of decision making by individual agents. Improved collection methods have enabled detailed analysis of trends and correlations among individual households, while advances in computer power have speeded up data collection and publication (Deaton, 1996). At the same time, the rise of behavioural and experimental economics has made the discipline much more empirical (Omerod, 2016).

Moreover, Angrist and Pischke (2010) argue that the design of research programmes has improved by using random assignment, where results are compared between groups that received and did not receive defined interventions. They cite the evaluation of a pioneering effort to improve child welfare, the Progresa programme in Mexico. This offered cash transfers to randomly selected mothers, contingent on participation in prenatal care, nutritional monitoring of children and the children's regular school attendance. The positive evaluation of Progresa is one reason why 30 countries worldwide now have conditional cash transfer programmes.

Progresa was emblematic of a wave of random assignment policy evaluations sweeping development economics. Randomised control trials (RCTs) are now extensively used to measure the impact of development interventions. Experiments have been undertaken to assess the effectiveness of micro-credit, and programmes targeting poverty, health and education. While useful, RCTs have their critics based on cost, ethics (withholding beneficial treatments from poor people) and external validity of the findings. RCTs have provided good evidence and arguments about the difficulties of empirically identifying causal impacts of policies and programmes without experimental data (Pritchett, 2014).

Empirical work in this spirit has produced a credibility revolution in development economics over the past 20 years (Angrist and Pischke, 2010) and RCTs have led to the development of a range of datasets at the micro level. Development economics has been strongly influenced by this method and indeed there are claims that the "best and brightest talent of a generation of development economists has been devoted to producing rigorous impact evaluations".[1] Yet the approach may not be a panacea. Critics warn it can lead to the selection of topics which are easy to randomise and to a "randomise or bust" attitude whereby many interesting research questions are ignored if they cannot be made the subject of a randomised trial (McKenzie, 2016).

From data for administration to data to improve lives

There has been a vast increase in the availability and quality of data from developing countries in recent years – measures of births and deaths, growth and poverty, taxes and trade, land and the environment, health, schooling, and the other data upon which national statistical systems are built. They are essential for statistical baselines, government administration and planning as well as resource allocation.

Maintaining and accelerating this progress will be essential to guide development policies. A basic requirement is to conduct a regular census, because estimates based on population growth models often turn out to be off target when new population census estimates are made available (Jerven, 2013). However, census data remain deficient in sub-Saharan Africa, in part due to limitations in technical know-how and qualified human resources, but also because of the barriers created by misaligned political and institutional incentives among governments and donors.

Some progress has been made in improving household surveys. But the data revolution can accelerate progress and dramatically improve the quality of the data. Rather than relying on surveys every few years to calculate the mortality rate, systems of civil registration and vital statistics can collect mortality data in real time, with the added benefit of information on cause of death (Sachs, 2015). Similarly, data on poverty could be collected in a low-cost way and with much higher frequency than today by using smartphones to replace paper-based surveys. Researchers with the UN Sustainable Development Solutions Network calculated that the use of mobile phones could bring down the cost of surveys by up to 60% in some east African countries over a ten-year period (SDSN, 2015). Scientists analysed data from billions of phone calls and text messages from 1.5 million subscribers to Rwanda's largest mobile phone network and combined this with phone surveys. The wealth and poverty maps their system generated agreed with those made using detailed surveys of the Rwandan population conducted in person by the Rwandan government (Blumenstock, Cadamuro and On, 2015).

The analysis of big data would allow decision makers to track development progress in real time, improve social protection, and understand where existing policies and programmes require adjustment.

The unprecedented innovations in data collection techniques and technologies have the capacity to distribute data widely and freely. A dense ecosystem of technologies – remote sensing and satellite imagery, biometric data, GIS tracking, facilities-based data, social media, crowd-sourcing, and other channels – has the power to integrate many different data sources. Fully exploiting the benefits will require collaboration between private companies and traditional public sector statistical offices to accelerate data collection. The companies are already collecting masses of data – indeed their business models are based on big data compiled by collecting information about individuals, including those living in developing countries.

The analysis of big data would allow decision makers to track development progress in real time, improve social protection, and understand where existing policies and programmes require adjustment. It presents a tremendous opportunity to gain richer, deeper insights that can complement the development indicators that are already collected. At the most general level, big data can provide snapshots of the well-being of populations at high frequency, high degrees of granularity, and from a wide range of angles, narrowing both time and knowledge gaps. Practically, analysing these data may provide real-time awareness of the status of a population and real-time feedback on the effectiveness of policy actions should in turn lead to a more agile and adaptive approach to international development, and ultimately, to greater resilience and better outcomes.

A true data revolution would draw on both existing and new sources of data to integrate statistics fully into decision making; promote open access to, and use of, data; and ensure increased support for statistical systems.

The OECD is supporting a broader effort to expand access to "smart data" – this includes big data as well as facilitating the use of administrative, commercial and geo-spatial data. The aim is to replace expensive survey collections while respecting privacy and confidentiality, and to develop new measures that will provide information on key aspects of well-being, such as trust, governance, the quality of the working environment, social connections, work-life balance and mental health.

Many of these new indicators may also help fill key information gaps to monitor the 17 goals and 169 targets of the SDGs. An OECD study has already measured the distance to SDG targets,[2] which has helped guide many countries in developing their national SDG implementation plans and reporting strategies, but this work also highlighted the extent of information gaps. Even for OECD countries, only 57% of the SDG targets could be monitored with the available indicators, and even these were not necessarily available for all countries and years.

Stronger government systems, and in particular strong statistical systems that can measure and incentivise progress across the 17 goals, will be essential. Donors have traditionally spent little on supporting national data systems, although human resources are in short supply and many countries lack trained statisticians and data scientists (Melamed, 2016). Investments in data can pay off – in Liberia, a government survey to assess the country's water points proved invaluable in deciding where to set up health clinics to deal with the Ebola crisis.

Conclusions

Governments have been collecting data for millennia, but until recently the essential purpose was to assess what the population could do for them, particularly as regards taxes or military service. With the shift away from government "of the people" to government "for the people", data needs have changed. This is reflected in the nature of the goals that data must now help us achieve, such as improving well-being and the SDGs' focus on "leaving no one behind". Likewise, the OECD's New Approaches to Economic Challenges (NAEC) and Better Lives Initiatives aim to put well-being at the centre of policy advice, and to take account of the trade-offs, spillovers and alternatives related to any decision.

This means developing new metrics. A simple, one-figure measure like GDP cannot capture the multifaceted mix of objective and subjective factors that contribute to well-being. A range of different kinds of data are central to our understanding of the development process and for assessing the effectiveness of development policies and programmes beyond GDP growth. Their value though depends on their quality, representativeness and how they are used. The quality and availability of data used for development purposes has expanded and the data revolution holds out the promise of better administration and governance. Advances in technology have opened up new sources of information as well as analytical innovations. This is set to continue and will increasingly help development actors to prepare for an uncertain future of mounting global challenges and environmental pressures.

Data have already helped us understand backwards – they now may prepare policy makers in the developing world to live forward.

Policy messages

- Policy making can be improved by exploiting the massive streams of data generated by new technologies.
- However, technical and analytical capacities have to be updated.
- New measures beyond GDP are needed to capture well-being, and the data revolution can help provide this, given sufficient investment.

Notes

1. Esther Duflo has pointed out that in 2000 the top 5 journals published 21 articles on development, of which none were RCTs, while in 2015 there were 32, of which 10 were RCTs, meaning that virtually all the growth in development papers in top journals came from RCTs.
2. *www.oecd.org/std/measuring-distance-to-the-sdgs-targets.htm.*

References

Angrist, J.D. and J.S. Pischke (2010), "The credibility revolution in empirical economics: How better research design is taking the con out of econometrics", *Journal of Economic Perspectives*, Vol. 24/2, pp. 3-30.

Blumenstock, J., G. Cadamuro and R. On (2015), "Predicting poverty and wealth from mobile phone metadata", *Science*, Vol. 350/6264, pp. 1073-1076, *http://dx.doi.org/10.1126/science.aac4420.*

Deaton, A. (1996), *The Analysis of Household Surveys: A Microeconometric Approach to Development Policy*, The World Bank, Washington, DC, *http://documents.worldbank.org/curated/en/593871468777303124/The-analysis-of-household-surveys-a-microeconometric-approach-to-development-policy.*

Duflo, E. (2006), "Field experiments in development economics", in: Blundell, R., W. Newey and T. Persson (eds.), *Advances in Economics and Econometrics: Theory and Applications*, Ninth World Congress, Cambridge University Press.

Dum, R. and J. Johnson (2016), "Global systems science and policy", in: Johnson, J. et al. (eds.), *Non-Equilibrium Social Science and Policy: Introduction and Essays on New and Changing Paradigms in Socio-Economic Thinking*, Springer, Cham, Switzerland.

Emmerij, L. (2002), "Aid as a flight forward", *Development and Change*, Vol. 33/2, pp. 247-260, *http://dx.doi.org/10.1111/1467-7660.00251.*

Jerven, M. (2013), *Poor Numbers*, Cornell University Press, London and Ithaca.

Leamer, E. (1983), "Let's take the con out of econometrics", *The American Economic Review*, Vol. 73/1, pp. 31-43, *www.jstor.org/stable/1803924.*

McKenzie, D. (2016), "Have RCTs taken over development economics", World Bank Impact Evaluations Blog, *https://blogs.worldbank.org/impactevaluations/have-rcts-taken-over-development-economics.*

Melamed, C. (2016), "Data for development", in: *Sustainable Development Goals 2016*, Witan Media, London.

OECD (1985), *Development Co-operation Report*, OECD Publishing, Paris.

Omerod, P. (2016), "Economics", in: Johnson, J. et al. (eds.), *Non-Equilibrium Social Science and Policy: Introduction and Essays on New and Changing Paradigms in Socio-Economic Thinking*, Springer, Cham, Switzerland.

Pearson Report (1969), *Partners in Development: Report of the Commission on International Development*, Pall Mall Press, London.

Pritchett, L. (2014), "An homage to the randomistas on the occasion of the J-PAL 10th anniversary: Development as a faith-based activity", Centre for Global Development Blog, *www.cgdev.org/blog/homage-randomistas-occasion-j-pal-10th-anniversary-development-faith-based-activity*.

Rodrik, D. (2012), "Why we learn nothing from regressing economic growth on policies", *Seoul Journal of Economics*, Vol. 25, pp. 137-151.

Roodman, D. (2007), "The anarchy of numbers: Aid, development, and cross-country empirics", *World Bank Economic Review*, Vol. 21/2, pp. 255-277, *www.cgdev.org/publication/anarchy-numbers-aid-development-and-cross-country-empirics-working-paper-32*.

Sachs, J. (2015), "Data for development", Project Syndicate Blog, *www.project-syndicate.org*.

SDSN (2015), "Data for development: A needs assessment for SDG monitoring and statistical capacity development", United Nations Sustainable Development Solutions Network, *http://unsdsn.org/wp-content/uploads/2015/04/Data-for-Development-Full-Report.pdf*.

Sen, A. (1989), *Development as Freedom*, Anchor Books (Random House Inc.), New York.

Sy, A. (2015), "Are African countries rebasing GDP in 2014 finding evidence of structural transformation?", Brookings Africa in Focus Blog, *www.brookings.edu/blog/africa-in-focus/2015/03/03/are-african-countries-rebasing-gdp-in-2014-finding-evidence-of-structural-transformation*.

Williamson, J. (1993), "From reform agenda to damaged brand name", *Finance & Development*, Vol. 40/3, *www.imf.org/external/pubs/ft/fandd/2003/09/pdf/williams.pdf*.

Development Co-operation Report 2017
Data for Development

PART I

Chapter 3

The role of national statistical systems in the data revolution

by
Shaida Badiee, Johannes Jütting, Deirdre Appel, Thilo Klein *and* Eric Swanson*

The supply of relevant, timely and usable data is essential for countries to set priorities, make informed choices and implement better policies for sustainable development. This chapter looks at how national statistical systems in developing countries can and should harness the data revolution. It explores the opportunities, enablers and challenges countries face in using big data and other new sources of data. The chapter reviews developing country capacity, gaps and strategies for putting in place the right data for policy making. It also presents selected examples of how the data revolution is already fuelling better statistics in developing countries. The chapter considers the role of governments as well as the opportunities offered by public-private partnerships. It enumerates the key conditions for building capable statistical systems and proposes steps to be taken by national statistical offices, policy makers and international development partners.

* Shaida Badiee, Deirdre Appel and Eric Swanson from Open Data Watch; and Johannes Jütting and Thilo Klein from PARIS21.

Key facts

- The 2010 Population Census Round, conducted between 2005 and 2014, was one of the great successes of national and international statistical efforts. Only 21 countries did not conduct a census (UNFPA, 2016a). An estimated 6.4 billion people (93% of the world's population) were enumerated (UNFPA, 2016b).
- The 2020 census round has already begun. Thirty-nine countries (including some that missed earlier rounds) are expected to prepare for or conduct censuses in 2017; some 200 more will need to complete censuses between 2018 and 2024.
- Many low and middle-income countries are using outdated base years for national accounts and price statistics while the lack of recent agricultural surveys or censuses limit their ability to produce reliable economic statistics.
- According to the World Health Organization's Global Health Observatory, "Only 34 countries – representing 15% of the world population – produce high-quality cause-of-death data… A further 85 countries – representing 65% of the world population – produce lower quality cause-of-death data, while 75 countries lack such data altogether" (WHO, n.d.).
- To seize the opportunities presented by the data revolution, statistical offices will need to invest in new technology and production processes and establish partnerships with new actors.

Advances in the ability to manage, exchange, combine and analyse data of all types, and to disseminate statistical information on line, are changing the way traditional statistical processes are carried out. National statistical offices can and should play a critical role in harnessing the data revolution for sustainable development. To be effective in stimulating data use and evidence-based decision making, they must also improve data accessibility by adopting open data policies.

However, there are still large differences in the capabilities of statistical systems. Despite some progress made over the past decade, many countries still lack the means and infrastructure to produce high-quality data. To enable national statistical systems to respond to the demands of data users, notably policy makers, it is critical that providers of development co-operation and developing countries alike increase their support for national statistical offices, strengthen the use and production of statistics, and change their mind-sets towards producing and using more open, transparent and action-oriented data.

The data revolution is fuelling better data in developing countries

The size and scope of the data revolution can be gauged by the exponential increase of on line digital information; by the growth of new occupations described as data scientist, data activist or data evangelist; and by the manifold impacts of digital information on our daily lives. Revolutions are, by their nature, disruptive, and the data revolution has already disrupted traditional modes of production, human interaction and public discourse. Yet a revolution can also overcome enduring barriers and solve long-standing problems, bringing benefits to people previously left out, left behind or forgotten.

> *The data revolution has the potential to transform the operations of national statistical systems in rich and poor countries alike.*

The data revolution has the potential to transform the operations of national statistical systems in rich and poor countries alike. It is often described in terms of the vast increase in the volume of digital data, called "big data", but it is more than big data. Innovative technologies have decreased the cost and increased the speed of data collection and data dissemination, responding to the growing demand for actionable, empirical information. When, for example, a World Bank project in Guatemala used entry-level mobile phones and free web-based software for data collection, it cut the average cost per interview by 71%. The project could, as a result of lower costs, increase the survey's sample size from 200 to 700 respondents, including from remote and marginalised areas highly populated by indigenous people, making the survey nationally representative.[1]

There are signs that the national statistical systems of developing countries are already embracing the data revolution and starting to make use of new technologies and methods. Far from being reluctant followers, many statistical offices are enthusiastic leaders. The following examples illustrate the exciting opportunities for development partners to engage in new and fruitful enterprises.

Combining traditional and unconventional data sources can fill statistical gaps

The United Nations (UN) Global Working Group on Big Data for Official Statistics is working with countries and their private sector partners to demonstrate the use of unconventional data sources to supplement official statistics. While many projects are still in the pilot phase, they are already demonstrating that insights can be obtained by combining data from traditional sources – such as censuses, surveys or administrative data – with information from new, big data sources. Statistics South Africa, for example, is assessing the use of detailed scanner data from retail chains as inputs to the consumer price index (GWG, 2017a). Statistics Canada is investigating the use of data from smart metres to track electricity consumption (GWG, 2017b). The World Bank Group is partnering with the government of Colombia to assess use of call detail records to measure income and inequality (GWG, 2017c).

Geospatial data can help to include people who have been overlooked

The Data2X report, "Big data and the well-being of women and girls" (Data2X, 2017), illustrates the use of a large, geospatial database to improve the understanding of stunting, literacy and access to contraceptives in Bangladesh, Haiti, Kenya, Nigeria and the United Republic of Tanzania. Because many types of social and health data correlate with physical phenomena – such as elevation, land cover, and distance to roads and schools – it is possible to use geospatial data along with other sources of data to infer social and health conditions in communities not included in the sample design, ensuring that these groups are not left behind.

Innovative use of big data can improve Sustainable Development Goal outcomes

SDG Target 3.3 calls for the elimination of epidemic diseases, including malaria. Insecticide-treated bed nets offer a proven method of reducing malaria incidence, but it is expensive and ineffective to distribute bed nets widely in low-incidence areas. If measures are taken to protect privacy, big data can be used to identify target populations. In Namibia, the country's largest cell phone service provider shared anonymised call detail records for 1.2 million subscribers. This permitted the construction of maps documenting patterns of internal migration. To pinpoint areas with high risk of malaria infection, the data from these maps were combined with remote sensing data – collected by the Namibia National Vector-borne Diseases Control Programme – tracing the factors affecting the location of mosquitos. With this information in hand, Namibia's Ministry of Health can target the distribution of bed nets to the most likely sources of the spread of infections (Vaitla et al., 2017; Tatem et al., 2014).

Monitoring progress on half of the SDG targets depends on the availability of environmental statistics.

Citizen-generated data can help close gaps in environmental statistics

Monitoring progress on half of the SDG targets depends on the availability of environmental statistics, yet a large portion of the indicators under these targets require data that are not regularly produced by countries. It may be possible to compensate for these significant gaps in environmental data by engaging citizens in data collection. A case study in the People's Republic of China is exploring the use of citizen-generated data to address traditionally intractable gaps in environmental statistics, highlighting the possibilities and challenges (Hsu, Weinfurter and Yan, 2017).

New technologies can improve census and survey data collection

Another example of the application of new technology to generate statistics is the use of computer-assisted personal interview (CAPI) devices – such as tablet computers or other handheld devices – to improve the efficiency and accuracy of census and survey data collection. There are numerous examples of the transition to CAPI in developing countries, including Uganda's National Panel Survey in 2011/12; Ethiopia's Rural Socioeconomic Survey in 2013/14; South Africa's Community Survey in 2016; and Sri Lanka's pilot in 2017 using CAPI with sample surveys.

The preceding examples illustrate just some of the many opportunities presented by the data revolution. To seize these opportunities, however, statistical offices will need to invest in new technology and production processes; they will also need to establish partnerships with new actors from the private sector, the media and academia. Too many statistical offices are not yet in a position to benefit from these opportunities as they are under-resourced, have limited capacity, and are unable to obtain the skilled staff or the equipment needed.

It is time to create a virtuous data cycle

Securing the investments needed to improve data production will depend on a clear demonstration of the value of data.

Now is the time to make a big push for investments in better data. The poorest and least-equipped statistical systems are fully dependent on external support and struggle to produce the data needed to advance their societies. In these countries, the use of statistics by policy makers remains limited, leading to uninformed decision making that generates poor development outcomes. Indeed, national statistical systems are often trapped in a vicious cycle of statistical under-development, where limited awareness and appreciation of the importance of data – by policy makers and at all levels of society – has led to sustained under-funding for statistics. This vicious cycle needs to be turned into a virtuous one (Figure 3.1). For example, efforts in planning and production will only create value for society if they are followed by strong data dissemination, and if users understand and use the available information. Similarly, securing the investments needed to improve data production will depend on a clear demonstration of the value of data.

Figure 3.1. **The virtuous data cycle**

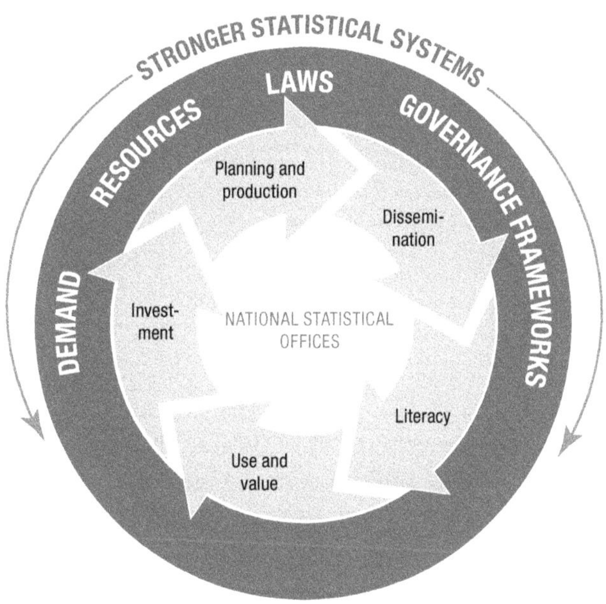

Source: OECD, based on PARIS21 and Open Data Watch.

The following section outlines various aspects of this virtuous cycle in detail, starting with the challenges emerging from the SDGs and the need to adjust national development and statistical plans to meet them.

The data challenges of the Sustainable Development Goals are both global and local

Recognising the importance of quality data for guiding social, economic and environmental policies, the high-level panel commissioned to make recommendations for the United Nations'

2030 Agenda for Sustainable Development proposed an ambitious programme of goals and targets, to be monitored using statistical indicators:

> The indicators that track them should be disaggregated to ensure no one is left behind and targets should only be considered "achieved" if they are met for all relevant income and social groups. We recommend that any new goals should be accompanied by an independent and rigorous monitoring system, with regular opportunities to report on progress and shortcomings at a high political level. We also call for a data revolution for sustainable development, with a new international initiative to improve the quality of statistics and information available to citizens. (UN, 2013: iv)

This vision of a data-driven programme of action to bring about "transformative shifts" in the well-being of people and the condition of the planet is embodied in the 17 SDGs, which comprise 169 targets and 232 indicators across a range of economic, social and environmental domains. This is a considerable step up from the 8 Millennium Development Goals (MDGs), which included 21 targets and 60 indicators, and puts pressure on countries to respond. Recognising these challenges, the Global Partnership for Sustainable Development Data (GPSDD), a broad coalition of governments, international agencies, non-governmental organisations and private sector firms, was established to help countries meet the challenges of monitoring the SDGs. The Data4SDGs Toolbox (GPSDD, n.d. *b*), for example, comprises a set of tools, methods and resources.

The 2015 report by the Sustainable Development Solutions Network (SDSN, 2015) lays out the programme of data collection and capacity development that will be needed to produce data for the core SDG indicators. It identifies six major categories of activity that are essential for producing SDG-relevant statistics: 1) national survey programmes; 2) decennial censuses; 3) administrative data, including civil registration and vital statistics systems; 4) economic statistics; 5) geospatial infrastructure; and 6) environmental monitoring. The investment and annual operating costs for 77 International Development Association (IDA)-eligible countries are estimated to be in the order of USD 925 million per year. When the cost of data collection to meet additional requirements for the SDGs is added to this figure, it brings the total to USD 1.2 billion per year (GPSDD, 2016).

In order to leave no one behind, data will have to be disaggregated by age, sex, disability and other relevant functional categories.

In addition to monitoring the sheer number of indicators comprised by the SDGs, **measuring progress towards these goals presents additional challenges to national statistical systems:**

- The need to compare data over time and to aggregate them across countries and regions requires adherence to common standards and methods. Where standards and methods already exist, baseline measurements are needed, coupled with an agreed programme of regular data collection. In addition, many of the proposed SDG indicators still lack clear definitions and may require new data collection instruments that will need to be tested and calibrated; staff will also require training in their use.
- To fulfil the SDGs' promise of leaving no one behind, data will have to be disaggregated by age, sex, disability status and other relevant functional categories. Administrative systems of central and local governments are important sources of information, which may be combined with data from censuses, surveys or new sources to provide more granular measurement and results. Some groups, such as nomadic populations, are difficult to reach and count accurately, especially if they move across borders. Other groups may live in areas affected by fragility, or with access to very limited communications.
- Developing countries face the challenge of producing more granular, local data related to each country's unique situation and challenges. The "data localisation" of the SDGs can be achieved only when the data revolution is accompanied by a capacity revolution that empowers data producers and users in developing countries to navigate through – and make full use of – the new emerging data ecosystem (see the "In my view" piece by Stefan Schweinfest).

In my view: We need a global data architecture for sustainable development

Stefan Schweinfest,
Director, United Nations Statistics Division

I was recently asked to name the three key elements of the data revolution. My answer was "capacity, capacity, capacity!"

The 2030 Agenda for Sustainable Development poses tremendous challenges for statisticians like me. At the same time, it offers an unprecedented opportunity. We need more data – covering all countries and relevant areas – more integrated data and disaggregated data.

In a remarkable effort, the global statistical community came together under the leadership of the United Nations (UN) Statistical Commission to develop a global indicator framework to underpin the new development goals and targets. Over the coming years, my office – the UN Statistics Division – will build a global data cube comprising 232 indicators for 193 countries over 15 years.

There are many reasons why achieving this is far from simple. Here, in my view, are what may be the two most important ones:

1. ***We need quality data and national ownership.***
   In addition to the usual standards of reliability, timeliness and relevance, in a global development database consistency is critical – over time, and over space. Only if data are sustained over time can we produce the series needed to measure what we truly wish to understand: development. And only if we apply consistent methodologies worldwide will we be able to compare countries and aggregate continents, ensuring that global support goes where it is most needed. Finally, only if politicians and people truly own and trust the data will they have the power to change policies and minds.
2. ***The global indicators are only the tip of the iceberg.***
   To realise the ambition of the 2030 Agenda, action will be needed at the local, subnational, national, regional, global and sectoral levels. This action has to be supported by data that are fit for purpose.

In my view, what is needed is a global data architecture, where data are produced at the local and national levels, reviewed for validity and then transported effectively to the various decision nodes.

What do we need to get there?

- investment in statistics and data at the national and international levels
- new methodologies and technical capacity building
- a transformation of national statistical systems to enable national statistical offices to play their new role as "chief data managers", co-ordinating and validating national information beyond official statistics and integrating geospatial information and big data
- a framework of knowledge-solidarity where diverse data stakeholders work together across the globe in an effective manner.

The recent UN resolution on the global indicator framework highlights all these elements. The UN High-Level Group for Partnership, Coordination and Capacity Building carries high ambitions in its name. Under its leadership, in January 2017 the first UN World Data Forum brought over 1 400 participants to Cape Town, South Africa to launch the Cape Town Global Action Plan, which addresses many of the challenges cited above.

I remain incurably optimistic. With this Cape Town Global Action Plan we are, collectively, on the right path. In this context, the partnership in statistics between the UN and the OECD, in particular the Statistics Directorate and the PARIS21 Secretariat, is key. I look forward to continuing this close and effective co-operation.

National statistical systems are the core of a larger, emerging data ecosystem

National statistical systems are ensembles of statistical organisations and units within a country that collect, process and disseminate "official statistics". Official statistics are derived from data produced by public bodies as part of their official function; they provide a record of the social, economic and environmental condition of the country. Governance of a national statistical system is determined by law and is regulated by adherence to professional standards (Box 3.1).

Box 3.1. **How are national statistical systems organised and governed?**

Typically, one unit within the national statistical system serves as the lead or co-ordinating agency. This agency is generically described as the national statistical office. To improve trust in data and ensure the independence and integrity of the national statistical system, the national statistical office should be structured as an autonomous body with a separate budget, accountable primarily to the legislature. In many countries, a designated board of governors or an advisory body provides independent advice on the standards and conduct of the national statistical office and the larger statistical system. When this office is not administratively autonomous, it may be located within the Ministry of Finance or Planning. Wherever situated, however, laws and regulations should protect statistical agencies from partisan influence.

National statistical systems are expected to be guided by the United Nations Fundamental Principles of Official Statistics (UNSC, 2014) and to govern themselves accordingly. Of the ten principles, Principle 1 describes the responsibility of statistical offices to make official statistics available to everyone: "Official statistics that meet the test of practical utility are to be compiled and made available on an impartial basis by official statistical agencies to honour citizens' entitlement to public information." Principle 2 speaks of maintaining trust in statistics through the exercise of professional and scientific judgement in the "collection, processing, storage, and presentation of statistical data". Principle 5 notes that "Data for statistical purposes may be drawn from all types of sources, be they statistical surveys or administrative records". Principle 6 states that individual data are to be kept "strictly confidential and used exclusively for statistical purposes".

The preamble to the Fundamental Principles tells us that "professional independence and accountability of statistical agencies are crucial", and that they "have to be guaranteed by legal and institutional frameworks and be respected at all political levels and by all stakeholders in national statistical systems". In most countries, specific legislation establishes the responsibilities of the national statistical office, its governance structure and its authority over the national statistical system (UNSD, 2013). National law should authorise national statistical offices to make data collection compulsory for certain purposes, to protect confidential information, and to release data or statistics in a form that preserves the privacy of individuals.

To respond to the call for greater transparency in government and to provide open access to data, countries may have to revise their statistical laws and regulations.

Source: Authors' compilation based on UNSC (2014), "Fundamental Principles of Official Statistics", *https://unstats.un.org/unsd/dnss/gp/fundprinciples.aspx* and UNSD (2013), "Implementation of the Fundamental Principles of Official Statistics", *http://unstats.un.org/unsd/statcom/doc13/BG-FP.pdf*.

In the past, the ecosystem of official statistics was limited to the national statistical system itself and the direct users of its outputs, principally other government agencies and a few non-governmental groups. International bodies set standards and provided an outlet for a limited set of statistics. In the context of the data revolution, however, national statistical systems operate increasingly as part of a larger, emerging data ecosystem. This data ecosystem is made up of multiple communities of data producers and users beyond the national statistical system, including civil society; the private sector; academic and scientific communities; as well as regional, international and UN agencies; and specialised data producers (Figure 3.2). The interactions among these

Figure 3.2. **The ecosystem of data production and use**

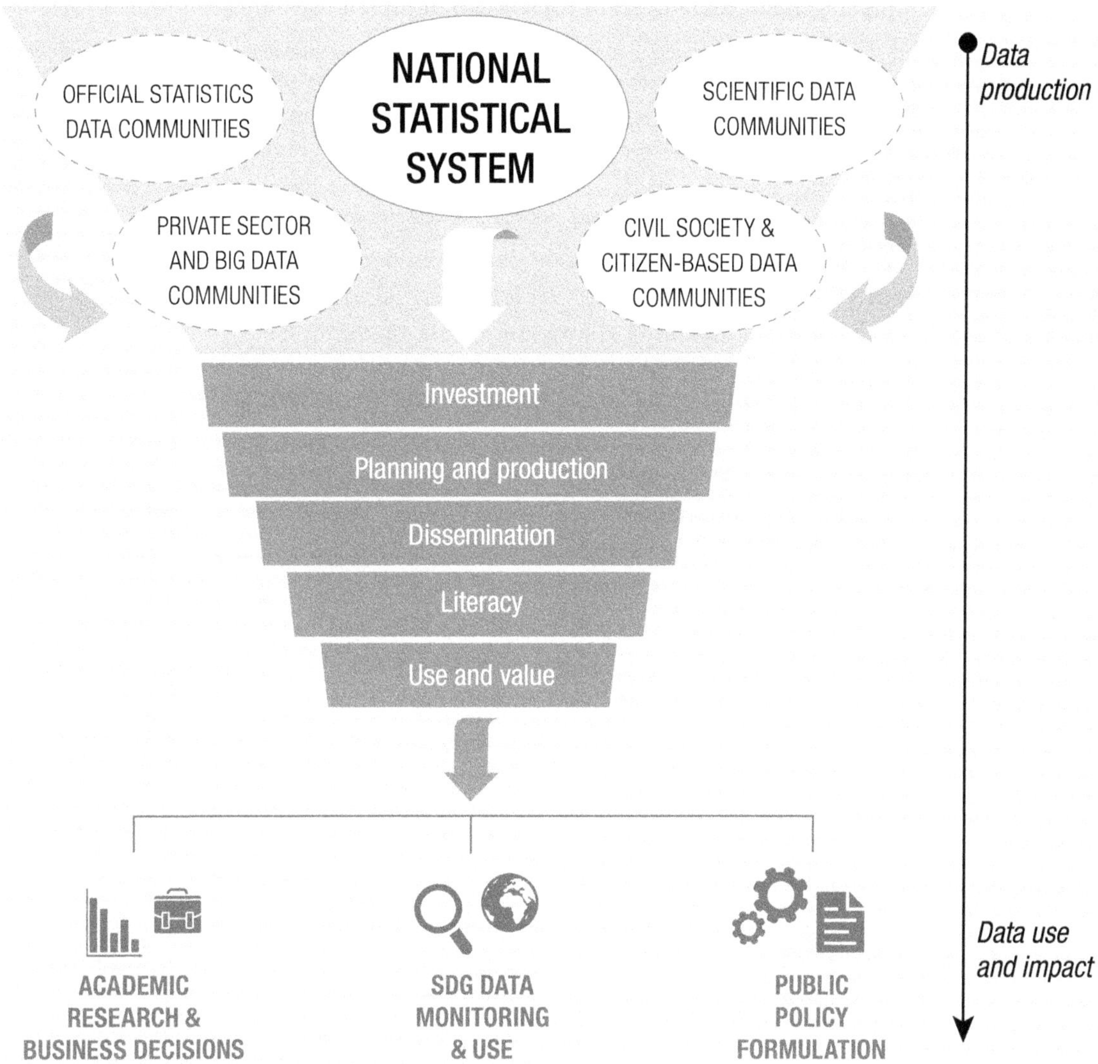

Source: Compiled by the authors, based on GPSDD (2016), "The state of development data funding 2016", *http://opendatawatch.com/wp-content/uploads/2016/09/development-data-funding-2016.pdf*.

communities are determined by each of their legal, political, technological and financial constraints, as well as by their shared interest in maximising the value of the data available to them through mutually beneficial exchanges.

Partnerships with new actors are essential to realise the full benefits of the data revolution and modernise national statistical systems.

As co-ordinators of their national statistical systems and custodians of large amounts of data, national statistical offices create value by overseeing the production of reliable statistics and by assisting others in the interpretation of those statistics. They play a critical role in leading the data revolution for sustainable development. As experts in the measurement of social, economic and environmental conditions, official statisticians deliver data that are trusted and useful for research, analysis and policy making. As independent agents committed to transparency and adherence to standards, national statistical offices ensure the quality of official statistics and engender trust in the policy-making process.

While national statistical offices remain at the centre of the data ecosystem, their role is changing as they reach out to new partners and adopt new methods. They may even find themselves working or competing with producers of data that are not part of the traditional remit of the national statistical system. In the future, these offices may become information brokers and "info-mediaries". In addition to their role as collectors and distributors of data, national statistical offices will actively co-ordinate work with non-governmental data producers, seeking the best sources of data to meet the needs of a variety of user communities. The national statistical office can also offer quality control services, advising on the correct implementation of standards and using data from censuses, surveys and administrative records to "ground-truth" estimates derived from big data or other non-standard sources. Partnerships with new data actors are essential to realise the full benefits of the data revolution and modernise the functions of national statistical systems.

Public-private partnerships for data can benefit business and the public good

As the data ecosystem expands and the demand for development data grows, taking advantage of new sources of data through public-private partnerships[2] can help fill existing data gaps. Private sector sources of non-official data – telecom data, social media, sensor and geospatial data – are gaining attention for their cost-effectiveness, timeliness, granularity and scope for constructing new indicators (Robin, Klein and Jütting, 2016). Harnessing the data, software and skillsets that the private sector can offer should be a top priority for national statistical offices and private actors alike.

Countries and businesses have recognised the potential benefits of public-private partnerships. For example, the Open Algorithms Project (OPAL)[3] is working with the telecom operators Orange Sonatel in Senegal and Telefónica in Colombia, employing big data analytics to mine telecom records in a manner that preserves privacy. In the OPAL model, algorithms developed by the co-operating partners are used to produce key development indicators in a secure environment controlled by the data owner.

Despite the recognised promise of public-private partnerships, however, there is still work to be done to find ways of navigating in this emerging space. For example, it is important to resolve issues concerning the perceived risks of sharing data and the protection of privacy. The World Economic Forum's "Data-driven development: Pathways for progress" report (2015) stresses the reluctance of many private actors to share their datasets because of these issues. National statistical offices, which already subscribe to high professional standards and have a good record of protecting confidentiality, have similar concerns. Mutually satisfactory solutions will increase the opportunities for public-private partnerships in the future. National statistical offices should take the lead in forging and sustaining public-private partnerships to improve the breadth and depth of official statistics. Although the legal and practical guidelines governing their interactions with private partners are still evolving, this should not stop them from engaging.

Klein and Verhulst have looked closely into how to incentivise the private sector to share their data. For example, benefits can accrue from working with national statistical offices, especially when this permits gaining access to official data sources that may be important to business decisions. Further incentives include "... the potential to develop new analytical skills, improve reputations, generate revenue, meet regulatory compliance measures and demonstrate corporate responsibility" (Klein and Verhulst, 2017: 8). Among many companies, there is growing recognition, albeit slowly, of the incentives for making data available for the public good (Klein, Galdin and Mohamedou, 2016).

All countries have room to increase statistical capacity, transparency and use

Harnessing the data revolution to achieve the ambitious SDGs will depend greatly on how national statistical systems respond to the challenges involved. They will need to:

- increase their capacity to produce timely and reliable data and statistics

- embrace a culture of openness, sharing data freely and forming partnerships with other data producers
- promote the use of data for decision making by engaging with users in and out of government and leading programmes to increase statistical literacy and use.

Despite 15 years of progress during the implementation of the MDGs, there remain large differences in the capabilities of national statistical systems to produce timely and reliable data and statistics.

Building statistical capacity is a long-term process

One way to understand the differences in capacity is to look at the statistical methods and data sources used by countries. For this report, we have selected 15 indicators from the World Bank's *Statistical Capacity Indicators* database (World Bank, 2017), which covers 131 low and middle-income countries: 10 indicators record the methodological standards employed to produce important datasets and 5 indicators record the timeliness or availability of data sources.[4] We rank the 131 countries according to their aggregate scores for methodological standards and indicators on data sources, grouping the countries into:

- low-capacity countries (51) ranking in the bottom third on one or both methodology and source measures
- mid-level capacity countries (50), ranking in the middle or upper third on one but not both of the measures
- high-capacity countries (30), ranking in the upper third on both measures.

Figure 3.3 shows the number of countries meeting basic standards for core statistical activities by capacity group. The analysis shows that most countries, whatever their capacity level (about 70% of the sample) lack complete civil registration and vital statistics systems, so many births and deaths go unrecorded. This means that demographic data must be estimated from models. It also means that many children lack birth certificates and that the causes of death go unreported. Many of these countries also lack data from national vaccination programmes that are consistent with World Health Organization standards, and are not able to report education statistics regularly to the United Nations Educational, Scientific and Cultural Organization.

Outdated statistics limit a country's ability to measure growth, productivity and poverty.

Outdated base years for national accounts and price statistics, as well as the lack of recent agricultural surveys or censuses, limit a country's ability to produce the reliable economic statistics needed to measure growth, productivity and poverty. In poorer countries, these surveys are often supported by bilateral providers of development co-operation or international organisations. But not all countries with weak capacity in this area are exceptionally poor: among the low-scoring countries for this type of data, almost one-third are classified as upper middle-income countries.

The countries that have a mid-level capacity score, for the most part, are able to conduct regular surveys, which combined with census and administrative data allow them to produce a range of sophisticated statistics, largely relying on their own resources. Still, more than 60% of these countries lack complete civil registration and vital statistics systems and almost 40% have outdated base years for their national accounts. This middle group can move to the next level by mobilising additional resources and adopting new methods and technologies, but they must also pay attention to their core statistical processes.

At the upper end are high-capacity countries. Most, but not all, are upper middle-income countries. Many have subscribed to the International Monetary Fund's Special Data Dissemination Standard, which sets criteria for their economic and financial statistics. They utilise data from multiple

Figure 3.3. **Number of countries with capacity to deliver fundamental statistics, 2016**

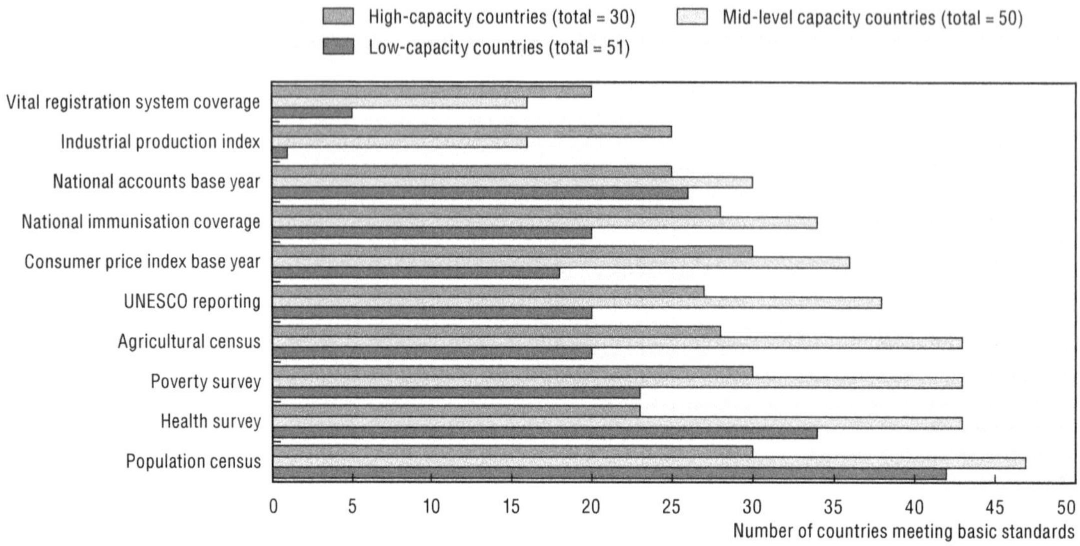

Source: Author's calculations based on World Bank (2017), *Statistical Capacity Indicators* (database), *http://databank.worldbank.org/data/reports.aspx?source=statistical-capacity-indicators#*.

StatLink http://dx.doi.org/10.1787/888933591803

sources and adopt new techniques to increase the scope and quality of their statistics; they also carry out their activities on a regular schedule, adhering to documented standards, and are largely financed by their own governments. Yet one-third of these countries still lack complete civil registration and vital statistics systems and one-quarter have not conducted a health survey in the past five years.

Increasing statistical capacity is a long-term process. It encompasses investing in people and institutions, and improving the environment in which national statistical offices work. The Partnership in Statistics for Development in the 21st Century (PARIS21) – a global partnership of data users and producers – has identified lessons for building statistical capacity. These include providing leadership training for senior management in national statistical offices, with specific components on change management and leadership; a more demand-led/user-driven focus in the data-production process; and a greater focus on the enabling environment, including governance structures.

Make data more open, transparent and accessible

To build trust in official statistics and increase their value, these should be provided to a wide audience in formats people can easily understand and use, at little or no cost. The report of the UN Secretary-General's Independent Expert Advisory Group, "A world that counts: Mobilizing the data revolution for sustainable development" (IEAG, 2014), called for open data standards to enable the data revolution to create a world of informed and empowered citizens who can hold decision makers accountable. The report recommends that all governments promote the release of open data – data that are available and useable by all data producers and statistical systems.

National statistical offices are joining the open data revolution by building partnerships with other statistical systems, civil society and the private sector.

Governments and their national statistical offices are joining the open data revolution by building partnerships with other statistical systems and with civil society and the private sector. For example, 22 national statistical offices shared their experiences in adopting international standards at the 2016 International Open Data Conference (OD4D, 2016). Sixteen national governments, including ten developing countries, have subscribed to the principles of the International Open Data

Charter (Box 3.2; ODC, n.d.) With the first principle governments commit to "develop and adopt policies and practices to ensure that all government data is made open by default..." Statistical offices can explicitly include open data in their national strategies for the development of statistics (PARIS21, n.d.) or in their SDG roadmaps (GPSDD, n.d. *a*).

Box 3.2. **Measuring openness through the Open Data Inventory**

The Open Data Charter defines open data as "... digital data that is made available with the technical and legal characteristics necessary for it to be freely used, reused, and redistributed by anyone, anytime, anywhere" (ODC, n.d.). Four principles define the technical characteristics of open data:

1. open by default
2. timely and comprehensive
3. accessible and usable
4. comparable and interoperable.

The Open Data Inventory (ODIN) applies similar criteria in assessing the coverage and openness of the statistics published by national statistical offices (Open Data Watch, 2017b).[1] The 2016 results show that all countries, from the poorest to the wealthiest, have room for improvement (Figure 3.4; Open Data Watch, 2017a). ODIN scores 173 countries on data coverage and openness in 20 data categories. The median country score in 2016 was 39, meaning that fewer than half the countries satisfied more than 39% of the ODIN criteria for data coverage and openness. Across all countries, ODIN scores ranged from 81 (Sweden) to 3 (Madagascar). While the high-income countries of Europe, North America and Asia achieved, on average, the highest scores, low and middle-income countries in many regions achieved higher results than their wealthier neighbours. Countries that have undertaken relatively simple reforms have made considerable improvements over the past years, but many have large deficits in coverage of important categories of statistics and have not taken the steps needed to make their data open.

Figure 3.4. **2016 Open Data Inventory average scores on data coverage and openness, by country income groups**

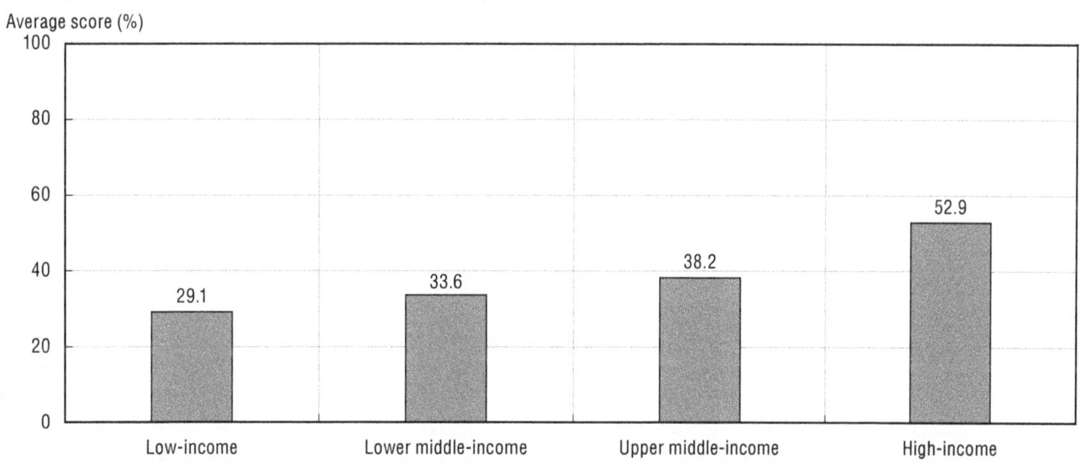

Source: Open Data Watch (2017a), "Data download", *2016 Open Data Inventory* (database), *http://odin.opendatawatch.com/data/download* (accessed 26 April 2017).

StatLink http://dx.doi.org/10.1787/888933591822

1. Two other indexes measure the openness of government data: the Open Data Barometer and the Global Open Data Index. However, these indexes include other types of data that are not usually within the provenance of national statistical systems, such as transportation timetables, mapping data, election outcomes and cadastral information.

Strengthen statistical literacy to increase the use of statistics

The power of data can only be realised when people can understand, analyse and explain them. Statistical literacy is often measured in terms of classroom statistical knowledge, but there are many other instances in which the ability to understand and use statistics is important.

Journalists play an important role by organising and interpreting statistical evidence. Klein, Galdin and Mohamedou (2016) argue that "… the writing of journalists can be seen as an image for a nation's demand for statistical facts as well as the depth of critical analysis". To assess the statistical literacy of journalists and journalists' expectations about the statistical literacy of their readers, Klein, Galdin and Mohamedou examined the use of statistics in newspaper articles in 32 countries and 4 languages, classifying 3 levels of sophistication.[5] Figure 3.5 shows the breakdown of scores by income group, based on the OECD Development Assistance Committee's (DAC) list of ODA recipients (OECD, n.d.). The results indicate a wide range of statistical literacy, from 2.5 in Chad to 28.6 in the Philippines. They also show that statistical literacy is not necessarily determined by national income; for example, lower middle-income countries with strong statistical institutes, such as the Philippines, rank very high on this index. The Philippines Statistics Authority is very engaged in monitoring the use of statistics by journalists, tracking references to their statistical products using Google news and by engaging actively with the media.

Figure 3.5. **Average statistical literacy scores, by country income groups**

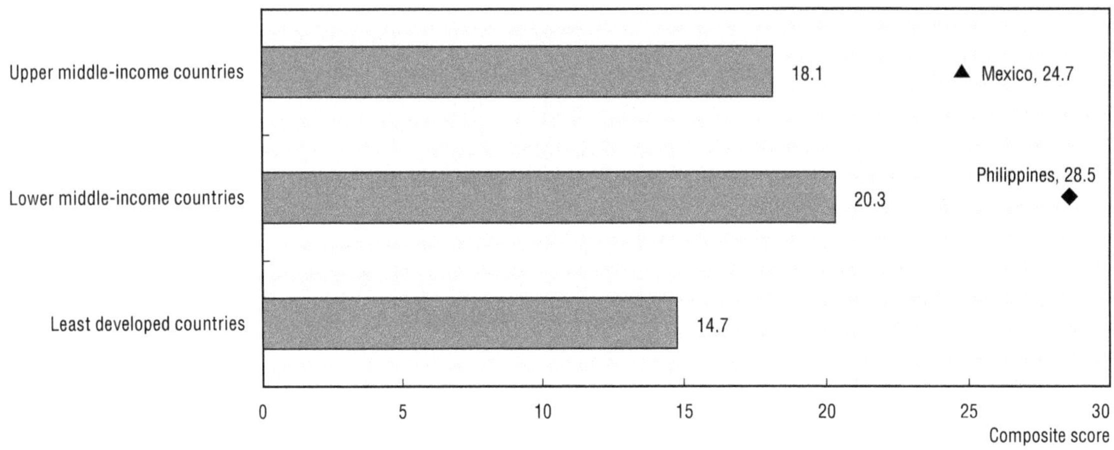

Note: Countries are classified according to the DAC List of ODA recipients, *www.oecd.org/dac/stats/documentupload/DAC%20List%20of%20ODA%20Recipients%202014%20final.pdf*.

Source: Klein, T., A. Galdin and E. Mohamedou (2016), "An indicator for statistical literacy based on national newspaper archives", *https://iase-web.org/documents/papers/rt2016/Klein.pdf*.

StatLink http://dx.doi.org/10.1787/888933591841

Producing and disseminating data and statistics means little if they are not used. Providing data in open formats with open licenses encourages their use. Yet data will have little impact unless user communities recognise their relevance for understanding the world around them or for informing decisions made by themselves or others. We have seen that statistics are used to varying degrees in newspaper articles, for instance, but are they used for planning and decision making? PARIS21 (2015) analysed the use of statistics in poverty reduction strategy papers, medium-term strategies and national development plans. Of the 20 countries that produced development plans in both periods analysed by the study (2001-07 and 2008-13), all but one increased their score on the use of statistics (Figure 3.6). The average score increased by 16 points between the two periods. These improvements reflect a growing emphasis on measuring development results, as well as an effort to incorporate

Figure 3.6. **The use of statistics for development planning in a sample of developing countries, 2001-07 and 2008-13**

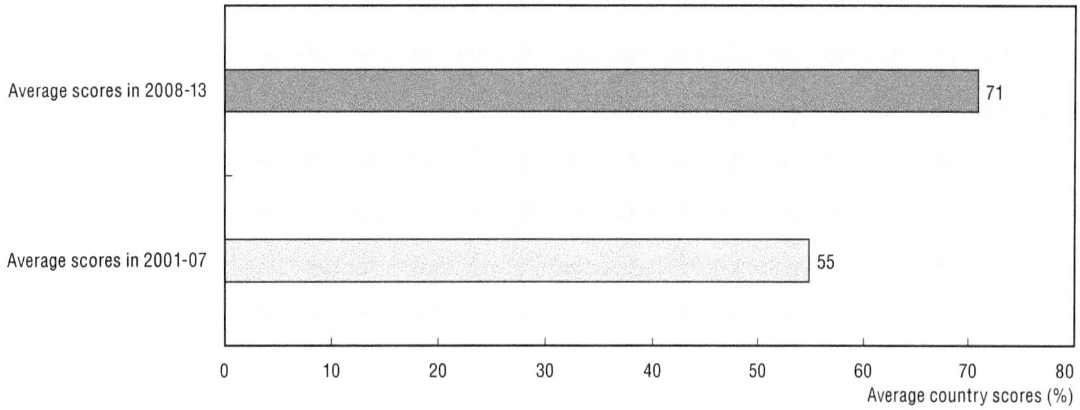

Note: The comparison is based on analysis of the use of statistics by 39 countries that published development/poverty reduction strategies and plans between 2001 and 2007 and 42 countries that published strategies and plans between 2008 and 2013.
Source: PARIS21 (2015), "A scoring system to measure the use of statistics in the policy-making process", *www.paris21.org/sites/default/files/Scoring_System_Use_Of_Data_2015_DFID.doc.*

StatLink http://dx.doi.org/10.1787/888933591860

quantified targets (e.g. the MDGs) into national development strategies. The evidence of increased use of statistics is encouraging. What remains unclear is the impact of this use of statistics on policy and programme outcomes.

For countries to realise the benefits of the data revolution, strategies for increasing statistical literacy must proceed on many fronts.

For countries to realise the benefits of the data revolution, the statistical literacy of citizens and government officials must increase. Enterprises, institutions and government agencies – the potential users of statistics – will have to recognise the value of statistics for guiding policies, assessing results and creating valuable products. Just as statistical literacy has multiple dimensions, strategies for increasing statistical literacy must proceed on many fronts. Over the long term, education is crucial. Students should be taught the basic skills needed to understand and utilise statistics. In the near term, partnerships between data producers and data users, including academic researchers and innovators, can create new uses and stimulate better understanding of statistical methods. National statistical offices should reach out to these groups and engage them in formal and informal programmes to spread statistical knowledge. Only by promoting widespread statistical literacy and the effective use of data can their full value be realised.

What needs to happen to build capable statistical systems?

By itself, the data revolution will not prompt institutional reform of national statistical systems, expand capacity, or lead to better use of and greater impact from statistics. Building capable national statistical systems is incremental: it depends as much on improving traditional core capacities as it does on using revolutionary technologies. The Cape Town Global Action Plan for Sustainable Development Data (UNSC, 2017), adopted by the United Nations Statistical Commission in March 2017, identifies national statistical systems and offices as the "necessary and appropriate leaders of this effort". It provides a framework for planning and implementing statistical capacity to match the scope of the 2030 Agenda.

The following section on what needs to happen is organised around four of the six strategic areas outlined in the Cape Town Global Action Plan: 1) leadership and governance; 2) strengthening core statistical programmes; 3) innovation and modernisation of national statistical systems; and 4) dissemination and use of statistics.[6]

Ensure better leadership and governance

To assert leadership within their own domain, national statistical offices need to work closely with national and subnational statistical agencies, facilitating communication with data users inside and outside of government. They need to modernise statistical standards and introduce new technologies and data sources into mainstream statistical activities. The national statistical agency of Tanzania offers a good example of how to do this: the Bureau of National Statistics played a critical role in championing the country's Open Government Partnership Action Plan. Tanzania was also one of the first countries to conduct an SDG Data Roadmap exercise in collaboration with the Global Partnership for Sustainable Development Data. Partnerships also offer an important opportunity for intra-governmental co-operation. The Philippines, for example, created an inter-agency committee on statistical data management and dissemination.

Many countries will need to update their statistical laws or regulations, authorising statistical offices to adopt new modes of data collection, engage in partnerships with external organisations and openly disseminate data from the statistical system. These regulations should be complemented by right-to-information laws that guarantee access by citizens to statistics and other forms of government information. Statistical offices can also provide guidance to other government agencies as they implement open data and freedom-of-information policies. For example, as part of a wider open government strategy to achieve a "Digital Mexico", open data was embraced as an enabler of economic and social growth, a lever to help fight corruption, and a mechanism to promote evidence-based policy making. The Coordination of National Digital Strategy of the Office of the President of Mexico partnered with the National Institute of Geography and Statistics to set up an Open Data Technical Committee, tasked with aligning national statistical plans with the implementation of open data policy across the government.

It is the responsibility of government, at the highest level, to recognise and support the production and use of reliable statistics.

Leadership must be earned, but it must also be nurtured. Many national statistical offices are unable to promote the use of recognised standards or to co-ordinate statistical activities throughout the larger data ecosystem. Under-resourced agencies find it hard enough to manage their own work without the added burden of co-ordinating their work with others. It is the responsibility of government, at the highest level, to recognise and support the production and use of reliable statistics. Likewise, international statistical bodies should encourage the full participation of all statistical systems in their processes, especially those from less developed countries. Finally, providers of development co-operation need to support statistical systems in a way that matches the value of the information they produce (Chapter 4).

Strengthen core statistical programmes

We have seen that many low and middle-income countries lack the capacity to produce the full range of statistical information needed to plan and monitor their development programmes and to inform citizens of their outcomes. Statistical planning and securing resources to deliver plans are integral functions of statistical systems. These plans need to ensure that core statistical programmes such as censuses, civil registration and vital statistics, and national accounts are prioritised.

Planning for the 2020 round of decennial censuses is an immediate concern. A few advanced statistical systems have replaced population censuses with data from civil registration and other administrative systems. Yet for most countries, the census is the only opportunity to anchor their demographic statistics to a complete enumeration of the population by sex, age, location and other important characteristics. The census is also a governance issue, as census results often determine legislative districts and the allocation of resources to communities. The 2010 census round, carried out between 2005 and 2014, was one of the great successes of national and international statistical efforts to date. With the support of the international development community, 214 countries and territories conducted national censuses, some for the first time in decades. However, 21 countries did not conduct a census, resulting in 7% of the world population not being enumerated. The 2020 census round has already begun. Based on the previous census dates for each country, 39 countries (including some that missed earlier rounds) should have begun preparing for or conducting censuses by 2017; some 200 more will need to complete censuses between 2018 and 2024.

Core statistical programmes such as censuses, civil registration and vital statistics, and national accounts should be prioritised.

Civil registration and vital statistics systems are essential for maintaining core demographic data. Through the registration of births, marriages, divorces and deaths, they also establish the legal basis for citizenship, inheritance and the right to public services; and they provide important information to the health system by recording cause of death. Complete registration of births and recording of cause of death should be the goal of every statistical system.

Timely and reliable statistics are needed to guide government policies and private economic and financial decisions. Although every country produces some form of national accounts, many lack adequate data on which to base their estimates of current or projected economic growth. The Cape Town Action Plan calls on countries to strengthen their national accounts; it also calls for implementing integrated systems of environmental economic accounts to capture the use of environmental resources and their possible depletion.

Modernise national statistical systems through innovation

To meet the demands of the SDGs and of domestic development programmes, national statistical systems will have to adopt new technologies and expand the scope of their work. The integration of geospatial data with conventional sources of environmental and socio-economic data is particularly important. Earth observations from satellites and aircraft or other remote sensors can be combined with geo-located data from censuses, surveys or other sources; these data can then be analysed and manipulated through geographic information systems. Geospatial data are crucial for monitoring environmental conditions and are rapidly becoming a core part of countries' data infrastructure. Combined with household surveys, they enable disaggregation by spatial characteristics such as proximity to roads or population density. Call detail records from mobile phones and other transaction data can add a dynamic component to geo-located data.

Geospatial data are crucial for monitoring environmental conditions and are rapidly becoming a core part of countries' data infrastructure.

The application of geospatial information and the analysis of big data will also require advances in information and communications technology (ICT). ICT is not only the foundation of the data revolution, it is also the key to improved government administration and e-government services, and to the widespread dissemination of data and statistics. The need for ICT capability is not limited to national statistical systems. The growth of the private sector and of its capacity to realise the benefits of the data revolution depend on modern ICT infrastructure. Public and private incentives for the development of ICT systems should, therefore, be aligned.

Focus more on disseminating and using statistics

As recommended by the Cape Town Action Plan, the work of statistical agencies should include programmes to increase data literacy, identify misuse of statistics and encourage knowledge sharing between producers and users. Potential allies of and clients for open and reliable development data include academic and research communities, news media and other information intermediaries, local governments and service providers, as well as the private sector and citizen groups. But data users are not uniform: each user group needs different kinds of data in different forms. It is also essential to accompany data with thorough and accurate metadata. Finally, open data policies must be supported by legal and regulatory frameworks that allow statistical agencies to disseminate data freely and without interference.

The way statistics are used is determined by historical factors, formal and informal institutional arrangements, the incentives of political elites and bureaucrats, external factors and global drivers.

Ultimately, the use and impact of statistics depend not only on their supply, but also on what Krätke and Byiers (2014) describe as the "political economy of official statistics". In addition to technical and governance factors, the way statistics are used is determined by historical factors, formal and informal institutional arrangements, the incentives of political elites and bureaucrats, external factors and global drivers. This means that many developing countries will need to overcome a legacy of statistics that served the interests only of colonial administrators or political and economic elites. Legal reforms that protect the independence of statistical offices and provide for effective co-ordination among them can help to overcome institutional roadblocks, but informal impediments may remain. The isolation of statistical offices from the decision-making process, or a lack of control over their own budgets and administrative processes, inhibits their ability to promote the effective use of statistics.

The way forward for national statistical systems in the data revolution

The data revolution has put new tools and sources of data in the hands of statisticians. These can serve national statistical offices, as well as the increasing number of data users and producers in the growing data ecosystem. Countries that seize opportunities can leap ahead, realising a rapid change in their capacity to produce high-quality statistics. In the future, national statistical systems will find themselves working with new partners, and their role within the data ecosystem may well change, but their core responsibilities for official statistics will remain.

We are at a critical juncture. The data revolution has demonstrated the value of data for the economy and society, as well as the opportunities for creating private and public returns on investment in data. Experience with the Millennium Development Goals has shown that statistical measurements can create incentives for better outcomes if national statistical systems are able to respond to the increasing demand for data. The growing popular demand for open data and government transparency further incentivises governments to produce and use trustworthy statistics. As these factors come together, there is a window of opportunity for development data to join the data revolution. Seizing this opportunity to have more and better data to achieve development results depends on the concerted action of statistical agencies and their governments, development co-operation providers, international agencies, civil society and the private sector.

Priority steps for making the data revolution work for development

Every statistical system is different and the details matter. Nevertheless, these priority steps can serve as guidance for national statistical offices and policy makers:

- Embrace the data revolution by using new sources of data, adopting innovative methods for producing and using statistics, and forging partnerships with other data producer and user communities.
- Strengthen the traditional systems of data collection – including censuses, surveys and administrative records – as they remain essential in the national statistical system; make them more efficient by using new technologies and methods.
- Support open data policies and the use of non-traditional sources of data, including through legal and regulatory reform; official data belong to everyone and should be open by default.
- Promote data dissemination and statistical literacy programmes to spur the use of statistics; promote active user communities.
- Identify the needs of the national statistical system and the resources available to address those needs.
- In strategic plans, data compacts and other joint agreements with providers of development co-operation and international agencies incorporate practical steps to address deficits in the production and use of statistics.

Notes

1. See: *http://siteresources.worldbank.org/INTLAC/Resources/257803-1269390034020/EnBreve_166_Web.pdf.*
2. Robin, Klein and Jütting (2016) define public-private partnerships as a "voluntary collaborative agreement between the public and private sectors, which is aimed at increasing a national statistical systems' capacity to provide new or better statistics".
3. See: *www.opalproject.org/about-us.*
4. Ten statistical capacity indicators that measured the availability of specific social and economic indicators were not included because they are based on data from international datasets that are often augmented by estimates from international agencies.
5. The three levels are: 1) consistent non-critical – appropriate but non-critical engagement with context, multiple aspects of terminology usage; 2) critical – critical, questioning engagement in contexts that do not involve proportional reasoning, but which do involve appropriate use of terminology; and 3) critical mathematical – critical, questioning engagement with context, using proportional reasoning particularly in chance contexts, showing appreciation of the need for uncertainty in making predictions, and interpreting subtle aspects of language (Klein, Galdin and Mohamedou, 2016: 4).
6. Chapter 4 covers the two remaining pillars of the Cape Town Global Action Plan: resource mobilisation and multi-stakeholder partnerships.

References

Data2X (2017), "Big data and the well-being of women and girls: Applications on the social scientific frontier", Data2X, *http://data2x.org/wp-content/uploads/2017/03/Big-Data-and-the-Well-Being-of-Women-and-Girls.pdf.*

GPSDD (2016), "The state of development data funding 2016", Global Partnership for Sustainable Development Data, *http://opendatawatch.com/wp-content/uploads/2016/09/development-data-funding-2016.pdf.*

GPSDD (n.d. *a*), "Data roadmaps for sustainable development guidelines", webpage, Global Partnership for Sustainable Development Data, *www.data4sdgs.org/data-roadmaps-for-sustainable-development-guidelines.*

GPSDD (n.d. *b*), "Data4SDGs toolbox", webpage, Global Partnership for Sustainable Development Data, *www.data4sdgs.org/toolbox.*

GWG (2017a), "Assessing use of scanner data for compiling the Consumer Price Index", Big Data Project Inventory, United Nations Global Working Group, *https://unstats.un.org/bigdata/inventory/?selectID=201431.*

GWG (2017b), "A big data pilot project: With smart meter data", Big Data Project Inventory, United Nations Global Working Group, *https://unstats.un.org/bigdata/inventory/?selectID=201429*.

GWG (2017c), "How good are CDR-derived measures of income and inequality, and can governments systematically use them?" Big Data Project Inventory, United Nations Global Working Group, *https://unstats.un.org/bigdata/inventory/?selectID=WB3*.

Hsu, A., A. Weinfurter and C. Yan (2017), "The potential for citizen-generated data in China", Yale ClimateWorks Foundation, *http://datadriven.yale.edu/wp-content/uploads/2017/01/Third_Wave_Citizen-Science_FINAL.pdf*.

IEAG (2014), "A world that counts: Mobilizing the data revolution for sustainable development", Independent Expert Advisory Group on a Data Revolution for Sustainable Development, United Nations, New York, *www.undatarevolution.org/wp-content/uploads/2014/11/A-World-That-Counts.pdf*.

Klein, T. and S. Verhulst (2017), "Access to new data sources for statistics: Business models and incentives for the corporate sector", *OECD Statistics Working Papers*, No. 82, OECD Publishing, Paris, *http://dx.doi.org/10.1787/9a1fa77f-en*.

Klein, T., A. Galdin and E. Mohamedou (2016), "An indicator for statistical literacy based on national newspaper archives", in: *Proceedings of the IASE Roundtable Conference on Promoting Understanding of Statistics about Society*, International Association of Statistics Education, Berlin, *https://iase-web.org/documents/papers/rt2016/Klein.pdf*.

Krätke, F. and B. Byiers (2014), "The political economy of official statistics: Implications for the data revolution in sub-Saharan Africa", *PARIS21 Discussion Papers*, No. 5, OECD, Paris, *www.paris21.org/sites/default/files/PARIS21-DiscussionPaper5_0.pdf*.

OD4D (2016), "International open data road map: Global goals, local impact", International Open Data Conference 2016, Summary Report and the Second Action Plan for International Collaboration, *http://od4d.com/roadmap/assets/files/report-iodc-2016-web.pdf?platform=hootsuite*.

ODC (n.d.), "Principles", Open Data Charter, *http://opendatacharter.net/principles*.

OECD (n.d.), "DAC List of ODA Recipients: Effective for reporting on 2014, 2015 and 2016 flows", OECD, Paris, *www.oecd.org/dac/stats/documentupload/DAC%20List%20of%20ODA%20Recipients%202014%20final.pdf*.

Open Data Watch (2017a), "Data download", *2016 Open Data Inventory* (database), *http://odin.opendatawatch.com/data/download* (accessed 26 April 2017).

Open Data Watch (2017b), "2016 Open Data Inventory: The ODIN annual report: Toward an open data revolution", Open Data Watch, Washington, DC, *http://odin.opendatawatch.com/report/pressReport*.

PARIS21 (2015), "A scoring system to measure the use of statistics in the policy-making process," *www.paris21.org/sites/default/files/Scoring_System_Use_Of_Data_2015_DFID.doc*.

PARIS21 (n.d.), "National strategies for the development of statistics", *www.paris21.org/NSDS*.

Robin, N., T. Klein and J. Jütting (2016), "Public-private partnerships for statistics: Lessons learned, future steps: A focus on the use of non-official data sources for national statistics and public policy", *OECD Development Co-operation Working Papers*, No. 27, OECD Publishing, Paris, *http://dx.doi.org/10.1787/5jm3nqp1g8wf-en*.

SDSN (2015), "Data for development: A needs assessment for SDG monitoring and statistical capacity development", United Nations Sustainable Development Solutions Network, *http://unsdsn.org/wp-content/uploads/2015/04/Data-for-Development-Full-Report.pdf*.

Tatem, A.J. et al. (2014), "Integrating rapid risk mapping and mobile phone call record data for strategic malaria elimination planning", *Malaria Journal*, Vol. 13, *https://malariajournal.biomedcentral.com/articles/10.1186/1475-2875-13-52*.

UN (2013), "A new global partnership: Eradicate poverty and transform economies through sustainable development", United Nations, New York, *www.post2015hlp.org/the-report*.

UNFPA (2016a), "Evaluation of UNFPA support to population and housing census data to inform decision-making and policy formulation 2005-2014", Evaluation Report, Evaluation Office, United Nations Population Fund, New York, *www.unfpa.org/sites/default/files/admin-resource/Evaluation_report_-_Volume.pdf*.

UNFPA (2016b), "Evaluation of UNFPA support to population and housing census data to inform decision-making and policy formulation 2005-2014", Evaluation Brief, Evaluation Office, United Nations Population Fund, New York, *www.unfpa.org/sites/default/files/admin-resource/Brief_1.pdf*.

UNICEF (2013), "Every child's birth right: Inequities and trends in birth registration", United Nations Children's Fund, New York, *www.unicef.org/publications/files/Birth_Registration_11_Dec_13.pdf*.

UNSC (2017), "Cape Town Global Action Plan for Sustainable Development Data", United Nations Statistics Commission, New York, *http://unstats.un.org/sdgs/hlg/Cape-Town-Global-Action-Plan*.

UNSC (2014), "Fundamental Principles of Official Statistics", A/RES/68/261, United Nations Statistics Commission, New York, *https://unstats.un.org/unsd/dnss/gp/fundprinciples.aspx*.

UNSD (2013), "Implementation of the Fundamental Principles of Official Statistics", United Nations Statistics Division, New York, *http://unstats.un.org/unsd/statcom/doc13/BG-FP.pdf*.

Vaitla, B. et al. (2017), "Phone records track malaria", in *Data Impacts: Case Studies from the Data Revolution*, Data Impacts, *http://dataimpacts.org/project/malaria*.

WHO (n.d.), "Civil registration of deaths", *Global Health Observatory*, World Health Organization, Geneva, *www.who.int/gho/mortality_burden_disease/registered_deaths/text/en*.

World Bank (2017), *Statistical Capacity Indicators* (database), *http://databank.worldbank.org/data/reports.aspx?source=statistical-capacity-indicators#* (accessed 22 May 2017).

World Economic Forum (2015), "Data-driven development: Pathways for progress", World Economic Forum, Geneva, *www3.weforum.org/docs/WEFUSA_DataDrivenDevelopment_Report2015.pdf*.

PART I

Chapter 4

Rethinking donor support for statistical capacity building

by
Shaida Badiee, Thilo Klein, Deirdre Appel, El Iza Mohamedou *and* Eric Swanson*

Investing in data brings returns. Development data are critical for policy making, planning, and monitoring and measuring impact nationally and globally. Yet statistical systems in developing countries are often under-resourced and under-staffed and traditional support to statistical capacity building is not fit for purpose. While political support to have and use more and better data is essential to realising the full potential of data for development, donor support needs to be increased, more effective and better co-ordinated by creating, for example, compacts for a country-led development data revolution. The chapter shows how support for building statistical capacity can be revitalised for greater impact over the long term and calls for a more comprehensive and transparent system for measuring international support to statistics. It also stresses the importance of country leadership, co-operation among providers of development co-operation for data and statistics, data literacy, and innovation. Finally, the chapter sets out priority steps in rethinking donor support for statistical capacity building.

* Shaida Badiee, Deirdre Appel and Eric Swanson from Open Data Watch; and El Iza Mohamedou and Thilo Klein from PARIS21.

Key facts

Investing in data brings returns, for example:

- Farmers' share of crop export prices in Ethiopia doubled to 70% within four years of opening the Ethiopian Commodity Exchange, which provides real-time, official price data; its dissemination mechanisms are tailored to the needs of small farmers (Vaitla et al., 2017).
- In the United Kingdom, a study has shown that every pound (GBP) invested in producing statistics on schools' performance leads to academic improvements equivalent to a GBP 16 increase in gross domestic product (Burgess et al., 2013).
- Censuses conducted in Mexico and Peru in 2000 showed that the proportion of births attended by health professionals among indigenous women was lower than among non-indigenous women (38% and 45%, respectively). These data were used to promote more effective interventions; by 2012, in both countries more than 80% of births by indigenous women were attended by health personnel (UN, 2015a).

Despite the evidence, however:

- In 2015, the share of official development assistance (ODA) dedicated to improving data for development was only 0.30% (USD 541 million) (PARIS21, 2017).
- A large share of global support to data for development continues to come from a very small number of providers: in 2015, five providers of development co-operation (the World Bank, Canada, the United Nations Population Fund, the European Commission/EUROSTAT and the African Development Bank) accounted for 75% of official development assistance for statistics (PARIS21, 2017).
- In 2015, USD 181 million was committed as bilateral aid for statistics. This aid accounted for one-third of total commitments to statistics. The top five bilateral providers by size of contribution are: Canada, Sweden, the United Kingdom, Korea and Australia, accounting for 78% of bilateral aid.
- Support to statistical capacity building has been supply driven and piecemeal, with little emphasis placed on partner countries' demand for data. There is greater emphasis on the data needed by development co-operation providers for their monitoring, reporting and accountability.

Development data give insights that are critical for policy making, planning, and monitoring and measuring impact nationally and globally. The demand for more and better data has increased in recent years as UN member states step up efforts to deliver and measure the Sustainable Development Goals (SDGs). Development data inform country strategies to attain these goals (UNJIU, 2016); at the same time, they are integral components of Agenda 2030 itself (SDGs 17.18 and 17.19).[1] To build high-functioning statistical systems capable of meeting the demands of the SDGs, it is essential to increase political and financial support from the international community (see the "In my view" piece by Sarah Hendriks). Despite the recognised contribution of development data to better outcomes,[2] the current levels of official development assistance (ODA) remain well below what is needed.

Statistical systems in developing countries are ofte81n under-staffed and under-resourced (see Chapter 3; UNJIU, 2016; UNECE 2016). Trends suggest that the share of ODA for data and statistics has stagnated in recent years. Many developing countries – especially the least developed countries, small island developing states and states in fragile situations – depend largely on international support to build statistical capacity. If the data revolution is to create a world of greater prosperity and sustainable development, increased and smarter investments by providers of development co-operation are needed. Effective international support can help change a vicious cycle of under-performance and inadequate resources in statistics to a virtuous one in which increased demand and improved quality lead to higher use and greater value. Better data can also help respond to the greater accountability expectation of citizens in both developed and developing countries.

Traditional support for development data has largely focused on technical assistance. Characterised by low levels of co-ordination among providers, this type of support has targeted specific sectors rather than whole-of-government approaches and has lacked country ownership; as a whole, these efforts have not yielded substantial increases in statistical capacity. In the context of the data revolution, providers must reshape their approach to statistical capacity development to promote country ownership, align support with country priorities, focus on data use and users, foster diverse public-private partnerships, utilise new funding mechanisms, and emphasise results-based support.

This chapter proposes several avenues for directing additional resources to improve statistical capacity building and in doing so, deliver on the 2030 Agenda for Sustainable Development (UN, 2015c).

New resources need to be raised to build statistical capacity

Developing statistical systems is a long-term process, and the results will live long beyond the SDGs. Building the statistical capacity to guide, monitor and track national development progress towards the SDGs must begin now and be reliably funded until 2030 and beyond. Calculating an aggregate cost for developing countries of building this statistical capacity is complex and a work in progress. Two recent studies (SDSN, 2015; GPSDD, 2016) have calculated the minimum cost of producing data for the SDGs in 144 developing countries to be about USD 2.8-3.0 billion per year up to 2030. The estimates include the cost of expanding the programme of surveys and censuses and of improving administrative data systems.

"The state of development data funding" report (GPSDD, 2016) estimated that developing countries face an annual funding gap, once domestic budgets for statistics are accounted for, of about USD 635-685 million to produce data for the SDGs up to 2030. To fill this gap countries would need to raise external sources of financing, notably from development co-operation. Assuming that aid to statistics, which reached USD 541 million in 2015, helps produce data for the SDGs in developing countries and thus helps fill this funding gap, an additional USD 200 million per year up to 2030 is needed to respond to the minimum financing needs.

In my view:
Closing the gender gap requires closing the data gap

Sarah Hendriks,
Director of Gender Equality, Bill & Melinda Gates Foundation

Nowhere in the world are males and females truly equal. Women learn less, earn less, have fewer rights and have less control over their assets. In 155 countries there is at least one law impeding women's economic opportunities. Women own less than 20% of the world's land despite producing the majority of its food. They represent 1.1 billion of the world's unbanked population and the World Economic Forum estimates that it will take 170 years to achieve economic gender equality. Harmful practices and policies around the world are grounded in the view that women and girls don't count. Even where good laws exist, implementation often falters.

Underpinning these gaps, one challenge is particularly acute for women and girls: data.

There are many data blind spots in global development. Even the most basic information on women and girls is often lacking: when they are born, how many hours they work, if and what they get paid, whether they've experienced violence, how they die. In too many areas, disaggregated data don't exist at all, or data collection is "sexist", leaving women and girls out or undercounting them. This perpetuates the undervaluation of women and girls in society, and leaves their huge potential untapped.

The problem is exacerbated by gaps in political will, funding and capacity. Only 13% of countries dedicate a budget to gender statistics and many lack the national strategies and training needed to ensure robust gender data collection. Data collection is often fragmented or conducted using outdated methods. Even when policies and programmes targeting women and girls are funded, they are often poorly evaluated. Consequently, policy makers don't learn about what is working and what isn't, making ill-informed decisions, trade-offs and resource allocations. Civil society groups are also ill-equipped to conduct data-driven advocacy.

In my view, closing the gender gap requires closing the data gap. Our foundation is investing USD 80 million in improving gender data, evidence and accountability. Critically, these resources will improve the way data and evidence are used to drive advocacy and inform policy.

Specifically, two new areas of partnership include:

1. Support for UN Women's flagship programme initiatives on gender data, which aim to improve the production, availability, accessibility, and use of quality gender data and statistics (*www.unwomen.org/en/how-we-work/flagship-programmes*).
2. The Initiative for What Works, which will build a network of in-country hubs to improve evidence on programmes and policies targeting women's economic empowerment and healthy adolescent transitions.

We call on donors and governments that care about advancing progress for women and girls to join us, prioritising and increasing investments in gender data and evidence. The needs are many – from filling data gaps; to strengthening national capacity; to gathering and tracking evidence in more timely, consistent ways; to reducing bias by harmonising approaches for data collection; to supporting access by women's organisations to data, as well as their capacity to advocate with it.

Better data are foundational to everything else we hope to achieve. Women and girls count, and they are counting on us to step up in the years ahead.

Trends in aid for statistics

In the early 2000s, there was a clear commitment from the international development community to improve data in support of the Millennium Development Goals. This commitment was matched by a steady increase in funding between 2005 and 2013. The latest trends in aid for statistics demonstrate that international calls to improve development data are not translating into a corresponding increase in predictable financing to produce data for the SDGs. According to the 2017 PARIS21 "Partner report on support to statistics"[4] – aid to statistics was USD 541 million in 2015 – this represents an increase of 12% (in real terms) compared to 2014 (PARIS21, 2017). However, at 0.30% of total ODA in 2015, aid for statistics remains a relatively low development co-operation priority for most donors. In 2015, bilateral aid for statistics (USD 181 million) was the equivalent of one-third of total support and five bilateral providers (Canada, Sweden, United Kingdom, Korea and Australia) accounted for 78% of this. Trends also show how financing fluctuates from year to year, undermining predictability for partners (Figure 4.1).

Figure 4.1. **Aid to statistics: Trends in volume and as a share of ODA, 2006-15, commitments**

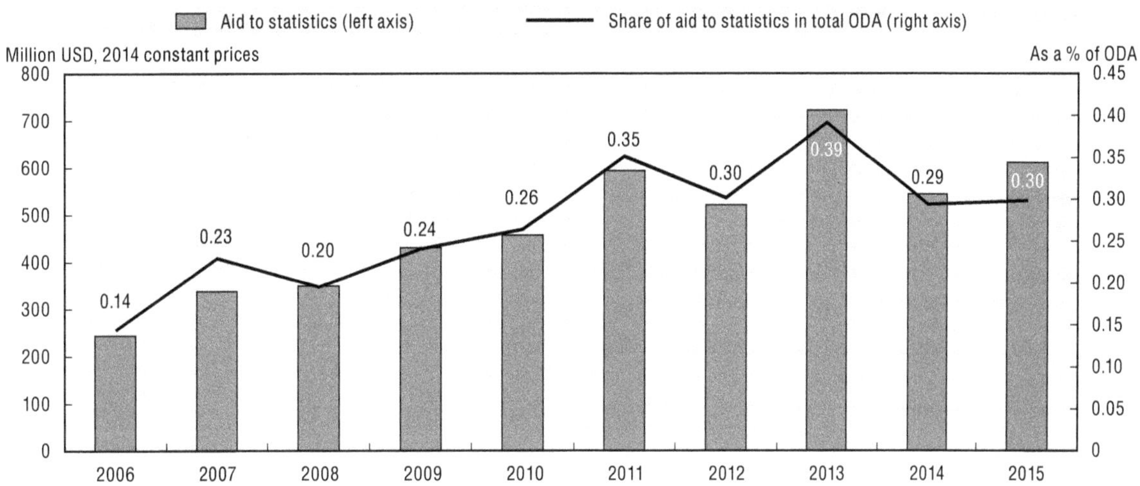

Source: PARIS21 (2017), "Partner report on support to statistics", *www.paris21.org/press2017*.

StatLink http://dx.doi.org/10.1787/888933591879

More detailed analysis of aid financing for statistics reveals interesting funding trends. For example, a large share of total ODA comes from a very small number of providers: five bilateral and multilateral providers accounted for 75% of total aid commitments to statistics in 2015 (PARIS21, 2017).[5] Between 2013-15, the countries with the lowest statistical capacity received the most support from members of the OECD Development Assistance Committee (DAC). The 2017 PRESS report found that when aid commitments were matched with the World Bank's Statistical Capacity Indicator (World Bank, 2017), low-capacity countries received on average more funding per capita (USD 0.87) than countries with high capacity (USD 0.36) (PARIS21, 2017). It is also promising to note that states with fragile situations receive considerably more support from the statistical development community: reported commitments for the 36 states with fragile situations included in the 2017 PRESS report were USD 507 million between 2013 and 2015 (Figure 4.2). This represents nearly one-third of global country-specific commitments during this period.[6]

The general trend for donor support is positive, as new providers of development co-operation beyond the DAC increasingly see the value of investments in development data. The United Arab Emirates, for examples, will host the second World Data Forum planned to take place in 2018. In 2016-17, donor support is expected to pick up, primarily driven by the changing donor landscape, with improved commitments from private foundations. The Bill & Melinda Gates and Hewlett Foundations are leading

Figure 4.2. **Aid to statistics for fragile situations, main recipients, 2013-15, commitments**

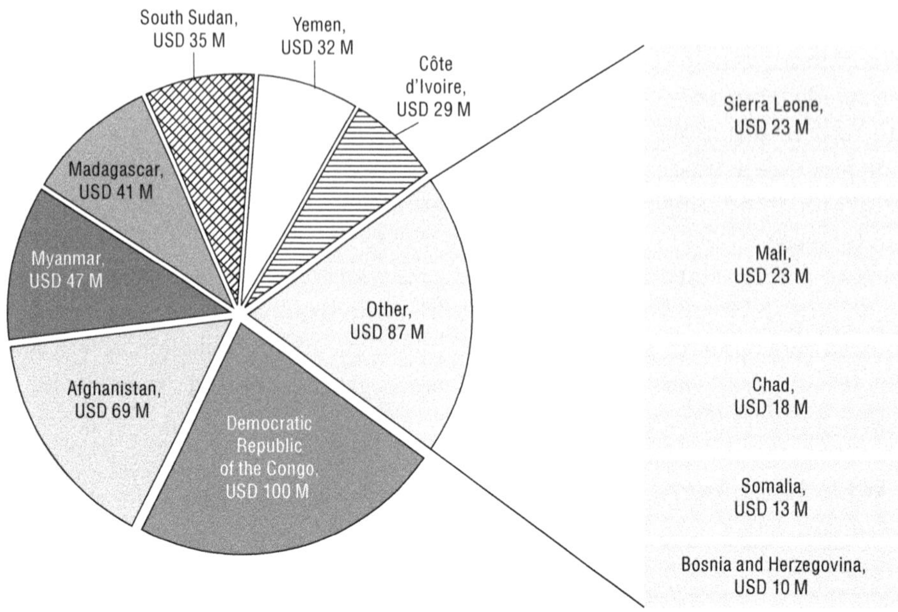

Source: PARIS21 (2017), "Partner report on support to statistics" *www.paris21.org/press2017.*

StatLink http://dx.doi.org/10.1787/888933591898

these efforts with commitments in 2016 of USD 13.2 million and USD 3 million, respectively (GPSDD, 2016). While these commitments are not yet reflected in the figures for 2015, the Bill & Melinda Gates Foundation is now one of the major providers for statistical development (see the "In my view" piece by Sarah Hendriks). According to the 2017 PRESS report (PARIS21, 2017), it ranks among the top nine global providers in 2015 with a total commitment of USD 14 million.

It is not only a question of how much support, but also of how it is given

The way development co-operation providers deliver their support is also critical. PRESS 2016 shows that while grants are the main financing instrument used, the choice between grants and loans or credit differs widely from region to region. While Open Data Watch's "Aid for statistics: 2016 inventory of financial instruments" also finds that trust-fund grants are the predominant type of funding used, its review of funding modalities notes that providers have several options for the delivery of increased funding (ODW, 2015). Table 4.1 summarises the strengths and weaknesses of each type of funding.

Traditional support to statistical capacity building is out of date

Statistical capacity building is described as a "process of changes at the levels of individuals, organisations, and enabling environments in a national statistical system through which the system obtains, strengthens, and maintains its capacities to set and achieve its own statistics development objectives over time" (UNJIU, 2016). Yet past efforts have not always yielded such outcomes. One of the main lessons of the past 20 years has been that top-down initiatives do not lead to sustained increases in capacity (Kiregyera, 2013). Today, the breadth and ambition of the SDGs have rendered past patterns of support outdated (Keijzer and Klingebiel, 2017).

What has gone wrong? Traditional efforts have been characterised by supply-driven, piecemeal approaches, with little emphasis placed on the endogenous demand for data. Rather, the emphasis was on the data needed by development co-operation providers for their monitoring, reporting and accountability. For instance, capacity building often prioritised making estimates of missing data values, such as HIV/AIDS prevalence rates, over building capacity in the national statistical office; or poverty lines were calculated by an external consultant that were impossible for anyone in the

Table 4.1. **Strengths and weaknesses of funding modalities for statistical capacity building**

Modality	Strengths	Weaknesses	Example
Domestic tax revenues	Create and strengthens domestic resource mobilisation for statistics, which can lead to a more sustainable system overall.	Countries may struggle with mobilising a tax base or fail to prioritise the use of funds for statistics.	National budgets.
Loans and credit (including multilateral lending)	Large size allows funding to cover many statistical domains, as well as the total overhaul of the national statistical system.	Lengthy approval processes, including loan preparation and design, and approval of projects.	World Bank lending for the Statistical Capacity Building Program.
Bilateral grants	Quick agreement between the provider and recipient, rapid disbursement.	Funds are often given to satisfy provider needs for data; high transaction costs for small funding.	European Commission or DFID support.
Technical assistance	Increases interaction between providers of development co-operation and national statistical offices; predictable timing and delivery.	High turnover of staff and low levels of results-based monitoring make it difficult to determine the impact of training; outdated approach to capacity building.	International Monetary Fund technical assistance for macro statistics.
Results-based aid	Links results directly to development activities; high potential for innovation; strong incentives for reform in developing countries.	Challenging for activities with less quantifiable impact.	Kenya Statistics Program-for-Results.
Pooling arrangements (basket funds, multi-donor trust funds)	Promotes co-ordination among providers; stable and predictable source of funding; reduces transaction costs through pools; promotes a more results-based financing culture.	Co-ordination and agreement can be challenging; procurement and disbursement rules of providers of development co-operation may differ, making pooling difficult.	World Bank Trust Fund for Statistical Capacity Building, Statistics for Results Facility; United Nations Statistical Division Evidence and Data for Gender Equality.

country to update or further analyse (Taylor, 2016). With this type of data production – driven by the desire to generate an immediate output needed by the external funder – short-term needs crowd out long-term effectiveness and sustainability.

What is needed is a demand-driven, holistic approach designed to strengthen the entire statistical system.

The results of a survey of DAC members' policies and practices to support national statistical capacities and systems in developing countries show that DAC members provide support to improve developing countries' statistical production mainly in the form of technical assistance (e.g. conducting training, designing surveys, building data management systems) (Sanna and Mc Donnell, 2017). While approaches such as these may identify and fix a broken piece in the data machine, they fail to consider the broader enabling environment or to reinforce the ability of the system to self-repair in the future. An approach addressing technical bottlenecks is not enough; what is needed is a demand-driven, holistic approach designed to strengthen the entire statistical system.

This is not to say that all previous efforts failed to yield results. The World Bank *Statistical Capacity Indicator* database shows slow but upward global and regional progress over the past 15 years. Yet the pace of this progress is not adequate if the global community is to match the scope and ambitions of the 2030 Agenda. Providers of development co-operation need to rethink how they provide support for statistics to address the remaining challenges and accelerate the pace.

To enable progress towards the Sustainable Development Goals, data need to be managed as a cross-cutting priority

In the context of the data revolution, two forces drive the need for donors and their partners to re-evaluate past methods. First, the data ecosystem is expanding to include new producers and users of development data. Second, the SDGs place increased demands on national and international statistical agencies, including robust disaggregation of data on vulnerable populations or collection of new data for the SDG indicators. Co-ordination, innovation and funding are essential if the global community is to measure and track progress towards the 232 SDG indicators. By recognising development data as a strategic cross-cutting priority, similar to the environment and gender equality and women's economic empowerment, and providing adequate funding, the international community can help to achieve this.

To be excluded from civil registration is, in many cases, synonymous with exclusion from public services.

Too often, support to statistics has been seen as an add-on to other sectoral projects. Over the years, the area of administrative data and civil registration has been neglected. For example, by one estimate, 83% of Africans live in countries without a complete and well-functioning birth registration system (Mo Ibrahim Foundation, 2016). There is a need to move beyond periodic surveys to continuous production of the data that enables countries to maintain complete records of births and deaths; these, in turn, dictate formal civic, personal, professional, business, and political activities and transactions. In many countries, civil registration enables individuals to be admitted into schools and hospitals, gain nationality and formal employment, vote or present themselves for electoral office, buy and transfer properties, or access financial and legal services. To be excluded from civil registration is, in many cases, synonymous with exclusion from public services.

The Cape Town Global Action Plan proposes a revitalised approach to statistical capacity development

There is international consensus around the principles that should guide a revitalised approach to statistical capacity development. In 2005, the Paris Declaration on Aid Effectiveness[7] stressed the importance of country ownership and harmonisation among providers of development co-operation. More recently, the Nairobi outcome document of the Second High-Level Meeting of the Global Partnership for Effective Development Co-operation (GPEDC, 2016) committed aid providers to strengthening the statistical capacity of developing countries. Several recent international commitments include a clear call to put these development principles into practice in their support to statistics as a sector in itself and a cross-cutting issue.

These pledges signal strong international support for data and lay the ground for concrete operational steps. Yet the question remains of whether the pledges are being translated into practice. Table 4.2 summarises the degree of delivery against goals for a sample of high-level commitments on statistics. Success is measured in different ways: some have generated increased financial or political support while others have championed innovation and collaboration.

The United Nations (UN) Cape Town Global Action Plan for Sustainable Development Data (UNSC, 2017) is the most recent roadmap for improving global data for sustainable development and defining the role of development co-operation providers. The Global Action Plan provides a framework for planning and implementing statistical capacity building to achieve the scope and intent of the 2030 Agenda. The plan acknowledges that this work will be country-led and will occur at the subnational, national and regional levels. It aims to fully communicate and co-ordinate existing efforts, as well as to identify new and strategic ways to efficiently mobilise resources from international organisations, national governments and other partners.

The Global Action Plan proposes action in six strategic areas, each associated with several objectives: 1) co-ordination and strategic leadership on data for sustainable development; 2) innovation and modernisation of national statistical systems; 3) strengthening of basic statistical activities and programmes; 4) dissemination and use of sustainable development data; 5) multi-stakeholder partnerships; and 6) mobilisation of resources and co-ordination of efforts for statistical capacity building. All of these aspects are integral to the capability to produce and use development data (Figure 4.3).

Table 4.2. **Implementation of high-level commitments to statistics**

Commitment	Goal	Outcome
2004: Marrakech Action Plan for Statistics (MAPS) (World Bank, 2004)	• Ensure sustainable improvements in national statistical capacity. • Mainstream and prepare national strategies for all low-income countries by 2006.	• Three major successes: 1. the International Household Survey Network 2. strong international political consensus for support to statistics with increased funding 3. broadened coverage of the 2010 census round.
2011: Busan Action Plan for Statistics (PARIS21, 2011)	• Fully integrate statistics into decision making. • Promote open access to statistics. • Emphasise the role of national statistical development strategies. • Increase resources for statistical systems.	• Helped to maintain momentum for collective action reaffirmed by the MAPS. • Was fully endorsed by the United Nations Statistical Commission (UNSC). ***but*** • Did not garner financial support needed to achieve the major action items of the plan.
2015: Addis Ababa Action Agenda (UN, 2015a)	• More than 100 concrete measures, including a pledge to improve data for monitoring the impact of development spending/progress towards the Sustainable Development Goals (SDGs).	• Launch of the Global Partnership for Sustainable Development Data with some commitments for its setup; few new commitments for statistical capacity development; focus on the need for domestic resource mobilisation and private sector investment in development.
2015: Sustainable Development Goals (UN, 2015c)	• Implement an extensive transformation of development data in all countries, rich or poor, to fill data gaps. • This includes developing new measures and improving data quality, access and use.	• SDG 17 on partnership includes a specific target (17.18) "to increase significantly the availability of high-quality, timely and reliable data disaggregated by income, gender, age, race, ethnicity, migratory status, disability, geographic location and other characteristics relevant in national contexts".
2015: Global Financing Facility Support for Strengthening Civil Registration and Vital Statistics (World Bank, 2016)	• Register all vital events in Africa, Asia and the Pacific during the "Decade of Civil Registration" (2015-24), as endorsed by ministers.	• Raised the profile of civil registration and vital statistics (CRVS), mobilised resources, incentivised countries to conduct assessments of CRVS systems and cost national plans. • Centre of excellence for CRVS established. • Canada committed CAD 16 million by 2030 for improving quality and availability of universal data on birth, death, cause of death and marriage.
2017: Cape Town Global Action Plan for Sustainable Development Data (UNSC, 2017)	• Undertake key actions under six strategic areas: 1. co-ordination and leadership 2. innovation and modernisation of national statistical systems 3. strengthening of basic statistics 4. dissemination and use 5. multi-stakeholder partnerships 6. resource mobilisation.	• Raised awareness and increased co-ordination among the technical data communities. • Adopted by the UNSC in March 2017; submission to the United Nations Economic and Social Council in July 2017.

Source: Author's compilation.

Lessons from research and evaluation on strengthening statistical systems

It is too soon to gauge the success of the Cape Town Global Action Plan. Nonetheless, several formal evaluations and other research conducted in recent years sheds light on some good practices for capacity building that link closely with strategic areas of the Cape Town Global Action Plan.[8] Some lessons include the following:

- **National strategies for the development of statistics should be the starting point for designing capacity building, ensuring that providers of development co-operation do not follow a one-size-fits-all approach.** As new approaches to strengthening statistical systems are explored it will be important to focus on comprehensive, co-ordinated interventions delivered through modalities that are appropriate for the entire set of stakeholders (Klingebiel, Casjen Mahn and Negre, 2016) and at the same time are aligned with the strategy and circumstances of the host country. The 2016 "Partner report on support to statistics" (PARIS21, 2016) showed good alignment of commitments with national strategies for the development of statistics and this alignment remains at an overall high level. Taking this good practice a step further, countries such as Sierra Leone are testing the idea of a "data compact" among all stakeholders in support of a well-articulated, results-based national plan (Box 4.1).

Figure 4.3. **Applying the Cape Town Global Action Plan to build development data capacity**

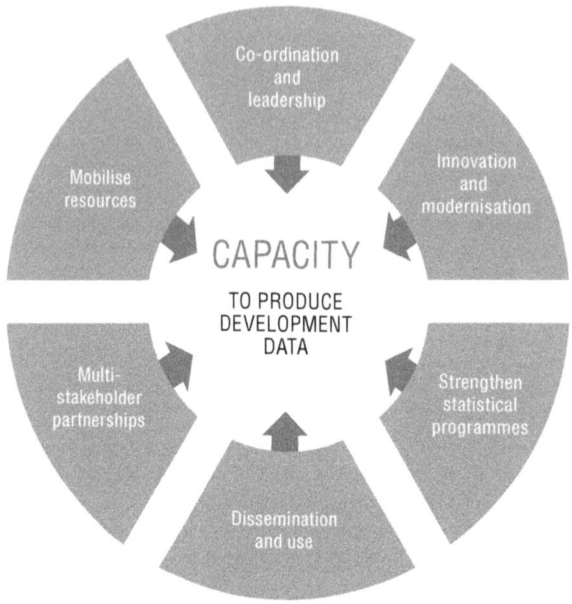

Source: Open Data Watch.

Box 4.1. **The benefits of data compacts**

In developing countries, data compacts can incite governments to:

- Commit to and implement a national strategy for the development of statistics that, as far as possible, meets the disaggregated data needs of the 2030 Agenda and explores the integration of non-traditional data providers and users.
- Ensure that statistical legislation is up to date and in line with the UN Fundamental Principles of Official Statistics.
- Ensure that the skills required to perform the data-related activities are available.
- Promote the effective co-ordination of data-related activities and ensure a proper scheduling of surveys to guarantee a regular data flow.
- Promote access to and use of data and statistics based on open data principles.
- Ensure data-related activities are adequately funded.

In turn, external funders – including bilateral providers of development co-operation, multilateral agencies, development banks and others – can be required to:

- Incentivise results-based financing and improve support for data-related activities, including funding based on demonstrated impact from or progress towards the production of high-quality data and the promotion of data use.
- Provide funding or in-kind support for technical assistance to strengthen the capacity of data providers and users.
- Ensure activities are aligned with the national strategy for the development of statistics and/or the national development plan, and that they are co-ordinated with other providers.
- Provide support in ways that minimise the burden on countries and make use of local processes and data.
- Support funding initiatives that increase domestic resources in support of statistics (e.g. new taxes, a national fund).
- Undertake research and development to promote and support innovation.

- **There is scope to increase focus on data literacy and use.** A United Nations Population Fund evaluation of its census work found that the 2010 census "had a pre-eminent focus on enhancing the production of census-related data, placing disproportionally less attention on data dissemination, analysis, and use in policy making" (UNFPA, 2016). The full potential of census data is not realised because of an over emphasis on data production rather than use. A recent survey conducted by the United Nations Economic Commission for Europe found that many national statistical offices actively promote user education – for example through publications and booklets tailored to specific user groups; seminars; user-friendly guides; and awareness campaigns such as National Statistics Month. Yet all of the developing countries participating in the survey reported that they lack resources for user education (UNECE, 2016).
- **Co-ordination of statistical capacity building reduces transaction costs.** Evaluations conducted by the World Bank Trust Fund for Statistical Capacity Building flagged the small size of individual stand-alone grants and the resulting loss of cost effectiveness (ODW, 2015). Methods such as pooling of resources among various providers reduce transaction costs and enable greater effectiveness and efficiency. One of the main challenges listed by DAC members in relation to making data work for sustainable development is the lack of systematic co-ordination among providers of development co-operation to support statistical capacity building (Sanna and Mc Donnell, 2017). An evaluation of capacity-building efforts by the International Monetary Fund found that giving responsibility for co-ordination to a single government institution was highly effective in increasing harmonisation among providers. In this way, a "lead donor" is identified by each country with the responsibility for the overall work strategy remaining with the country (ODW, 2015).
- **Multi-stakeholder partnerships can mobilise more resources for sustainable development data.** While domestic resources mobilised by individual countries can help close the funding gap for statistics (SDSN, 2015) public-private partnerships offer more room for innovation and risk-taking than traditional funding modalities. Innovative funding mechanisms – such as peer-to-peer support (e.g. the twinning partnership between the Japan International Cooperation Agency and Cambodia) and incentive funds (i.e. the World Bank's innovation fund) – can also offer valuable alternatives.

Moving from traditional to revitalised support

In addition to the Cape Town Global Action Plan, the revitalisation of statistical capacity development has been reinforced by recent international fora.[9] Table 4.3 compares the principles of a traditional donor approach to statistical capacity development with a vision of what a revitalised approach would entail.

Table 4.3. **Revitalising donor support for statistics**

Traditional approach	Revitalised approach
• Heavy reliance on technical aspects, such as support for survey design, supply of and assistance with a data management system.	• Expansion beyond technical assistance to building partnerships and fostering skills, such as management and leadership.
• Lopsided agenda of statistical activities with the focus on the supply side (data production/producer) and on donor priorities and needs.	• Support aligned with national statistical plans and priorities; focus on the use and user of data as well as on proper dissemination and format (disaggregated, open, geospatial integration).
• Low levels of official development assistance funding; little co-ordination among providers of development co-operation; limited results-based funding; view of statistics as technical aspects of funding.	• Increased support (domestic, international, private) for statistics; increased use of new funding mechanisms with a result-based focus; statistics seen as both key means of achieving the Sustainable Development Goals and as integral goals in themselves.
• Limited focus on national statistical offices, little attention given to external users.	• Country-driven strengthening of national systems; focus on data literacy and user groups.

Source: Authors' compilation.

The way forward for supporting statistical capacity building

The 2030 Agenda to end poverty, build sustainable growth and prosperity, and improve lives while leaving no one behind, combined with the untapped power of the data revolution, put us at an exceptional pivotal moment. To advance using the framework articulated in the Cape Town Global Action Plan, the shortcomings of donor support for development data outlined in this chapter must be addressed. In short, we need to raise the level of political support for the sustainable development data agenda; align donor support and country ownership; build a stronger culture of focus on results; and tackle donor co-ordination issues in the statistics sector. Among many possible actions, this chapter prioritises three sets of recommendations, largely motivated by the potential of these changes to yield high returns, combined with a focus on goals that are achievable in three to five years.

1. Raise the level of political support for sustainable development data

Policy and technical discussions on data to support sustainable development occur mostly within the statistical community. Technical discussions have been fruitful in articulating the data infrastructure needed at the national level, highlighting the capacity challenges in developing countries, estimating the required level of investment and reviewing the support mechanisms for data for development. While this information is invaluable for understanding the current state of affairs within the data revolution, deliberations need to move to the political sphere.

In developing countries, senior officials from the Finance and Planning Ministries as well as central government units such as the Chancellery or Office of the President need to be more involved and engaged in national data production discussions. The SDG data indicator debate, which has just started to unfold, offers a good opportunity for the heads of national statistical offices to "step up, step forward and step on the gas", as John Pullinger, the National Statistician for the United Kingdom, has eloquently put it, raising data in the public debate. Most senior government officials will understand the need to engage in data for development debates, in particular if they have seen concrete examples of how national data can be instrumental in demonstrating the impact of their policies.

The "data" topic is universal, cross-cutting and highly underrated.

In countries that provide development co-operation, the heads of aid agencies and ministries need to be made aware that the "data" topic is universal, cross-cutting and highly underrated – comparable to gender equality some ten years ago. In many DAC countries the issue of "data" is dealt with either in the "sector" department – much as health, education or agriculture – and/or are part of the "governance/public sector" portfolio. In the new age of data, data for development have an intrinsic and instrumental value, and development co-operation needs to adjust to this reality. DAC countries could make an important contribution to improving the production of data that matters for people; for example, a work stream within the OECD DAC could look at good practices and develop guidelines for how to best engage in this new field.

Data for development should be recognised as part of the essential infrastructure for delivering on national, regional and global development commitments. The OECD DAC, the G20, the UN General Assembly, and other high-level strategic and political fora can lead efforts to build awareness of and support for the data for development agenda. Data for development discussions at high-level fora can also be used to review the status of work towards existing commitments.

2. Establish co-ordinated and effective donor support for development data

A business-as-usual approach will not suffice to enable the urgent changes needed in national statistical capacity and the related support systems. Analyses of how ODA is distributed for development data projects show that statistics are in fact underfunded despite the widespread discussions of their central role in the implementation of the 2030 Agenda. Furthermore, the evidence suggests that funding for data for development is not strategically allocated or efficiently used. Rather, it is largely concentrated among a few providers and goes to a relatively small number of countries (PARIS21, 2017).

Build an alliance for improved effectiveness of assistance for development data

One way of responding to the need for increased donor co-ordination would be to build a formal alliance among providers in support of development data. A Development Data Donors' Alliance (hereafter referred to as "the Alliance") could share strategic plans as well as information on focus countries, sectors, support for specialised activities, tools and portals. Such an alliance could produce marked improvements in the distribution, sequencing and monitoring of support for development data. Providers would need to remain flexible and open to make needed adjustments over time in setting their priorities.

An alliance could produce marked improvements in the distribution, sequencing and monitoring of support for development data.

The Alliance could also help to bring in new partners and ways of delivering support. The data revolution includes many new players who have much to contribute to the functioning of official statistical systems. The private sector, particularly information and communications technology firms, have unique datasets and technical expertise to share. As users of official statistics, businesses can be incentivised to join with traditional providers in funding improvements in statistical systems.

Create data compacts for a country-led development data revolution

Improved management of aid for data and statistics in the form of a data compact, where both parties agree on a set of criteria, could address some of the current stumbling blocks to ensuring holistic demand-driven support. A data compact can facilitate such interactions, allowing all the stakeholders involved in a country's statistical development – national governments, external funders, citizen groups, media and technical agencies – the opportunity to come together at an early stage of planning and jointly establish a development data action plan (Box 4.1). By signing and committing to a data compact they establish a performance agreement based on the individual country's own national plans. Through the data compact, the plan is underpinned by financing from domestic and international sources and can build in incentives for data quality improvements, open data, promoting data use and data impact. The agreement can also create momentum for bringing new stakeholders, partners and providers of development co-operation into the data compact discussions.

The data compact idea has been discussed in several studies of development data funding and capacity-building needs (PARIS21, 2015; GPSDD, 2016; CGD, 2014; UNECA, 2016). However, the concept has not been fully tested or implemented. This is mainly because no one development agency so far has been able to take on the convening role among the diverse group of stakeholders. PARIS21 is in a good position to pilot data compacts in a few countries and, based on the outcome, help to scale up the concept as a natural next step for countries that are updating an older national strategy for the development of statistics or establishing a new one.

Improve monitoring and establish a marker for development data

Measuring support to statistics comes with many methodological challenges. The PARIS21 Secretariat has identified best practices in reporting and begun to promote their implementation. If followed by more aid providers, their use would result in considerable improvements of current reporting and co-ordination, for example:

- To circumvent the issue of double counting that arises when providers and implementing agencies report the same activity twice, multilateral reporters to the PRESS questionnaire indicate their role as "implementer" (rather than "donor") when they manage or implement a project financed by another donor. Such reporting allows the PARIS21 Secretariat to ensure that these commitments appear only once in the global number, resulting in a more accurate estimate.
- To solve the problem of counting project totals for multi-recipient projects, some OECD-DAC Creditor Reporting System (CRS) reporters already split their projects into sub-projects – one per recipient country – with each specifying the respective share of the total project commitment that goes to statistics. PARIS21 has incorporated this practice in its methodology and encourages its use.
- Finally, with the current call for a substantial increase in support to statistics, it is important to assess each country's absorptive capacity, ensuring that it can make effective use of an increase in funding. To this end, ODA reporting needs to go beyond commitments, also recording actual disbursements of funding as well as domestic resources invested in statistics. The PARIS21 Secretariat provides technical support to countries in producing complete budgets.

To establish a fully functional system that measures the real support to statistics, however, a marker for development data in the CRS will be indispensable. Although there is a CRS sector code for statistical capacity building, it fails, for example, to identify multi-sector projects that comprise only a small statistics component. Aside from improving the identification of the many related projects in ODA reporting, this would also acknowledge the strategic importance of statistical capacity building. A marker would also help systems that build on the CRS system, such as the International Aid Transparency Initiative and AidData, to track aid data. At the same time, it is important that there be wide participation in efforts to increase the transparency of funding for development data. This includes the participation of philanthropic organisations, which should follow the example of the Bill & Melinda Gates Foundation by providing data on their funding. A task force could be established to consider ways for funding agencies to make data on support to statistics more open and accessible.

3. Support the 2030 Agenda through the 2020 census round

Developing countries require prompt action on many fronts, and needs vary from country to country. One area, however, requires immediate global support: the preparation of the 2020 census round. The 2020 global census is critical for the implementation of the SDGs.

The Millennium Development Goals created global momentum behind planning and financing the 2010 census round, and this was one of their significant successes. Without a concerted global effort to replicate this success in 2020, many people will be left behind. Censuses yield population numbers, and these are the denominator of a large portion of the 232 agreed-upon SDG indicators. However, no one community or organisation alone, be it senior development policy makers, providers of development co-operation, technical specialists, non-governmental organisations or operational teams, can move the needle on this agenda. It requires collective action by all stakeholders (Box 4.2).

Box 4.2. **Guiding principles for the 2020 census round**

Established principles can guide the 2020 census to ensure its effectiveness in contributing to the implementation of the Sustainable Development Goals (SDGs):

- **Collect the data once – use it many times:** Tap into existing data sources; build data analysis skills nationally and regionally; focus on improving the frequency of updating and the level of disaggregation of the existing data.
- **Focus on filling core gaps:** Make sure that all countries produce core statistics for monitoring their economic, social and environmental progress.
- **Ensure essential rights:** Make data part of the right to be counted; to access information; to participate (through citizen-generated data); and to privacy and ownership of personal data (anonymity and quality standards).
- **Support co-ordination:** Ensure new data ecosystems (new collaborative and co-operative arrangements) do not disrupt the governance of data at the country level; fund alternative data collections in co-ordination with national representatives.
- **Uphold diversity:** Each country has a unique national data ecosystem, depending on its socio-economic, political and legal environment.
- **Leverage innovation:** New data technologies can help to fill the data gaps identified in national strategies.
- **Move away from projects and programmes:** Manage for development results by investing in whole-of-government approaches through national strategies.
- **Look beyond the SDGs:** Promote systemic improvement by embedding action in national statistical systems and not only generating information on specific indicators.
- **Focus on outcomes:** Make sure issues are monitored from a results-based perspective (for instance, that school enrolment rates are accompanied by learning assessments).

Priority steps in rethinking donor support for statistical capacity building

- Raise the profile of data for development at the highest political level.
- Treat data for development as a cross-cutting priority, viewing it as both a key means of achieving the SDGs and as an integral goal in itself.
- Revitalise support to development data; acknowledge the need for building the statistical capacity of developing countries.
- Increase domestic, international and private support for statistics and align support with national statistical plans and priorities.
- Ensure that strengthening of national systems is country driven.
- Focus on data use and users, as well as on dissemination and format.
- Establish co-ordinated and effective donor support for development data; build partnerships and co-operation.
- Increase the use of new funding mechanisms with a result-based focus.
- Improve monitoring, tracking and transparency of investments in development data.
- Contribute to the 2030 Agenda by supporting preparations for the 2020 census round.

Notes

1. Target 17.18: "By 2020, enhance capacity-building support to developing countries, including for least developed countries and small island developing states, to increase significantly the availability of high-quality, timely and reliable data disaggregated by income, gender, age, race, ethnicity, migratory status, disability, geographic location and other characteristics relevant in national contexts." Target 17.19: "By 2030, build on existing initiatives to develop measurements of progress on sustainable development that complement gross domestic product, and support statistical capacity-building in developing countries."
2. The United Nations Secretary-General's report, "A world that counts", says "Data are the lifeblood of decision-making and the raw material for accountability. Without high-quality data providing the right information on the right things at the right time, designing, monitoring and evaluating effective policies becomes almost impossible" (IEAG, 2014). More recently, the Cape Town Global Action Plan for Sustainable Development Data calls for a "global pact or alliance that recognises the funding of national statistical system modernisation efforts is essential to the full implementation of Agenda 2030" (UNSC, 2017).
3. The study focuses exclusively on the Tier I and Tier II SDG indicators for which there are existing data or known collection methodologies (GPSDD, 2016).
4. The 2017 PARIS21 "Partner report on support to statistics" uses data from an annual donor survey and from the OECD-DAC Creditor Reporting System to report on commitments to statistical capacity building from 2006 to 2015. It measures financial support from multilateral and bilateral providers covering all areas of statistics, from national accounts to human resources and training (PARIS21, 2017).
5. The top five providers of support for statistics in 2015 were the African Development Bank, Canada, the European Commission/EUROSTAT, the United Nations Population Fund and the World Bank. The International Monetary Fund, which was one of the top five donors in 2014, did not make the deadline to report to PRESS 2017. Its commitments to statistical development will be included in PRESS 2018.
6. For the purposes of this report, the definition for fragility and the identification of countries satisfying those criteria are drawn from the World Bank's harmonised list of fragile states, available at: *http://go.worldbank.org/BNFOS8V3S0*.
7. See: *www.oecd.org/dac/effectiveness/parisdeclarationandaccraagendaforaction.htm*.
8. In 2015, Open Data Watch released a report highlighting lessons learnt from 27 evaluations of statistical capacity programmes (ODW, 2015). The UN has also published a document on the implementation of the Fundamental Principles of Official Statistics, which helps illustrate the needs of national statistical offices and highlight what they find works well (UNSD, 2015). Another evaluation looks at lessons learnt from international statistical capacity building during the era of the Millennium Development Goals and applies these lessons to the 2030 Agenda (UNJIU, 2016).
9. These include the Capacity Development track at the 2017 United Nations World Data Forum in Cape Town, the 2017 PARIS21 Annual Meeting on "Revisiting Capacity Development to Deliver on the SDGs", and several events during the 48th Session of the United Nations Statistical Commission.

References

Burgess, S. et al. (2013), "A natural experiment in school accountability: The impact of school performance information on pupil progress", *Journal of Public Economics*, Vol. 106, pp. 57-67, *https://doi.org/10.1016/j.jpubeco.2013.06.005*.

CGD (2014), *Delivering on the Data Revolution in Sub-Saharan Africa: Final Report of the Data for African Development Working Group*, Center for Global Development, Washington, DC, *www.cgdev.org/publication/delivering-data-revolution-sub-saharan-africa-0*.

GPEDC (2016), "Nairobi outcome document" of the Second High-Level Meeting of the Global Partnership for Effective Development Co-operation, Global Partnership for Effective Development Co-operation, *http://effectivecooperation.org/wp-content/uploads/2016/12/OutcomeDocumentEnglish.pdf*.

GPSDD (2016), "The state of development data funding 2016", Global Partnership for Sustainable Development Data, *http://opendatawatch.com/wp-content/uploads/2016/09/development-data-funding-2016.pdf*.

IEAG (2014), "A world that counts: Mobilizing the data revolution for sustainable development", Independent Expert Advisory Group on a Data Revolution for Sustainable Development, United Nations, New York, *www.undatarevolution.org/wp-content/uploads/2014/11/A-World-That-Counts.pdf*.

Keijzer, N. and S. Klingebiel (2017), "Realising the data revolution for sustainable development: Towards capacity development 4.0", *PARIS21 Discussion Paper*, No. 9, Partnership in Statistics for Development in the 21st Century, Paris, *www.paris21.org/sites/default/files/CapacityDevelopment4.0_FINAL_0.pdf*.

Kiregyera, B. (2013), "The emerging data revolution in Africa: Strengthening the statistics, policy and decision-making chain", Sun Press.

Klingebiel, S., T. Casjen Mahn and M. Negre (eds.) (2016), "Fragmentation: A key concept for development cooperation", in: *The Fragmentation of Aid: Concepts, Measurements and Implications for Development Cooperation*, Palgrave Macmillan, United Kingdom, *www.palgrave.com/de/book/9781137553560*.

Mo Ibrahim Foundation (2016), "Strength in numbers: Africa's data revolution", Mo Ibrahim Foundation, *http://s.mo.ibrahim.foundation/u/2016/05/16162558/Strength-in-Numbers.pdf*.

ODW (2015), "Aid for statistics: An inventory of financial instruments", Open Data Watch, Washington, DC, *http://opendatawatch.com/wp-content/uploads/2016/02/Aid-For-Statistics-An-Inventory-of-Financial-Instruments.pdf*.

PARIS21 (2017), "Partner report on support to statistics: PRESS 2017", Partnership in Statistics for Development in the 21st Century, OECD, Paris, *www.paris21.org/press2017*.

PARIS21 (2016), "Partner report on support to statistics: PRESS 2016", Partnership in Statistics for Development in the 21st Century, OECD, Paris, *www.paris21.org/sites/default/files/PRESS-2016-web-final.pdf*.

PARIS21 (2015), *A Road Map for a Country-led Data Revolution*, OECD Publishing, Paris, *http://dx.doi.org/10.1787/9789264234703-en*.

PARIS21 (2011), *Statistics for Transparency, Accountability, and Results: A Busan Action Plan for Statistics*, Partnership in Statistics for Development in the 21st Century, OECD, Paris, *www.paris21.org/sites/default/files/Busanactionplan_nov2011.pdf*.

Sanna, V. and I. Mc Donnell (2017), "Data for development: DAC member priorities and challenges", *OECD Development Co-operation Working Papers*, No. 35, OECD Publishing, Paris, *http://dx.doi.org/10.1787/6e342488-en*.

SDSN (2015), "Data for development: A needs assessment for SDG monitoring and statistical capacity development", United Nations Sustainable Development Solutions Network, New York, *http://unsdsn.org/wp-content/uploads/2015/04/Data-for-Development-Full-Report.pdf*.

Taylor, M. (2016), "The political economy of statistical capacity: A theoretical approach", *Inter-American Development Bank Discussion Paper*, IDB-DP-471, Inter-American Development Bank, *https://publications.iadb.org/bitstream/handle/11319/7794/ThePolitical-Economy-of-Statistical-Capacity-A-Theoretical-Approach.pdf?sequence=2*.

UN (2015a), "Addis Ababa Action Agenda of the Third International Conference on Financing for Development (Addis Ababa Action Agenda)", United Nations, New York, *www.un.org/esa/ffd/wp-content/uploads/2015/08/AAAA_Outcome.pdf*.

UN (2015b), *The Millennium Development Goals Report*, United Nations, New York, *www.un.org/millenniumgoals/2015_MDG_Report/pdf/MDG%202015%20rev%20(July%201).pdf*.

UN (2015c), "Transforming our world: The 2030 Agenda for Sustainable Development", United Nations, New York, *https://sustainabledevelopment.un.org/post2015/transformingourworld/publication*.

UNECA (2016), "The Africa data revolution report 2016: Highlighting developments in African data ecosystems", United Nations Economic Commission for Africa, *www.africa.undp.org/content/rba/en/home/library/reports/the_africa_data_revolution_report_2016.html*.

UNECE (2016), "Value of official statistics – interim report", United Nations Economic Commission for Europe, *www.unece.org/fileadmin/DAM/stats/documents/ece/ces/2016/mtg/CES_11_-ENG_G1602756.pdf*.

UNFPA (2016), "Evaluation of UNFPA support to population and housing census data to inform decision-making and policy formulation 2005-2014", Evaluation Brief, Evaluation Office, United Nations Population Fund, New York, *www.unfpa.org/sites/default/files/admin-resource/Evaluation_report_-_Volume.pdf*.

UNJIU (2016), "Independent system-wide evaluation of operational activities for development: Evaluation of the contribution of the United Nations development system to strengthening national capacities for statistical analysis and data collection to support the achievement of the Millennium Development Goals and other internationally agreed development goals: Technical appendix", United Nations Joint Inspection Unit, *www.unjiu.org/en/reports-notes/CEB%20and%20organisation%20documents/Technical%20Appendix_JIU_REP_2016_5_Final.pdf*.

UNSC (2017), "Cape Town Global Action Plan for Sustainable Development Data", United Nations Statistics Commission, New York, *http://undataforum.org/WorldDataForum/wp-content/uploads/2017/01/Cape-Town-Action-Plan-For-Data-Jan2017.pdf*.

UNSD (2015), *UN Fundamental Principles of Official Statistics – Implementation Guidelines 2015*, United Nations Statistics Division, United Nations, New York, *https://unstats.un.org/unsd/dnss/gp/Implementation_Guidelines_FINAL_without_edit.pdf*.

Vaitla, B. et al. (2017), "Phone records track malaria", in: *Data Impacts: Case Studies from the Data Revolution*, Data Impacts, *http://dataimpacts.org/project/malaria*.

World Bank (2017), *Statistical Capacity Indicators* (database), *http://databank.worldbank.org/data/reports.aspx?source=statistical-capacity-indicators#*.

World Bank (2016), Global Financing Facility website, *www.globalfinancingfacility.org*.

World Bank (2004), "Marrakech Action Plan for Statistics", World Bank Group, Washington, DC, *www.worldbank.org/en/data/statistical-capacity-building/marrakech-action-plan-for-statistics*.

Further reading

GPSDD (n.d.), "Data roadmaps for sustainable development guidelines", webpage, Global Partnership for Sustainable Development Data, *www.data4sdgs.org/data-roadmaps-for-sustainable-development-guidelines*.

GWG (2015) , "Principles for Access to Big Data Sources", United Nations Global Working Group on Big Data for Official Statistics, United Nations, New York, *https://unstats.un.org/unsd/trade/events/2015/abudhabi/gwg/GWG%202015%20-%20item%202%20(ii)%20-%20Draft%20Access%20Principles%20-%20TTAP%20deliverable%202.pdf*.

Klein, T. and S. Verhulst (2017), "Access to new data sources for statistics: Business models and incentives for the corporate sector", *PARIS21 Discussion Paper*, No. 10, Partnership in Statistics for Development in the 21st Century, Paris, *www.paris21.org/sites/default/files/Paper_new-data-sources_final.pdf*.

Robin, N., T. Klein and J. Jütting (2016), "Public-private partnerships for statistics: Lessons learned, future steps: A focus on the use of non-official data sources for national statistics and public policy", *OECD Development Co-operation Working Papers*, No. 27, OECD Publishing, Paris, *http://dx.doi.org/10.1787/5jm3nqp1g8wf-en*.

UN (2016), *Framework for the Development of Environment Statistics (FDES 2013)*, United Nations Statistics Division, Department of Economic and Social Affairs, New York, *https://unstats.un.org/unsd/ENVIRONMENT/FDES/FDES-2015-supporting-tools/FDES.pdf*.

UN (2014), "Fundamental Principles of Official Statistics", United Nations General Assembly, New York, *https://unstats.un.org/unsd/dnss/gp/FP-New-E.pdf*.

PART I

Chapter 5

Making better use of results data in development co-operation

by
Rosie Zwart *and* John Egan, OECD Development Co-operation Directorate

Under pressure to account for the use of taxpayers' money, providers of development co-operation tend to report on the immediate outputs of their development co-operation efforts. By focusing instead on outcomes and change, they can support developing countries in securing the long-term impact envisaged in their own development priorities and, ultimately, achieving the Sustainable Development Goals. This chapter examines how better use of results data can improve the contribution of development co-operation to national and global development goals. It looks at who produces results data, who uses it and how. The chapter reviews the factors that influence choices about data collection and the unintended consequences these choices can have. Finally, it examines the gap between donor commitments and action. It makes suggestions for a more co-ordinated and country-led approach, utilising the Sustainable Development Goal targets and indicators as a shared framework.

Key facts

- More than half (16 out of 30) of the members of the OECD Development Assistance Committee (DAC) find it challenging to base development co-operation decisions on evidence from statistics and data (Sanna and Mc Donnell, 2017).
- While 17 DAC members try to use partner country data by default, their success in doing so varies from country to country (Sanna and Mc Donnell, 2017).
- In 2015, 81% of new projects agreed by DAC members were aligned with developing country objectives. Yet just 58% drew on developing country results indicators and only 50% relied on country data sources (OECD/UNDP, 2016).
- Since 2015, six DAC member agencies[1] have introduced new or updated standard indicator sets for agency-wide results reporting; the next step is to align these indicators with what is measured by developing countries and to make efforts to harmonise the indicators among providers (OECD, 2017a).

The 2030 Agenda for Sustainable Development is ultimately about development results.[2] Data can be used to demonstrate progress towards these results – the Sustainable Development Goals (SDGs) and their targets – evidencing the development outcomes that are being achieved and the change that is occurring.[3] Each country (developed and developing) has its own political goals and priorities and is focusing on those SDGs which align to these priorities. Yet the SDGs and their targets are integrated and indivisible. While countries prioritise the goals and targets that are most important for their own sustainable development, the United Nations is mandated to monitor and promote the 2030 Agenda as a whole (OECD, 2017b; 2017c).

To contribute to achieving results in developing countries, providers of development co-operation are attempting to:

- maximise their contribution to the SDG results that developing countries have prioritised within their national systems and frameworks
- better understand the linkages between progress towards SDG targets, and the allocation and use of development co-operation resources
- use results data to inform decisions about their development co-operation interventions and make course corrections
- safeguard ODA budgets by demonstrating impact to their constituencies.

Development data that demonstrate change are crucial in these efforts. They come from a variety of sources, including data collected in countries through national and subnational statistical systems; data collected and verified by multilateral institutions; data from research and evaluations; and data collected on activities funded by providers to monitor their specific development interventions.

Politicians and the public in provider countries are demanding evidence of how taxpayers' money is being used and what it is achieving.

Politicians and the public in provider countries are demanding evidence that aid is being well spent. They want to know how taxpayers' money is being used and what it is achieving. In other words, they want to know the results of development co-operation (OECD, 2016). Under pressure to be accountable for their use of taxpayer money, providers are reporting on the outputs of development co-operation using data from the projects they have funded. They report, for example, on numbers of people trained, facilities built, children educated, mothers reached during pregnancy, and households provided with safe water or reliable electricity (OECD, 2017a).

The focus on the outputs of development co-operation efforts explains what is delivered as a result of aid, but does not explain what has been achieved in terms of advancing development in the countries where development co-operation providers work and, ultimately, of progress towards the SDGs. To do so requires a focus on outcomes, impact[4] and change. While data showing outcomes may be generated during project implementation, data on impact and change are normally obtained from a country's national statistical system or from multilateral institutions (for example, on infant mortality rates, employment rates, CO_2 emissions). Research and evaluations also generate information about outcomes and impact.

Where results data are lacking, providers may invest directly in data collection. However, data generated through provider efforts may or may not be available to their partners in developing countries and to other development actors, and their collection and use of these data may also duplicate or overlap similar efforts by others.

Much can be done to improve the quantity, quality and accessibility of data. Doing so can enable data to be used more effectively to demonstrate the contribution of development co-operation to sustainable development, and can help countries and the global community measure and steer their policies and interventions towards the goals they have set.

This chapter explains what is meant by "results data" in the context of development co-operation. It examines who uses these data and in what contexts. The chapter explores how providers source results data and the factors influencing their choices about data collection and use. It then explores the unintended consequences of these choices at the country level, before setting out suggestions for a more co-ordinated effort, utilising the SDG targets and indicators as a shared framework.[5]

What are results data?

Providers of development co-operation use data collected at all stages along the "results chain", from inputs and activities, through outputs and outcomes, to impact (Figure 5.1).

Figure 5.1. **The results chain and the relevant categories of results data**

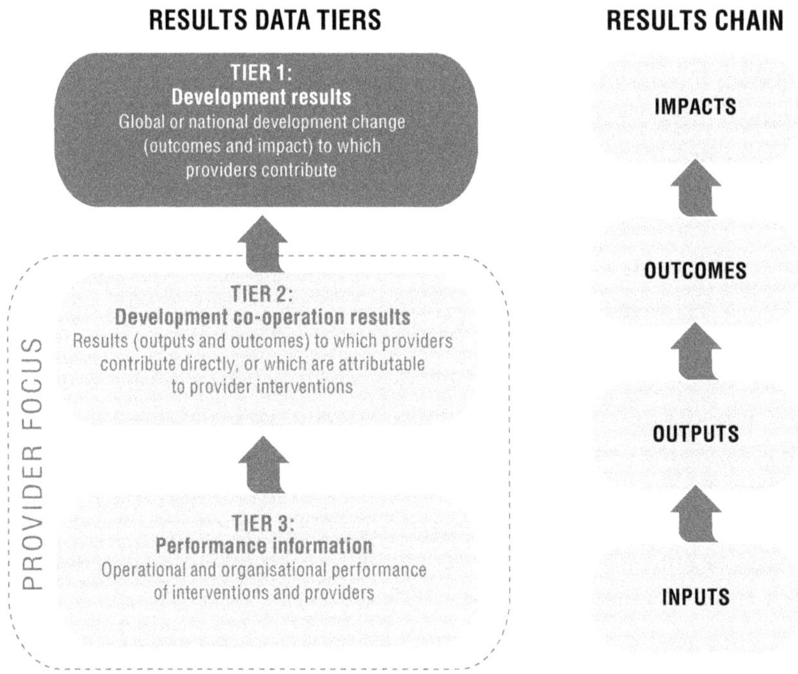

Source: OECD (2017a), "Strengthening the results chain: Synthesis of results-based management by providers", *http://dx.doi.org/10.1787/544032a1-en*.

In previous chapters, development data are referred to as those data collected for reference or analysis of progress towards sustainable development. In this chapter, the term "results data" refers to the use of these data for the analysis of progress at each stage of the results chain, as follows:

- "Development results data" illustrate impact and change in global or national development (Tier 1) resulting from the collective effort of all development actors, including providers and their country partners.
- "Development co-operation results data" show progress achieved through development co-operation efforts, whether these results are directly attributable to a specific provider, or reflect the contributions of the provider together with other development actors (Tier 2).

Providers increasingly favour data from Tier 2, and also frequently use data demonstrating the operational and organisational performance of their interventions (Tier 3 – performance information; see Figure 5.1). This is largely because data from Tiers 2 and 3 can be directly attributed[6] to the aid provided.

Providers' approaches to managing results can draw data from all three tiers. At Tier 3, input data drawn from financial, aid and human resource management systems show how well activities are performing – for example the number of projects funded, the quality of delivery, the amount of ODA spent, the percentage of ODA delivered as planned, the use made of developing country systems and the turnover of staff. These input data are not classified as results data.

In Tier 2, data from projects funded show the outputs and immediate outcomes that have been delivered as a result of the support given. In the education sector, for example, this may include the number of children enrolled in primary school, the number of classrooms constructed and the number of teachers trained. If a single provider funds the total cost of a project, these outputs can be directly attributed to that support. Otherwise, the provider is seen as having contributed to the outputs. Providers also use data on the immediate outcomes resulting from these outputs to demonstrate the effectiveness of their support.

In Tier 1, providers may use data drawn from a country's national statistical system to show the change that has occurred in the country. This may include, for example, literacy and numeracy rates, the percentage of females in secondary and tertiary education, or student achievement rates. They may also use data collected and verified by multilateral agencies to demonstrate change that has occurred globally, for example the percentage of men and women worldwide having access to affordable and quality technical, vocational and tertiary education. Providers use these data to highlight the contributions of their specific development co-operation efforts to national and global development results.

Development co-operation results are the direct outputs or outcomes of provider-funded projects. They contribute to the achievement of development results, including long-term impact or change such as that articulated in the SDGs.

Who produces and uses results data?

Results data are produced and used by a wide range of actors. The focus in this chapter is on data that inform development co-operation, and on the use of these data by providers.

Data on development results are generated by the national statistical system in each country: the ensemble of organisations and units within a country that collect, process and disseminate official statistics (see Chapter 3). In this chapter, these are referred to as "country-led results data". Relevant data are also collected by multilateral institutions tasked with producing and verifying global data and statistics. The 2030 Agenda focus on leaving no one behind will require increasing disaggregation of data, drawing in particular on subnational data (Box 5.1).

Data on development co-operation results are generated by actors involved in delivering development co-operation, including developing countries, providers and implementing partners. When these data are not available from a country's national statistical system, subnational systems or third parties (civil society organisations, academia, etc.), they are generated and collected through the projects that are funded (i.e. at the point of service delivery).

Box 5.1. **What types of results data are most important?**

All too often, discussions about managing for results fail to specify who is managing, or what results data are being used. Identifying the who and what is critical, as understanding the context of decisions informs what types of tools, processes and information are needed by decision makers.

At the **global** level, data related to Sustainable Development Goal (SDG) indicators may be among the most important types of results data. They can be used at an aggregate level to measure country, regional and global progress (for example towards Target 3.1, maternal mortality[1]), or to enable cross-country comparisons. They also can contribute to decision making by countries and development agencies on resource allocation. Each indicator has, or is expected to have, definitions and methodologies, as well as a clear designation of the United Nations agency responsible for reporting on it.

At the **country** level, the most important indicators within the national monitoring and evaluation framework are those that measure progress against the national development plan. These may overlap with the SDGs, or may be distinct. The data on these indicators primarily support national decision makers in assessing ministerial, sectoral or national progress against the priorities set by the government. For example, the Tanzania Five Year Development Plan (2016/17-2020/21) has a goal related to maternal mortality.[1] Data on progress towards this goal are used annually in the national planning and policy-making processes, and (to some extent) quarterly by line ministries. Providers can also use these data to align their aid to the development needs of their partners.

At the **community** or subnational level, data on service delivery, inputs and disaggregated outcomes are the most important. This information is used to monitor service delivery and facility reporting; plan capacity-building programmes; support supervision visits; and evaluate staff performance. In countries where there is a high level of decentralisation, these data also contribute to district budget and planning processes. For example, the Tanzanian district medical officers use reports from the reproductive, maternal, neonatal, adolescent and child health programmes to monitor service delivery related to maternal health in their district's facilities. The District Council Health Management team also uses annual and monthly programme reports to plan district health budget and allocation activities. These data may also be used by providers to monitor the outcomes of projects.

Contributed by Vinisha Bhatia-Murdach, Development Gateway.

1. Bring [the] maternal mortality rate to 250 per 100 000 by 2020/21 and to 220 per 100 000 by 2025/26.

What results data do providers use and what drives their choices?

Two factors have an important influence on the results data that providers use in their development co-operation: 1) the quality and availability of country-led results data; and 2) the information that providers need to meet their domestic accountability requirements (see the "In my view" piece by Ellen Cathrine Kiøsterud).

Providers of development co-operation have committed to using developing countries' own results data and systems.

Providers of development co-operation have committed to using developing countries' own results data and systems[7] to determine whether development co-operation interventions are contributing to the impact and change for which countries are striving (OECD, 2005; 2011). In 2016 in Nairobi, they agreed to support countries in developing and implementing their own country-led

In my view: International development partners face the challenge of good practice

Ellen Cathrine Kiøsterud,
Division for Development Co-operation, Statistics Norway

When capacity building in national statistics systems is discussed by the international community, questions concerning the challenges of co-ordination among supporters and alignment with national priorities often headline the deliberations.

Despite these debates, however, many resources continue to be channelled to parallel processes of data collection and analysis, with limited participation by national statistical offices. If involved at all, their role may be reduced to that of data collectors, while the processing and analysis takes place elsewhere. Even when there are workshops for national institutions, these may not be sufficient to enable them to take charge of the process. In extreme cases, the knowledge of the methods and quality factors behind core indicators is held by international consultants who have moved on to their next assignment.

Coverage is another challenge. To make statistics useful for national policy development and monitoring, many areas must be covered; national statistical systems need coherent and relevant data on the whole population. Yet these are not necessarily of interest to survey programmes reporting on international indicators or covering the limited geographical area of a specific programme. What's more, when national systems and international organisations produce similar statistics, confusion arises.

The World Food Programme provides a good example of how the statistical community can approach these challenges. Moving away from implementing costly surveys on food security and vulnerability, instead it is using data collected through national household budget surveys to feed into nationwide baseline reports on food security. This process is cost efficient, avoids duplication and supports national systems.

Experience shows that the international community can benefit from supporting national survey programmes rather than creating alternatives. This does not mean that all information needs can be met by national systems and that all statistics need to be official. For example, there may be a need for quick and limited surveys for programme purposes. Channelling the demand for these ad hoc statistics to the national system may overload the system and delay regular production.

Another issue is trust. Distrust in the independence of government approved statistics is not uncommon, and international organisations hold an equally biased interest in the results of the statistics production they support. It is therefore crucial to strengthen the independence, capacity and transparency of those organisations whose task it is to produce and deliver statistics of high quality.

In my view, donors should begin by doing the following:

- Support statistics production aligned with national information needs.
- Co-ordinate with other organisations to channel core statistics production through national statistical offices/ organisations.
- Avoid parallel and ad hoc surveys; indicators should be monitored for all and over time.
- Invest in administrative data, which improves planning and monitoring at the subnational level and reduces the cost of statistics production over time.
- Support the delivery of timely and high-quality statistics by national entities, including by building capacity and reducing the dependence on consultants.

When donors receive applications for support to statistics, the first question they should ask is whether this information is of national interest and if the project will contribute to strengthening national, sustainable structures.

results frameworks and associated systems (e.g. health and education information management systems).[8] Providers also offered to assist countries in integrating the SDGs into their national development plans, results frameworks and data collection efforts.

To strengthen the focus on results, we will:

further develop, support and use country-level results frameworks; progressively adapt results frameworks to reflect the targets and indicators of the SDGs; and make data on results publicly available.

further develop, support and use national statistical systems, and generate disaggregated data to report on progress (GPEDC, 2016).

In addition, providers agreed to minimise the use of additional or parallel frameworks, and to refrain from pressuring countries to add performance indicators that are not consistent with the country's own priorities (GPEDC, 2016).

Unfortunately, the 2016 progress report of the Global Partnership for Effective Development Co-operation (GPEDC) found that while country data are being used to establish development priorities and plan development co-operation interventions, providers are making limited use of country results data and systems in the implementation, monitoring and evaluation of these interventions (OECD/UNDP, 2016). In 2015, the objectives of 81% of DAC members' new development co-operation interventions were aligned with the development priorities set by countries. However, only 58% of their new interventions drew their results indicators from those included in country results frameworks and only 50% intended to use countries' data and monitoring systems (OECD/UNDP, 2016).[9]

To explain their unwillingness to use countries' indicators, data and monitoring systems, providers cite the unreliability of national reporting and mismatches between provider and country reporting requirements and indicators (OECD, 2012). Furthermore, in a survey of DAC members undertaken for this report (Sanna and Mc Donnell, 2017), 16 of the 22 respondents indicated that they face challenges in having the right evidence from statistics and data for development co-operation decisions, programming, monitoring and reporting. The survey also found that while 17 of the 22 respondents tried to use partner country data by default, their actual use varies depending on the national system they are working with (Figure 5.2).

Figure 5.2. **Do Development Assistance Committee members use development data produced by their partners?**

Is it possible to rely on and use data produced by partner countries in development co-operation decision making, programming, monitoring and reporting?

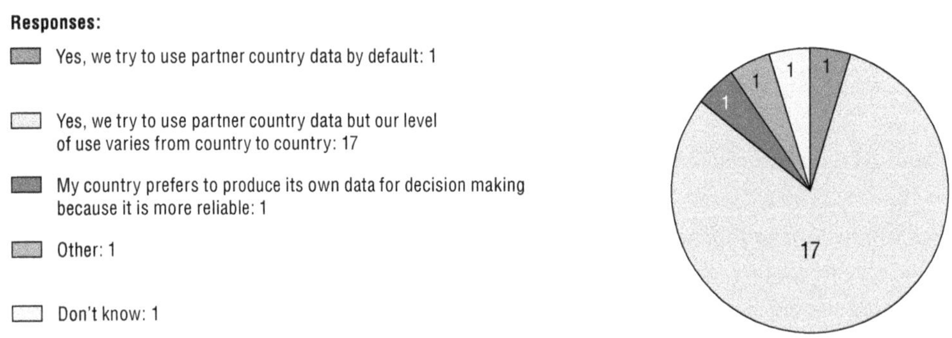

Note: Number of DAC members who responded: 21

Source: Sanna, V. and I. Mc Donnell (2017), "Data for development: DAC member priorities and challenges", *http://dx.doi.org/10.1787/6e342488-en*.

StatLink http://dx.doi.org/10.1787/888933591917

As described in Chapter 3, the quality of national statistical systems is variable. This affects the level of use of country data by providers of development co-operation. Poor data quality can result from delays in publication, episodic data collection, limited data management at the subnational level, insufficient disaggregation and gaps in coverage (Custer and Sethi, 2017a; 2017b). When they are not able to use country data, a number of DAC members attempt to fill the gaps with data from multilateral institutions or generated by the projects that they fund (Sanna and Mc Donnell, 2017). If these data are insufficient, they undertake one-off surveys and data collection efforts. This, as we will see below, has consequences for countries and other development actors.

Developing countries recognise that there are concerns regarding the coverage, quality, regularity and availability of their data and acknowledge that their national monitoring and evaluation frameworks are weak. They expect providers and other partners to work with them in addressing these challenges, rather than seeking other solutions (DCF, 2016).

Another driver of providers' choice of results data is their need to demonstrate performance and be accountable to parliament and taxpayers. To meet accountability needs, providers turn to results data on the outputs of development co-operation from the projects they fund. Project-level data are chosen to show that outputs are being delivered and, where possible, that outcomes are being achieved. When these data are used for programme or agency-wide reporting, ease of aggregation (i.e. the ability to group data from multiple projects under common indicators) and of attribution also influence which data are used (OECD, 2017a). Providers also use data for communication purposes, which are intrinsically linked to accountability (Box 5.2), and to a much lesser extent for learning, policy formulation and strategic decision making (OECD, 2016; 2017a).

Standard indicator sets, which are designed to aggregate project-level data and summarise agency-wide achievements, are increasingly used by providers for their reporting. The data are often derived from "reach indicators" – for example, the number of people reached by a service or intervention, or the amount of infrastructure installed. This type of results data is collected at the point of service delivery (at the project level), easily aggregated (i.e. data from multiple projects can be grouped by country or at an agency-wide level) and can readily be attributed to individual providers, thus meeting domestic accountability and communication requirements. For many providers, data from these indicators, alongside input or finance data, are key for reporting to both domestic parliaments and taxpayers (OECD, 2017a). Figure 5.3 sets out the main attributes of agency-wide results approaches among a selection of development co-operation providers. Recent DAC peer reviews indicate similar approaches exist among a wider group of DAC members.

Box 5.3 shows how the European Commission used standard indicators to report the results of the European Union's (EU) development co-operation in its 2015 results report.

To collect, aggregate and analyse project-level results data, providers are creating their own internal information management systems with increasingly sophisticated "results modules".[10] In theory, this enables greater use of data for decision making within development co-operation agencies, while still allowing aggregation for reporting purposes (OECD, 2017a). Several bilateral providers – including Austria, Canada, Ireland, the Netherlands, New Zealand and the United Kingdom – have established, or plan to establish, new donor-specific information technology solutions for the capture and analysis of results data (OECD, 2016; 2017a). Often the goal is to establish systems that can capture and code project-level data, which are then aggregated to the country, sector and agency-wide levels.[11]

Box 5.2. **Communicating about development results: Not just numbers**

There are important reasons for development agencies to communicate about results. Providers of development co-operation need to build public trust, showing taxpayers that aid is being put to good use. They also need to build public awareness, educating citizens about development and the role of development co-operation.

Since the turn of the century, providers have made considerable progress in communicating about their work. Aid data have become more transparent and increasingly accessible on line. Annual reports to parliament now include impressive numbers, not just on money spent, but also on the outcomes and impact of that spending. More and more information is also available on the activities of private development actors, such as non-governmental organisations and philanthropic foundations.

If you are interested in development, you will find interesting data on results.

But what about people who are not interested enough to seek out the facts? Surveys tell us that, despite communication efforts, the general public knows very little about the reality of life in developing countries or about international efforts to promote development.

According to a 2016 Glocalities Report, only 1% of people know that extreme poverty has been cut in half in the past 20 years; 87% of people think it has increased or stayed the same (Lampert and Papadongonas, 2016). In a 2015 survey of 17 traditional and emerging provider countries, 4 out of 10 people thought aid represented 3-10% of their country's annual budget (Ipsos Public Affairs, 2015). In reality, only five of the countries surveyed spent more than 1% on aid, and only one country – the United Arab Emirates – spent more than 3%.

If donors want the general public to know more about results and have an informed voice in the debate, they need to communicate differently. Drawing on recent discussions in the OECD Development Communication Network (DevCom, *oecd.org/dev/devcom*), here are five starting points:

1. Craft results messages that appeal to both hearts and minds. Citizens want to hear the real stories behind development. Numbers alone will not resonate with most people.
2. Choose results messengers to whom people can relate. Citizens want to hear from the beneficiaries of aid or from passionate field workers, not just politicians, diplomats or celebrities.
3. Use countries' own frameworks to find results data and stories. The most compelling stories come from the programmes and projects that local actors care about.
4. Build public trust over time by telling it how it is: development is complicated, risky and long term. Donors need a confident, but humbler, narrative about the role and impact of aid.
5. Use data to understand your audiences. Web analytics, public attitudes research and consultations can shed light on how to reach different constituencies. They can also tell communicators whether their work has been effective.

The late Professor Hans Rosling inspired millions of people to engage with development results, delivering tremendous data visualisations with charm, gentle provocation and humour. Data are an essential part of development communications, but narratives and emotions help bring them to life.*

Contributed by Felix Zimmermann, OECD Development Communication Network.

* Hans Rosling, was the co-founder and chairman of the Gapminder Foundation, which is an independent Swedish foundation which uses facts to fight misconceptions about global development, *www.gapminder.org/about-gapminder*.

Figure 5.3. **A comparison of results approaches**

	NETHERLANDS MINISTRY OF FOREIGN AFFAIRS	NEW ZEALAND MINISTRY OF FOREIGN AFFAIRS AND TRADE	SWISS AGENCY FOR DEVELOPMENT CO-OPERATION	WORLD BANK GROUP	UNITED KINGDOM DEPARTMENT FOR INTERNATIONAL DEVELOPMENT
Tier 1 Results	✖	✔	✖	✔	✖
Tier 2 Results	✔	✔	✔	✔	✔
Tier 3 Results	✖	✔	✖	✔	✔
No. of standard output/outcome indicators at Tier 2[1]	15	36	40	15	6
Attribution of Tier 2 results	✔	✔	✔	✖	✔
Aggregate targets used	✔	✖	✖	✖	✔
Year current approach introduced	2016	2016 (second generation)	2016	2011	2017

✔ YES ✖ NO

1. See Figure 5.1.

Source: OECD (2017a) "Strengthening the results chain: Synthesis of results-based management by providers", *http://dx.doi.org/10.1787/544032a1-en*.

Box 5.3. **Examples of European Union reporting**

The *EU International Cooperation and Development: First Report on Selected Results, July 2013-June 2014* (EC, 2017a) presents the results of the most financially important EU-funded projects and programmes completed between mid-2013 and mid-2014. It shows that, with the contribution of EU development co-operation:

- Over 4.5 million women of reproductive age and children under five benefited from nutrition-related programmes.
- Over 1.1 million births were attended by skilled health personnel, helping to reduce maternal mortality.
- Over 29 million children were enrolled in school, with over 19 million in primary education and 9.5 million in secondary education.
- More than 19 elections were supported, where the electoral process was perceived by independent observers as free and fair.
- Almost 14 million hectares of protected areas were managed to help ensure biological diversity and preserve natural heritage.
- More than 325 000 people benefited from training and skills development intended to improve their employability, productivity and competitiveness.

Source: EC (2017b), "EU publishes key results of its international cooperation and development activities", *http://europa.eu/rapid/press-release_IP-16-2543_en.htm*.

What are the unintended consequences of choices about results data?

We have seen that lack of trust in, and ultimately reluctance to use, country-led results data can lead providers to compensate by creating parallel mechanisms for data collection in developing countries. There is a risk that collection and use of project-level results data for standard indicator sets, and also for stand-alone project monitoring and reporting, can divert attention and resources away from measuring development change and outcomes at the country level (OECD, 2017a).

Attribution of results clashes with the principle of country ownership espoused by DAC members and their partners.

A growing body of evidence-based literature critiques approaches that focus on aggregating results data against standard indicator sets. The authors argue that such efforts have contributed to a range of unintended consequences, for example increased reporting burdens, poor data quality, perverse incentives (in both reporting and programming), failure to capture the totality of the results achieved, and loss of focus on learning (Holzapfel, 2016; Shutt, 2016; ICAI, 2015; World Bank, 2016). Attribution of results and use of targets imposed by provider headquarters also clash with the principle of country ownership espoused by DAC members and their partners for over a decade. Despite these findings, however, domestic pressures and requirements increasingly push providers towards the use of data that enables them to "brand" or claim ownership of the results.

Furthermore, aid providers are using standard indicators (and systems) at the country level that are distinct from, but similar to, those used by other providers, and, importantly, by developing countries themselves. The use of such standard project-level indicators for domestic accountability purposes complicates and fragments the country-level data landscape. Providers often cite the need to rationalise across their portfolios, avoiding the proliferation of multiple indicators, as an internal driver for the creation of standard indicator sets (OECD, 2017a).[12] However, when the standard indicators used by providers of development co-operation are compared, they are often similar, although with subtle differences. Table 5.1 compares, by sector, a sample of standard indicators used by the five providers profiled in Figure 5.3.

Table 5.1. **A comparison of standard indicators by sector**

Indicator	Netherlands Ministry of Foreign Affairs	New Zealand Ministry of Foreign Affairs and Trade	Swiss Agency for Development Co-operation	World Bank Group	UK Department for International Development (DFID)
Health sector	The additional number of women or their partners of reproductive age using a modern contraceptive method.	Number of people who have received essential medicines and care at primary health facilities (Number M/F).	Number of people reached through health education sessions related to the prevention of non-communicable diseases.	Number of people who have received essential health, nutrition and population services.	Number of additional women using modern methods of family planning through DFID support.
Education sector	n.a.	Number of children assisted in primary and secondary education (through sector support) (Number M/F, per year).	Number of children (< 15 years old) and number of persons > 15 years old who have gained access to quality basic education (M/F).	Number of students benefiting from direct interventions to enhance learning.	Number of children supported to gain a decent education.
Climate change/energy	Number of people with access to renewable energy.	Number of people provided with new or improved electricity supply (Number M/F).	Number of energy-related policies, laws, strategies and plans developed at the national level.	Number of people provided with new or improved electricity service.	DFID spending on climate.
Water sector	Number of people with access to safe and affordable drinking water.	Number of people provided with new or improved water supply (Number M/F).	Number of people who have gained new access to safe and affordable drinking water (M/F).	Number of people provided with access to improved water sources.	Number of people with sustainable access to clean water and/or sanitation through DFID support.

Source: OECD (2017a) "Strengthening the results chain: Synthesis of results-based management by providers", *http://dx.doi.org/10.1787/544032a1-en*.

The use of numerous related, but different, indicators inevitably leads to overlapping systems and reporting at the country level. This is challenging for implementing partners. In addition, these efforts may act against co-ordination and alignment around measurement of the SDG indicators that each country prioritises, undermining country ownership.

Low trust in country data combined with provider accountability requirements leads to overlapping data collection efforts that are not well shared.

Overall, the evidence suggests that there is a vicious cycle operating in some countries. Low trust in country data combined with provider accountability requirements leads to independent and often overlapping data collection efforts that are not well shared. When data are not shared, there is duplication and overlap; and when country data are not used, their quality does not improve, further diminishing the chances that they will be used (Custer and Sethi, 2017a, 2017b; Homer, Bhatia and Powell, 2016). As a recent OECD mutual accountability study in Timor-Leste found, while national governments want providers to use their systems and strengthen them over time, most providers want to see better systems in place before they start to use them (OECD, forthcoming).

How can results data better inform the contribution of development co-operation to the Sustainable Development Goals?

A focus on aggregated and attributed results data may provide domestic audiences with a tangible sense of what their aid dollar has purchased, but these data do not provide sufficient information about the outcomes, impact and change envisaged in the SDGs. By drawing on additional data and analysis, providers can tell an equally compelling story – and gain important insights – about the long-term changes their development co-operation efforts are helping to make happen.

The results of development co-operation are not limited to outputs and immediate outcomes. Development co-operation contributes to long-term outcomes in the countries in which it is delivered and this, in turn, contributes to real change. While providers may not be able to claim full responsibility for these changes as a result of their interventions, they can explain the contributions they make alongside their partner countries and other actors. It is important, therefore, that providers identify, support and use data that provide evidence of such change.

National statistical systems capture data on long-term outcomes, impact and change. To fill the gaps resulting from the limited capabilities of some national statistical systems, providers can draw on multilateral institutions; however, this is unlikely to fill all the gaps. For the time being, providers are supplementing these sources; but in order to have lasting impact, it is important that providers do so in a way that builds the capacity of national statistical systems.

The SDGs can serve as a platform for the shared generation and use of results data, enabling mutual accountability among all stakeholders.

Investments in and use of country-level results data will contribute to the monitoring and achievement of the SDGs at the country level. In turn, the SDGs can serve as a platform for the shared generation and use of results data, including for development co-operation, enabling mutual accountability among all stakeholders (OECD, forthcoming).

Developing countries are working to ensure that their national development plans reflect the SDGs, and that providers align with these priorities in their strategies and commitments. At a 2017 workshop jointly hosted by the OECD and the EU, partner country officials demonstrated how they are aligning their country results frameworks, budgeting and planning processes to selected SDGs.

Partners then urged providers to map aid resources to the SDG results defined in national strategies (OECD, 2017c; Savedoff, 2017). As one workshop participant observed: "the SDGs provide an opportunity to link domestic agendas to SDGs and then use that linkage as leverage to get co-operation from donors who are publicly committed to the same SDGs" (Savedoff, 2017). Collection and use of results data aligned with the SDG indicators is integral to ensuring such efforts remain on track (Box 5.4).

Box 5.4. **How Timor-Leste is using the Sustainable Development Goals as a shared results framework**

Timor-Leste is considered an early adopter of the Sustainable Development Goals (SDGs). Six SDGs have been prioritised and 21 indicators will be used to guide national action. Four ministries have been given responsibility for implementation of the selected SDGs and the Prime Minister's Office leads on monitoring progress. Timor-Leste has asked for donor champions on specific goals. In response, development partners have supported the government's approach to implementing the goals and to monitoring progress. Several partners (including the European Union and New Zealand) plan to adopt some of Timor-Leste's sustainable development plan indicators to help measure how their assistance contributes to SDG progress in the country.

The OECD study on mutual accountability notes that development of a shared results framework around Timor-Leste's progress towards the SDGs should create a pragmatic incentive for strategic dialogue, partnership, co-ordination and accountability among the government and its partners.

Source: OECD (forthcoming) "Going beyond the rhetoric: Mutual accountability in practice".

What can be done to increase the use of results data?

There is clearly scope for providers to increase their use of country results data and systems and, where they are not using these, to better harmonise indicators and ensure that results data from independent data collection efforts are co-ordinated with and made available to all stakeholders, in particular to the developing countries.

Development co-operation providers have commited to invest in, align with and use results data generated by developing countries' frameworks and systems. These commitments are intended to reduce the transaction costs that parallel systems place on countries, and to strengthen and improve national systems through their use. Providers must weigh up the benefits of investing in and using government data sources even when the data they provide are not completely accurate or do not have full coverage. The alternative – conducting separate primary data collection efforts – is counterproductive. Support for the collection and use of country-led data that measure outcomes and change can promote the purposeful use of evidence by providers and their partners.[13]

The Post 2015 Data Test[14] recommends investment in national priorities and systems, taking stock of and harnessing existing data sources, and ensuring long-term and predictable support for national statistics (Kindornay, Bhattacharya and Higgins, 2016). Investment in country-led data collection efforts should be guided by country priorities (including SDG priorities). Providers can make efforts to align their indicator sets to the indicators prioritised by developing countries while supporting these countries in streamlining their own indicators (Homer et al., 2016).

The SDGs can be used as a common framework. Alignment around the SDGs, and the targets and indicators prioritised by each country, enables a more co-ordinated and strategic approach to data measurement and management at the country level. Ultimately, this will enable development co-operation to better contribute to the achievement of the goals.

Alongside support for country-led generation of results data, providers should also invest in capacity building for using these data through results-based management, analysis and decision making.[15] Developing countries do not just need data. They need data that can be analysed and interpreted in a way that facilitates insights and decision making; they need the tools and capacity to enable this analysis; and they need the ability to meaningfully link aid data, budgets and results to provide greater insights (Homer, Bhatia and Powell, 2016; Custer and Sethi, 2017b).[16] In order to inform planning, budgeting, implementation, monitoring and evaluation, results data and systems need to be high quality, accurate and available.

Providers may wish to rethink attribution and work to ensure a do-no-harm approach to data collection.

It is important to acknowledge that despite the best efforts to support and strengthen country systems, providers will, for their own purposes, continue to support some data collection outside of country systems. However, data generated from these efforts are not always accessible to partner country governments or other development actors, and can draw resources from country-led data collection. In measuring progress towards the SDG targets, Kindornay, Bhattacharya and Higgins (2016) recommend ensuring that at the country level, unofficial data sources be accessed and used strategically – but not at the expense, or to the detriment, of official data. As such, providers may wish to rethink their approach to attribution and work instead to ensure a do-no-harm approach to the collection of data for standard indicators and other project-level needs. Moreover, any results data generated by providers should be considered, and treated as, a public good (World Bank, 2015).

Overall, a more strategic approach to data generation and access is required. Better alignment of indicators for results data collection is an important first step. While good practice examples exist, they are often project or relationship-specific. Providers must recognise that at the country level they "should be better co-ordinated among themselves to avoid duplication, promote synergies and increase impact through collective action" (OECD, forthcoming).

The way forward for making better use of results data

A stronger focus on outcomes and change will enable providers to tell a more compelling story about the contribution of development co-operation to achieving the SDGs. It will also enable them to focus development co-operation efforts on helping countries achieve their own sustainable development priorities. Data contribute to the achievement of the SDGs by enabling learning, insights, analysis, comparison, identification of needs, prioritisation, and a platform for dialogue and decision making throughout the implementation cycle.

Development results and development co-operation results represent a shared effort in which developing countries have the greatest stake.

Reconsidering how data on the results of development co-operation are generated and used, both at headquarters and in-country, would enable providers to find ways to better harmonise their data requirements with those of other development actors and their country partners. An important first step would be to acknowledge that development results and development co-operation results represent a shared effort in which developing countries have the greatest stake. An exclusive focus on attribution of results solely for reporting purposes limits the ability to heighten development co-operation's contribution to achieving the SDGs and runs against the grain of the underlying development effectiveness principles.

Co-ordinating and aligning results data and indicator requirements at the country and sectoral levels will strengthen country systems. Providers of development co-operation are ideally placed to support national data and statistics at all levels by using country data to demonstrate and contextualise the contribution of development co-operation to achieving development results. The SDG targets and indicators prioritised by developing countries can increase the focus on impact while enhancing alignment and harmonisation among providers and with their country partners.

Priority steps for providers of development co-operation to make better use of results data

- Honour commitments to invest in and use country results data; support developing countries in their use of results data.
- Refocus the collection and use of results data; place a stronger focus on outcomes, linking project results to change and progress towards SDG priorities at the country level.
- Be realistic about attribution. If attribution is essential for domestic accountability, keep it minimal based on a small number of output indicators, and use narratives to explain how results contribute to change and outcomes.
- Harmonise and streamline indicators among providers and countries, using the SDG targets and indicators as a framework wherever possible.
- Make sure the results from any independent data collection efforts are accessible to all development actors and co-ordinated with the statistical objectives of developing country governments.

Notes

1. These are the Netherlands, New Zealand, Switzerland, the United Kingdom, Finland and the European Union. See OECD (2017a) and OECD (2017c).
2. Development results are defined as the output, outcome or impact (intended or unintended, positive and/or negative) of a development intervention (OECD, 2010).
3. It is important to note that not all 17 SDGs and 169 SDG targets are about outcomes and change on the ground. Some are about the necessary policies and partnerships to achieve the goals and outcomes. The 2030 Agenda is explicit about this difference between SDG outcomes and processes. In a results context, the SDG targets that focus on outcomes and change present intended results, while other SDG targets focus on the means of implementation. A recent OECD assessment suggests that approximately half of the SDG targets are about outcome change, and therefore constitute a set of results to be achieved by 2030 (OECD, 2017c).
4. In the context of development results, impact is defined as: positive and negative, primary and secondary long-term effects produced by development interventions, directly or indirectly, intended or unintended (OECD, 2010).
5. This chapter draws evidence on the management and use of data from a range of sources, including OECD case studies and surveys, DAC peer reviews, and the 2016 progress report of the Global Partnership for Effective Development Co-operation (OECD/UNDP, 2016).
6. From a results perspective, attribution of results refers to instances where providers claim outputs (or in some cases immediate outcomes) from projects as a direct result of their funding, taking a *pro rata* approach to calculate the quantity of results that can be directly attributed based on the share of their inputs. For example, if a project that is 50% funded by donor A and 50% by donor B results in 500 teachers trained, then donor A directly attributes and reports 250 trained teachers as a result of its support. In this chapter, attribution refers to this method of "direct attribution". Providers may take a softer approach to attribution. For example, in the case of the World Bank Group, the results reported by clients implementing operations supported by the World Bank Group are attributable to the World Bank Group, though not on a *pro rata* basis.
7. By country results data and systems we refer both to the government's national statistical system and the country-led results framework.
8. "A country-led results framework is understood as one that is led or originated by the government of the country itself. [...] This can include any form of government-led planning instrument that defines a country's approach to development, sets out its development priorities and establishes the results expected to be achieved. It also outlines the systems and tools that will be used to monitor and evaluate progress towards

these targets, establishes the indicators of progress and determines the baseline against which results will be measured" (OECD/UNDP, 2016).

9. DAC members scored just below the average for all providers in each of these three areas. The objectives of 85% of all new development co-operation interventions were aligned with country objectives. Only 62% of all new interventions drew on country results indicators and only 52% of new interventions intended to use partner countries' data and monitoring systems (OECD/UNDP, 2016).

10. A results module sits within an aid management system; it collates and enables analysis of data on the outputs and outcomes of development co-operation.

11. A new aid management system in New Zealand (to be launched at the end of 2017) will include a significant results capture and reporting element. The system will enable staff to track and monitor progress at the programme, country and sector levels through standardised results reports in a dashboard format. This will make it possible to measure and report against both aggregated and project-level non-aggregated results. In the United Kingdom, DFID is building new platforms to strengthen and support project-level results-based management. This involves analysis to identify what is currently collected at the project level, and to explore ways of standardising or summarising upwards. The standardisation may involve using a system to code or tag the indicators used by diverse partners into a set of standard indicators. DFID's goal is to generate data that can be cut and sliced at different levels, thus enhancing the use of results information to manage interventions at the project and country levels, and for learning and decision making (OECD, 2017a).

12. For example, a recent internal study by the Swiss Agency for Development Cooperation found that there were over 150 different indicators in use across its food security and nutrition sector; thanks to the introduction of four aggregated reference indicators and four thematic reference indicators, it is hoped that there will be a reduction in the number of indicators (OECD, 2017a).

13. For example, AidData's interviews with development co-operation providers in three countries found that where country systems were used, the most useful type of data were found to be geo-referenced and sector-specific administrative data produced by line ministries, and through surveys and censuses by national statistical offices (Custer and Sethi, 2017b). Similarly, AidData's recent *Listening to Leaders* report found that 24% of development partners rated national statistics as the most useful types of data from domestic sources; 21% gave top ranking to survey data (AidData, forthcoming).

14. The Post 2015 Data Test involved teams of researchers in seven countries examining issues related to the availability and quality of data for tracking progress on the SDGs relevant to that country. The countries involved in the test were Bangladesh, Canada, Peru, Senegal, Sierra Leone, the United Republic of Tanzania and Turkey (Kindornay, Bhattacharya and Higgins, 2016).

15. As noted by Development Gateway, "efforts to improve the data eco-system should focus as much on the political economy of decision-making as on promoting skills and technology" (Homer et al., 2016: 18).

16. Development Gateway found that overall, there was limited use of results data in partner country governments, a lack of incentives for using results data and a tendency for local priorities to overshadow data use for decision making.

References

AidData (forthcoming), *2017 Listening to Leaders Survey*, preliminary findings, draft provided to the OECD.

Custer, S. and T. Sethi (eds.) (2017a), "Executive summary: Avoiding data graveyards: Insights from data producers and users in three countries", AidData at the College of William & Mary, Williamsburg, Virginia, *http://aiddata.org/sites/default/files/avoiding_data_graveyards_executive_summary.pdf.*

Custer, S. and T. Sethi (eds.) (2017b), "Avoiding data graveyards: Insights from data producers and users in three countries", AidData at the College of William & Mary, Williamsburg, Virginia, *http://aiddata.org/sites/default/files/avoiding_data_graveyards_full_report.pdf.*

DCF (2016), "National mutual accountability and transparency in development cooperation: Study on the findings of the fourth DCF Survey", Development Cooperation Forum, *www.un.org/ecosoc/sites/www.un.org.ecosoc/files/files/en/dcf/dcf-accountability-study-v4.pdf.*

EC (2016a), *EU International Cooperation and Development: First Report on Selected Results, July 2013-June 2014*, European Union, Luxembourg, *https://ec.europa.eu/europeaid/sites/devco/files/eu-results-report_2013-14_en.pdf.*

EC (2016b), "EU publishes key results of its international cooperation and development activities", press release, 22 July, European Commission, Brussels, *http://europa.eu/rapid/press-release_IP-16-2543_en.htm.*

GPEDC (2016), "Nairobi outcome document" of the Second High-Level Meeting of the Global Partnership for Effective Development Co-operation, Global Partnership for Effective Development Co-operation, *http://effectivecooperation.org/wp-content/uploads/2016/12/OutcomeDocumentEnglish.pdf.*

Holzapfel, S. (2016), "Boosting or hindering aid effectiveness? An assessment of systems for measuring donor agency results", *Public Administration and Development*, Vol. 36/1, pp. 3-19, *http://dx.doi.org/10.1002/pad.1749.*

Homer, D., V. Bhatia and J. Powell (2016), "Increasing the impact of results data", Policy Brief, Development Gateway, *www.developmentgateway.org/sites/default/files/2017-02/RDI-PolicyBrief.pdf.*

Homer, D. et al. (2016), "Results Data Initiative: Findings from Ghana", Development Gateway, *www.developmentgateway.org/sites/default/files/2017-02/RDI-Ghana.pdf.*

ICAI (2015), "DFID's approach to delivering impact", Report 45, Independent Commission for Aid Impact, United Kingdom, *http://icai.independent.gov.uk/wp-content/uploads/ICAI-report-DFIDs-approach-to-Delivering-Impact.pdf.*

Ipsos Public Affairs (2015), "Ipsos Public Affairs findings from a global poll on the Sustainable Development Goals", *www.ipsos.com/en-us/17-country-study-foreign-aid-and-sustainable-development-goals* (accessed 6 July 2017).

Kindornay, S., D. Bhattacharya and K. Higgins (2016), *Implementing Agenda 2030: Unpacking the Data Revolution at Country Level*, Centre for Policy Dialogue, Dhaka, Bangladesh, *www.post2015datatest.com/wp-content/uploads/2016/07/Implementing-Agenda-2030-Unpacking-the-Data-Revolution-at-Country-Level.pdf.*

Lampert, M. and P. Papadongonas (2016), "Towards 2030 without poverty: Increasing knowledge of progress made and opportunities for engaging frontrunners in the world population with the global goals", PowerPoint presentation, Motivaction International B.V., Amsterdam, Netherlands, *www.glocalities.com/reports/towards-2030-without-poverty.html.*

OECD (forthcoming), "Going beyond the rhetoric: Mutual accountability in practice", peer learning exercise on mutual accountability, OECD, Paris.

OECD (2017a), Strengthening the results chain: Synthesis of results-based management by providers, OECD, Paris, *http://dx.doi.org/10.1787/544032a1-en.*

OECD (2017b), Strengthening providers' results frameworks through targets & indicators of the Sustainable Development Goals (SDGs), OECD, Paris, *www.oecd.org/dac/results-development/docs/strengthening-providers-results-frameworks.pdf.*

OECD (2017c), "Development co-operation results under the 2030 Agenda: Challenges and opportunities in results monitoring", draft January 2017, OECD, Paris, *www.oecd.org/dac/results-development/docs/Results%20and%20development%20co-operation%20for%202030.pdf.*

OECD (2017d), "Mutual accountability through results: Supporting partner countries' development goals and results frameworks: Key messages", OECD, Paris, *www.oecd.org/dac/peer-reviews/Results workshop February 2017 Key Messages.pdf.*

OECD (2016), "Providers' use of results information for accountability, communication, direction and learning: Survey results", OECD, Paris,*www.oecd.org/dac/results-development/docs/Providers'_use_of_results_information_for_accountability_communication_direction_and_learning.pdf.*

OECD (2012), *Aid Effectiveness 2011: Progress in Implementing the Paris Declaration*, OECD Publishing, Paris, *http://dx.doi.org/10.1787/9789264125780-en.*

OECD (2011), "Busan Partnership for Effective Development Co-operation", Fourth High-Level Forum on Aid Effectiveness, Busan, *www.oecd.org/dac/effectiveness/49650173.pdf.*

OECD (2010), "Glossary of key terms in evaluation and results-based management", OECD, Paris, *www.oecd.org/dac/evaluation/2754804.pdf.*

OECD (2005), *Paris Declaration on Aid Effectiveness*, OECD Publishing, Paris, *http://dx.doi.org/10.1787/9789264098084-en.*

OECD/UNDP (2016), *Making Development Co-operation More Effective: 2016 Progress Report*, OECD Publishing, Paris, *http://dx.doi.org/10.1787/9789264266261-en.*

Sanna, V. and I. Mc Donnell (2017), "Data for development: DAC member priorities and challenges", *OECD Development Co-operation Working Papers*, No. 35, OECD Publishing, Paris, *http://dx.doi.org/10.1787/6e342488-en.*

Savedoff, W. (2017), "Insights from experience: Practical effects of the SDGs on public administration and aid", Views from the Center Blog, 8 March, Center for Global Development, *www.cgdev.org/blog/insights-experience-practical-effects-sdgs-public-administration-and-aid.*

Shutt, C. (2016), *Towards an Alternative Development Management Paradigm?*, Elanders Sverige AB, Stockholm, *http://eba.se/wp-content/uploads/2016/08/Rapport2016_07_webb.pdf.*

World Bank (2016), "Behind the mirror: A report on the self-evaluation systems of the World Bank Group", World Bank Group, Washington, DC, *http://ieg.worldbankgroup.org/evaluations/roses.*

World Bank (2015), "The poverty focus of country programs: Lessons from World Bank experience", *Working Paper*, World Bank Group, Washington, DC, *https://openknowledge.worldbank.org/bitstream/handle/10986/22486/TheOpovertyOfoOorldOBankOexperience.pdf?sequence=1&isAllowed=y.*

Development Co-operation Report 2017
Data for Development

PART I

Chapter 6

Getting development finance data right

by
Jens Sedemund *and* Naeeda Crishna Morgado, OECD Development Co-operation Directorate

Over the past two decades, financing for development has undergone fundamental changes in terms of sources, volumes and patterns of flows. This chapter focuses on data related to development finance, setting out the current landscape and looking at how data systems are evolving in the context of the Addis Ababa Action Agenda and the 2030 Agenda for Sustainable Development. It reviews the outstanding gaps in data on international development finance, presenting challenges and priorities going forward as well as lessons from past experience. The chapter also examines the changing needs of developing countries and other development partners, and the actions being taken to address them, including clarifying the inter-linkages between climate and development finance. Finally, it highlights areas for further work to improve the understanding and use of development finance data in support of sound policy making, and as an incentive for increasing public and private flows for development.

Key messages

- A better understanding of financing for the Sustainable Development Goals (SDGs) in developing countries and globally requires modernised measures, new data series and, crucially, a framework for capturing this information systematically.
- Total official support for sustainable development (TOSSD) is designed to harvest the full range of official development finance data, including private resources mobilised through official interventions. Agreement in 2018 on the scope and method of TOSSD reporting, in particular for cross-border flows, will enable TOSSD data to contribute to international reporting on SDG implementation at the United Nations-hosted High Level Political Forum in 2019.
- Financial flows from providers of development finance beyond the membership of the Development Assistance Committee (DAC) are estimated at around USD 300 billion. There is scope to increase international recognition and enhance transparency of development finance provided by actors such as South-South providers of development co-operation, civil society organisations and philanthropic foundations, through better accounting to agreed measures, standards and reporting systems.
- Recent surveys found that in 2012-15, official development finance mobilised USD 81.1 billion from the private sector. The main instrument used was guarantees, which mobilised USD 39.5 billion (44% of the total). This and similar data will be collected by the OECD regularly from 2017, thereby filling a major gap in development finance data.
- Development finance and climate finance grapple with similar data challenges and gaps. The analysis of financing patterns, modalities and trends for both climate and development goals can be improved by exploiting synergies between existing statistical systems for climate-related development finance and country reporting on climate finance to the UNFCCC.

Over the past two decades, financing for development has undergone fundamental changes in terms of sources, volumes and patterns of flows. Looking forward, significant volumes of investment will be required to meet the SDGs. OECD (2017a) estimates that building the needed infrastructure alone will require USD 6.9 trillion per year over the next 15 years. The 2030 Agenda for Sustainable Development (UN, 2015a), the Addis Ababa Action Agenda (UN, 2015b) and the Paris Agreement on Climate Change (hereafter the "Paris Agreement"; UNFCCC, 2015) reflect the need for a comprehensive approach to financing so as to mobilise the unprecedented amounts that will be required, and to align funding from all sources.

Addressing this financing challenge starts with data. Data on development finance support good decision making for development outcomes by providing evidence on the reality of resource flows. They also help to shed light on how successfully the international community and individual countries mobilise resources to meet their commitments, and how they collectively work together to leave no one behind. In addition, data incentivise official providers of development co-operation and other investors to step up efforts to fill financing gaps, leveraging a range of resources to deliver the 2030 Agenda (UN, 2015a).

Investing in data – including development finance data – is investing in evidence. Data on development finance need to better capture the full picture of resource flows for implementing the SDGs to enable all stakeholders, and especially developing countries, to plan, target and mobilise the resources they need to deliver their development priorities. Getting the full picture requires modernised data systems and a dedicated effort to enhance the compilation, availability and use of data.

This chapter presents priorities, challenges and key lessons for getting development finance data right. The initial sections highlight why it is important to upgrade data on international development finance. This is followed by a discussion of the significant gaps in development finance in light of changing data needs and a review of actions underway to address them. Finally, the chapter highlights areas where further work is needed to improve the understanding and use of development finance data in support of sound policy making.

Development finance data are central to financing for development

Financing alone will not achieve development outcomes. Yet to be implemented, development policies and projects must be backed by appropriate, dedicated and predictable resources. Indeed, in 1970, decades before the international community agreed on the Millennium Development Goals – the first global results framework for development – the United Nations set a funding goal for economically advanced countries: to provide 0.7% of gross national income as official development assistance (ODA). Similarly, even before the SDGs were agreed, the Addis Ababa Action Agenda provided the framework for financing for development in the era of the 2030 Agenda.

Data are fundamental to understanding the overall picture of SDG financing.

Data are fundamental to understanding the state of SDG financing, from current flows and gaps to specific needs, shortfalls and opportunities. Governments and public actors rely on financial data to plan and prioritise the deployment of resources internationally and at the country and subnational levels. Data are the basis for holding public and private investors to account for their financial commitments and for gauging the effectiveness and efficiency of public expenditure. Data also are important for incentivising efforts to mobilise additional resources for development (OECD/UNDP, 2016). In the private sector, data provide market information and price signals; they underpin investment decisions at all levels, from foreign direct investment to the purchase of seeds by smallholder farmers.

A vast range of data sources and series are relevant to development finance. Funding that supports development outcomes includes an increasingly broad array of flows raised publicly and privately by diverse actors (Box 6.1). Having comprehensive development finance data is crucial to ensure that this financing is transparent and accountable for meeting stated objectives. This chapter focuses on official development finance data, including their role in catalysing additional private flows and supporting developing countries. The chapter also touches on data issues related to private financing for development.

Box 6.1. **What are development finance data?**

While there is no official definition of development finance data, its scope can be derived from the concept of development finance. Whereas the broad concept of financing for development, as reflected in the Addis Ababa Action Agenda covers a comprehensive range of financing sources, development finance is narrower in scope. The defining criterion for development finance is the intentionality of the flow, i.e. it is based on an explicit development mandate or purpose. At the international level, this comprises official development finance which is concessional and non-concessional bilateral and multilateral finance in support of development; private development finance relates to private funds that are governed by a development mandate, e.g. financing provided by philanthropic organisations for development purposes in developing countries. While there are also domestic flows in developing countries that can fall under this concept, they are beyond the scope of this chapter. On this basis, development finance data relates to data that describe and characterise the financial flows, terms and conditions of development finance.

Sound measurement underpins good development finance data

The Addis Ababa Action Agenda stresses the need for high-quality disaggregated data as "an essential input for smart and transparent decision-making, including in support of the post-2015 agenda and its means of implementation, and policy-making at all levels". The OECD's "Quality framework and guidelines for OECD statistical activities" (2011) helps assess data quality in seven dimensions: relevance, accuracy, credibility, timeliness, accessibility, interpretability and coherence. Ideally, any dataset should strive to score as high as possible on all these dimensions. In practice, however, trade-offs are often made among the dimensions, especially when considering what the data will be used for. For example, to provide accountability for commitments and transparency on spending, accuracy, credibility and accessibility are crucial. Timeliness commands a particularly high premium in certain contexts; for example when decision makers face urgent and fast-evolving crises (e.g. the Ebola epidemic) they need up-to-date information on the availability and allocation of resources; or fishermen may depend on volatile and fluctuating information to enable them to sell their catch at the best price.

The fundamental condition for ensuring the quality of development finance data, however, is a sound measurement system with clear definitions and methodologies, which makes the collected data comparable across providers. In this regard, data on official development finance, and in particular on ODA, are well known for their quality as a result of the solid and high standards used to generate and collect the data (Box 6.2). ODA data inform development co-operation policy making, facilitate co-ordination of aid, and allow comparisons of providers' performance as well as assessments of progress against individual or collective commitments. The definitions and categories of the ODA measurement system are also closely followed by the International Aid Transparency Initiative (IATI), which provides a register of data on flows from a range of aid providers.

Box 6.2. **Official development assistance is a quality standard for development finance data**

Data on official development assistance (ODA) are based on a system of official reporting to the Creditor Reporting System (CRS) by 30 OECD Development Assistance Committee (DAC) members and some 35 multilateral agencies. The CRS captures detailed information on about 250 000 transactions per year. Twenty non-DAC providers and one foundation also report on their development co-operation to the OECD DAC.[1] Although the CRS database does not include all global development data, OECD-DAC statistics are the only source of accurate, comparable data providing a global picture of official cross-country resource flows for development.

DAC members are required to provide the OECD with data on their official and private resource flows to developing countries. The OECD verifies and validates the data, for example for completeness and for reporting against key fields (e.g. type of aid, sector classification, tying status, channels of delivery). Reporting errors are corrected, contributing to improvements in the data.

The OECD-DAC statistical directives, which cover all definitions and methodologies, are agreed by consensus among DAC members and form the basis for comparable aid statistics. The directives have evolved over time to take into account decisions on reporting techniques and changing forms of assistance, and to track flows to new policy priorities.

All OECD-DAC statistics – including databases, tables, charts, reports and analyses – as well as the methodology used to compile these statistics are publicly and freely available.[2] In 2016, there were over 1.2 million page views of OECD-DAC development databases, with about 60 000 downloads of CRS data. The OECD-DAC aid statistics website (*www.oecd.org/dac/financing-sustainable-development*) attracts over 260 000 unique visitors per year.

These data enable macro and disaggregated analysis of aid flows. For example, DAC statistics show that overall aid flows reached USD 142.6 billion in 2016, an increase of 8.9% over 2015 (OECD, 2017c). Likewise, over the past ten years sub-Saharan Africa was the region with the highest ratio of disbursements to commitments (101%); the region with the lowest ratio during this period was South and Central Asia, with a disbursement ratio of 78%.

ODA statistics also support monitoring of progress on international conventions and agreements, including ten targets of nine Sustainable Development Goals. The statistics are also used to monitor progress on G8 commitments for food security, international coalitions such as the Addis Tax Initiative (see the following chapter on development finance and policy trends), and aid for strengthening statistical capacity (see Chapter 4).

1. As of December 2016.
2. *www.oecd.org/dac/financing-sustainable-development.*

Source: Authors' compilation.

Every year, the OECD reviews the quality, completeness and timeliness of reporting by DAC members and ranks their performance (OECD, 2017b). In addition, it provides individual guidance in areas where data reporting could be improved. The timeliness of many DAC members' statistical reporting has significantly improved in the past few years. However, most members face challenges in meeting the statistical reporting requirements which change frequently to reflect new types and channels or to give more detail of ODA in line with changing priorities. Staff turnover in ministries and development agencies or complex and decentralised reporting systems can also have an impact on quality and accuracy. To support DAC members in meeting the increasing demand for comprehensive, reliable and accessible statistics on development finance, and to enhance the quality and use of the data, the OECD will begin to undertake statistical peer reviews. These reviews will be a source of peer learning and recommendations for improving data collection, processing, reporting and transparency.

Transparency, which plays a key role in enabling development finance data to serve their purpose, has risen to the top of the global development agenda. In 2011, participants at the Fourth High Level Forum on Aid Effectiveness in Busan agreed to establish a common open standard for the electronic publication of timely, comprehensive and forward-looking information on resources for development co-operation by end-2015. This standard comprises detailed activity-level data from the OECD-DAC Creditor Reporting System (CRS), data from the OECD-DAC forward spending survey and IATI data. Moreover, initiatives such as AidData[1] aim to make these data more accessible and provide additional tools for their use, e.g. by geocoding data that are sourced from the OECD-DAC database.

To mobilise more financing for development, data gaps and challenges need to be addressed

Gaps in development finance data constitute a key bottleneck to assessing resource needs, as well as to targeting and mobilising financing for the implementation of the financing for development agenda (UN, 2015b). Many statistics and datasets tracking financial resources for development are not comprehensive, comparable or consolidated. This poor coverage and weak quality make it difficult to form a cohesive picture of the sources, volume and allocation of resources.

> *Many statistics and datasets tracking financial resources for development are not comprehensive, comparable or consolidated.*

Data gaps exist for every type of financing for development (IATF, 2017). For example, while central banks and the International Monetary Fund (IMF) compile national macroeconomic and financial statistics, there are critical gaps in data on contingent liabilities, which are important for debt financing and sustainability, or on financing by national development banks. Similarly, there are data gaps on domestic private investment in developing countries, as well as on civil society funding (Box 6.3); foreign direct investment data vary across institutions, and remittances through informal channels are not recorded reliably (IATF, 2017; Alvarez et al., 2015). Such gaps mean that that the international community lacks key evidence to inform strategies for mobilising the resources needed to deliver the SDGs (see the "In my view" piece by Lisa Grace S. Bersales).

Although much granular project-level data are available on official development finance, gaps and challenges still exist. For example, there is a need for more data from providers of development co-operation beyond the DAC membership, including major international development partners such as Brazil, the People's Republic of China (hereafter "China"), India or Indonesia. Existing data series, for example relating to the SDGs, need to be modernised and improved. Expanded coverage of and reporting on key development finance categories, for example to include more detailed information about bilateral aid that is allocated regionally, is important. And updated data standards and methodologies for some data series, for example on in-donor refugee costs, need to be developed.

There is no one-size-fits-all approach to managing the challenges to getting the data right. In some instances, individual countries will need to take the lead; in others, political consensus has to be brokered, which takes time; and yet in others new technology initiatives by the private sector, improvements in the rigour of coding and systems, combined with training, can make a significant contribution. Nevertheless, it is crucial to maintain credible, objective and transparent processes for defining common standards and updating them to ensure that they are fit for changing demands, as this enhances data usability and sustains relevance for all data users.

The following sections outline several development finance data gaps and challenges. It explores efforts underway to build and enhance data systems, including OECD data work in support of the SDGs.

In my view: Strong data partnerships are needed to ensure the right data for development

Lisa Grace S. Bersales,
PhD, Vice Minister, National Statistician and Civil Registrar General, Philippines

A diverse range of stakeholders is rallying behind the commitment to leave no one behind that is embedded in the 2030 Agenda for Sustainable Development. This agenda reflects our global ambition to achieve peace and prosperity by 2030 for our planet and its people. But how will we turn ambition into reality? Do we even know if we are on the right track to achieve the development goals and targets? How can we be sure that by 2030 we will have achieved what we committed to?

Everyone seems to agree that more and better data are needed to answer these questions. But in reality, producing and using the data we need is a challenge for chief statisticians like myself who are not always well equipped to manage the political aspects of data and to lock in financial support. While there is strong demand from my government for data to inform policy decisions, this is not the case in many other countries. That is why we need to have political champions advocating for improving and using data.

How can we make partnerships for data strong?

Multi-stakeholder engagement and partnerships are vital, but it is also notoriously challenging to manage and make them work given the different interests and capacities. In my experience, effective partnerships must be truly inclusive, involving different data generation communities, such as official statistics and government data, earth and geospatial sciences, information and communications technology as well as users and possible producers of data – such as policy makers, development partners, media, business, academia and civil society. National statistical offices should be at the centre of these partnerships, ensuring good co-ordination and alignment to national priorities and needs. However, national statistical offices need to be capable of playing their central role.[1] This requires having access to adequate resources, which could be financial, technical or international knowledge sharing. South-South co-operation should be encouraged even as North-South co-operation is expanded.

Developing countries must participate in international initiatives on data and statistics

This report makes a clear case for the need to improve development finance data so that developing countries receive the data they need for financial planning to deliver development plans and the Sustainable Development Goals (SDGs). Developing countries need to be involved in international processes to establish new statistical measures on development finance, such as total official support for sustainable development (TOSSD).[2] That is why the Philippines continues to engage in designing TOSSD, most recently as co-chair of the special TOSSD International Task Force. The TOSSD has great potential to contribute to international reporting on SDG implementation, but more developing country governments need to help shape this new measure by engaging in the international process for agreeing on its scope and the method of reporting.

In my view, only strong and inclusive data partnerships will survive to 2030 and beyond. I welcome efforts by the OECD and the United Nations to design the TOSSD in this way and call on other countries to get involved because we need to understand, track and assess all development finance better.

1. See 2017 Cape Town Global Action Plan (*https://undataforum.org/WorldDataForum/launch-of-the-cape-town-global-action-plan-for-sustainable-development-data*).
2. TOSSD: A statistical measurement framework for tracking the means of implementation to achieve the SDGs, presentation made at UN Statistical Commission side event, 6 March 2017.

Box 6.3. **The incomplete picture of development finance raised by civil society organisations**

Civil society organisations (CSOs) are independent development and humanitarian actors in their own right. They make a significant contribution to development finance through funds that they raise from the public sector, the general public and the private sector, including philanthropic foundations. According to current, but incomplete, OECD data, total flows in 2015 for both development and humanitarian relief handled by non-governmental organisations (NGOs) amounted to approximately USD 53 billion.

The OECD's development finance database gathers data on three types of NGO flows: contributions made by NGOs based in OECD countries from their own resources, contributions by governments to NGO programmes and government aid programmes administered by NGOs.

Reporting by member countries on the first type of flow – contributions by NGOs from their own resources (also called net private grants) – is less complete than for the other types of flows. OECD-DAC data indicate that NGOs from OECD countries raised about USD 35 billion from private sources in 2015; USD 29 billion of this amount is attributable to NGOs in the United States. OECD-DAC data on these flows understate the level of funding that CSOs raise from private sources for development, as several DAC member countries (about one-third) do not report these flows. A number of NGO-platform organisations state that there is a mismatch between OECD-DAC data on net private grants and their own calculations. The real amount of development finance raised by NGOs is likely to be much higher than what the official data show.

By providing more complete and consistent reporting on these flows to the OECD-DAC database, members – in collaboration with civil society – can make a significant contribution to increasing the transparency of the development finance raised by NGOs, thereby increasing understanding of civil society organisations as important development finance actors.

Source: OECD Creditor Reporting System.

Ensure official development assistance accounting is fit for responding to the greatest needs

The way in which ODA is measured influences providers' allocation of resources. This in turn relates directly to the central 2030 Agenda principle of leaving no one behind and targeting funding to those most in need. By modernising the ODA measure and creating stronger incentives to allocate aid to where the needs are greatest, the OECD DAC ensures that ODA and other development finance statistics remain relevant for delivering on the 2030 Agenda.

At the end of 2014, DAC members agreed to move from a flow-based system for counting ODA to a grant-equivalent approach.

To qualify as ODA, minimum requirements of concessionality must be met. Yet ODA has historically been measured on a flow basis, recording the face value of grants and concessional loans. Better reflecting the actual terms of lending to account for "donor effort" can incentivise development spending and improve its targeting. In 2014, DAC members agreed to modernise the measurement of ODA by moving from a flow-based system of accounting to a grant-equivalent approach. The decision is currently being phased in and will become the standard for reporting from 2018 onwards. This new system will count grants and the "grant portion" of concessional loans as ODA (Table 6.1), better capturing differences in the levels of concessionality of different financing instruments and the provider's effort at the time of disbursing a loan, and thereby enabling a more realistic comparison of loans and grants.

Table 6.1. **Modernised ODA measurement – what are the changes?**

	Before	After
Grant element	≥ 25%	≥ 45% for LDCs and other LICs ≥ 15% for LMICs ≥ 10% for UMICs
Discount rate	= 10% (used for assessing the concessionality of a loan)	= 5% base (IMF discount rate) + adjustment factors of: → 4% for LDCs and other LICs → 2% for LMICs → 1% for UMICs. Used both for assessing the concessionality of a loan and for calculating its ODA grant equivalent.
Measurement of flows	Face value of loan counted as ODA when disbursed. Face value of loan subtracted from ODA when repaid.	Grant equivalent of loan (grant element multiplied by amount disbursed) counted when disbursed. Not subtracted from ODA when loan is repaid. More ODA credit for softer loan terms and conditions.
Debt sustainability safeguard	No explicit measure.	Linked to IMF debt limits policy and non-concessional borrowing policy.

Note: ODA: official development assistance; LDC = least developed country; LIC = low-income country; LMIC = lower middle-income country; UMIC = upper middle-income country; IMF = International Monetary Fund.
Source: OECD (2015a), "Why modernise official development assistance?", *www.oecd.org/dac/financing-sustainable-development/Addis%20flyer%20-%20ODA.pdf*.

A second step was taken to make ODA fit for purpose and strengthen incentives for allocating it to the least developed countries, which rely most heavily on concessional finance. This involves differentiating the discount rate according to developing country groups. In addition to responding to greater need, lending to poorer countries demands greater effort by providers in terms of risk. In the future, differentiated discount rates will result in a loan to a least developed country or other low-income country being recorded as a higher level of ODA than a loan extended under the same conditions to other country groups.[2]

Increase recognition of the contribution of South-South co-operation through better accounting

The rapid growth of the major emerging economies, and their growing capacity for co-operation, has heightened the focus on South-South co-operation and its contribution to promoting development, as stated in the Addis Ababa Action Agenda (UN, 2015b).[3] Despite this increased attention, however, there is no internationally agreed definition of South-South co-operation and little systematised reporting on it. The resulting data gaps lead to this important and growing contribution to promoting development being undervalued by the international community. Similarly, reporting on triangular co-operation needs to be stepped up by all providers to increase the evidence base and strengthen the modality as a means to achieve the Sustainable Development Goals.

The High-level United Nations Conference on South-South Cooperation in Nairobi (UN, 2010) highlighted the need for internationally comparable data on South-South financial flows and co-operation. Many countries publish information on international co-operation, with some countries, including Brazil, China, Mexico and Qatar, publishing detailed reports on their activities (see also chapter the "Profiles of other development co-operation providers"). In addition, 24 South-South providers have participated in the country-level monitoring processes carried out by the Global Partnership for Effective Development Co-operation (GPEDC). The latest report found that these providers had good quality reporting about their co-operation and delivery (OECD/UNDP, 2016).

South-South co-operation is not yet integrated into global reporting systems, although it has played an important role in international development for decades.

Coming up with an appropriate and acceptable measure for South-South co-operation, which often takes the form of technical co-operation, training, exchanges of experts and other low-cost activities, is a key challenge. Quality and value added are difficult to quantify in financial terms. In addition, the salary costs of developing country experts can be considerably lower than those of experts from many DAC member countries. This can make South-South co-operation appear to be relatively "low-cost", even though the experience and knowledge shared may be more relevant and timely, and may have a substantial development impact.

South-South providers are beginning to take action to remedy this situation. An increasing number of providers from emerging economies are adopting reporting practices that enable data comparability and allow a better appreciation of their efforts, as can be seen in the "Profiles of other development co-operation providers". While the OECD recognises that many providers of South-South co-operation do not consider their efforts to be ODA,[4] South-South providers can report their activities to the OECD statistical system on a voluntary basis. Twenty provider countries that are not members of the DAC are doing so using OECD reporting standards. Their development co-operation programmes reached USD 17.7 billion in net terms, or 11% of total bilateral development co-operation, in 2015; broader international development funding from providers outside the DAC, both concessional and non-concessional, was estimated at USD 300 billion (Luijkx and Benn, 2017).

Increase the transparency of financing raised privately by foundations through systematic reporting

Global private philanthropy is a growing source of financing for development worldwide and foundations are important actors in achieving the 2030 Agenda. Yet the potential of foundations will not be fully realised, nor their influence fully understood, unless a key weakness is addressed – that is, the paucity of information available about philanthropic resources and their deployment at the national, regional and international levels. The lack of available data on philanthropic funding makes budgeting of public policies and social investments difficult for countries. Indeed, very few countries require private philanthropic organisations to disclose financing information. In addition, the definitions, legal status and regulations underpinning philanthropic giving vary dramatically from country to country, which hampers efforts to map the philanthropic sector accurately by comparing or aggregating data.

To address these data gaps, the OECD has undertaken a large-scale survey of private philanthropy for development. The survey contains detailed (activity-level) information from more than 100 private philanthropic foundations involved in development co-operation, based in both developing and developed countries in Africa, the Americas, Asia and Europe. The survey applies OECD-DAC reporting standards, making the data gathered unique in that they are comparable to official development assistance. Even if well below volumes of official flows, the amounts are significant and constitute a key source of innovation. The OECD is currently engaging with a broader range of philanthropic foundations globally to continue to expand the survey coverage, with a final report to be released in 2018.

The preliminary survey results show that during 2013-15, philanthropic giving amounted to USD 22.7 billion with an upward trend over the survey period (OECD, 2017d). India was the largest recipient country, resulting particularly from significant giving by the Bill & Melinda Gates Foundation, Tata Trusts and the IKEA Foundation. While Africa was by far the most targeted region, at 29%, the largest share of giving (45%) was global or multi-continental in scope (Figure 6.1). In terms of sectoral allocation, philanthropic giving predominantly targeted health and reproductive health, which together accounted for 53% of the three-year total, followed by education (9%), agriculture (9%), and government and civil society (8% – including human rights, gender, civil society development, and transparency and accountability). Health and reproductive health benefited mainly from the Bill & Melinda Gates Foundation's giving (76% of sector total), while flows to education, government and civil society, and general environmental protection came mainly from other foundations.

Figure 6.1. **Geographical distribution of philanthropic giving, 2013-15**

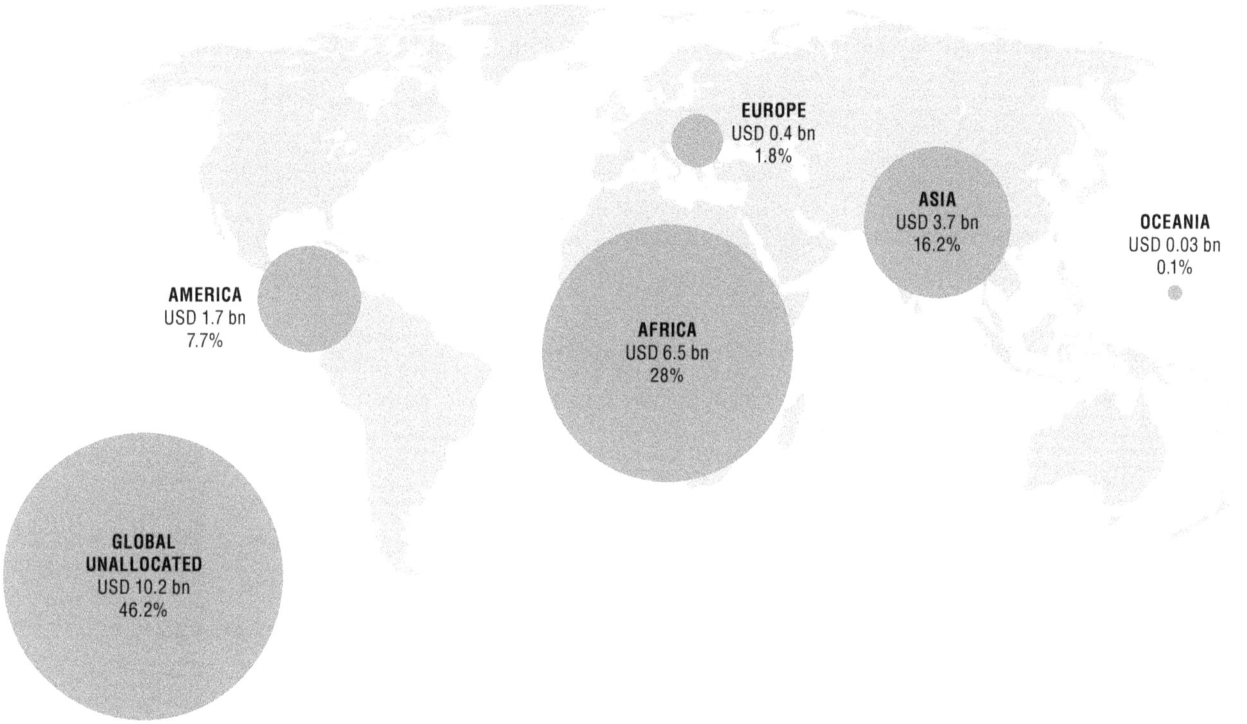

Source: OECD (2017d), "Global private philanthropy for development: Results of the OECD data survey as of 19 June 2017", *www.oecd.org/dac/financing-sustainable-development/development-finance-data/Flyer_update_June_2017.pdf.*

StatLink http://dx.doi.org/10.1787/888933591936

Improve coverage of non-concessional official development finance

Non-concessional bilateral development finance has serious data gaps as reporting is not comprehensive or sufficiently systematic. Reported net volumes of non-concessional official development finance from DAC members averaged USD 5 billion per year between 2006 and 2015. Reported ODA volumes are much higher than those of non-concessional bilateral development finance, though there is considerable anecdotal evidence that non-concessional development finance is growing.

Under-reporting impedes policy understanding of this critical SDG finance source and makes it difficult for policy makers to gain crucial insights into their magnitude. As long as data coverage remains poor, a key part of the picture of development finance will be missing. There seems to be little political interest in improving reporting on this financing, however, as it is not perceived to be relevant for international and national accountability mechanisms on development commitments, even though these official financial resources are deployed with a development objective. Quality non-concessional data need to be made available to enable a comprehensive overview of development finance and to assess effectiveness. In addition, as the development finance agenda evolves to capture the mobilisation of private finance for development (in particular through blended finance), and as countries graduate from concessional development finance, the relevance of these flows is likely to grow – as will demands for greater transparency. By shedding light on these flows, the development picture will become clearer and ODA targeting will be more effective and relevant.

Develop a methodology for counting resources mobilised by private sector instruments

In order to mobilise increased development financing from private sources, many providers have established specialised private sector instruments that use a range of financial vehicles and arrangements. These instruments play a key role in the direct mobilisation of private investment and their importance is expected to increase in the future. However, existing official development finance data do not capture the effort involved in mobilising private finance for development, primarily because the methodology for collecting the data related to these instruments has yet to be agreed.

> *Private sector instruments play a key role in the direct mobilisation of private investment, and their importance is expected to increase in the future.*

Intensive work is underway at the OECD to develop a methodology for capturing data on these instruments in official development finance data systems. DAC members have agreed a set of guiding principles for developing the methodology:

- remove disincentives for using private sector instruments
- ensure that development finance data support the balanced, coherent and efficient use of scarce public funds, as well as the targeting of projects with high expected social returns
- avoid distorting competition rules
- maintain a clear distinction between ODA and commercially motivated flows.

Data on mobilisation need to be consistent and based on a clear methodology

Measuring the official effort involved in mobilising private finance is pointless unless there is a measure of the success of the effort. Individual organisations have routinely used "leverage ratios" to report on their progress in mobilising additional resources. In the past, however, the absence of a clear methodology has resulted in significant double counting, precluding a meaningful understanding of the extent to which official development finance has succeeded in mobilising private finance for development efforts. The OECD has focused on establishing an international standard for measuring the volume of private finance mobilised by official development finance interventions. Multilateral development banks have also established a task force on mobilisation. Both approaches have common underlying principles (e.g. only include amounts mobilised for which a concrete link with or a direct and active involvement of a public institution can be demonstrated), but the scope of application and the formulas used are different.

Multilateral development banks have developed a common methodology for their institutions to calculate and report mobilisation of private investment, differentiating between direct and indirect mobilisation, co-financing and "catalysation". The OECD measures mobilisation from all public actors, while avoiding double counting at the international level. It attributes the private finance mobilised to all public institutions involved in a transaction (i.e. to multilateral and bilateral providers, as well as to local actors if applicable), while the multilateral development bank approach prorates the amounts mobilised among the multilateral development banks only (i.e. no attribution to potential bilateral providers or local actors). So far, the OECD measure covers five types of instruments/mechanisms: guarantees, syndicated loans, shares in collective investment vehicles, credit lines and direct investment in companies (Box 6.4). Work is scheduled in 2017/18 to cover a

Box 6.4. **OECD instrument-specific surveys to pilot methodologies for measuring mobilisation**

To date, the OECD has conducted a series of surveys to pilot methodologies for measuring mobilisation using five instruments: guarantees, syndicated loans, shares in collective investment vehicles, credit lines and direct investment in companies. Overall, the results show that in 2012-15, USD 81.1 billion was mobilised from the private sector by official development finance (ODA and other official flows) using these five instruments. The surveys show a continued upward trend in the amounts mobilised, increasing from USD 15.0 billion to USD 26.8 billion between 2012 and 2015 (Figure 6.2). The results confirm that the main leveraging instrument to date is guarantees (USD 35.9 billion mobilised, representing 44% of the total), while also evidencing the mobilisation effect of the other instruments: syndicated loans and credit lines (19% each), shares in collective investment vehicles (12%), and direct investment in companies (6%).

Figure 6.2. **Private finance mobilised in 2012-15, billion USD**

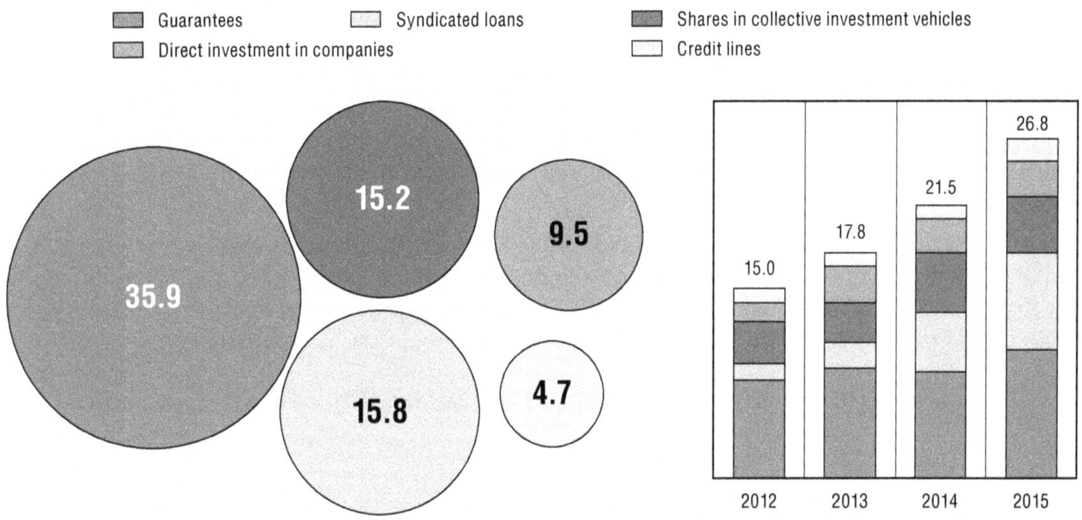

Source: Benn, J. et al. (forthcoming), "Amounts mobilised from the private sector by official development finance interventions: Guarantees, syndicated loans, shares in collective investment vehicles, direct investment in companies and credit lines".

StatLink http://dx.doi.org/10.1787/888933591955

broader range of leveraging instruments, such as standard loans and grants in co-financing schemes with the private sector. This work is carried out in close collaboration with the OECD-hosted Research Collaborative on Tracking Private Climate Finance to also meet the needs of the climate community.

Reporting on mobilisation is now being integrated into the OECD statistical system and regular reporting by DAC members and other institutions on amounts mobilised will begin with 2016 data (available at the end of 2017). Providing high-quality, systematised data on mobilised private finance will be a key contribution to filling data gaps for the financing for development agenda, while also being of immediate relevance to the Paris Agreement.

Data on performance and risk are crucial for crowding-in private finance

Whereas measuring mobilisation is key to improving the understanding of the broader picture of development finance, the actual effective mobilisation of private finance hinges, to a very large extent, on a sophisticated understanding of risk and financial performance. Assessment of risks and expected financial performance is essential to any financial investment, whether for commercial investors interested in optimising financial returns or for development institutions aiming to enhance the development impact of their financing. Better gauges of risk are critical to realise the potential of blended finance in unlocking private financing for SDG-aligned investments (Box 6.5).

Better data on risk are indispensable, both for optimising financial returns and for enhancing the development impact of their financing.

Box 6.5. **Pooling data to create the *Global Emerging Markets Risk Database***

The *Global Emerging Markets (GEMs) Risk Database* (2017) is a comprehensive database of credit risk information derived from the emerging market operations of multilateral development banks and development finance institutions. The GEMs database collects, on an anonymous basis, risk data on loans provided by these organisations in emerging market countries to derive default and recovery rates. It covers loans to sovereigns, public entities and the private sector.

Why GEMs? Multilateral development banks and development finance institutions, by the nature of their business, often operate in markets that are less accessible to private investors and to the capital markets sector. The lack of adequate quality data can become problematic in terms of computing risk parameters such as default rates and recovery rates. By pooling the data of these organisations in a consistent and methodologically accepted manner, the GEMs database derives risk parameters that are statistically significant and can be used by members when making lending decisions in emerging markets.

By the end of 2015, the database contained 7 693 entries on transactions made since 1988, 88% of which relate to private counterparts. The data collected are anonymous and are broken down by region and sector. The participating institutions map their internal ratings to a common scale based on an agreed methodology, ensuring that data from all members are harmonised.

Figure 6.3. **Geographic breakdown of the availability of credit risk data**

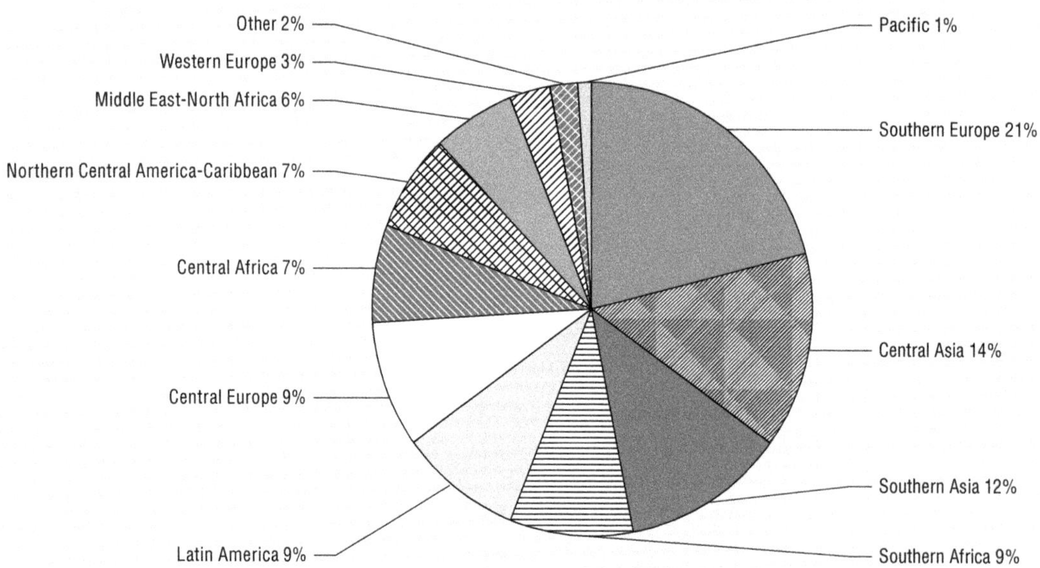

StatLink http://dx.doi.org/10.1787/888933591974

Beyond data pooling. Whilst the primary objective of the consortium is to pool data and derive risk parameters, GEMs has been used as a platform for co-operation and discussion. GEMs members are considering making the database available to a broader set of users in the future, including regulatory bodies, commercial financial institutions and private investors.

Source: European Investment Bank.

A mapping survey of 140 blended finance funds and facilities[5] identified more than USD 30 billion in blended finance between 2000 and 2014. A follow-on survey, currently underway, focuses on capturing more in-depth financial information together with insights on how funds and facilities are evaluated and how they are evolving. Better data on all blended finance instruments are indispensable for policy makers to allocate ODA resources effectively so as to encourage private investment in the sectors and economies where it is most needed. Appropriate safeguards will have to be put in place to protect confidential proprietary information, for example through anonymisation and aggregation. A particularly promising initiative in this regard is the *Global Emerging Markets Risk Database* (see Box 6.5), which captures risk and performance data from over 7 000 investments by multilateral development banks.

Agree on common definitions and data standards for social impact investment

Social impact investment mobilises investment for specific development outcomes and impact. Social impact investors seek explicit social/environmental returns as well as financial returns. In the context of developing countries, this implies a high degree of commonality with bilateral and multilateral development finance institutions, which also operate on a development mandate while seeking financial returns. Development finance institutions are among the three largest providers of capital with an impact focus in developing countries, next to banks and pension funds.

Social impact investment's impact capital is expected to grow by 17% yearly on average.

The social impact investment market has grown rapidly in recent years. According to one global survey, it had assets of USD 114 billion under management in 2016 and its impact capital is expected to grow by 17% yearly on average (GIIN, 2017). The survey found that there were over 8 000 impact investments globally in 2016, totalling USD 22.1 billion. There are, however, limited market data available on social impact investment. In addition, the data that exist are not internationally comparable. There are a number of reasons for this: definitions of social impact investment vary; and the data on impact and financial returns are collected on a project-by-project or investor-by-investor basis. The lack of comparable definitions and data is an obstacle for the further development of this market, making it difficult for practitioners and policy makers to understand its actual financial flows.

To promote the social impact investment market and enable further scaling up, greater transparency and accountability are essential. Global data standards are critical for addressing this issue and for capturing the potential of social impact investment for achieving the SDGs. The OECD is working to create a roadmap for social impact investment, convening key players and data aggregators to agree on definitions, data segmentation and the initial set of data standards for reporting.

Clarify the links between development and climate finance

Finance for climate action in developing countries and development finance are intrinsically linked. Both are critical sources of support for developing countries working towards the SDGs and the Paris Agreement on climate change. Practically all gaps and challenges set out so far in this chapter are relevant to data on both development finance and climate finance. Considering the linkages between these flows, the synergies among the methodologies for tracking them need to be strengthened and the corresponding data harmonised and aligned.

Developed countries have committed to mobilising USD 100 billion per year by 2020 to support climate action in developing countries (OECD, 2015b). Data, underpinned by sound methodologies and systems to track climate finance, are essential to enable countries to track and report progress against this commitment, and to assess whether the financing mobilised is effective in addressing climate change challenges. Two sets of data are important in this regard: data on international, public, climate finance (bilateral and multilateral); and data on private finance mobilised through international public interventions.

In recent years, bilateral and multilateral finance providers, think tanks and international organisations have made increasing efforts to improve the data on climate finance by developing and harmonising definitions, methodologies and reporting (Box 6.6). These combined efforts have, in turn, enabled several high-profile assessments of progress against the commitments of developed country bilateral providers (UNFCCC, 2016; OECD, 2015b, 2016a; Department for Business, Energy & Industrial Strategy, 2016). These assessments have supported negotiations within the context of the United Nations Framework Convention on Climate Change (UNFCCC), while also contributing to a better understanding of priority areas for action.

Box 6.6. **Recent progress in tracking climate finance**

Significant efforts have been made to improve climate finance tracking. These include:

- Tracking and reporting **official development finance targeting the Rio Conventions** through the OECD Creditor Reporting System's standardised "Rio markers" approach. This includes definitions of what constitutes financing in support of adaptation, mitigation, biodiversity and desertification, as well as guidance to improve reporting.
- Development of methodologies, by the Research Collaborative on Tracking Private Climate Finance and the OECD, to track **publicly mobilised private climate finance** and produce first estimates.*
- Development of a joint **climate finance tracking methodology** by multilateral development banks, for reporting on support for climate action (including a joint annual report).
- Development of **Common Principles on Climate Finance Tracking** among multilateral development banks and the International Development Finance Club, a group of bilateral, multilateral and national development finance institutions.

Various initiatives by think tanks, such as the Climate Policy Initiative (CPI) and the Overseas Development Institute (ODI), also support climate finance tracking. The ODI maintains the Climate Funds Update (ODI, n.d.), which analyses funding provided by various multilateral climate funds that have been set up in support of the goals of the UNFCCC. The CPI produces the "Global landscape of climate finance" (e.g. CPI, 2015), which contextualises international public climate finance among other sources of climate finance: domestic, South-South, private, etc.

* *www.oecd.org/env/researchcollaborative* and *www.oecd.org/development/stats/mobilisation.htm*.

There is no internationally agreed definition of what constitutes climate finance.

Despite these advances, however, data on climate finance face several political and technical barriers to their broader use. In particular, within the context of the UNFCCC, there is no internationally agreed definition of what constitutes climate finance, which means that no estimates of progress are accepted by all countries. Furthermore, there is a need for more transparency on what providers report to the UNFCCC as climate finance. Beyond tracking, coherent and transparent data on climate finance are also critical for assessments of the effectiveness of how climate finance is programmed and spent, which in turn are key to scaling up implementation. The availability of more granular, project-level data can facilitate this process by allowing detailed analysis of the distribution of climate-related development finance, for example by country, sector, income group or instrument. The OECD statistical system contains project-level detail by provider country and institution, which facilitates such analysis (Figure 6.4).

Figure 6.4. **Climate-related international development finance, by income group and instrument, 2013-14 average**

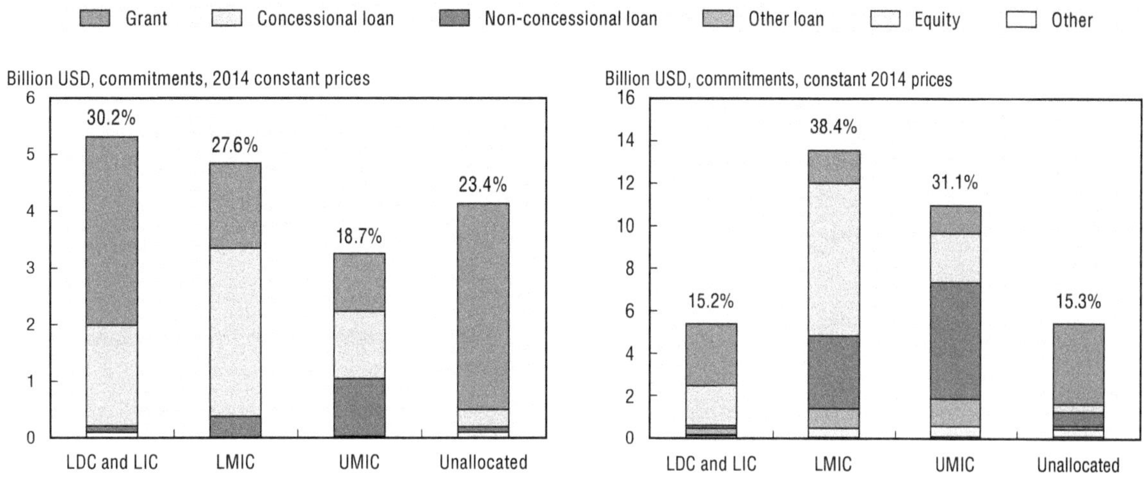

Notes: "Other loan" includes loans for which information on concessionality is not available. "Other" includes interest subsidy, other securities/claims and unclassified instruments. LDC = least developed country; LIC = low-income country; LMIC = lower middle-income country; UMIC = upper middle-income country.

Source: OECD (2016b), "Climate-related development finance in 2015", *www.oecd.org/dac/environment-development/Climate-related%20development%20finance%20in%202015%20-%20FINAL%20(2).pdf.*

StatLink http://dx.doi.org/10.1787/888933591993

There is potential to exploit synergies among existing statistical systems. Linking what countries report to the UNFCCC as climate finance with what is reported to the OECD as climate-related development finance, in a disaggregated data format, will allow for a substantially improved analysis of financing patterns, modalities and trends for both climate and development goals.

Understanding and linking up development finance data is essential

Ensuring that development finance data contribute to improved evidence and decision making depends not only on the generation of more and better data, it is also fundamental that data are relevant and useful to actual users, notably the developing country governments that rely on this information for financial planning. As development finance grows in complexity, the availability of quality data will facilitate a growing number of analyses, in turn generating increased demand for more and better information while improving the understanding of the relationships and inter-linkages among different types of finance.

Development finance data must be made available to developing countries

Global transparency efforts are improving the availability and quality of development finance data. ODA data are publicly available at a very detailed and granular level. Nonetheless, it is not always easy to match what is reported by providers of development co-operation internationally with the flows observed or recorded by developing countries through their aid management and information systems. One reason for the mismatch is that ODA statistical reporting was designed, initially, to measure provider effort; it therefore includes some financing that does not flow across borders, for example, administrative costs or in-donor refugee costs.

Getting a complete picture of all development finance flows to countries is a major challenge. Country programmable aid, also known as "core" aid, is the portion of aid programmed by bilateral and multilateral providers for individual countries and regions; it approximates actual aid flows entering developing countries. While country programmable aid is a useful indicator of the aid that is destined for countries, it would need to be complemented by country-level data to be useful for local policy and accountability purposes.[6]

The limited availability of forward-looking data is a crucial hurdle for medium-term planning and budgeting in developing countries.

The limited availability of forward-looking development finance data also constrains developing countries' medium-term planning and budgeting processes. Developing country governments need country-specific, demand-driven, timely and comprehensive data on aid. A core priority of the GPEDC is to strengthen the flow and quality of development finance data at the country level. Yet as shown in Box 6.7, responding to this need is a work in progress for providers.

Box 6.7. **There is scope to provide more and better development finance data to developing countries**

Under the auspices of the Global Partnership for Effective Development Co-operation, every two years developing countries take stock of progress on agreed development effectiveness commitments. In this data-intensive exercise, each national government leads the process, building on data available through its own information management platforms. Development co-operation providers are requested to share their disaggregated financing data to ensure data comprehensiveness and reliability. This includes information on current and forward-looking disbursements of development finance provided to the public sector, the private sector and civil society organisations for in-country development programmes and projects.

The latest monitoring exercise in 2016 involved a data-gathering process led by 81 low and middle-income countries (OECD/UNDP, 2016). The average DAC provider responded to 77% of developing countries' requests for data, although with differing levels of engagement across providers (Figure 6.5). Overall, the shared data were fairly comprehensive (84.3% of data requests by national co-ordinators were met). Aggregated data (e.g. at the country-programme level) were more frequently available than disaggregated data (e.g. at the project level). Yet out of 2 819 major development projects approved in 2015, representing USD 72 billion in development funding, developing country governments were able to access the project documents of just 40% of the reported projects (1 133 projects).

Data from new types of development finance project documents and information regarding financing delivered to/through civil society organisations and private sector entities were less readily or publicly available. In countries where the predominant development financing modalities (e.g. official lending) require legislative approval, or where local aid information management systems are well used by the provider community, data gathering and validation by the government was easier.

Figure 6.5. **Are providers ready for country-led data gathering?**

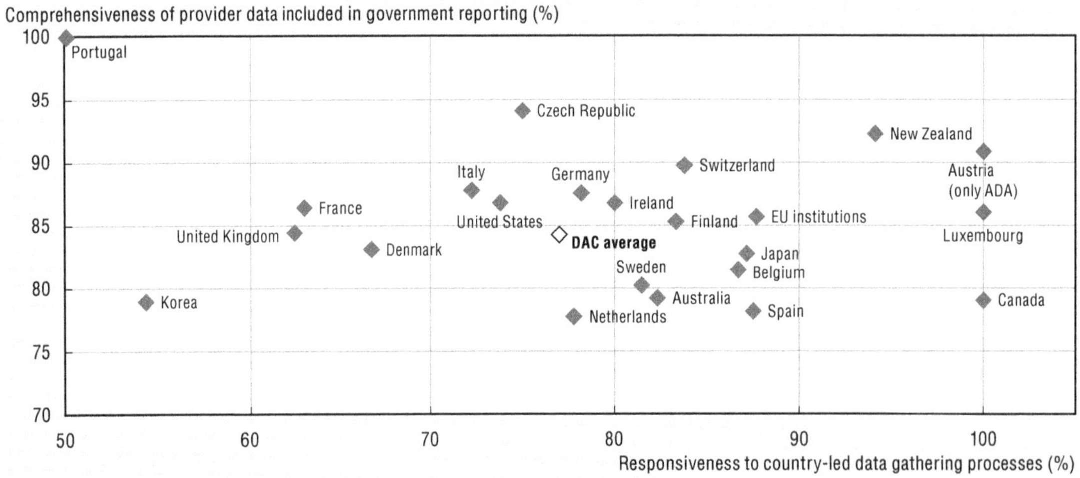

Source: Based on data reported in OECD/UNDP (2016), *Making Development Co-operation More Effective: 2016 Progress Report*, *http://dx.doi.org/10.1787/9789264266261-en*.

StatLink *http://dx.doi.org/10.1787/888933592012*

A more coherent picture of all development financing requires viewing all flows as part of a whole

Arriving at a better understanding of how SDG financing is coming together, both at the country level and globally, requires the international community to know the full volume of resources invested in development and where they are deployed. In order to fulfil this ambition, a new common international framework that captures information far beyond traditional aid in a systematic manner is required. Total official support for sustainable development (TOSSD) is being designed to harvest the full range of official development finance data, including private resources mobilised through official interventions.

Work on the TOSSD framework aims to facilitate understanding of:

- the scale and scope of officially supported SDG financing that crosses the borders of developing countries
- how the international community is supporting development enablers and the provision of global public goods
- how to access and combine financial resources most effectively
- collaboration and joint financing for the SDGs across development partners.

An initial estimate by the OECD based on a preliminary statistical breakdown of the TOSSD in 2014 stands at USD 580 billion. In addition to yielding a richer picture at the global level, however, a key objective of the TOSSD framework is to provide enhanced information on development finance at the country level. Two recent TOSSD pilots, in the Philippines and Senegal (OECD, 2017e), substantiated the value-added of the framework.[7] Some of the findings from these pilots included:

- the TOSSD presents high potential as an international standard, including for ensuring comparability of data across different sources
- the TOSSD framework and measure can be a useful tool to enhance transparency and unpack complex financial packages
- a framework such as the TOSSD is very much needed to reflect all contributions to sustainable development, including those made by emerging economies in developing countries
- better tracking of triangular and South-South co-operation, NGO activities or subnational co-operation would strengthen the TOSSD framework as a tool in line with recipient countries' needs
- it is critical to develop the technical features and boundaries of the TOSSD measure.

Work to establish the TOSSD as an international statistical standard, against which official bilateral and multilateral institutions and South-South providers will be able to report SDG-relevant data on resource flows, will be taken forward in close association with a wide range of actors, including relevant UN bodies. As a first step, a special the TOSSD Task Force has been established; it held its first meeting in July 2017 to elaborate the statistical features of the TOSSD and prepare a first set of reporting instructions. Agreement in 2018 on the scope and method of TOSSD reporting, in particular for cross-border flows,[8] will enable TOSSD data to contribute to international reporting on SDG implementation at the UN-hosted High Level Political Forum in 2019.

The effective financing of the 2030 Agenda requires putting together the increasingly complex development finance puzzle in a way that combines seemingly disparate components into a coherent picture. The role of each resource, in terms of its ability to contribute to closing the overall financing gap, has to be seen as a part of a whole that addresses the full range of financing needs. The TOSSD is designed to harvest all official development finance data, including private resources mobilised through official interventions, so as to enhance their impact on and contribution to international development goals.

The way forward for getting development finance data right

Data on development finance play a central role in advancing sustainable development: they are fundamental to understanding the state of SDG financing and designing strategies to fill the financing gaps. Yet, as presented in this chapter, there continue to be major challenges to getting the data right. Making progress on addressing these fundamental challenges to come up with new measures, methods and systems requires political will, leadership and consensus building. Financial and human resources as well as new technical resources are needed to build the capacity to collect, report and analyse development finance data so that they can play their transformative role. The appreciation by providers and other development finance actors that their efforts will be better recognised offers an incentive to invest in getting the data right. Yet the needs of developing countries for comprehensive, timely and predictable data should drive and shape the work.

Priority actions to improve development finance data

- Increase the availability and transparency of quality data on development finance, including concessional and non-concessional official flows, private finance mobilised through official interventions, private flows at market terms, South-South and triangular co-operation, and giving by philanthropic foundations and civil society organisations.
- Improve methodologies and standards, including: the TOSSD statistical standard, through an inclusive, international process so that the data can contribute to international reporting on SDG implementation; the methodologies for measurement of private sector ODA instruments; and global data standards for social impact investment.
- Improve analysis of financing patterns, modalities and trends for both climate and development goals by exploiting synergies between existing systems for climate-related development finance and country reporting on climate finance to UNFCCC.

Notes

1. AidData is a partnership between the College of William & Mary, Development Gateway and Brigham Young University. AidData publishes a comprehensive development finance data portal, and invests in creating tools and conducting analyses and training that make this information useful in research, programme planning and advocacy.
2. See: *www.oecd.org/dac/financing-sustainable-development/concessional-sovereign-loans.htm.*
3. Paragraph 57 of the Addis Ababa Action Agenda (UN, 2015b) states the following about South-South and triangular co-operation: "We welcome the increased contributions of South-South co-operation to poverty eradication and sustainable development. We encourage developing countries to voluntarily step up their efforts to strengthen South-South co-operation, and to further improve its development effectiveness in accordance with the provisions of the Nairobi outcome document of the High-level United Nations Conference on South-South Cooperation. We also commit to strengthening triangular co-operation as a means of bringing relevant experience and expertise to bear in development co-operation."
4. The ODA definition itself does not specify the country classification of the origin funding source. It does, however, limit the eligible recipients to developing countries. See: *www.oecd.org/dac/stats/daclist.htm.*
5. The Funds and Facilities Survey is based on a combination of surveys by the Commons Consultants on behalf of the association of European Development Finance Institutions, and by the World Economic Forum under the WEF-OECD Redesigning Development Finance Initiative.
6. For instance, it does not include cross-border flows that are not programmable, such as debt relief or humanitarian aid.
7. For more information see OECD (2017e) and OECD (forthcoming).
8. For more information on the architecture of the TOSSD framework, please see: *https://www.oecd.org/dac/financing-sustainable-development/development-finance-standards/TOSSD%20Flyer%20crops.pdf.*

References

Alvarez, S.P. et al. (2015), "Remittances: How reliable are the data?", *Migration Policy Practice*, Vol. V/2, pp. 42-46, *www.un.org/en/development/desa/population/migration/events/other/workshop/2015/docs/MPP_Issue_21.pdf.*

Benn, J. et al. (2017), "Amounts mobilised from the private sector by official development finance interventions: Guarantees, syndicated loans, shares in collective investment vehicles, direct investment in companies and credit lines", *OECD Development Co-operation Working Papers*, OECD Publishing, Paris.

CPI (2015), "Global landscape of climate finance 2015", Climate Policy Initiative, *http://climatepolicyinitiative.org/wp-content/uploads/2015/11/Global-Landscape-of-Climate-Finance-2015.pdf.*

Department for Business, Energy & Industrial Strategy (2016), "Roadmap to US$100 billion", prepared by a group of developed countries lead by the UK and Australia in advance of COP22, UK Department for Business, Energy & Industrial Strategy, London, *www.gov.uk/government/publications/climate-finance-roadmap-to-us100-billion.*

Global Emerging Market Risk Database (2017), official website, *www.gems-riskdatabase.org.*

GIIN (2017), "Annual Impact Investor Survey 2017, The Seventh Edition", Global Impact Investing Network, New York, *https://thegiin.org/assets/GIIN_AnnualImpactInvestorSurvey_2017_Web_Final.pdf.*

IATF (2017), *Financing for Development: Progress and Prospects, Report of the Inter-agency Task Force on Financing for Development 2017*, United Nations, New York, *https://developmentfinance.un.org/financing-development-progress-and-prospects-2017.*

Luijkx, W. and J. Benn (2017), "Emerging providers' international co-operation for development", *OECD Development Co-operation Working Papers*, No. 33, OECD Publishing, Paris, *http://dx.doi.org/10.1787/15d6a3c7-en.*

ODI (n.d.), "Climate funds update", Overseas Development Institute, London, *www.climatefundsupdate.org.*

OECD (forthcoming), "The total official support for sustainable development (TOSSD) pilot study in the Philippines", OECD, Paris, forthcoming.

OECD (2017a), *Investing in Climate, Investing in Growth*, OECD Publishing, Paris, *http://dx.doi.org/10.1787/9789264273528-en.*

OECD (2017b), "DAC statistical reporting issues in 2016", DCD/DAC/STAT(2017)15, OECD, Paris, *www.oecd.org/officialdocuments/publicdisplaydocumentpdf/?cote=DCD/DAC/STAT(2017)15&docLanguage=En.*

OECD (2017c), "Development aid rises again in 2016 but flows to poorest countries dip", OECD, Paris, *www.oecd.org/dac/development-aid-rises-again-in-2016-but-flows-to-poorest-countries-dip.htm.*

OECD (2017d), "Global private philanthropy for development: Results of the OECD data survey as of 19 June 2017", OECD, Paris, *www.oecd.org/dac/financing-sustainable-development/development-finance-data/Flyer_update_June_2017.pdf.*

OECD (2017e), "A recipient perspective on TOSSD: The case of Senegal", OECD, Paris, *www.oecd.org/dac/financing-sustainable-development/development-finance-standards/2017-03%20-%20recipient%20perspective%20on%20TOSSD_Senegal%20%20wirh%20crops%20for%20opsFINAL.pdf.*

OECD (2016a), "2020 projections of climate finance towards the USD 100 billion goal: Technical note", OECD, Paris, *www.oecd.org/environment/cc/Projecting%20Climate%20Change%202020%20WEB.pdf.*

OECD (2016b), "Climate-related development finance in 2015", statistical flyer, OECD, Paris, *www.oecd.org/dac/environment-development/Climate-related%20development%20finance%20in%202015%20-%20FINAL%20(2).pdf.*

OECD (2015a), "Why modernise official development assistance?", A flyer for the Third International Conference on Financing for Development, Addis Ababa, July 2015, OECD, Paris, *www.oecd.org/dac/financing-sustainable-development/Addis%20flyer%20-%20ODA.pdf.*

OECD (2015b), *Climate Finance in 2013-14 and the USD 100 billion Goal: A Report by the OECD in Collaboration with Climate Policy Initiative*, OECD Publishing, Paris, *http://dx.doi.org/10.1787/9789264249424-en.*

OECD (2011), "Quality framework and guidelines for OECD statistical activities: Version 2011/1", OECD, Paris, *www.oecd.org/officialdocuments/publicdisplaydocumentpdf/?cote=std/qfs(2011)1&doclanguage=en.*

OECD/UNDP (2016), *Making Development Co-operation More Effective: 2016 Progress Report*, OECD Publishing, Paris, *http://dx.doi.org/10.1787/9789264266261-en.*

UN (2015a), "Transforming our world: The 2030 Agenda for Sustainable Development", United Nations, New York, *https://sustainabledevelopment.un.org/content/documents/21252030%20Agenda%20for%20Sustainable%20Development%20web.pdf.*

UN (2015b), "Addis Ababa Action Agenda of the Third International Conference on Financing for Development (Addis Ababa Action Agenda)", United Nations, New York, *www.un.org/esa/ffd/wp-content/uploads/2015/08/AAAA_Outcome.pdf.*

UN (2010), "Nairobi outcome document of the High-level United Nations Conference on South-South Cooperation", A/RES/64/222, United Nations General Assembly, New York, *http://ssc.undp.org/content/dam/ssc/documents/Key%20Policy%20Documents/Nairobi%20Outcome%20Document.pdf.*

UNFCCC (2016), "UNFCCC Standing Committee on Finance: 2016 biennial assessment and overview of climate finance flows report", United Nations Framework Convention on Climate Change, Bonn, Germany, *http://unfccc.int/cooperation_and_support/financial_mechanism/standing_committee/items/10028.php*.

UNFCCC (2015), "Adoption of the Paris Agreement", FCCC/CP/2015/L.9/Rev.1, 21st Conference of the Parties, United Nations Framework Convention on Climate Change, *https://unfccc.int/resource/docs/2015/cop21/eng/l09r01.pdf*.

PART II

Profiles of development co-operation providers

Development Co-operation Report 2017
Data for Development

Development finance and policy trends

This chapter highlights emerging trends in official development assistance (ODA) from members of the Development Assistance Committee (DAC) and other providers of development assistance. It draws on DAC statistics, the findings and recommendations of DAC peer reviews conducted since 2015 and the results of the Global Partnership for Effective Development Co-operation's 2016 progress report. According to preliminary data, in 2016 net ODA reached yet another peak, at USD 142.6 billion, or 0.32% of gross national income, driven in part by increased spending on in-donor refugee costs. Country programmable aid and flows to least developed countries and small island developing states are declining, while the percentage of humanitarian assistance and aid channelled through the multilateral system and civil society organisations has risen. DAC members are improving the quality of their development co-operation but most still have a long way to go to meet their international commitments.

This chapter was prepared by Yasmin Ahmad, John Egan and Alejandro Guerrero Ruiz of the Development Co-operation Directorate, OECD.

Key trends

- Official development assistance (ODA) reached an all-time high of USD 142.6 billion in 2016, representing 0.32% of gross national income.
- ODA has doubled since the turn of the century and in 2016 rose by 8.9% in real terms compared to 2015.
- Aid spending on in-donor refugees rose by 27.5% in real terms to USD 15.4 billion in 2016.
- Multilateral co-operation rose to USD 41 billion in 2016, representing 28% of total net ODA.
- The share of concessional loans has increased over the past decade, from 10% of gross bilateral ODA in 2005 to 16% in 2015.
- Humanitarian assistance rose from 9% to 13% of gross bilateral ODA between 2010 and 2015.
- The quality of aid is improving but much remains to be done to achieve the four development effectiveness principles: Ownership, a focus on results, partnerships, and transparency and shared responsibility.

Despite commitments made by Development Assistance Committee (DAC) members in 2014:

- Bilateral ODA to least developed countries fell by 3.9% in real terms in 2016.
- Bilateral ODA to small island developing states fell by 17% in real terms between 2011 and 2015.
- Bilateral ODA to fragile and conflict-affected contexts fell by nearly 10% in real terms between 2011 and 2015.

ODA support is critical for the 2030 Agenda

ODA is critical to achieving the 2030 Agenda for Sustainable Development, filling key financing gaps where no alternatives exist. Given the unprecedented volume of public and private resources to be mobilised in order to achieve the ambition of the Sustainable Development Goals (SDGs), ODA must evolve and be used as effectively as possible within the broader development finance landscape.

The 2014 *Development Co-operation Report* (OECD, 2014a) suggested a range of smart approaches through which ODA could have a multiplier effect on the resources needed to deliver sustainable development in the Agenda 2030 era, including: supporting developing countries, especially fragile states, to mobilise their own domestic revenue; helping countries to create a conducive environment for investment, including in infrastructure; leveraging resources from the private sector by diversifying and sharing risk; and supporting developing countries to make their growth green and inclusive.

In December 2014, members of the DAC agreed to allocate more ODA to countries most in need – least developed countries (LDCs), low-income countries, small island developing states (SIDS), landlocked developing countries, and fragile and conflict-affected states. Central to this agreement was reversing the declining trend of ODA to LDCs. Members of the DAC also agreed on changes to their reporting of the concessional element of loans to incentivise lending on highly concessional terms to LDCs and other low-income countries. These changes will become the standard for reporting from 2018 (OECD, 2014b).

Hungary became the 30th DAC Member on 6 December 2016. Because its accession to the DAC was so late in the calendar year, the Secretariat was not able to include its data in the 2015 figures for DAC members published in December 2016. Therefore it still appears as a non-DAC provider in this release of the data. Figures for Hungary will be incorporated in the DAC total as reporting in 2017 on flows in 2016.

In February 2016, the DAC agreed on a series of principles to ensure that the DAC statistical system reflects the effort of the official sector in providing private sector instruments in a credible and transparent manner; it also agreed on a number of updates to the way development finance is measured (OECD, 2016a).

DAC statistics provide a framework for monitoring and for accountability for providers, recipients and the broader international development community on ODA volumes and allocations. Tracking and analysing ODA allocations plays an important role in monitoring the implementation of international agreements to ensure the effective deployment of development expenditures in response to developing countries' needs. A fit-for-purpose ODA standard is crucial for the implementation of the 2030 Agenda (see Chapter 6).

DAC peer reviews add to the analysis of statistics, describing the strategic orientations, organisation and operations of DAC members' development co-operation and offering insight into the future direction of ODA.

Every two years, the Global Partnership for Effective Development Co-operation (GPEDC) monitors progress towards achieving the development effectiveness principles in developing countries by development partners, including DAC members. The latest progress report was released in 2016 ahead of the Second High Level Meeting of the GPEDC in Nairobi (OECD/UNDP, 2016).

This chapter examines trends in development financing and highlights what countries are doing to fulfil their development co-operation objectives and commitments, drawing on findings from DAC statistics, recent OECD-DAC peer reviews* and the GPEDC 2016 progress report.

Financial flows to developing countries are changing

ODA has been the steadiest source of development financing for developing countries over the past 45 years and the largest source of finance until the mid-1970s (Figure 7.1). Since then, private flows have been larger in volume most years, but also more volatile and subject to market fluctuations. After 1974, lending by banks (other private capital flows in Figure 7.1) increased, and along with foreign direct investment (FDI) constituted more than half of resource flows to developing

Figure 7.1. **DAC countries' total net resource flows to developing countries, 1970-2015**

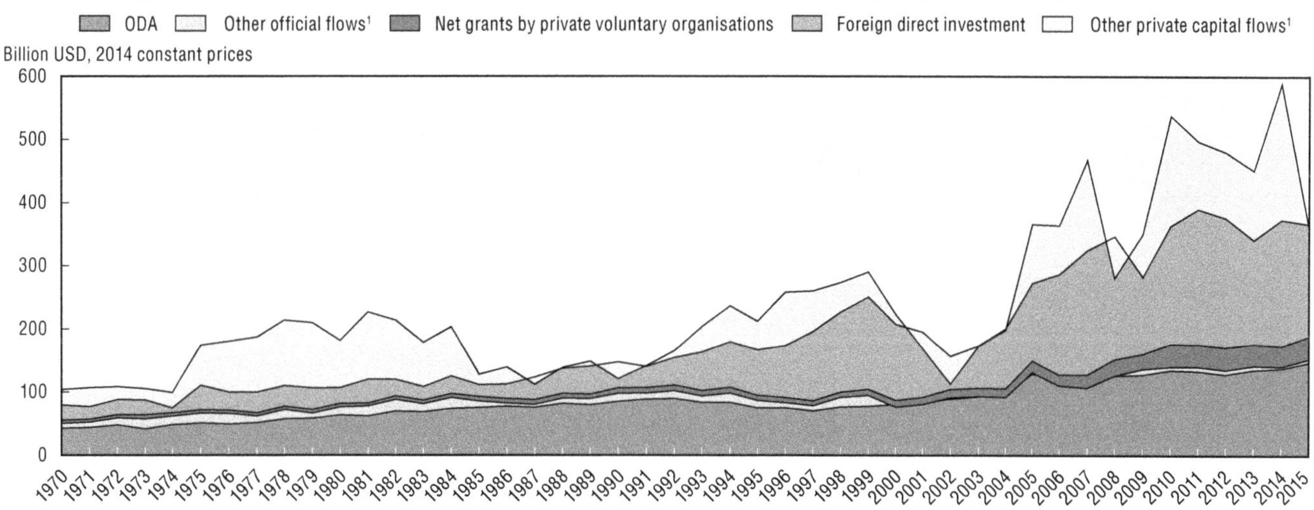

Note: ODA: Official development assistance.

1. Net other official flows were negative in 2000-01, 2004 and 2006-07; other private capital flows were negative in 1987, 1990, 2001-04, 2008 and 2015.

StatLink http://dx.doi.org/10.1787/888933491230

* Full peer reviews include: Belgium, the Czech Republic, Denmark, Germany, Iceland, New Zealand, Poland, Portugal, Spain and the United States. Mid-term reviews include: France, Ireland, Korea, Luxembourg, Norway, the Slovak Republic, Sweden and Switzerland.

countries. These fell after the Mexican debt crisis in 1982. Since 2005, FDI has become the most significant source of private external financing, reflecting investors' long-term confidence in developing countries' investment opportunities and growth. Remittances, which are perceived to mostly finance consumption rather than investment, are also an important flow of finance to developing countries and have been growing steadily.[1] Aid by private voluntary organisations, including non-governmental organisations, has risen, doubling in volume between 2005 and 2015.

ODA flows are increasing steadily

Since the turn of the 21st century, ODA flows have been on the rise, doubling since 2000. There are several reasons for this: the agreement of the Millennium Development Goals in 2000, the Monterrey Conference on Financing for Development in 2002, the Gleneagles G8 Summit and other fora in 2005 where donors made specific commitments to scale up their ODA by 2010. Since then ODA has continued to grow, with slips in 2011 and 2012 due to the financial crisis and the euro area turmoil. Nevertheless, few donors have delivered fully on their commitments, such as achieving 0.7% ODA/GNI by 2015.

In adopting the 2030 Agenda, world leaders called on developed countries to fully implement their existing ODA commitments, including to provide 0.7% of gross national income (GNI) in ODA to developing countries, of which 0.15% to 0.2% should be provided to LDCs. While many DAC members have committed to increase ODA volumes in order to reach the target of 0.7% of GNI, and others, particularly the newer European Union members, have agreed to reach 0.33% of GNI, peer reviews show that very few have a clear plan for doing so.

Figure 7.2. **Official development assistance over the past 50 years**

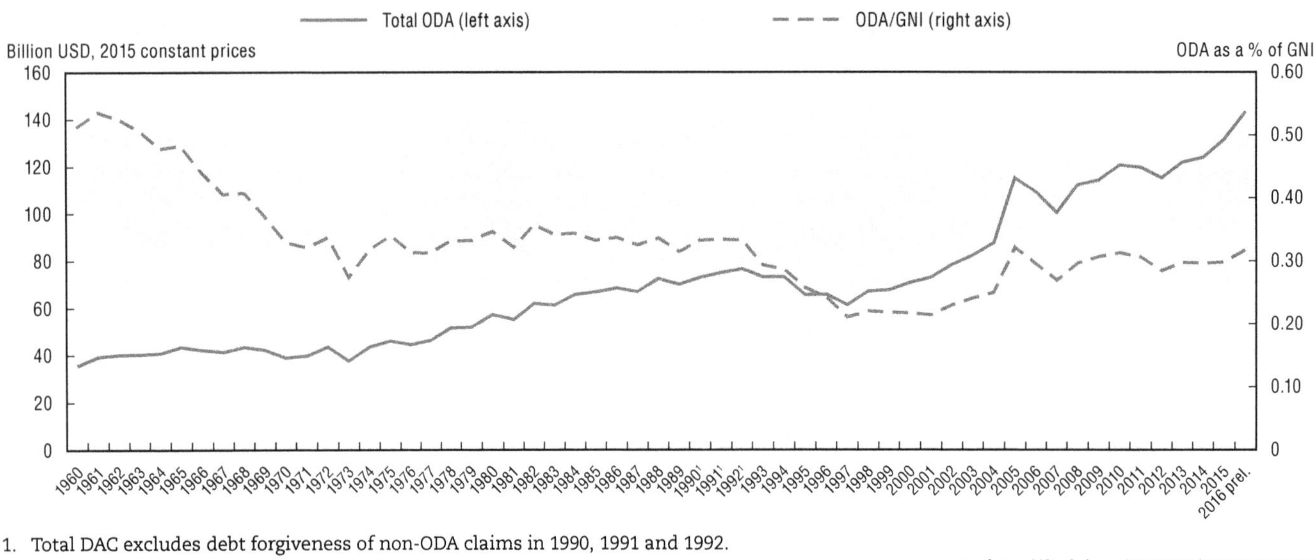

1. Total DAC excludes debt forgiveness of non-ODA claims in 1990, 1991 and 1992.

StatLink http://dx.doi.org/10.1787/888933491241

Refugee costs in donor countries are on the rise

Preliminary data (Figure 7.3) show that ODA reached a new peak in 2016 at USD 142.6 billion, representing an increase of 8.9% in real terms compared to 2015. Net ODA as a share of GNI also rose, from 0.30% in 2015 to 0.32% in 2016.

Net ODA rose in 22 DAC member countries, with the largest increases recorded in Austria, Belgium, the Czech Republic, Germany, Greece, Iceland, Ireland, Italy, Poland, the Slovak Republic, Slovenia and Spain (OECD, 2017a). For several members the increases were due to the impact of in-donor refugee costs (for example for Austria, Germany and Switzerland). France has increased its ODA but has not yet recovered its 2010 level.

Figure 7.3. **Net ODA from DAC donors in volume and as a share of GNI, 2016**

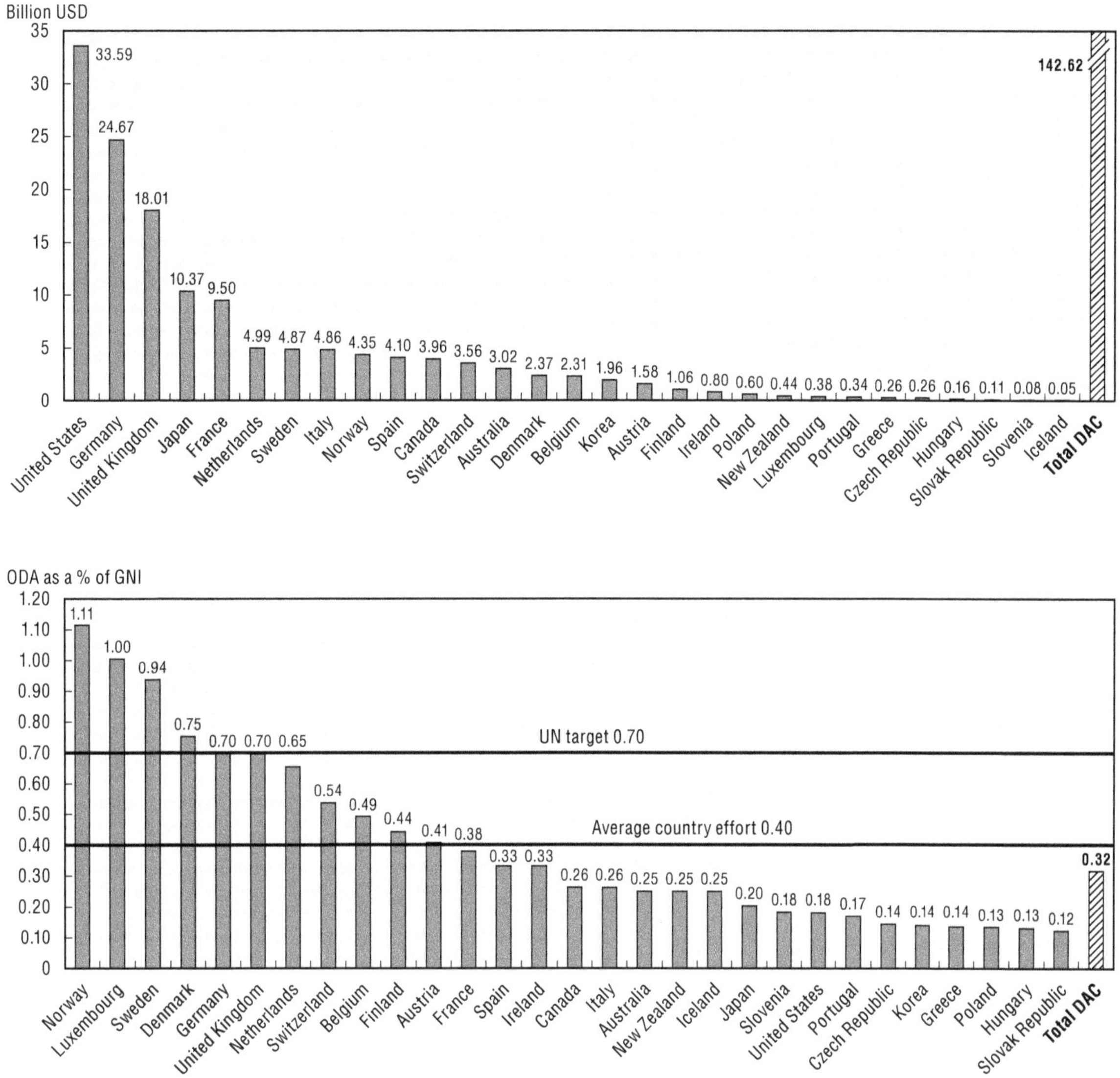

Note: Preliminary data for 2016.

StatLink http://dx.doi.org/10.1787/888933491252

The largest DAC donors by volume in 2016 were the United States, Germany, the United Kingdom, Japan and France (Figure 7.3). Denmark, Luxembourg, Norway, Sweden and the United Kingdom met or exceeded the United Nations target of 0.7% of GNI and Germany reached this target for the first time in 2016 (Figure 7.3). The United Arab Emirates, a participant in the DAC, provided 1.12% of GNI as ODA and Turkey provided 0.79%.

In real terms, ODA fell in seven countries, with the largest decreases noted in Australia, Finland, the Netherlands and Sweden due mainly to overall budgetary cuts and fluctuations in in-donor refugee costs (Sweden).

In 2016, DAC countries' core contributions to multilateral organisations rose by nearly 10%. Support for bilateral projects, programmes and technical co-operation rose by nearly 3% but their share of total net ODA fell from 58% on average during the period 2010-12 to 49% in 2016.

The overall increase in ODA in 2016 is also explained by higher in-donor refugee costs (see Box 7.1). These costs rose by 27.5% in real terms from USD 12.1 billion in 2015 to USD 15.4 billion in 2016. Their share of total net ODA also increased, from 9.2% in 2015 to 10.8% in 2016. However, when expenditure on refugee costs is excluded, net ODA still rose by 7.1% in real terms. Excluding in-donor refugee costs and debt relief, mainly for Cuba, net ODA rose by 5.4% in real terms.

Box 7.1. **Reporting on in-donor refugee costs**

Specific instructions on the reporting of in-donor refugee costs were first introduced in the Development Assistance Committee (DAC) statistical reporting directives in 1988. These instructions have changed little since then.

In-donor refugee costs:

- "A refugee is a person who is outside his/her home country because of a well-founded fear of persecution on account of his race, religion, nationality, social group or political opinion. Assistance to persons who have fled from their homes because of civil war or severe unrest may also be counted under this item.
- Official sector expenditures for the sustenance of refugees in donor countries can be counted as ODA during the first twelve months of their stay.[1] This includes payments for refugees' transport to the host country and temporary sustenance (food, shelter and training); these expenditures should not be allocated geographically. However, this item also includes expenditures for voluntary resettlement of refugees in a developing country; these are allocated geographically according to the country of resettlement. Expenditures on deportation or other forcible measures to repatriate refugees should not be counted as ODA. Amounts spent to promote the integration of refugees into the economy of the donor country, or resettle them elsewhere than in a developing country, are also excluded.[2]"

To improve transparency in members' reporting of in-donor refugee costs, the DAC is undertaking work to clarify the Reporting Directives pertaining to in-donor country refugee costs in order to enhance comparability, transparency and credibility of official development assistance spent on in-donor refugee costs. For further information see: *www.oecd.org/dac/refugees-migration-working-group.htm*.

1. Contributions by one donor to another donor to cover such expenditures should be recorded as ODA by the contributing country. The receiving country should reduce the expenditure reported under this item by the same amount.
2. Extract from DAC Statistical Reporting Directives (see: *www.oecd.org/dac/financing-sustainable-development/development-finance-standards/DCDDAC(2016)3FINAL.pdf*, paragraphs 92-93).

While European Union (EU) DAC member states spent USD 9.7 billion on some 1.2 million asylum seekers in 2015, they spent just USD 3.1 billion in ODA to the Syrian Arab Republic, Afghanistan, Somalia, South Sudan and Sudan, the top five countries from which those asylum seekers had fled.

Country programmable aid appears to be declining

About half of bilateral ODA in 2015 was country programmable aid (CPA), also known as "core" aid. CPA is the portion of aid that providers can programme for individual countries and regions, and over which partner countries could have a significant say. This measure provides an estimate of actual aid flows that go to partner countries.

While DAC member countries' CPA has fluctuated between 53% and 55% of total gross bilateral ODA over the past five years, in 2015 it fell to 49%, representing USD 52 billion. However, the relatively stable percentage of total CPA disguises significant differences among DAC members.

Twenty-one DAC member countries reduced their volume of CPA between 2010 and 2015, with the biggest falls in the United States (USD 3.3 billion), Spain (USD 1.6 billion) and the Netherlands (USD 577 million).

These falls were offset by significant increases in CPA for Germany (USD 3.4 billion) and the United Kingdom (USD 1.2 billion), reflecting an overall scaling up of their ODA in recent years, as well as France, Korea, Japan and Switzerland. The ratio of CPA to bilateral ODA diverges markedly amongst DAC members, with Korea (83%), Portugal and Japan (76% each) having the highest share in 2015 and Austria (9%) and Greece (6%) the lowest. While Austria's CPA averaged 15% in the period 2010-15 as a result of large contributions to debt relief, it fell in 2015 as a result of high in-donor refugee costs.

DAC peer reviews since 2015 have flagged a number of changes in how DAC members are allocating their aid, which are likely to have a continuing impact on the share of CPA. For example, a significant reorientation of Dutch development co-operation has led to the use of centrally managed thematic budgets disbursed through global or regional partnerships and competitive grant mechanisms open to broad alliances of civil society, knowledge institutions, the private sector and multilateral agencies. As a result, 73% of gross bilateral ODA is now unspecified by region and 81% is unspecified by income group (OECD, 2017b). Reductions to CPA in Spain and Sweden result from cuts to the ODA budget. Similar cuts have been signalled for Denmark and Finland. On the other hand, diminishing CPA in the United States reflects the significant rise in humanitarian aid between 2013 and 2015 (which rose by nearly 22% in real terms to USD 6 billion in 2015) and greater use of multilateral channels in recent years.

Figure 7.4. **Composition of DAC countries' bilateral ODA, 2015, gross disbursements**

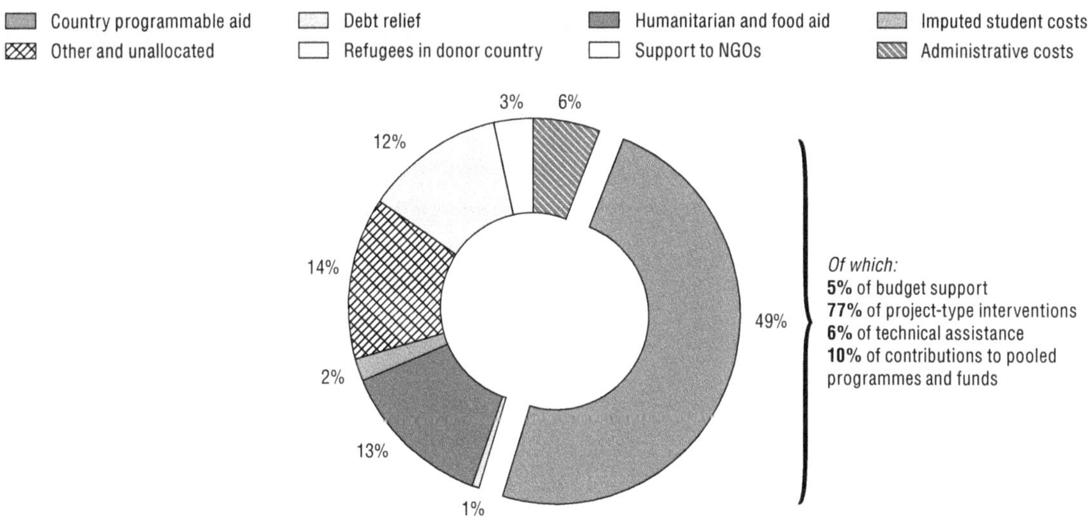

StatLink http://dx.doi.org/10.1787/888933491264

Concessional lending is growing

Most DAC members provide ODA only in the form of grants; however, low interest rates and fiscal constraints have led to the share of concessional loans increasing over the past decade, from 10% of gross bilateral ODA in 2005 to 16% in 2015. While most DAC members provided their ODA in the form of grants, concessional loans represented a third or more of some providers' bilateral gross ODA in 2015 (France: 44%; Germany: 34%; Japan: 58%; Korea: 41%; Portugal: 38% and Poland: 33%).

While loans are a major feature of Japanese development co-operation, Japan has taken action to ensure its ODA portfolio meets the requirements of the *DAC Recommendation on the Terms and Conditions of Aid* (OECD, 1978) in which members agreed to raise the overall grant element of ODA to 86%. Japan's grant element of total ODA was 87.3% in 2014-15. France first failed to comply with the DAC recommendation in 2010 and with a grant element of 82.8% in 2014-15 France remains non-compliant as does Germany (85.6%). The peer review of Germany in 2015 noted that its portfolio of loans shows a disconnect between its stated focus on the poorest countries and the volume of German ODA going to middle-income countries. German loans accounted for 34% of gross bilateral ODA disbursements in 2015, largely to middle-income countries. The last peer review of France commented that it should ensure an appropriate balance between grants and loans. Korea's emphasis on highly concessional loans can be explained by its own positive experience as a recipient of this kind of aid in the past.

As part of the ODA measure, the DAC has moved towards recording the grant equivalent of concessional loans rather than recording the full amount of the loan and netting out repayments in future years (OECD, 2014b). This recognises a higher level of ODA for those loans with higher concessionality, and may incentivise more concessional lending for poorer countries (e.g. a loan provided to least developed or low-income countries will need to have a grant element of at least 45% compared to 15% and 10% for lower and upper-middle countries respectively). In turn, this allows these countries to reduce their average cost of borrowing.

Such changes are seen as important in a post-financial crisis context. Looking ahead, gross public and private non-financial sector debt reached a record high in 2015 of USD 152 trillion (IMF, 2016). While the bulk of this increase is in advanced economies, debt levels across developing economies are also increasing, including in LDCs and SIDS (United Nations, 2017). The collaboration between provider and recipient countries has long been important in the upstream assurance of debt sustainability as well as in the downstream resolution of debt distress. Moreover, debt issues could affect both the public and private sectors. While concessional lending has not itself been driving debt accumulation, steps to modernise ODA recording is one way in which concessional lenders have been "playing their part" in mitigating these risks. Debt issues will be discussed further in the upcoming *Global Outlook on Financing for Development* (to be released in 2018).

Bilateral ODA to least developed countries is falling

The increase in ODA since the turn of the millennium benefitted countries in all income groups, especially least developed countries (Figure 7.5). However, since 2011 bilateral ODA flows to these countries have fallen (the increase in 2013 was due to debt relief for Myanmar), and between 2014 and 2015 they increased only slightly. Preliminary data for 2016 show that bilateral flows to the LDCs fell by 3.9% in real terms compared to 2015.

While 19 DAC members provided less ODA to LDCs in 2015 than in 2010, there were significant increases in gross bilateral ODA to LDCs from Poland (461%), Korea (62%), New Zealand (65%), Switzerland (61%) and the United Kingdom (38%). Austria's support to LDCs dropped from 25% of total ODA in 2014 to 6% in 2015 and budget projections for 2016 indicate further reductions ahead. DAC members with a low percentage of total ODA to LDCs in 2015 include Germany (14%), Greece (16%), the Netherlands (18%), Sweden (21%) and Italy (22%). The fact that just 15% of Slovenia's ODA goes to LDCs is explained by a focus on middle-income countries in its immediate neighbourhood of the Western Balkans. The Czech Republic (21%) and Slovak Republic (22%) are in a similar situation, with their support to LDCs being provided primarily through contributions to the European Union and multilateral agencies. While many DAC members use the multilateral system to reach out to LDCs, it

Figure 7.5. **Bilateral ODA by income group, 2000-15, gross disbursements**

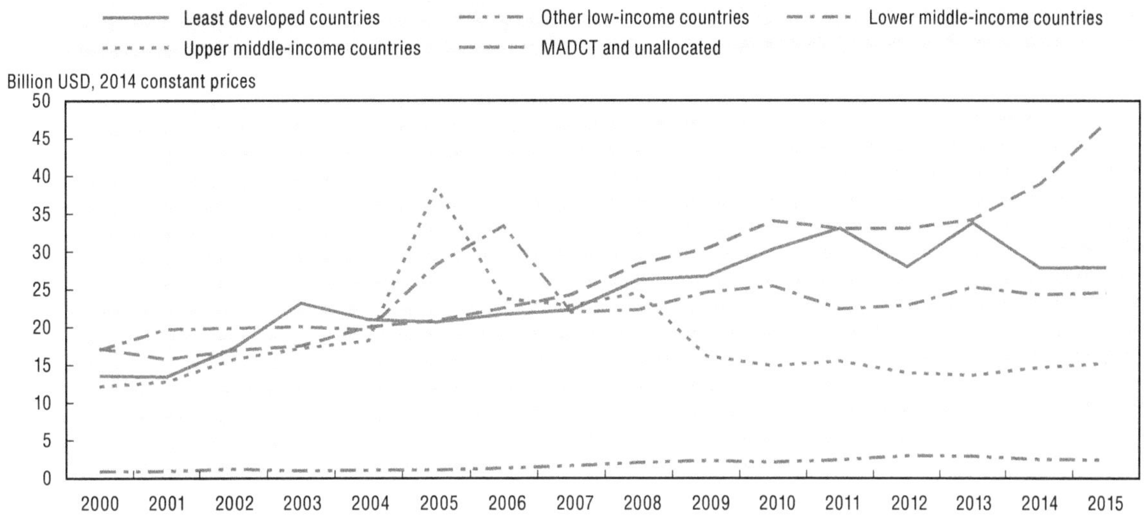

MADCT: More advanced developing countries.

StatLink http://dx.doi.org/10.1787/888933491273

is worth noting that imputed multilateral contributions to LDCs dropped from 45% in 2006 to 35% in 2015 largely as a result of reductions in the percentage provided by UN agencies and European Union institutions.

Peer reviews of DAC members highlight that stronger efforts will be needed if DAC members are to meet their December 2014 agreement to reverse the declining trend of ODA to LDCs (OECD, 2014b). Ireland and Belgium have exceeded their commitments to allocate at least 50% of ODA to LDCs, and the United Kingdom will allocate 50% of DFID spending to fragile states and regions, many of which are LDCs. Korea has set targets of allocating 50% of grants to LDCs and other low-income countries and 40% of ODA loan commitments from its Economic Development Co-operation Fund to LDCs.

The share of bilateral ODA that is not allocated by country has increased, from 31% in 2010 to 40% in 2015. Part of this increase is due to higher costs reported for in-donor refugees, which are not allocated by country. However, some donors report higher shares of aid that is not allocated by country due to regional programmes or, as suggested by the Netherlands in its recent peer review, by a lack of detailed reporting by DAC members of increased contributions to non-governmental organisations (NGOs). Some of the unallocated funding may be directed to LDCs, although the exact volume is not known.

On average, nearly half of the ODA flows to LDCs were directed to 7 out of the 48 LDCs in 2014 and 2015 (Afghanistan, Bangladesh, the Democratic Republic of the Congo, Ethiopia, Myanmar, South Sudan and the United Republic of Tanzania). Of these, Afghanistan accounted for about 15% of gross bilateral ODA flows to LDCs (with nearly 80% from Germany, Japan, the United Kingdom and the United States) and the four African countries accounted for about a quarter. The remaining 41 LDCs received half of the aid, although some of these are very small countries where smaller volumes may still translate into relatively high per capita levels. For example, in 2015 Afghanistan received around USD 130 per capita in aid, a significant amount which was dwarfed only by a number of SIDS such as Kiribati and Tonga which received some USD 600 per capita and Tuvalu USD 5 000 per capita.

In terms of volume, the United States has been the most generous donor since 2000, and its gross ODA to the group of LDCs has increased, even when its flows to Afghanistan, its largest recipient, are discounted. Aid to the LDCs from the United Kingdom also increased substantially, and although aid from Japan did not grow overall, it was redirected towards the LDCs.

Figure 7.6. **Bilateral ODA to the least developed countries from top DAC donors, 2000-15, gross disbursements**

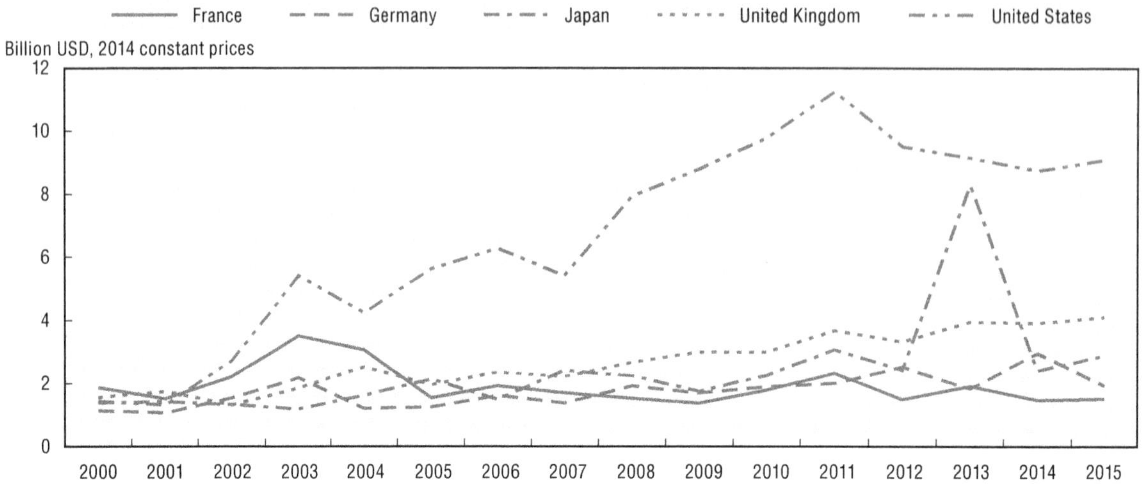

StatLink http://dx.doi.org/10.1787/888933491284

While the larger donors provide a greater volume of ODA, a number of medium-sized donors tend to provide a larger share of their country allocable ODA to LDCs. Over the period from 2013 to 2015, ten DAC donors provided more than half of their gross bilateral country allocable aid to LDCs. Peer reviews show that countries such as Finland, Ireland, Luxembourg and Sweden prioritise LDCs in their ODA policy.

Table 7.1. **Top ten providers of country allocable aid to least developed countries, gross disbursements**

	2013	2014	2015	3 year average	LDCs as a % of total country allocable ODA
	Million USD, 2014 constant prices				2013-15
1 Iceland	16	13	14	14	80
2 Ireland	325	309	297	311	78
3 Netherlands	702	593	556	617	67
4 Belgium	508	480	454	481	65
5 Finland	296	325	281	301	60
6 Sweden	1 049	995	1 053	1 032	60
7 Denmark	710	650	507	622	60
8 Luxembourg	121	135	140	132	57
9 United Kingdom	3 954	3 917	4 103	3 992	54
10 Canada	1 134	1 039	1 156	1 110	52

StatLink http://dx.doi.org/10.1787/888933491410

The majority of DAC countries still fall short of the United Nations target to allocate 0.15% of their gross national income as ODA to LDCs. Only seven countries attained this target in 2015 (Figure 7.7). That same year, DAC countries combined provided 0.08% of their GNI to LDCs, down from 0.09% in 2014 and 0.10% in 2013.

With respect to types of financing, in the period 2014-15, LDCs received 48% of country allocable grants extended by DAC donors; 29% went to lower middle-income countries (LMICs) and 19% to upper middle-income countries (UMICs). By contrast, just 9% of loans went to LDCs, with 47% to LMICs and 43% to UMICs. In 2014-15, the bulk of loans to LDCs came from France, Japan and Korea; almost half of Korea's support to LDCs was by way of loans followed by France (31%) and Japan (29%).

Figure 7.7. **Total net ODA to least developed countries as a percentage of the donor's gross national income, 2015**

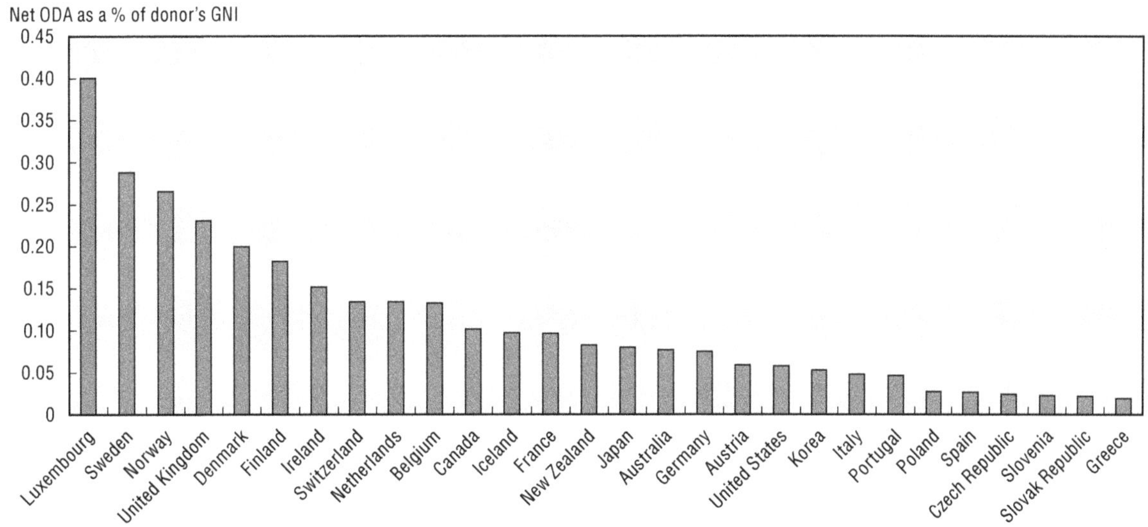

StatLink http://dx.doi.org/10.1787/888933491296

Over the last decade, the share of grants in gross ODA to the group of least developed countries fell slightly – from 96% of gross bilateral ODA flows from DAC donors in 2005 to 93% in 2015. However, there are some marked differences for some donors: the share of grants to LDCs from France fell from 94% to 71% between 2005 and 2015, from Japan from 82% to 66% , from Poland from 100% to 8%, and from Portugal from 100% to 74%. By contrast, some countries increased their grant share, like Italy (from 64% in 2005 to 98% in 2015) and Korea (from 32% to 53%), increased their grant share.

The share of loans to middle-income countries increased compared to grants, from an average of 15% in 2005 to 37% in 2015, with large increases from France, Germany, Japan and Korea. Peer reviews indicate that for some DAC members, the use of loans within overall portfolios is increasing (Germany) or likely to increase (France) as total ODA levels rise.

Declining volumes of bilateral ODA to small island developing states

Small island developing states face significant challenges in attracting external private finance as well as in accessing concessional finance.[2] Concessional finance to SIDS remained fairly constant between 2000 and 2009 and peaked in 2010, largely due to exceptional relief aid to Haiti after the earthquake. However, it started to decrease in 2011. In 2015, gross bilateral ODA to SIDS from DAC members amounted to USD 3.3 billion, representing a decrease of 17% in real terms since 2011. A recent study by the OECD and the World Bank noted that between 2011 and 2014, the volume of concessional finance in support of climate and disaster resilience to SIDS nearly doubled, reaching USD 1.01 billion in 2014. This represented 14% of the total concessional finance directed to SIDS during this period (OECD/The World Bank, 2016).

In 2015, the top DAC providers of gross bilateral ODA to SIDS were: Australia (USD 857 million), the United States (USD 636 million), EU institutions (USD 461 million) and France (USD 340 million). Together these donors provided more than two-thirds of gross bilateral ODA to SIDS in 2015. They are also the largest providers of climate and disaster resilience finance to SIDS along with Japan, Canada, Germany, New Zealand, Norway and Spain.

Australia is a top donor in most Pacific SIDS, where, along with New Zealand, it accounts for the bulk of the concessional finance that these countries receive. The United States is an important donor for Caribbean SIDS, while the EU is a top provider to SIDS.

Figure 7.8. **External finance in small island developing states**

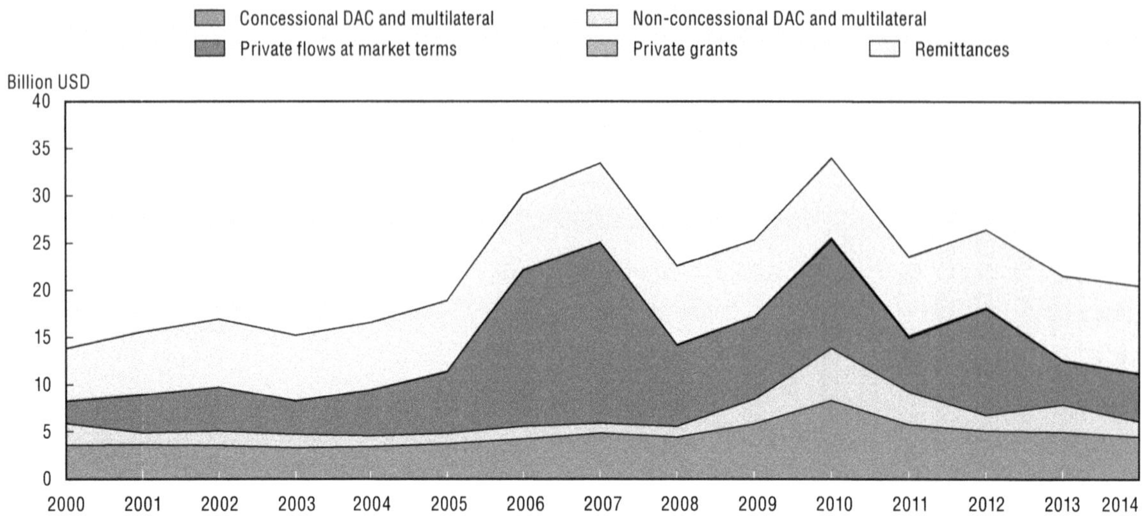

StatLink http://dx.doi.org/10.1787/888933491309

However, compared to other developing countries, SIDS do seem to have a greater reliance on one or two donors for the bulk of their concessional financing, which increases the vulnerability of these countries to changes in donor priorities. For some SIDS this is partly explained by their remoteness and limited geopolitical interest (e.g. for Pacific SIDS). For other SIDS the reasons are less clear.

The special development needs of SIDS have also been widely recognised internationally, most recently through the SIDS Accelerated Modalities of Action Pathway, the Sendai Framework for Disaster Risk Reduction, the Addis Ababa Action Agenda, the SDGs and the Paris Agreement.

Increased targeting of ODA to fragile contexts

Fragile contexts are more dependent on aid on average, but the extent of aid dependence varies significantly. While ODA remains an important source of finance for fragile contexts, some of it tends to be unevenly distributed and targeted at the symptoms rather than the real drivers of fragility (OECD, 2016c). In 2015, DAC members provided USD 41 billion in bilateral gross ODA to fragile contexts.

Table 7.2. **Gross official development assistance to fragile contexts from DAC members**

Current million USD

	2010	2011	2012	2013	2014	2015
Developing countries, total	116 005	127 561	119 646	127 582	126 724	121 070
Fragile states	45 863	49 982	45 024	52 679	44 773	40 541
% fragile states	40	39	38	41	35	33
Humanitarian ODA in fragile states	7 607	8 380	6 755	8 584	9 039	9 400
% humanitarian ODA in fragile states	17	17	15	16	20	23

StatLink http://dx.doi.org/10.1787/888933491425

The top DAC providers of ODA to fragile contexts in 2015 were the United States (USD 12.7 billion), the United Kingdom (USD 5.7 billion) and the EU institutions (USD 5 billion). Together these donors provided more than half of gross bilateral ODA to fragile contexts.

The total volume of gross bilateral ODA from DAC members to fragile states fell by nearly 7% in real terms between 2010 and 2015, due mainly to decreased spending from Belgium, Canada, France and the United States; some donors – Germany, Japan and the United Kingdom – increased their funding.

ODA allocated to and through the multilateral aid system has increased

On average for 2014 and 2015, DAC countries channelled 40% of their ODA to and through the multilateral aid system, a slight increase from the 2008-09 average of 38%. This increase was mainly due to larger ODA shares allocated to the multilateral system for specific themes, sectors or countries.

While the share of bilateral aid channelled through the multilateral system increased slightly from 11% in 2008-09 to 13% in 2014-15, the share of core contributions to multilateral organisations remained at 27%.

Figure 7.9. **ODA channelled to and through the multilateral system, two year averages, gross disbursements, DAC countries**

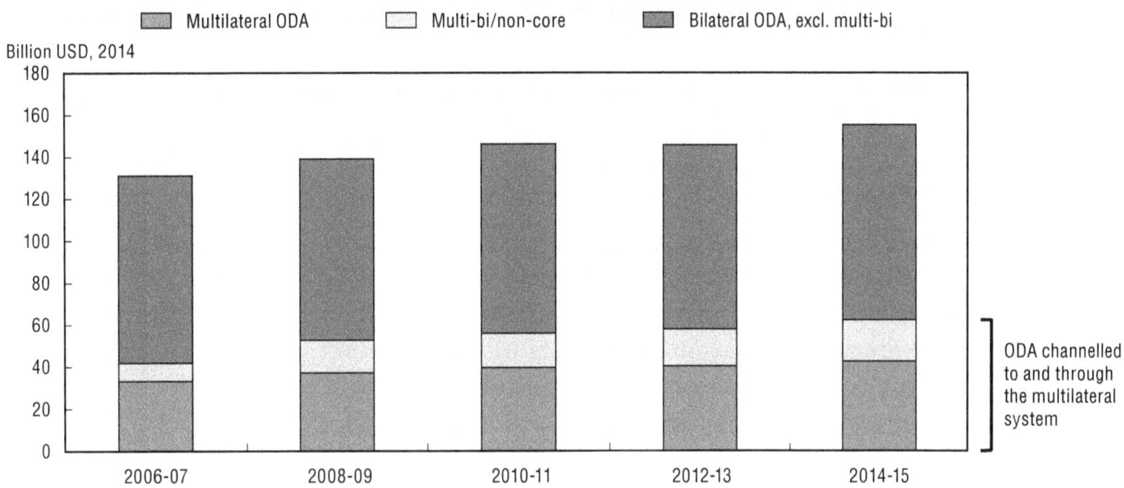

StatLink http://dx.doi.org/10.1787/888933491315

Recent peer reviews of DAC members note that many lack a strategic approach to their engagement with multilateral organisations and that their financing of the UN system can be fragmented. A number of members have decreased their contributions with, for example, Denmark's share of core and non-core resources falling since 2010. The United States, which is the second-largest DAC contributor to the core budget of multilateral organisations after the United Kingdom, saw a sharp increase in its multilateral aid between 2011 and 2014. A significant portion of the United States' bilateral aid has also been channelled through multilateral organisations of late, notably to finance flash appeals through the World Food Programme, the United Nations High Commissioner for Refugees, the UN Office for the Coordination of Humanitarian Affairs and the International Organisation for Migration. Peer reviews have recommended that members concentrate resources on a few strategic multilateral partners and increase synergies with bilateral programmes. As earmarking of contributions increases, DAC members have been encouraged to focus on streamlining their monitoring and reporting procedures for multilateral organisations to increase efficiency, notably by reducing the number of similar accountability processes that the organisations should manage.

ODA allocated to and through civil society organisations remains stable

In 2015, DAC members channelled USD 22 billion in official development assistance to and through civil society organisations (CSOs). This represented 16% of total bilateral aid. While the share of bilateral aid allocated to and through CSOs differs widely among DAC members, the average share of total bilateral aid for all DAC countries over the last three years has been around 16%. In 2015, the top donors of bilateral ODA to and through CSOs were the United States (USD 7.1 billion), the United Kingdom (USD 2.7 billion), EU institutions (USD 2.1 billion), the Netherlands (USD 1.3 billion) and Germany (USD 1.2 billion).

Peer reviews of DAC members show that a number, including Finland and Slovenia, use funding to CSOs to broaden their geographical footprint, engage the domestic taxpayers and the broader public in development co-operation, and support activities promoting democracy and freedom of speech beyond their long-term partners. Luxembourg works with CSOs to support developing contexts where it cannot engage via government channels. The nature of relationships between the Netherlands and Dutch CSOs has changed significantly in recent years. While the Netherlands' 2013 strategy signalled reduced funding, it sought to preserve the independence of CSOs in relation to government spending and the need to strengthen CSOs in their role as watchdogs for global issues. CSOs are able to bid for thematic funding from the Netherlands alongside other development actors. Overall, there is need for greater clarity and understanding of how DAC members support and partner with developing country/southern NGOs.

Sector allocations are changing with more investment in economic sectors

The DAC Creditor Reporting System (CRS) collects data on individual aid activities. Each activity is assigned a sector code. These are organised by broad sector categories (social, economic, production, multisector) and non-sector aid (programme assistance, debt relief, humanitarian aid, administrative costs of donors, in-donor refugee costs and aid that is not allocated). Each broad sector has more granular sub-sectors. For example, the social sector comprises expenditure on education, health, population programmes and policies, water and sanitation, government and civil society, and other social sectors.

Figure 7.10. **Share of ODA to and through CSOs by DAC members, 2015**

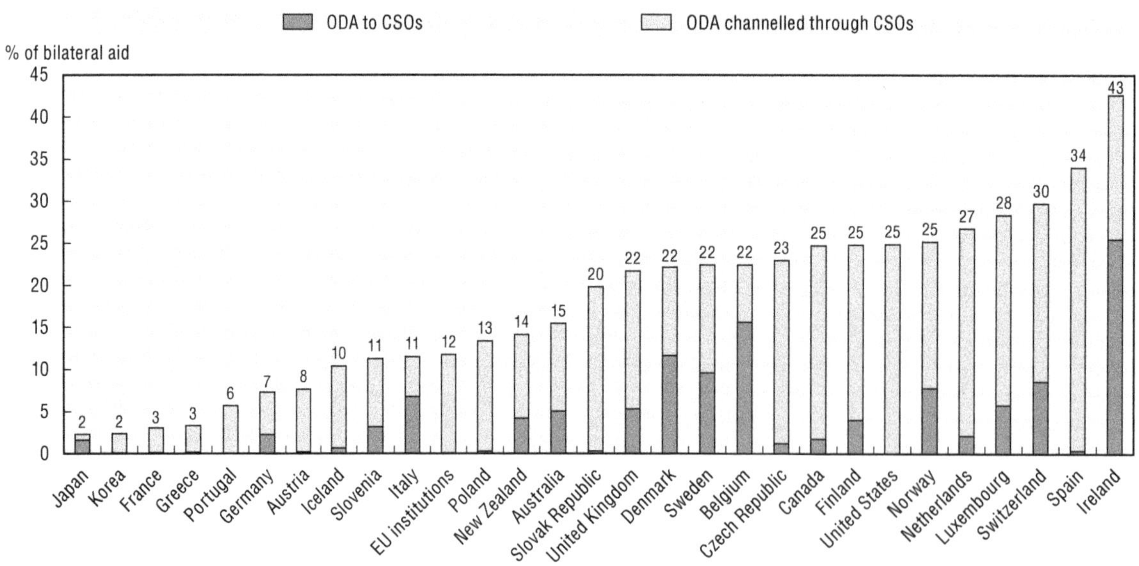

Note: The value at each bar represents the share of aid to and through non-governmental organisations (%).

StatLink http://dx.doi.org/10.1787/888933491322

Figure 7.11 shows shifts in aid for particular sectors over the past decade as DAC members have responded to changes in the development co-operation landscape. Commitments to population, government and civil society, and other social sectors were larger in 2010-11 than in 2006-07, but had declined by 2014-15. Investments in transport and storage, energy, and other economic sectors have risen steadily as have multi sector aid, humanitarian aid and expenditure on refugees in donor countries. While debt relief was significant in 2005 and 2006 due to exceptional relief for Iraq and Nigeria, this has tapered off, and was insignificant in 2014-15.

Figure 7.11. **Trends in ODA commitments by sector**

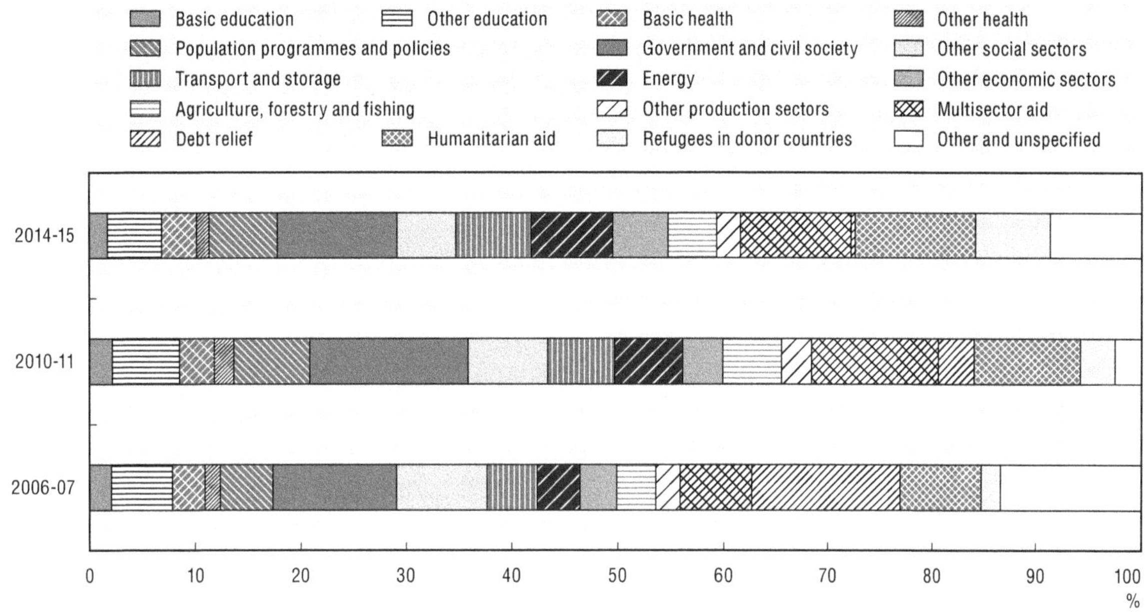

StatLink http://dx.doi.org/10.1787/888933491337

According to DAC peer reviews, DAC members' ODA mostly reflects their stated sector priorities. The United States' support for economic infrastructure and services remains important in volume even if it is proportionately less than its significant investments in health and good governance. The mainstay of Japanese ODA remains support to developing countries' economic infrastructure, for which it allocates more than 50% of its bilateral ODA, provided mostly as loans. New Zealand is meeting its target of 40% of sector allocable aid to the theme of sustainable economic development and 37% to human development. The United Kingdom more than doubled its investment in economic development following its 2014 Economic Development Strategic Framework.

Spain, on the other hand, has decreased ODA to the productive sector, which is in line with its strategy of focusing on social infrastructure and services, government and civil society, water and sanitation, and education. In line with its priority to water, food security, sexual and reproductive health and rights, and security and rule of law, one-third of the Netherlands' bilateral ODA went to social infrastructure and services and 12% to economic infrastructure and services. Denmark's ODA allocations have followed the four priority areas set out in its 2012 strategy: human rights and democracy, inclusive green growth, social progress, and stability and protection. Recent moves away from social sectors towards economic sectors are expected to continue in line with the government's new development co-operation priorities.

DAC members are increasingly developing partnerships with the private sector to leverage private capital, expertise, innovation and core business to benefit sustainable development. Box 7.2 lists good practice and key lessons for engaging with the private sector that emerged from an in-depth, thematic peer learning review on working with and through the private sector that was conducted in 2016..

Box 7.2. **Good practice and key lessons for engaging with the private sector**

Members of the Development Assistance Committee (DAC) are increasingly working with the private sector to realise sustainable development outcomes. A peer learning review on working with and through the private sector in development co-operation examined the politics, policies and institutions behind private sector engagement, the focus and delivery of private sector engagements, private sector engagement portfolios, effective partnership and thematic issues including risk, leverage and ensuring results. Drawing on the practical experiences of DAC members, the review highlighted good practice and outlined key lessons:

- Communicate the who, what, when, where and how.
- Engage the private sector as a means, not an end.
- Integrate aid effectiveness principles in private sector engagements.
- Ensure institutions are fit for purpose.
- Invest in the business-enabling environment.
- Develop a holistic, flexible portfolio of private sector engagement mechanisms that harness core business.
- Facilitate private sector engagements with a wide range of stakeholders.
- Make it easy to engage.
- See partnership as a relationship not a contract.
- Take risks if you want others to do so.
- Establish systems to ensure and measure additionality.
- Invest in results measurement and systems for monitoring and evaluation.

For further information see: OECD (2016d), *Private Sector Engagement for Sustainable Development: Lessons from the DAC*, *http://dx.doi.org/10.1787/9789264266889-en*.

Better co-ordination is needed amongst donors as humanitarian aid rises

From 2010 to 2015 DAC members' humanitarian aid rose from 9% to 13% of gross bilateral ODA, with significant differences among members (up to 22% for Canada and the United States). The overall amount of humanitarian aid rose at a slower pace than total ODA. The United States remains the largest donor by volume followed by the European Union and the United Kingdom, but members such as Germany, Japan, Korea and the Netherlands have more than doubled their humanitarian budgets since 2010.

While the top ten recipients of humanitarian aid were located in Africa, the Syrian crisis alone accounted for 36% of humanitarian aid in 2015, a sharp increase from 2014 (24%) and previous years.

Since 2015, peer reviews have found that DAC members are increasingly looking for greater coherence between humanitarian and development aid. Humanitarian aid is divided between the use of foreign policy tools such as resilience and integration and emergency response, which are regulated by humanitarian principles. While co-ordination amongst donors is generally weak, DAC members

Table 7.3. **Humanitarian aid, gross disbursements**

Current million USD

	2010	2011	2012	2013	2014	2015
DAC members, total	115 977	127 528	119 624	127 547	126 694	121 022
Humanitarian aid	10 795	11 374	10 124	12 547	15 392	15 143
% humanitarian aid	9	9	8	10	12	13

StatLink http://dx.doi.org/10.1787/888933491434

have strengthened their whole-of-government co-ordination. The role of Ministries of Foreign Affairs is changing from that of sole humanitarian provider to a co-ordination role, ensuring a coherent whole-of-government approach to humanitarian aid. While relations between civilians and the military are now well regulated, this is not the case for new actors (e.g. border control, police) in the migration crisis. Most DAC members need to improve their monitoring of humanitarian responses.

Increasing focus on domestic resource mobilisation, but more aid is needed

The Addis Ababa Action Agenda recognised the importance of domestic resource mobilisation in financing for development. Over recent years there has been an increased focus on ODA being allocated to supporting tax systems development. This focus was most evident in the Addis Tax Initiative which 19 DAC members have joined. Signatory donors collectively agreed to double their spending on supporting domestic resource mobilisation by 2020.[3] To help monitor spending in this priority area, a new CRS purpose code was introduced for 2015, which shows that commitments on domestic resource mobilisation in 2015 were USD 190 million, representing just 0.14% of ODA.[4] Previous attempts to estimate ODA to tax, before introducing the new purpose code, had identified similar levels of spending.

The United Kingdom is by far the largest provider of ODA supporting partner countries' tax systems. Together with Germany, they provided nearly 50% of all funding (Table 7.4). The majority of the funding is targeted at LDCs (56%) and LMICs (24%). Afghanistan is the largest recipient (USD 41 million) followed by Pakistan (USD 13 million). Tax to GDP ratios in LDCs are increasing. Ratios have increased from under 10% in 2001 to 14.8% in 2015 on average and are approaching 15% which is generally thought to be the minimum level necessary to fund basic state functions. It is critical that donors deliver on their commitments to increase funding to tax in the coming years and improve efforts to monitor the impact of aid to tax, which is still in its infancy.

Table 7.4. **Top donors and top recipients of domestic resource mobilisation**

Donor	2015 commitments (million USD)	Recipient country	2015 commitments (million USD)
1 United Kingdom	61.0	Afghanistan	40.8
2 Germany	31.7	Pakistan	12.8
3 United States	26.9	Mozambique	9.2
4 Norway	14.1	Indonesia	7.2
5 Switzerland	7.8	Burundi	6.7
6 Australia	7.7	Tanzania	6.4
7 Finland	7.1	Zambia	5.2
8 Denmark	7.0	Guatemala	5.0
9 Belgium	6.7	Ghana	4.9
10 France	5.8	Somalia	4.6

StatLink http://dx.doi.org/10.1787/888933491443

Political commitment to gender equality is not reflected well in aid allocations

Gender equality and women's empowerment is included in the 2030 Agenda as a stand-alone goal in its own right and a cross-cutting issue in achieving sustainable development. In the Nairobi Outcome Document, participants committed to accelerating efforts in this area (GPEDC, 2016). Adequate financing for gender equality and women's rights will be critical for making the gender equality commitments of the Busan Partnership Agreement a reality and accelerating progress towards gender equality and women's rights beyond 2015.

While DAC peer reviews find that DAC countries' political commitment to gender equality and women's empowerment is strong, implementation remains difficult. This is partly a result of the inability of DAC members to ensure mainstreaming of gender equality and women's empowerment across their development co-operation programmes. Recommendations focus on operationalising the political commitment, noting that DAC members need leadership, guidance, resources, capacity and a stronger focus on the results of investment in gender.

In 2014-15, DAC countries committed a total of USD 40 billion for gender equality and women's empowerment. The DAC country average for the share of development co-operation that had a gender equality and women's empowerment objective was 35% in 2014-15, with some DAC members well above the average – Sweden (86%), Iceland (83%) and Belgium (75%) – whereas others are well below the average: the Czech Republic (17%), France (16%), Switzerland (14%), Slovenia (13%), Poland (2%) and the Slovak Republic (1%).[5]

Development co-operation for the environment, including the Rio Conventions, is increasing

Since 1998, the DAC has monitored ODA commitments targeting the objectives of the Rio Conventions through the CRS using the "Rio markers". Every bilateral development co-operation activity reported to the CRS should be screened and marked as either: targeting the conventions as a "principal objective" or a "significant objective", or not targeting the objective. The Rio markers are descriptive and allow for an approximate quantification of financial flows targeting the objectives of the Rio Conventions. Finance reported to the United Nations Framework Convention on Climate Change and the Convention on Biological Diversity may be based on alternative definitions and measurement methodologies, and may not be comparable with Rio marker data.

In 2015, total commitments of bilateral ODA by OECD-DAC members in support of the environment, including the Rio Conventions, was USD 36 billion, representing 31% of total ODA. This represented a real increase of 19% over 2014. Of the various global environmental objectives, climate-related ODA totalled USD 28 billion, of which 47% addressed mitigation only; 31% addressed adaptation only; and 22% addressed both adaptation and mitigation.

As is the case with support for gender equality and women's empowerment, while DAC members allocate significant amounts of aid to the environment and climate change, peer reviews indicate that they continue to struggle with mainstreaming protection of the environment across their development co-operation programmes.

Development finance from providers beyond the DAC is becoming increasingly important

The development co-operation landscape has changed significantly over the past 50 years impacting the composition of providers of ODA flows.

The present 20 DAC-EU members have provided about half of net ODA flows over the past 25 years. The United States has been the largest single donor, except when it was surpassed by Japan for several years in the 1990s. Net ODA from Arab donors rose substantially in the 1970s until the early 1980s, due to the petrodollars gained from oil prices after the "oil shocks" in 1974 and 1979. Since then, their aid has fallen; however, aid by Saudi Arabia has been increasing and more recently from the United Arab Emirates (UAE) which surpassed the UN ODA/GNI target of 0.7% from 2013 and was the most generous donor that year, mostly due to a large concessional loan provided to Egypt. The UAE provided USD 4.4 billion in 2015, which represented 1.18% of its gross national income and in 2016 launched its development co-operation strategy for 2017-21.

Many providers beyond the DAC have long traditions of development co-operation and have played a key role that continues to grow. Development co-operation by countries beyond DAC membership amounted to about USD 18 billion in 2015.[6] Some donors have modest programmes, at around USD 10 million, while others spend over USD 300 million annually (e.g. Kuwait, Saudi Arabia and Turkey; see Benn and Luijkx, 2017). The characteristics of development co-operation differ from one donor to another in terms of priority sectors, partner countries and instruments. Moreover, according to preliminary figures for 2016, two non-DAC development providers, Turkey and the UAE, exceeded the 0.7% target, with net ODA as a percentage of GNI amounting to 0.79% and 1.12%, respectively.

Private philanthropy is also making an important contribution to the global development landscape. Since 2009, the Bill & Melinda Gates Foundation has been reporting to the OECD on its grants under its Global Health and Global Development Programs, and more recently has begun reporting its loans and equities under its programme-related investments. In 2015, with USD 3.3 billion of disbursements, the Bill & Melinda Gates Foundation was the third-largest provider in the health and reproductive health sectors.

Global concessional development finance exceeds USD 155 billion

Figure 7.13 provides an overview, in both volume and as a percentage of GNI, of concessional financing for development (grants and concessional loans) provided by the 30 countries – both DAC members and countries beyond the DAC membership – with the largest development co-operation programmes in 2015. In total, the OECD estimates that global net concessional development finance reached USD 156 billion in 2015, of which 15.8% was provided by countries that are not members of the DAC (Table 7.5). It should be stressed that for countries that do not report to the OECD, this number is based on an estimate of their development co-operation.

Figure 7.12. **Donor shares in net ODA**

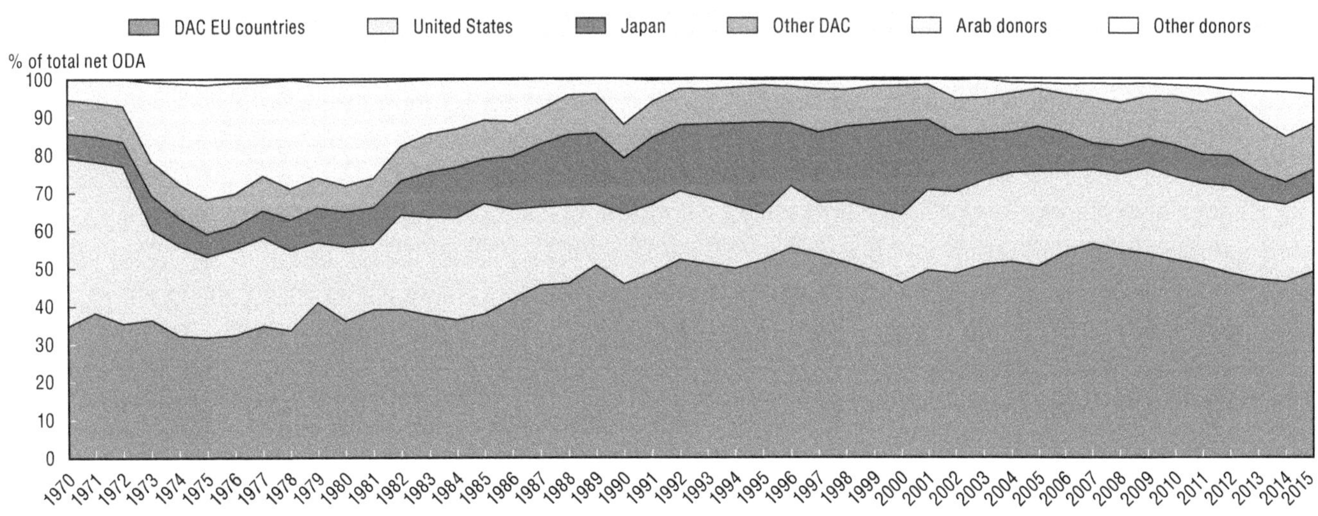

StatLink http://dx.doi.org/10.1787/888933491341

Table 7.5. **Estimated global development co-operation flows, 2011-15**

Billion USD

	2011	2012	2013	2014	2015	2015 (% of total)
ODA from 28 DAC countries	135.0	126.9	134.7	137.4	131.4	84.2
ODA from 20 reporting countries beyond the DAC	8.9	6.2	16.4	24.7	17.7	11.3
Estimated development co-operation flows from ten non-reporting countries beyond the DAC	5.2	5.6	6.8	7	6.9	4.4
Subtotal flows from non-DAC providers	14.1	11.8	23.2	31.7	24.6	15.8
Estimated global total	**149.1**	**138.7**	**157.9**	**169.1**	**156.0**	**100.0**

Notes: Hungary joined the DAC on 6 December 2016. Data for Hungary are included under "reporting countries beyond the DAC".

StatLink http://dx.doi.org/10.1787/888933491458

Figure 7.13. **Thirty largest providers of gross concessional financing for development, 2015**

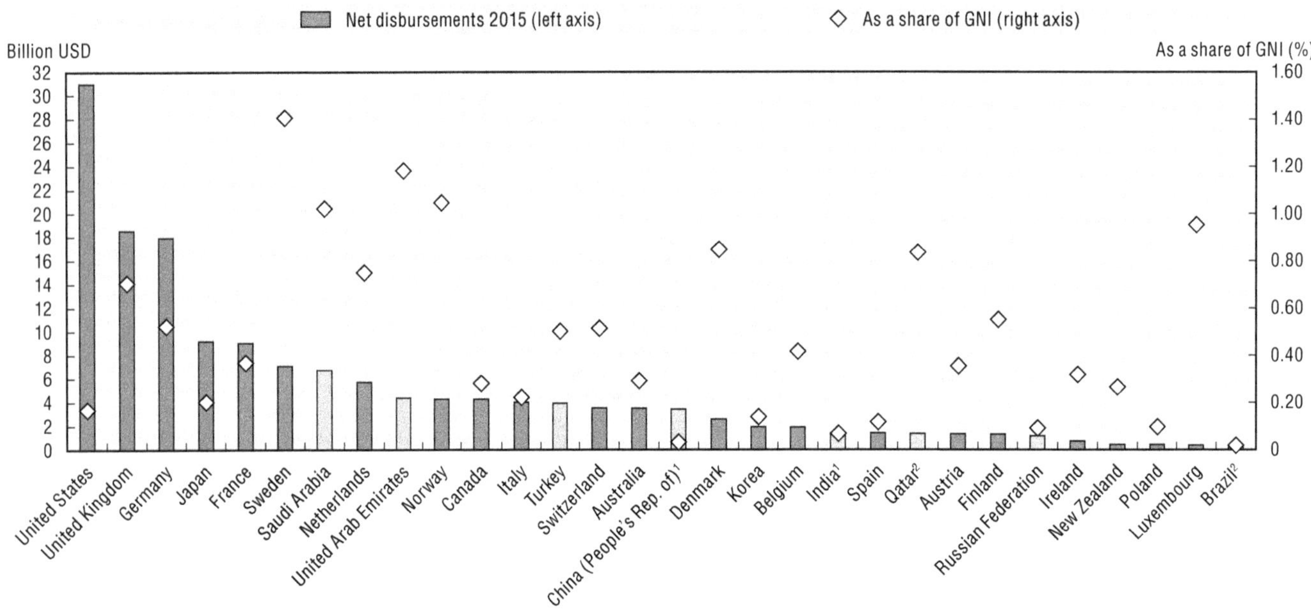

Notes: Countries that are not members of the DAC are represented by grey bars.

1. Estimates based on available 2015 data.
2. Estimates based on latest data available.

StatLink http://dx.doi.org/10.1787/888933491353

Greater attention to triangular co-operation

Triangular co-operation brings together the best of different actors that support development – bilateral providers of development co-operation, partners in South-South co-operation and international organisations – to share knowledge and implement projects that support the common goal of reducing poverty and promoting development in developing countries. Triangular co-operation continues to be a highly relevant way to support development.

The OECD has been promoting dialogue on triangular co-operation over recent years while also building the evidence base of how and where it happens, notably through surveys conducted in 2012 and 2015.[7] Triangular co-operation is important for many Latin American and Caribbean donors, such as Brazil, Chile or Mexico, which work with some DAC members (e.g. Germany, Spain or the United States) to implement triangular co-operation. Other donors, such as Japan, engage in triangular co-operation, notably in southeast Asia. Some Arab donors, especially the Islamic Development Bank, have mainstreamed triangular co-operation within their activities. More data are now available on the activities and point to an increase in the number and length of projects as well as the size of the budgets. There is a great variety of triangular co-operation in terms of scale, scope, region, sector and project type. Moreover, respondents to the 2015 survey mentioned a more strategic use of triangular co-operation by pooling different actors' expertise and resources. In the long run, triangular co-operation can prove to be effective in achieving greater ownership of development results by the actors involved and has the potential to be scaled-up to reinforce joint action to achieve the Sustainable Development Goals.

Aid quality is improving but there is still some unfinished business

The Addis Ababa Action Agenda welcomed continued efforts to improve the quality, impact and effectiveness of development co-operation. While peer reviews of DAC members and the Global Partnership for Effective Development Co-operation's 2016 monitoring round, which was carried out in 81 partner countries, show important progress towards achieving the effectiveness principles agreed in Busan[8] there remains a long way to go.

Providers of development assistance have made particular progress in increasing the transparency of development co-operation and in aligning with partner countries' development priorities. While these gains are encouraging, they are coupled with an overall need for development co-operation to adapt to a dynamic and evolving development landscape. There are also specific areas where concerted effort is required to unlock bottlenecks to increasing the predictability of development co-operation, untying aid, and strengthening and using partner countries' own systems for implementing, monitoring and evaluating aid. Providing effective development co-operation is still unfinished business. While DAC members state that they remain committed to the four development effectiveness principles – ownership, results, inclusive partnerships, transparency and accountability – greater efforts are needed to achieve the behaviour change required by these principles.

Donor alignment with partner countries' priorities and results can improve

Strengthening the results focus of development co-operation and responding to partner countries' defined priorities is critical for development co-operation to be effective. The Global Partnership monitoring process reveals that 85% of new aid interventions are aligned with partner countries' results frameworks and plans. However, providers only use government sources and systems to track results for 52% of interventions – meaning that broadly half continue to rely on project-specific sources of information. Similarly, while 77% of the new interventions incorporate some form of final evaluation, partner governments are engaged in the evaluation of results for only 49% of new projects and programmes – typically in defining the scope of the evaluation.

Peer reviews and the OECD-DAC workstream on results-based decision making indicate that managing for development results remains a priority of providers and partner countries and that results information is widely used for accountability and communication. However, using results information for strategic policy making and learning, including quality assurance, is more challenging. There is scope for providers of development assistance to improve how they use partner country results data and systems as part of their commitment to deliver the SDGs.

Figure 7.14. **State of play in focusing on results**

All countries reporting in the 2016 monitoring round

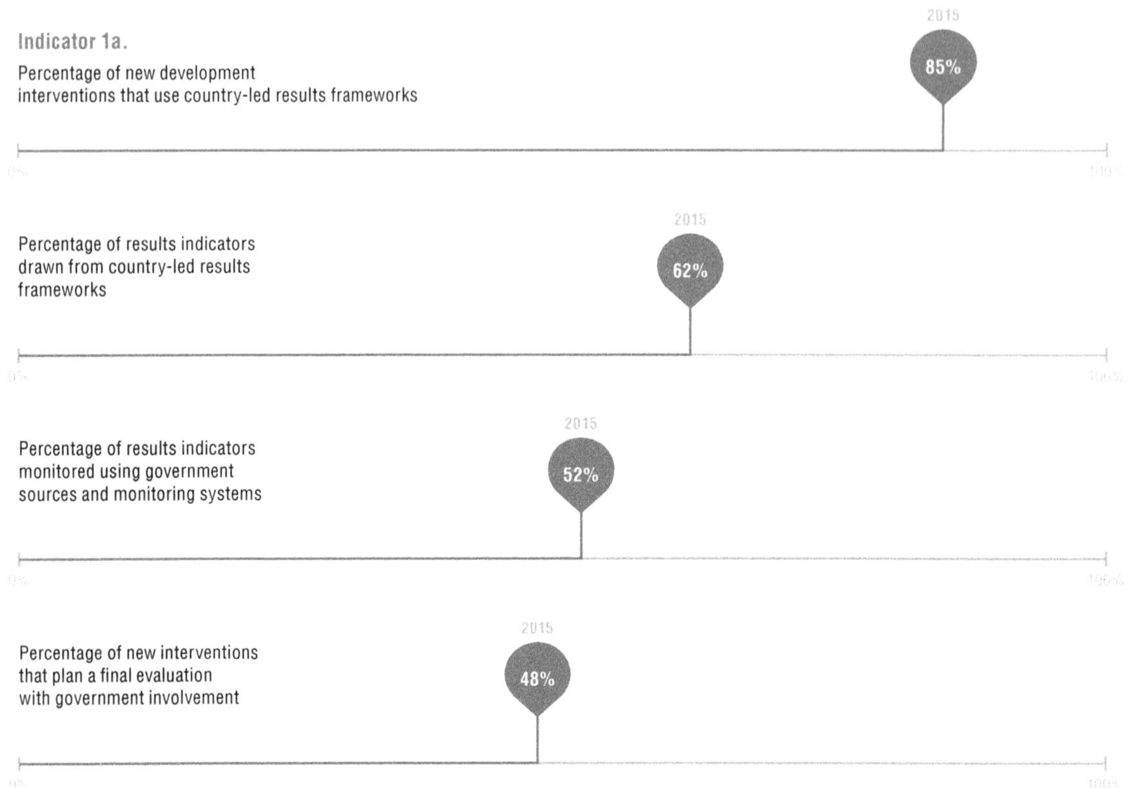

StatLink http://dx.doi.org/10.1787/888933491367

The predictability of development co-operation needs to increase

Partner countries need to manage diverse financing flows in a complementary and strategic manner. Yet development partners are making limited progress in increasing the predictability of development co-operation. Development co-operation flows to partner countries continue to be either below or above scheduled disbursements for the year, which undermines governments' capacity to plan public finance and manage external support. Annual predictability declined by 1% in 2015, to 84%. Similarly, the increase in medium-term predictability of development co-operation (i.e. three-year horizon) was moderate, reaching just 74% in 2016. While the latest spending plans of the bilateral and multilateral providers of development co-operation reveal a shift in aid allocations towards the poorest and most fragile countries (OECD, 2016b), a major institutional and cultural shift is needed to arrive at regular publication of real-time information that meets country needs for planning and managing development co-operation.

Peer reviews reveal that while some DAC members always include multi-year indicative budgets in their country strategy papers, several others do not do so consistently. The use of multi-year budgets is diminished by changes to scheduled disbursements or by lack of clear communication with partner countries.

Figure 7.15. **State of play in annual and medium-term predictability**

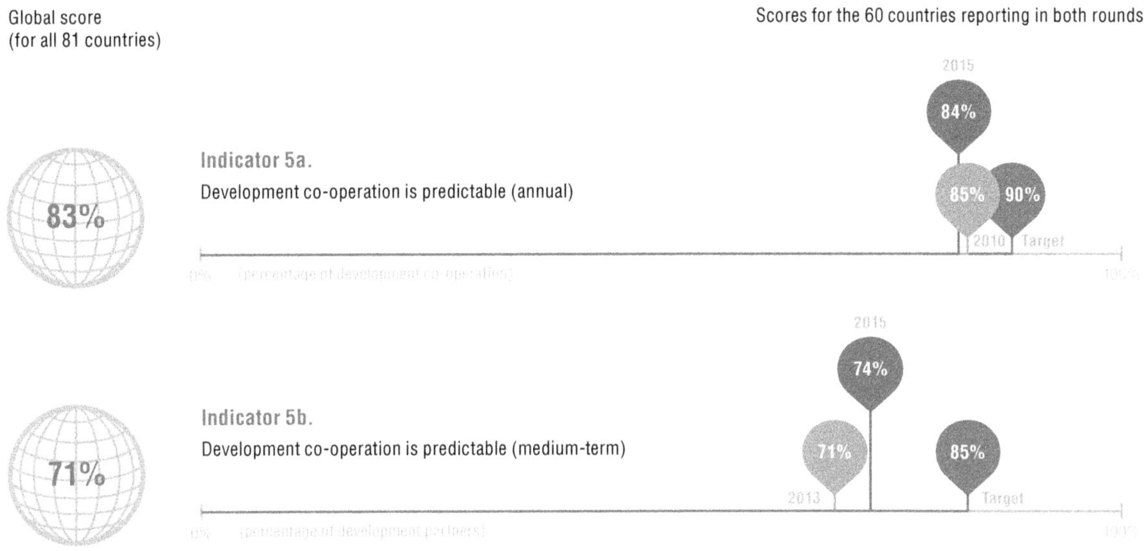

StatLink http://dx.doi.org/10.1787/888933491375

The use of partner country systems and level of untied aid need to increase

The use of partner countries' public financial management and procurement systems to channel development co-operation slightly increased from 45% in 2010 to 51% in 2015. Bilateral partners have driven this increase in the use of country systems – particularly those beyond the DAC, who increased their use from 4% to 40%. Providers are finding diverse ways to use specific systems by, for example, increasingly relying on countries' own budget execution procedures, financial reporting and auditing mechanisms. In contrast, the use of partner countries' procurement systems has decreased since 2010.

Peer reviews note a number of reasons for reduced use of country systems amongst DAC countries. These include the steady decline in the use of general budget support in recent years (down from 2% of bilateral ODA in 2004-05 to 0.6% in 2015) coupled with an increasing use of project aid (investment projects made up 13% of bilateral ODA in 2015) as well as the use of centrally managed funds addressing thematic issues and increased delivery of aid by the private sector and CSOs.

The DAC recommends that its members should untie their aid for greater effectiveness and value for money. Since 2010 the share of untied aid has marginally increased, with the global average hovering around the peak value of 78.6% which was achieved in 2014. In 2015, Australia, Canada, Denmark, Iceland, Ireland, Luxembourg, Norway and the United Kingdom maintained fully or almost fully untied aid; on the other hand, ten DAC members have not achieved the 2010 level of 74% untied development co-operation (OECD, 2015).

The DAC Chair recently expressed concern at the rise in the share of ODA that is tied to companies in donor countries, noting that it is like protectionism – "it may be a nice sell with some audiences at home... but we know it doesn't work".[9] Peer reviews consistently recommend to DAC members to meet the terms of the *DAC Recommendation on Untying ODA to the Least Developed Countries and Heavily Indebted Poor Countries* (OECD, 2014c) and to fully untie their development co-operation in line with the commitment made at Busan in 2011.

Figure 7.16. **Progress in using country systems to deliver development co-operation**

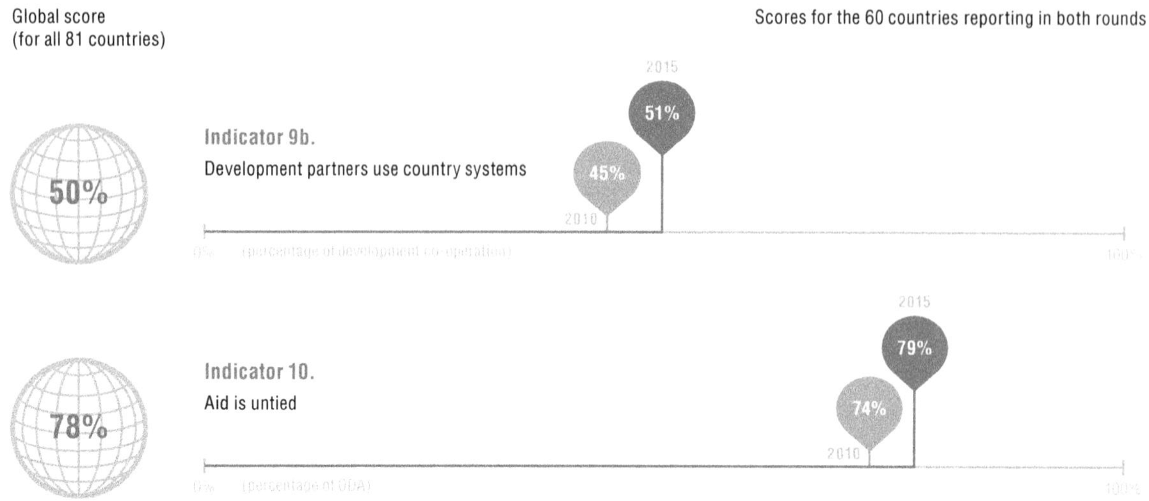

StatLink http://dx.doi.org/10.1787/888933491386

Improved transparency of development co-operation

Transparency is growing with more publicly available information on development co-operation than ever before: 72% of providers assessed for transparency achieved a "good" score in their reporting to at least one of the three international databases on development co-operation[10] and 39% achieved "excellent" in reporting to one or more systems. Progress was most notable on the timeliness and comprehensiveness of publicly available development co-operation data, while the publication of forward-looking information continues to be a challenge. Some providers experienced a trade-off between data timeliness and accuracy that needs to be managed.

Figure 7.17. **Transparency of providers' reporting to international databases on development co-operation**

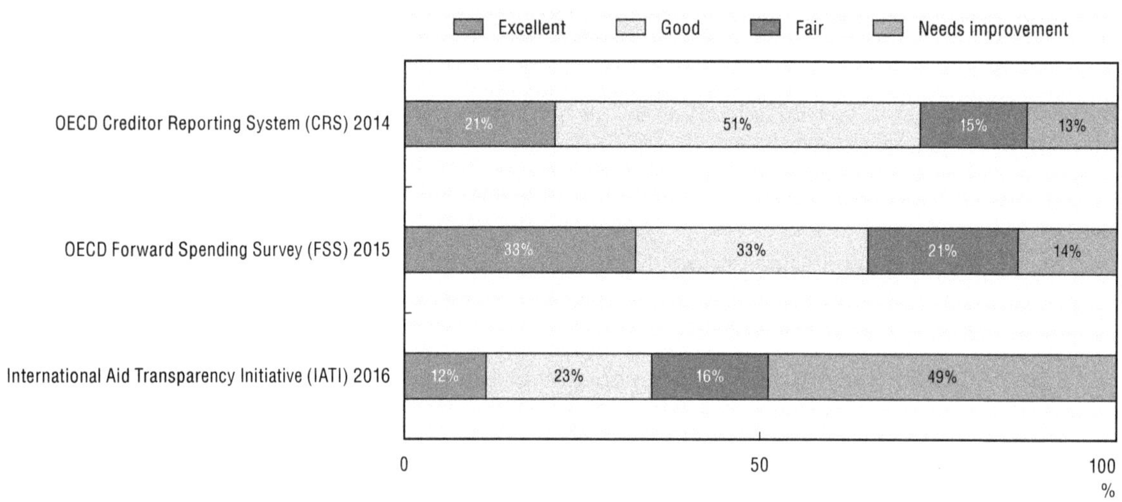

StatLink http://dx.doi.org/10.1787/888933491399

Peer reviews note that DAC members such as Belgium, Denmark and Switzerland are creating whole-of-government country strategies as a mechanism for greater transparency with partner countries. While improvements in transparency among DAC members has been aided by good use of open websites, much less information is published about the results and risks of development co-operation.

Providers and partner countries have taken joint strides to increase the recording of development co-operation finance in national budgets that are subject to the oversight of partner countries' parliaments, with an increase from 54% to 66% since 2010.

Figure 7.18. **Development co-operation recorded in national budgets**

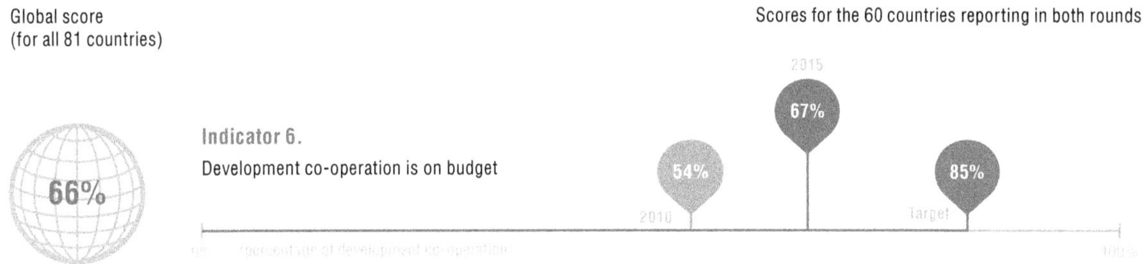

StatLink http://dx.doi.org/10.1787/888933491403

The 2016 Global Partnership monitoring evidence has shown that strong institutionalised partnerships at the country level can build mutual trust and underpin transparency and accountability. It also confirmed that there are countries, providers and non-state stakeholders that demonstrate the capacity to progress on agreed effectiveness principles and commitments. This indicates great potential for identifying success factors, sharing lessons and facilitating mutual learning to accelerate the global development community's efforts to deliver on the Sustainable Development Goals by 2030.

Notes

1. Remittances are not included in DAC statistics as they are primarily used to finance consumption rather than investment in developing countries. In 2015, remittances to developing countries are estimated to have been about USD 441 billion, (World Bank, 2016).
2. For more information see: *www.oecd.org/dac/financing-sustainable-development/Flyer%20-%202016%20-%20the%20case%20of%20SIDS.pdf*.
3. The spending in 2015 is to be used as the baseline against which the spending commitment will be measured.
4. The data for 2015 are based on CRS reporting against the purpose Code 15114 on "Domestic revenue mobilisation", except for: Australia, EU institutions, Ireland and Portugal, which provided the OECD with an aggregate figure on their spending.
5. See country profiles and the latest data at: *www.oecd.org/development/gender-development/Aid-to-Gender-Equality-Donor-Charts-2017.pdf*.
6. Many providers beyond the DAC report their flows for development co-operation to the DAC. For further details see Table 33: *www.oecd.org/dac/financing-sustainable-development/development-finance-data/statisticsonresourceflowstodevelopingcountries.htm*.
7. See: *www.oecd.org/dac/dac-global-relations/triangular-cooperation.htm*.
8. The Fourth High-Level Forum on Aid Effectiveness in Busan (OECD, 2011) agreed on four principles of effective development co-operation and tasked the Global Partnership for Effective Development Co-operation with measuring progress against each principle. The four principles are: ownership of development priorities by developing countries; focus on results; inclusive development partnerships; transparency and accountability to each other.
9. *www.indepthnews.net/index.php/opinion/1103-we-must-be-serious-about-untying-aid-for-the-sake-of-credibility-and-private-sector-engagement*.
10. The OECD-DAC's Creditor Reporting System and Forward Spending Survey, and the International Aid Transparency Initiative.

References

Benn, J. and W. Luijkx (2017), "Emerging providers' international co-operation for development", *OECD Development Co-operation Working Papers*, No. 33, OECD Publishing, Paris, *http://dx.doi.org/10.1787/15d6a3c7-en*.

GPEDC (2016), "Nairobi outcome document", Second High Level Meeting of the Global Partnership for Effective Development Co-operation, 1 December 2016, Nairobi, Kenya, *http://effectivecooperation.org/wp-content/uploads/2016/12/OutcomeDocumentEnglish.pdf*.

IMF (2016), *Fiscal Monitor: Debt – Use It Wisely*, International Monetary Fund, Washington, DC, *www.imf.org/en/Publications/FM/Issues/2016/12/31/Debt-Use-it-Wisely*.

OECD (2017a), "Development aid rises again in 2016", 11 April, OECD, Paris, *www.oecd.org/dac/financing-sustainable-development/development-finance-data/ODA-2016-detailed-summary.pdf*.

OECD (2017b), *Peer Review of the Netherlands, 2017*, OECD Publishing, Paris.

OECD (2016a), "DAC High Level Meeting: Communiqué", 19 February, OECD, Paris, *www.oecd.org/dac/DAC-HLM-Communique-2016.pdf*.

OECD (2016b), "2016 global aid prospects and projections: From words to action", OECD Publishing, Paris, *www.oecd.org/dac/financing-sustainable-development/development-finance-standards/FSS%202016%20flyer.pdf*.

OECD (2016c), *States of Fragility 2016: Understanding Violence*, OECD Publishing, Paris, *http://dx.doi.org/10.1787/9789264267213-en*.

OECD (2016d), *Private Sector Engagement for Sustainable Development: Lessons from the DAC*, OECD Publishing, Paris, *http://dx.doi.org/10.1787/9789264266889-en*.

OECD (2015), "Creditor Reporting System: Aid activities", *OECD International Development Statistics* (database), *http://stats.oecd.org/Index.aspx?DataSetCode=TABLE7B*.

OECD (2014a), "How to better mobilise resources for sustainable development", in *Development Co-operation Report 2014: Mobilising Resources for Sustainable Development*, OECD Publishing, Paris, *http://dx.doi.org/10.1787/dcr-2014-5-en*.

OECD (2014b), "DAC High Level Meeting: Final communiqué", 16 December, OECD, Paris, *www.oecd.org/dac/OECD%20DAC%20HLM%20Communique.pdf*.

OECD (2014c), *Revised DAC Recommendation on Untying ODA to the Least Developed Countries and Heavily Indebted Poor Countries*, OECD, Paris, *www.oecd.org/dac/untied-aid*.

OECD (2011), "Busan Partnership for Effective Development Co-operation", Fourth High Level Forum on Aid Effectiveness, Busan, Republic of Korea, 29 November-1 December 2011, *www.oecd.org/dac/effectiveness/49650173.pdf*.

OECD (1978), DAC Recommendation on the Terms and Conditions of Aid, OECD Publishing, Paris *www.oecd.org/dac/stats/recommendationontermsandconditionsofaid.htm*

OECD/The World Bank (2016), *Climate and Disaster Resilience Financing in Small Island Developing States*, OECD Publishing, Paris, *http://dx.doi.org/10.1787/9789264266919-en*.

OECD/UNDP (2016), *Making Development Co-operation More Effective: 2016 Progress Report*, OECD Publishing, Paris, *http://dx.doi.org/10.1787/9789264266261-en*.

United Nations (2017), *Financing for Development: Progress and Prospects*, report of the Inter-Agency Task Force on Financing for Development 2017, *http://developmentfinance.un.org*.

World Bank (2016), "Migration and remittances factbook 2016", Third edition, World Bank Group, Washington, DC, *https://siteresources.worldbank.org/INTPROSPECTS/Resources/334934-1199807908806/4549025-1450455807487/Factbookpart1.pdf*.

Profiles of Development Assistance Committee members

The profiles of Development Assistance Committee (DAC) members, which are presented in alphabetical order in this section, give key data on official development assistance (ODA) flows, channels, and thematic and geographic allocations. In line with the overall focus of the Development Co-operation Report 2017, *the profiles also show how DAC members contribute to data for sustainable development, in particular through strengthening statistical capacities and systems in developing countries.*

This section was prepared by Valentina Sanna, in collaboration with Yasmin Ahmad, Joëlline Bénéfice, Elena Bernaldo, Pierre Blanchard, Emily Bosch, Olivier Bouret, John Egan, Kerri Elgar, Mags Gaynor, Alejandro Guerrero-Ruiz, Karen Jorgensen, Thilo Klein, Rahul Malhotra, Ragini Malik, Ida Mc Donnell, Valentina Orrú, Joseph Stead, Andrzej Suchodolski, Valérie Thielemans, Yu Tian and Talisa Zur Hausen.

AUSTRALIA

Australia's contribution to data for development

Australia focuses on collecting and using quality data to inform decision making. Its capacity building, including through the Pacific Islands Statistics Strengthening Programme, focuses on improving statistical production and literacy and strengthening data dissemination and use by policy makers, civil society and citizens. Australia works with national statistics offices and other actors to build comparable data that enables global dialogue and better targeting of resources.

On gender statistics, Australia invests in the enabling environment for accessible data, in developing gender-sensitive and multidimensional measures of poverty as well as indicators on the prevalence of violence against women and girls and on unpaid work. It advocates for the need to interrogate household-level data, build capacity to analyse and use data on violence against women, and invest in disability statistics.

Its regional and bilateral sector programmes provide targeted capacity building for relevant ministries to collect, manage and disseminate data to inform decision making. In collaboration with partners, Australia is also working with big data, using mobile technology to collect vital health data.

According to the 2017 Partner Report on Support to Statistics (PRESS) dataset, Australia committed on average USD 12.4 million per year to finance national statistical capacities and systems in developing countries in 2013-15.

Financial flows from Australia to developing countries

Figure 8.1. **Net resource flows to developing countries, 2005-15, Australia**

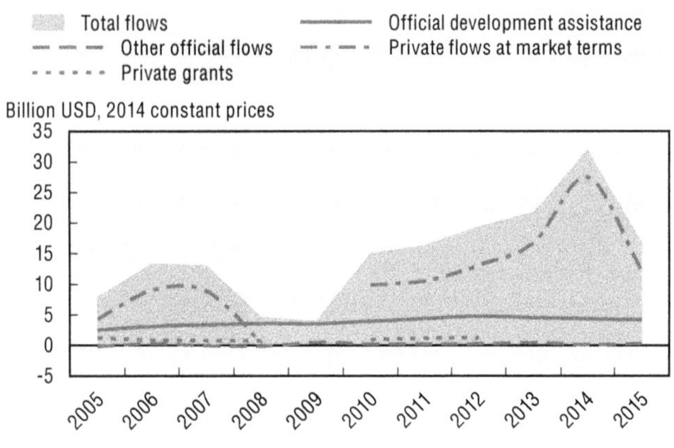

Note: Data on private flows at market terms are not available for 2009. Data on private grants are not available for 2009 or 2013-15.

StatLink http://dx.doi.org/10.1787/888933479674

Australia's use of ODA to mobilise other resources for sustainable development

- **USD 7.7 million** of official development assistance (ODA) was committed to the mobilisation of domestic resources in developing countries, e.g. to support the development of their tax systems, in 2015.
- **USD 386 million** of ODA (+21.5% in real terms from 2014) was committed to promote aid for trade and improve developing countries' trade performance and integration into the world economy in 2015.

Australia's performance against commitments for effective development co-operation

Table 8.1. **Results of the 2016 Global Partnership monitoring round, Australia**

	Alignment and ownership by partner country (%)				Predictability (%)		Transparency		
	Use of country-led results frameworks	Funding recorded in countries' national budgets	Funding through countries' systems	Untied ODA	Annual predictability	Medium-term predictability	Retrospective statistics (OECD CRS)	Information for forecasting (OECD FSS)	Publishing to IATI
2016	71.9	50.2	32.8	100.0	95.9	79.9	Needs improvement	Needs improvement	Fair
Baseline	-	34.8	23.5	98.5	68.9	51.5	Needs improvement	Good	-
Trend	-	⇑	⇑	⇑	⇑	⇑	=	⇓	-

Note: Please refer to Annex B for details on the indicators.

StatLink http://dx.doi.org/10.1787/888933482979

Australia's official development assistance

Australia provided USD 3 billion in net ODA in 2016 (preliminary data), which represented 0.25% of gross national income (GNI) and a fall of 12.7% in real terms from 2015, due to cuts in the bilateral aid programme. Australia's share of untied ODA (excluding administrative costs and in-donor refugee costs) was 100% in 2015 (up from 89.1% in 2014), while the DAC average was 78.1%. The grant element of total ODA was 99.9% in 2015.

Australia did not report expenditure on in-donor refugee costs as ODA in 2016. It considers that its processing of irregular migrants does not align with DAC rules for in-donor refugee costs.

Figure 8.2. **Net ODA: Trends in volume and as a share of GNI, 2000-16, Australia**

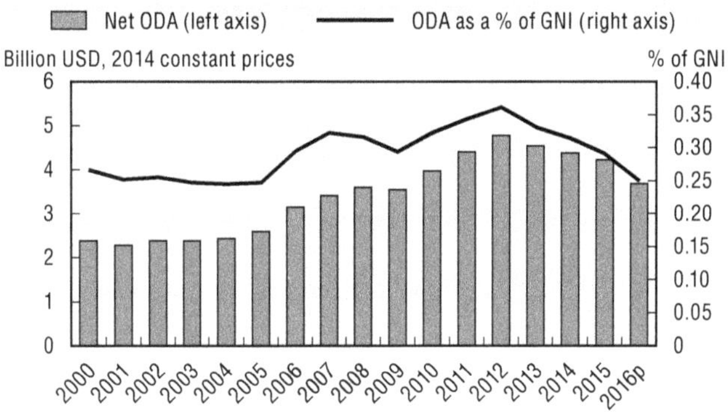

p: Preliminary data.

StatLink http://dx.doi.org/10.1787/888933479683

In 2015, 78.8% of ODA was provided bilaterally. Australia allocated 21.2% of total ODA as core contributions to multilateral organisations, compared with the DAC country average of 26.2%. In addition, it channelled 23.2% of its bilateral ODA for projects implemented by multilateral organisations (multi-bi/non-core).

Figure 8.3. **Share of ODA channelled to and through the multilateral system, two year averages, gross disbursements, Australia**

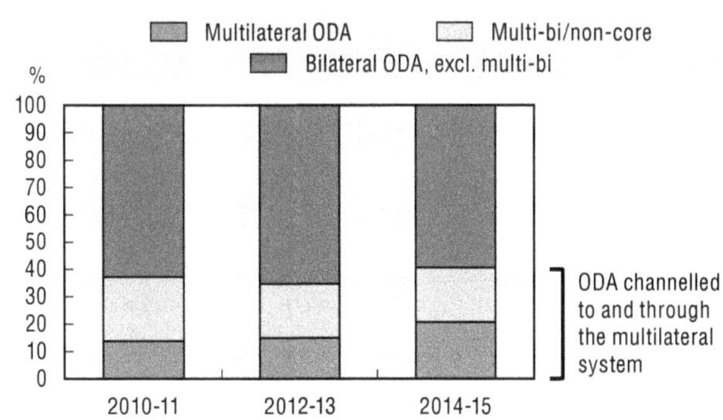

StatLink http://dx.doi.org/10.1787/888933479696

In 2015, 69.3% of bilateral ODA was programmed with partner countries. Australia's share of country programmable aid was above the DAC country average (48.8%) and 47% of this aid consisted of project-type interventions.

Figure 8.4. **Composition of bilateral ODA, 2015, gross disbursements, Australia**

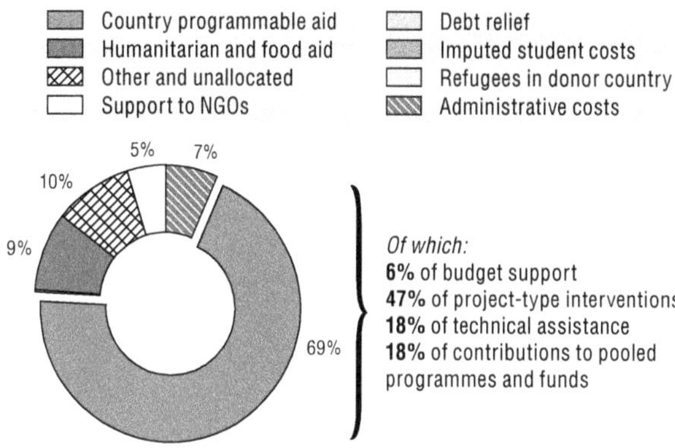

StatLink http://dx.doi.org/10.1787/888933479708

In 2015, USD 406.6 million of bilateral ODA was channelled to and through civil society organisations (CSOs). This was equivalent to 14.8% of bilateral ODA, compared with the DAC average of 16.9%. Aid to and through CSOs has decreased since 2014, both in volume (-13.2%) and as a share of bilateral ODA (from 16.1% to 14.8%).

Figure 8.5. **Bilateral ODA to and through CSOs, two year averages, gross disbursements, Australia**

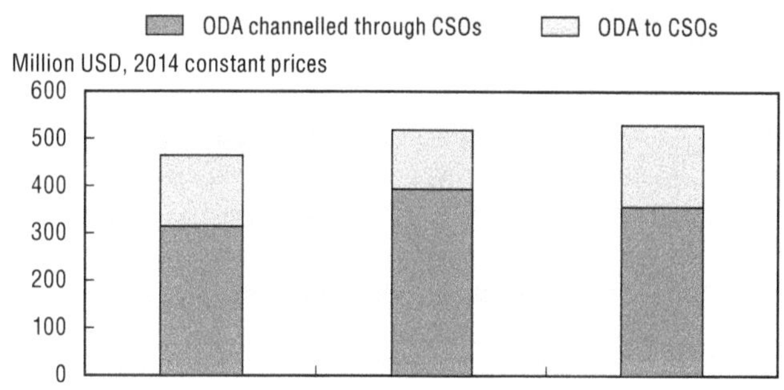

StatLink http://dx.doi.org/10.1787/888933479710

In 2015, bilateral ODA was primarily focused on Asia and Oceania. USD 852.1 million was allocated to Oceania, USD 759.8 million to Far East Asia, and USD 329 million to south and central Asia. USD 91 million was allocated to sub-Saharan Africa. Bilateral allocations to sub-Saharan Africa are decreasing in line with government policy.

Figure 8.6. **Share of bilateral ODA by region, 2014-15 average, gross disbursements, Australia**

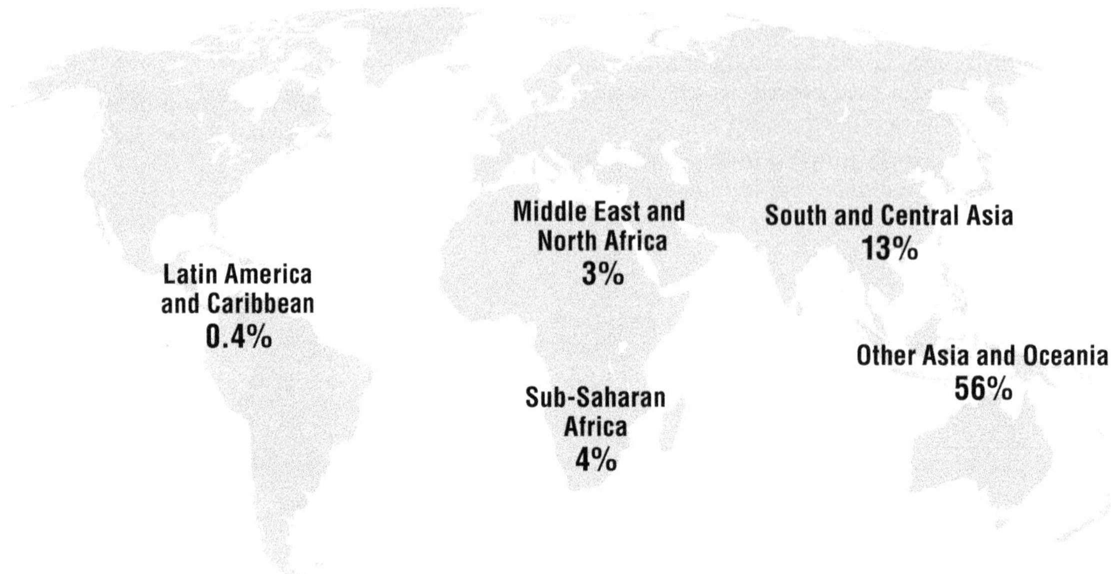

Note: 23% of bilateral ODA allocated was unspecified by region in 2014-15. This share is not represented on the map.

StatLink http://dx.doi.org/10.1787/888933479727

In 2015, 52.5% of bilateral ODA went to Australia's top 10 recipients. Its top 10 recipients are in the Asia-Pacific region, where Australia has programmes with 25 countries, in line with its focus on its immediate neighbourhood. Its support to fragile contexts reached USD 1.1 billion in 2015 (38.6% of gross bilateral ODA).

Figure 8.7. **Bilateral ODA to top recipients, 2014-15 average, gross disbursements, Australia**

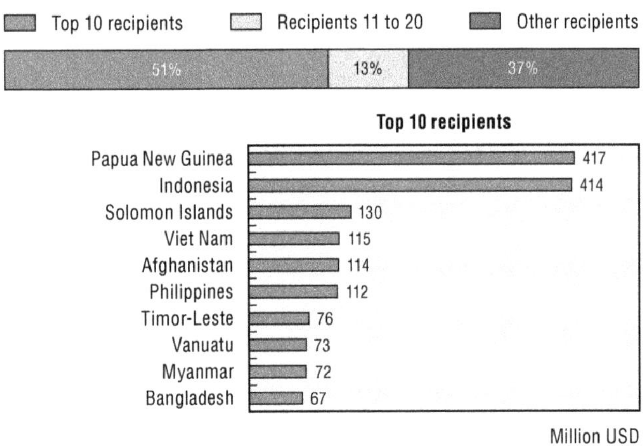

StatLink http://dx.doi.org/10.1787/888933479737

In 2015, 24.6% of Australia's bilateral ODA was allocated to least developed countries (LDCs), corresponding to USD 678.8 million. This is down from 25.2% in 2014 and is in line with the DAC average of 24.3%. Lower middle-income countries received the highest share of bilateral ODA in 2015 (42.1%).

At 0.08% of GNI in 2015, total ODA to LDCs was lower than the UN target of 0.15% of GNI.

Figure 8.8. **Bilateral ODA by income group, two year averages, gross disbursements, Australia**

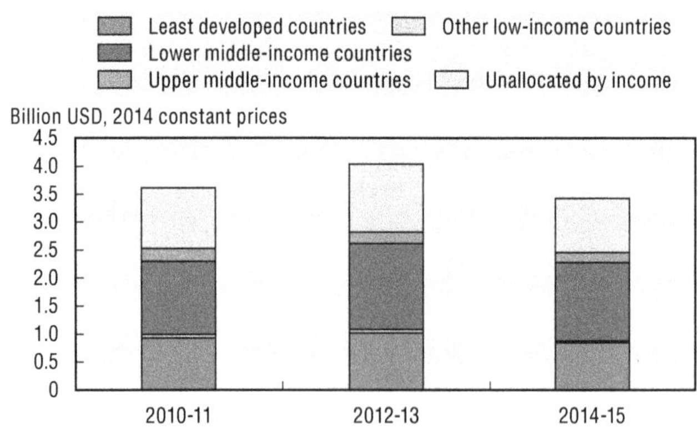

StatLink http://dx.doi.org/10.1787/888933479741

In 2015, 45.3% of bilateral ODA was allocated to social infrastructure and services, representing USD 1.2 billion. There was a strong focus on support to government and civil society (USD 512.6 million), education (USD 333.5 million), and health (USD 166.2 million). Humanitarian aid amounted to USD 238.7 million.

Figure 8.9. **Share of bilateral ODA by sector, 2014-15 average, commitments, Australia**

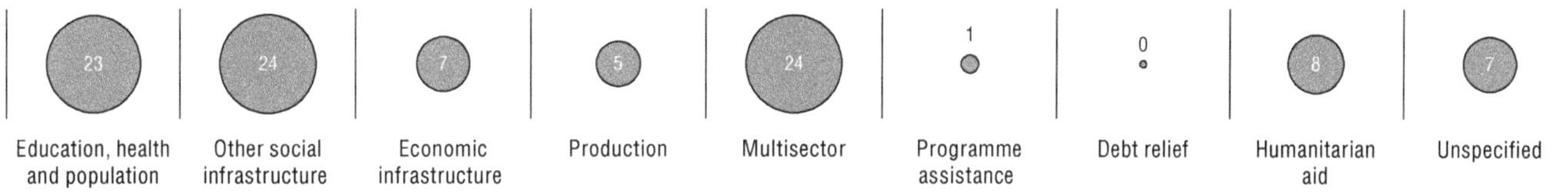

StatLink http://dx.doi.org/10.1787/888933479755

USD 1.3 billion of bilateral ODA supported gender equality in 2015. Empowering women and girls and promoting gender equality are central to Australia's development co-operation and international diplomacy. Australia has a strategic target of 80% of investments performing satisfactorily on gender equality, as measured through its aid quality check process. In 2016, it rated 78% of aid investments as effectively addressing gender equality in their implementation. OECD data show that in 2015, 54.1% of Australia's bilateral allocable aid had gender equality and women's empowerment as a principal or significant objective. This is lower than the 2014 level of 57% but remains higher than the 2015 DAC country average of 36.3%. Australia's aid to population, reproductive health and education focuses on gender.

Figure 8.10. **Share of bilateral allocable ODA in support of gender equality by sector, 2015, commitments, Australia**

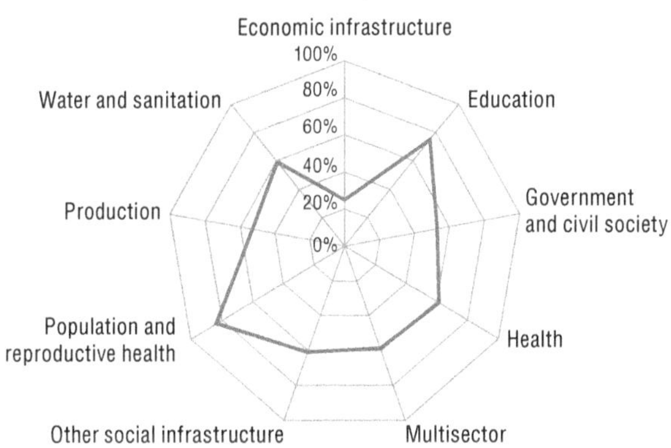

StatLink http://dx.doi.org/10.1787/888933479769

USD 378 million of bilateral ODA supported the environment in 2015. Australia's development policy commits Australia's aid programme to "... actively manage risk by mitigating adverse environmental and social impacts in the aid programme through the application of mandatory safeguard policies..." (Commonwealth of Australia, 2014). In 2015, 14.7% of its bilateral allocable aid focused on the environment, compared with the DAC country average of 33.2%. In 2015, 13% of Australian bilateral allocable aid (USD 334.7 million) focused particularly on climate change, compared with the DAC country average of 26.2%.

Figure 8.11. **Bilateral allocable ODA in support of global and local environment objectives, two year averages, commitments, Australia**

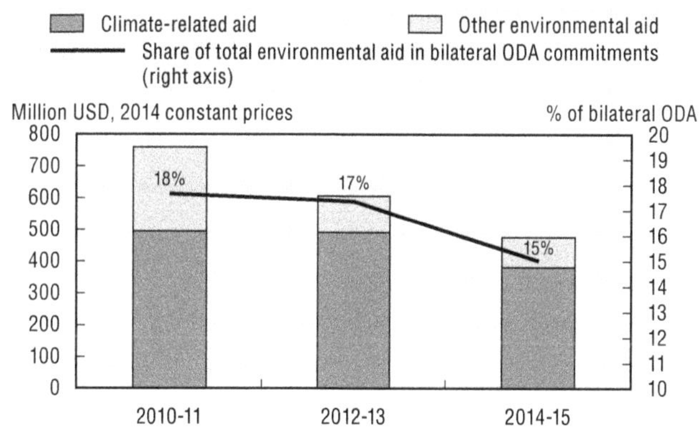

StatLink http://dx.doi.org/10.1787/888933479776

Note to reader: Annex B provides "Methodological notes on the profiles of Development Assistance Committee members".

Reference

Commonwealth of Australia (2014), *Australian Aid: Promoting Prosperity, Reducing Poverty, Enhancing Stability*, Department of Foreign Affairs and Trade, Canberra, *www.dfat.gov.au/about-us/publications/Documents/australian-aid-development-policy.pdf*.

AUSTRIA

Austria's contribution to data for development

According to the 2017 Partner Report on Support to Statistics (PRESS) dataset, Austria committed on average USD 0.96 million per year to finance national statistical capacities and systems in developing countries in 2013-15.

Financial flows from Austria to developing countries

Figure 9.1. **Net resource flows to developing countries, 2005-15, Austria**

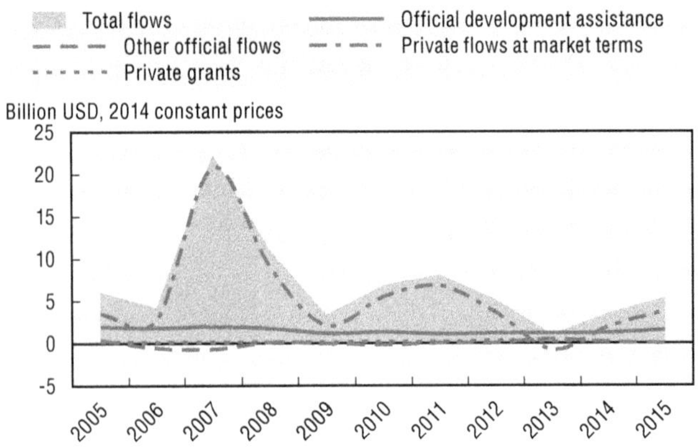

Note: Data on private grants are not available for 2015.

StatLink http://dx.doi.org/10.1787/888933479784

Austria's use of ODA to mobilise other resources for sustainable development

- **USD 68.2 million** of ODA (+17.2% in real terms from 2014) was committed to promote aid for trade and improve developing countries' trade performance and integration into the world economy in 2015.

Austria's performance against commitments for effective development co-operation

Table 9.1. **Results of the 2016 Global Partnership monitoring round, Austria**

	Alignment and ownership by partner country (%)				Predictability (%)		Transparency		
	Use of country-led results frameworks	Funding recorded in countries' national budgets	Funding through countries' systems	Untied ODA	Annual predictability	Medium-term predictability	Retrospective statistics (OECD CRS)	Information for forecasting (OECD FSS)	Publishing to IATI
2016	83.8	62.3	32.7	36.4	88.1	58.1	Excellent	Good	-
Baseline	-	76.7	59.0	57.9	99.7	73.2	Excellent	Excellent	-
Trend	-	⇓	⇓	⇓	⇓	⇓	=	⇓	

Note: Please refer to Annex B for details on the indicators.

StatLink http://dx.doi.org/10.1787/888933482987

Austria's official development assistance

In 2016, Austria provided USD 1.6 billion in net ODA (preliminary data), which represented 0.41% of gross national income (GNI) and an 18.3% increase in real terms from 2015, due largely to an increase in in-donor refugee costs and multilateral contributions. Austria plans to double its budget for bilateral co-operation by 2021. Austria's share of untied ODA (excluding administrative costs and in-donor refugee costs) was 36.4% in 2015 (down from 48.2% in 2014), while the DAC average was 78.1%. The grant element of total ODA was 100% in 2015.

In 2016, in-donor refugee costs were USD 596 million, an increase of 34.3% in real terms over 2015, and represented 37.7% of Austria's total net ODA.

Figure 9.2. **Net ODA: Trends in volume and as a share of GNI, 2000-16, Austria**

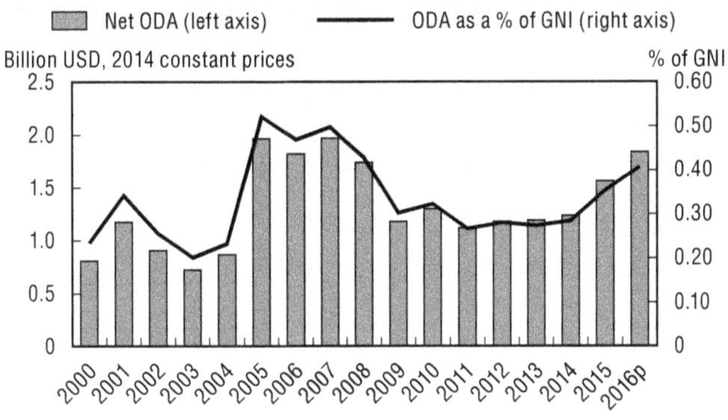

p: Preliminary data.

StatLink http://dx.doi.org/10.1787/888933479795

In 2015, 59.3% of Austria's ODA was provided bilaterally. Austria allocated 40.7% of total ODA as core contributions to multilateral organisations, compared with the DAC country average of 26.2%. In addition, it channelled 7.7% of its bilateral ODA for specific projects implemented by multilateral organisations (multi-bi/non-core).

Figure 9.3. **Share of ODA channelled to and through the multilateral system, two year averages, gross disbursements, Austria**

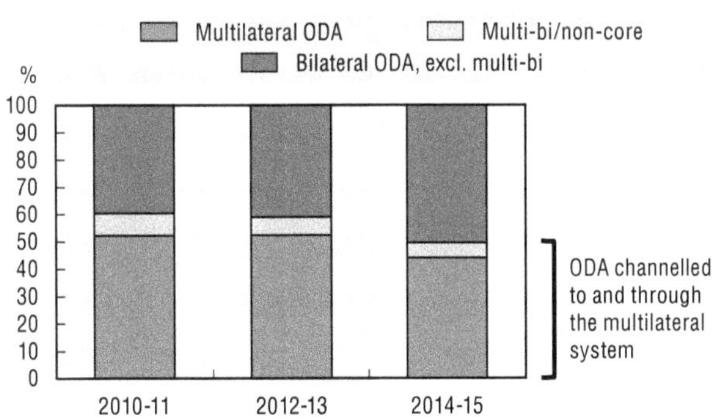

StatLink http://dx.doi.org/10.1787/888933479801

In 2015, only 8.7% of Austria's bilateral ODA was programmed with partner countries, making Austria's share of country programmable aid lower than the DAC country average of 48.8% in 2015. Project-type interventions accounted for 52% of this aid. Fifty-six per cent of bilateral ODA was allocated to refugees in donor country.

Figure 9.4. **Composition of bilateral ODA, 2015, gross disbursements, Austria**

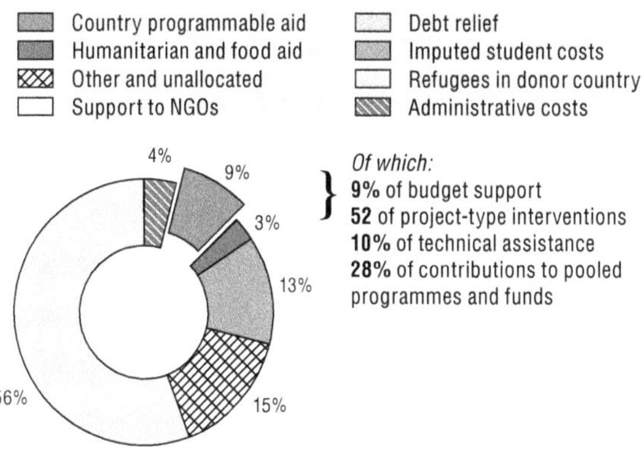

StatLink http://dx.doi.org/10.1787/888933479816

In 2015, USD 49.3 million of bilateral ODA was channelled to and through civil society organisations (CSOs). ODA channelled to and through CSOs decreased by 15.5% in volume compared to 2014. As a share of bilateral ODA, support for CSOs decreased from 10.7% in 2014 to 6.3% in 2015. The DAC average was 16.9%.

Figure 9.5. **Bilateral ODA to and through CSOs, two year averages, gross disbursements, Austria**

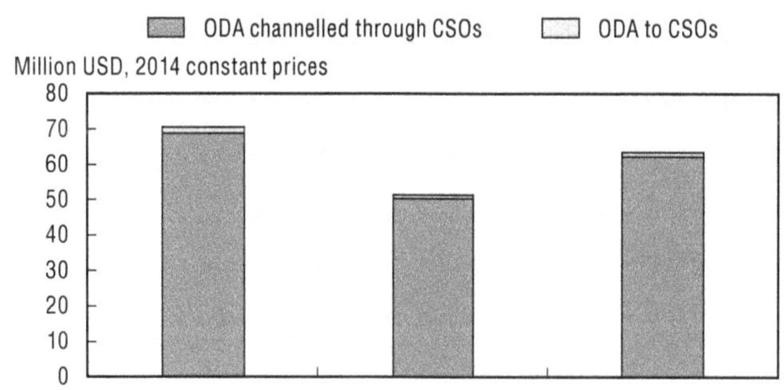

StatLink http://dx.doi.org/10.1787/888933479821

In 2015, bilateral ODA was primarily focused on Eastern Europe, sub-Saharan Africa, and south and central Asia. This represented USD 107.3 million to Eastern Europe, USD 50.3 million to sub-Saharan Africa, and USD 32 million to south and central Asia. ODA to south and central Asia decreased significantly (-76% in real terms) between 2014 and 2015.

Figure 9.6. **Share of bilateral ODA by region, 2014-15 average, gross disbursements, Austria**

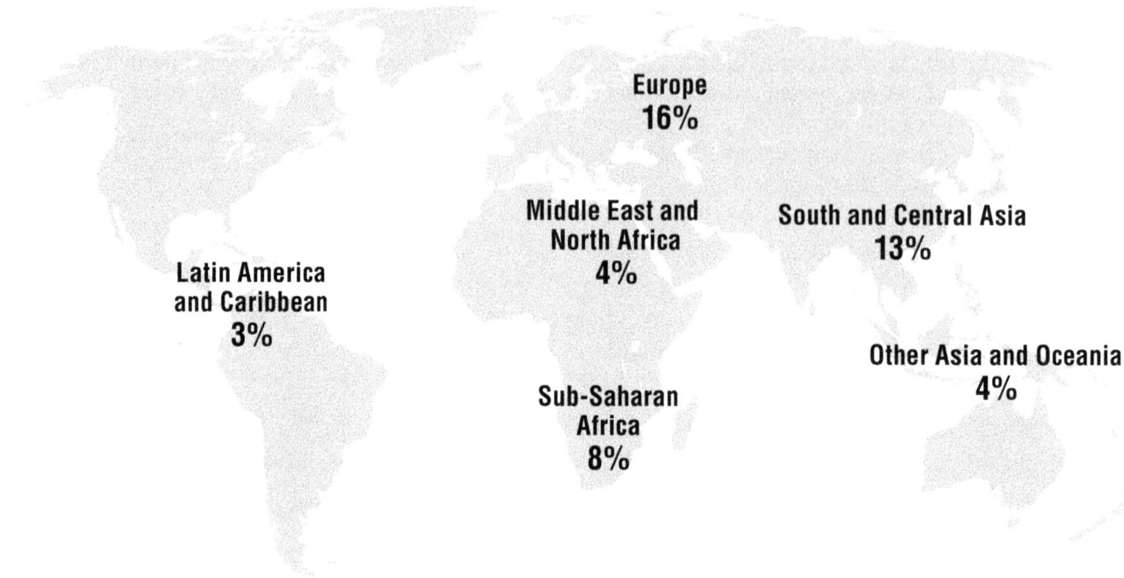

Note: 51% of bilateral ODA allocated was unspecified by region in 2014-15. This share is not represented on the map.

StatLink http://dx.doi.org/10.1787/888933479831

Austria allocated 15.5% of its bilateral ODA to its top 10 recipients. Three of its 11 priority partner countries are among its top 10 recipients (Albania, Kosovo and Uganda). Austria's support to fragile contexts reached USD 63.4 million in 2015 (8% of gross bilateral ODA).

Figure 9.7. **Bilateral ODA to top recipients, 2014-15 average, gross disbursements, Austria**

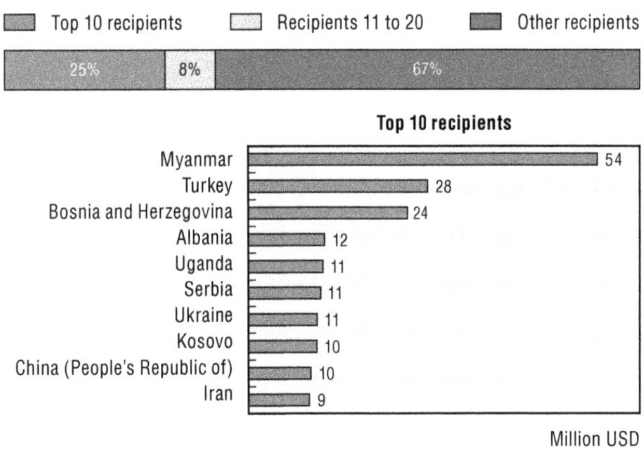

StatLink http://dx.doi.org/10.1787/888933479845

In 2015, 5.6% of Austria's bilateral ODA (USD 44.2 million) was allocated to least developed countries (LDCs), which is below the 2015 DAC average of 24.3%. As a share of bilateral ODA, aid to LDCs dropped dramatically in 2015, after increasing up until 2014, when it was 24.9%. Upper middle-income countries received the highest share of bilateral ODA in 2015 (13.4%), noting that 70.1% was unallocated by income group.

At 0.06% of GNI in 2015, Austria's total ODA to LDCs was less than the UN target of 0.15% of GNI.

Figure 9.8. **Bilateral ODA by income group, two year averages, gross disbursements, Austria**

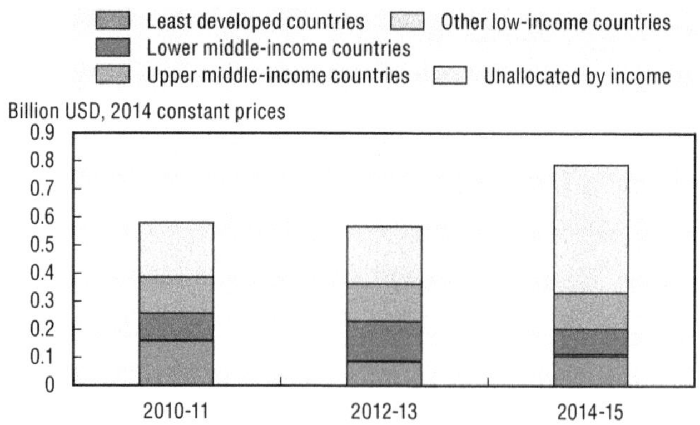

StatLink http://dx.doi.org/10.1787/888933479850

In 2015, 26.9% of bilateral ODA was allocated to social infrastructure and services. A total of USD 220.8 million of bilateral ODA was allocated to social sectors, with a strong focus on support to education (USD 136.9 million) and health (USD 28.7 million). Humanitarian aid amounted to USD 23.2 million. In 2015, in line with its commitments to the 2030 Agenda for Sustainable Development, Austria announced a new focus area of renewable energy.

Figure 9.9. **Share of bilateral ODA by sector, 2014-15 average, commitments, Austria**

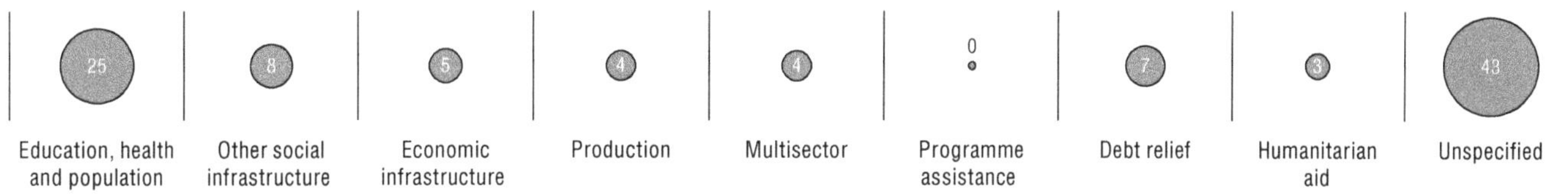

StatLink http://dx.doi.org/10.1787/888933479862

USD 72.6 million of bilateral ODA supported gender equality in 2015. Support for gender equality is a priority cross-cutting issue for Austrian development co-operation. The 2015 DAC Peer Review recommended that Austria clarify its priorities for mainstreaming cross-cutting themes, and ensure that it has the tools and resources to follow through on these priorities. In 2015, 44.9% of bilateral allocable aid had gender equality and women's empowerment as a principal or significant objective, which is an increase from 29.3% in 2014 and is higher than the DAC country average of 36.3% in 2015. Austria's aid to population, reproductive health, and water and sanitation focuses on gender.

Figure 9.10. **Share of bilateral allocable ODA in support of gender equality by sector, 2015, commitments, Austria**

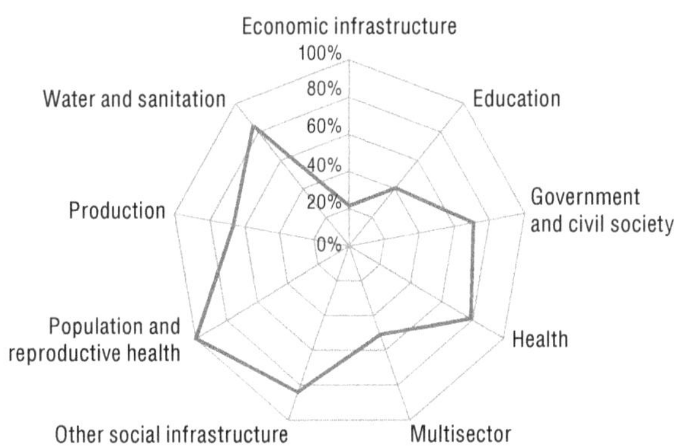

StatLink http://dx.doi.org/10.1787/888933479877

USD 77.2 million of bilateral ODA supported the environment in 2015. Tackling global environmental issues is a top priority for Austria, although mainstreaming the environment throughout the programme remains work in progress and Austria needs to ensure that it has the tools and resources to follow through on these priorities. In 2015, 33% of its bilateral allocable aid focused on the environment and 22.9% (USD 53.6 million) focused particularly on climate change, compared with the respective DAC country averages of 33.2% and 26.2%.

Figure 9.11. **Bilateral allocable ODA in support of global and local environment objectives, two year averages, commitments, Austria**

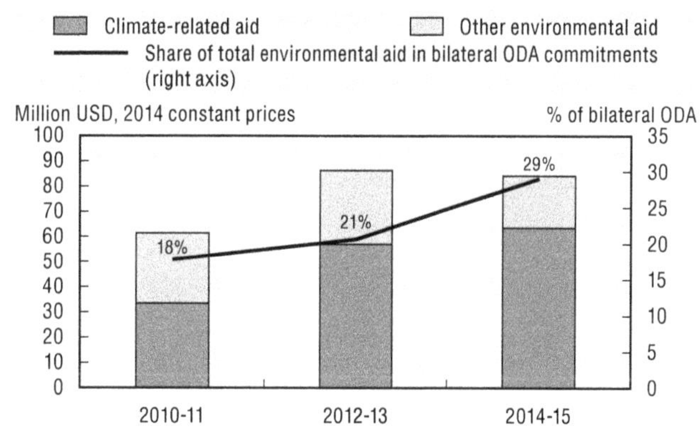

StatLink http://dx.doi.org/10.1787/888933479886

Note to reader: Annex B provides "Methodological notes on the profiles of Development Assistance Committee members".

Reference

OECD (2015), *OECD Development Co-operation Peer Reviews: Austria 2015*, OECD Publishing, Paris, *http://dx.doi.org/10.1787/9789264227958-en*.

BELGIUM

Belgium's contribution to data for development

Belgium plans to engage more actively in statistical capacity building in developing countries to improve their statistical production; to promote the use of data by policy makers, civil society and citizens; and to strengthen co-ordination among development partners. Belgium provides support mainly through technical assistance and funding for equipment.

Collecting reliable "big data" and providing more open and accessible data to the public is a new strategic priority for Belgian Development Cooperation. In Uganda, Belgium supports two innovative "big data" programmes: 1) the Pulse Lab Kampala that is developing applications to monitor, in real time, the quality of the public health and education service in Uganda; and 2) Mobile Money for the Poor that aims to support Kampala's public transport planning, to map financial inclusion and promote the expansion of mobile money transfers among the poor. In several of its sectoral programmes (e.g. agriculture, water, health and rural infrastructure), Belgium also works to strengthen capacities on geographic data processing, which are important for modern data management.

According to the 2017 Partner Report on Support to Statistics (PRESS) dataset, Belgium committed on average USD 0.18 million per year to finance national statistical capacities and systems in developing countries in 2013-15.

Financial flows from Belgium to developing countries

Figure 10.1. **Net resource flows to developing countries, 2005-15, Belgium**

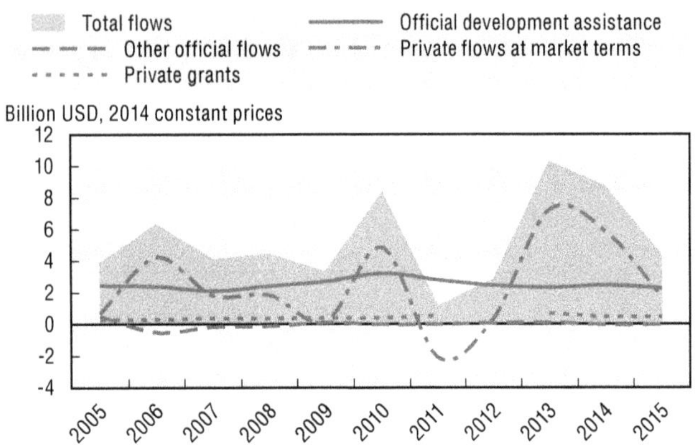

Note: Data on private grants are not available for 2012.

StatLink http://dx.doi.org/10.1787/888933479892

Belgium's use of ODA to mobilise other resources for sustainable development

- **USD 6.7 million** of official development assistance (ODA) was committed to the mobilisation of domestic resources in developing countries, e.g. to support the development of their tax systems, in 2015.
- **USD 205 million** of ODA (-11.9% in real terms from 2014) was committed to promote aid for trade and improve developing countries' trade performance and integration into the world economy in 2015.

Belgium's performance against commitments for effective development co-operation

Table 10.1. **Results of the 2016 Global Partnership monitoring round, Belgium**

	Alignment and ownership by partner country (%)				Predictability (%)		Transparency		
	Use of country-led results frameworks	Funding recorded in countries' national budgets	Funding through countries' systems	Untied ODA	Annual predictability	Medium-term predictability	Retrospective statistics (OECD CRS)	Information for forecasting (OECD FSS)	Publishing to IATI
2016	77.7	35.3	53.2	96.7	63.4	59.8	Good	Excellent	Good
Baseline	-	30.3	23.2	94.9	79.6	77.7	Good	Good	-
Trend	-	⇑	⇑	⇑	⇓	⇓	=	⇑	-

Note: Please refer to Annex B for details on the indicators.

StatLink http://dx.doi.org/10.1787/888933482994

Belgium's official development assistance

In 2016, Belgium provided USD 2.3 billion in net ODA (preliminary data), which represented 0.49% of gross national income (GNI) and a rise of 19.6% in real terms from 2015, mostly because of increased in-donor refugee costs. There is a negative outlook for Belgium's ODA. The government's commitment to reach the target of 0.7% ODA/GNI is included in law; however, the 2015 budget announced significant cuts up until 2019. Belgium's share of untied ODA (excluding administrative costs and in-donor refugee costs) was 96.7% in 2015 (remaining stable since 2014). The 2015 DAC average was 78.1%. The grant element of total ODA was 99.8% in 2015.

In 2016, in-donor refugee costs were USD 386 million, an increase of 67.3% in real terms over 2015, and represented 16.8% of Belgium's total net ODA.

Figure 10.2. **Net ODA: Trends in volume and as a share of GNI, 2000-16, Belgium**

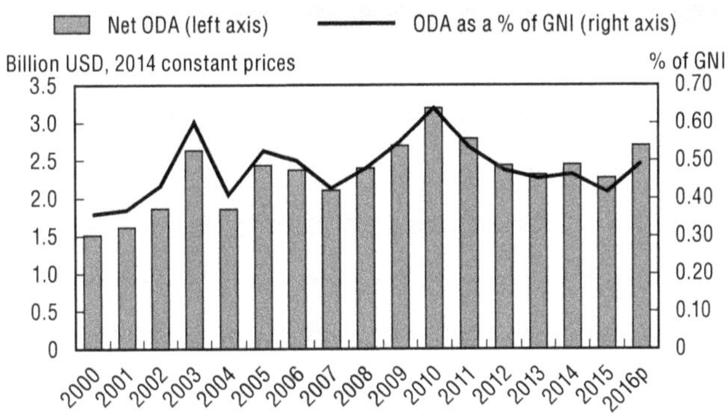

p: Preliminary data.

StatLink http://dx.doi.org/10.1787/888933479902

In 2015, 59.9% of ODA was provided bilaterally. Belgium allocated 40.1% of total ODA as core contributions to multilateral organisations, compared with the DAC country average of 26.2%. In addition, it channelled 10.7% of its bilateral ODA for specific projects implemented by multilateral organisations (multi-bi/non-core).

Figure 10.3. **Share of ODA channelled to and through the multilateral system, two year averages, gross disbursements, Belgium**

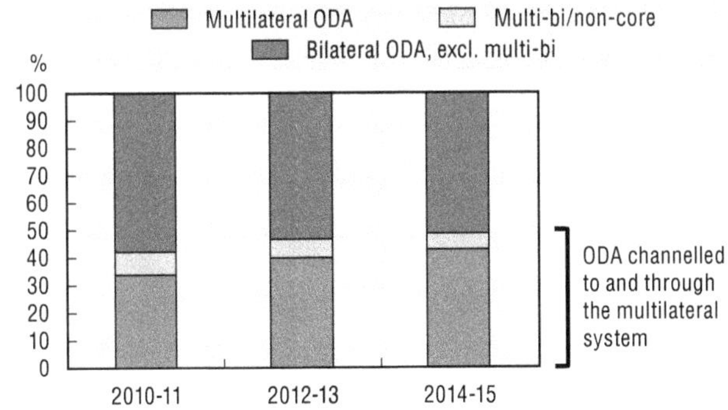

StatLink http://dx.doi.org/10.1787/888933479914

In 2015, 25.7% of bilateral ODA was programmed with partner countries. The share of country programmable aid was low compared with the DAC country average (48.8%) in 2015. Project-type interventions accounted for 87% of this aid.

Figure 10.4. **Composition of bilateral ODA, 2015, gross disbursements, Belgium**

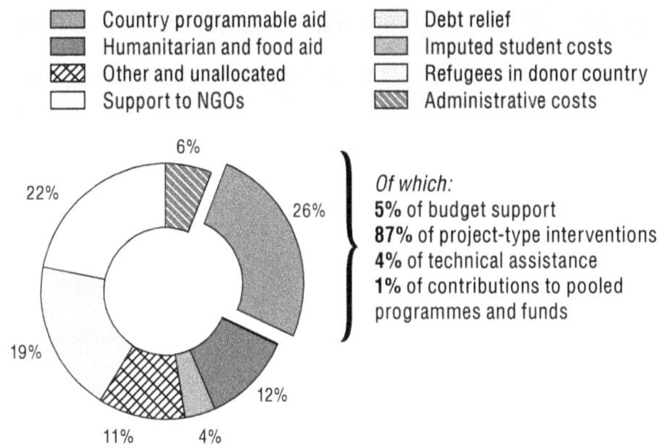

StatLink http://dx.doi.org/10.1787/888933479925

In 2015, USD 262.6 million of bilateral ODA was channelled to and through civil society organisations (CSOs). This was equivalent to 22.2% of Belgium's bilateral ODA, compared with the DAC average of 16.9%. Between 2014 and 2015, Belgium's aid channelled to and through CSOs increased slightly in terms of volume (0.7%), and remained stable as a share of bilateral aid (it was 22.7% in 2014).

Figure 10.5. **Bilateral ODA to and through CSOs, two year averages, gross disbursements, Belgium**

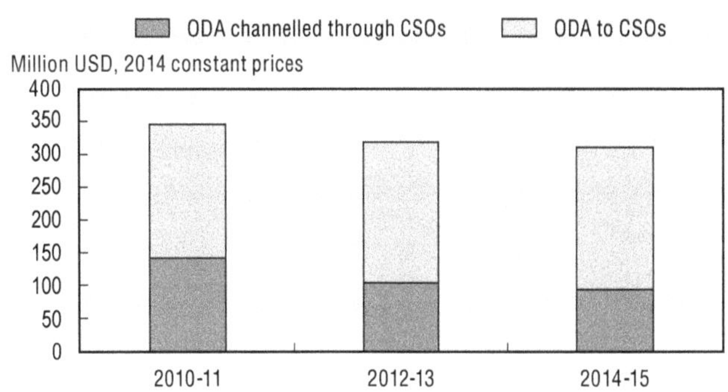

StatLink http://dx.doi.org/10.1787/888933479936

Bilateral ODA in 2015 was primarily focused on sub-Saharan Africa, with USD 406.5 million allocated to this region. USD 295 million of Belgium's aid to sub-Saharan Africa was allocated to the Great Lakes region, which is a priority for Belgian Development Cooperation.

Figure 10.6. **Share of bilateral ODA by region, 2014-15 average, gross disbursements, Belgium**

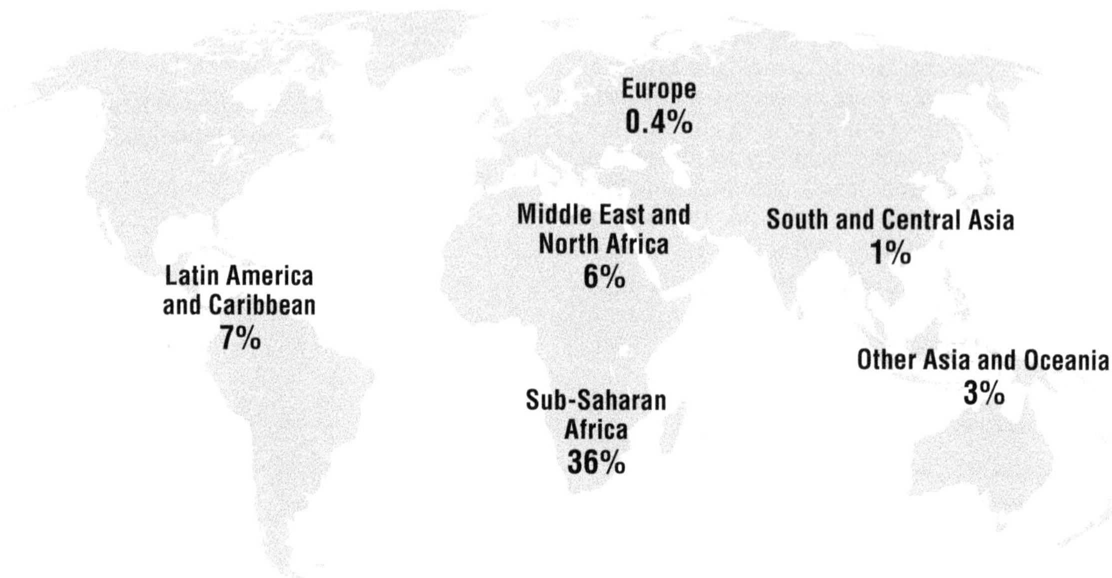

Note: 46% of bilateral ODA allocated was unspecified by region in 2014-15. This share is not represented on the map.

StatLink http://dx.doi.org/10.1787/888933479941

In 2015, 27.4% of bilateral ODA went to Belgium's top 10 recipients. Eight of its 14 priority partner countries are among its top 10 recipients. The Democratic Republic of the Congo, Burundi and Rwanda are among its top 5 recipients. Belgium's support to fragile contexts reached USD 417 million in 2015, accounting for 35.2% of gross bilateral ODA.

Figure 10.7. **Bilateral ODA to top recipients, 2014-15 average, gross disbursements, Belgium**

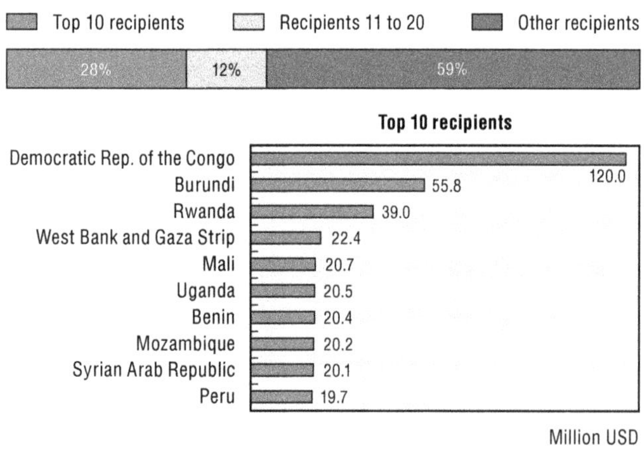

StatLink http://dx.doi.org/10.1787/888933479951

In 2015, 32.2% of Belgium's bilateral ODA was allocated to least developed countries (LDCs), amounting to USD 381.2 million. This is a decrease from 35.1% in 2014, but remains higher than the 2015 DAC average of 24.3%. LDCs received the highest share of bilateral ODA in 2015, noting that 48.1% was unallocated by income group.

At 0.13% of GNI in 2015, Belgium's total ODA to LDCs was below the UN target of 0.15% of GNI.

Figure 10.8. **Bilateral ODA by income group, two year averages, gross disbursements, Belgium**

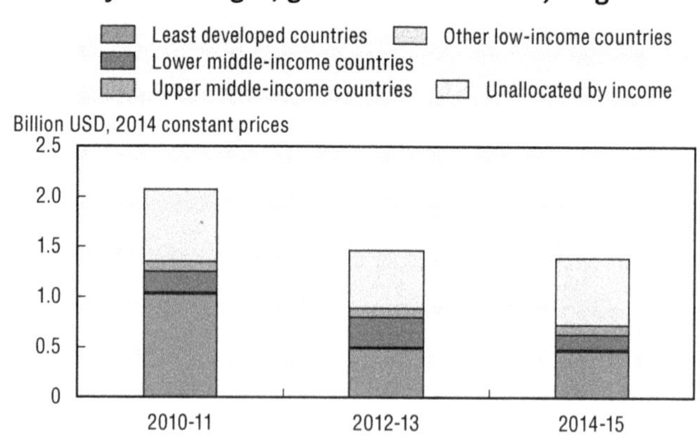

StatLink http://dx.doi.org/10.1787/888933479960

In 2015, 28% of bilateral ODA was allocated to social infrastructure and services, for a total of USD 368.1 million. There was a strong focus on health (USD 109.5 million), government and civil society (USD 79.7 million), and education (USD 89.4 million). Humanitarian aid amounted to USD 235.7 million.

Figure 10.9. **Share of bilateral ODA by sector, 2014-15 average, commitments, Belgium**

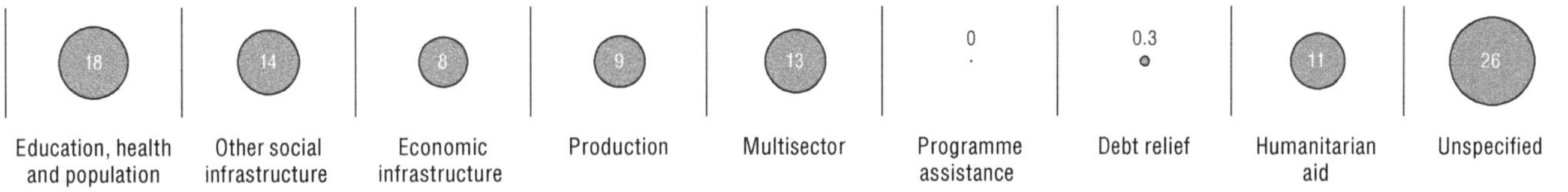

StatLink http://dx.doi.org/10.1787/888933479975

USD 718 million of bilateral ODA supported gender equality in 2015. Gender equality is a cross-cutting theme for Belgian Development Cooperation, which in 2013 approved its second National Action Plan for Women, Peace and Security. This plan places a strong emphasis on preventing and combating gender-based violence in conflict and post-conflict zones. In 2015, 75.9% of Belgium's bilateral allocable aid had gender equality and women's empowerment as a principal or significant objective, compared with the DAC country average of 36.3%. This is an increase from 73.6% in 2014. Belgium's aid to education, productive sectors, government and civil society, and population and reproductive health focuses on gender.

Figure 10.10. **Share of bilateral allocable ODA in support of gender equality by sector, 2015, commitments, Belgium**

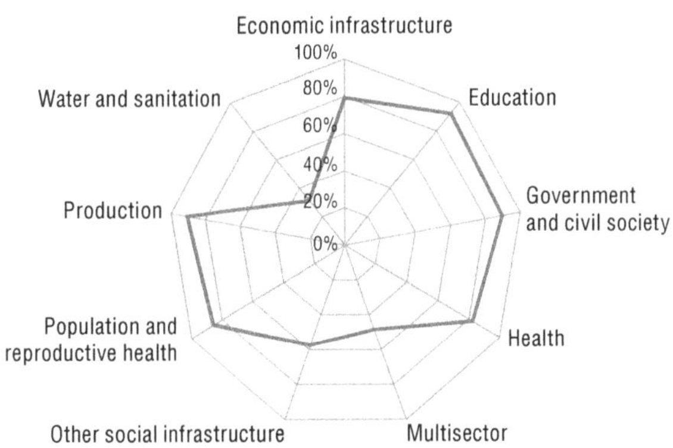

StatLink http://dx.doi.org/10.1787/888933479985

USD 541 million of bilateral ODA supported the environment in 2015. The environment and climate change are cross-cutting themes for Belgium, which is also reinforcing its strategy and resources for making progress. The share of environment-focused bilateral aid has been increasing since 2010. In 2015, 56.2% of its bilateral allocable aid supported the environment and 32.1% focused particularly on climate change, compared with the respective DAC country averages of 33.2% and 26.2%.

Figure 10.11. **Bilateral allocable ODA in support of global and local environment objectives, two year averages, commitments, Belgium**

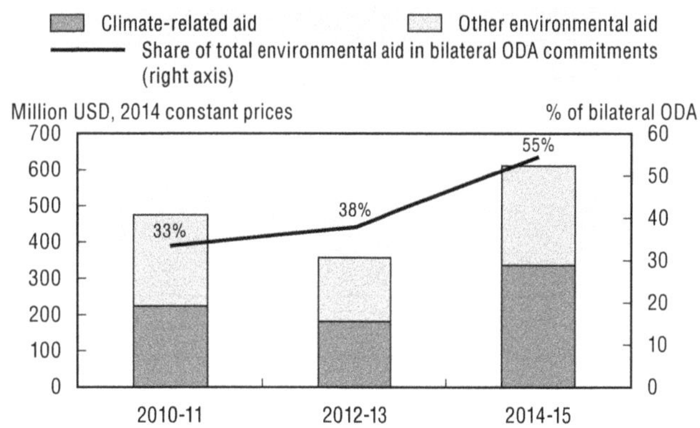

StatLink http://dx.doi.org/10.1787/888933479992

Note to reader: Annex B provides "Methodological notes on the profiles of Development Assistance Committee members".

Reference

OECD (2015), *OECD Development Co-operation Peer Reviews: Belgium 2015*, OECD Publishing, Paris, *http://dx.doi.org/10.1787/9789264239906-en*.

CANADA

Canada's contribution to data for development

Canada believes that national statistical systems that provide quality and disaggregated data for evidence-based decision making are a cornerstone of good governance and strong democratic institutions. It supports statistical production; data dissemination; use of data by policy makers, civil society and citizens; and capacity to measure progress, including towards the Sustainable Development Goals. Support is provided mainly in the form of technical assistance.

Canada's capacity building in the health sector focuses on information management systems and civil registration and vital statistics. It supports partner governments to strengthen nutrition surveillance, tracking of vaccination coverage, pandemic preparedness and evaluation platforms. Canada has also established a global network of partners around the Open Data for Development initiative. Through the International Aid Transparency Initiative, it works to make more and better data available on development co-operation and promotes the use of data for results.

Statistics Canada is actively involved in statistical capacity building. For instance, it provides technical assistance to the National Agency of Statistics and Demography of Senegal to improve the quality of statistics.

According to the 2017 Partner Report on Support to Statistics (PRESS) dataset, Canada committed on average USD 52.28 million per year to finance national statistical capacities and systems in developing countries in 2013-15.

Financial flows from Canada to developing countries

Figure 11.1. **Net resource flows to developing countries, 2005-15, Canada**

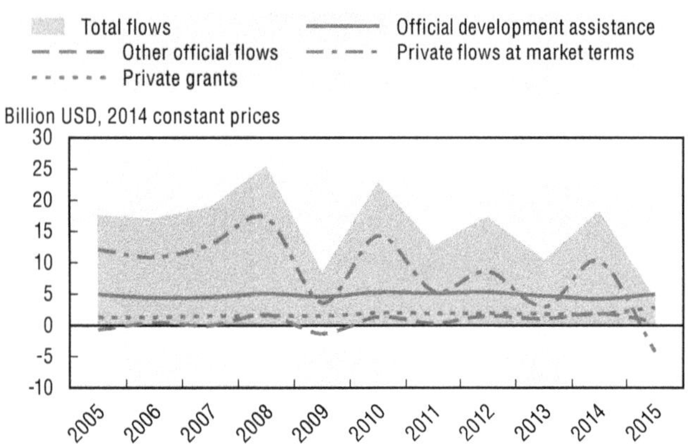

StatLink http://dx.doi.org/10.1787/888933480003

Canada's use of ODA to mobilise other resources for sustainable development

- **USD 4.5 million** of official development assistance (ODA) was committed to the mobilisation of domestic resources in developing countries, e.g. to support the development of their tax systems, in 2015.
- **USD 713.2 million** of ODA (+78.3% in real terms from 2014) was committed to promote aid for trade and improve developing countries' trade performance and integration into the world economy in 2015.

Canada's performance against commitments for effective development co-operation

Table 11.1. **Results of the 2016 Global Partnership monitoring round, Canada**

	Alignment and ownership by partner country (%)				Predictability (%)		Transparency		
	Use of country-led results frameworks	Funding recorded in countries' national budgets	Funding through countries' systems	Untied ODA	Annual predictability	Medium-term predictability	Retrospective statistics (OECD CRS)	Information for forecasting (OECD FSS)	Publishing to IATI
2016	54.5	68.3	51.7	98.5	82.9	59.2	Excellent	Excellent	Excellent
Baseline	-	73.4	64.5	86.7	81.6	65.2	Excellent	Excellent	-
Trend	-	⇓	⇓	⇑	⇑	⇓	=	=	-

Note: Please refer to Annex B for details on the indicators.

StatLink http://dx.doi.org/10.1787/888933483008

Canada's official development assistance

In 2016, Canada provided USD 4 billion in net ODA (preliminary data). This represented 0.26% of gross national income (GNI) and a decrease of 4.4% in real terms from 2015 due to the timings of payments, although it has increased support to in-donor refugees. The 2016 budget allocated an additional CAD 256 million for 2016-17 and 2017-18. Canada's share of untied ODA (excluding administrative costs and in-donor refugee costs) was 98.5% in 2015 (up from 93% in 2014), which is above the DAC average of 78.1%. The grant element of total ODA was 97.3% in 2015.

In 2016, in-donor refugee costs were USD 390 million, an increase of 89.2% in real terms over 2015, and represented 9.9% of Canada's total net ODA.

Figure 11.2. **Net ODA: Trends in volume and as a share of GNI, 2000-16, Canada**

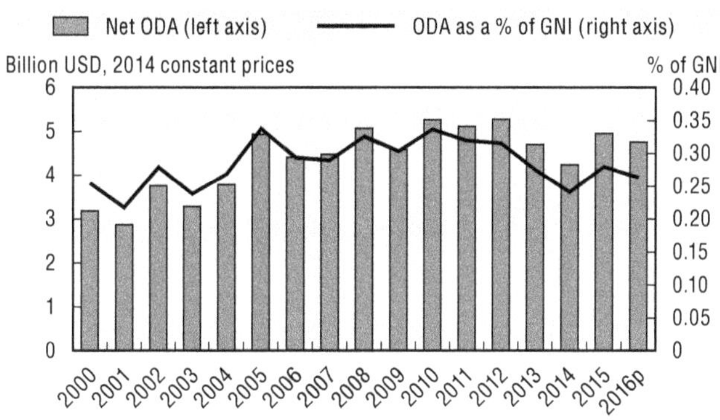

p: Preliminary data.

StatLink http://dx.doi.org/10.1787/888933480012

In 2015, 69.8% of bilateral ODA was provided bilaterally. In 2015, Canada allocated 30.2% of total ODA as core contributions to multilateral organisations, compared with the DAC country average of 26.2%. In addition, it channelled 34.3% of its bilateral ODA for specific projects implemented by multilateral organisations (multi-bi/non-core).

Figure 11.3. **Share of ODA channelled to and through the multilateral system, two year averages, gross disbursements, Canada**

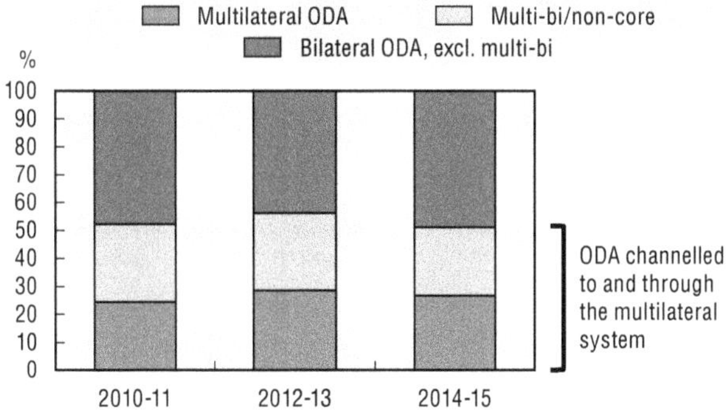

StatLink http://dx.doi.org/10.1787/888933480020

In 2015, 31.2% of bilateral ODA was programmed with partner countries. Canada's share of country programmable aid was lower than the DAC country average (48.8%) in 2015 and contributions to pooled programmes and funds accounted for 43% of this aid. Twenty-seven per cent of Canada's bilateral ODA was categorised as "other and unallocated".

Figure 11.4. **Composition of bilateral ODA, 2015, gross disbursements, Canada**

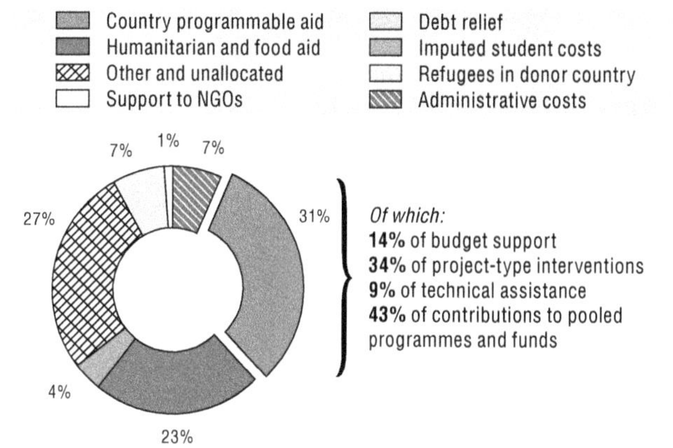

StatLink http://dx.doi.org/10.1787/888933480039

In 2015, USD 750.3 million of bilateral ODA was channelled to and through civil society organisations (CSOs). Aid channelled to and through CSOs increased between 2014 and 2015 in terms of volume (+6.6%) and remained stable as a share of bilateral ODA (it was 24.5% in 2014 and 24.9% in 2015). This share was higher than the DAC country average of 16.9%.

Figure 11.5. **Bilateral ODA to and through CSOs, two year averages, gross disbursements, Canada**

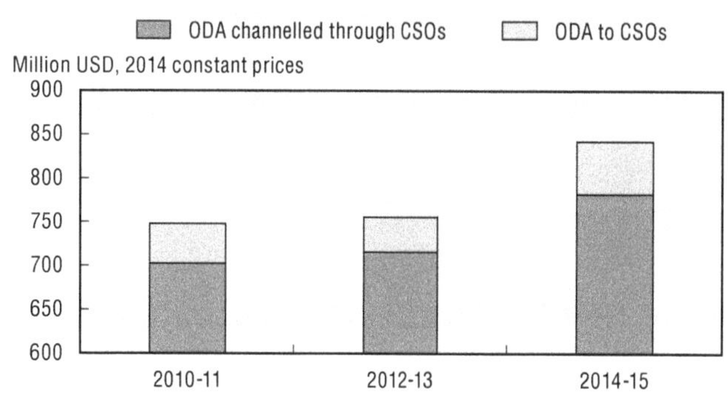

StatLink http://dx.doi.org/10.1787/888933480045

In 2015, bilateral ODA primarily focused on sub-Saharan Africa and the Middle East. USD 944.3 million of bilateral ODA was allocated to sub-Saharan Africa, and USD 379.4 million to the Middle East.

Figure 11.6. **Share of bilateral ODA by region, 2014-15 average, gross disbursements, Canada**

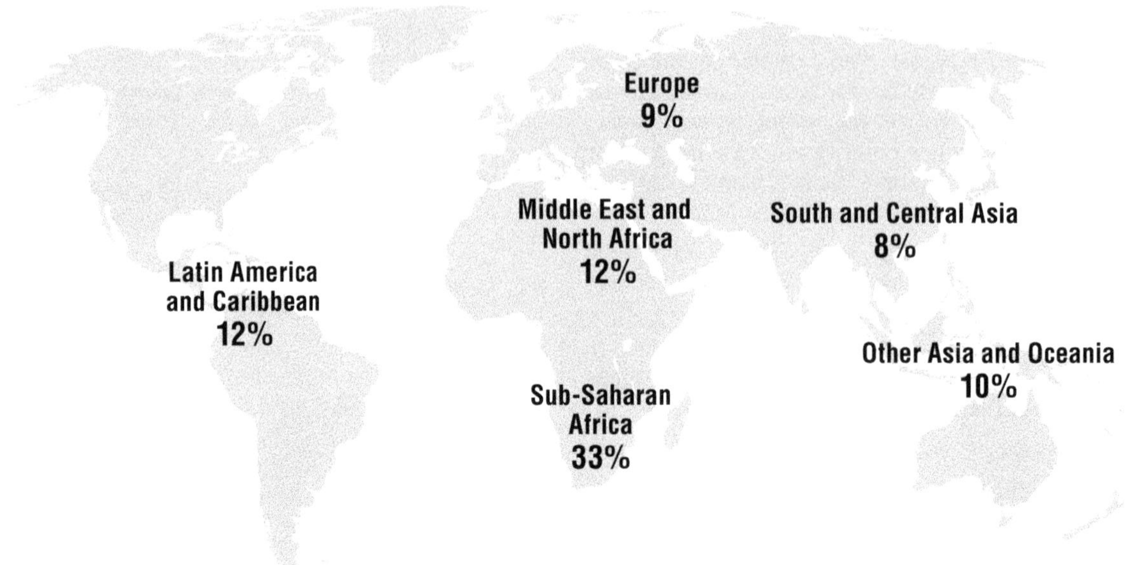

Note: 16% of bilateral ODA allocated was unspecified by region in 2014-15. This share is not represented on the map.

StatLink http://dx.doi.org/10.1787/888933480059

In 2015, 34.9% of bilateral ODA went to Canada's top 10 recipients. Nine of the top 10 recipients of Canadian aid were from Canada's 25 "countries of focus". Its support to fragile contexts reached USD 1.2 billion (40.9% of gross bilateral ODA) in 2015.

Figure 11.7. **Bilateral ODA to top recipients, 2014-15 average, gross disbursements, Canada**

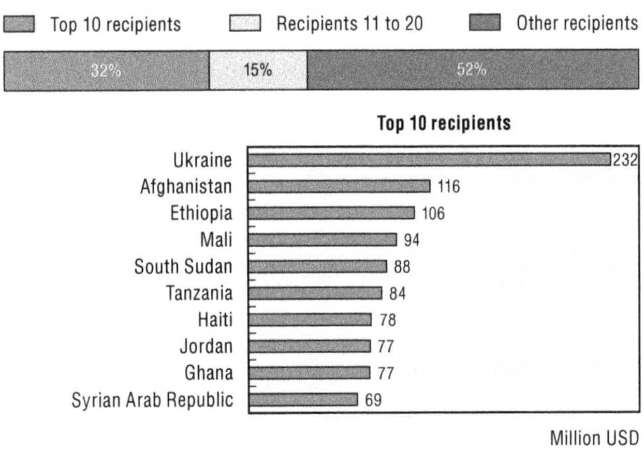

StatLink http://dx.doi.org/10.1787/888933480066

In 2015, 33.1% of bilateral ODA was allocated to least developed countries (LDCs), amounting to USD 998.4 million. The share has increased from 31.3% in 2014 and remains higher than the 2015 DAC average of 24.3%. LDCs received the highest share of bilateral ODA in 2015, noting that 32.9% was unallocated by income group.

At 0.1% of GNI in 2015, total ODA to LDCs was lower than the UN target of 0.15% of GNI.

Figure 11.8. **Bilateral ODA by income group, two year averages, gross disbursements, Canada**

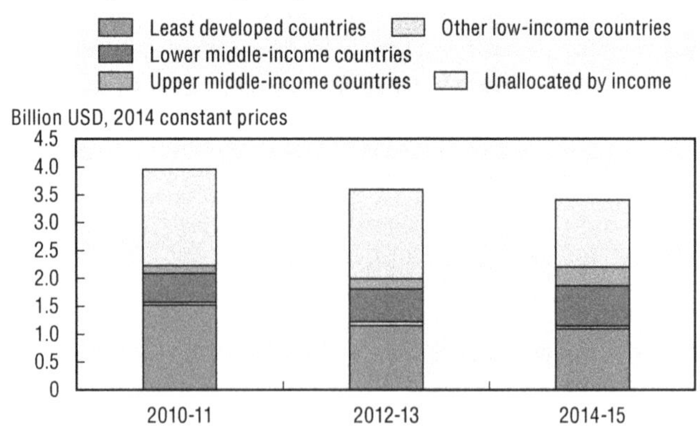

StatLink http://dx.doi.org/10.1787/888933480070

In 2015, 39.7% of bilateral ODA was allocated to social infrastructure and services, amounting to USD 1.4 billion. There was a strong focus on support to health (USD 471 million), government and civil society (USD 351.9 million), and education (USD 292.2 million). Humanitarian aid amounted to USD 631.4 million.

Figure 11.9. **Share of bilateral ODA by sector, 2014-15 average, commitments, Canada**

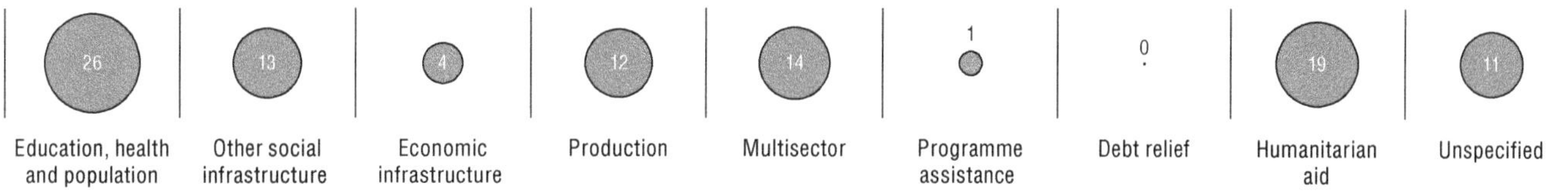

StatLink http://dx.doi.org/10.1787/888933480085

USD 2.2 billion of bilateral ODA supported gender equality and the empowerment of women and girls in 2015. Canada has a long track record of mainstreaming gender equality across its programmes and raising the issue in policy dialogue with partners. In 2015, 71.7% of its bilateral allocable aid had gender equality and the empowerment of women and girls as either a principal or significant objective (up from 60.2% in 2014), compared with the DAC country average of 36.3%. Moving forward, Canada is committed to taking a feminist approach to international assistance, by putting gender equality and the empowerment of all women and girls at the heart of its efforts. A high share of Canada's aid to population and reproductive health focuses on gender.

Figure 11.10. **Share of bilateral allocable ODA in support of gender equality by sector, 2015, commitments, Canada**

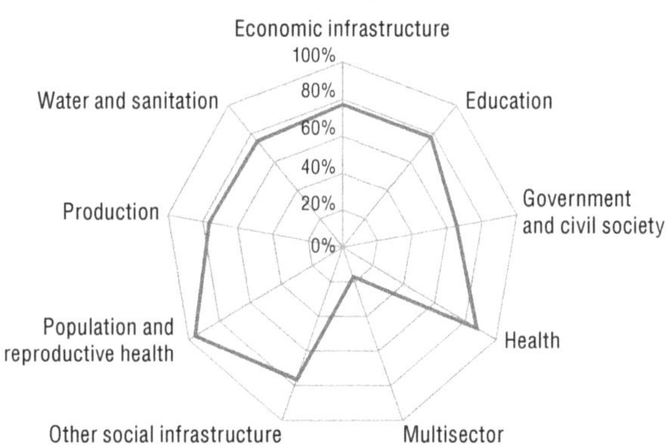

StatLink http://dx.doi.org/10.1787/888933480091

USD 885.6 million of bilateral ODA supported the environment in 2015. Environmental sustainability is a cross-cutting priority for Canada. In 2015, 28.5% of Canadian bilateral allocable aid supported the environment and 10.6% (USD 328.3 million) focused particularly on climate change (up from 4.5% in 2014), compared with the respective DAC country averages of 33.2% and 26.2%.

Figure 11.11. **Bilateral allocable ODA in support of global and local environment objectives, two year averages, commitments, Canada**

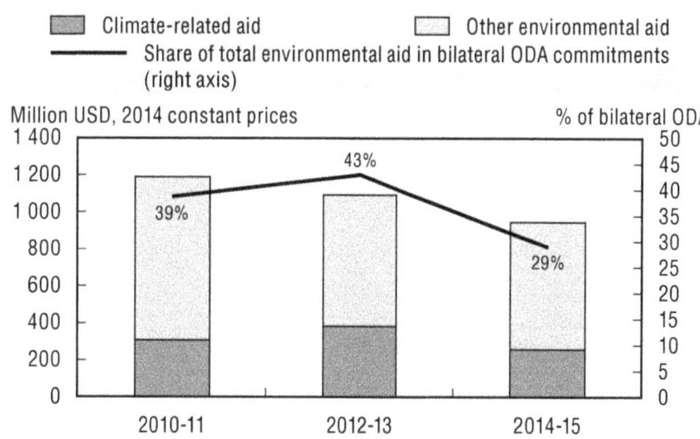

StatLink http://dx.doi.org/10.1787/888933480103

Note to reader: Annex B provides "Methodological notes on the profiles of Development Assistance Committee members".

CZECH REPUBLIC

The Czech Republic's contribution to data for development

The Czech Republic engages in statistical capacity building in developing countries through its State Statistical Office, which participated in several World Bank and European Union projects in 2016. For instance, the Czech State Statistical Office provided expertise within the context of a World Bank project to help Kazakhstan strengthen its national statistical system. It also supported a European Union project to help the modernisation of Azerbaijan's National Statistical System and the alignment of this system with European standards. The Czech State Statistical Office has also provided technical assistance for statistical capacity building in Armenia.

According to the 2017 Partner Report on Support to Statistics (PRESS) dataset, the Czech Republic committed on average USD 0.16 million per year to support national statistical capacities and systems in developing countries in 2013-15.

Financial flows from the Czech Republic to developing countries

Figure 12.1. **Net resource flows to developing countries, 2005-15, Czech Republic**

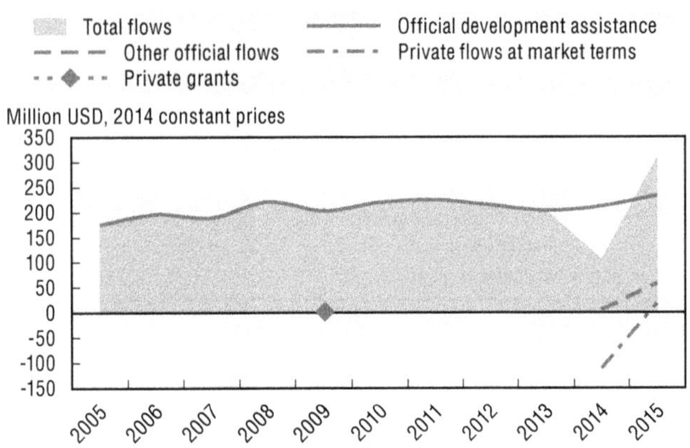

Note: Data on other official flows and private flows at market terms are only available from 2014 onwards. Data on private grants are only available for 2009.

StatLink http://dx.doi.org/10.1787/888933480110

The Czech Republic's use of ODA to mobilise other resources for sustainable development

- **USD 17 945** of official development assistance (ODA) was committed to the mobilisation of domestic resources in developing countries, e.g. to support the development of their tax systems, in 2015.
- **USD 10.4 million of ODA** (+65.3% in real terms from 2014) was committed to promote aid for trade and improve developing countries' trade performance and integration into the world economy in 2015.

The Czech Republic's performance against commitments for effective development co-operation

Table 12.1. **Results of the 2016 Global Partnership monitoring round, Czech Republic**

	Alignment and ownership by partner country (%)				Predictability (%)		Transparency		
	Use of country-led results frameworks	Funding recorded in countries' national budgets	Funding through countries' systems	Untied ODA	Annual predictability	Medium-term predictability	Retrospective statistics (OECD CRS)	Information for forecasting (OECD FSS)	Publishing to IATI
2016	61.1	100.0	0.0	44.3	72.5	66.7	Excellent	Excellent	-
Baseline	-	13.3	6.9	-	100.0	67.5	Good	Good	-
Trend	-	⇑	⇓	-	⇓	⇓	⇑	⇑	-

Note: Please refer to Annex B for details on the indicators.

StatLink http://dx.doi.org/10.1787/888933483019

The Czech Republic's official development assistance

In 2016, the Czech Republic provided USD 261 million in net ODA (preliminary data). This represented 0.14% of gross national income (GNI) and an increase of 29.3% in real terms from 2015, due to the increased contributions to the EU budget for development. It plans to increase its ODA to reach an intermediary target of 0.17% of ODA/GNI by 2020. The 2016 DAC Peer Review of the Czech Republic recommended that it should prepare a more ambitious plan for reaching its commitment of 0.33% ODA/GNI by 2030 (OECD, 2016). Its share of untied ODA (excluding administrative costs and in-donor refugee costs) increased from 32.4% in 2014 to 44.3% in 2015, but is below the 2015 DAC average of 78.1%. The grant element of total ODA was 100% in 2015.

In 2016, in-donor refugee costs were USD 19 million, an increase of 31.6% in real terms over 2015, and represented 7.2% of the Czech Republic's total net ODA.

Figure 12.2. **Net ODA: Trends in volume and as a share of GNI, 2000-16, Czech Republic**

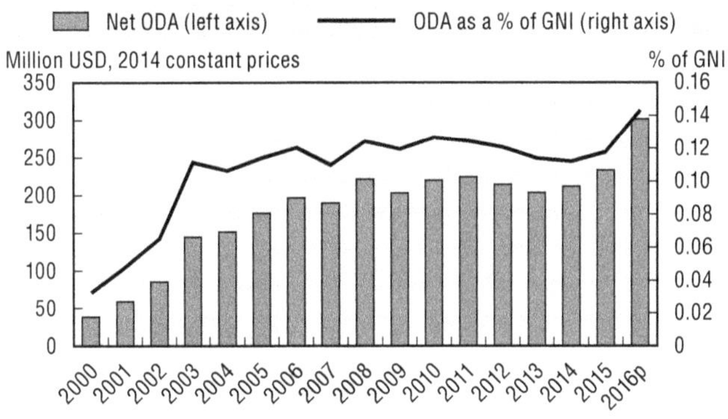

p: Preliminary data.

StatLink http://dx.doi.org/10.1787/888933480124

In 2015, 35.2% of ODA was provided bilaterally. In 2015, the Czech Republic allocated 64.8% of total ODA as core contributions to multilateral organisations, compared with the DAC country average of 26.2%. In addition, it channelled 18.5% of its bilateral ODA for specific projects implemented by multilateral organisations (multi-bi/non-core).

Figure 12.3. **Share of ODA channelled to and through the multilateral system, two year averages, gross disbursements, Czech Republic**

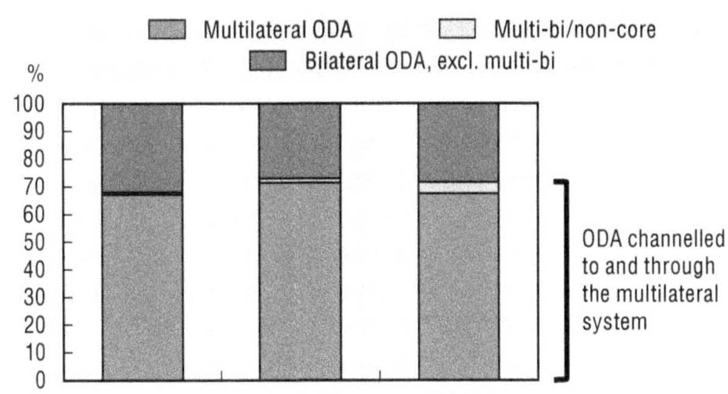

Note: Data on multi-bi/non-core ODA are not available prior to 2011.

StatLink http://dx.doi.org/10.1787/888933480131

In 2015, 58.8% of bilateral ODA was programmed with partner countries. The Czech Republic's share of country programmable aid was above the DAC country average of 48.8% in 2015. Project-type interventions made up 56% of this aid.

Figure 12.4. **Composition of bilateral ODA, 2015, gross disbursements, Czech Republic**

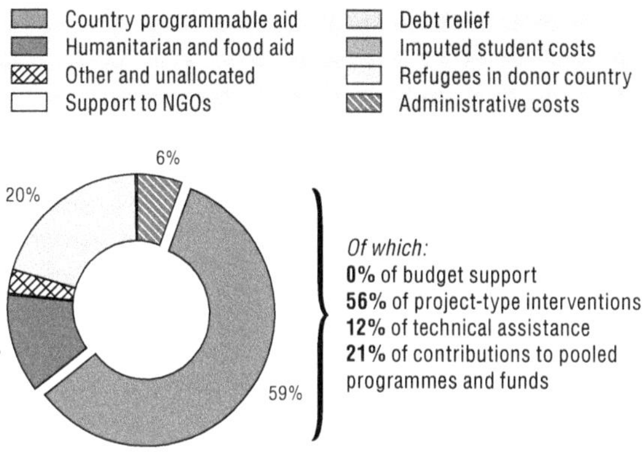

StatLink http://dx.doi.org/10.1787/888933480142

In 2015, USD 15.2 million of bilateral ODA was channelled to and through civil society organisations (CSOs). Between 2014 and 2015, the Czech Republic's ODA channelled to and through CSOs increased in terms of volume (+15%), but decreased as a share of bilateral aid, from 24.6% to 21.6%. This share was higher than the 2015 DAC country average of 16.9%.

Figure 12.5. **Bilateral ODA to and through CSOs, two year averages, gross disbursements, Czech Republic**

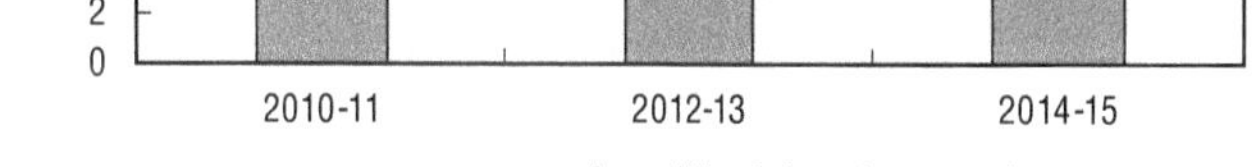

StatLink http://dx.doi.org/10.1787/888933480153

In 2015, bilateral ODA was primarily focused on Eastern Europe, south and central Asia, and the Middle East. USD 20.5 million of bilateral ODA was allocated to Eastern Europe, USD 10.6 million to the Middle East, and USD 8.9 million to south and central Asia.

Figure 12.6. **Share of bilateral ODA by region, 2014-15 average, gross disbursements, Czech Republic**

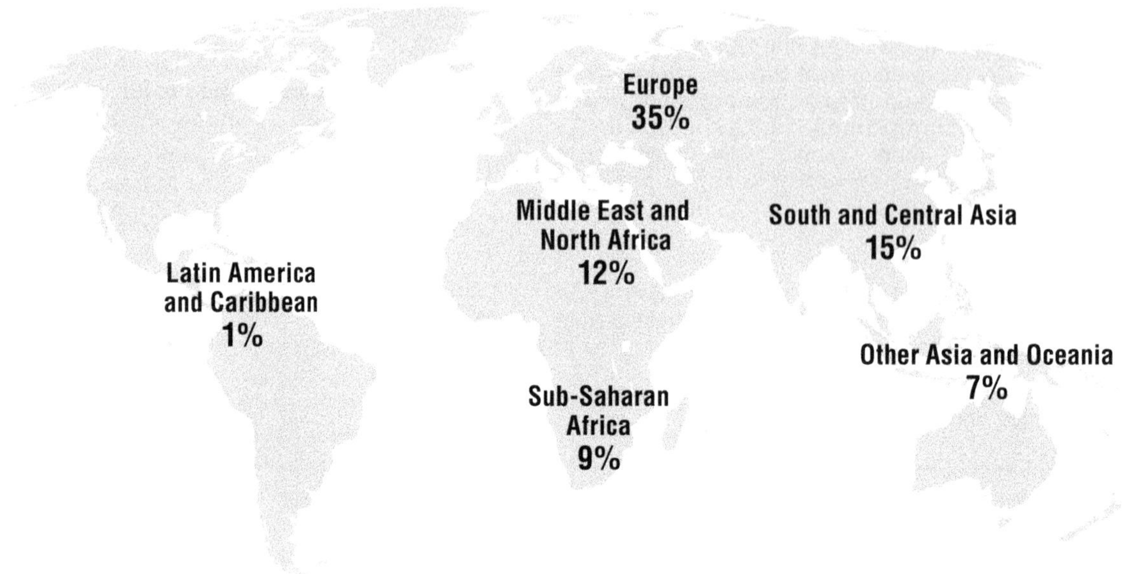

Note: 21% of bilateral ODA allocated was unspecified by region in 2014-15. This share is not represented on the map.

StatLink http://dx.doi.org/10.1787/888933480164

In 2015, 41.9% of bilateral ODA went to the Czech Republic's top 10 recipients. Eight of its priority countries are among its top 10 recipients. Its support to fragile contexts reached USD 14.4 million in 2015 (20.6% of gross bilateral ODA).

Figure 12.7. **Bilateral ODA to top recipients, 2014-15 average, gross disbursements, Czech Republic**

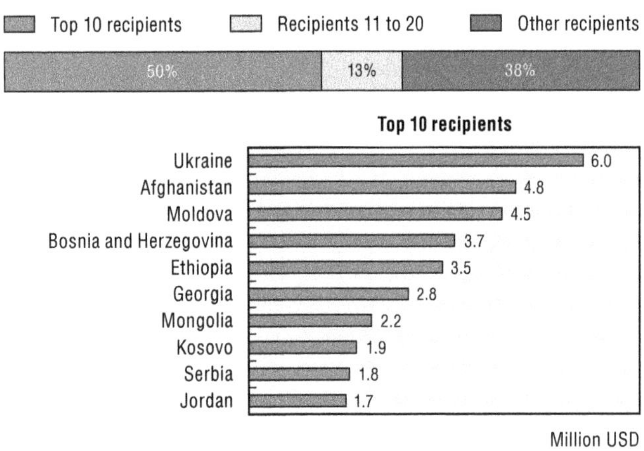

StatLink http://dx.doi.org/10.1787/888933480174

In 2015, 16.4% of bilateral ODA was allocated to least developed countries (LDCs), amounting to USD 11.5 million. The share of ODA to LDCs decreased from 22.9% in 2014 and remains lower than the 2015 DAC average of 24.3%. Lower middle-income countries received the highest share of bilateral ODA in 2015 (24%), noting that 39.8% was unallocated by income group.

At 0.02% of GNI in 2015, total ODA to LDCs was below the UN target of 0.15% of GNI.

Figure 12.8. **Bilateral ODA by income group, two year averages, gross disbursements, Czech Republic**

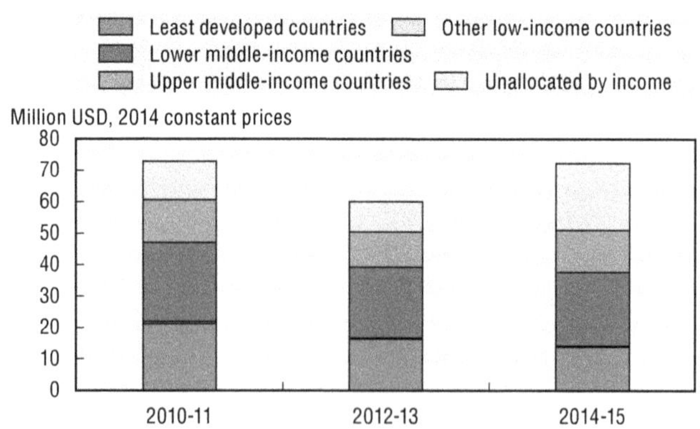

StatLink http://dx.doi.org/10.1787/888933480189

In 2015, 37.3% of bilateral ODA was allocated to social infrastructure and services, amounting to USD 27.1 million, with a strong focus on support to education (USD 9.7 million) and government and civil society (USD 8.7 million). Humanitarian aid amounted to USD 8.6 million.

Figure 12.9. **Share of bilateral ODA by sector, 2014-15 average, commitments, Czech Republic**

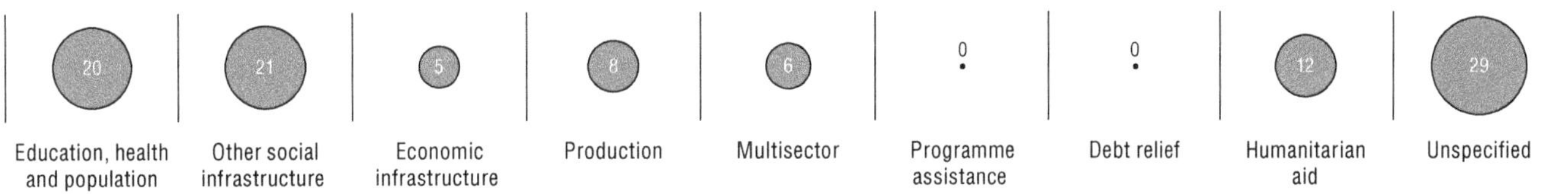

StatLink http://dx.doi.org/10.1787/888933480198

The amount of bilateral ODA that supported gender equality reached USD 5.6 million in 2015. Gender equality is one of the cross-cutting priorities in the Czech Republic's development co-operation. It is trying to develop a methodology for integrating gender equality into projects more systematically (OECD, 2016). In 2015, 14.6% of Czech bilateral allocable aid had gender equality and women's empowerment as a principal or significant objective, compared with the DAC country average of 36.3%. The Czech Republic's aid to health has an important focus on gender.

Figure 12.10. **Share of bilateral allocable ODA in support of gender equality by sector, 2015, commitments, Czech Republic**

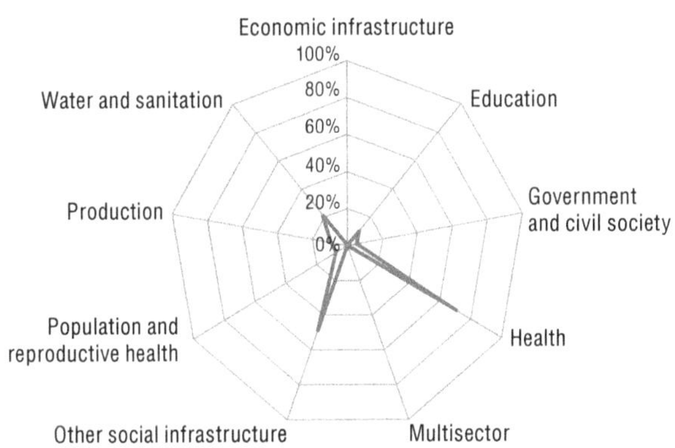

StatLink http://dx.doi.org/10.1787/888933480203

USD 9 million of bilateral ODA supported the environment in 2015. Respect for the environment and the climate are priority cross-cutting issues for the Czech Republic, which screens and monitors projects for their environment focus (OECD, 2016). In 2015, 17.2% of Czech bilateral allocable aid supported the environment (down from 21.1% in 2014) and 11.5% (USD 6 million) focused particularly on climate change, compared with the respective DAC country averages of 33.2% and 26.2%.

Figure 12.11. **Bilateral allocable ODA in support of global and local environment objectives, two year averages, commitments, Czech Republic**

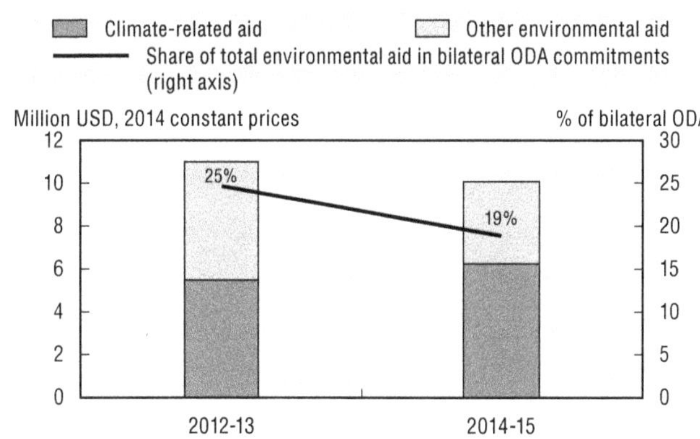

Note: Data are not available prior to 2011.

StatLink http://dx.doi.org/10.1787/888933480216

Note to reader: Annex B provides "Methodological notes on the profiles of Development Assistance Committee members".

Reference

OECD (2016), *OECD Development Co-operation Peer Reviews: Czech Republic 2016*, OECD Publishing, Paris, *http://dx.doi.org/10.1787/9789264264939-en*.

DENMARK

Denmark's contribution to data for development

Supporting statistical capacity building has not been a high priority for Denmark. However, investing in more and better data is increasingly important in line with Denmark's focus on delivering the Sustainable Development Goals and discussions on how to report on these. Denmark offers some support for statistical capacity building with the aim to improve statistical production and promote the use of data by policy makers, civil society and citizens. Statistical capacity building is provided in a few countries through Denmark's support to household surveys.

According to the 2017 Partner Report on Support to Statistics (PRESS) dataset, Denmark committed on average USD 12.72 million per year to finance national statistical capacities and systems in developing countries in 2013-15.

Financial flows from Denmark to developing countries

Figure 13.1. **Net resource flows to developing countries, 2005-15, Denmark**

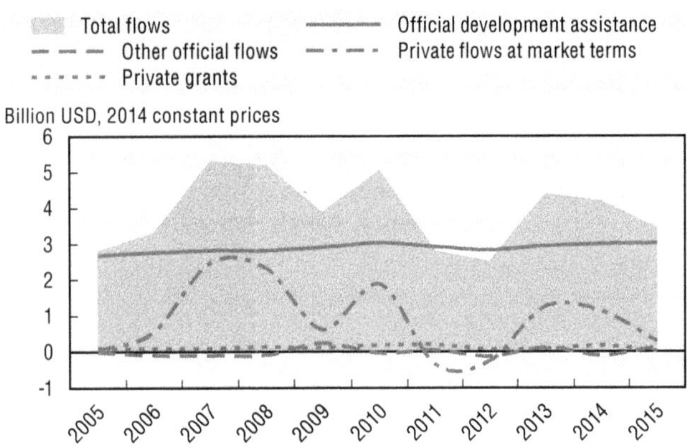

StatLink http://dx.doi.org/10.1787/888933480224

Denmark's use of ODA to mobilise other resources for sustainable development

- **USD 7 million** of official development assistance (ODA) was committed to the mobilisation of domestic resources in developing countries, e.g. to support the development of their tax systems, in 2015.
- **USD 119.8 million** of ODA (-68.2% in real terms from 2014) was committed to promote aid for trade and improve developing countries' trade performance and integration into the world economy in 2015.

Denmark's performance against commitments for effective development co-operation

Table 13.1. **Results of the 2016 Global Partnership monitoring round, Denmark**

	Alignment and ownership by partner country (%)				Predictability (%)		Transparency		
	Use of country-led results frameworks	Funding recorded in countries' national budgets	Funding through countries' systems	Untied ODA	Annual predictability	Medium-term predictability	Retrospective statistics (OECD CRS)	Information for forecasting (OECD FSS)	Publishing to IATI
2016	56.4	86.3	89.1	100.0	77.1	66.7	Needs improvement	Good	Good
Baseline	-	55.8	65.7	100.0	92.1	71.8	Needs improvement	Excellent	-
Trend	-	⇑	⇑	=	⇓	⇓	=	⇓	-

Note: Please refer to Annex B for details on the indicators.

StatLink http://dx.doi.org/10.1787/888933483021

Denmark's official development assistance

In 2016, Denmark provided USD 2.4 billion in net ODA (preliminary data), which represented 0.75% of gross national income (GNI), and a 7.6% decrease in real terms from 2015, due to cuts in its bilateral aid programme. Denmark is one of six DAC members to achieve the UN target of 0.7% ODA/GNI. From 2016, Denmark's ODA is expected to drop to approximately 0.7%, in line with government policy. Denmark's share of untied ODA (excluding administrative costs and in-donor refugee costs) was 100% in 2015 (up from 95.1% in 2014), compared to the DAC average of 78.1%. The grant element of total ODA was 100% in 2015.

In 2016, in-donor refugee costs were USD 420 million, an increase of 5.9% in real terms over 2015, and represented 17.7% of Denmark's total net ODA.

Figure 13.2. **Net ODA: Trends in volume and as a share of GNI, 2000-16, Denmark**

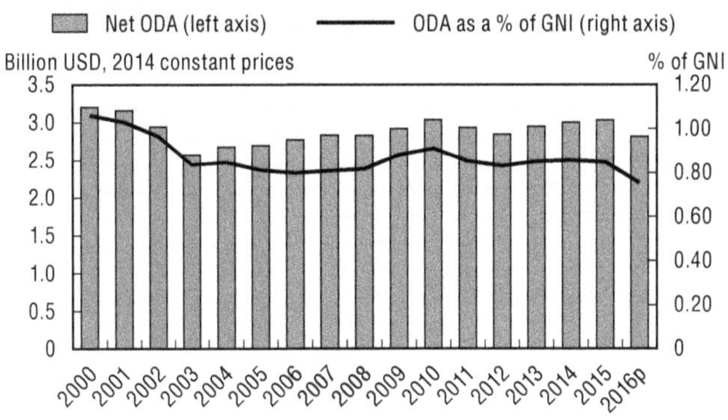

p: Preliminary data.

StatLink http://dx.doi.org/10.1787/888933480238

In 2015, 74.3% of ODA was provided bilaterally. Denmark allocated 25.7% of total ODA as core contributions to multilateral organisations, compared to the DAC country average of 26.2%. In addition, it channelled 18.6% of its bilateral ODA for specific projects implemented by multilateral organisations (multi-bi/non-core).

Figure 13.3. **Share of ODA channelled to and through the multilateral system, two year averages, gross disbursements, Denmark**

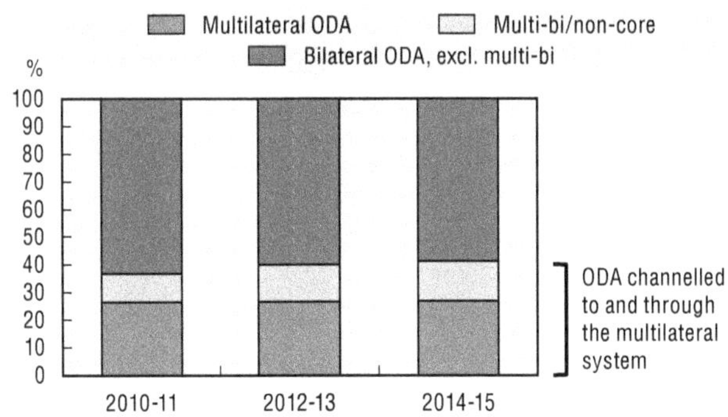

StatLink http://dx.doi.org/10.1787/888933480241

In 2015, 38.2% of bilateral ODA was programmed with partner countries. Denmark's share of country programmable aid was lower than the DAC country average (48.8%). Project-type interventions made up 67.2% of this aid.

Figure 13.4. **Composition of bilateral ODA, 2015, gross disbursements, Denmark**

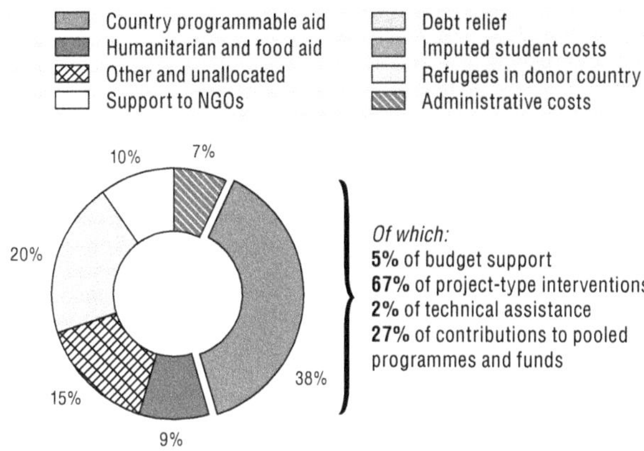

StatLink http://dx.doi.org/10.1787/888933480254

In 2015, USD 424.4 million of bilateral ODA was channelled to and through civil society organisations (CSOs). Denmark channelled 21.4% of its bilateral ODA to and through CSOs in 2015, compared with the DAC country average of 16.9%. Aid to and through CSOs decreased from 2014 both in volume (-4% between 2014 and 2015) and as a share of bilateral ODA (it was 23% in 2014).

Figure 13.5. **Bilateral ODA to and through CSOs, two year averages, gross disbursements, Denmark**

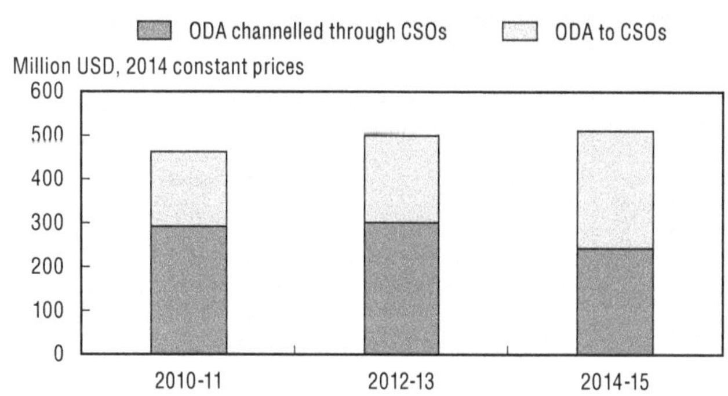

StatLink http://dx.doi.org/10.1787/888933480264

Bilateral ODA was primarily focused on sub-Saharan Africa and south and central Asia. In 2015, Denmark allocated USD 419.5 million to sub-Saharan Africa and USD 164.9 million to south and central Asia.

Figure 13.6. **Share of bilateral ODA by region, 2014-15 average, gross disbursements, Denmark**

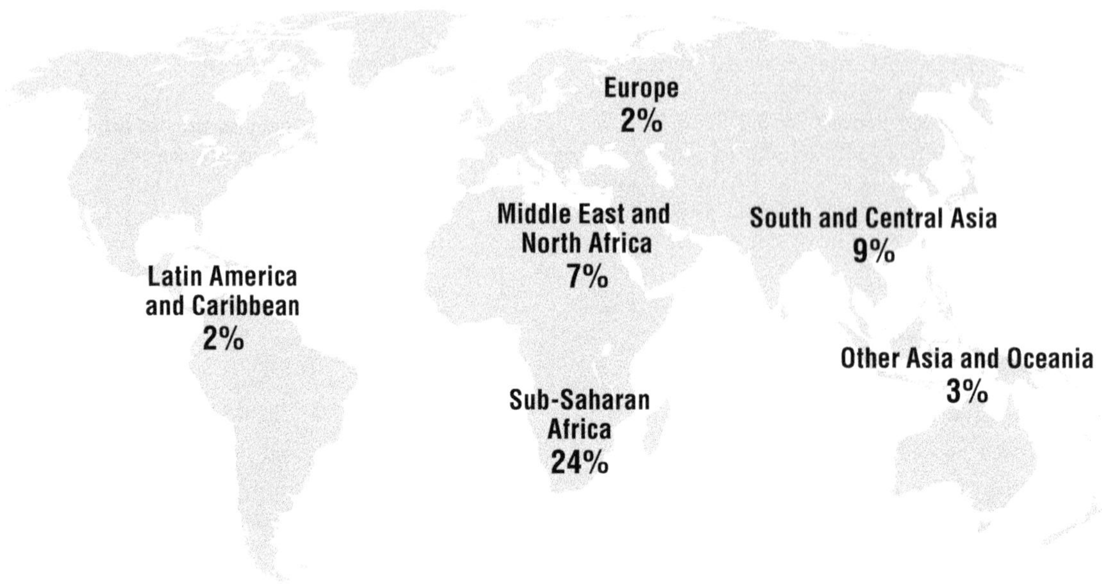

Note: 53% of bilateral ODA allocated was unspecified by region in 2014-15. This share is not represented on the map.

StatLink http://dx.doi.org/10.1787/888933480279

In 2015, 23.5% of bilateral ODA went to Denmark's top 10 recipients. Nine of the top 10 recipients of Danish aid were priority countries, with the exception being the Syrian Arab Republic. In 2015, Denmark had a total of 21 priority countries which was reduced to 14 in 2016. In 2015, its support to fragile contexts reached USD 591.5 million (29.9% of gross bilateral ODA).

Figure 13.7. **Bilateral ODA to top recipients, 2014-15 average, gross disbursements, Denmark**

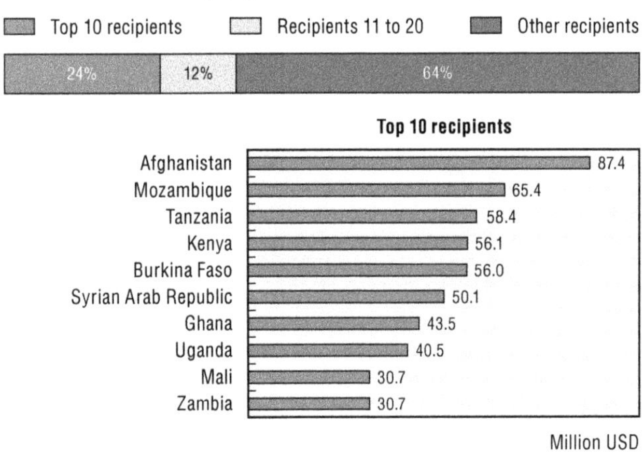

StatLink http://dx.doi.org/10.1787/888933480285

In 2015, 21.7% of bilateral ODA was allocated to least developed countries (LDCs), amounting to USD 429.4 million. This is a decrease from 2013 (30.5%) and 2014 (28.6%) and is now lower than the 2015 DAC average of 24.3%. LDCs still received the highest share of bilateral ODA in 2015, noting that 60.6% was unallocated by income group.

At 0.20% of GNI in 2015, total ODA to LDCs was above the UN target of 0.15% of GNI.

Figure 13.8. **Bilateral ODA by income group, two year averages, gross disbursements, Denmark**

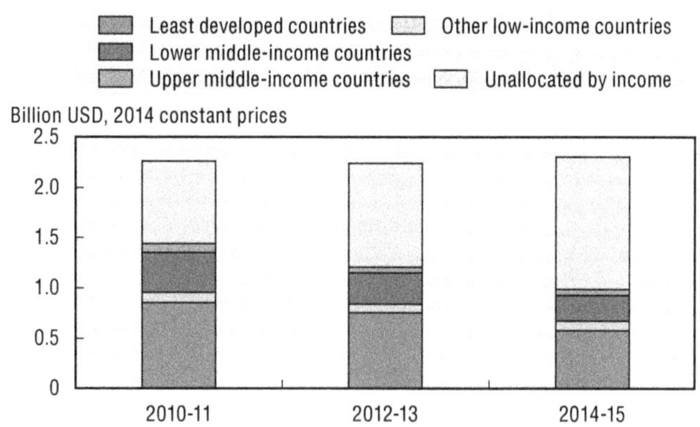

StatLink http://dx.doi.org/10.1787/888933480290

In 2015, 34.5% of bilateral ODA was allocated to social infrastructure and services, reaching USD 641.8 million. There was a strong focus on support to government and civil society (USD 446.8 million) and education (USD 96.4 million). USD 220.9 million was allocated to humanitarian aid.

Figure 13.9. **Share of bilateral ODA by sector, 2014-15 average, commitments, Denmark**

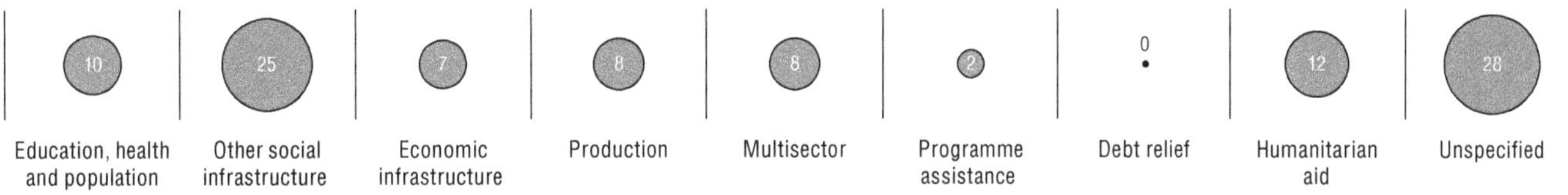

StatLink http://dx.doi.org/10.1787/888933480302

USD 698.4 million of bilateral ODA supported gender equality in 2015. Advancing gender equality and women's rights is a major strategic priority for Denmark. In line with the overall 2014 Strategy for Denmark's Development Co-operation (*The Right to a Better Life*), the Strategic Framework for Gender Equality, Rights and Diversity is integrated across Denmark's four priority areas: human rights and democracy, inclusive green growth, social progress, and stability and protection. In 2015, 56.8% of Danish bilateral allocable aid had gender equality and women's empowerment as a principal or significant objective, compared with the DAC country average of 36.3%. It is, however, lower than in 2014 (59.5%). Denmark's aid to population and reproductive health, health and other social infrastructure also focuses on gender.

Figure 13.10. **Share of bilateral allocable ODA in support of gender equality by sector, 2015, commitments, Denmark**

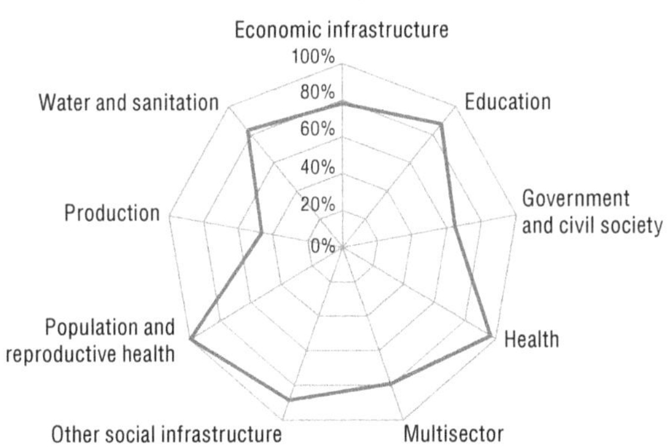

StatLink http://dx.doi.org/10.1787/888933480310

USD 305.8 million of bilateral ODA supported the environment in 2015. Promoting inclusive green growth based on the sustainable management and use of natural resources is one of four overall goals for Danish development co-operation. In 2015, 22.7% of Danish bilateral allocable aid supported the environment and 16.3% (USD 219.7 million) focused particularly on climate change, compared with the respective DAC country averages of 33.2% and 26.2%.

Figure 13.11. **Bilateral allocable ODA in support of global and local environment objectives, two year averages, commitments, Denmark**

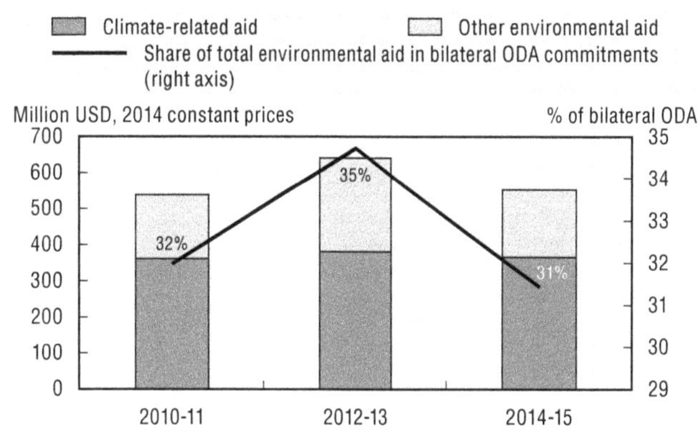

StatLink http://dx.doi.org/10.1787/888933480320

Note to reader: Annex B provides "Methodological notes on the profiles of Development Assistance Committee members".

Reference

OECD (2016), *OECD Development Co-operation Peer Reviews: Denmark 2016*, OECD Publishing, Paris, *http://dx.doi.org/10.1787/9789264259362-en*.

EUROPEAN UNION INSTITUTIONS

The European Union institutions' contribution to data for development

Strengthening partner country statistical capacities is part of the overall capacity-building activities of the European Union, which emphasises the need for reliable statistics for macroeconomic management, project management and the evaluation of objectives, for example for budget support programmes. The EU's statistical capacity-building activities in developing countries focus mostly on improving statistical production, strengthening data dissemination and improving co-ordination among development partners. Support focuses, in particular, on statistics for key societal variables which are often needed as performance indicators in budget support programmes – but also on trade and fiscal statistics. Support is provided mainly through funding for equipment and technical assistance.

According to the 2017 Partner Report on Support to Statistics (PRESS) dataset, the European Commission committed on average USD 51.74 million per year to finance national statistical capacities and systems in developing countries in 2013-15.

Financial flows from the European Union institutions to developing countries

Figure 14.1. **Net resource flows to developing countries, 2005-15, EU institutions**

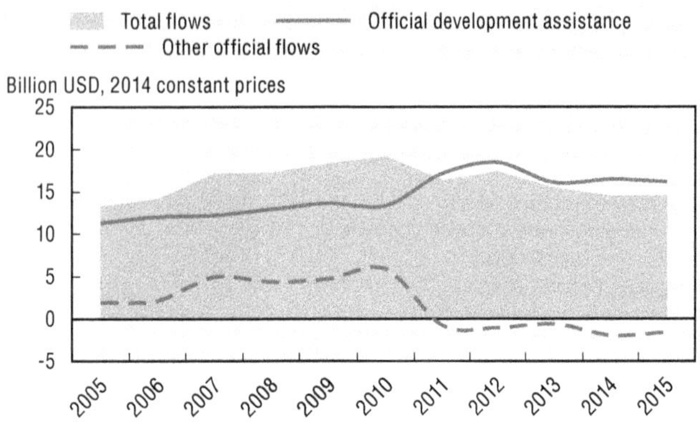

StatLink http://dx.doi.org/10.1787/888933480332

The European Union institutions' use of ODA to mobilise other resources for sustainable development

- **USD 0.17 million** of official development assistance (ODA) was committed to the mobilisation of domestic resources in developing countries, e.g. to support the development of their tax systems, in 2015.
- **USD 6.7 billion** of ODA (+6% in real terms from 2014) was committed to promote aid for trade and improve developing countries' trade performance and integration into the world economy in 2015.

The European Union institutions' performance against commitments for effective development co-operation

Table 14.1. **Results of the 2016 Global Partnership monitoring round, EU institutions**

	Alignment and ownership by partner country (%)				Predictability (%)		Transparency		
	Use of country-led results frameworks	Funding recorded in countries' national budgets	Funding through countries' systems	Untied ODA	Annual predictability	Medium-term predictability	Retrospective statistics (OECD CRS)	Information for forecasting (OECD FSS)	Publishing to IATI
2016	70.3	60.2	45.0	62.3	72.6	84.6	Good	Excellent	Good
Baseline	-	67.8	47.9	47.7	87.3	69.4	Good	Good	-
Trend	-	⇓	⇓	⇑	⇓	⇑	=	⇑	-

Note: Please refer to Annex B for details on the indicators.

StatLink http://dx.doi.org/10.1787/888933483037

The European Union institutions' official development assistance

In 2016, the EU institutions provided USD 15.7 billion in net ODA (preliminary data), which represented a 14.3% increase in real terms from 2015, mostly due to increased bilateral projects with developing countries and increased humanitarian aid. The EU institutions' ODA budget is determined within the EU multi-year financial framework. The EU institutions' share of untied ODA (excluding administrative costs and in-donor refugee costs) was 62.3% in 2015 (down from 65.6% in 2014).

Figure 14.2. **Net ODA: Trends in volume, 2000-16, EU institutions**

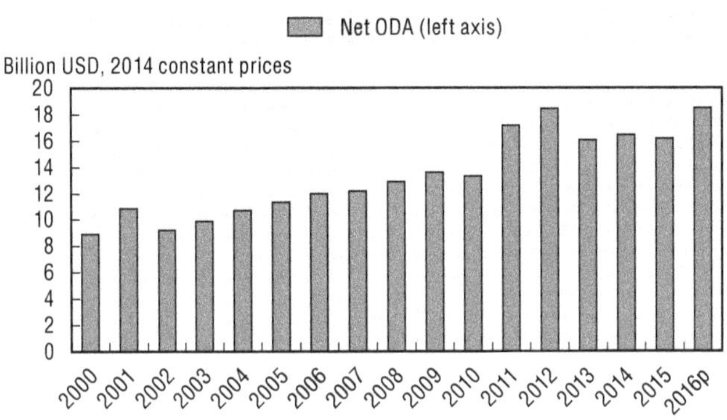

p: Preliminary data.

StatLink http://dx.doi.org/10.1787/888933480346

In 2015, almost all of the EU's gross ODA (99.1%) was provided bilaterally. The EU channelled 16.1% of its bilateral ODA for projects implemented by multilateral organisations (multi-bi/non-core).

Figure 14.3. **Share of ODA channelled to and through the multilateral system, two year averages, gross disbursements, EU institutions**

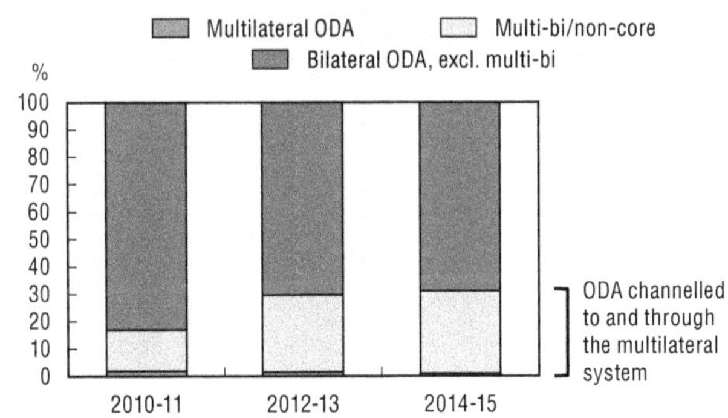

StatLink http://dx.doi.org/10.1787/888933480354

In 2015, 52.6% of the EU institutions' bilateral ODA was programmed with partner countries. Project-type interventions accounted for 65.1% of country programmable aid, while budget support accounted for 22%. Thirty-one per cent of bilateral ODA was categorised as "other and unallocated".

Figure 14.4. **Composition of bilateral ODA, 2015, gross disbursements, EU institutions**

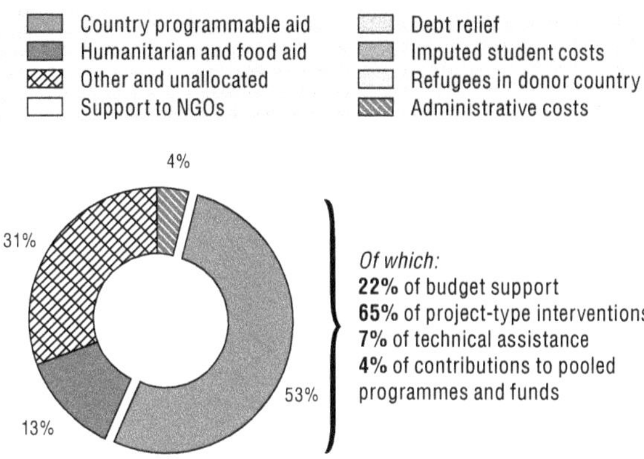

StatLink http://dx.doi.org/10.1787/888933480361

In 2015, USD 1.8 billion of bilateral ODA was channelled to and through civil society organisations (CSOs), corresponding to 11.6% of bilateral ODA. Between 2014 and 2015, aid to and through CSOs decreased in terms of volume (by -2.4%), but it remained relatively stable as a share of bilateral aid.

Figure 14.5. **Bilateral ODA to and through CSOs, two year averages, gross disbursements, EU institutions**

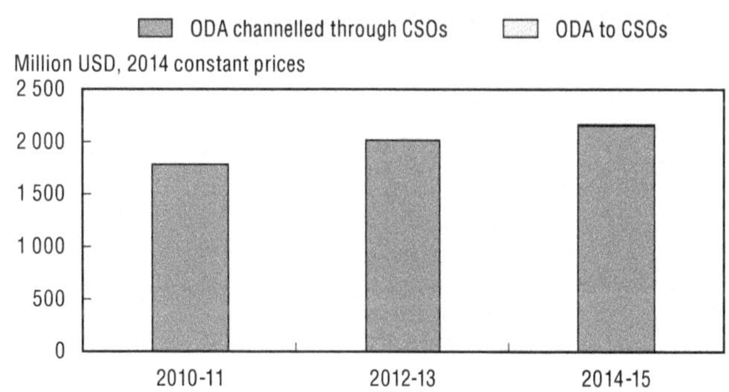

Note: Data on CSOs are not available for 2010-11.

StatLink http://dx.doi.org/10.1787/888933480370

Bilateral ODA focused primarily on Eastern Europe and sub-Saharan Africa. In 2015, USD 4.4 billion was allocated to Eastern Europe and USD 4 billion to sub-Saharan Africa.

Figure 14.6. **Share of bilateral ODA by region, 2014-15 average, gross disbursements, EU institutions**

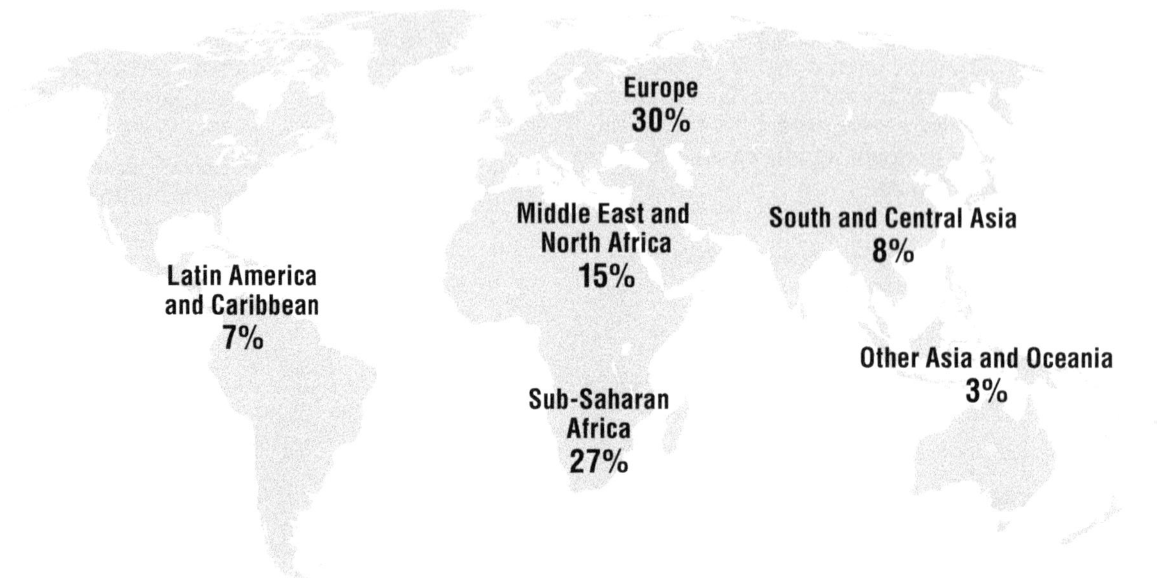

Note: 9% of bilateral ODA allocated was unspecified by region in 2014-15. This share is not represented on the map.

StatLink http://dx.doi.org/10.1787/888933480389

In 2015, 35.2% of bilateral ODA went to the top 10 recipients. The European Union has specific agreements and instruments with 79 African, Caribbean and Pacific countries, and 9 European accession countries. In 2015, its support to fragile contexts reached USD 5 billion (32.1% of gross bilateral ODA).

Figure 14.7. **Bilateral ODA to top recipients, 2014-15 average, gross disbursements, EU institutions**

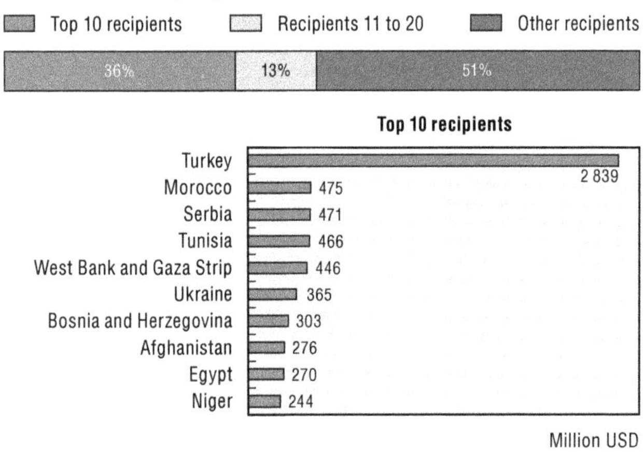

StatLink http://dx.doi.org/10.1787/888933480395

In 2015, 22.4% of bilateral ODA was allocated to least developed countries (LDCs), which amounted to USD 3.5 billion. The share decreased from 24.7% in 2014. Upper middle-income countries still received the highest share of bilateral ODA in 2015 (37.2%). This is partly due to the instrument for pre-accession with nine European countries.

Figure 14.8. **Bilateral ODA by income group, two year averages, gross disbursements, EU institutions**

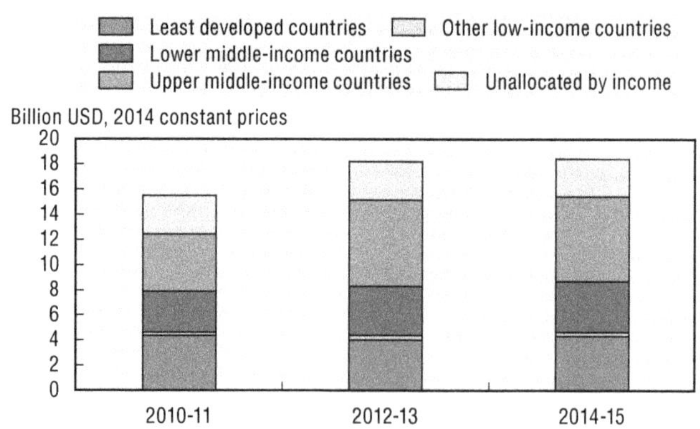

StatLink http://dx.doi.org/10.1787/888933480406

In 2015, 24.3% of bilateral ODA was allocated to social and economic infrastructure and services (USD 4.8 billion), with a strong focus on government and civil society (USD 3 billion). Twenty-four per cent of bilateral ODA was allocated to economic infrastructure and services, with a focus on energy generation and supply (USD 1.7 billion), and banking and financial services (USD 1.6 billion). USD 2 billion was allocated to humanitarian aid.

Figure 14.9. **Share of bilateral ODA by sector, 2014-15 average, commitments, EU institutions**

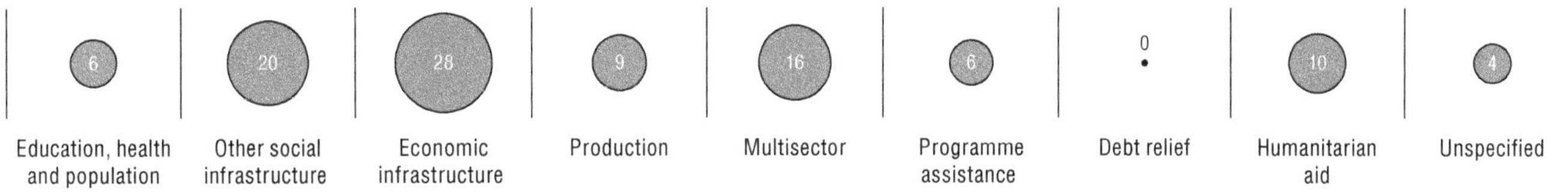

StatLink http://dx.doi.org/10.1787/888933480418

USD 7 billion of bilateral ODA supported gender equality in 2015. The EU's commitment to promoting gender equality continues to grow. Its new Gender Action Plan (GAP II) for 2016-20 aims to place gender equality and the empowerment of girls and women at the heart of the EU's external actions, focusing on four priority areas: ensuring girls' and women's physical and psychological integrity, promoting their economic and social rights, strengthening their voice and participation, and changing the EU institutional culture to integrate gender equality as a shared responsibility in all external relations activities and initiatives. In 2015, 52.7% of the EU's bilateral allocable aid had gender equality and women's empowerment as a principal or significant objective, compared to 17.4% in 2014.

Figure 14.10. **Share of bilateral allocable ODA in support of gender equality by sector, 2015, commitments, EU institutions**

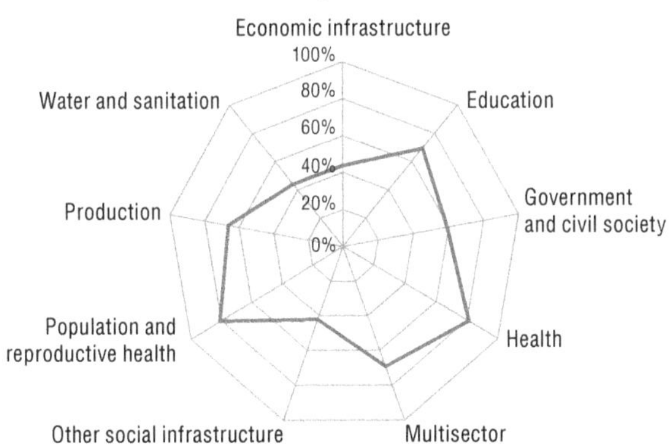

StatLink http://dx.doi.org/10.1787/888933480429

USD 3.8 billion of bilateral ODA supported the environment in 2015. This represented 20.8% of bilateral allocable aid (up from 14% in 2014). The EU institutions' tools and services developed to support mainstreaming in its programme include guidance documents, systematic screening and review of action documents, quality control on the use of Rio markers, training seminars and technical assistance, in addition to the knowledge-sharing platform available on Capacity4Dev. In line with the 2030 Agenda for Sustainable Development and the UN Paris Agreement on Climate Change, the EU has undertaken to step up its efforts to integrate environment and climate change into EU co-operation, through the development of new guidelines, enhanced engagement with EU delegations in partner countries and continued support to partner countries, notably through the new phase of the EU Global Climate Change Alliance flagship initiative (GCCA+) and the UN Poverty-Environment Initiative. In 2015, 17.5% (USD 3.2 billion) of the EU's bilateral allocable aid focused particularly on climate change.

Figure 14.11. **Bilateral allocable ODA in support of global and local environment objectives, two year averages, commitments, EU institutions**

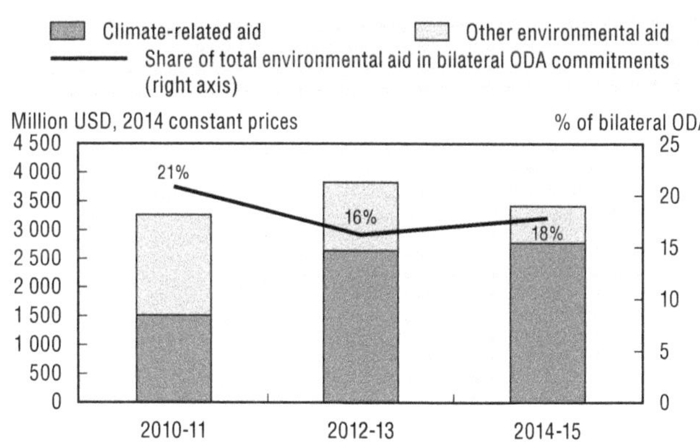

StatLink http://dx.doi.org/10.1787/888933480439

Note to reader: Annex B provides "Methodological notes on the profiles of Development Assistance Committee members".

FINLAND

Finland's contribution to data for development

According to the 2017 Partner Report on Support to Statistics (PRESS) dataset, Finland committed on average USD 1.51 million per year to finance national statistical capacities and systems in developing countries in 2013-15.

Financial flows from Finland to developing countries

Figure 15.1. **Net resource flows to developing countries, 2005-15, Finland**

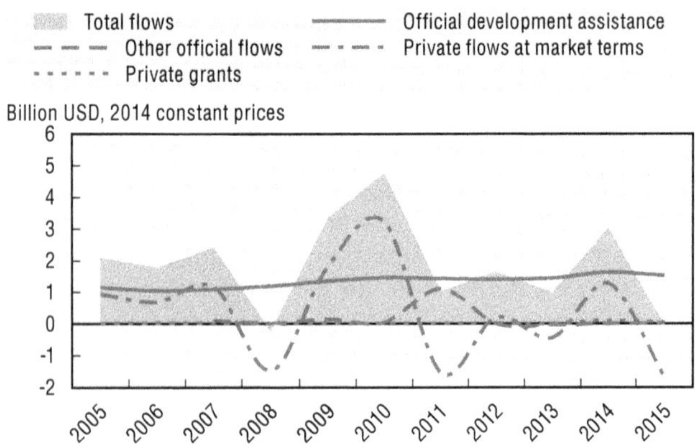

Note: Data on other official flows are not available for 2005 or 2006.

StatLink http://dx.doi.org/10.1787/888933480443

Finland's use of ODA to mobilise other resources for sustainable development

- **USD 7.1 million** of official development assistance (ODA) was committed to the mobilisation of domestic resources in developing countries, e.g. to support the development of their tax systems, in 2015.
- **USD 89.2 million of ODA** (-36.3% in real terms from 2014) was committed to promote aid for trade and improve developing countries' trade performance and integration into the world economy in 2015.

Finland's performance against commitments for effective development co-operation

Table 15.1. **Results of the 2016 Global Partnership monitoring round, Finland**

	Alignment and ownership by partner country (%)				Predictability (%)		Transparency		
	Use of country-led results frameworks	Funding recorded in countries' national budgets	Funding through countries' systems	Untied ODA	Annual predictability	Medium-term predictability	Retrospective statistics (OECD CRS)	Information for forecasting (OECD FSS)	Publishing to IATI
2016	67.0	60.7	37.3	92.6	92.7	43.7	Fair	Good	Needs improvement
Baseline	-	63.3	56.7	89.4	82.8	64.5	Fair	Excellent	-
Trend	-	⇓	⇓	⇑	⇑	⇓	=	⇓	-

Note: Please refer to Annex B for details on the indicators.

StatLink http://dx.doi.org/10.1787/888933483046

Finland's official development assistance

In 2016, Finland provided USD 1.1 billion in net ODA (preliminary data), which represented 0.44% of gross national income (GNI) and a fall of 18.7% in real terms from 2015 due to cuts in the ODA budget, which were partly offset by increases in its contributions to the EU development budget and in-donor refugee costs. At the same time, Finland, like other EU member countries, committed in 2015 to provide 0.7% of GNI as ODA by 2030. The share of Finnish ODA that is untied (excluding administrative costs and in-donor refugee costs) has slightly increased, from 90.4% in 2014 to 92.6% in 2015, compared to the 2015 DAC average of 78.1%. The grant element of total ODA was 100% in 2015.

In 2016, in-donor refugee costs were USD 130 million, an increase of 230.5% in real terms over 2015, and represented 12.3% of Finland's total net ODA.

Figure 15.2. **Net ODA: Trends in volume and as a share of GNI, 2000-16, Finland**

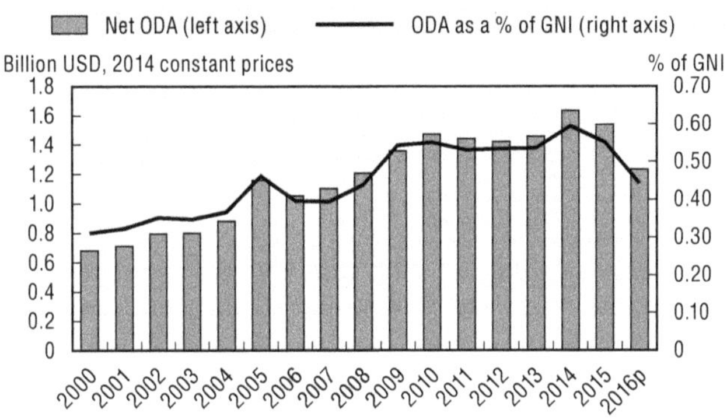

p: Preliminary data.

StatLink http://dx.doi.org/10.1787/888933480459

In 2015, 54.9% of ODA was provided bilaterally. Finland allocated 45.1% of total ODA as core contributions to multilateral organisations, above the DAC country average of 26.2%. In addition, it channelled 31.6% of its bilateral ODA for specific projects implemented by multilateral organisations (multi-bi/non-core).

Figure 15.3. **Share of ODA channelled to and through the multilateral system, two year averages, gross disbursements, Finland**

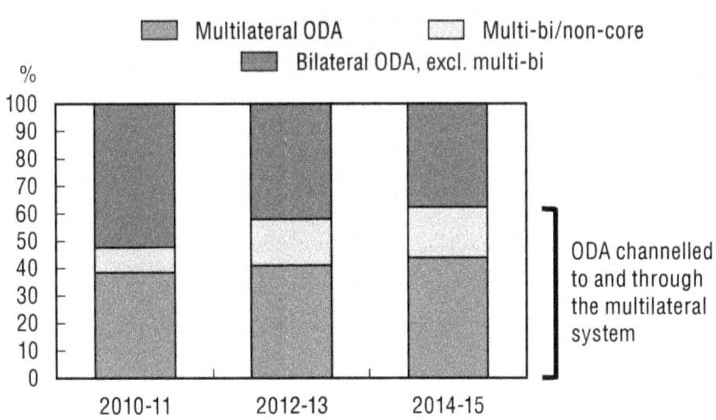

StatLink http://dx.doi.org/10.1787/888933480468

In 2015, 49% of bilateral ODA was programmed with partner countries. Finland's share of country programmable aid was above the DAC country average (48.8%) in 2015. Project-type interventions accounted for 66.3% of this aid.

Figure 15.4. **Composition of bilateral ODA, 2015, gross disbursements, Finland**

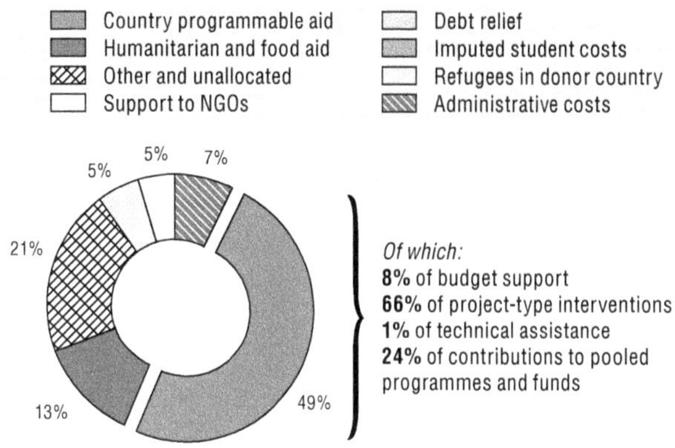

StatLink http://dx.doi.org/10.1787/888933480470

In 2015, USD 193.2 million of bilateral ODA was channelled to and through civil society organisations (CSOs). ODA channelled to and through CSOs increased between 2014 and 2015 both in terms of volume (+7.4%) and as a share of bilateral aid (from 22.9% in 2014 to 26.9% in 2015). The share provided in 2015 is higher than the DAC average of 16.9%.

Figure 15.5. **Bilateral ODA to and through CSOs, two year averages, gross disbursements, Finland**

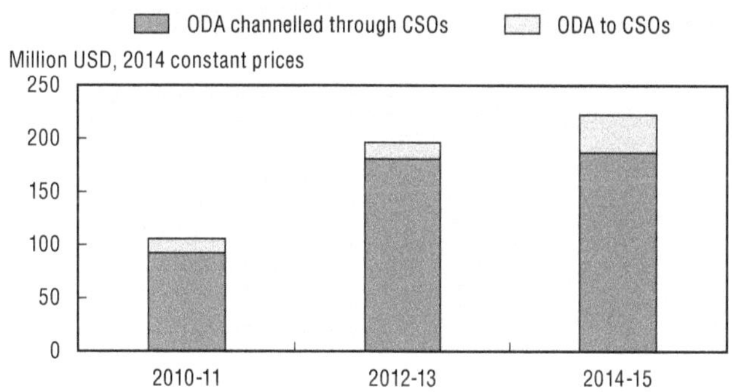

StatLink http://dx.doi.org/10.1787/888933480487

Bilateral ODA was primarily focused on sub-Saharan Africa and south and central Asia. In 2015, USD 222.9 million was allocated to sub-Saharan Africa and USD 82.9 million to south and central Asia.

Figure 15.6. **Share of bilateral ODA by region, 2014-15 average, gross disbursements, Finland**

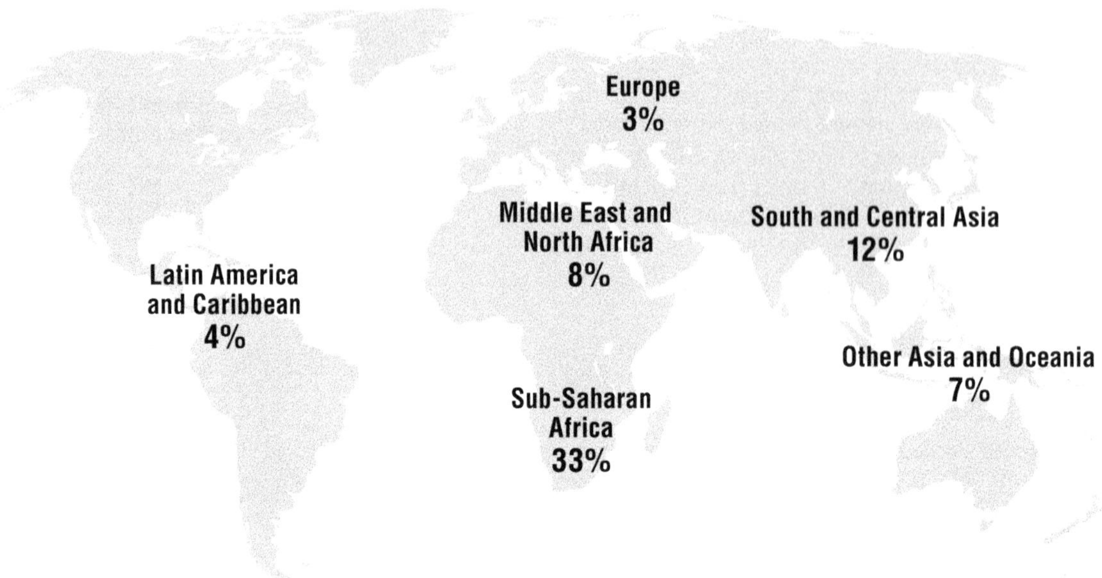

Note: 33% of bilateral ODA allocated was unspecified by region in 2014-15. This share is not represented on the map.

StatLink http://dx.doi.org/10.1787/888933480491

In 2015, 31.6% of bilateral ODA went to Finland's top 10 recipients. Eight of its nine long-term partner countries are among its top 10 recipients of bilateral ODA. In 2015, Finland's support to fragile contexts reached USD 278.3 million (38.8% of gross bilateral ODA).

Figure 15.7. **Bilateral ODA to top recipients, 2014-15 average, gross disbursements, Finland**

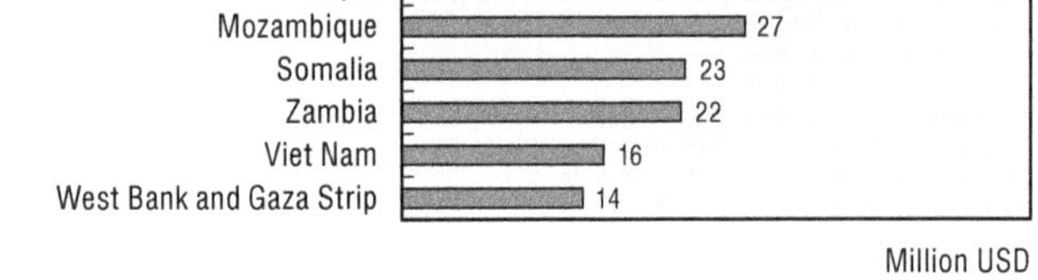

StatLink http://dx.doi.org/10.1787/888933480504

The share of bilateral ODA that was allocated to least developed countries (LDCs) was 32.8%, amounting to USD 235.7 million in 2015. The share decreased from 34.7% in 2014, but remains higher than the 2015 DAC average of 24.3%. LDCs received the highest share of bilateral ODA compared with other income groups in 2014, noting that 45.8% was unallocated by income group.

At 0.18% of GNI in 2015, total ODA to LDCs was above the UN target of 0.15% of GNI.

Figure 15.8. **Bilateral ODA by income group, two year averages, gross disbursements, Finland**

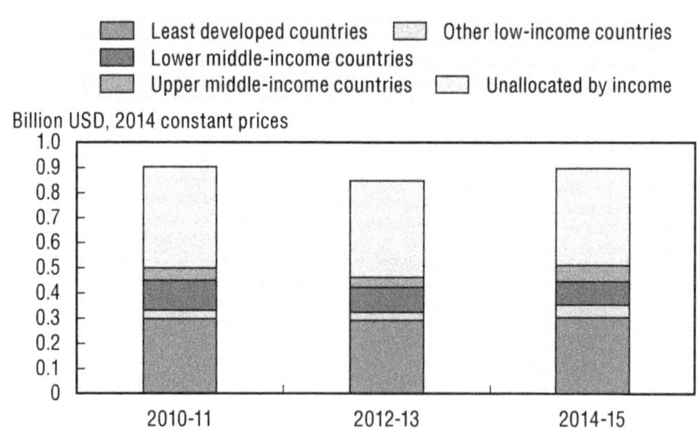

StatLink http://dx.doi.org/10.1787/888933480516

In 2015, 45.6% of bilateral ODA was allocated to social infrastructure and services, amounting to USD 262.8 million, with a strong focus on support to government and civil society (USD 117.7 million) and education (USD 72.4 million). USD 75.2 million was allocated to humanitarian aid.

Figure 15.9. **Share of bilateral ODA by sector, 2014-15 average, commitments, Finland**

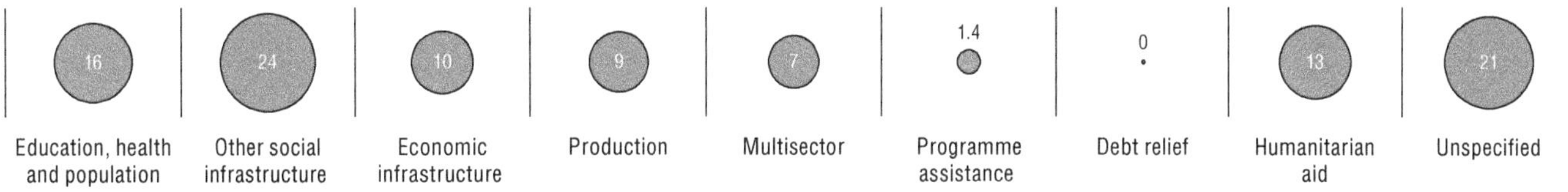

StatLink http://dx.doi.org/10.1787/888933480528

USD 235.1 million of bilateral ODA supported gender equality in 2015. Gender equality is mainstreamed across Finland's development programme, and the rights and status of women and girls feature as one of Finland's four priority areas in its 2016 development policy. Finland strives to ensure that women and girls are better educated with diversified skills; have better access to high-quality basic services; have more opportunities to influence decision making; and have greater agency over their own lives. In 2015, 49.9% of its bilateral allocable aid had gender equality and women's empowerment as a principal or significant objective, compared with the DAC country average of 36.3%. This is an increase from 44% in 2014. A high share of Finland's aid to water and sanitation and education focuses on gender.

Figure 15.10. **Share of bilateral allocable ODA in support of gender equality by sector, 2015, commitments, Finland**

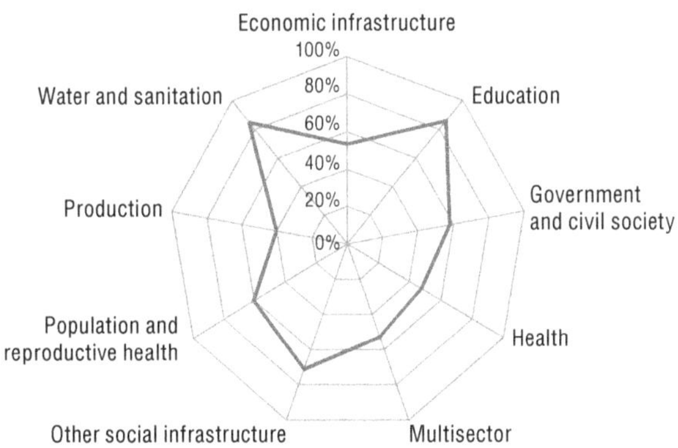

StatLink http://dx.doi.org/10.1787/888933480532

USD 98.6 million of bilateral ODA supported the environment in 2015. Sustainable use of natural resources, including food security and access to water and energy, is one of the four priorities of Finland's development policy updated in 2016. This priority is in line with Sustainable Development Goals 2, 6, 7, 13 and 15. Adaptation and mitigation measures to climate change are an important part of this work. In 2015, 20.9% of Finland's bilateral allocable aid focused on the environment and 15.2% (USD 71.9 million) focused on climate change, compared with respective DAC country averages of 33.2% and 26.2%. There was a sharp decrease in the share and volume of total aid supporting the environment between 2010-11 and 2012-13.

Figure 15.11. **Bilateral allocable ODA in support of global and local environment objectives, two year averages, commitments, Finland**

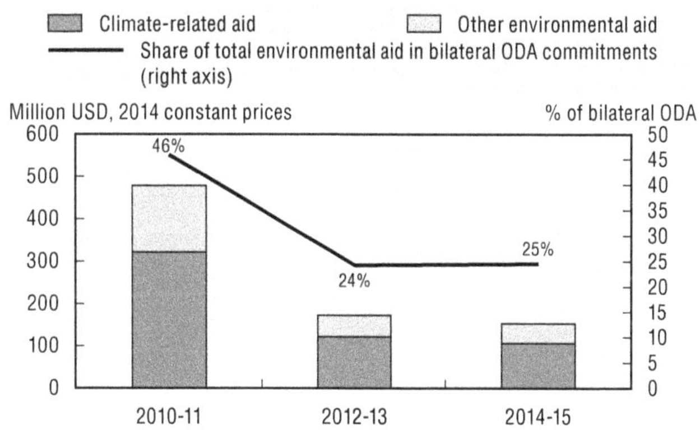

StatLink http://dx.doi.org/10.1787/888933480546

Note to reader: Annex B provides "Methodological notes on the profiles of Development Assistance Committee members".

FRANCE

France's contribution to data for development

Investing in having more and better data for sustainable development is becoming a greater priority for France's development co-operation. France engages in statistical capacity building through the multilateral and bilateral channels with the objective to strengthen statistical production, data dissemination, and statistical literacy and to advocate and promote the use of data for better decision making. France supports developing countries' national statistical systems through technical assistance and funding for equipment, but also through direct financing to national statistical offices.

France has started to look at the potential contribution of big data to development co-operation. For instance, the Agence Française de Développement supports the Open Algorithms (OPAL) Project through a EUR 1.5 million grant in 2017 for projects in Colombia and Senegal. This project aims to unleash the power of big data held by private companies for the public good. OPAL provides an open platform and algorithms that can be run on the servers of business partners to extract accurate, timely and reliable key development indicators that are relevant for a wide range of potential users, while at the same time preserving privacy at multiple levels: personal, group/community and commercial.

According to the 2017 Partner Report on Support to Statistics (PRESS) dataset, France committed on average USD 0.69 million per year to finance national statistical capacities and systems in developing countries in 2013-15.

Financial flows from France to developing countries

Figure 16.1. **Net resource flows to developing countries, 2005-15, France**

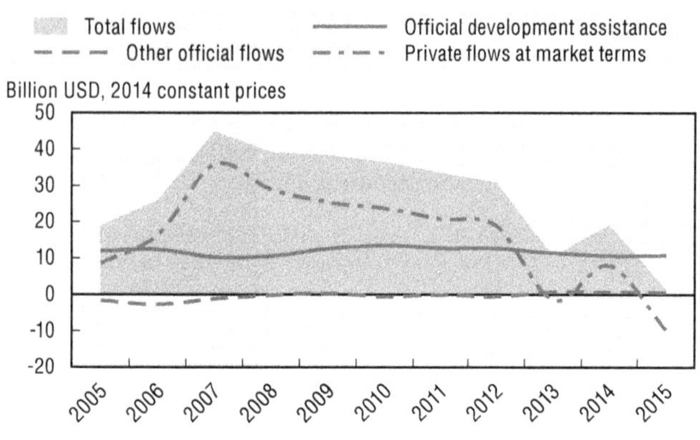

StatLink http://dx.doi.org/10.1787/888933480557

France's use of ODA to mobilise other resources for sustainable development

- **USD 5.8 million** of official development assistance (ODA) was committed to the mobilisation of domestic resources in developing countries, e.g. to support the development of their tax systems, in 2015.
- **USD 2.8 billion** of ODA (+29.4% in real terms from 2014) was committed to promote aid for trade and improve developing countries' trade performance and integration into the world economy in 2015.

France's performance against commitments for effective development co-operation

Table 16.1. **Results of the 2016 Global Partnership monitoring round, France**

	Alignment and ownership by partner country (%)				Predictability (%)		Transparency		
	Use of country-led results frameworks	Funding recorded in countries' national budgets	Funding through countries' systems	Untied ODA	Annual predictability	Medium-term predictability	Retrospective statistics (OECD CRS)	Information for forecasting (OECD FSS)	Publishing to IATI
2016	60.0	63.9	67.3	95.6	80.3	58.7	Good	Good	Needs improvement
Baseline	-	57.1	70.3	95.0	86.1	82.2	Good	Fair	-
Trend	-	⇑	⇓	⇑	⇓	⇓	=	⇑	-

Note: Please refer to Annex B for details on the indicators.

StatLink http://dx.doi.org/10.1787/888933483055

France's official development assistance

In 2016, France provided USD 9.5 billion in net ODA (preliminary data), which represented 0.38% of gross national income (GNI) and a 4.6% increase in real terms from 2015, due to an increase in bilateral lending. France is committed, at European level, to collectively achieve a 0.7% ODA/GNI ratio by 2030. France's share of untied ODA (excluding administrative costs and in-donor refugee costs) was 95.6% in 2015 (increasing from 92.3% in 2014), compared to the DAC average of 78.1%. The grant element of total ODA was 79.6% in 2015, lower than in 2014 (when it stood at 85.6%) and below the DAC compliance grant element norm of 86%.

In 2016, in-donor refugee costs were USD 428 million, an increase of 17.2% in real terms over 2015, and represented 4.5% of France's total net ODA.

Figure 16.2. **Net ODA: Trends in volume and as a share of GNI, 2000-16, France**

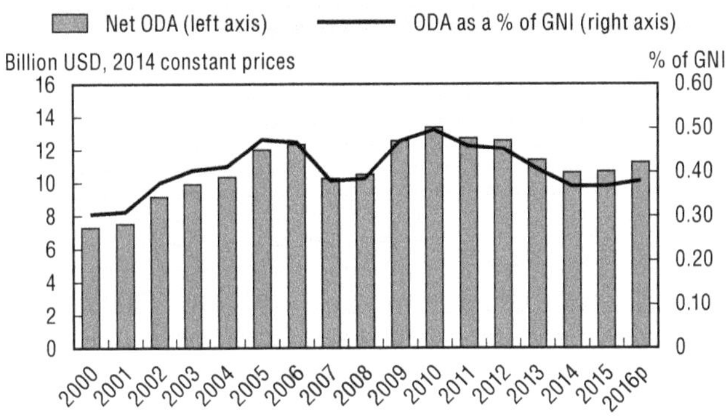

p: Preliminary data.

StatLink http://dx.doi.org/10.1787/888933480566

In 2015, 62.1% of ODA was provided bilaterally. France allocated 37.9% of total ODA as core contributions to multilateral organisations, compared with the DAC country average of 26.2%. In addition, it channelled 1.7% of its bilateral ODA for specific projects implemented by multilateral organisations (multi-bi/non-core).

Figure 16.3. **Share of ODA channelled to and through the multilateral system, two year averages, gross disbursements, France**

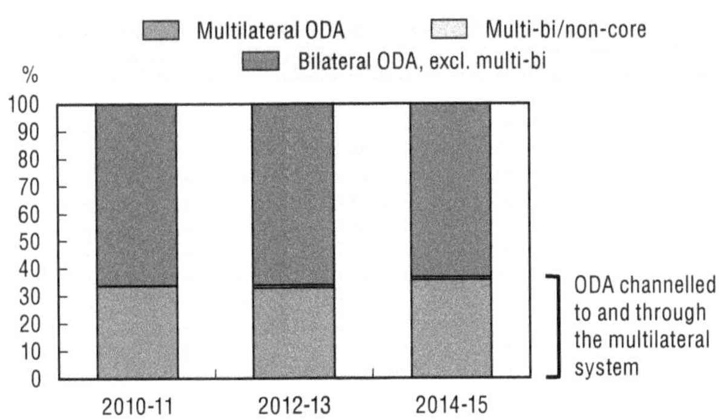

StatLink http://dx.doi.org/10.1787/888933480574

In 2015, 67.6% of French gross bilateral ODA was programmed with partner countries. France's share of country programmable aid was higher than the DAC country average (48.8%) in 2015. Project-type interventions made up 80.9% of this aid.

Figure 16.4. **Composition of bilateral ODA, 2015, gross disbursements, France**

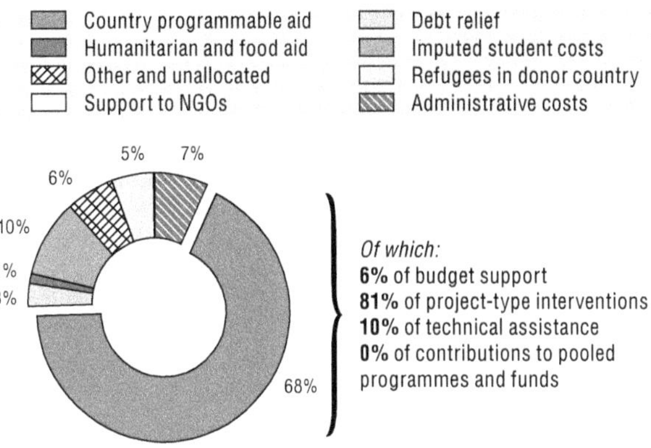

StatLink http://dx.doi.org/10.1787/888933480582

In 2015, USD 198.2 million of bilateral ODA was channelled to and through civil society organisations (CSOs). France's ODA to and through CSOs decreased between 2014 and 2015 in terms of volume (-13%), and as a share of bilateral aid. This share (2.9% in 2015) was lower than the DAC country average of 16.9%.

Figure 16.5. **Bilateral ODA to and through CSOs, two year averages, gross disbursements, France**

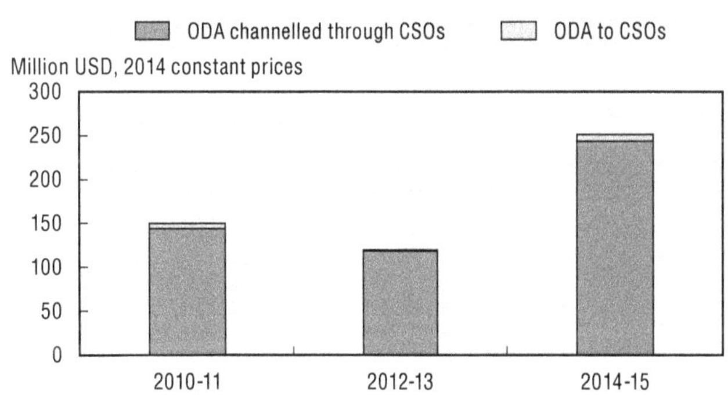

Note: Data on ODA to CSOs are not available for 2012 or 2014.

StatLink http://dx.doi.org/10.1787/888933480599

In 2015, bilateral ODA primarily focused on sub-Saharan Africa, South America and North Africa. In 2015, France allocated USD 2.4 billion to sub-Saharan Africa, USD 954.3 million to South America and USD 748.7 million to North Africa.

Figure 16.6. **Share of bilateral ODA by region, 2014-15 average, gross disbursements, France**

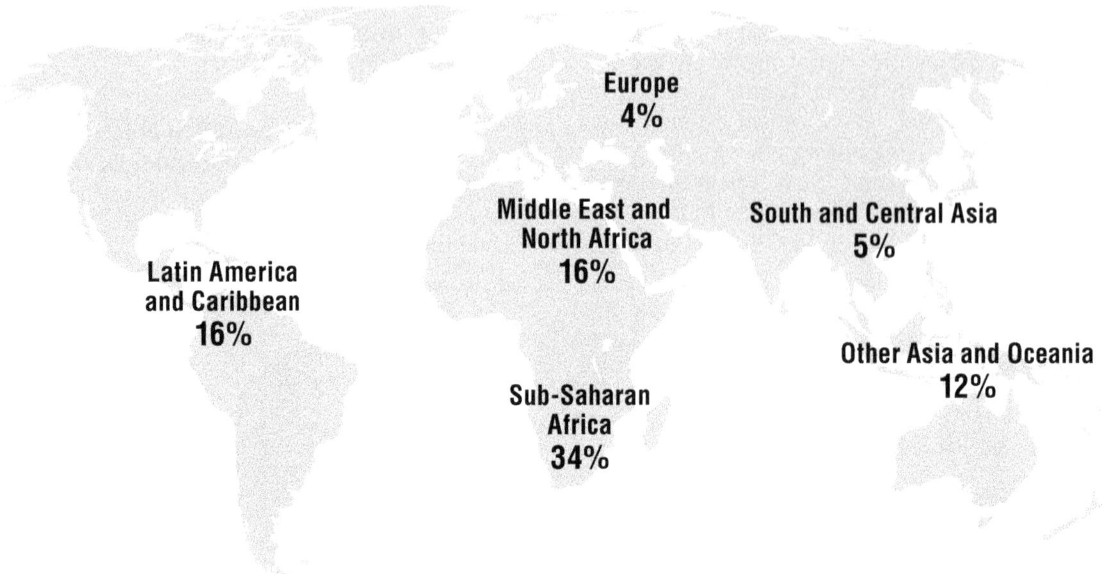

Note: 13% of bilateral ODA allocated was unspecified by region in 2014-15. This share is not represented on the map.

StatLink http://dx.doi.org/10.1787/888933480600

In 2015, 35.5% of bilateral ODA went to France's top 10 recipients. The French government has decided that at least 50% of France's grant ODA should go to its 16 priority partner countries, all in sub-Saharan Africa. In 2014-15 just one of these priority countries (Senegal) was on the list of top 10 recipients. France's support to fragile contexts reached USD 1.9 billion in 2015 (27.7% of gross bilateral ODA).

In 2015, 18.8% of gross bilateral ODA was allocated to least developed countries (LDCs), amounting to USD 1.3 billion. This is a slight increase from 2014 (17.7%), and is lower than the 2015 DAC average of 24.3%. Upper middle-income countries received the highest share of bilateral ODA in 2015 (32%).

At 0.10% of GNI in 2015, ODA to LDCs was lower than the UN target of 0.15% of GNI.

Figure 16.7. **Bilateral ODA to top recipients, 2014-15 average, gross disbursements, France**

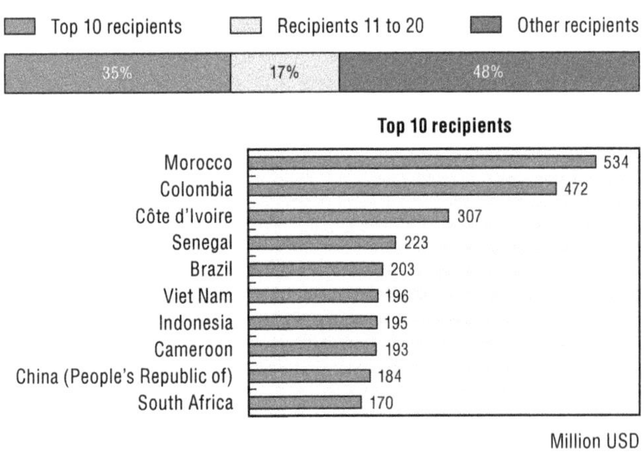

StatLink http://dx.doi.org/10.1787/888933480616

Figure 16.8. **Bilateral ODA by income group, two year averages, gross disbursements, France**

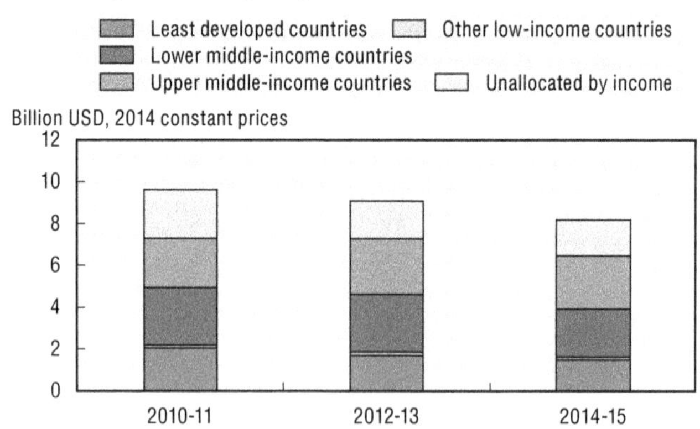

StatLink http://dx.doi.org/10.1787/888933480629

In 2015, 31.1% of France's bilateral ODA was committed to social infrastructure and services, amounting to USD 2.7 billion, with a strong focus on education (USD 1.2 billion) and water and sanitation (USD 826.8 million). USD 2.2 billion (25.3% of bilateral ODA) was allocated to economic infrastructure and services, mainly to energy generation and supply (USD 1.6 billion) and transport and storage (USD 399.2 million). Humanitarian aid amounted to USD 36 million.

Figure 16.9. **Share of bilateral ODA by sector, 2014-15 average, commitments, France**

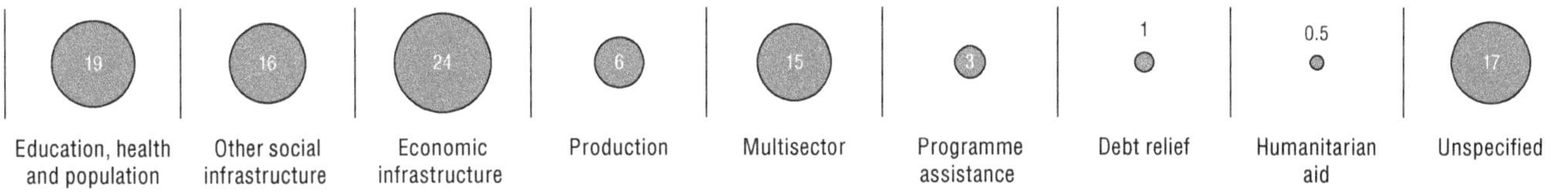

StatLink http://dx.doi.org/10.1787/888933480632

USD 1 billion of bilateral ODA supported gender equality in 2015. France has made positive steps to integrate gender equality into its development co-operation with a new Gender and Development Strategy (2013-17) and the Cross-cutting Intervention Framework, the Agence Française de Développement's own gender strategy adopted in 2014 (OECD, 2014). In 2015, 17% of French bilateral allocable aid had gender equality and women's empowerment as a principal or significant objective, compared with the DAC country average of 36.3%. Education, population and reproductive health, and health are the only sectors in which the focus on gender is strong.

Figure 16.10. **Share of bilateral allocable ODA in support of gender equality by sector, 2015, commitments, France**

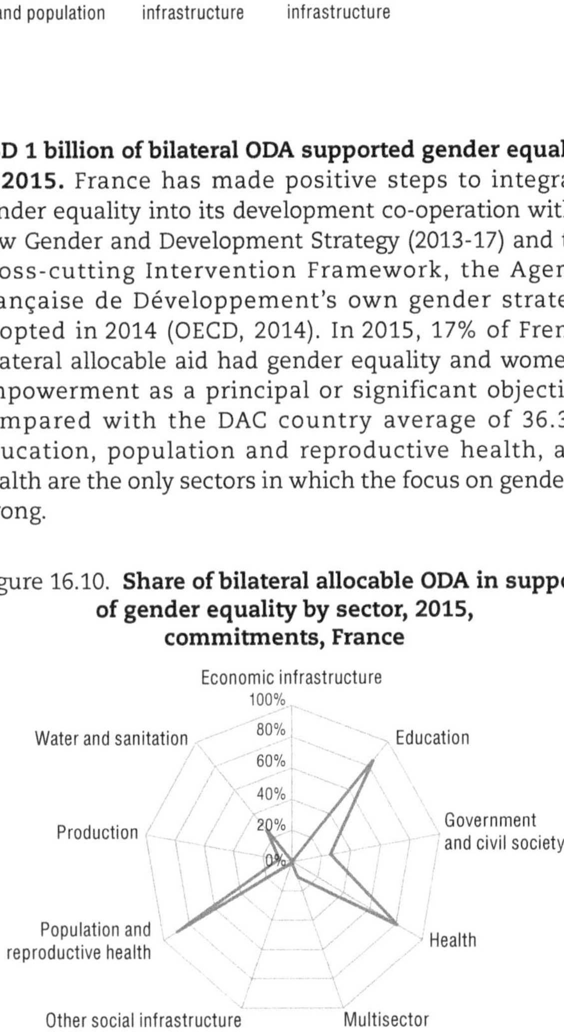

StatLink http://dx.doi.org/10.1787/888933480641

USD 4.2 billion of bilateral ODA supported the environment in 2015. France has taken positive steps to integrate the environment and climate change into its development co-operation (OECD, 2014). This is reflected in its upward funding trend in recent years in bilateral ODA supporting the environment. In 2015, 60.5% of French bilateral allocable aid supported the environment and 48.3% (USD 3.3 billion) focused on climate change, compared with the respective DAC country averages of 33.2% and 26.2%.

Figure 16.11. **Bilateral allocable ODA in support of global and local environment objectives, two year averages, commitments, France**

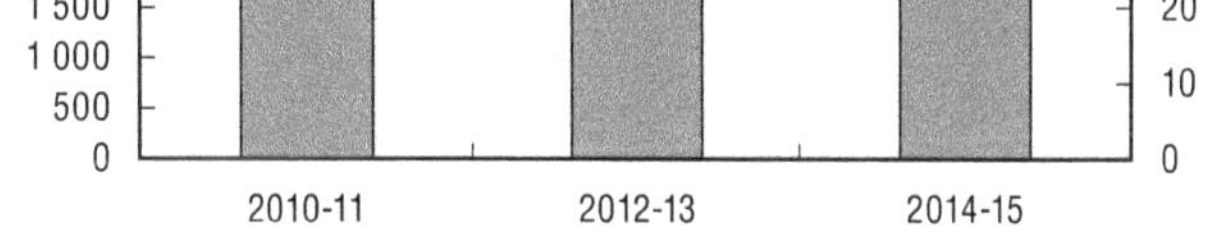

StatLink http://dx.doi.org/10.1787/888933480657

Note to reader: Annex B provides "Methodological notes on the profiles of Development Assistance Committee members".

Reference

OECD (2014), *OECD Development Co-operation Peer Reviews: France 2013*, OECD Publishing, Paris, *http://dx.doi.org/10.1787/9789264196193-en*.

GERMANY

Germany's contribution to data for development

Statistical capacity building is one of the pillars of Germany's efforts to support the Sustainable Development Goals in its partner countries. Given the centrality of reliable statistical systems to effective planning, it focuses on the environment in which statistical capacity building takes place, in particular the relationship between state and society and the flow of data between subnational and national levels. Ensuring civil society can use relevant data for accountability is also a priority. Moreover, it considers that the use of more and better data is important for evidence-based development co-operation planning and allocating resources effectively.

Germany engages directly in capacity building to promote the use of data by policy makers, civil society and citizens and works to improve co-ordination among development partners. It has, for example, supported Pakistan's national and provincial bureaus of statistics to produce up-to-date, harmonised and internationally comparable statistics while also providing advice on Pakistan's General Statistics Act. Germany is examining how "big" and "open data" can serve development co-operation, notably in relation to real-time monitoring of multidimensional poverty.

According to the 2017 Partner Report on Support to Statistics (PRESS) dataset, Germany committed on average USD 12.29 million per year to finance national statistical capacities and systems in developing countries in 2013-15.

Financial flows from Germany to developing countries

Figure 17.1. **Net resource flows to developing countries, 2005-15, Germany**

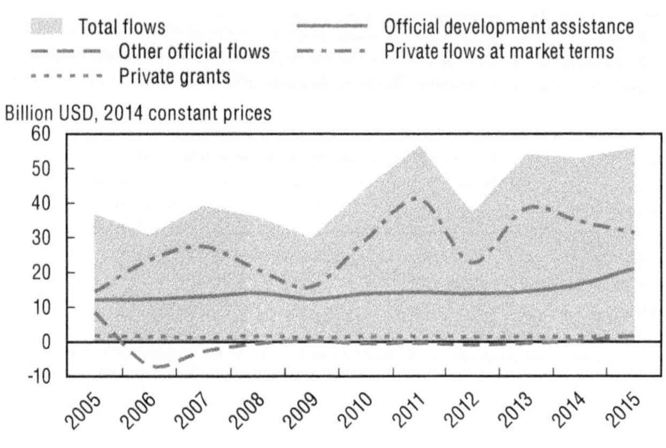

StatLink http://dx.doi.org/10.1787/888933480664

Germany's use of ODA to mobilise other resources for sustainable development

- **USD 31.7 million** of official development assistance (ODA) was committed to the mobilisation of domestic resources in developing countries, e.g. to support the development of their tax systems, in 2015.
- **USD 5.6 billion** of ODA (-14.2% in real terms from 2014) was committed to promote aid for trade and improve developing countries' trade performance and integration into the world economy in 2015.

Germany's performance against commitments for effective development co-operation

Table 17.1. **Results of the 2016 Global Partnership monitoring round, Germany**

	Alignment and ownership by partner country (%)				Predictability (%)		Transparency		
	Use of country-led results frameworks	Funding recorded in countries' national budgets	Funding through countries' systems	Untied ODA	Annual predictability	Medium-term predictability	Retrospective statistics (OECD CRS)	Information for forecasting (OECD FSS)	Publishing to IATI
2016	62.8	47.7	31.0	84.0	79.8	62.1	Excellent	Good	Needs improvement
Baseline	-	44.8	47.9	75.3	92.8	46.8	Excellent	Excellent	-
Trend	-	⇓	⇓	⇑	⇓	⇑	=	⇓	-

Note: Please refer to Annex B for details on the indicators.

StatLink http://dx.doi.org/10.1787/888933483069

Germany's official development assistance

In 2016, Germany provided USD 24.7 billion in net ODA (preliminary data). This represented 0.70% of gross national income (GNI) and a 36.1% increase in real terms from 2015, due to the overall scaling up of its aid programme and doubling of in-donor refugee costs. In 2016 Germany's ODA hit a record high and reached the 0.7% ODA/GNI target for the first time. It is just one of six DAC members to do so. Germany's share of untied ODA (excluding administrative costs and in-donor refugee costs) was 84% in 2015 (up from 83.6% in 2014), compared to the DAC average of 78.1%. The grant element of total ODA was 86.6% in 2015 (increasing from 83.6% in 2014), meeting the DAC compliance grant element norm of 86%.

In 2016, in-donor refugee costs were USD 6.22 billion, an increase of 103.8% in real terms over 2015, and represented 25.2% of Germany's total net ODA.

Figure 17.2. **Net ODA: Trends in volume and as a share of GNI, 2000-16, Germany**

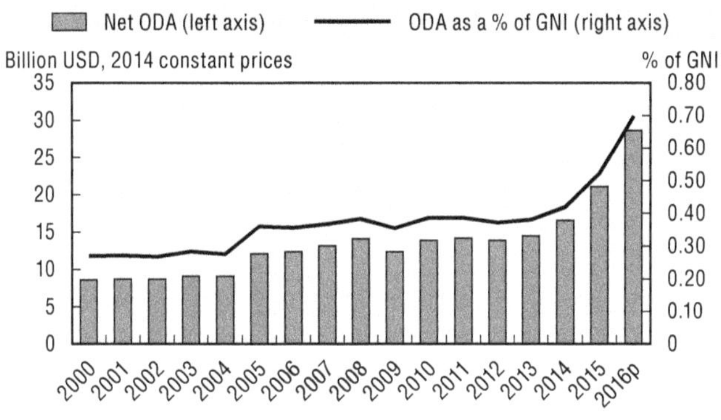

p: Preliminary data.

StatLink http://dx.doi.org/10.1787/888933480675

In 2015, 80.6% of ODA was provided bilaterally. Germany allocated 19.4% of total ODA as core contributions to multilateral organisations, compared with the DAC country average of 26.2%. In addition, it channelled 6.8% of its bilateral ODA for specific projects implemented by multilateral organisations (multi-bi/non-core contributions).

Figure 17.3. **Share of ODA channelled to and through the multilateral system, two year averages, gross disbursements, Germany**

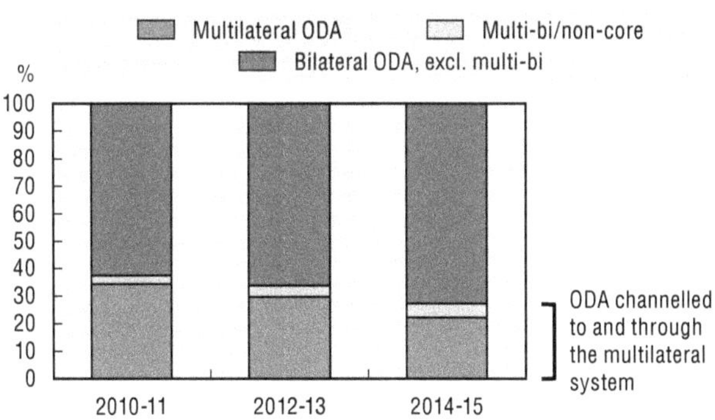

StatLink http://dx.doi.org/10.1787/888933480689

In 2015, 48.2% of bilateral ODA was programmed with partner countries. Germany's share of country programmable aid was below the DAC country average (48.8%) in 2015 and project-type interventions accounted for 79% of this aid.

Figure 17.4. **Composition of bilateral ODA, 2015, gross disbursements, Germany**

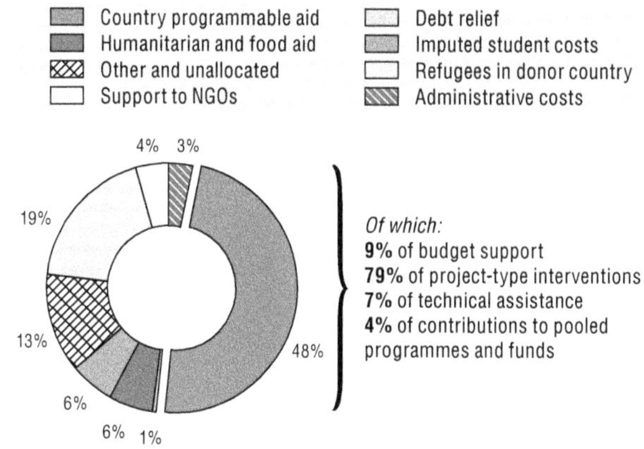

StatLink http://dx.doi.org/10.1787/888933480696

In 2015, USD 1.1 billion of bilateral ODA was channelled to and through civil society organisations (CSOs), corresponding to 6.6% of bilateral aid, compared with the DAC country average of 16.9%. Between 2014 and 2015, ODA through CSOs increased in terms of volume (+4%), but decreased as a share of bilateral ODA (it was 8.2% in 2014).

Figure 17.5. **Bilateral ODA to and through CSOs, two year averages, gross disbursements, Germany**

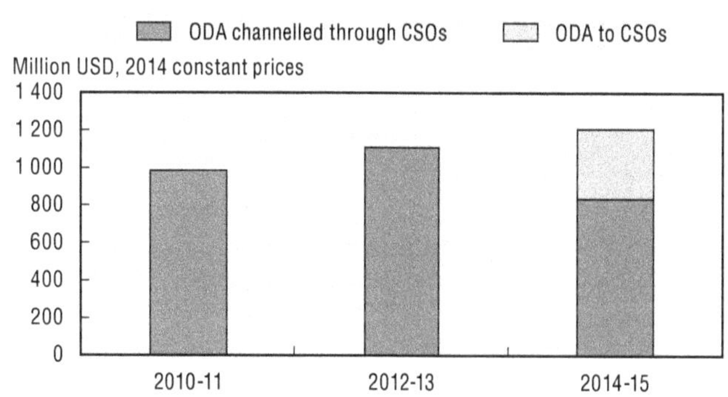

Note: Data on ODA to civil society organisations are not available before 2015.

StatLink http://dx.doi.org/10.1787/888933480702

In 2015, Germany's bilateral ODA had a broad geographical coverage. USD 2.1 billion was allocated to south and central Asia and USD 2 billion was allocated to sub-Saharan Africa.

Figure 17.6. **Share of bilateral ODA by region, 2014-15 average, gross disbursements, Germany**

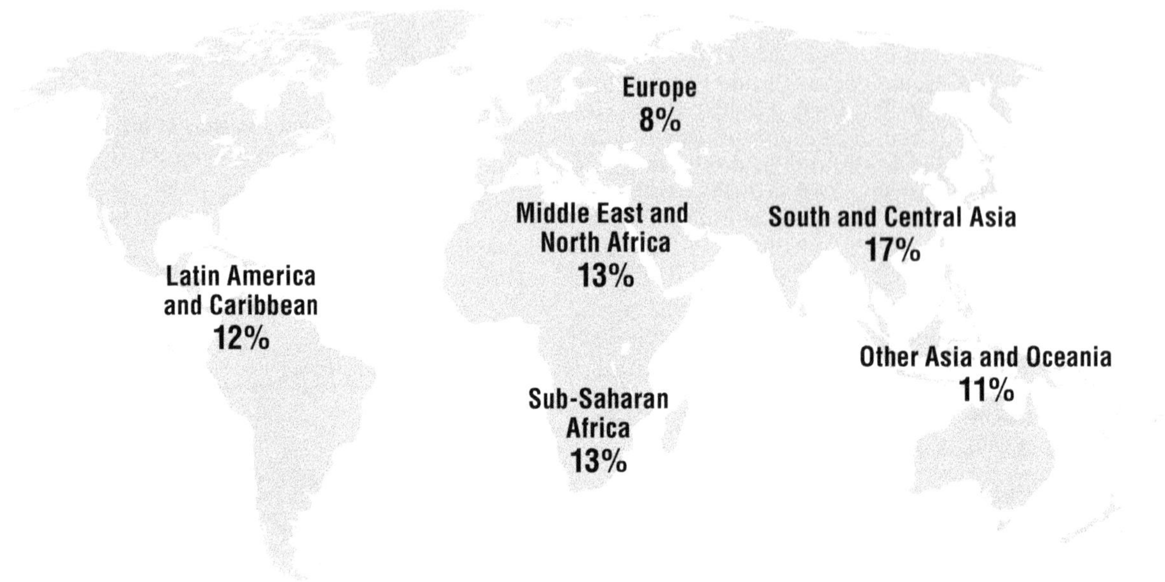

Note: 27% of bilateral ODA allocated was unspecified by region in 2014-15. This share is not represented on the map.

StatLink http://dx.doi.org/10.1787/888933480717

In 2015, 30.6% of bilateral ODA went to Germany's top 10 recipients. Germany has 67 partner countries which it supports through bilateral or regional programmes. All top 10 recipients of German ODA are partner countries. The 2015 DAC Peer Review of Germany found that there has been an increase in German funds which are not allocated geographically. In 2015, its support to fragile contexts reached USD 2.7 billion (16.8% of gross bilateral ODA).

Figure 17.7. **Bilateral ODA to top recipients, 2014-15 average, gross disbursements, Germany**

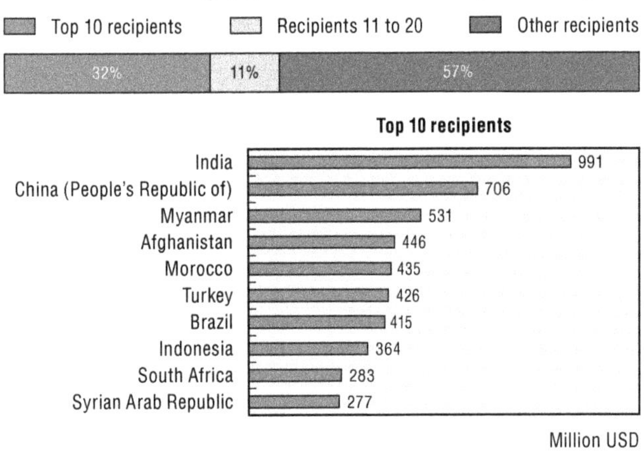

StatLink http://dx.doi.org/10.1787/888933480729

In 2015, 10.4% of bilateral ODA was allocated to least developed countries (LDCs), amounting to USD 1.6 billion. This is a sharp decrease from 20.6% in 2014 and is lower than the 2015 DAC average (24.3%). In 2015, lower middle-income countries received the highest share of bilateral ODA (23.6%), noting that 43.9% was unallocated by income group.

At 0.08% of GNI in 2015, total ODA to LDCs was far lower than the UN target of 0.15% of GNI.

Figure 17.8. **Bilateral ODA by income group, two year averages, gross disbursements, Germany**

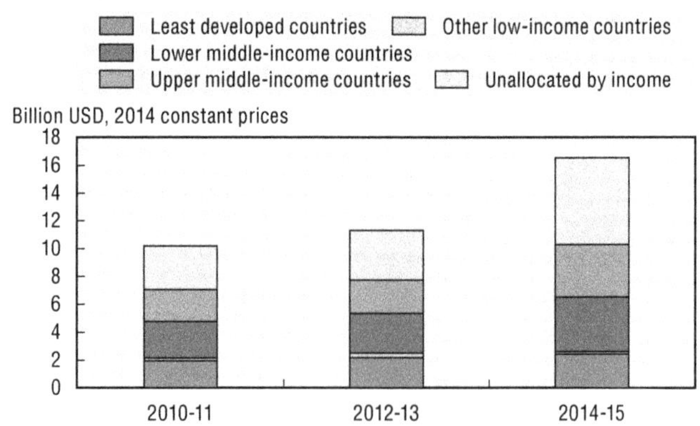

StatLink http://dx.doi.org/10.1787/888933480737

In 2015, 30.1% of Germany's bilateral ODA was allocated to social infrastructure and services, amounting to USD 5.3 billion, with a strong focus on education (USD 2 billion) and government and civil society (USD 1.6 billion). USD 4.6 billion was allocated to economic infrastructure and services, with a focus on energy generation and supply (USD 2.2 billion) and banking and financial services (USD 1.4 billion). USD 810.3 million was allocated to humanitarian aid.

Figure 17.9. **Share of bilateral ODA by sector, 2014-15 average, commitments, Germany**

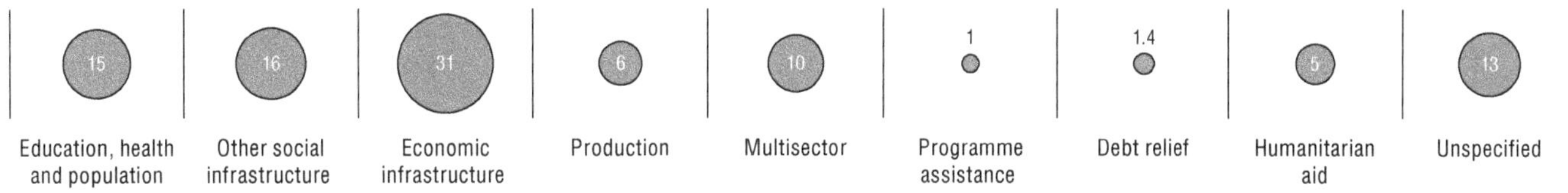

StatLink http://dx.doi.org/10.1787/888933480741

USD 5.7 billion of bilateral ODA supported gender equality in 2015. The Federal Ministry for Economic Cooperation and Development integrates gender equality into programming through political dialogue, empowerment and gender mainstreaming. The 2015 DAC Peer Review recommended that Germany should match its commitment to gender equality with adequate leadership, resources and tools (OECD, 2015). In 2015, 46.5% of German bilateral allocable aid had gender equality and women's empowerment as a principal or significant objective, compared with 39% in 2014. The DAC country average was 36.3% in 2015. Germany's aid to population and reproductive health and other social infrastructure focuses on gender.

Figure 17.10. **Share of bilateral allocable ODA in support of gender equality by sector, 2015, commitments, Germany**

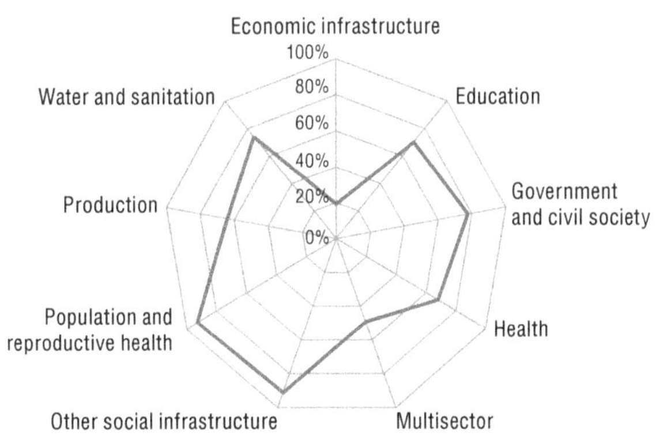

StatLink http://dx.doi.org/10.1787/888933480757

USD 6.4 billion of bilateral ODA supported the environment in 2015. Climate change is well embedded in the development co-operation programme along with the environment and natural resource issues (OECD, 2015). Germany helps partner countries to identify the causes of environmental and climate risks, strengthen their governance structures and policies, and develop regional co-operation. Capacity building and technology transfer are key components of Germany's support (ibid.). In 2015, the share of German bilateral allocable aid focusing on the environment reached 48.9%, compared to the DAC country average of 33.2%. Germany's financial commitment to climate change-related activities has decreased since 2014, when the share was 46.9%. Its share of bilateral allocable aid to climate-related aid reached 39.9% in 2015 (USD 5.2 billion), compared to the DAC country average of 26.2%.

Figure 17.11. **Bilateral allocable ODA in support of global and local environment objectives, two year averages, commitments, Germany**

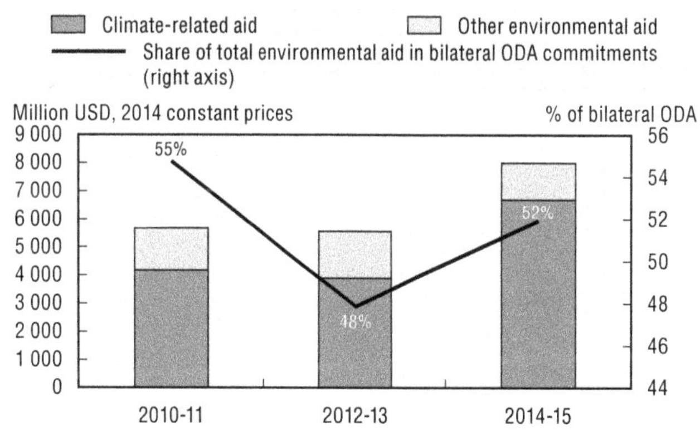

StatLink http://dx.doi.org/10.1787/888933480768

Note to reader: Annex B provides "Methodological notes on the profiles of Development Assistance Committee members".

Reference

OECD (2015), *OECD Development Co-operation Peer Reviews: Germany 2015*, OECD Publishing, Paris, *http://dx.doi.org/10.1787/9789264246133-en*.

GREECE

Greece's contribution to data for development

Greece considers that the development of national statistical systems in partner countries is important to provide quality data in support of decision making, which can enhance governance. Supporting statistical capacity building in developing countries has not been a high priority for Greece since its development programme has diminished at all levels due to the severe fiscal constraints the country is facing. It will strive to improve its development co-operation in this sector when it has the budgetary capacity to do so.

Financial flows from Greece to developing countries

Figure 18.1. **Net resource flows to developing countries, 2005-15, Greece**

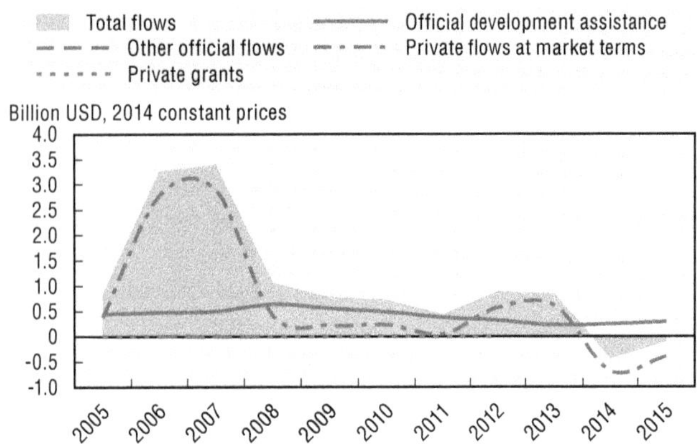

Note: Data on other official flows are only available for 2006, 2007 and 2008. Data on private grants are not available for 2013-15.

StatLink http://dx.doi.org/10.1787/888933480776

Greece's use of ODA to mobilise other resources for sustainable development

- **USD 4 900** of ODA (-64.1% in real terms from 2014) was committed to promote aid for trade and improve developing countries' trade performance and integration into the world economy in 2015.

Greece's performance against commitments for effective development co-operation

Table 18.1. **Results of the 2016 Global Partnership monitoring round, Greece**

	Alignment and ownership by partner country (%)				Predictability (%)		Transparency		
	Use of country-led results frameworks	Funding recorded in countries' national budgets	Funding through countries' systems	Untied ODA	Annual predictability	Medium-term predictability	Retrospective statistics (OECD CRS)	Information for forecasting (OECD FSS)	Publishing to IATI
2016	-	-	-	14.5	-	-	Needs improvement	-	-
Baseline	-	0.0	0.0	47.9	100.0	0.0	-	-	-
Trend	-	-	-	⇓	-	-	-	-	-

Note: Please refer to Annex B for details on the indicators.

StatLink http://dx.doi.org/10.1787/888933483074

Greece's official development assistance

In 2016, Greece provided USD 264 million in net ODA (preliminary data), which represented 0.14% of gross national income (GNI) and an increase of 10.8% in real terms from 2015 partly due to increased contributions to the EU development budget. Greece's ODA decreased between 2009-14 as a consequence of the economic crisis. Greece's share of untied ODA (excluding administrative costs and in-donor refugee costs) was 14.5% in 2015, thus below the 2015 DAC average of 78.1%, decreasing from 22% in 2014. The high share of tied aid reflects the composition of Greece's aid portfolio, which has a high share of tied technical co-operation (i.e. scholarships, imputed students costs – considered by the DAC as tied by definition). The grant element of total ODA was 100% in 2015.

In 2016, in-donor refugee costs were USD 59 million, a decrease of 0.5% in real terms over 2015, and represented 22.3% of Greece's total net ODA.

Figure 18.2. **Net ODA: Trends in volume and as a share of GNI, 2000-16, Greece**

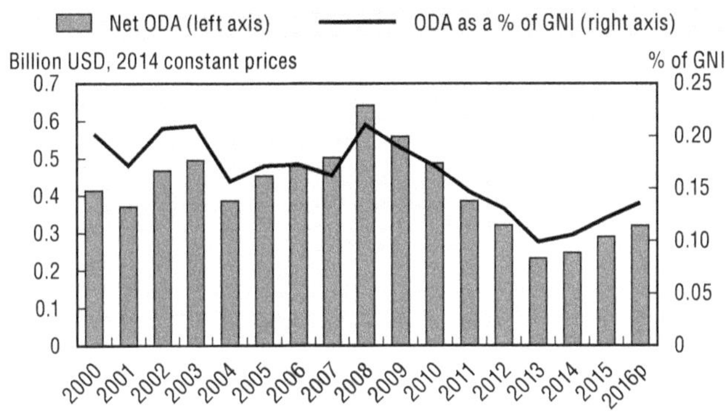

p: Preliminary data.

StatLink http://dx.doi.org/10.1787/888933480780

In 2015, 30.1% of Greece's ODA was provided bilaterally. Greece allocated 69.9% of total ODA as core contributions to multilateral organisations, compared with the DAC country average of 26.2%. This high share reflects the maintenance of payments of assessed contributions to the EU and other multilateral organisations within an overall declining ODA budget. Greece also channelled 0.1% of its bilateral ODA for specific projects implemented by multilateral organisations (multi-bi/non-core contributions).

Figure 18.3. **Share of ODA channelled to and through the multilateral system, two year averages, gross disbursements, Greece**

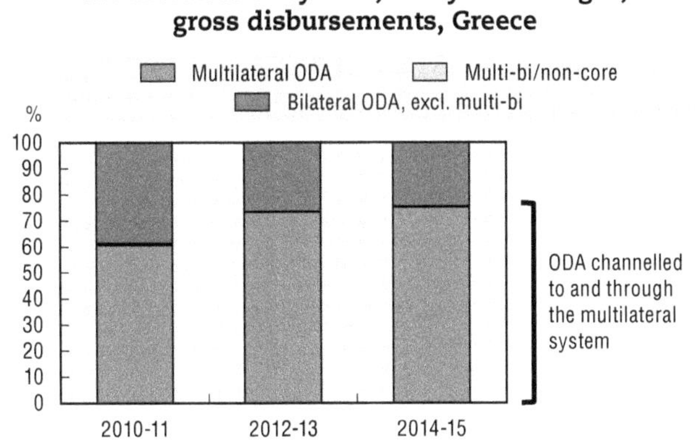

StatLink http://dx.doi.org/10.1787/888933480797

In 2015, only 5.7% of Greece's bilateral ODA was programmed with partner countries. Greece's share of country programmable aid was low compared to the DAC country average (48.8%) in 2015. This is explained by its limited funding for grants, its high spending for refugees in Greece (82.7% of bilateral aid) and imputed student costs. "Scholarships/training in donor country" accounted for 47.9% of country programmable aid.

Figure 18.4. **Composition of bilateral ODA, 2015, gross disbursements, Greece**

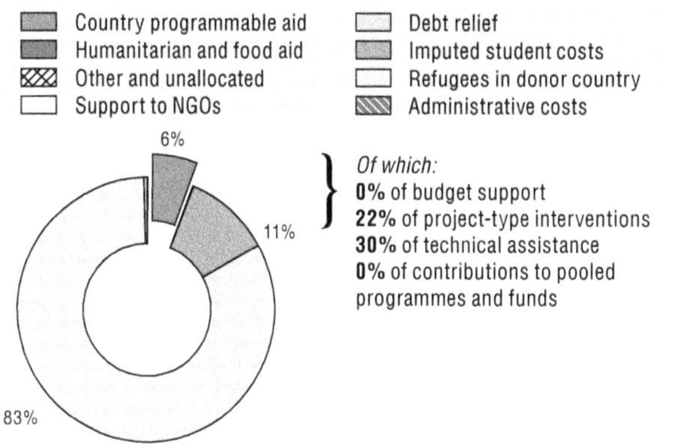

StatLink http://dx.doi.org/10.1787/888933480807

In 2015, USD 0.2 million of bilateral ODA was channelled to and through civil society organisations (CSOs), corresponding to 0.2% of bilateral aid (compared to the DAC country average of 16.9%). Overall, aid to and through civil societies has decreased since 2014, both in volume (-95%) and as a share of bilateral ODA (from 9.2% in 2014).

Figure 18.5. **Bilateral ODA to and through CSOs, two year averages, gross disbursements, Greece**

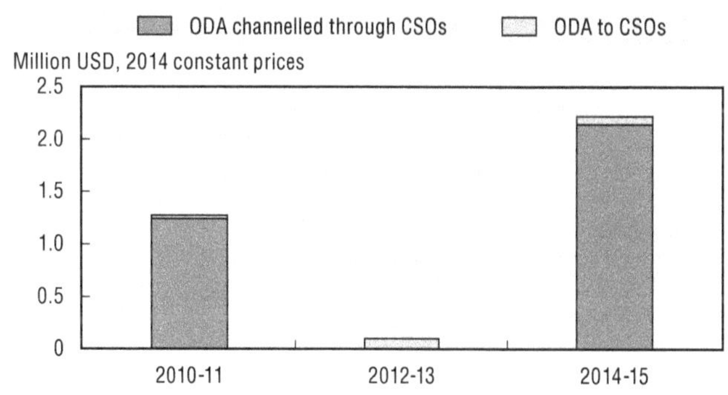

StatLink http://dx.doi.org/10.1787/888933480814

Bilateral ODA primarily focused on Eastern Europe. In 2015, USD 6.1 million was allocated to Eastern Europe and USD 2.1 million to the Middle East.

Figure 18.6. **Share of bilateral ODA by region, 2014-15 average, gross disbursements, Greece**

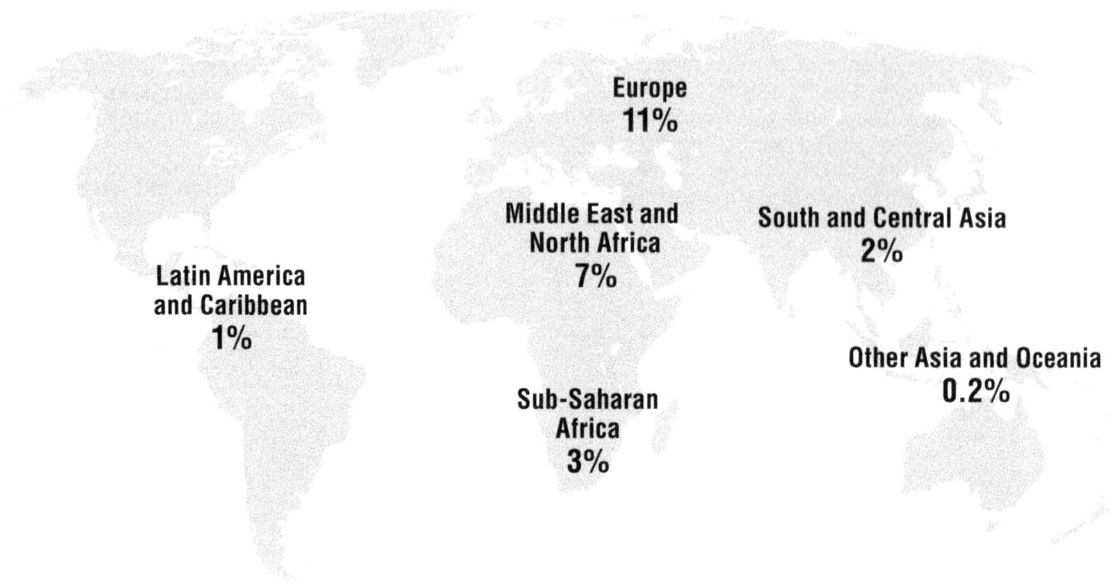

Note: 76% of bilateral ODA allocated was unspecified by region in 2014-15. This share is not represented on the map.

StatLink http://dx.doi.org/10.1787/888933480822

In 2015, 10.6% of bilateral ODA went to Greece's top 10 recipients. Greece has 18 priority partner countries. Seven of these priority countries featured on its list of top 10 recipients in 2014-15. In 2015, its support to fragile contexts reached USD 3.5 million (4.9% of gross bilateral ODA).

Figure 18.7. **Bilateral ODA to top recipients, 2014-15 average, gross disbursements, Greece**

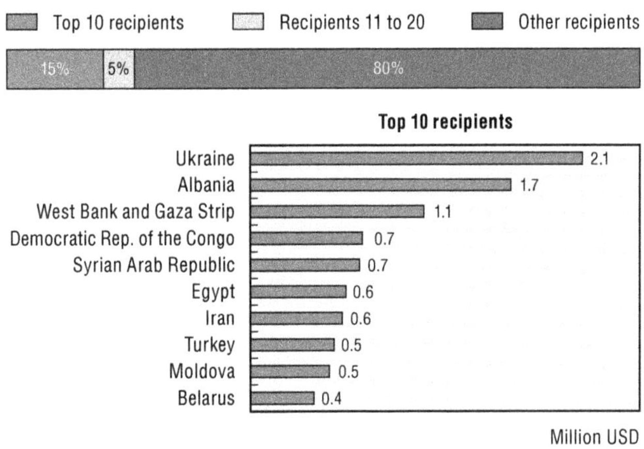

StatLink http://dx.doi.org/10.1787/888933480834

In 2015, 1.6% of bilateral ODA was allocated to least developed countries (LDCs), amounting to USD 1.2 million. This is a decrease from 4% in 2014 and is below the DAC average of 24.3% in 2015. Lower middle-income countries received the highest share of bilateral ODA in 2015 (7.6%), noting that 84% was unallocated by income group.

At 0.02% of GNI in 2015, total ODA to LDCs was below the UN target of 0.15% of GNI.

Figure 18.8. **Bilateral ODA by income group, two year averages, gross disbursements, Greece**

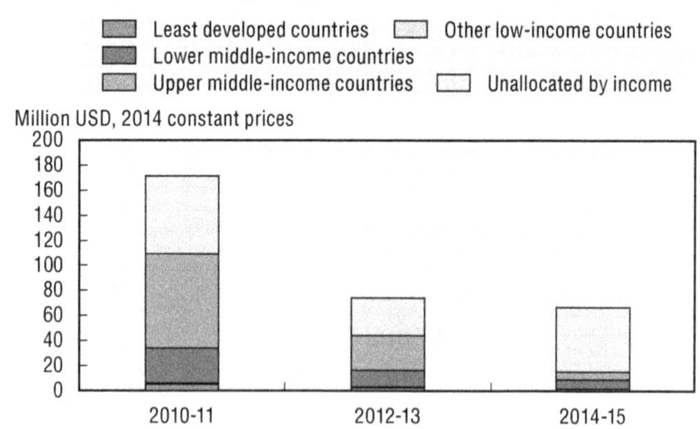

StatLink http://dx.doi.org/10.1787/888933480847

In 2015, 14.2% of bilateral ODA was allocated to social infrastructure and services, equal to USD 10.2 million, with a strong focus on education (USD 9.2 million).

Figure 18.9. **Share of bilateral ODA by sector, 2014-15 average, commitments, Greece**

StatLink http://dx.doi.org/10.1787/888933480857

USD 3.2 million of bilateral ODA supported gender equality in 2015. Gender equality is a priority issue for Greece, which provides equal opportunities to male and female students from developing countries granted tertiary scholarships and studying in Greek universities. In 2015, 71.6% of its bilateral allocable aid had gender equality and women's empowerment as a principal or significant objective, compared to the DAC country average of 36.3%. This is down from 2014 when it stood at 75.9%.

Figure 18.10. **Share of bilateral allocable ODA in support of gender equality by sector, 2015, commitments, Greece**

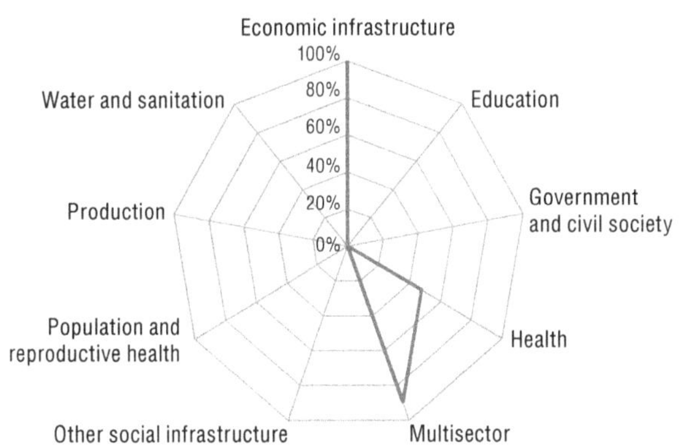

StatLink http://dx.doi.org/10.1787/888933480863

USD 0.2 million of bilateral ODA supported the environment in 2015. The share of Greek bilateral allocable aid focusing on the environment reached 4.3% in 2015, compared to 8% in 2010 and a 2015 DAC country average of 33.2%. The share of its bilateral allocable aid focusing on climate change was 4.3% in 2015 (USD 0.2 million), compared to the DAC country average of 26.2%.

Figure 18.11. **Bilateral allocable ODA in support of global and local environment objectives, two year averages, commitments, Greece**

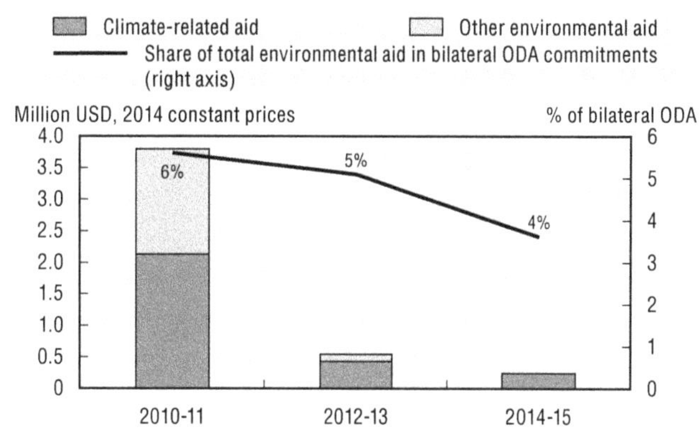

StatLink http://dx.doi.org/10.1787/888933480879

Note to reader: Annex B provides "Methodological notes on the profiles of Development Assistance Committee members".

HUNGARY

Hungary became the Development Assistance Committee's 30th member in December 2016.

Hungary's contribution to data for development

Hungary is not currently engaged in activities related to data for development such as statistical capacity building in developing countries.

Financial flows from Hungary to developing countries

In 2016, Hungary provided USD 155 million in net ODA (preliminary data), which represented 0.13% of gross national income (GNI) and a 0.5% increase in real terms from 2015. As all member states that have joined the European Union since 2002, Hungary has committed to attain a 0.33% ODA/GNI ratio by 2030. At present, data on other official flows, private grants (funds raised by non-governmental organisations and foundations) and private flows at market terms from Hungary to developing countries are not available.

Figure 19.1. **Net ODA: Trends in volume and as a share of GNI, 2003-16, Hungary**

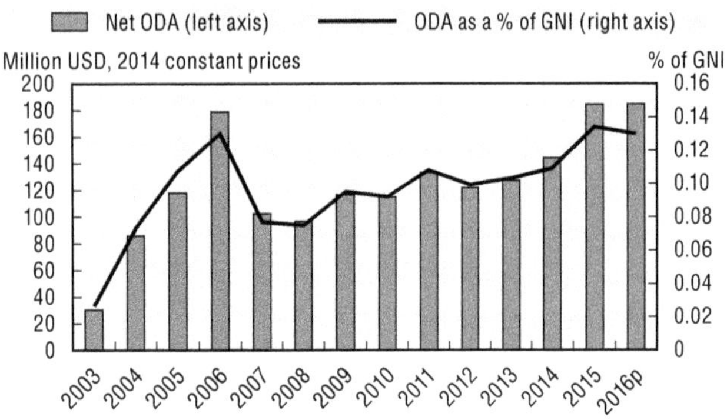

p: Preliminary data.

StatLink http://dx.doi.org/10.1787/888933480887

Hungary's use of ODA to mobilise other resources for sustainable development

- **USD 10 400** of official development assistance (ODA) was committed to the mobilisation of domestic resources in developing countries, e.g. to support the development of their tax systems, in 2015.
- **USD 0.4 million** of ODA was committed to promote aid for trade and improve developing countries' trade performance and integration into the world economy in 2015.

Hungary's official development assistance

In 2015, 30.4% of Hungary's ODA was provided bilaterally, amounting to USD 47.3 million. Hungary channelled 69.6% of its ODA, or USD 108.2 million, as core contributions to multilateral organisations in 2015, compared with the DAC country average of 26.2%. Its multilateral aid consisted mainly of mandatory assessed contributions to the European Union and other international organisations. In addition, Hungary channelled 18.1% of its bilateral ODA for specific projects implemented by multilateral organisations (multi-bi/non-core).

In 2016, in-donor refugee costs were USD 10 million, an increase of 2% in real terms over 2015, and represented 6.3% of Hungary's total net ODA.

Figure 19.2. **Share of ODA channelled to and through the multilateral system, two year averages, gross disbursements, Hungary**

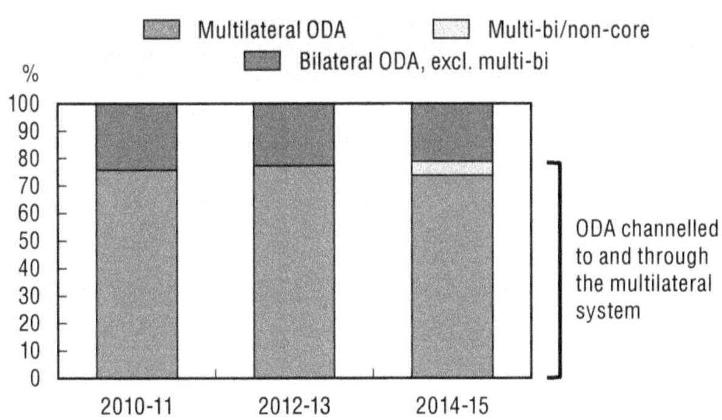

StatLink http://dx.doi.org/10.1787/888933480897

In 2015, 19.9% of bilateral ODA was programmed with partner countries. Hungary's share of country programmable aid was lower than the DAC country average (48.8%) in 2015. Project-type interventions made up 88% of this aid. Imputed student costs (38%) and in-donor refugee costs (20%) amounted to more than half of bilateral ODA.

Figure 19.3. **Composition of bilateral ODA, 2015, gross disbursements, Hungary**

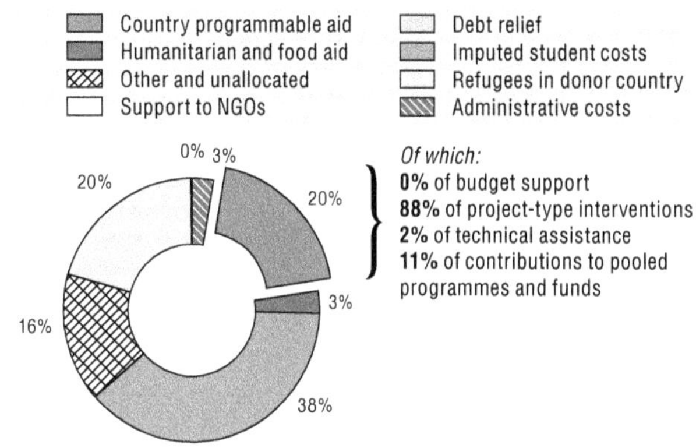

StatLink http://dx.doi.org/10.1787/888933480900

In 2015, USD 1.6 million of bilateral ODA was channelled to and through civil society organisations (CSOs), amounting to 3.4% of bilateral aid. The DAC country average was 16.9% in 2015.

Figure 19.4. **Bilateral ODA to and through CSOs, 2014-15 average, gross disbursements, Hungary**

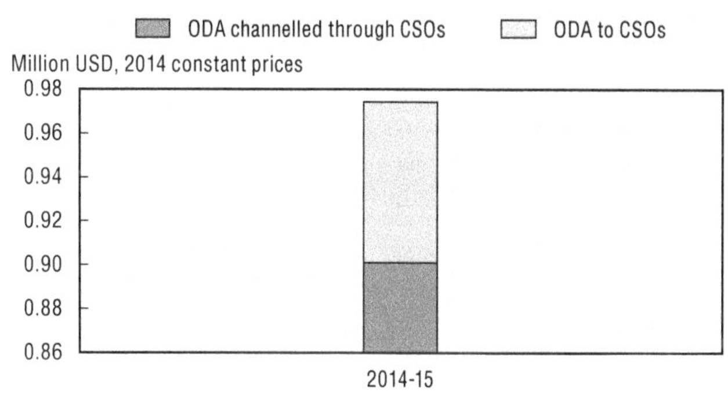

StatLink http://dx.doi.org/10.1787/888933480918

In 2015, bilateral ODA primarily focused on Europe and Asia. USD 6.9 million was allocated to Eastern Europe, USD 6.2 million to south and central Asia, USD 6.2 million to Far East Asia, and USD 5.3 million to the Middle East.

Figure 19.5. **Share of bilateral ODA by region, 2014-15 average, gross disbursements, Hungary**

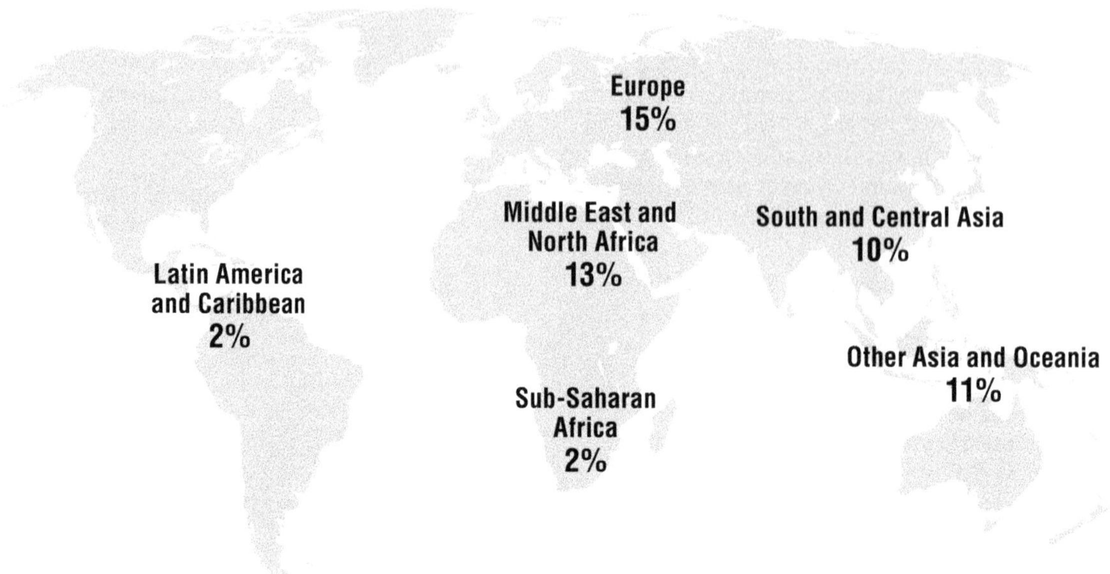

Note: 48% of bilateral ODA allocated was unspecified by region in 2014-15. This share is not represented on the map.

StatLink http://dx.doi.org/10.1787/888933480929

In 2015, 73% of bilateral ODA went to Hungary's top 10 recipients. Hungary focuses on 8 strategic partners and 12 project-based partners. Support for the strategic partners involves more intensive co-operation and higher levels of funding, compared to the project-based partners. Three of its 20 priority partners were among its top 10 recipients in 2014-15. Its support to fragile contexts reached USD 15.2 million in 2015 (32.2% of gross bilateral ODA).

Figure 19.6. **Bilateral ODA to top recipients, 2014-15 average, gross disbursements, Hungary**

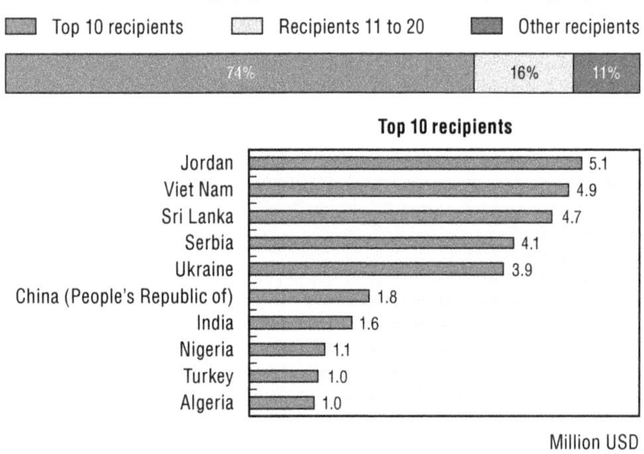

StatLink http://dx.doi.org/10.1787/888933480934

In 2015, 2.9% of bilateral ODA was allocated to least developed countries (LDCs), amounting to USD 1.4 million. The DAC country average share of bilateral ODA allocated to LDCs was 24.3% in 2015. Lower middle-income countries and upper middle-income countries received the highest share of bilateral ODA in 2015, representing 28.9% and 28.4% respectively, noting that 39.7% was unallocated by income.

At 0.02% of GNI in 2015, total ODA to LDCs was below the UN target of 0.15% of GNI.

Figure 19.7. **Bilateral ODA by income group, two year averages, gross disbursements, Hungary**

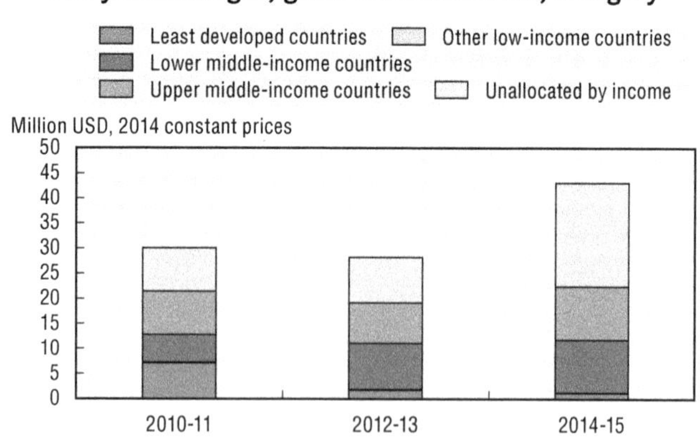

StatLink http://dx.doi.org/10.1787/888933480948

In 2015, 53.5% of bilateral ODA was allocated to social infrastructure and services, reaching USD 25.3 million, with a strong focus on education, which amounted to USD 18.5 million. Humanitarian aid amounted to USD 1.3 million in 2015. A high share (40%) of bilateral ODA was unspecified by sector in 2015.

Figure 19.8. **Share of bilateral ODA by sector, 2014-15 average, commitments, Hungary**

StatLink http://dx.doi.org/10.1787/888933480958

Environmental protection is among the priority areas of Hungary's bilateral development co-operation. Cross-cutting principles, notably gender equality and environmental sustainability, are still to be incorporated into Hungary's development co-operation strategy and activities in a systematic way.

Note to reader: Annex B provides "Methodological notes on the profiles of Development Assistance Committee members".

ICELAND

Iceland's contribution to data for development

Iceland is not currently engaged in activities related to data for development such as statistical capacity building in developing countries.

Financial flows from Iceland to developing countries

In 2016, Iceland delivered USD 50 million in net ODA (preliminary data), which represented 0.25% of its gross national income (GNI) and an 11.6% increase in real terms from 2015 due in part to increased support for in-donor refugee costs. Iceland has a long-standing commitment to joining the ranks of those countries which have achieved 0.7% ODA/GNI. However, following the 2008-11 financial and banking crisis, Iceland has revised its ambitious timetable for achieving this target, with the parliament adopting a revised plan for ODA levels to reach 0.26% by 2018 and to remain at this level until 2021.

Iceland untied 100% of its ODA (excluding administrative costs and in-donor refugee costs) in 2015, compared to the DAC average of 78.1%. Its ODA was also fully untied in 2014 and 2013. The grant element of total ODA was 100% in 2015. At present, data on other official flows and on private grants (funds raised by non-governmental organisations and foundations) from Iceland to developing countries are not available. Data on private flows at market terms are available for 2015 (amounting to USD 0.2 million).

In 2016, in-donor refugee costs were USD 8 million, an increase of 58.5% in real terms over 2015, and represented 16.8% of Iceland's total net ODA.

Figure 20.1. **Net ODA: Trends in volume and as a share of GNI, 2000-16, Iceland**

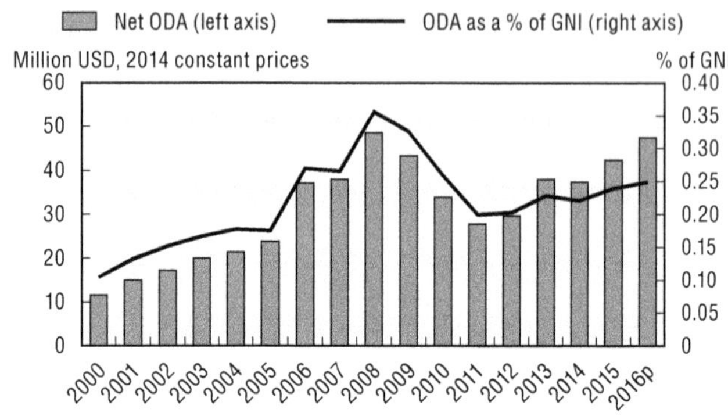

p: Preliminary data.

StatLink http://dx.doi.org/10.1787/888933480967

Iceland's use of ODA to mobilise other resources for sustainable development

- **USD 6.6 million** of ODA (-25.6% in real terms from 2014) was committed to promote aid for trade and improve developing countries' trade performance and integration into the world economy in 2015.

Iceland's performance against commitments for effective development co-operation

Table 20.1. **Results of the 2016 Global Partnership monitoring round, Iceland**

	Alignment and ownership by partner country (%)				Predictability (%)		Transparency		
	Use of country-led results frameworks	Funding recorded in countries' national budgets	Funding through countries' systems	Untied ODA	Annual predictability	Medium-term predictability	Retrospective statistics (OECD CRS)	Information for forecasting (OECD FSS)	Publishing to IATI
2016	100.0	50.9	25.0	100.0	100.0	100.0	Good	Fair	
Baseline	-	0.0	52.8	-	72.4	83.5	Good	-	-
Trend	-	⇑	⇓	-	⇑	⇑	=	-	-

Note: Please refer to Annex B for details on the indicators.

StatLink http://dx.doi.org/10.1787/888933483082

Iceland's official development assistance

In 2015, 77.9% of ODA was provided bilaterally, totalling USD 31 million. Iceland allocated 22.1% of total ODA as core contributions to multilateral organisations, compared with the DAC country average of 26.2%. In addition, it channelled 31.6% of its bilateral ODA for specific projects implemented by multilateral organisations (multi-bi/ non-core contributions). Iceland provides contributions to multilateral organisations such as the United Nations agencies and the World Bank.

Figure 20.2. **Share of ODA channelled to and through the multilateral system, two year averages, gross disbursements, Iceland**

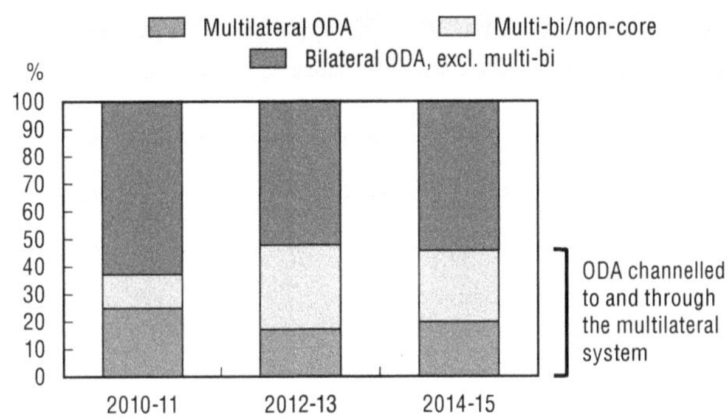

Note: Data on multi-bi/non-core ODA are not available prior to 2011.

StatLink http://dx.doi.org/10.1787/888933480974

In 2015, 45.6% of bilateral ODA was programmed with partner countries. Iceland's share of country programmable aid was lower than the DAC country average (48.8%) in 2015 and project-type interventions made up 66.4% of this aid. The proportion of bilateral ODA categorised as other and unallocated equalled 19.1%.

Figure 20.3. **Composition of bilateral ODA, 2015, gross disbursements, Iceland**

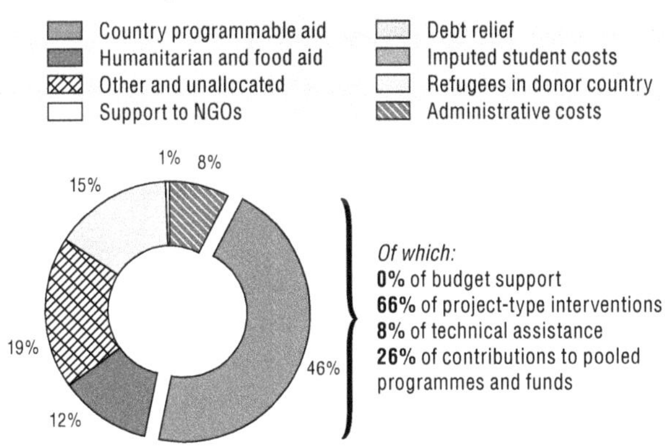

StatLink http://dx.doi.org/10.1787/888933480989

In 2015, USD 3.7 million of bilateral ODA was channelled to and through civil society organisations (CSOs). Between 2014 and 2015 Iceland's aid channelled to and through CSOs increased both in volume (41.9%) and as a share of bilateral ODA, from 8.9% in 2014 to 11.8% in 2015. This share was lower than the DAC average of 16.9%.

Figure 20.4. **Bilateral ODA to and through CSOs, two year averages, gross disbursements, Iceland**

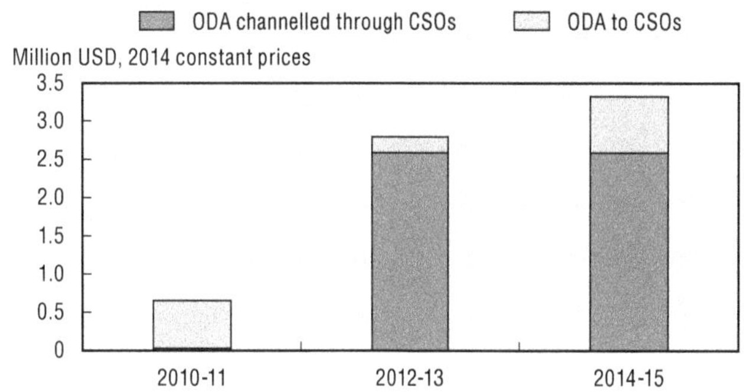

Note: Data on ODA to CSOs are not available prior to 2011.

StatLink http://dx.doi.org/10.1787/888933480996

Bilateral ODA was primarily focused on sub-Saharan Africa, which received USD 13.1 million in 2015.

Figure 20.5. **Share of bilateral ODA by region, 2014-15 average, gross disbursements, Iceland**

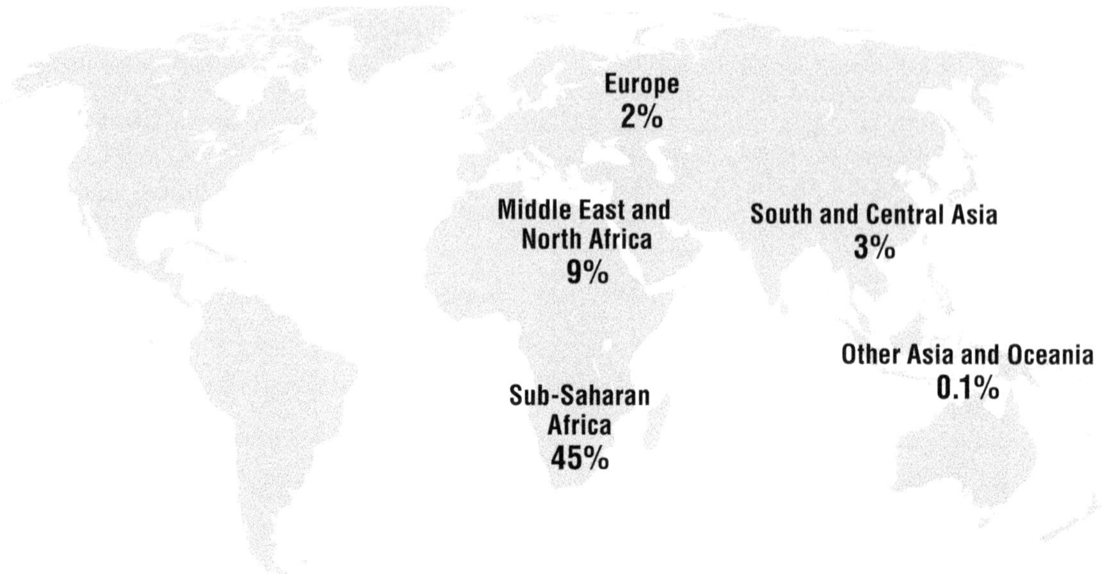

Note: 41% of ODA allocated was unspecified by region in 2014-15. This share is not represented on the map.

StatLink http://dx.doi.org/10.1787/888933481009

In 2015, 50.6% of bilateral ODA went to Iceland's top 10 recipients. Its three priority partner countries – Malawi, Uganda and Mozambique – are the top three recipients of its ODA. In 2015, its support to fragile contexts reached USD 14.3 million (46.2% of gross bilateral ODA).

Figure 20.6. **Bilateral ODA to top recipients, 2014-15 average, gross disbursements, Iceland**

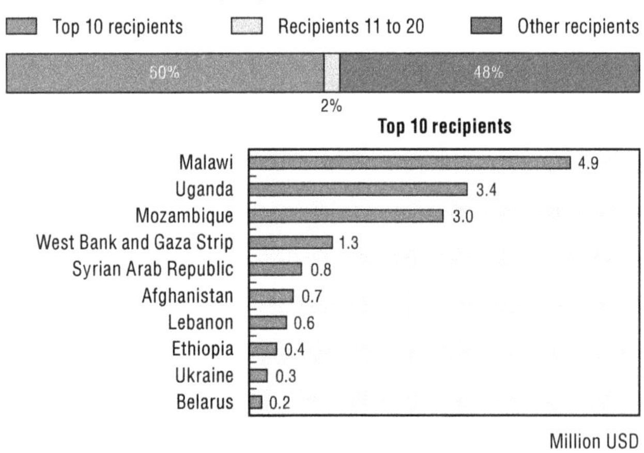

StatLink http://dx.doi.org/10.1787/888933481015

In 2015, 41.6% of bilateral ODA was allocated to least developed countries (LDCs), amounting to USD 12.9 million. This is a slight decrease from 42.1% in 2014, but is still above the DAC average of 24.3% in 2015. LDCs received the highest share of bilateral ODA in 2015, noting that 46.9% was unallocated by income group.

At 0.10% of GNI in 2015, total ODA to LDCs was below the UN target of 0.15% of GNI.

Figure 20.7. **Bilateral ODA by income group, two year averages, gross disbursements, Iceland**

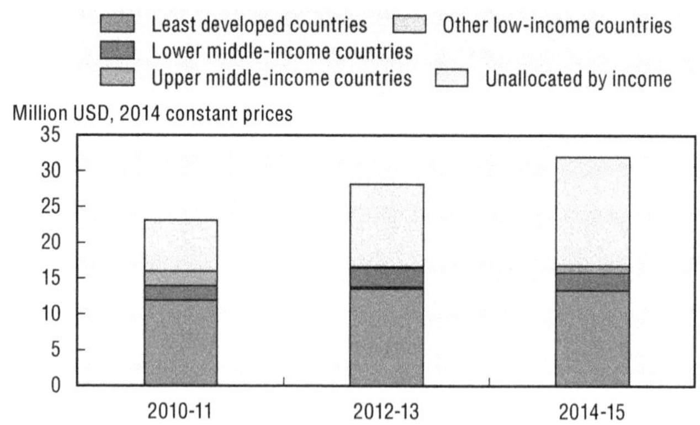

Note: Data concerning other low-income countries are only available for 2009.

StatLink http://dx.doi.org/10.1787/888933481029

In 2015, 42.2% of bilateral ODA was allocated to social infrastructure and services, amounting to USD 13.1 million, with a strong focus on government and civil society (USD 2.9 million) and water and sanitation (USD 2.7 million). USD 3.4 million was allocated to the production sectors, in particular to fishing (USD 2.8 million) and USD 3.2 million to economic infrastructure and services. Humanitarian aid amounted to USD 3.6 million.

Figure 20.8. **Share of bilateral ODA by sector, 2014-15 average, commitments, Iceland**

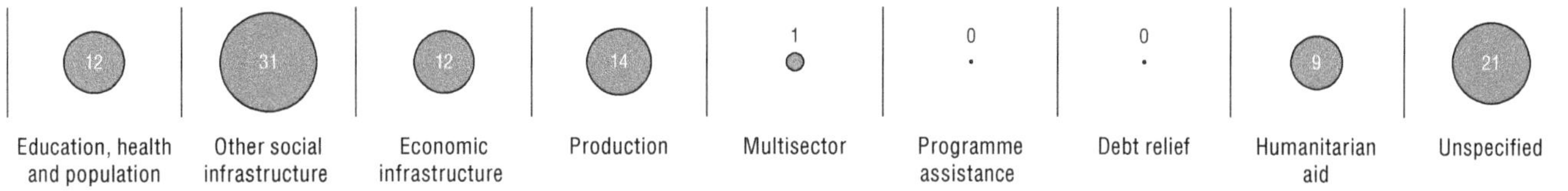

StatLink http://dx.doi.org/10.1787/888933481037

USD 20.4 million of bilateral ODA supported gender equality in 2015. Gender equality is one of two cross-cutting themes (with environment) in Iceland's development co-operation and is solidly integrated into its projects and programmes. In 2015, 86.1% of Iceland's bilateral allocable aid had gender equality and women's empowerment as a principal or significant objective, above the DAC country average of 36.3%. This is up from 80.6% in 2014. Iceland has also worked to promote gender equality in its multilateral support, mainly through the United Nations and the World Bank, including through innovative approaches such as the "HeForShe" campaign, and supports gender equality through investments in nearly all sectors.

Figure 20.9. **Share of bilateral allocable ODA in support of gender equality by sector, 2015, commitments, Iceland**

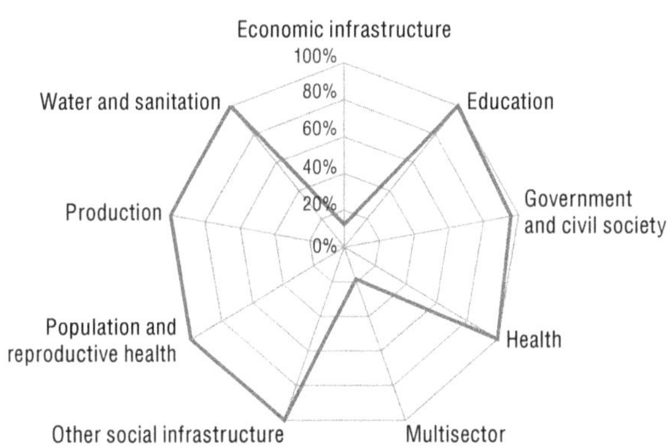

StatLink http://dx.doi.org/10.1787/888933481045

USD 17.4 million of bilateral ODA supported the environment in 2015. The environment is the second cross-cutting theme in Iceland's development co-operation and is integrated into its projects and programmes, although the 2017 DAC Peer Review found Iceland could put greater emphasis on reporting against the DAC Rio markers. In 2015, Iceland reported that 73.4% of its bilateral allocable aid supported the environment and 37.1% (USD 8.8 million) focused particularly on climate change, compared with the respective DAC country averages of 33.2% and 26.2%.

Figure 20.10. **Bilateral allocable ODA in support of global and local environment objectives, two year averages, commitments, Iceland**

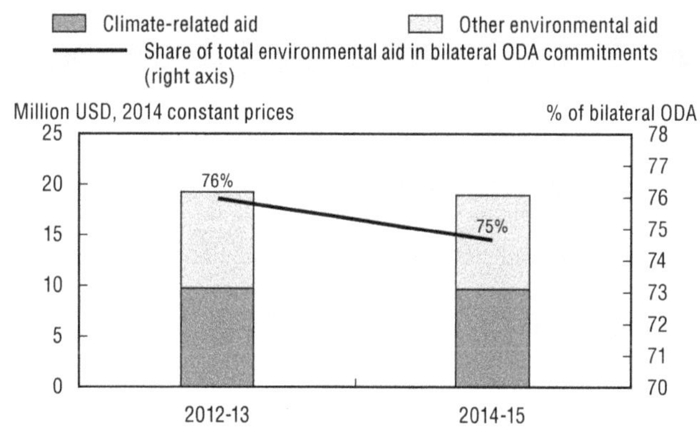

StatLink http://dx.doi.org/10.1787/888933481051

Note to reader: Annex B provides "Methodological notes on the profiles of Development Assistance Committee members".

Reference

OECD (2017), *OECD Development Co-operation Peer Reviews: Iceland 2017*, OECD Publishing, Paris, *http://dx.doi.org/10.1787/9789264274334-en*.

IRELAND

Ireland's contribution to data for development

According to the 2017 Partner Report on Support to Statistics (PRESS) dataset, Ireland committed on average USD 0.44 million per year to finance national statistical capacities and systems in developing countries in 2013-15.

Financial flows from Ireland to developing countries

Figure 21.1. **Net resource flows to developing countries, 2005-15, Ireland**

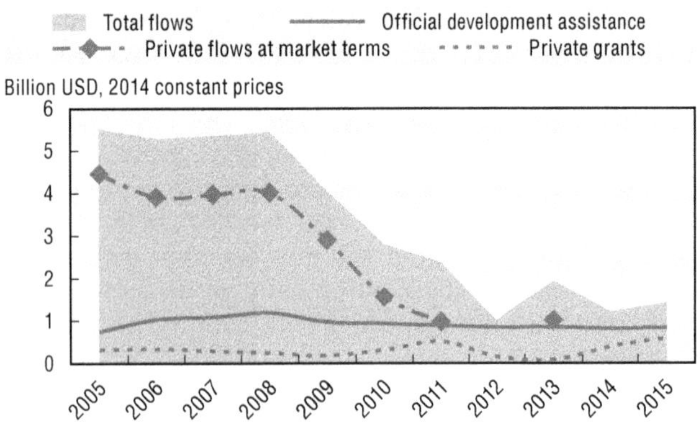

Note: Data on other official flows are not available; data on private flows are not available for 2012, 2014 or 2015.

StatLink http://dx.doi.org/10.1787/888933481065

Ireland's use of ODA to mobilise other resources for sustainable development

- **USD 332 779** of official development assistance (ODA) was committed to the mobilisation of domestic resources in developing countries, e.g. to support the development of their tax systems, in 2015.
- **USD 32.6 million** of ODA (-23.8% in real terms from 2014) was committed to promote aid for trade and improve developing countries' trade performance and integration into the world economy in 2015.

Ireland's performance against commitments for effective development co-operation

Table 21.1. **Results of the 2016 Global Partnership monitoring round, Ireland**

	Alignment and ownership by partner country (%)				Predictability (%)		Transparency		
	Use of country-led results frameworks	Funding recorded in countries' national budgets	Funding through countries' systems	Untied ODA	Annual predictability	Medium-term predictability	Retrospective statistics (OECD CRS)	Information for forecasting (OECD FSS)	Publishing to IATI
2016	68.8	90.7	62.0	100.0	88.7	51.7	Needs improvement	Excellent	Needs improvement
Baseline	-	75.5	82.2	100.0	91.7	84.6	Needs improvement	Excellent	-
Trend	-	⇑	⇓	=	⇓	⇓	=	=	-

Note: Please refer to Annex B for details on the indicators.

StatLink http://dx.doi.org/10.1787/888933483090

Ireland's official development assistance

In 2016, Ireland provided USD 802 million in net ODA (preliminary data), which represented 0.33% of gross national income (GNI) and an 11.9% increase in real terms from 2015 due mainly to an increase in its contributions to multilateral organisations. For the first time in seven years, in 2016 the government increased the ODA budget. Ireland, like other EU member countries, made a new commitment to meeting the 0.7% ODA/GNI target by 2030. Its share of untied ODA (excluding administrative costs and in-donor refugee costs) was 100% in 2015 (up from 98.2% in 2014), compared with the DAC average of 78.1%. The grant element of total ODA was 100% in 2015.

In 2016, in-donor refugee costs were USD 1 million, an increase of 72.9% in real terms over 2015, and represented 0.1% of Ireland's total net ODA.

Figure 21.2. **Net ODA: Trends in volume and as a share of GNI, 2000-16, Ireland**

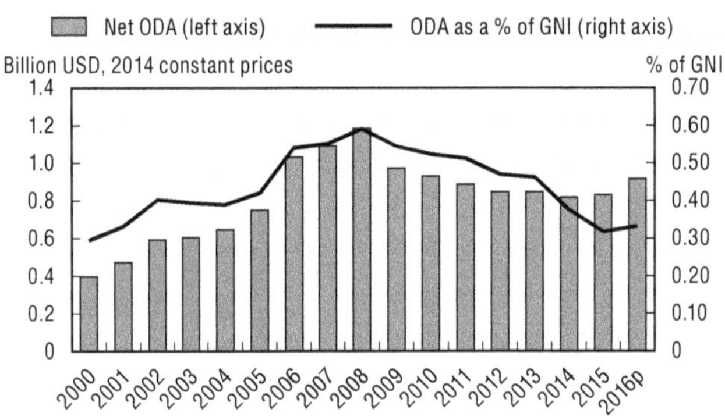

p: Preliminary data.

StatLink http://dx.doi.org/10.1787/888933481070

In 2015, 59.5% of ODA was provided bilaterally. In 2015, Ireland allocated 40.5% of total ODA as core contributions to multilateral organisations, compared with the DAC country average of 26.2%. In addition, it channelled 18.5% of its bilateral ODA for specific projects implemented by multilateral organisations (multi-bi/non-core contributions).

Figure 21.3. **Share of ODA channelled to and through the multilateral system, two year averages, gross disbursements, Ireland**

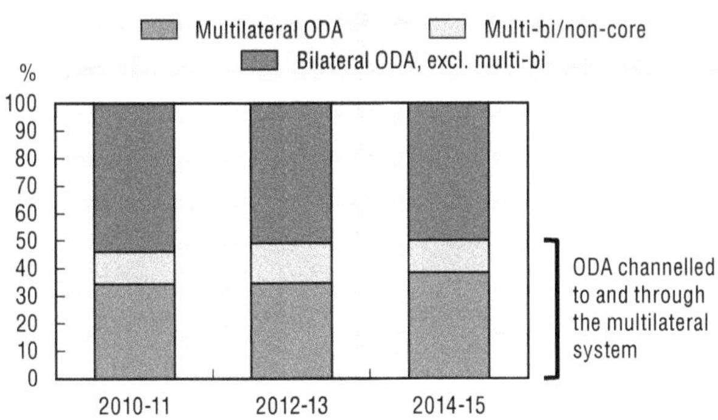

StatLink http://dx.doi.org/10.1787/888933481085

In 2015, 38.1% of bilateral ODA was programmed with partner countries. Ireland's share of country programmable aid was lower than the DAC country average (48.8%) in 2015; 41.9% of this aid consisted of project-type interventions. Core aid to non-governmental organisations and humanitarian assistance accounted for almost half of bilateral ODA.

Figure 21.4. **Composition of bilateral ODA, 2015, gross disbursements, Ireland**

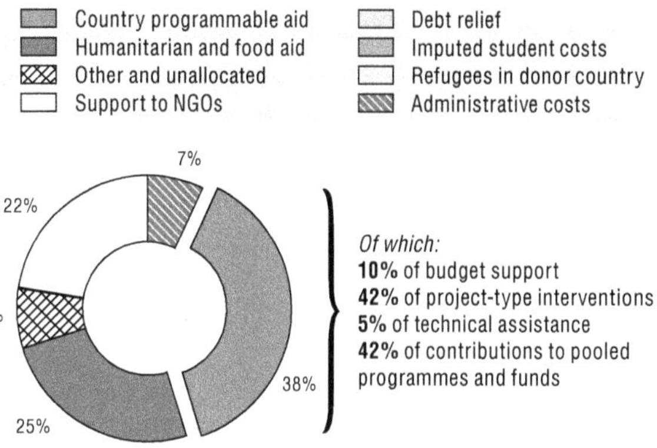

StatLink http://dx.doi.org/10.1787/888933481091

In 2015, USD 183.8 million of bilateral ODA was channelled to and through civil society organisations (CSOs). This equalled 43% of bilateral ODA, compared with the DAC average of 16.9%. Between 2014 and 2015, Irish aid channelled through and to CSOs decreased, both in volume (-46%) and as a share of bilateral aid (from 75.2% in 2014).

Figure 21.5. **Bilateral ODA to and through CSOs, two year averages, gross disbursements, Ireland**

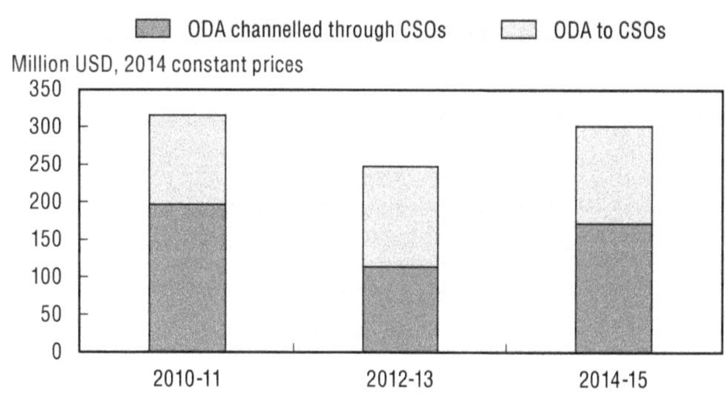

StatLink http://dx.doi.org/10.1787/888933481108

Bilateral ODA was primarily focused on sub-Saharan Africa. In 2015, Ireland allocated USD 271.9 million to sub-Saharan Africa, USD 25.4 million to the Middle East and USD 15.2 million to Far East Asia.

Figure 21.6. **Share of bilateral ODA by region, 2014-15 average, gross disbursements, Ireland**

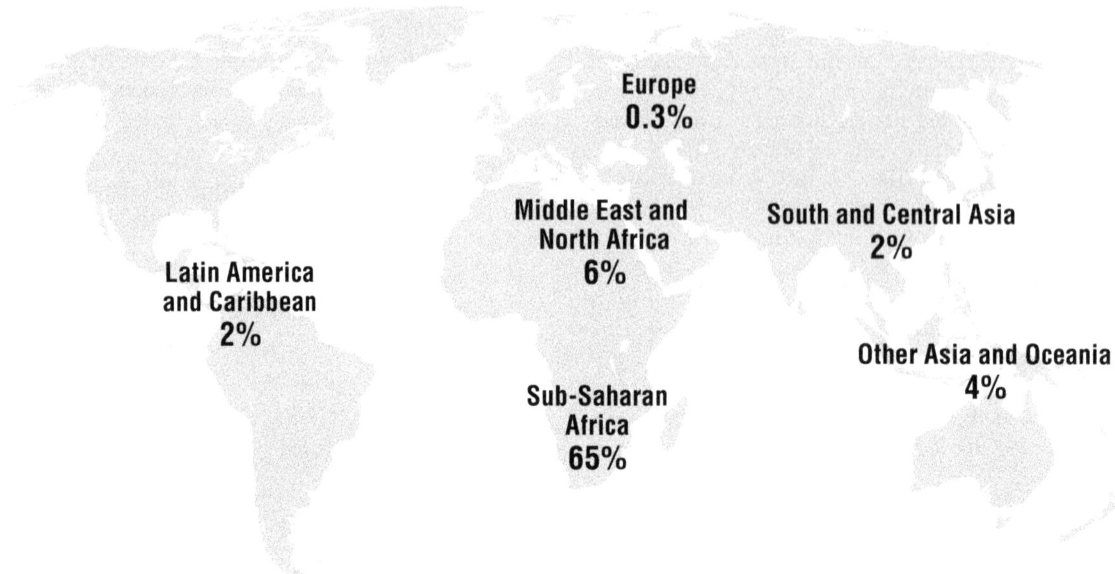

Note: 20% of bilateral ODA allocated was unspecified by region in 2014-15. This share is not represented on the map.

StatLink http://dx.doi.org/10.1787/888933481116

In 2015, 52.4% of bilateral ODA went to Ireland's top 10 recipients. Seven of its eight key partners are among its top 10 recipients, showing that it concentrates its aid allocations on partner countries. Irish support to fragile contexts was USD 297.8 million in 2015 (69.7% of gross bilateral ODA).

Figure 21.7. **Bilateral ODA to top recipients, 2014-15 average, gross disbursements, Ireland**

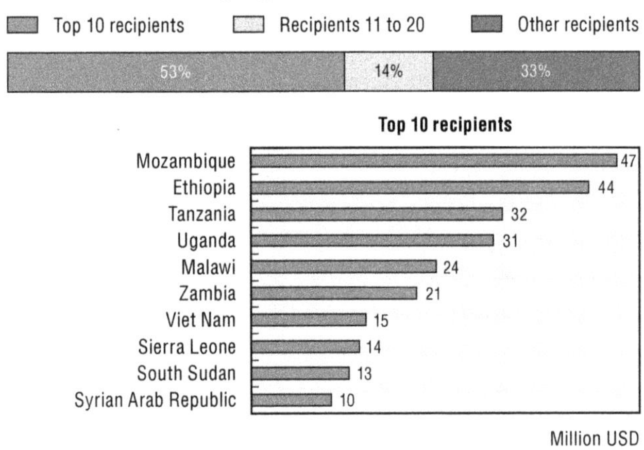

StatLink http://dx.doi.org/10.1787/888933481124

In 2015, 60.1% of bilateral ODA was allocated to least developed countries (LDCs), amounting to USD 256.7 million. The share allocated to LDCs has remained relatively stable since 2012 (62.4%) with a slight decrease in 2014 (59.6%). Ireland ranked highest among DAC members for the share of bilateral ODA allocated to LDCs in 2015 (the DAC average was 24.3%).

At 0.15% of GNI in 2015, total ODA to LDCs achieved the UN target of 0.15% of GNI.

Figure 21.8. **Bilateral ODA by income group, two year averages, gross disbursements, Ireland**

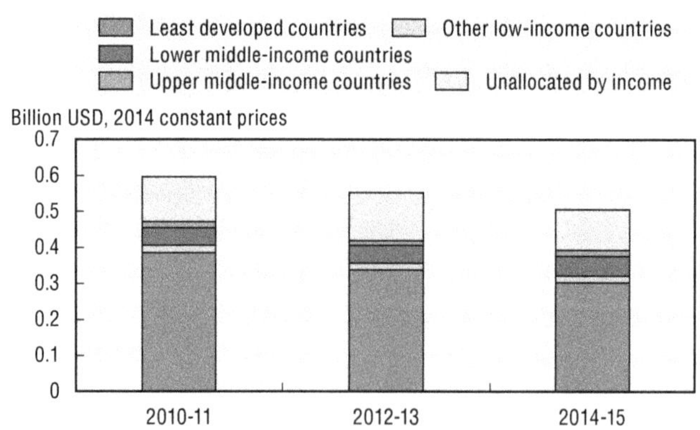

StatLink http://dx.doi.org/10.1787/888933481131

In 2015, 46.4% of bilateral ODA, or USD 198.3 million, was allocated to social infrastructure and services, with a strong focus on government and civil society (USD 64 million) and support to health (USD 56 million) and education (USD 39.8 million). Humanitarian aid amounted to USD 89.7 million.

Figure 21.9. **Share of bilateral ODA by sector, 2014-15 average, commitments, Ireland**

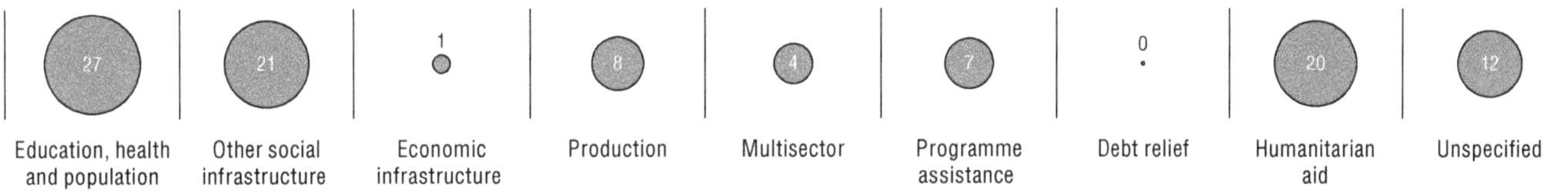

StatLink http://dx.doi.org/10.1787/888933481144

USD 289.9 million of bilateral ODA supported gender equality in 2015. Ireland plays an agenda-setting role on gender equality and women's empowerment as evidenced by its advocacy for the theme when negotiating the 2030 Agenda. In 2015, 79% of its bilateral allocable aid had gender equality and women's empowerment as a principal or significant objective (up from 48.7% in 2014), compared with the DAC country average of 36.3%. Ireland's aid to population and reproductive health, education, other social infrastructure, and health focuses on gender equality.

Figure 21.10. **Share of bilateral allocable ODA in support of gender equality by sector, 2015, commitments, Ireland**

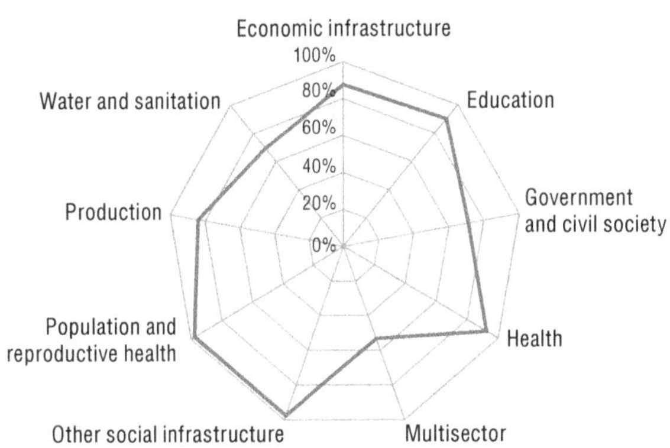

StatLink http://dx.doi.org/10.1787/888933481156

USD 78 million of bilateral ODA supported the environment in 2015. Environmental sustainability, climate change and development have been growing priority policy issues for Ireland. In 2015, 20.7% of its bilateral allocable aid supported the environment, compared with the DAC country average of 33.2%. Also, 17.3% (USD 65.2 million) of Irish bilateral allocable aid focused on climate change, compared with the DAC country average of 26.2%.

Figure 21.11. **Bilateral allocable ODA in support of global and local environment objectives, two year averages, commitments, Ireland**

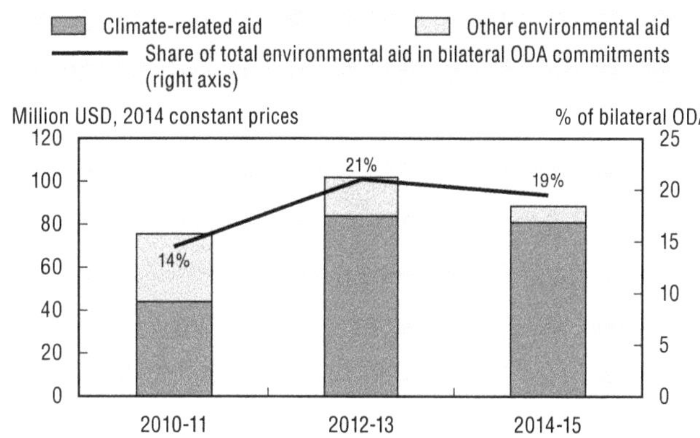

StatLink http://dx.doi.org/10.1787/888933481165

Note to reader: Annex B provides "Methodological notes on the profiles of Development Assistance Committee members".

ITALY

Italy's contribution to data for development

Italian Development Co-operation has been promoting a "culture of statistics" since the 1990s, providing statistical assistance to developing countries (including Albania, Bosnia and Herzegovina, Cabo Verde, Egypt, Ethiopia, Lebanon, Mozambique, Myanmar, Senegal and the Caribbean Community). In 2015, Italy published an action plan on statistics outlining its commitment to co-operate with the international community to reinforce and modernise the capacity of developing countries' national statistical offices to support population and agricultural censuses and vital statistics.

Italy provides support to developing countries mainly through bilateral government to government technical assistance and funding for equipment. It focuses on improving statistical production, strengthening data dissemination and improving statistical literacy of data users. Italy considers that the technical assistance provided to the new Central Statistical Organisation of Myanmar to help it implement business surveys and improve data dissemination and vital statistics is a successful example of statistical capacity building with a limited budget and a well-co-ordinated donor group.

According to the 2017 Partner Report on Support to Statistics (PRESS) dataset, Italy committed on average USD 0.96 million per year to finance national statistical capacities and systems in developing countries in 2013-15.

Financial flows from Italy to developing countries

Figure 22.1. **Net resource flows to developing countries, 2005-15, Italy**

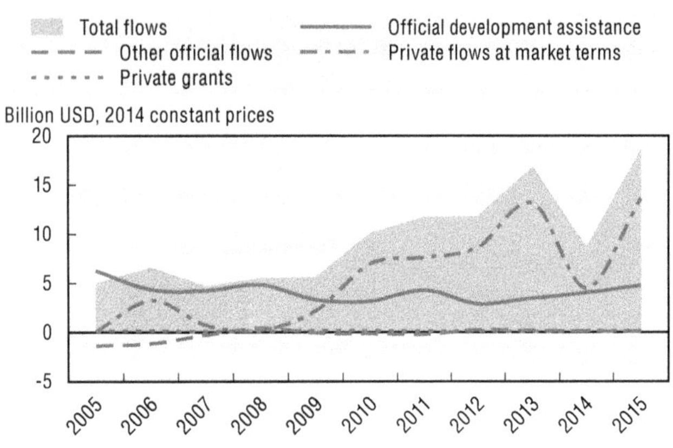

StatLink http://dx.doi.org/10.1787/888933481173

Italy's use of ODA to mobilise other resources for sustainable development

- **USD 0.61 million** of official development assistance (ODA) was committed to the mobilisation of domestic resources in developing countries, e.g. to support the development of their tax systems, in 2015.
- **USD 184.2 million** of ODA (doubling in real terms from 2014) was committed to promote aid for trade and improve developing countries' trade performance and integration into the world economy in 2015.

Italy's performance against commitments for effective development co-operation

Table 22.1. **Results of the 2016 Global Partnership monitoring round, Italy**

	Alignment and ownership by partner country (%)				Predictability (%)		Transparency		
	Use of country-led results frameworks	Funding recorded in countries' national budgets	Funding through countries' systems	Untied ODA	Annual predictability	Medium-term predictability	Retrospective statistics (OECD CRS)	Information for forecasting (OECD FSS)	Publishing to IATI
2016	60.4	52.9	50.8	95.1	57.8	60.6	Fair	Good	-
Baseline	-	32.9	38.4	58.3	56.6	77.5	Fair	Good	-
Trend	-	⇑	⇑	⇑	⇑	⇓	=	=	-

Note: Please refer to Annex B for details on the indicators.

StatLink http://dx.doi.org/10.1787/888933483108

Italy's official development assistance

In 2016, Italy provided USD 4.9 billion in net ODA (preliminary data), which represented 0.26% of gross national income (GNI) and a 20.2% increase in real terms from 2015 due to increased in-donor refugee costs as well as a rise in its contributions to multilateral organisations. In line with Italy's commitment to scale up its aid, ODA has increased both in terms of volume and as a percentage of GNI over the last three years. Italy's share of untied ODA (excluding administrative costs and in-donor refugee costs) was 95.1% in 2015 (up from 93.5% in 2014), while the DAC average was 78.1%. The grant element of total ODA was 99.6% in 2015.

In 2016, in-donor refugee costs were USD 1.67 billion, an increase of 67.9% in real terms over 2015, and represented 34.3% of Italy's total net ODA.

Figure 22.2. **Net ODA: Trends in volume and as a share of GNI, 2000-16, Italy**

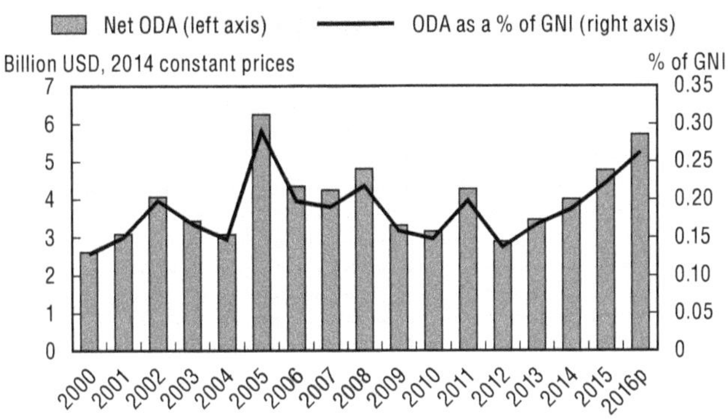

p: Preliminary data.

StatLink http://dx.doi.org/10.1787/888933481185

In 2015, 46.4% of ODA was provided bilaterally. Italy allocated 53.6% of total ODA as core contributions to multilateral organisations, compared with the DAC country average of 26.2%. In addition, it channelled 14.6% of its bilateral ODA for specific projects implemented by multilateral organisations (multi-bi/non-core contributions).

Figure 22.3. **Share of ODA channelled to and through the multilateral system, two year averages, gross disbursements, Italy**

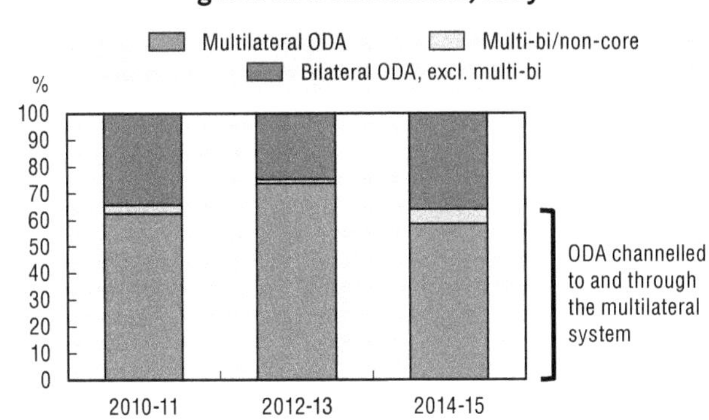

StatLink http://dx.doi.org/10.1787/888933481198

In 2015, 21.5% of bilateral ODA was programmed with partner countries. Italy's share of country programmable aid was low compared with the DAC country average (48.8%) in 2015. Project-type interventions accounted for 62.3% of this aid. Fifty-two per cent of bilateral ODA was allocated to refugees in donor country.

Figure 22.4. **Composition of bilateral ODA, 2015, gross disbursements, Italy**

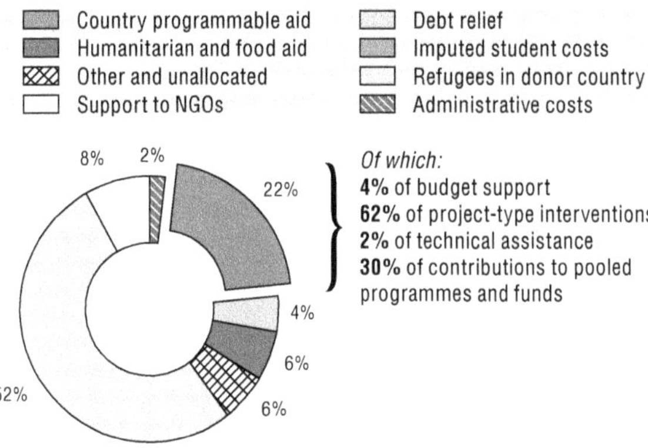

StatLink http://dx.doi.org/10.1787/888933481203

In 2015, USD 201.4 million of bilateral ODA was channelled to and through civil society organisations (CSOs). Between 2014 and 2015, Italy's aid channelled to and through CSOs increased in terms of volume (+29.2%), but decreased as a share of bilateral ODA (from 12.7% in 2014 to 10.7% in 2015). The DAC country average was 16.9% in 2015.

Figure 22.5. **Bilateral ODA to and through CSOs, two year averages, gross disbursements, Italy**

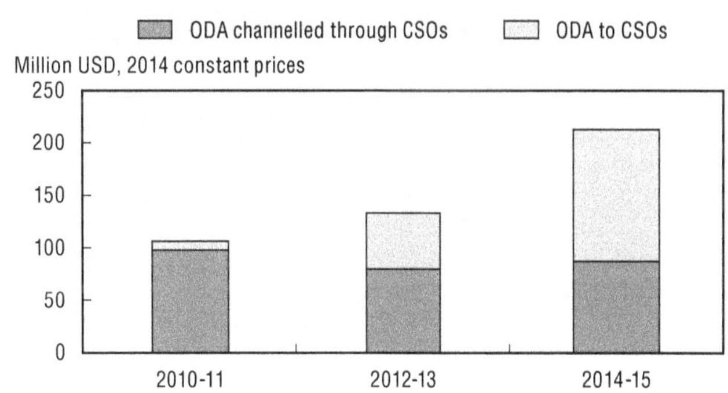

StatLink http://dx.doi.org/10.1787/888933481218

In 2015, bilateral ODA mainly focused on sub-Saharan Africa and south and central Asia. USD 222 million was allocated to sub-Saharan Africa, USD 172.8 million to south and central Asia, and USD 136.3 million to the Middle East.

Figure 22.6. **Share of bilateral ODA by region, 2014-15 average, gross disbursements, Italy**

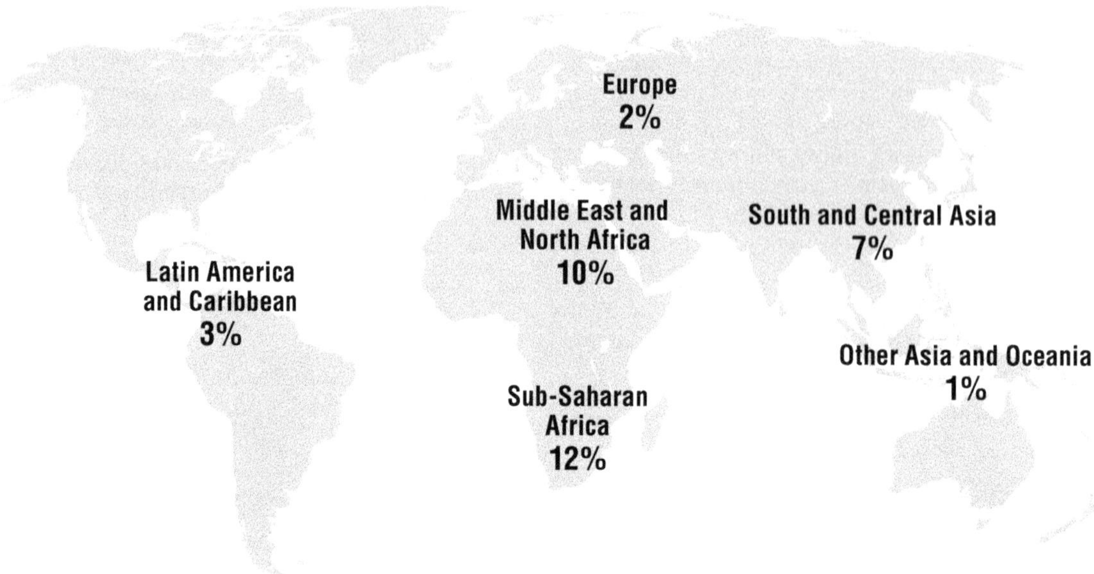

Note: 64% of bilateral ODA allocated was unspecified by region in 2014-15. This share is not represented on the map.

StatLink http://dx.doi.org/10.1787/888933481224

In 2015, 21.1% of bilateral ODA went to Italy's top 10 recipients. Italy has 20 priority countries; 9 of them feature on the list of its top 10 recipients. Its support to fragile contexts reached USD 471.2 million in 2015 (25% of gross bilateral ODA).

Figure 22.7. **Bilateral ODA to top recipients, 2014-15 average, gross disbursements, Italy**

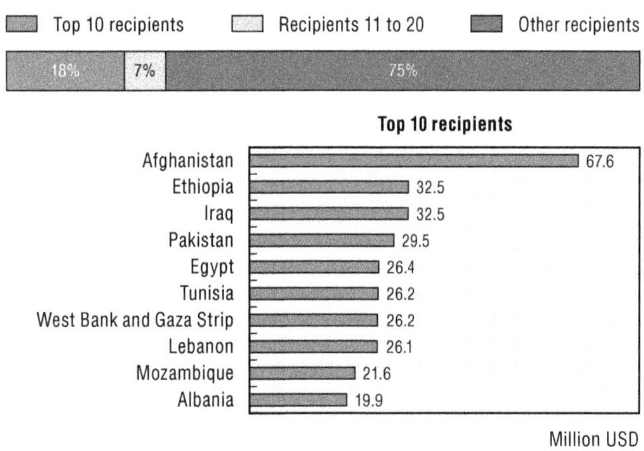

StatLink http://dx.doi.org/10.1787/888933481235

In 2015, 15.7% of bilateral ODA was allocated to least developed countries (LDCs), amounting to USD 296.5 million. Aid to LDCs as a share of bilateral ODA has slightly increased since 2014 (13.3%); however, it still falls below Italy's peak in 2011 when it stood at 47.8% (due to debt relief to the Democratic Republic of the Congo). The 2015 DAC country average was 24.3%. LDCs received the highest share of bilateral ODA, noting that 63.9% was unallocated by income group.

At 0.05% of GNI in 2015, total ODA to LDCs was below the UN target of 0.15% of GNI.

Figure 22.8. **Bilateral ODA by income group, two year averages, gross disbursements, Italy**

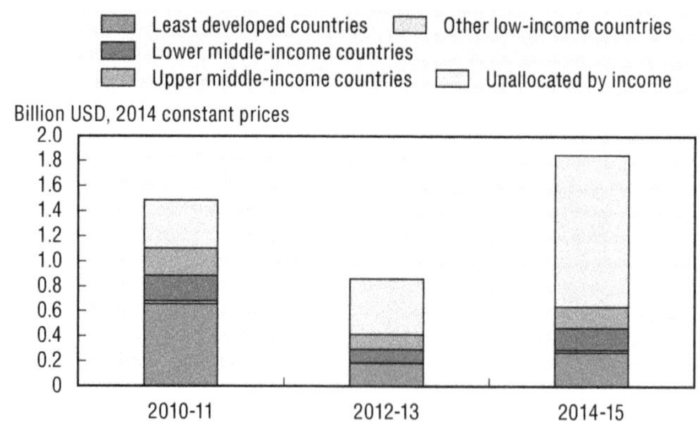

StatLink http://dx.doi.org/10.1787/888933481241

In 2015, 20.2%, or USD 405.5 million, of bilateral ODA was allocated to social infrastructure and services, with a strong focus on government and civil society (USD 131.6 million), education (USD 105.2 million), and health (USD 92.2 million). Humanitarian aid amounted to USD 98.5 million.

Figure 22.9. **Share of bilateral ODA by sector, 2014-15 average, commitments, Italy**

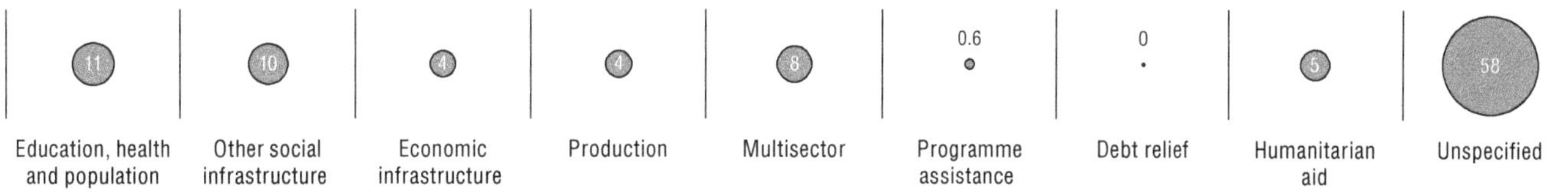

StatLink http://dx.doi.org/10.1787/888933481256

USD 290.2 million of Italy's bilateral ODA supported gender equality in 2015. Gender equality and women's empowerment is both a thematic priority and a cross-cutting issue for Italy's development co-operation. Italy approved specific guidelines for gender equality in 2010. Nevertheless, mainstreaming gender remains challenging (OECD, 2014). In 2015, 32.5% of Italian bilateral allocable aid had gender equality and women's empowerment as a principal or significant objective, a decrease compared with 69.3% in 2014. The DAC country average was 36.3% in 2015.

Figure 22.10. **Share of bilateral allocable ODA in support of gender equality by sector, 2015, commitments, Italy**

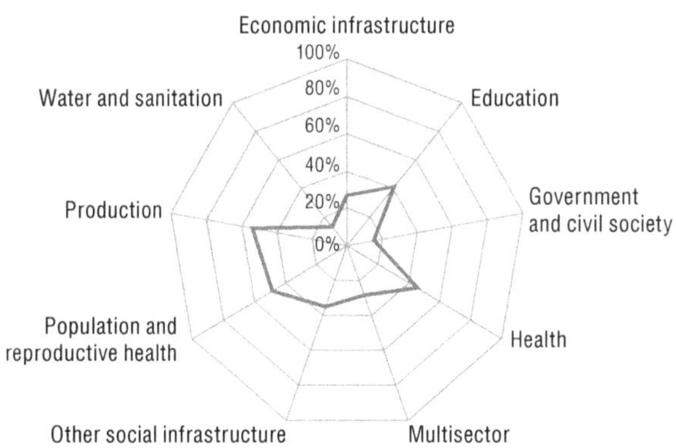

StatLink http://dx.doi.org/10.1787/888933481260

USD 391.1 million of bilateral ODA supported the environment in 2015. Protecting the environment is both a priority and a cross-cutting issue of Italy's development co-operation. In 2015, 43.8% of Italian bilateral allocable aid supported the environment and 27.9% (USD 248.8 million) focused particularly on climate change, compared with respective DAC country averages of 33.2% and 26.2%. This represents an increase since 2014, when the contribution to the environment (29% of bilateral allocable aid) and climate change (16%) was significantly lower. Italy issued environmental guidelines in 2011. However, mainstreaming environment throughout its development co-operation remains a challenge for Italy (OECD, 2014).

Figure 22.11. **Bilateral allocable ODA in support of global and local environment objectives, two year averages, commitments, Italy**

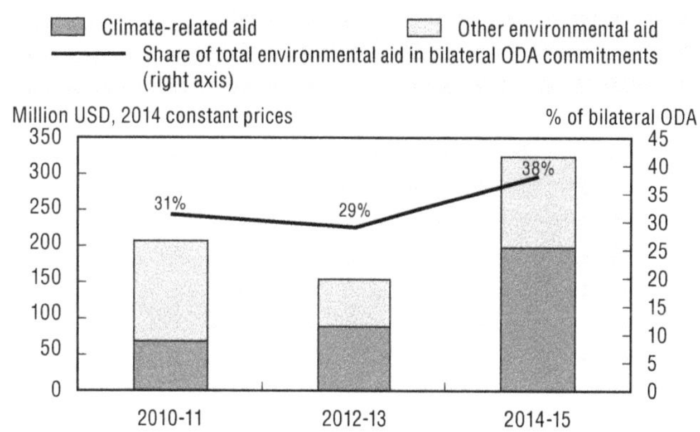

StatLink http://dx.doi.org/10.1787/888933481276

Note to reader: Annex B provides "Methodological notes on the profiles of Development Assistance Committee members".

Reference

OECD (2014), *OECD Development Co-operation Peer Reviews: Italy 2014*, OECD Publishing, Paris, *http://dx.doi.org/10.1787/9789264213241-en*.

JAPAN

Japan's contribution to data for development

Japan has been providing support to strengthen statistical capacities and systems in developing countries for many years. Support focuses on national statistical systems and is offered through technical assistance and funding for equipment, in particular with the aim of contributing to improve statistical production and the statistical literacy of data users and to strengthen data dissemination.

Japan offers its support through bilateral and multilateral channels. Bilateral assistance is offered by the Statistics Bureau of Japan and Japan International Cooperation Agency (JICA), which provide capacity building to developing countries' national statistical offices to help them carry out population and economic censuses, other surveys, and statistical studies. Japan's Statistics Bureau has been providing expertise in particular to the national statistical offices of Cambodia, Egypt, Indonesia and Nepal. Japan has also made both cash and in-kind contributions to the United Nations Statistical Institute for Asia and the Pacific, which has implemented training and other activities to build the capacities of 16 139 participants from national statistical offices of 137 developing countries/regions since 1970.

According to the 2017 Partner Report on Support to Statistics (PRESS) dataset, Japan committed on average USD 4.3 million per year to finance national statistical capacities and systems in developing countries in 2013-15.

Financial flows from Japan to developing countries

Figure 23.1. **Net resource flows to developing countries, 2005-15, Japan**

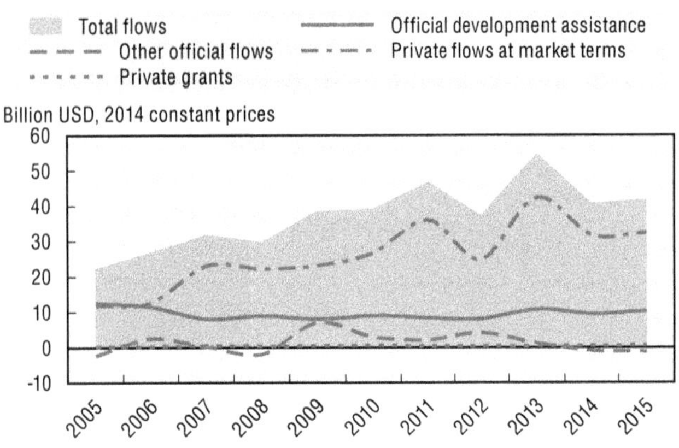

StatLink http://dx.doi.org/10.1787/888933481286

Japan's use of ODA to mobilise other resources for sustainable development

- **USD 2.9 million** of official development assistance (ODA) was committed to the mobilisation of domestic resources in developing countries, e.g. to support the development of their tax systems, in 2015.
- **USD 11.8 billion** of ODA (+37.6% in real terms from 2014) was committed to promote aid for trade and improve developing countries' trade performance and integration into the world economy in 2015.

Japan's performance against commitments for effective development co-operation

Table 23.1. **Results of the 2016 Global Partnership monitoring round, Japan**

	Alignment and ownership by partner country (%)				Predictability (%)		Transparency		
	Use of country-led results frameworks	Funding recorded in countries' national budgets	Funding through countries' systems	Untied ODA	Annual predictability	Medium-term predictability	Retrospective statistics (OECD CRS)	Information for forecasting (OECD FSS)	Publishing to IATI
2016	75.9	83.0	67.9	74.6	98.4	63.0	Excellent	Needs improvement	Needs improvement
Baseline	-	64.9	68.8	78.6	99.8	79.4	Excellent	Fair	-
Trend	-	⇑	⇓	⇓	⇓	⇓	=	⇑	-

Note: Please refer to Annex B for details on the indicators. For untied ODA please refer to the footnote on the next page.

StatLink http://dx.doi.org/10.1787/888933483117

Japan's official development assistance

In 2016, Japan provided USD 10.4 billion in net ODA (preliminary data). This represented 0.20% of gross national income (GNI) and a 0.9% increase in real terms from 2015 due to a slight increase in its bilateral ODA. In 2015, the untied share of Japanese total bilateral ODA, excluding technical co-operation, was 82.3%, a decrease of 7.3 percentage points from 2014. Japan's ODA includes a large technical co-operation programme, but Japan does not report its tying status. The share of total Japanese bilateral aid reported as untied was 74.6% in 2015.* The grant element of total ODA was 87.5% in 2015.

Japan did not report in-donor refugee costs as ODA in 2016.

Figure 23.2. **Net ODA: Trends in volume and as a share of GNI, 2000-16, Japan**

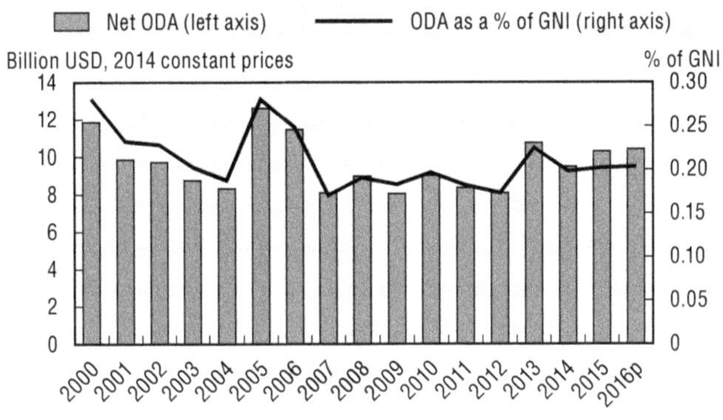

p: Preliminary data.

StatLink http://dx.doi.org/10.1787/888933481291

In 2015, 79.7% of ODA was provided bilaterally. Japan allocated 20.3% of total ODA as core contributions to multilateral organisations, compared with the DAC country average of 26.2%. In addition, it channelled 13.9% of its bilateral ODA for specific projects implemented by multilateral organisations (multi-bi/non-core contributions).

Figure 23.3. **Share of ODA channelled to and through the multilateral system, two year averages, gross disbursements, Japan**

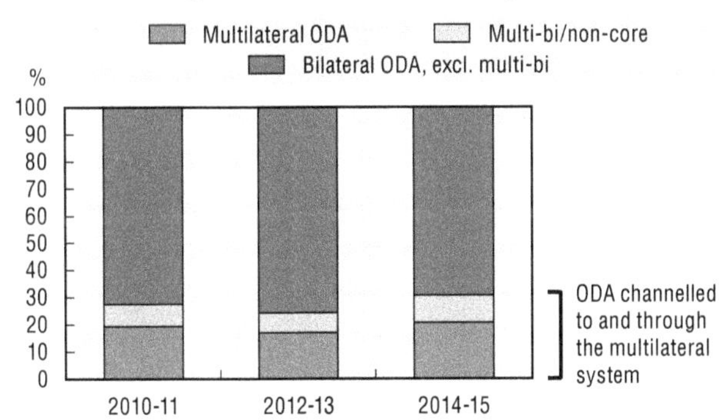

StatLink http://dx.doi.org/10.1787/888933481308

In 2015, Japan programmed 76.2% of bilateral ODA with partner countries. Japan's share of country programmable aid was above the DAC country average of 48.8% in 2015. Project-type interventions totalled 89.4% of this aid.

Figure 23.4. **Composition of bilateral ODA, 2015, gross disbursements, Japan**

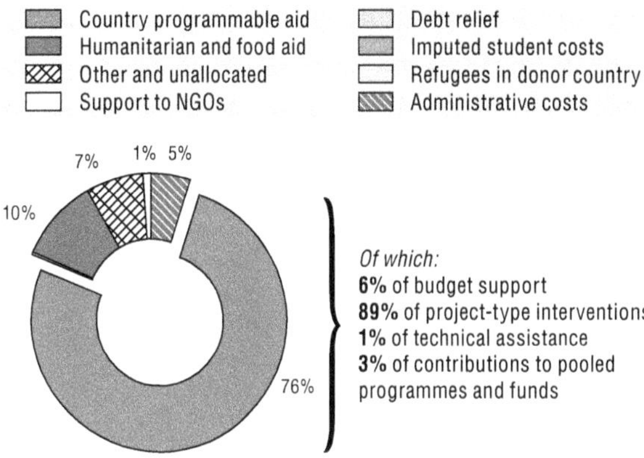

StatLink http://dx.doi.org/10.1787/888933481314

In 2015, USD 280.3 million of bilateral ODA was channelled to and through civil society organisations (CSOs). Between 2014 and 2015 Japan's aid channelled to and through CSOs increased in terms of volume (+7.5%) and remained stable as a share of bilateral ODA (2.3% in 2014 and 2015). The DAC country average for aid to and through CSOs was 16.9% in 2015.

Figure 23.5. **Bilateral ODA to and through CSOs, two year averages, gross disbursements, Japan**

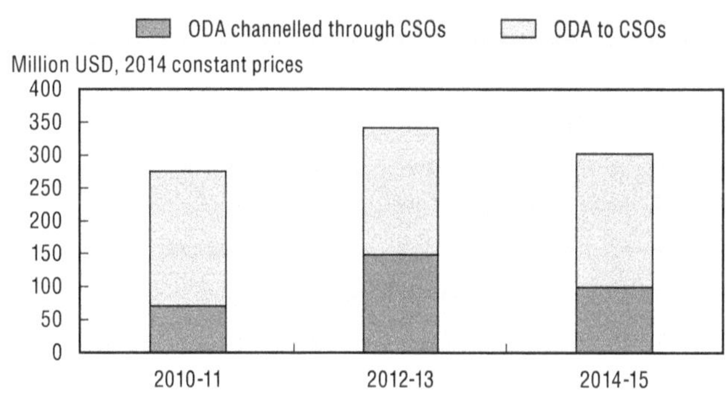

StatLink http://dx.doi.org/10.1787/888933481329

* Japan interprets the Accra and Busan commitments on untying to be restricted only to ODA covered by the *DAC Recommendation on Untying ODA to Least Developed Countries and Heavily Indebted Poor Countries* (OECD, 2008). With respect to the implementation of the recommendation, Japan notified the DAC during the 2014 Peer Review that, in accordance with paragraph 21 of this recommendation, it reserves the right to use tied aid as part of its ODA to all non-LDC highly-indebted poor countries (HIPCs).

Bilateral ODA was heavily focused on Asia. In 2015, USD 3.4 billion was allocated to south and central Asia and USD 3.2 billion to Far East Asia. USD 1.5 billion was allocated to sub-Saharan Africa.

Figure 23.6. **Share of bilateral ODA by region, 2014-15 average, gross disbursements, Japan**

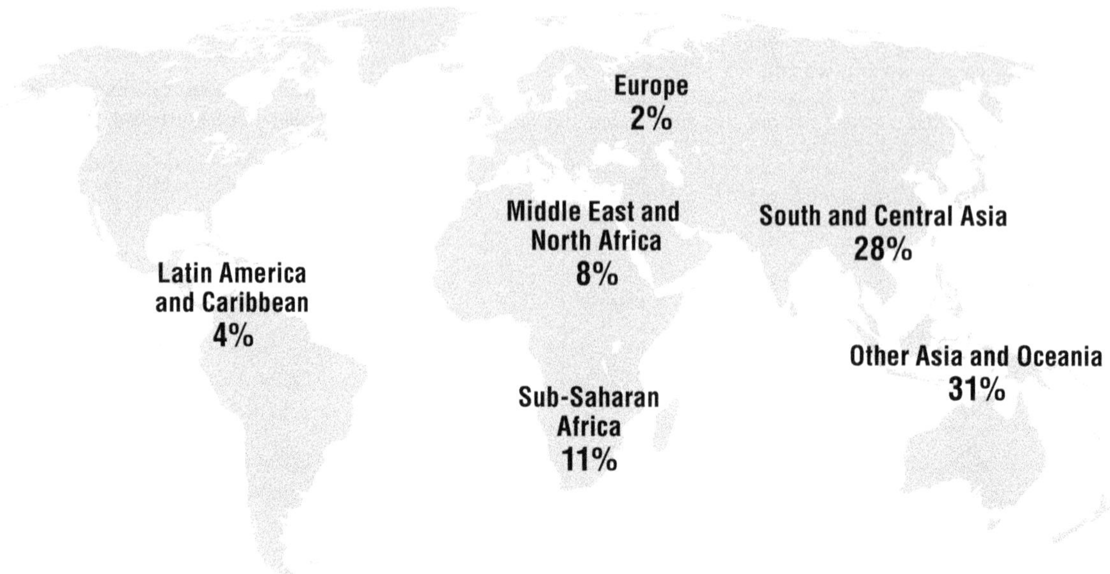

Note: 15% of bilateral ODA allocated was unspecified by region in 2014-15. This share is not represented on the map.

StatLink http://dx.doi.org/10.1787/888933481336

In 2015, 49.5% of bilateral ODA went to Japan's top 10 recipients. In line with its stated use of ODA as a diplomatic tool, Japan has a bilateral programme in over 140 countries. In 2011-12, 37% of Japanese bilateral ODA went to 5 recipient countries and 66% to the top 20 recipients. Japan's support to fragile contexts reached USD 3.6 billion in 2015 (29.7% of gross bilateral ODA).

Figure 23.7. **Bilateral ODA to top recipients, 2014-15 average, gross disbursements, Japan**

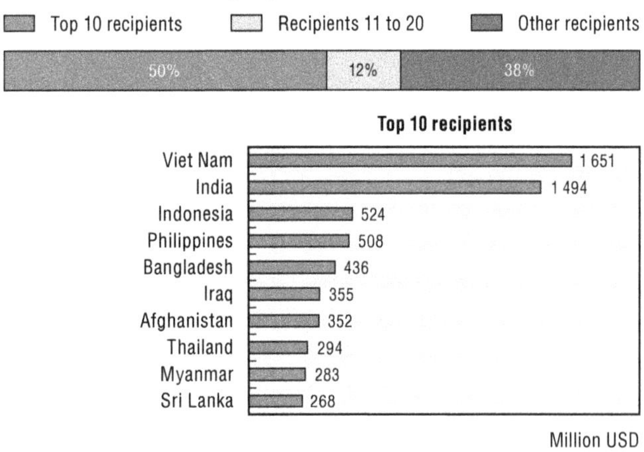

StatLink http://dx.doi.org/10.1787/888933481340

In 2015, 21.6% of bilateral ODA was provided to least developed countries (LDCs), amounting to USD 2.6 billion. This is an increase from 2014 (19.2%), but remains lower than the 2015 DAC country average of 24.3%. Lower middle-income countries received the highest share of bilateral ODA in 2015 (44.8%).

At 0.08% of GNI in 2015, total ODA to LDCs was lower than the UN target of 0.15% of GNI.

Figure 23.8. **Bilateral ODA by income group, two year averages, gross disbursements, Japan**

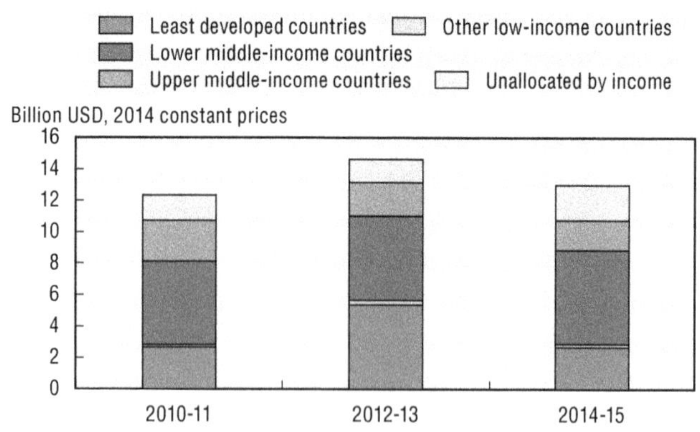

StatLink http://dx.doi.org/10.1787/888933481352

In 2015, 52.9% of bilateral ODA was allocated to economic infrastructure and services, or a total of USD 10.3 billion, with a strong focus on transport and storage (USD 6.4 billion) and energy generation and supply (USD 3.8 billion). USD 1.7 billion was allocated to water and sanitation, USD 712.4 million to health, and USD 530.7 million to education, as a part of social infrastructure and services. Humanitarian aid amounted to USD 1.1 billion.

Figure 23.9. **Share of bilateral ODA by sector, 2014-15 average, commitments, Japan**

StatLink http://dx.doi.org/10.1787/888933481369

USD 7.2 billion of bilateral ODA supported gender equality in 2015. In 2015, 41.2% of Japan's bilateral allocable aid had gender equality and women's empowerment as a principal or significant objective, compared to the DAC country average of 36.3%. This was up from 2014 when it was at 22.6%. Japan's aid to health and government and civil society focuses on gender. In 2013, the government of Japan announced a new and significant emphasis on women's empowerment in its development co-operation. This was further emphasised in the 2015 Development Co-operation Charter.

Figure 23.10. **Share of bilateral allocable ODA in support of gender equality by sector, 2015, commitments, Japan**

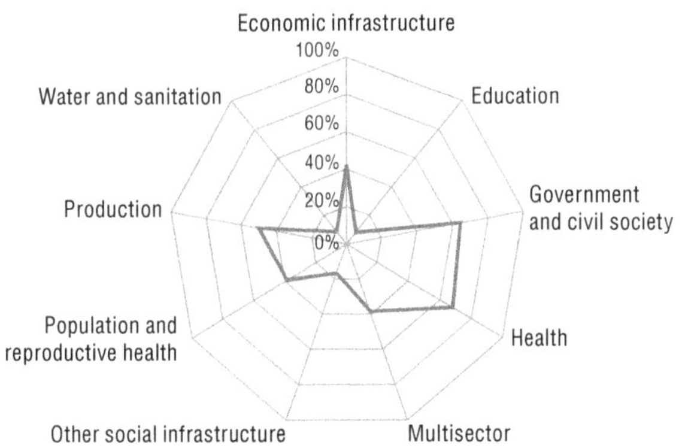

StatLink http://dx.doi.org/10.1787/888933481379

USD 9.7 billion of bilateral ODA supported the environment in 2015. Japan has maintained strong financial commitments to the environment and climate change. In 2015, 52.7% of its bilateral allocable aid supported the environment and 48.8% (USD 9 billion) focused particularly on climate change, compared with the respective DAC country averages of 33.2% and 26.2%.

Figure 23.11. **Bilateral allocable ODA in support of global and local environment objectives, two year averages, commitments, Japan**

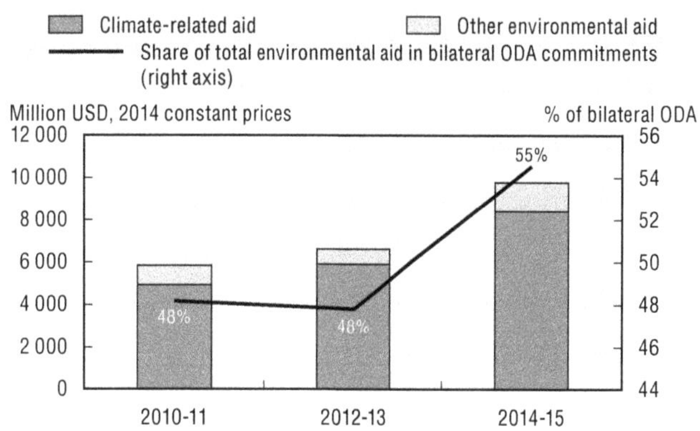

StatLink http://dx.doi.org/10.1787/888933481389

Note to reader: Annex B provides "Methodological notes on the profiles of Development Assistance Committee members".

References

OECD (2014), *OECD Development Co-operation Peer Reviews: Japan 2014*, OECD Publishing, Paris, *http://dx.doi.org/10.1787/9789264218161-en.*

OECD (2008), *DAC Recommendation on Untying ODA to the Least Developed Countries and Heavily Indebted Poor Countries*, OECD, Paris, *www.oecd.org/dac/41707972.pdf.*

KOREA

Korea's contribution to data for development

Korea engages in statistical capacity building in developing countries with the aim to improve statistical production and statistical literacy of data users and to promote the use of data by policy makers, civil society and citizens. Korea also works to improve co-ordination among development partners. Its support focuses on national statistical systems and is offered mainly in the form of bilateral government to government capacity-building programmes, assistance to establish statistical data systems and funding for equipment, software and consumables. Korea also indirectly supports statistical capacity building in partner countries by enhancing understanding and knowledge on monitoring and evaluation.

According to the 2017 Partner Report on Support to Statistics (PRESS) dataset, Korea committed on average USD 6.06 million per year to finance national statistical capacities and systems in developing countries in 2013-15.

Financial flows from Korea to developing countries

Figure 24.1. **Net resource flows to developing countries, 2005-15, Korea**

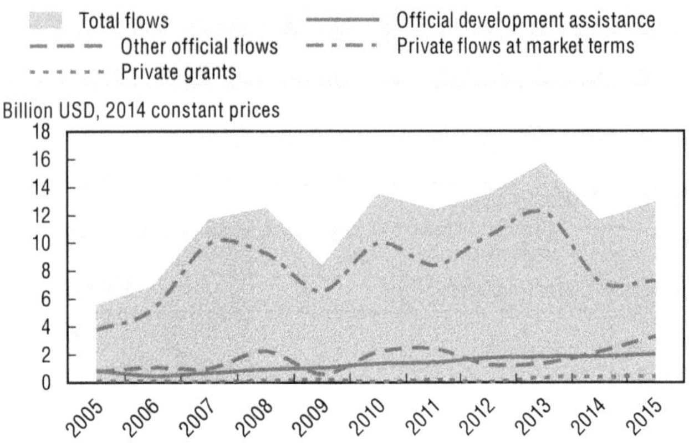

StatLink http://dx.doi.org/10.1787/888933481396

Korea's use of ODA to mobilise other resources for sustainable development

- **USD 0.35 million** of official development assistance (ODA) was committed to the mobilisation of domestic resources in developing countries, e.g. to support the development of their tax systems, in 2015.
- **USD 892 million** of ODA (-12.1% in real terms from 2014) was committed to promote aid for trade and improve developing countries' trade performance and integration into the world economy in 2015.

Korea's performance against commitments for effective development co-operation

Table 24.1. **Results of the 2016 Global Partnership monitoring round, Korea**

	Alignment and ownership by partner country (%)				Predictability (%)		Transparency		
	Use of country-led results frameworks	Funding recorded in countries' national budgets	Funding through countries' systems	Untied ODA	Annual predictability	Medium-term predictability	Retrospective statistics (OECD CRS)	Information for forecasting (OECD FSS)	Publishing to IATI
2016	67.9	60.0	45.5	50.2	92.8	78.5	Excellent	Good	-
Baseline	-	52.5	16.2	32.3	73.6	45.9	Excellent	Fair	-
Trend	-	⇑	⇑	⇑	⇑	⇑	=	⇑	-

Note: Please refer to Annex B for details on the indicators.

StatLink http://dx.doi.org/10.1787/888933483124

Korea's official development assistance

In 2016, Korea provided USD 2 billion in net ODA (preliminary data), which represented 0.14% of gross national income (GNI) and a 3.4% increase in real terms from 2015* due to an increase in its bilateral aid. Korea missed its ODA/GNI target of 0.25% by 2015 but has set a new target of 0.30% ODA/GNI by 2030. To help reach this target Korea plans to publish an ODA growth plan with milestones. Korea's share of untied ODA (excluding administrative costs and in-donor refugee costs) was 50.2% in 2015 (down from 53.2% in 2014), compared to the DAC average of 78.1%. The grant element of total ODA was 95.3% in 2015. Korea did not report in-donor refugee costs as ODA in 2016.

Figure 24.2. **Net ODA: Trends in volume and as a share of GNI, 2000-16, Korea**

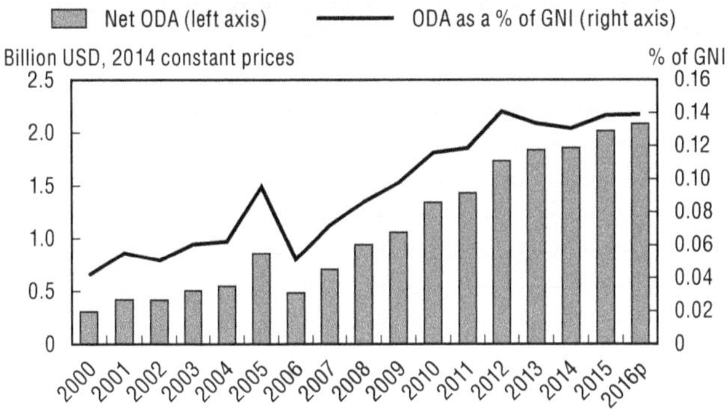

p: Preliminary data.

StatLink http://dx.doi.org/10.1787/888933481403

In 2015, 80.7% of ODA was provided bilaterally. Korea allocated 19.3% of total ODA as core contributions to multilateral organisations, compared with the DAC country average of 26.2%. In addition, it channelled 15.2% of its bilateral ODA for specific projects implemented by multilateral organisations (multi-bi/non-core contributions).

Figure 24.3. **Share of ODA channelled to and through the multilateral system, two year averages, gross disbursements, Korea**

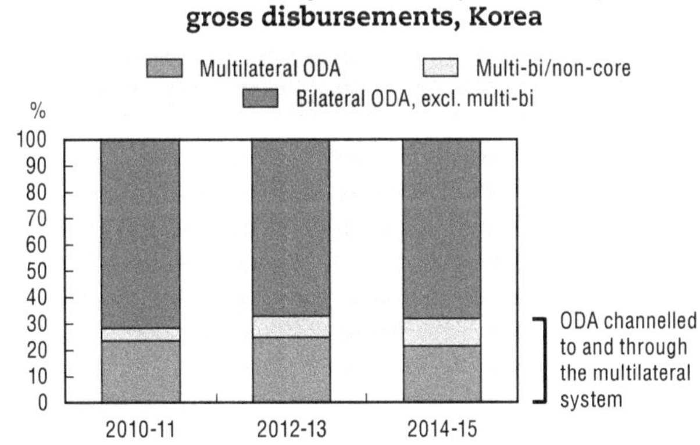

StatLink http://dx.doi.org/10.1787/888933481418

In 2015, 79.9% of bilateral ODA was programmed with partner countries. Korea's bilateral programme is characterised by a high proportion of country programmable aid, which was above the DAC country average of 48.8% in 2015. This is explained mainly by its low levels of other bilateral expenditures, such as in-donor refugee costs, humanitarian assistance and debt relief. Project-type interventions amounted to 77.9% of country programmable aid .

Figure 24.4. **Composition of bilateral ODA, 2015, gross disbursements, Korea**

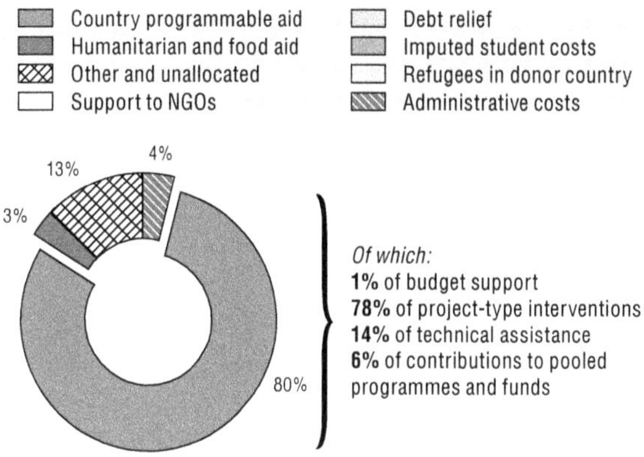

StatLink http://dx.doi.org/10.1787/888933481420

In 2015, USD 38.6 million of bilateral ODA was channelled to and through civil society organisations (CSOs). Korea's ODA channelled to and through CSOs has increased in volume in recent years (+17.3% between 2014 and 2015). It has, however, been a consistently low share of bilateral ODA. This share amounted to 2.4% in 2015, compared with the DAC country average of 16.9%.

Figure 24.5. **Bilateral ODA to and through CSOs, two year averages, gross disbursements, Korea**

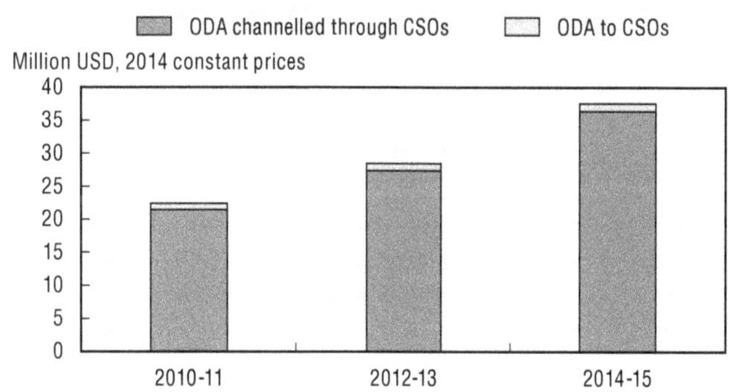

StatLink http://dx.doi.org/10.1787/888933481439

* Korea does not report to the DAC on ODA-eligible assistance to the Democratic People's Republic of Korea (DPRK). The ODA-eligible portion of its assistance to the DPRK was estimated at approximately USD 12.4 million in 2015.

Bilateral ODA was primarily focused on Asia. In 2015, USD 518.5 million was allocated to Far East Asia and USD 231.5 million to south and central Asia. USD 344.2 million was allocated to sub-Saharan Africa.

Figure 24.6. **Share of bilateral ODA by region, 2014-15 average, gross disbursements, Korea**

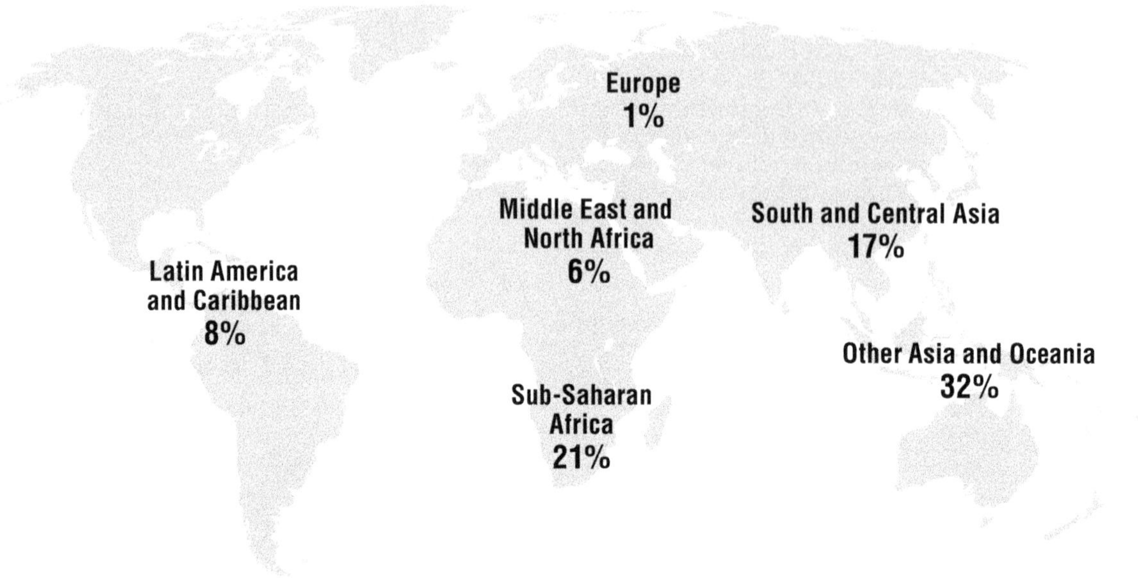

Note: 16% of bilateral ODA was unspecified by region in 2014-15. This share is not represented on the map.

StatLink http://dx.doi.org/10.1787/888933481447

In 2015, 46.5% of bilateral ODA went to Korea's top 10 recipients. Eight of its 26 priority partner countries are among its top 10 recipients. Korea's support to fragile contexts reached USD 648.5 million in 2015 (40.2% of gross bilateral ODA).

Figure 24.7. **Bilateral ODA to top recipients, 2014-15 average, gross disbursements, Korea**

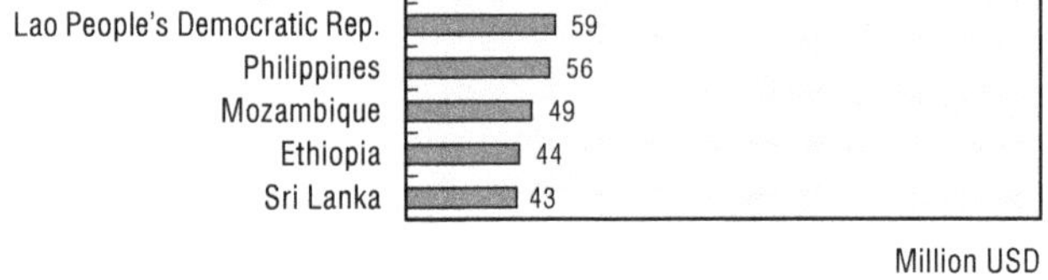

StatLink http://dx.doi.org/10.1787/888933481453

In 2015, 37% of bilateral ODA was allocated to least developed countries (LDCs), reaching USD 595.4 million. The share remained relatively stable from 2013 to 2014 (38.1%) and is higher than the 2015 DAC average of 24.3%. LDCs received the highest share of bilateral ODA in 2015.

At 0.05% of GNI in 2015, total ODA to LDCs was lower than the UN target of 0.15% of GNI.

Figure 24.8. **Bilateral ODA by income group, two year averages, gross disbursements, Korea**

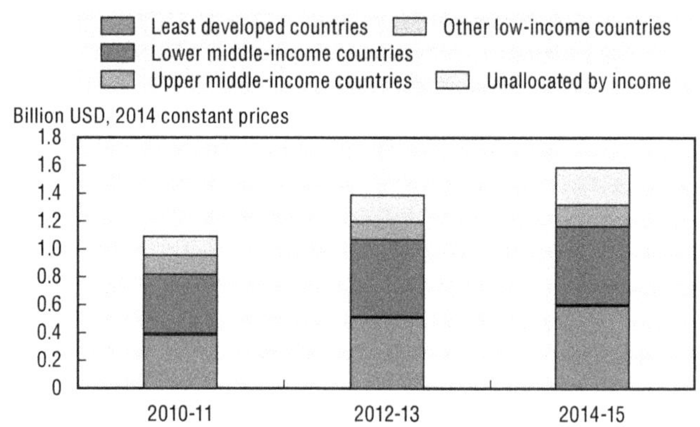

StatLink http://dx.doi.org/10.1787/888933481463

In 2015, 47% of Korea's bilateral ODA was allocated to social infrastructure and services, amounting to USD 1.1 billion, with a strong focus on support to health (USD 273.7 million), education (USD 260.3 million), and water and sanitation (USD 251.9 million). USD 760.2 million (32% of bilateral ODA) was allocated to economic infrastructure and services, with a strong focus on transport and storage (USD 600.9 million).

Figure 24.9. **Share of bilateral ODA by sector, 2014-15 average, commitments, Korea**

StatLink http://dx.doi.org/10.1787/888933481473

USD 218.7 million of bilateral ODA supported gender equality. In 2015, 9.8% of Korea's bilateral allocable aid had gender equality and women's empowerment as a principal or significant objective, compared with the DAC country average of 36.3%. This is down from 13.4% in 2014. Population and reproductive health is the only sector in which the focus on gender is evident. With the introduction of new Gender Awareness Guidelines, Korea is stepping up efforts to better mainstream gender equality into its projects and to report on the gender marker.

Figure 24.10. **Share of bilateral allocable ODA in support of gender equality by sector, 2015, commitments, Korea**

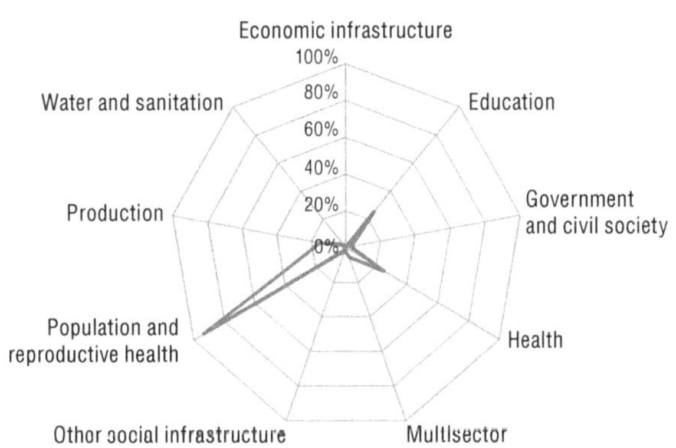

StatLink http://dx.doi.org/10.1787/888933481483

USD 392.1 million of bilateral ODA supported the environment in 2015. Korea committed to increase its environment-relevant ODA to 30% by 2020 and is making an effort to improve the integration of the environment and climate change into its development co-operation. In 2015, 17.1% of its bilateral allocable aid supported the environment and 13.2% (USD 301.2 million) focused specifically on climate change, compared with the DAC country averages of 33.2% and 26.2% respectively.

Figure 24.11. **Bilateral allocable ODA in support of global and local environment objectives, two year averages, commitments, Korea**

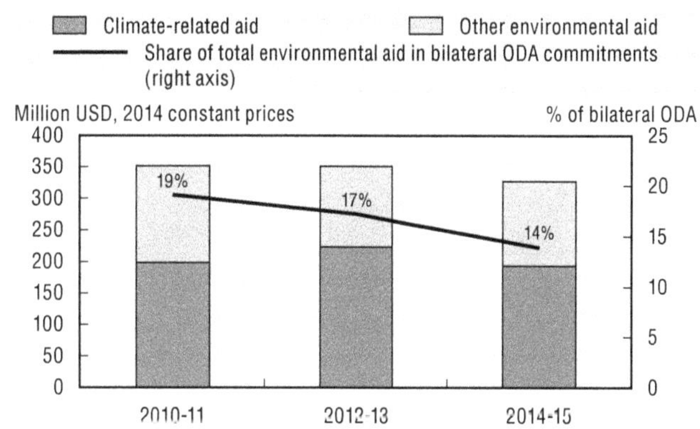

StatLink http://dx.doi.org/10.1787/888933481494

Note to reader: Annex B provides "Methodological notes on the profiles of Development Assistance Committee members".

LUXEMBOURG

Luxembourg's contribution to data for development

According to the 2017 Partner Report on Support to Statistics (PRESS) dataset, Luxembourg committed on average USD 0.13 million per year to finance national statistical capacities and systems in developing countries in 2013-15.

Financial flows from Luxembourg to developing countries

Figure 25.1. **Net resource flows to developing countries, 2005-15, Luxembourg**

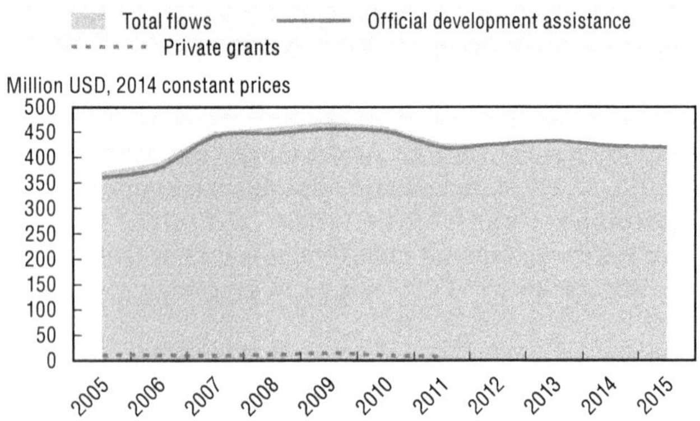

Note: Data on private grants are not available from 2012.

StatLink http://dx.doi.org/10.1787/888933481502

Luxembourg's use of ODA to mobilise other resources for sustainable development

- **USD 0.48 million** of official development assistance (ODA) was committed to the mobilisation of domestic resources in developing countries, e.g. to support the development of their tax systems, in 2015.
- **USD 32.3 million** of ODA (-16.1% in real terms from 2014) was committed to promote aid for trade and improve developing countries' trade performance and integration into the world economy in 2015.

Luxembourg's performance against commitments for effective development co-operation

Table 25.1. **Results of the 2016 Global Partnership monitoring round, Luxembourg**

	Alignment and ownership by partner country (%)				Predictability (%)		Transparency		
	Use of country-led results frameworks	Funding recorded in countries' national budgets	Funding through countries' systems	Untied ODA	Annual predictability	Medium-term predictability	Retrospective statistics (OECD CRS)	Information for forecasting (OECD FSS)	Publishing to IATI
2016	95.9	79.0	36.2	98.8	88.1	84.5	Good	Excellent	-
Baseline	-	33.1	7.3	99.2	74.0	70.4	Good	Good	-
Trend	-	⇑	⇑	⇓	⇑	⇑	=	⇑	-

Note: Please refer to Annex B for details on the indicators.

StatLink http://dx.doi.org/10.1787/888933483139

Luxembourg's official development assistance

In 2016, Luxembourg provided USD 384 million in net ODA (preliminary data), which represented 1% of gross national income (GNI) and an increase of 7.7% in real terms from 2015 in line with increases in its overall aid programme. Luxembourg is one of only six DAC members to have met the UN target of 0.7% in 2016. Luxembourg's share of untied ODA (excluding administrative costs and in-donor refugee costs) increased from 97.5% in 2014 to 98.8% in 2015, and is above the DAC average of 78.1%. The grant element of total ODA was 100% in 2015. Luxembourg did not report in-donor refugee costs as ODA in 2016.

Figure 25.2. **Net ODA: Trends in volume and as a share of GNI, 2000-16, Luxembourg**

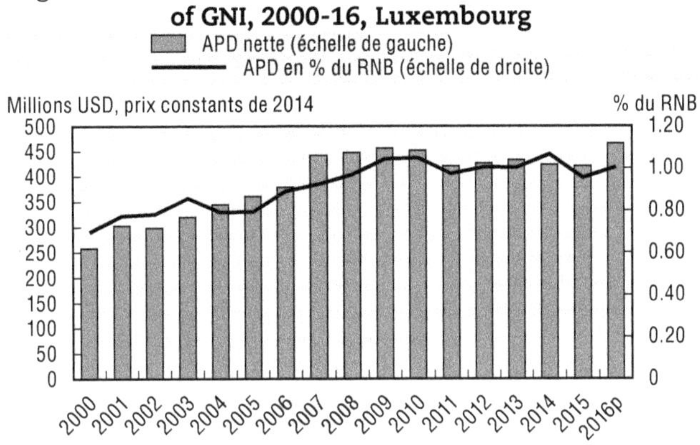

p: Preliminary data.

StatLink http://dx.doi.org/10.1787/888933481510

In 2015, 72.4% of ODA was provided bilaterally. Luxembourg allocated 27.6% of total ODA as core contributions to multilateral organisations, in line with the DAC country average of 26.2%. In addition, it channelled 24.9% of its bilateral ODA for specific projects implemented by multilateral organisations (multi-bi/non-core contributions).

Figure 25.3. **Share of ODA channelled to and through the multilateral system, two year averages, gross disbursements, Luxembourg**

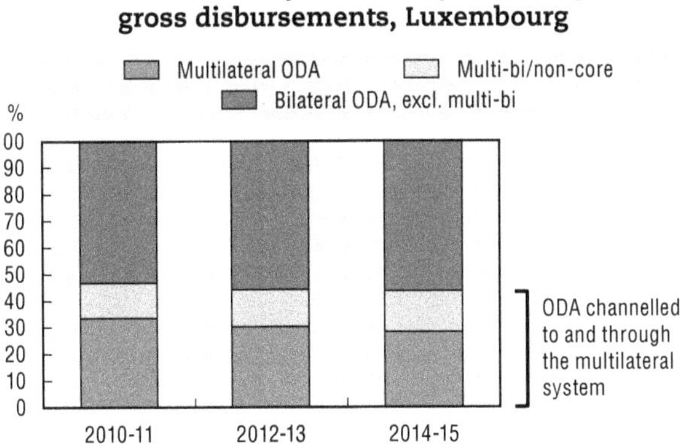

StatLink http://dx.doi.org/10.1787/888933481520

In 2015, 62% of bilateral ODA was programmed with partner countries. Luxembourg's share of country programmable aid was above the 2015 DAC country average of 48.8% in 2015 and project-type interventions made up 84.5% of this aid. Humanitarian and food aid amounted to 17.5% of bilateral aid.

Figure 25.4. **Composition of bilateral ODA, 2015, gross disbursements, Luxembourg**

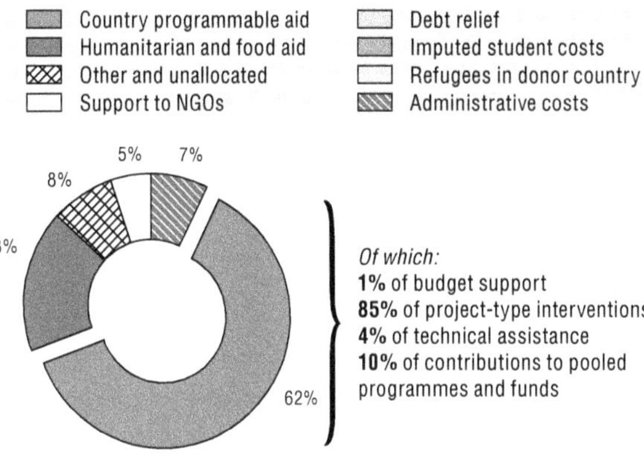

StatLink http://dx.doi.org/10.1787/888933481539

In 2015, USD 72.5 million of bilateral ODA was channelled to and through civil society organisations (CSOs). ODA channelled to and through CSOs decreased between 2014 and 2015 both in volume (-3%) and as a share of bilateral ODA (from 28.4% in 2014 to 27.6% in 2015). The DAC country average was 16.9% in 2015.

Figure 25.5. **Bilateral ODA to and through CSOs, two year averages, gross disbursements, Luxembourg**

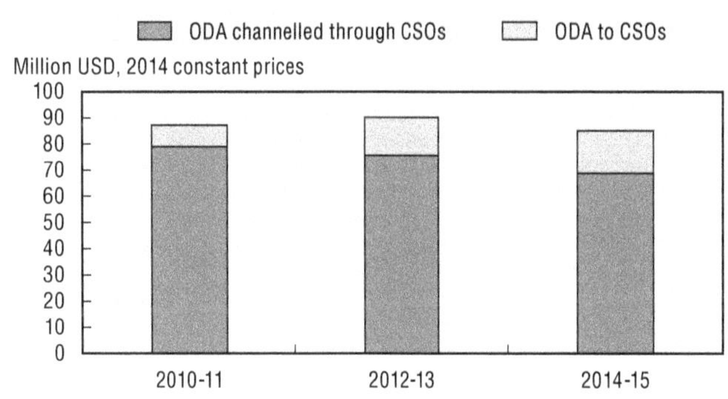

StatLink http://dx.doi.org/10.1787/888933481543

Bilateral ODA was primarily focused on sub-Saharan Africa. In 2015, USD 120.9 million was allocated to sub-Saharan Africa and USD 33.2 million to Far East Asia.

Figure 25.6. **Share of bilateral ODA by region, 2014-15 average, gross disbursements, Luxembourg**

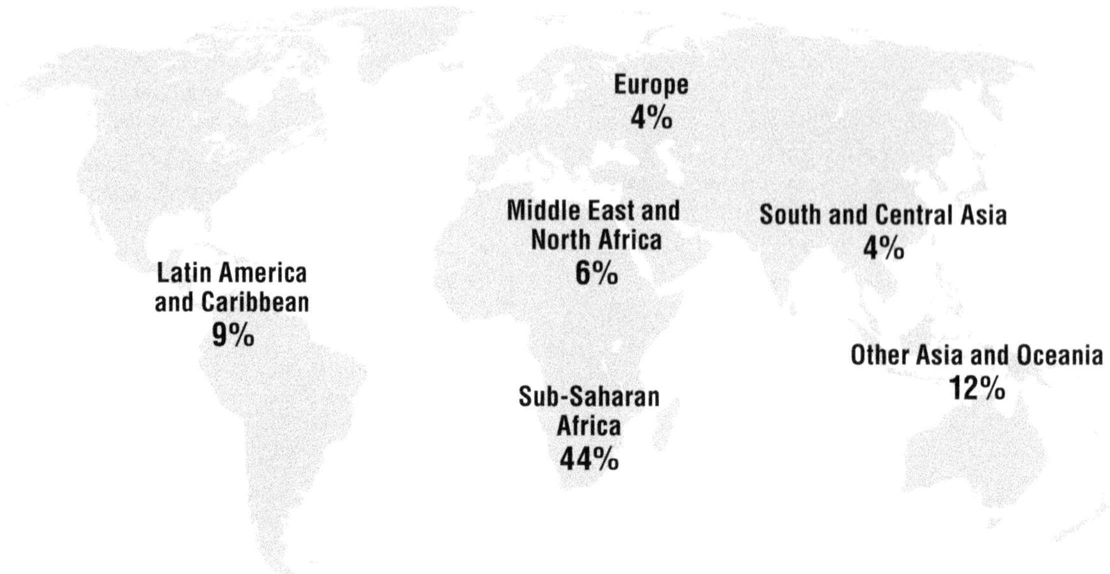

Note: 21% of bilateral ODA allocated was unspecified by region in 2014-15. This share is not represented on the map.

StatLink http://dx.doi.org/10.1787/888933481556

In 2015, 54.9% of bilateral ODA went to Luxembourg's top 10 recipients. Luxembourg has nine priority partner countries, eight of them are among its top 10 recipients. In 2015, its support to fragile contexts reached USD 115.2 million (43.9% of gross bilateral ODA).

Figure 25.7. **Bilateral ODA to top recipients, 2014-15 average, gross disbursements, Luxembourg**

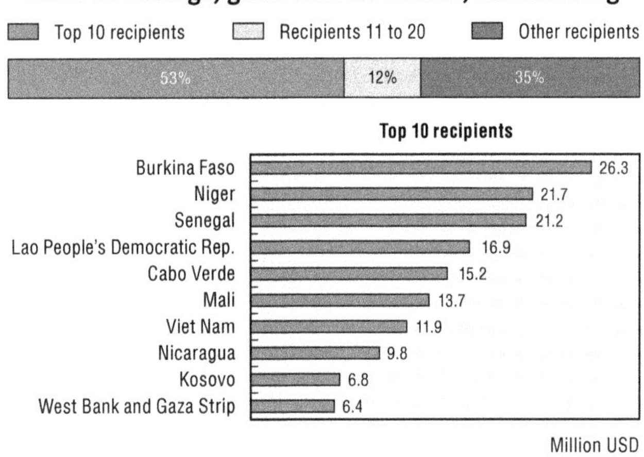

StatLink http://dx.doi.org/10.1787/888933481562

In 2015, 46.2% of bilateral ODA was allocated to least developed countries (LDCs), amounting to USD 121.4 million. The share has increased from 44.4% in 2014 and is above the 2015 DAC average of 24.3%. LDCs received the highest share of bilateral ODA in 2015 compared with other income groups.

At 0.4% of Luxembourg's GNI in 2015, total ODA to LDCs exceeds the UN target of 0.15% of GNI.

Figure 25.8. **Bilateral ODA by income group, two year averages, gross disbursements, Luxembourg**

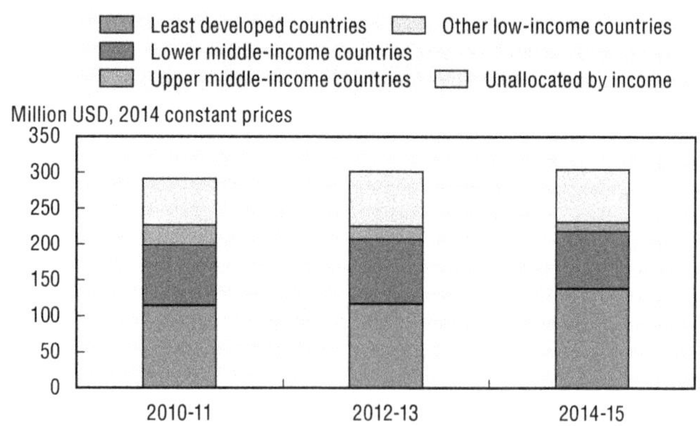

StatLink http://dx.doi.org/10.1787/888933481575

In 2015, 47% of bilateral ODA was allocated to social infrastructure and services, or USD 122.3 million, with a strong focus on education (USD 44.3 million) and health (USD 29.3 million). Humanitarian aid amounted to USD 42.6 million.

Figure 25.9. **Share of bilateral ODA by sector, 2014-15 average, commitments, Luxembourg**

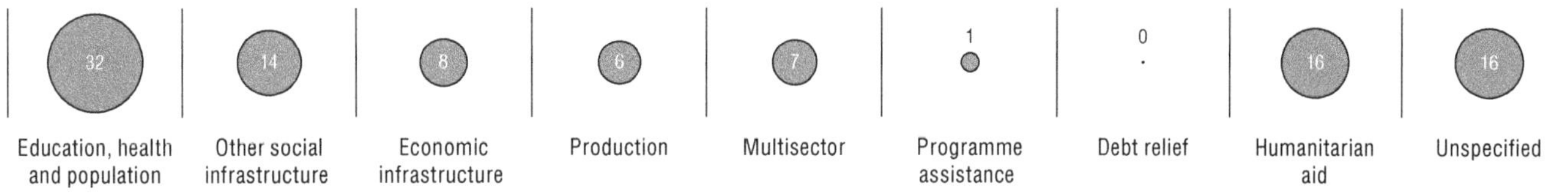

StatLink http://dx.doi.org/10.1787/888933481588

USD 78.4 million of bilateral ODA supported gender equality in 2015. Luxembourg mainstreams gender in its programmes while also advocating gender equality in international bodies as experienced under its EU presidency. In 2015, 33.2% of its bilateral allocable aid had gender equality and women's empowerment as a principal or significant objective, compared with the DAC country average of 36.3%. This is up from 30.5% in 2014. Luxembourg's aid to education and productive sectors has an important focus on gender.

Figure 25.10. **Share of bilateral allocable ODA in support of gender equality by sector, 2015, commitments, Luxembourg**

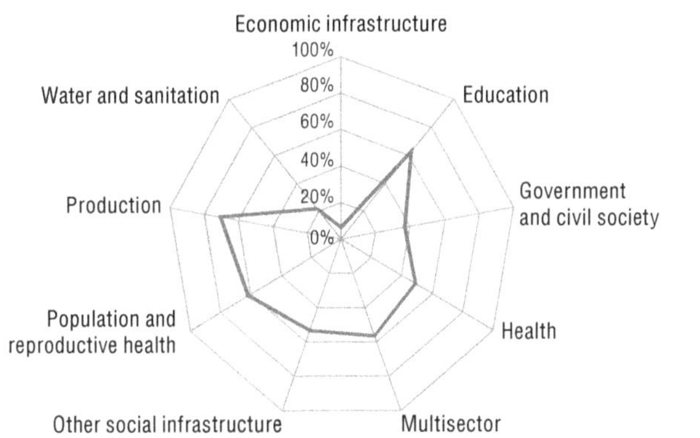

StatLink http://dx.doi.org/10.1787/888933481591

USD 61.8 million of bilateral ODA supported the environment in 2015. Luxembourg has developed a holistic approach to the environment and climate change in its development co-operation and will commit an additional USD 127 million of ODA to climate change activities between 2014 and 2020. It is using impact analysis and environmental evaluation more systematically. In 2015, 25.7% of its bilateral allocable aid supported the environment and 12.9% (USD 31 million) focused particularly on climate change, compared with the respective DAC country averages of 33.2% and 26.2%.

Figure 25.11. **Bilateral allocable ODA in support of global and local environment objectives, two year averages, commitments, Luxembourg**

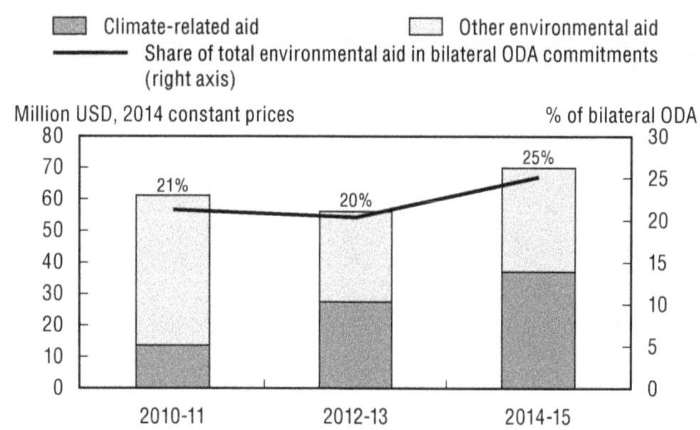

StatLink http://dx.doi.org/10.1787/888933481600

Note to reader: Annex B provides "Methodological notes on the profiles of Development Assistance Committee members".

NETHERLANDS

The Netherlands's contribution to data for development

The Netherlands engages in strengthening statistical capacities and systems in developing countries through contributions to multilateral organisations and some bilateral capacity building. For instance, the Netherlands has supported the Statistics for Results Facility – Catalytic Fund of the World Bank since 2008, providing a total of EUR 5.25 million.

The government is following up on a commitment made by the Minister for Development Co-operation, Ms Ploumen, to provide technical assistance for disaggregated data collection and analysis within the context of the Leave No One Behind Agenda of the Sustainable Development Goals. It is looking into offering bilateral assistance to support the collection and analysis of disaggregated data – in particular on income, access to education and health services – on the poorest and most marginalised groups in partner countries. The Netherlands plans to focus its support on national statistical systems and other data producers as well as the interaction between these different actors. Promoting the use of data by policy makers, civil society and citizens will also be an important objective.

According to the 2017 Partner Report on Support to Statistics (PRESS) dataset, the Netherlands committed on average USD 4.36 million per year to finance national statistical capacities and systems in developing countries in 2013-15.

Financial flows from the Netherlands to developing countries

Figure 26.1. **Net resource flows to developing countries, 2005-15, Netherlands**

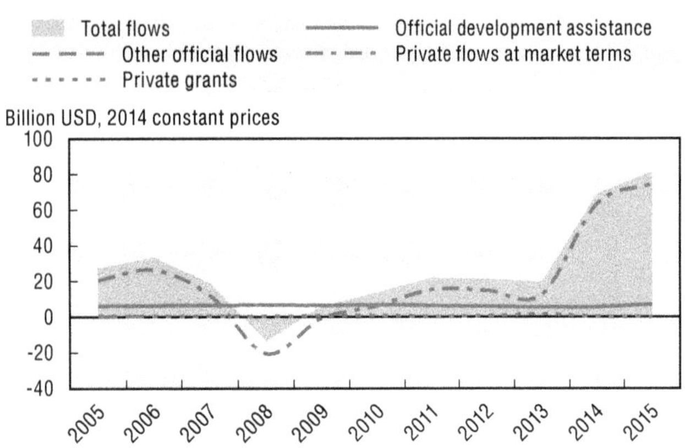

Note: Data on other official flows are not available from 2007.

StatLink http://dx.doi.org/10.1787/888933481617

The Netherlands' use of ODA to mobilise other resources for sustainable development

- **USD 0.63 million** of official development assistance (ODA) was committed to the mobilisation of domestic resources in developing countries, e.g. to support the development of their tax systems, in 2015.
- **USD 588.2 million** of ODA (-33.7% in real terms from 2014) was committed to promote aid for trade and improve developing countries' trade performance and integration into the world economy in 2015.

The Netherlands' performance against commitments for effective development co-operation

Table 26.1. **Results of the 2016 Global Partnership monitoring round, Netherlands**

	Alignment and ownership by partner country (%)				Predictability (%)		Transparency		
	Use of country-led results frameworks	Funding recorded in countries' national budgets	Funding through countries' systems	Untied ODA	Annual predictability	Medium-term predictability	Retrospective statistics (OECD CRS)	Information for forecasting (OECD FSS)	Publishing to IATI
2016	63.8	71.7	44.4	92.7	58.9	73.0	Needs improvement	Fair	Excellent
Baseline	-	48.9	64.9	100.0	68.5	41.7	Needs improvement	Fair	-
Trend	-	⇑	⇓	⇓	⇓	⇑	=	=	-

Note: Please refer to Annex B for details on the indicators.

StatLink http://dx.doi.org/10.1787/888933483144

The Netherlands' official development assistance

In 2016, the Netherlands provided USD 5 billion in net ODA (preliminary data), which represented 0.65% of gross national income (GNI) and a decrease of 13.1% in real terms from 2015, mostly due to lower expenditures for in-donor refugees compared to 2015. The Netherlands' ODA/GNI ratio slipped below the UN target of 0.7% in 2016 – the third time since 1974. The Netherlands' share of untied ODA (excluding administrative costs and in-donor refugee costs) was 92.7% in 2015 (down from 98.4% in 2014), above the DAC average of 78.1%. The grant element of total ODA was 100% in 2015.

In 2016, in-donor refugee costs were USD 461 million, a decrease of 65.3% in real terms over 2015, and represented 9.3% of the Netherlands' total net ODA.

Figure 26.2. **Net ODA: Trends in volume and as a share of GNI, 2000-16, Netherlands**

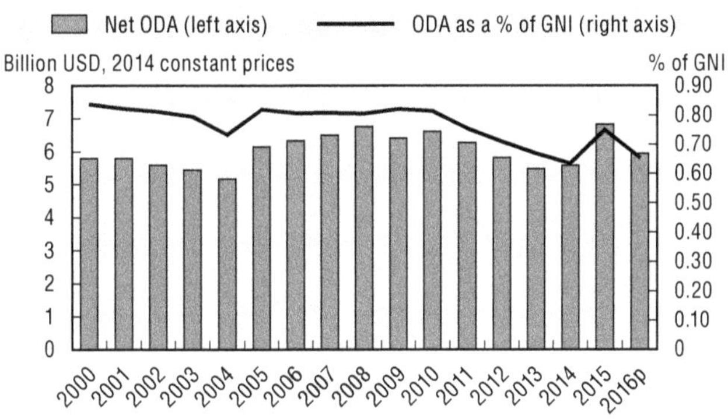

p: Preliminary data.

StatLink http://dx.doi.org/10.1787/888933481625

In 2015, 73.1% of ODA was provided bilaterally. The Netherlands allocated 26.9% of total ODA as core contributions to multilateral organisations, above the DAC country average of 26.2%. In addition, it channelled 15.5% of its bilateral ODA for specific projects implemented by multilateral organisations (multi-bi/non-core contributions).

Figure 26.3. **Share of ODA channelled to and through the multilateral system, two year averages, gross disbursements, Netherlands**

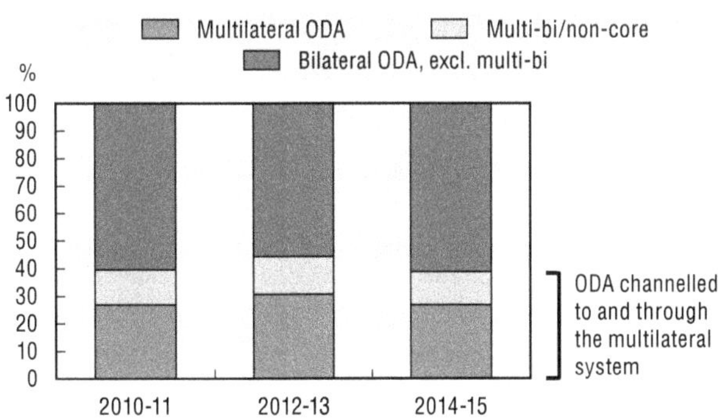

StatLink http://dx.doi.org/10.1787/888933481639

In 2015, only 16.5% of bilateral ODA was programmed with partner countries. The Netherlands' share of country programmable aid was lower than the DAC country average of 48.8% in 2015. Project-type interventions accounted for 65% of this aid. Twenty-nine per cent of the Netherlands' bilateral ODA was reported as "other and unallocated" by category, and 31.1% was allocated to refugee costs in the Netherlands.

Figure 26.4. **Composition of bilateral ODA, 2015, gross disbursements, Netherlands**

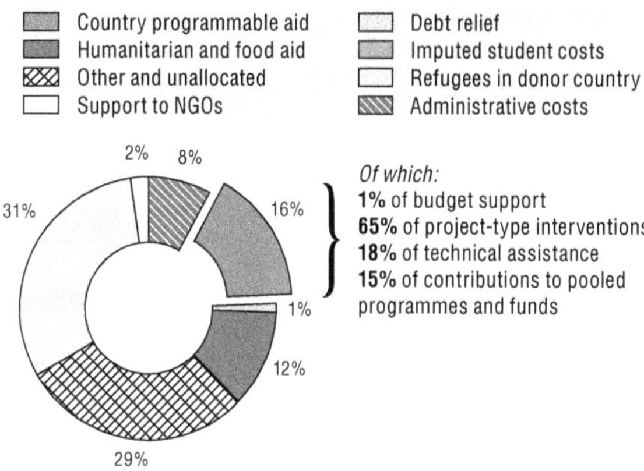

StatLink http://dx.doi.org/10.1787/888933481640

In 2015, USD 1.1 billion of bilateral ODA was channelled to and through civil society organisations (CSOs). Between 2014 and 2015, aid channelled to and through CSOs increased in volume (3%) but decreased as a share of bilateral aid (from 29.2% to 24.7%). This share was higher than the 2015 DAC country average (16.9%).

Figure 26.5. **Bilateral ODA to and through CSOs, two year averages, gross disbursements, Netherlands**

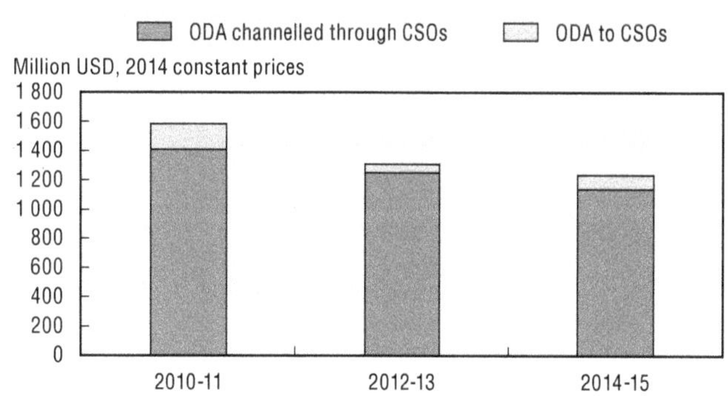

StatLink http://dx.doi.org/10.1787/888933481659

The largest share of Dutch allocable bilateral ODA was directed towards sub-Saharan Africa. In 2015, USD 620.8 million was allocated to sub-Saharan Africa and USD 219.8 million to the Middle East, noting that 72% of Dutch bilateral ODA is unallocated by region.

Figure 26.6. **Share of bilateral ODA by region, 2014-15 average, gross disbursements, Netherlands**

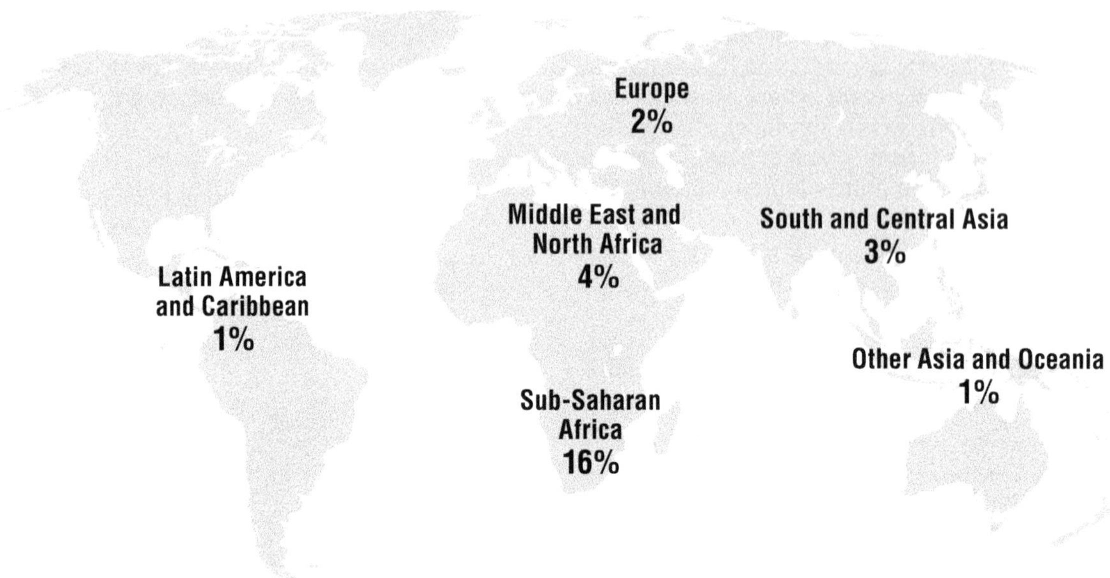

Note: 73% of bilateral ODA allocated was unspecified by region in 2014-15. This share is not represented on the map.

StatLink http://dx.doi.org/10.1787/888933481664

In 2015, 10.9% of bilateral ODA went to the Netherlands' top 10 recipients. Nine of its 15 priority partner countries are on the list of its top 10 recipients. In 2015, its support to fragile contexts reached USD 580.5 million (13.6% of gross bilateral ODA).

Figure 26.7. **Bilateral ODA to top recipients, 2014-15 average, gross disbursements, Netherlands**

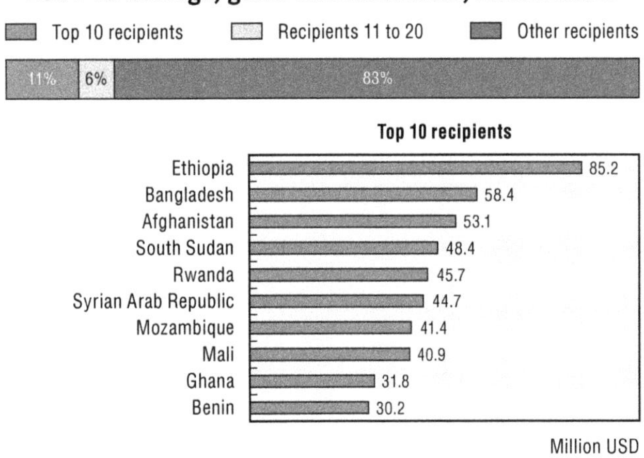

StatLink http://dx.doi.org/10.1787/888933481676

In 2015, 11% of bilateral ODA was allocated to least developed countries (LDCs), amounting to USD 466.4 million. This is a decrease from 18.2% in 2013 and 14.2% in 2014 and is well below the 2015 DAC average of 24.3%. LDCs received the highest share of bilateral ODA in 2015, noting that 81.8% of bilateral ODA was unallocated by income group.

At 0.14% of the Netherlands' GNI in 2015, total ODA to LDCs was below the UN target of 0.15% of GNI.*

Figure 26.8. **Bilateral ODA by income group, two year averages, gross disbursements, Netherlands**

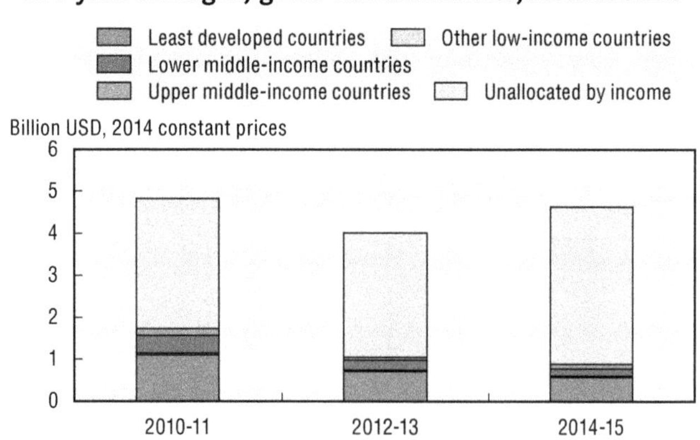

StatLink http://dx.doi.org/10.1787/888933481687

* The Netherlands' Ministry of Foreign Affairs estimates that 0.26% of GNI was directly or indirectly targeted at LDCs in 2015.

In 2015, 37.8% of the Netherlands' bilateral ODA was allocated to social and economic infrastructure and services. USD 1.9 billion was allocated to social sectors, with a strong focus on support to government and civil society (USD 1.4 billion), population and reproductive health (USD 211.3 million), and water and sanitation (USD 152.4 million). USD 424.1 million was allocated to production services, with a strong focus on agriculture (USD 165.2 million). Humanitarian aid amounted to USD 549.5 million.

Figure 26.9. **Share of bilateral ODA by sector, 2014-15 average, commitments, Netherlands**

StatLink http://dx.doi.org/10.1787/888933481696

USD 2.1 billion of bilateral ODA supported gender equality. In 2015, 61.3% of the Netherlands' bilateral allocable aid had gender equality and women's empowerment as a principal or significant objective, compared with the DAC country average of 36.3%. This is up from 57.1% in 2014. The Netherlands' aid to population and reproductive health, government and civil society, and water and sanitation has a strong focus on gender equality and the Netherlands is among the biggest donors to women's organisations.

Figure 26.10. **Share of bilateral allocable ODA in support of gender equality by sector, 2015, commitments, Netherlands**

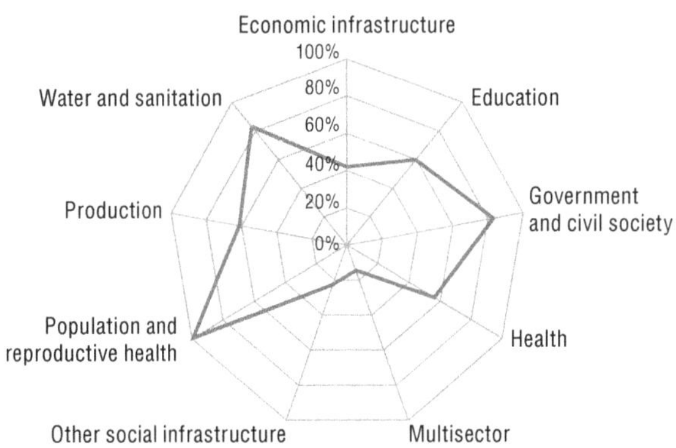

StatLink http://dx.doi.org/10.1787/888933481700

USD 1.2 billion of Dutch bilateral ODA commitments supported environmental outcomes in 2015. The Netherlands has a strong focus on climate change and sustainable use of natural resources, with a focus on water management and access to energy. It invests in both mainstreaming climate change into development co-operation programmes and direct support to climate mitigation and adaptation. The share of bilateral allocable aid supporting the environment was significantly higher than in 2014 (35.3% vs. 15.8%), and above the DAC country average of 33.2%. In 2015, 29.9% of bilateral allocable aid (USD 1 billion) focused on climate change, above the DAC country average of 26.2%.

Figure 26.11. **Bilateral allocable ODA in support of global and local environment objectives, two year averages, commitments, Netherlands**

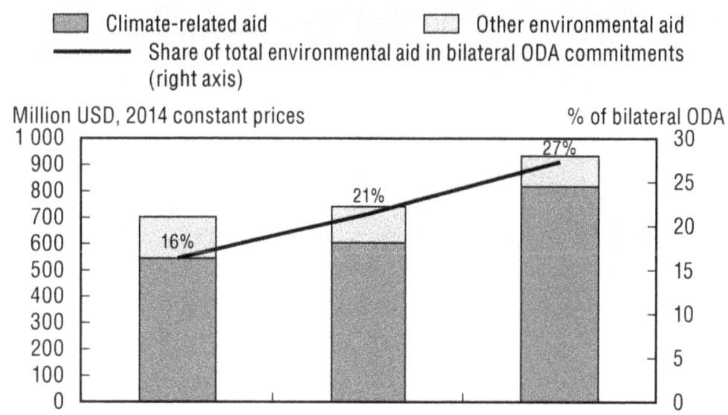

StatLink http://dx.doi.org/10.1787/888933481711

Note to reader: Annex B provides "Methodological notes on the profiles of Development Assistance Committee members".

Reference

OECD (2017), *OECD Development Co-operation Peer Reviews: The Netherlands 2017*, OECD Publishing, Paris.

NEW ZEALAND

New Zealand's contribution to data for development

New Zealand supports statistical capacity building in developing countries with the aim to improve national statistical production and statistical literacy of data users, and to promote the use of data by policy makers, civil society and citizens.

New Zealand engages in strengthening statistical capacities through bilateral initiatives and through funding multilateral and regional (in the Pacific more specifically) initiatives. Support takes the form of technical assistance and funding for equipment but also of direct financial support to national statistical offices or other government departments. An example of a relatively small but successful capacity-building initiative supported by New Zealand is a course offering certificates in official statistics to government officials. The course aims to improve understanding of official statistics, and their use in policy settings. The emphasis on using statistics in planning processes helps drive the demand for statistics, the dissemination of information and to improve the quality from national statistical offices.

According to the 2017 Partner Report on Support to Statistics (PRESS) dataset, New Zealand committed on average USD 0.22 million per year to finance national statistical capacities and systems in developing countries in 2013-15.

Financial flows from New Zealand to developing countries

Figure 27.1. **Net resource flows to developing countries, 2005-15, New Zealand**

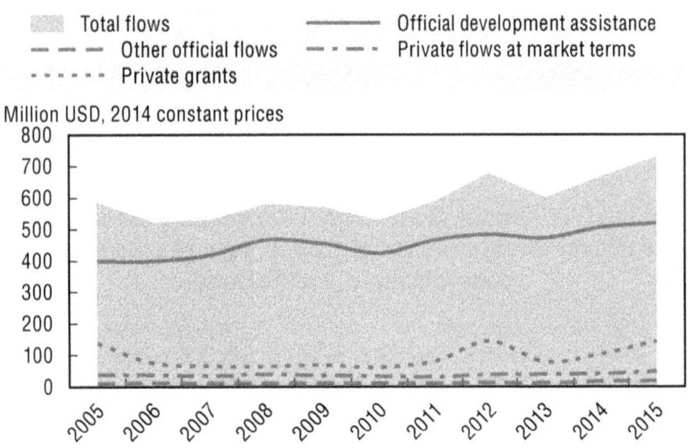

StatLink http://dx.doi.org/10.1787/888933481729

New Zealand's use of ODA to mobilise other resources for sustainable development

- **USD 135.2 million** of ODA (-19.6% in real terms from 2014) was committed to promote aid for trade and improve developing countries' trade performance and integration into the world economy in 2015.

New Zealand's performance against commitments for effective development co-operation

Table 27.1. **Results of the 2016 Global Partnership monitoring round, New Zealand**

	Alignment and ownership by partner country (%)				Predictability (%)		Transparency		
	Use of country-led results frameworks	Funding recorded in countries' national budgets	Funding through countries' systems	Untied ODA	Annual predictability	Medium-term predictability	Retrospective statistics (OECD CRS)	Information for forecasting (OECD FSS)	Publishing to IATI
2016	58.2	91.7	51.1	84.7	83.7	79.6	Fair	Excellent	Needs improvement
Baseline	-	39.0	36.1	81.1	78.6	59.6	Fair	Excellent	-
Trend	-	⇑	⇑	⇑	⇑	⇑	=	=	-

Note: Please refer to Annex B for details on the indicators.

StatLink http://dx.doi.org/10.1787/888933483153

New Zealand's official development assistance

In 2016, New Zealand provided USD 438 million in net ODA (preliminary data), which represented 0.25% of gross national income (GNI) and a decrease of 2.5% in real terms from 2015, due to annual fluctuations in its increased three-year aid budget. New Zealand has committed to a NZD 220 million increase in ODA over the 2015/16-2017/18 triennium. New Zealand's share of untied ODA (excluding administrative costs and in-donor refugee costs) was 84.7% in 2015 (up from 81.8% in 2014), compared with the DAC average of 78.1%. The grant element of total ODA was 100% in 2015.

In 2016, in-donor refugee costs were USD 17 million, a decrease of 1.4% in real terms over 2015, and represented 3.8% of New Zealand's total net ODA.

Figure 27.2. **Net ODA: Trends in volume and as a share of GNI, 2000-16, New Zealand**

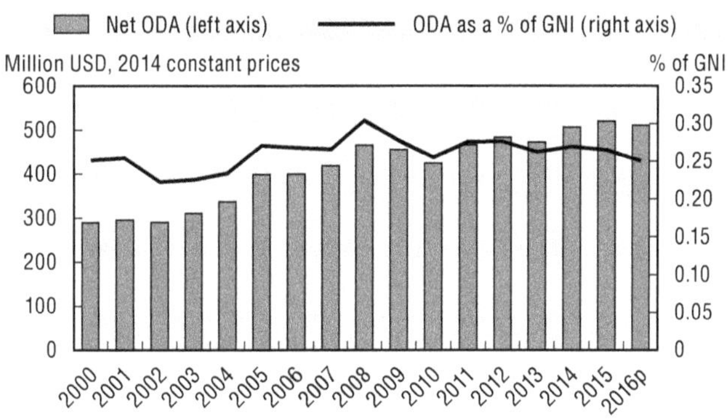

p: Preliminary data.

StatLink http://dx.doi.org/10.1787/888933481730

In 2015, 81.1% of ODA was provided bilaterally. New Zealand allocated 18.9% of total ODA as core contributions to multilateral organisations, compared with the DAC country average of 26.2%. In addition, it channelled 12.6% of its bilateral ODA for specific projects implemented by multilateral organisations (multi-bi/ non-core contributions).

Figure 27.3. **Share of ODA channelled to and through the multilateral system, two year averages, gross disbursements, New Zealand**

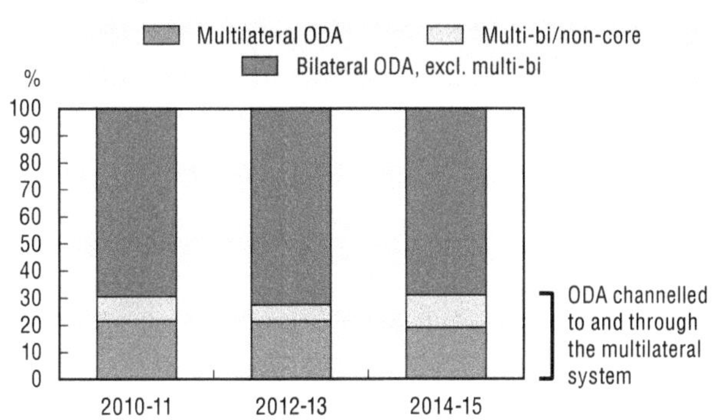

StatLink http://dx.doi.org/10.1787/888933481749

In 2015, New Zealand programmed 72.6% of bilateral ODA with partner countries. New Zealand's share of country programmable aid was above the DAC country average 48.8% in 2015. Project-type interventions accounted for 35% of this aid.

Figure 27.4. **Composition of bilateral ODA, 2015, gross disbursements, New Zealand**

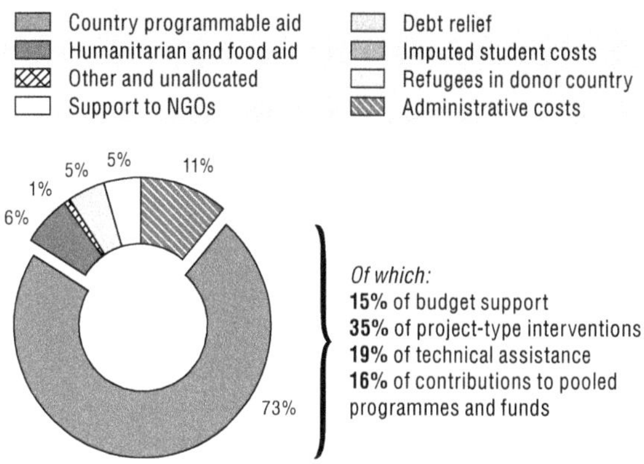

StatLink http://dx.doi.org/10.1787/888933481750

In 2015, USD 48.6 million of bilateral ODA was channelled to and through civil society organisations (CSOs). ODA channelled to and through CSOs decreased between 2014 and 2015 in terms of volume (-12%) and as a share of bilateral ODA (from 15.9% in 2014 to 13.6% in 2015). This share was lower than the 2015 DAC country average of 16.9%.

Figure 27.5. **Bilateral ODA to and through CSOs, two year averages, gross disbursements, New Zealand**

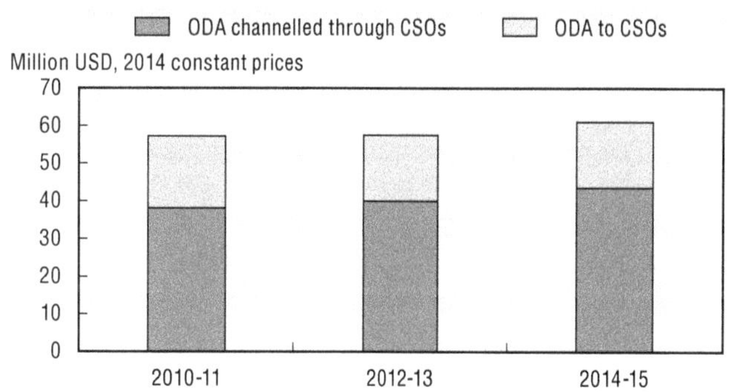

StatLink http://dx.doi.org/10.1787/888933481762

Bilateral ODA was strongly focused on Oceania and Asia. In 2015, USD 227.7 million was allocated to Oceania and USD 54.8 million to Far East Asia.

Figure 27.6. **Share of bilateral ODA by region, 2014-15 average, gross disbursements, New Zealand**

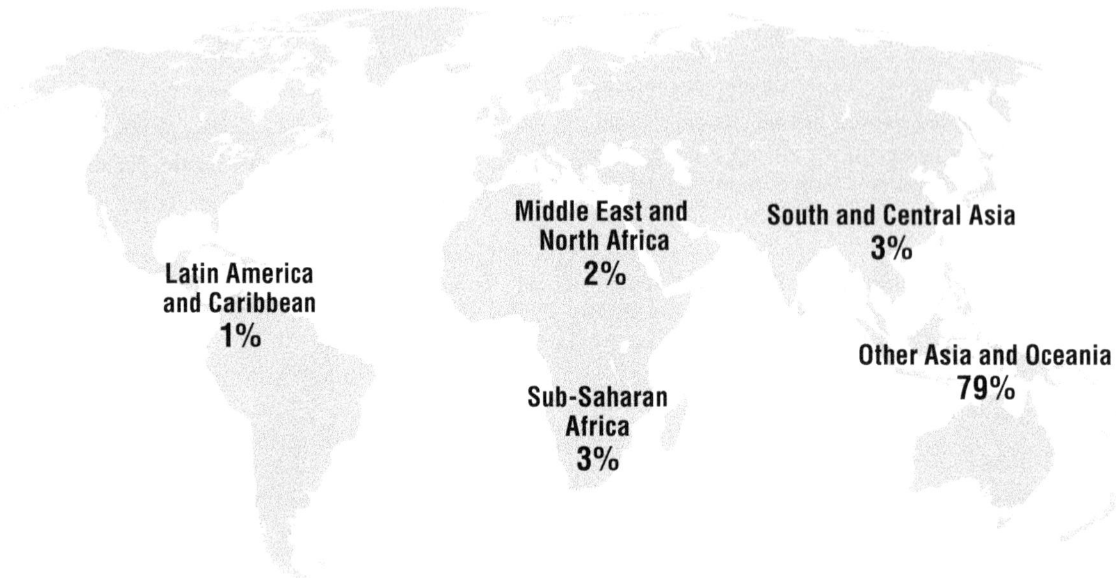

Note: 12% of bilateral ODA allocated was unspecified by region in 2014-15. This share is not represented on the map.

StatLink http://dx.doi.org/10.1787/888933481772

In 2015, 47.5% of bilateral ODA went to New Zealand's top 10 recipients. All of its top 10 recipients are priority partner countries. Its support to fragile contexts reached USD 82.2 million in 2015 (22.9% of its gross bilateral ODA).

Figure 27.7. **Bilateral ODA to top recipients, 2014-15 average, gross disbursements, New Zealand**

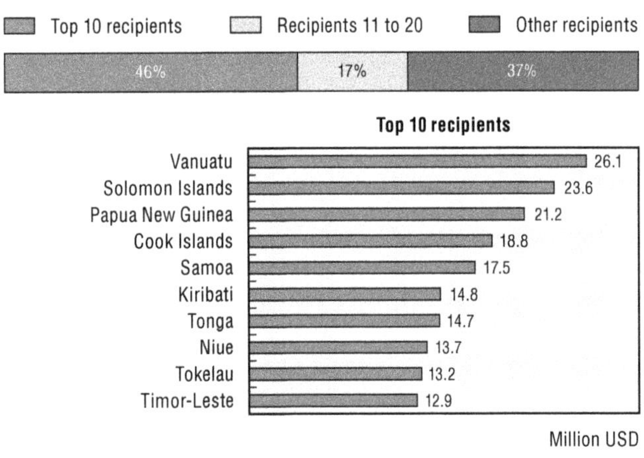

StatLink http://dx.doi.org/10.1787/888933481785

In 2015, 31.7% of bilateral ODA was allocated to least developed countries (LDCs), reaching USD 113.4 million. This is an increase from 27.7% in 2014 and is higher than the 2015 DAC average of 24.3%. Compared with other income groups, LDCs received the highest share of bilateral ODA in 2015, noting that 30.9% was unallocated by income group.

At 0.08% of New Zealand's GNI in 2015, total ODA to LDCs was lower than the UN target of 0.15% of GNI. This reflects the geographical focus of New Zealand's ODA on small island developing states in Oceania and Asia, many of which are not LDCs.

Figure 27.8. **Bilateral ODA by income group, two year averages, gross disbursements, New Zealand**

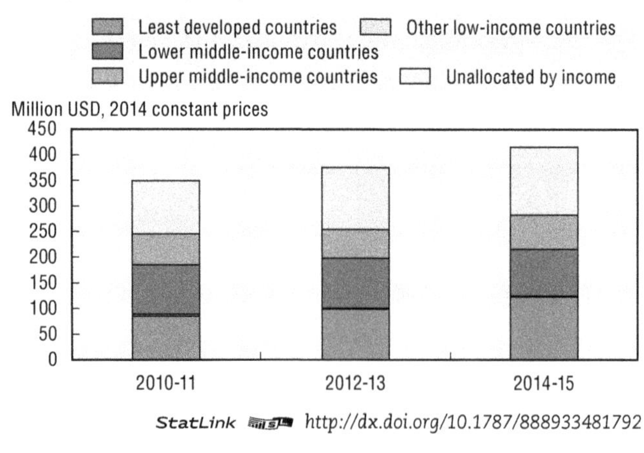

StatLink http://dx.doi.org/10.1787/888933481792

In 2015, 39% of bilateral ODA was allocated to social infrastructure and services, representing USD 139.7 million, with a strong focus on education (USD 74 million) and government and civil society (USD 35.7 million). USD 62.5 million was allocated to production sectors, in particular to agriculture (USD 32.3 million) and tourism (USD 16.4 million). USD 21.9 million was allocated to humanitarian aid.

Figure 27.9. **Share of bilateral ODA by sector, 2014-15 average, commitments, New Zealand**

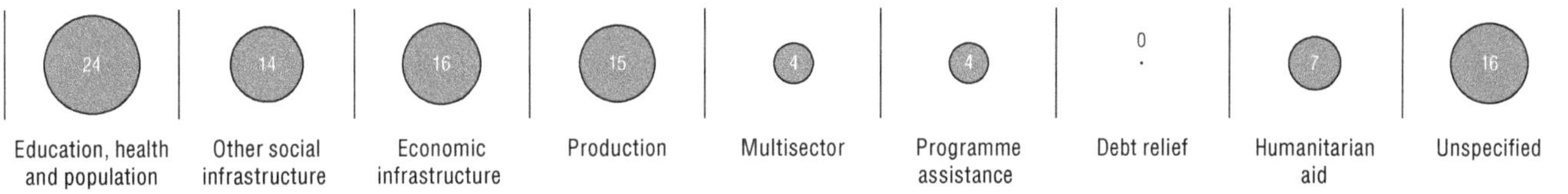

StatLink http://dx.doi.org/10.1787/888933481806

USD 174.6 million of bilateral ODA supported gender equality. In 2015, 58% of New Zealand's bilateral allocable aid had gender equality and women's empowerment as a principal or significant objective, compared with the DAC country average of 36.3%, reversing the decline observed since 2007-08. New Zealand's aid to population and reproductive health and education focuses on gender.

Figure 27.10. **Share of bilateral allocable ODA in support of gender equality by sector, 2015, commitments, New Zealand**

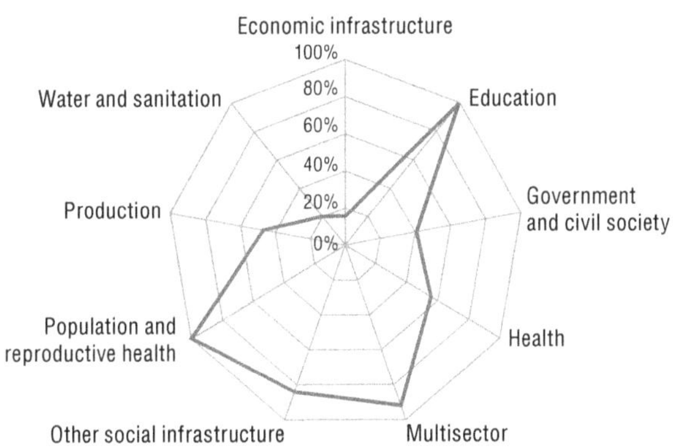

StatLink http://dx.doi.org/10.1787/888933481819

USD 138.6 million of bilateral ODA contributed to environmental outcomes in 2015. The share of New Zealand's bilateral allocable aid that focused on the environment was 46% and 15% (USD 45.1 million) concentrated on climate change (mostly on adaptation), compared with the respective DAC country averages of 33.2% and 26.2%.

Figure 27.11. **Bilateral allocable ODA in support of global and local environment objectives, two year averages, commitments, New Zealand**

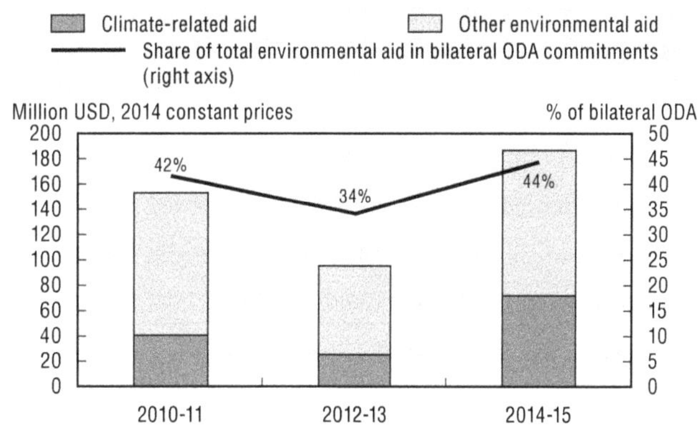

StatLink http://dx.doi.org/10.1787/888933481820

Note to reader: Annex B provides "Methodological notes on the profiles of Development Assistance Committee members".

NORWAY

Norway's contribution to data for development

Norway has been engaged in strengthening national statistical capacities and systems in developing countries through its national institute for statistics – Statistics Norway – for the past 23 years. Norway is currently finalising a new white paper with the aim of bringing increased focus on the need for good data and statistics in its development co-operation.

Norway engages in statistical capacity building in developing countries to improve statistical production and data literacy and to strengthen co-ordination among development partners. Its support focuses on national statistical systems and is provided mainly through bilateral government to government technical assistance. In particular, Norway brings its added value by helping developing countries to build up civil registration and vital statistics – an area in which it has gained considerable experience over many years. Statistics Norway is also collaborating with the United Nations High Commissioner for Refugees and other partners to establish international guidelines for collecting and producing statistics on refugees and on internally displaced people.

According to the 2017 Partner Report on Support to Statistics (PRESS) dataset, Norway committed on average USD 15.05 million per year to finance national statistical capacities and systems in developing countries in 2013-15.

Financial flows from Norway to developing countries

Figure 28.1. **Net resource flows to developing countries, 2005-15, Norway**

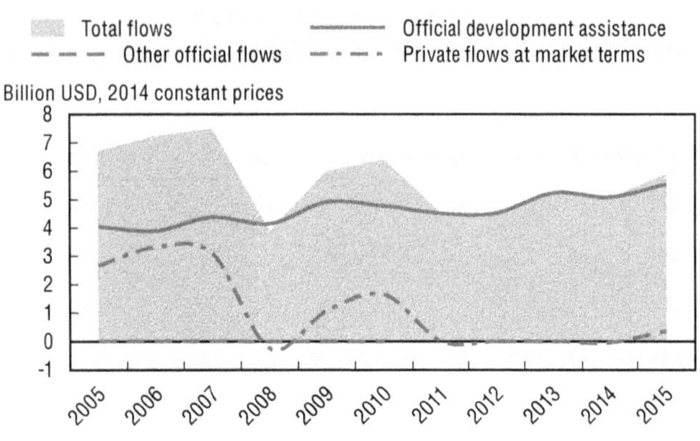

Note: Data on other official flows are not available for 2011. Data on private flows at market terms are not available for 2014.

StatLink http://dx.doi.org/10.1787/888933481839

Norway's use of ODA to mobilise other resources for sustainable development

- **USD 14.1 million** of official development assistance (ODA) was committed to the mobilisation of domestic resources in developing countries, e.g. to support the development of their tax systems, in 2015.
- **USD 337.6 million** of ODA (-35.5% in real terms from 2014) was committed to promote aid for trade and improve developing countries' trade performance and integration into the world economy in 2015.

Norway's performance against commitments for effective development co-operation

Table 28.1. **Results of the 2016 Global Partnership monitoring round, Norway**

	Alignment and ownership by partner country (%)				Predictability (%)		Transparency		
	Use of country-led results frameworks	Funding recorded in countries' national budgets	Funding through countries' systems	Untied ODA	Annual predictability	Medium-term predictability	Retrospective statistics (OECD CRS)	Information for forecasting (OECD FSS)	Publishing to IATI
2016	61.6	85.7	56.4	100.0	85.4	54.5	Good	Fair	Needs improvement
Baseline	-	68.0	62.4	100.0	85.5	52.5	Good	Fair	-
Trend	-	⇑	⇓	=	⇓	⇑		=	-

Note: Please refer to Annex B for details on the indicators.

StatLink http://dx.doi.org/10.1787/888933483167

Norway's official development assistance

In 2016, Norway provided USD 4.4 billion in net ODA (preliminary data), which represented 1.11% of gross national income (GNI) and a 7.8% increase in real terms from 2015, due mainly to increased in-donor refugee costs. Norway is one of only six DAC members to have met the UN target of 0.7% and it has consistently spent about 1% of GNI on ODA every year since 2009. All of Norway's ODA was untied in 2015 (excluding administrative costs and in-donor refugee costs), while the DAC average was 78.1%. Its ODA was also fully untied in 2013 and 2014. The grant element of total ODA was 100% in 2015.

In 2016, in-donor refugee costs were USD 800 million, an increase of 83% in real terms over 2015, and represented 18.4% of Norway's total net ODA.

Figure 28.2. **Net ODA: Trends in volume and as a share of GNI, 2000-16, Norway**

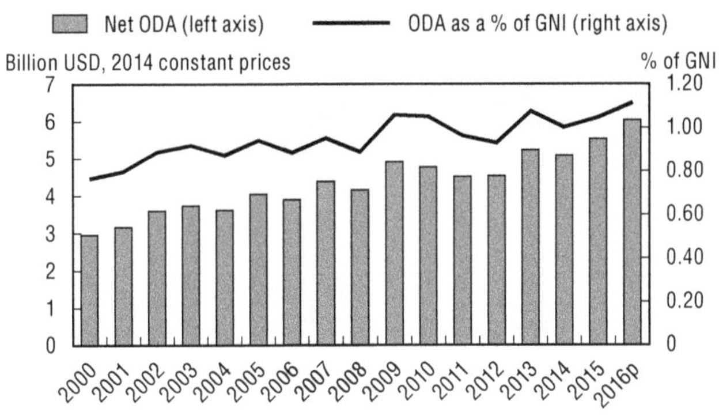

p: Preliminary data.

StatLink http://dx.doi.org/10.1787/888933481843

In 2015, 77.4% of ODA was provided bilaterally. Norway allocated 22.6% of total ODA as core contributions to multilateral organisations, compared with the DAC country average of 26.2%. In addition, it channelled 29.7% of its bilateral ODA for specific projects implemented by multilateral organisations (multi-bi/non-core contributions).

Figure 28.3. **Share of ODA channelled to and through the multilateral system, two year averages, gross disbursements, Norway**

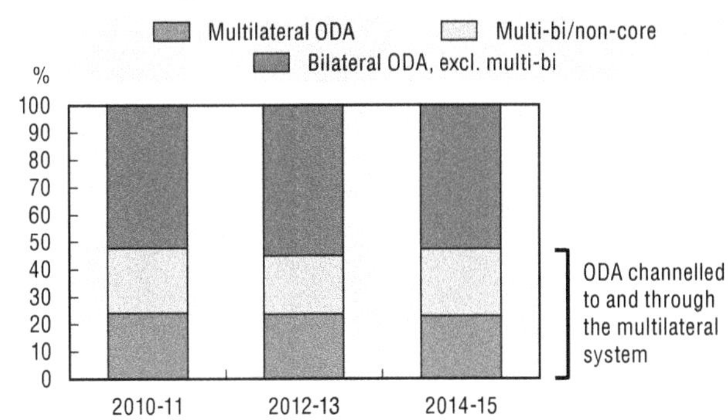

StatLink http://dx.doi.org/10.1787/888933481859

In 2015, 33.2% of bilateral ODA was programmed with partner countries. Norway's share of country programmable aid was lower than the DAC country average 48.8% in 2015. Project-type interventions accounted for 53% of this aid. A large share (25%) of bilateral aid was classified as "other and unallocated".

Figure 28.4. **Composition of bilateral ODA, 2015, gross disbursements, Norway**

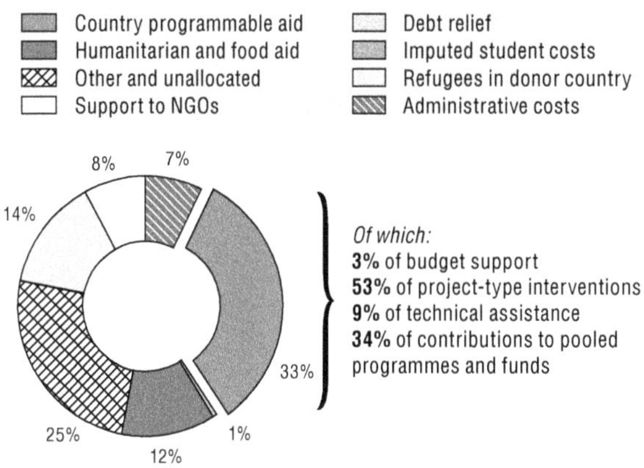

StatLink http://dx.doi.org/10.1787/888933481860

In 2015, USD 813.5 million of Norway's bilateral ODA was channelled to and through civil society organisations (CSOs). Norway's ODA channelled to and through CSOs increased in volume between 2014 and 2015 (+3.3%) but slightly decreased as a share of bilateral ODA (from 26% to 24.4%). This share was higher than the DAC country average of 16.9%.

Figure 28.5. **Bilateral ODA to and through CSOs, two year averages, gross disbursements, Norway**

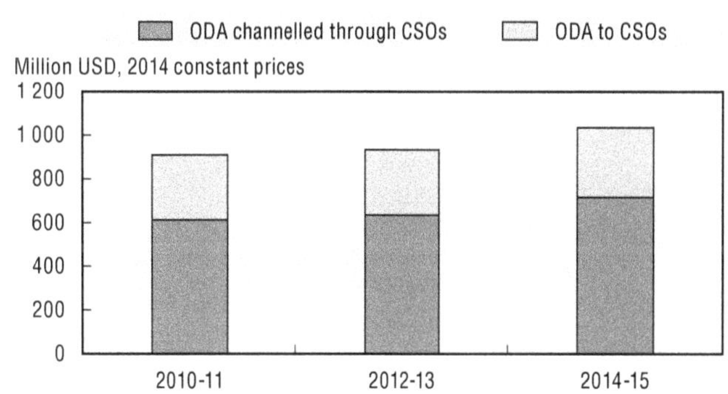

StatLink http://dx.doi.org/10.1787/888933481871

Bilateral ODA primarily focused on sub-Saharan Africa and the Middle East. In 2015, USD 629.2 million was allocated to sub-Saharan Africa, USD 297.7 million to the Middle East, and USD 243.7 million to south and central Asia.

Figure 28.6. **Share of bilateral ODA by region, 2014-15 average, gross disbursements, Norway**

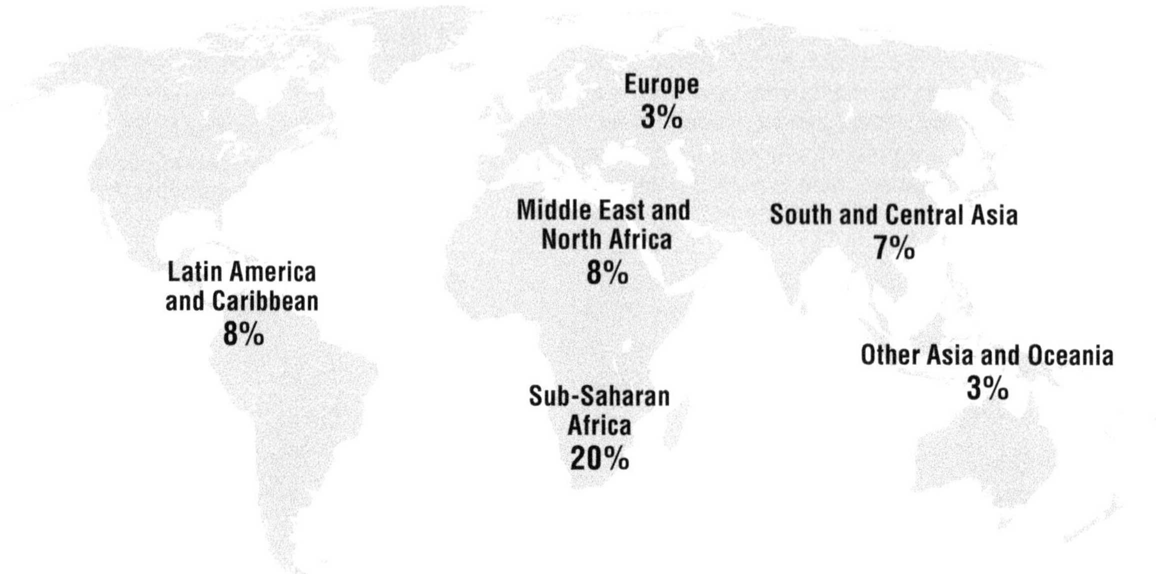

Note: 50% of bilateral ODA allocated was unspecified by region in 2014-15. This share is not represented on the map.

StatLink http://dx.doi.org/10.1787/888933481881

In 2015, 21.8% of bilateral ODA went to Norway's top 10 recipients. Seven of its 12 focus countries are among its top 10 recipients. In 2015, its support to fragile contexts reached USD 938.9 million (28.2% of gross bilateral ODA).

Figure 28.7. **Bilateral ODA to top recipients, 2014-15 average, gross disbursements, Norway**

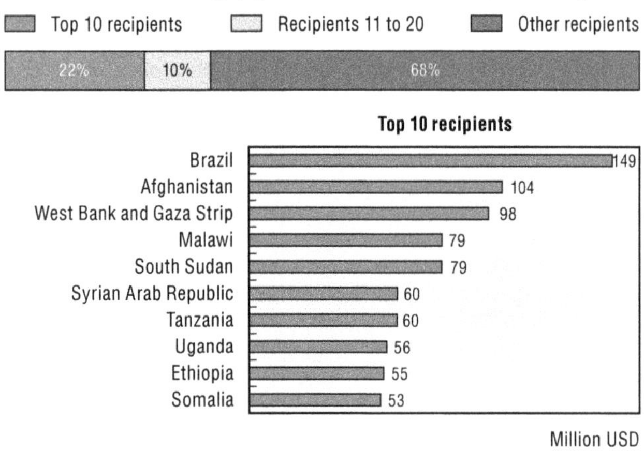

StatLink http://dx.doi.org/10.1787/888933481895

In 2015, 22.3% of bilateral ODA was allocated to least developed countries (LDCs), amounting to USD 744.2 million. The share has fallen, from 30% in 2011 to 25% in 2014, and is below the 2015 DAC average of 24.3%. LDCs received the highest share of bilateral ODA in 2015, noting that 56.2% was unallocated by income group.

At 0.27% of GNI in 2015, total ODA to LDCs exceeded the UN target of 0.15% of GNI.

Figure 28.8. **Bilateral ODA by income group, two year averages, gross disbursements, Norway**

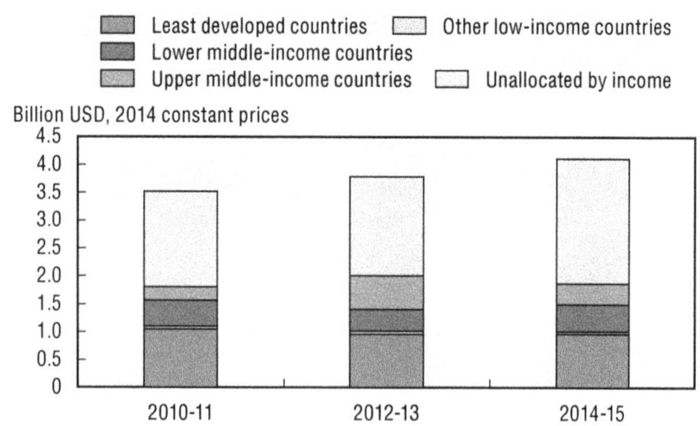

StatLink http://dx.doi.org/10.1787/888933481903

In 2015, 32.3% of bilateral ODA was allocated to social infrastructure and services, reaching USD 1.2 billion, with a strong focus on support to government and civil society (USD 497.2 million) and education (USD 458.7 million). Humanitarian aid amounted to USD 377.4 million.

Figure 28.9. **Share of bilateral ODA by sector, 2014-15 average, commitments, Norway**

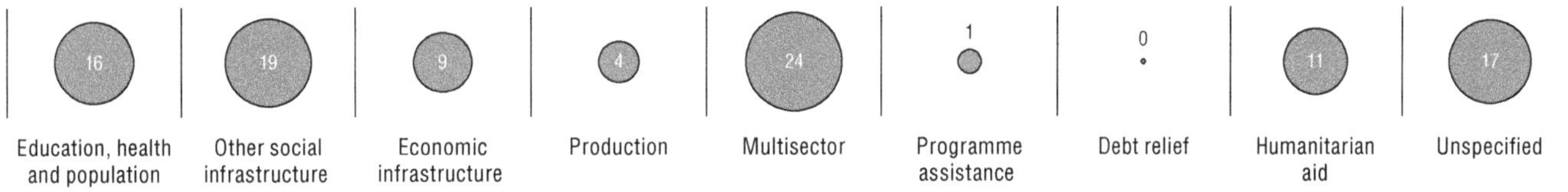

StatLink http://dx.doi.org/10.1787/888933481919

USD 701.3 billion of bilateral ODA supported gender equality in 2015. Gender is a long-standing focus of Norway's development programme, both as a thematic priority and a cross-cutting issue (OECD, 2014). Norway has already geared up its support to important gender-related Sustainable Development Goal targets and is committed to include them in its development co-operation. In 2015, 22.8% of its bilateral allocable aid had gender equality and women's empowerment as a principal or significant objective, compared with the DAC country average of 36.3%. This is a decrease from 2014 when it stood at 31.7%. Norway's aid to population, reproductive health and education focuses on gender.

Figure 28.10. **Share of bilateral allocable ODA in support of gender equality by sector, 2015, commitments, Norway**

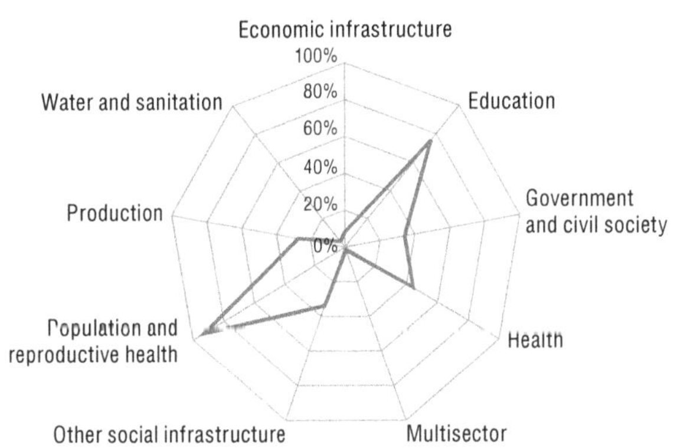

StatLink http://dx.doi.org/10.1787/888933481927

USD 829.7 million of bilateral ODA supported the environment in 2015. Norway is strongly committed to supporting environmental and climate change activities. It is making progress with mainstreaming these issues in its development co-operation (OECD, 2014). In 2015, 27% of its bilateral allocable aid focused on the environment and 24.3% (USD 748.1 million) focused specifically on climate change, compared with the respective DAC country averages of 33.2% and 26.2%.

Figure 28.11. **Bilateral allocable ODA in support of global and local environment objectives, two year averages, commitments, Norway**

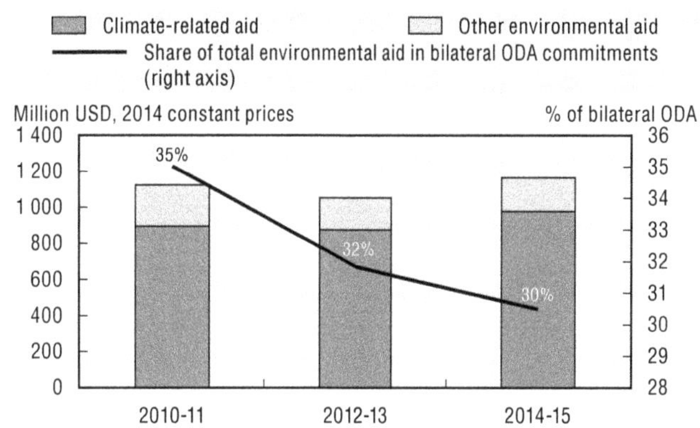

StatLink http://dx.doi.org/10.1787/888933481936

Note to reader: Annex B provides "Methodological notes on the profiles of Development Assistance Committee members".

Reference

OECD (2014), *OECD Development Co-operation Peer Reviews: Norway 2013*, OECD Publishing, Paris, *http://dx.doi.org/10.1787/9789264196315-en*.

POLAND

Poland's contribution to data for development

Poland provides some support for national statistical capacities and systems in developing countries, mainly through hosting internships and study visits in its Central Statistical Office from neighbouring countries – Albania, Armenia, Belarus Bosnia and Herzegovina, Kosovo, Moldova, Romania and Turkey.

Poland also supports bilateral government to government interventions which are approved on a case by case basis, taking into account the interest expressed by developing countries and the capacity of Poland's Central Statistical Office to respond. Poland's Central Statistical Office has, for example, implemented a project in Georgia to support the development of a system of public statistics in the field of environmental statistics.

According to the 2017 Partner Report on Support to Statistics (PRESS) dataset, Poland committed on average USD 0.14 million per year to finance national statistical capacities and systems in developing countries in 2013-15.

Financial flows from Poland to developing countries

In 2016, Poland provided USD 603 million in net ODA (preliminary data), which represented 0.13% of gross national income (GNI) and a 42.6% increase in real terms from 2015, due to increased contributions to the EU development budget. Scaling up its ODA to deliver on its international commitment to achieve an ODA to GNI ratio of 0.33% by 2030 will be challenging without a plan. Poland's share of untied ODA (excluding administrative costs and in-donor refugee costs) was 33.6% in 2015 (up from 31% in 2014), compared to the DAC average of 78.1%. The grant element of total ODA was 98.6% in 2015. At present, data on other official flows and private grants (funds raised by non-governmental organisations and foundations) from Poland to developing countries are not available. Data on private flows at market terms are available for 2015 (amounting to USD 58.3 million).

In 2016, in-donor refugee costs were USD 6 million, a decrease of 35.1% in real terms over 2015, and represented 1.0% of Poland's total net ODA.

Figure 29.1. **Net ODA: Trends in volume and as a share of GNI, 2003-16, Poland**

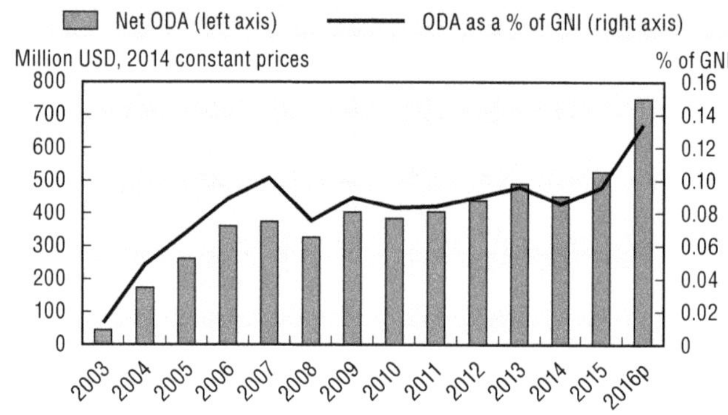

p: Preliminary data.

StatLink http://dx.doi.org/10.1787/888933481949

Poland's use of ODA to mobilise other resources for sustainable development

- According to the DAC Peer Review of Poland's development co-operation, Poland supports domestic resources mobilisation in developing countries by organising workshops, study visits and technical assistance to help them to improve their tax administrations and customs procedures (OECD, 2017).
- **USD 31.2 million** of ODA (+38.5% in real terms from 2014) was committed to promote aid for trade and improve developing countries' trade performance and integration into the world economy in 2015.

Poland's performance against commitments for effective development co-operation

Table 29.1. **Results of the 2016 Global Partnership monitoring round, Poland**

	Alignment and ownership by partner country (%)				Predictability (%)		Transparency		
	Use of country-led results frameworks	Funding recorded in countries' national budgets	Funding through countries' systems	Untied ODA	Annual predictability	Medium-term predictability	Retrospective statistics (OECD CRS)	Information for forecasting (OECD FSS)	Publishing to IATI
2016	-	-	-	33.6	-	-	-	Needs improvement	-

Note: Please refer to Annex B for details on the indicators.

StatLink http://dx.doi.org/10.1787/888933483179

Poland's official development assistance

Poland delivered 26.8% of ODA bilaterally in 2015. It channelled 73.2% of its ODA to multilateral organisations in 2015, compared with the DAC country average of 26.2%. Its multilateral aid consisted mainly of mandatory assessed contributions to the European Union and other international organisations. In addition, it channelled 6% of its bilateral ODA to specific projects implemented by multilateral organisations (multi-bi/non-core contributions).

Figure 29.2. **Share of ODA channelled to and through the multilateral system, two year averages, gross disbursements, Poland**

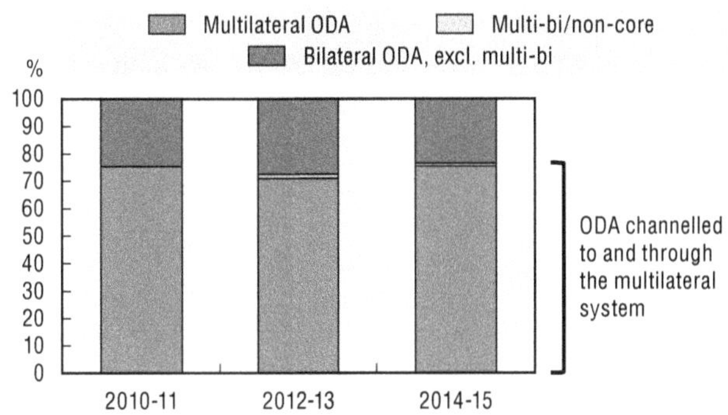

StatLink http://dx.doi.org/10.1787/888933481952

In 2015, 62.9% of bilateral ODA was programmed with partner countries. Poland's share of country programmable aid was higher than the DAC country average (48.8%) in 2015 and project-type interventions made up 83% of this aid. Imputed student costs (19%) and in-donor refugee costs (7.4%) amounted to 26.4% of bilateral ODA.

Figure 29.3. **Composition of bilateral ODA, 2015, gross disbursements, Poland**

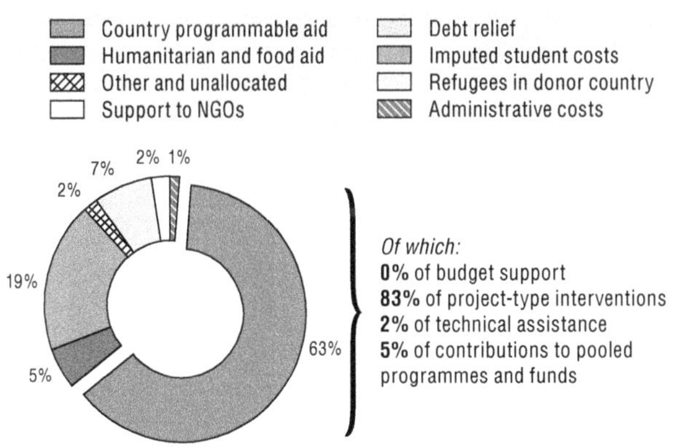

StatLink http://dx.doi.org/10.1787/888933481960

In 2015, USD 15.3 million of bilateral ODA was channelled to and through civil society organisations (CSOs). Poland's ODA to and through CSOs increased between 2014 and 2015 in volume (+17.4%) but decreased as a share of bilateral aid (from 15% to 12.2%). The DAC country average was 16.9% in 2015.

Figure 29.4. **Bilateral ODA to and through CSOs, two year averages, gross disbursements, Poland**

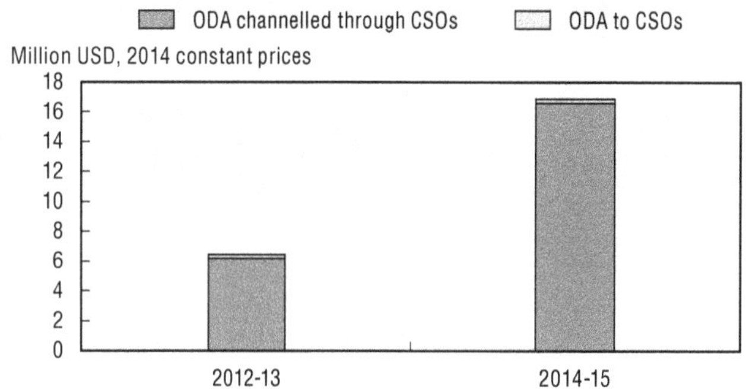

StatLink http://dx.doi.org/10.1787/888933481974

In 2015, bilateral ODA primarily focused on Europe and sub-Saharan Africa. USD 51.4 million was allocated to Eastern Europe, USD 43.9 million to sub-Saharan Africa, and USD 5.9 million to south and central Asia.

Figure 29.5. **Share of bilateral ODA by region, 2014-15 average, gross disbursements, Poland**

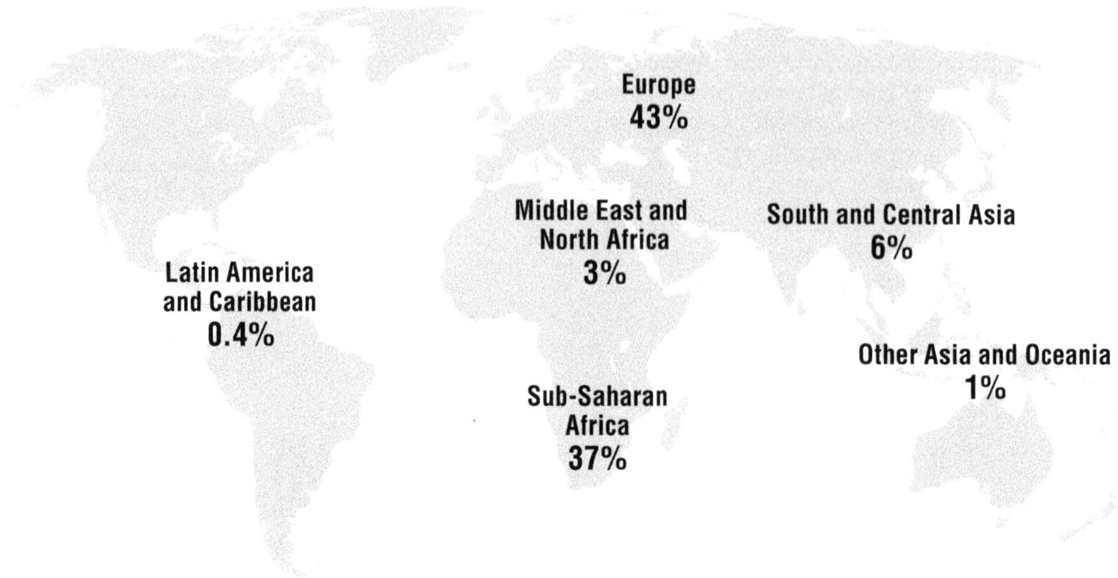

Note: 9% of bilateral ODA allocated was unspecified by region in 2014-15. This share is not represented on the map.

StatLink http://dx.doi.org/10.1787/888933481983

In 2015, 80.3% of bilateral ODA went to Poland's top 10 recipients. Poland divides its geographical priorities into two groups: Eastern Partnership countries and selected countries of Africa, Asia and the Middle East. Six of its ten priority countries are among its top 10 recipients. Its support to fragile contexts reached USD 50.4 million in 2015 (40.4% of gross bilateral ODA).

Figure 29.6. **Bilateral ODA to top recipients, 2014-15 average, gross disbursements, Poland**

StatLink http://dx.doi.org/10.1787/888933481991

In 2015, 36.2% of bilateral ODA was allocated to least developed countries (LDCs), amounting to USD 45.2 million. This purports a slight decrease from 2014, when the share reached a peak of 39.8%. It is still higher than the 2015 DAC average of 24.3%. LDCs received the highest share of bilateral ODA in 2015, followed by lower middle-income countries receiving 32.3%.

At 0.03% of GNI in 2015, total ODA to LDCs was below the UN target of 0.15% of GNI.

Figure 29.7. **Bilateral ODA by income group, two year averages, gross disbursements, Poland**

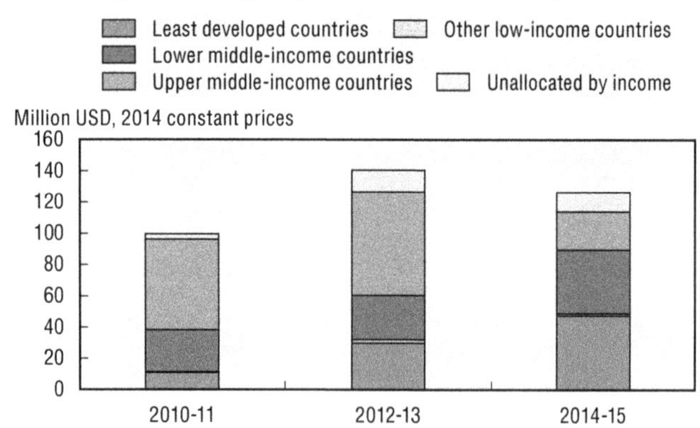

StatLink http://dx.doi.org/10.1787/888933482001

In 2015, 59.6% of bilateral ODA was allocated to social infrastructure and services, reaching USD 74.7 million, with a strong focus on education (USD 49.3 million) and government and civil society (USD 19.2 million). USD 28.2 million went to production sectors, mainly to agriculture (USD 27.8 million).

Figure 29.8. **Share of bilateral ODA by sector, 2014-15 average, commitments, Poland**

StatLink http://dx.doi.org/10.1787/888933482017

USD 1.6 million of bilateral ODA supported gender equality in 2015. Gender equality is a cross-cutting issue for Poland. The 2017 DAC Peer Review of Poland found that clearer objectives and guidance to mainstream gender equality and women's empowerment could help translate this general commitment into practice and ensure it is addressed systematically in programming and policy dialogue (OECD, 2017). In 2015, 1.7% of Poland's bilateral allocable aid had gender equality and women's empowerment as a principal or significant objective, compared with the DAC country average of 36.3%. Sectors where Poland has a gender focus are population and reproductive health.

Figure 29.9. **Share of bilateral allocable ODA in support of gender equality by sector, 2015, commitments, Poland**

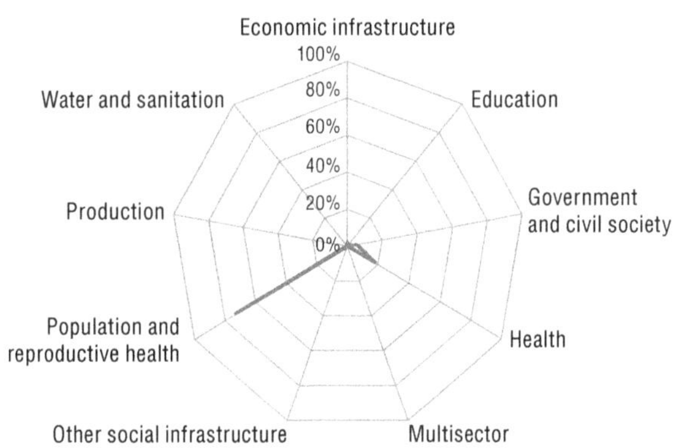

StatLink http://dx.doi.org/10.1787/888933482020

USD 5.5 million of bilateral ODA supported the environment in 2015. Protecting the environment, promoting the sustainable use of natural resources and preventing climate change are all thematic priorities and cross-cutting issues of Polish development co-operation. The 2017 DAC Peer Review found that Poland would need more precise objectives and guidance to mainstream the environment in its interventions and that it should ensure that environment mainstreaming tools, such as environmental impact assessments, are applied systematically to Poland's support, particularly for infrastructure-related activities (OECD, 2017). In 2015, 6.1% of Poland's bilateral allocable aid supported the environment and 3.3% (USD 3 million) focused on climate change, compared with the respective DAC country averages of 33.2% and 26.2%.

Figure 29.10. **Bilateral allocable ODA in support of global and local environment objectives, 2014-15 average, commitments, Poland**

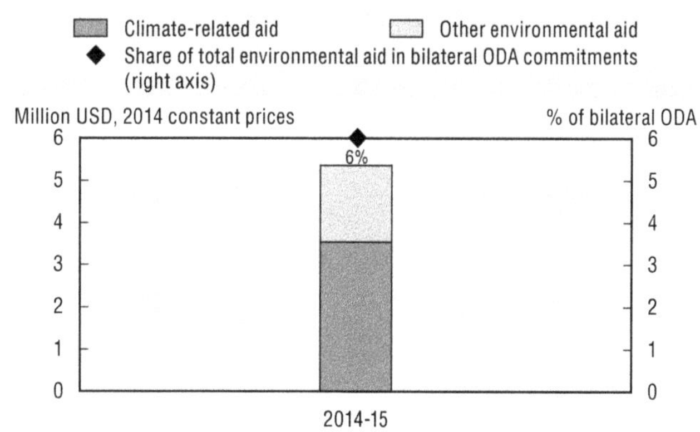

StatLink http://dx.doi.org/10.1787/888933482034

Note to reader: Annex B provides "Methodological notes on the profiles of Development Assistance Committee members".

Reference

OECD (2017), *OECD Development Co-operation Peer Reviews: Poland 2017*, OECD Publishing, Paris, *http://dx.doi.org/10.1787/9789264268869-en*.

PORTUGAL

Portugal's contribution to data for development

Strengthening statistical capacities and systems in developing countries is an explicit strategic priority of Portugal's development co-operation. Portugal provides support mainly through bilateral government to government technical assistance to national statistical institutions, giving priority to co-operation with Portuguese-speaking countries. Portugal focuses on improving statistical production, strengthening data dissemination and co-ordination among development partners. Support covers a wide range of activities, including the production of short-term indicators, geo-referencing, institutional support and improvement of statistical methodology.

Portugal considers its support to the regular production of the Consumer Price Index for Cabo Verde and Mozambique, the implementation of census cartography systems, and the publication of a brochure with the main development indicators for all Portuguese-speaking countries to be examples of successful initiatives in strengthening statistical capacity. In Mozambique and Timor-Leste, Portugal also supports the Aid Transparency Portals/Databases. Portugal plans to publish a Handbook on Good Practices in Statistical Co-operation in 2017.

According to the 2017 Partner Report on Support to Statistics (PRESS) dataset, Portugal committed on average USD 0.45 million per year to finance national statistical capacities and systems in developing countries in 2013-15.

Financial flows from Portugal to developing countries

Figure 30.1. **Net resource flows to developing countries, 2005-15, Portugal**

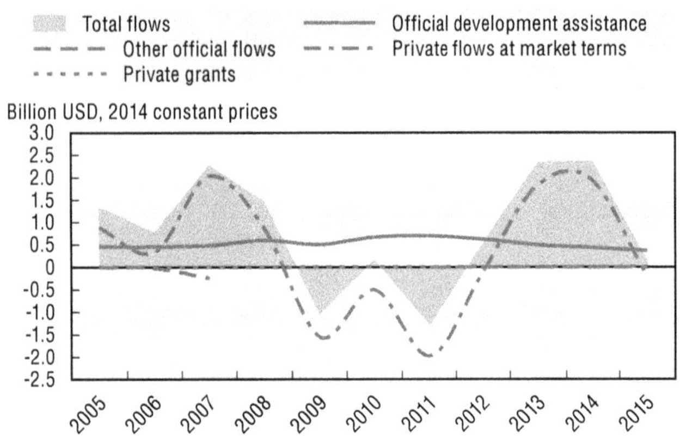

Note: Data on other official flows are not available for 2008-10.

StatLink http://dx.doi.org/10.1787/888933482048

Portugal's use of ODA to mobilise other resources for sustainable development

- **USD 109 000** of official development assistance (ODA) was committed to the mobilisation of domestic resources in developing countries, e.g. to support the development of their tax systems, in 2015.
- **USD 24.1 million** of ODA (-39.5% in real terms from 2014) was committed to promote aid for trade and improve developing countries' trade performance and integration into the world economy in 2015.

Portugal's performance against commitments for effective development co-operation

Table 30.1. **Results of the 2016 Global Partnership monitoring round, Portugal**

	Alignment and ownership by partner country (%)				Predictability (%)		Transparency		
	Use of country-led results frameworks	Funding recorded in countries' national budgets	Funding through countries' systems	Untied ODA	Annual predictability	Medium-term predictability	Retrospective statistics (OECD CRS)	Information for forecasting (OECD FSS)	Publishing to IATI
2016	73.4	82.6	17.1	49.0	100.0	18.3	Excellent	Fair	-
Baseline	-	75.9	21.1	42.6	100.0	80.5	Excellent	Good	-
Trend	-	⇑	⇓	⇑	=	⇓	=	⇓	-

Note: Please refer to Annex B for details on the indicators.

StatLink http://dx.doi.org/10.1787/888933483187

Portugal's official development assistance

In 2016, Portugal provided USD 340 million in net ODA (preliminary data), which represented 0.17% of gross national income (GNI) and a rise of 8.9% in real terms from 2015 due to an increase in its contributions to the EU development budget. Portugal's ODA increased in 2016 for the first time since 2011. Portugal intends to meet its ODA target when its economy begins to recover (OECD, 2015) and is committed, at the European level, to collectively achieve a 0.7% ODA/GNI ratio by 2030. Portugal's share of untied ODA (excluding administrative costs and in-donor refugee costs) was 49% in 2015 (up from 34.5% in 2014), compared to the DAC average of 78.1%. The grant element of total ODA was 93.7% in 2015 (increasing from 89.7% in 2014).

In 2016, in-donor refugee costs were USD 2 million, a decrease of 40.2% in real terms over 2015, and represented 0.5% of Portugal's total net ODA.

Figure 30.2. **Net ODA: Trends in volume and as a share of GNI, 2000-16, Portugal**

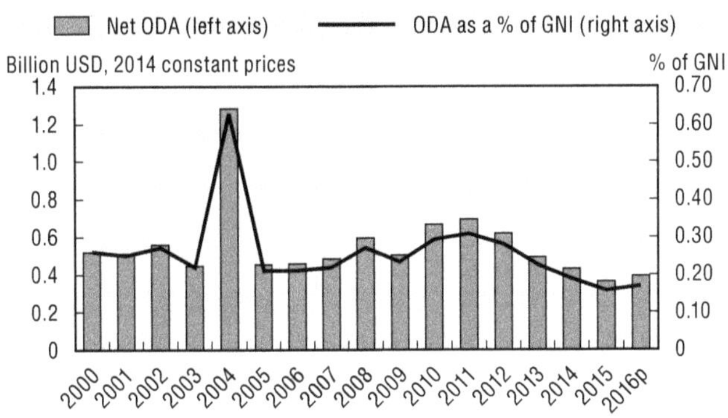

p: Preliminary data.

StatLink http://dx.doi.org/10.1787/888933482052

In 2015, 54.2% of ODA was provided bilaterally. Portugal allocated 45.8% of total ODA as core contributions to multilateral organisations, compared with the DAC country average of 26.2%. In addition, it channelled 6% of its bilateral ODA to specific projects implemented by multilateral organisations (multi-bi/non-core contributions).

Figure 30.3. **Share of ODA channelled to and through the multilateral system, two year averages, gross disbursements, Portugal**

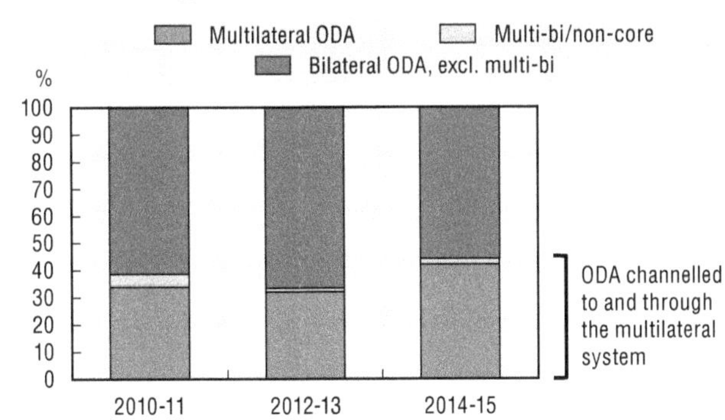

StatLink http://dx.doi.org/10.1787/888933482061

In 2015, 75.7% of bilateral ODA was programmed with partner countries. The share of country programmable aid was high compared with the 2015 DAC country average of 48.8% and project-type interventions made up 93.4% of this aid.

Figure 30.4. **Composition of bilateral ODA, 2015, gross disbursements, Portugal**

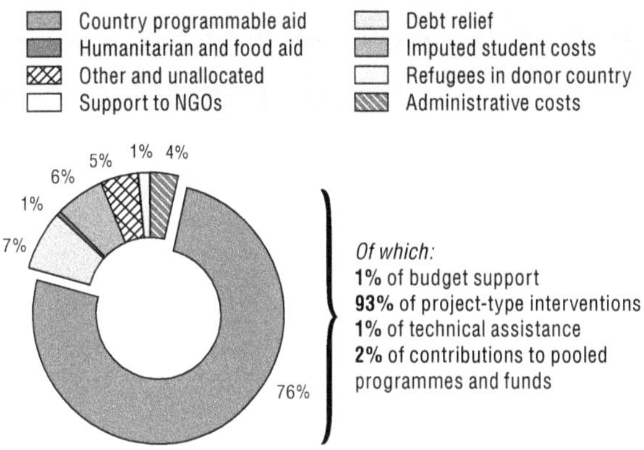

StatLink http://dx.doi.org/10.1787/888933482071

In 2015, USD 12.2 million of bilateral ODA was channelled to and through civil society organisations (CSOs). Portugal's ODA to and through CSOs increased between 2014 and 2015 as a share of bilateral ODA (from 5.2% to 6.4%), but decreased in terms of volume (-5.2%). The DAC country average was 16.9% in 2015.

Figure 30.5. **Bilateral ODA to and through CSOs, two year averages, gross disbursements, Portugal**

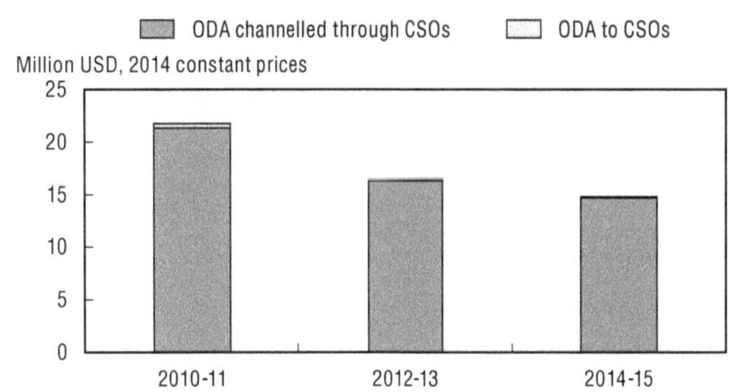

StatLink http://dx.doi.org/10.1787/888933482089

Bilateral ODA was heavily focused on sub-Saharan Africa. In 2015, USD 137.9 million was allocated to this region and USD 17.1 million was allocated to Far East Asia.

Figure 30.6. **Share of bilateral ODA by region, 2014-15 average, gross disbursements, Portugal**

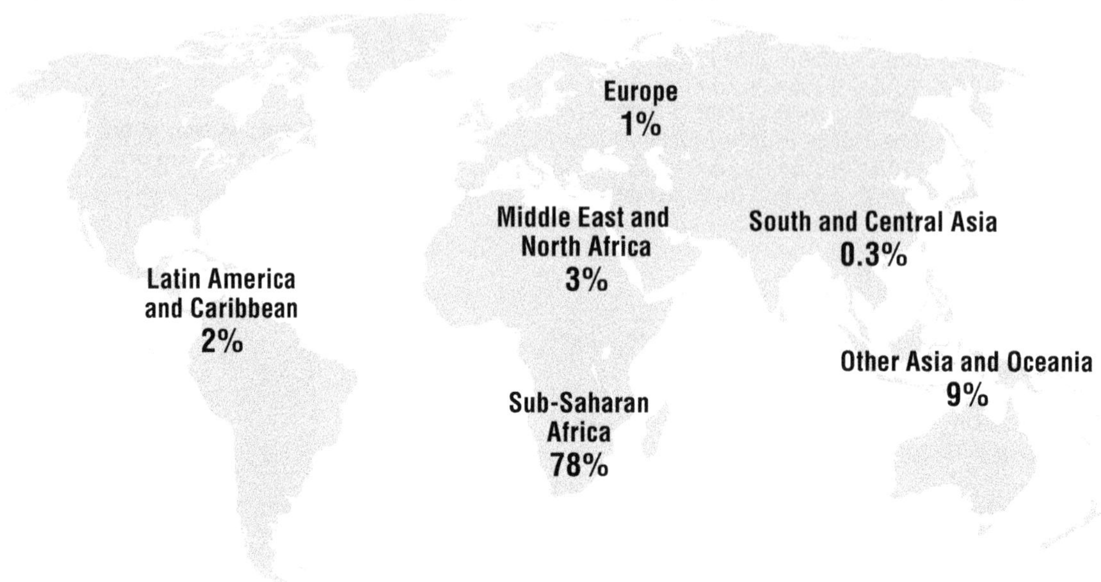

Note: 6% of bilateral ODA allocated was unspecified by region in 2014-15. This share is not represented on the map.

StatLink http://dx.doi.org/10.1787/888933482099

In 2015, 86.5% of bilateral ODA went to Portugal's top 10 recipients. Portugal's programme is focused on its six Lusophone priority partner countries, which are its top ODA recipients. Its support to fragile contexts reached USD 71.1 million in 2015 (37.1% of gross bilateral ODA).

Figure 30.7. **Bilateral ODA to top recipients, 2014-15 average, gross disbursements, Portugal**

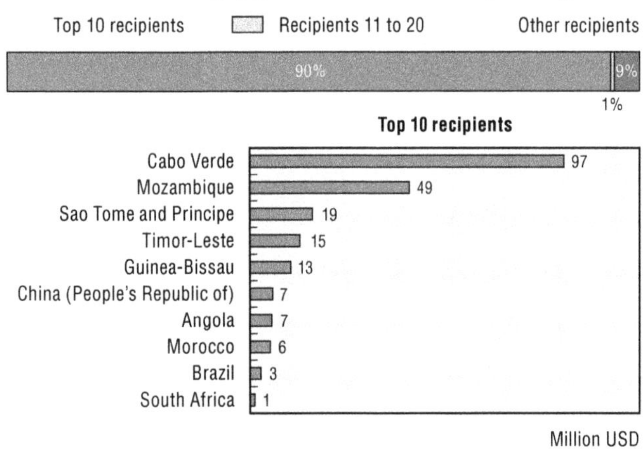

StatLink http://dx.doi.org/10.1787/888933482106

In 2015, 49.7% of bilateral ODA was allocated to least developed countries (LDCs), amounting to USD 95.3 million. This is an increase from 38.9% in 2014 and is higher than the 2015 DAC average of 24.3%. LDCs received the highest share of bilateral ODA in 2015.

At 0.05% of GNI in 2015, total ODA to LDCs was below the UN target of 0.15% of GNI.

Figure 30.8. **Bilateral ODA by income group, two year averages, gross disbursements, Portugal**

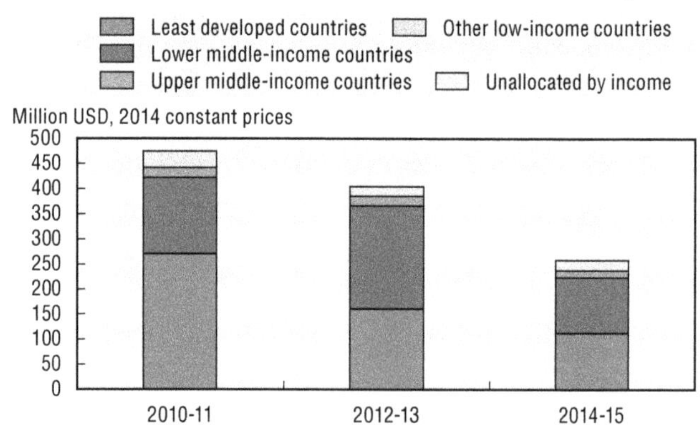

StatLink http://dx.doi.org/10.1787/888933482111

In 2015, 58.7% of bilateral ODA was allocated to social infrastructure and services, amounting to USD 105.1 million, with a strong focus on education (USD 41.6 million) and health (USD 22.5 million). USD 22.2 million was allocated to economic infrastructure and services, in particular to energy generation and supply (USD 16.5 million).

Figure 30.9. **Share of bilateral ODA by sector, 2014-15 average, commitments, Portugal**

StatLink http://dx.doi.org/10.1787/888933482128

USD 30.8 million of bilateral ODA supported gender equality in 2015. Portugal is strongly committed to gender equality and the empowerment of women and girls. However, this commitment is not yet reflected in its development co-operation programmes (OECD, 2015). In 2015, 19.8% of Portuguese bilateral allocable aid had gender equality and women's empowerment as a principal or significant objective, compared with the DAC country average of 36.3%. This is an increase from 14.6% in 2014 and 8.7% in 2010. Portugal's aid to population and reproductive health, water and sanitation, and education focuses on gender.

Figure 30.10. **Share of bilateral allocable ODA in support of gender equality by sector, 2015, commitments, Portugal**

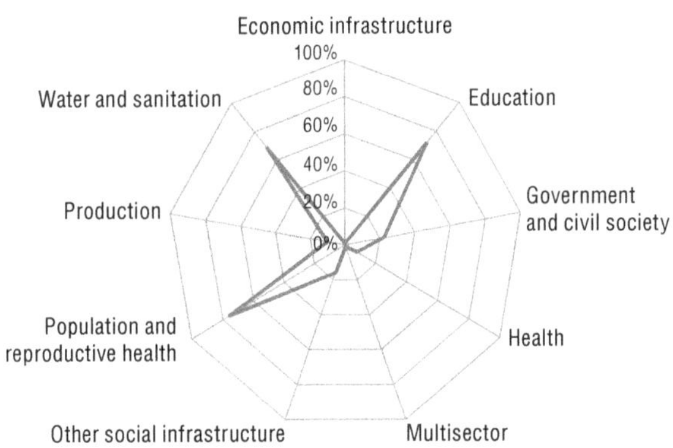

StatLink http://dx.doi.org/10.1787/888933482132

USD 22 million of bilateral ODA supported the environment in 2015. Portugal's share of environment-focused ODA has increased in recent years, and the country's vision for its development co-operation – the Strategic Concept 2014-20 – places greater emphasis on the environment. Nevertheless, integrating the environment and climate change across its development co-operation remains a challenge (OECD, 2015). In 2015, 14.1% of its bilateral allocable aid supported the environment and 13.1% (USD 20.4 million) focused specifically on climate change (up from 5% in 2014), compared with the respective DAC country averages of 33.2% and 26.2%.

Figure 30.11. **Bilateral allocable ODA in support of global and local environment objectives, two year averages, commitments, Portugal**

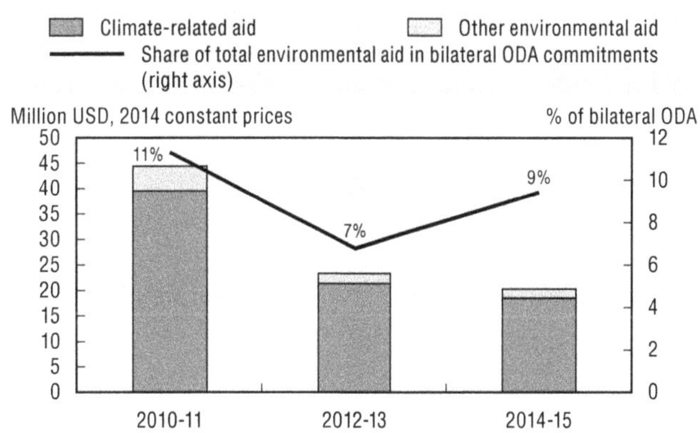

StatLink http://dx.doi.org/10.1787/888933482141

Note to reader: Annex B provides "Methodological notes on the profiles of Development Assistance Committee members".

Reference

OECD (2015), *OECD Development Co-operation Peer Reviews: Portugal 2016*, OECD Publishing, Paris, *http://dx.doi.org/10.1787/9789264248571-en.*

SLOVAK REPUBLIC

The Slovak Republic's contribution to data for development

According to the 2017 Partner Report on Support to Statistics (PRESS) dataset, the Slovak Republic committed on average USD 0.59 million per year to finance national statistical capacities and systems in developing countries in 2013-15.

Financial flows from the Slovak Republic to developing countries

In 2016, the Slovak Republic provided USD 107 million in net ODA (preliminary data), which represented 0.12% of gross national income (GNI) and a rise of 26.8% in real terms from 2015 due to increased contributions to the EU development budget. The Slovak Republic is committed to gradually meeting the official development assistance (ODA) target of 0.33% adopted at the EU level, as its economy recovers. The Slovak Republic's share of untied ODA (excluding administrative costs and in-donor refugee costs) was 47.5% in 2015 (up from 1.2% in 2014), compared to the DAC average of 78.1%. The grant element of total ODA was 100% in 2015. At present, data on other official flows, private grants (funds raised by non-governmental organisations and foundations) and private flows at market terms from the Slovak Republic to developing countries are not available.

In 2016, in-donor refugee costs were USD 1 million, a decrease of 23.2% in real terms over 2015, and represented 1.2% of the Slovak Republic's total net ODA.

Figure 31.1. **Net ODA: Trends in volume and as a share of GNI, 2006-16, Slovak Republic**

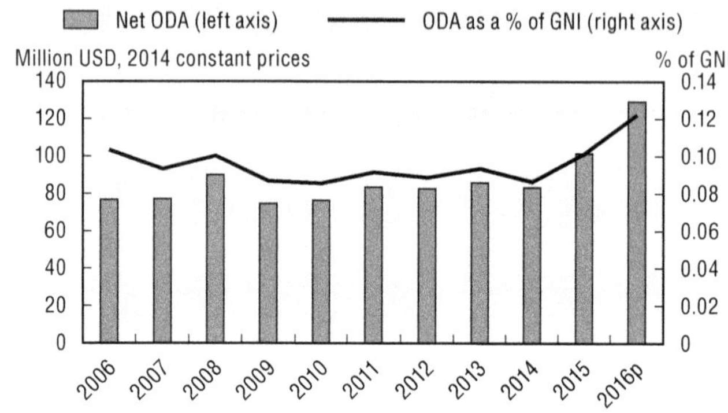

p: Preliminary data.

StatLink http://dx.doi.org/10.1787/888933482151

The Slovak Republic's use of ODA to mobilise other resources for sustainable development

- **USD 23 300** of ODA was committed to the mobilisation of domestic resources in developing countries, e.g. to support the development of their tax systems, in 2015.
- **USD 1 million** of ODA (+14.4% in real terms from 2014) was committed to promote aid for trade and improve developing countries' trade performance and integration into the world economy in 2015.

The Slovak Republic's performance against commitments for effective development co-operation

Table 31.1. **Results of the 2016 Global Partnership monitoring round, Slovak Republic**

	Alignment and ownership by partner country (%)				Predictability (%)		Transparency		
	Use of country-led results frameworks	Funding recorded in countries' national budgets	Funding through countries' systems	Untied ODA	Annual predictability	Medium-term predictability	Retrospective statistics (OECD CRS)	Information for forecasting (OECD FSS)	Publishing to IATI
2016	50.0	100.0	1.7	47.5	100.0	33.3	Fair	Excellent	-

Note: Please refer to Annex B for details on the indicators.

StatLink http://dx.doi.org/10.1787/888933483197

The Slovak Republic's official development assistance

In 2015, 20.3% of the Slovak Republic's ODA was provided bilaterally, while 79.7% of total ODA was allocated as core contributions to multilateral organisations (above the DAC country average of 26.2%). The major share of its multilateral aid (89%) went to fulfil its assessed contribution to the EU (including the European Development Fund). It also contributed to several other international organisations, notably the European Investment Bank, the United Nations system and the World Bank Group. In addition, it channelled 20.3% of its bilateral ODA to specific projects implemented by multilateral organisations (multi-bi/non-core contributions).

Figure 31.2. **Share of ODA channelled to and through the multilateral system, two year averages, gross disbursements, Slovak Republic**

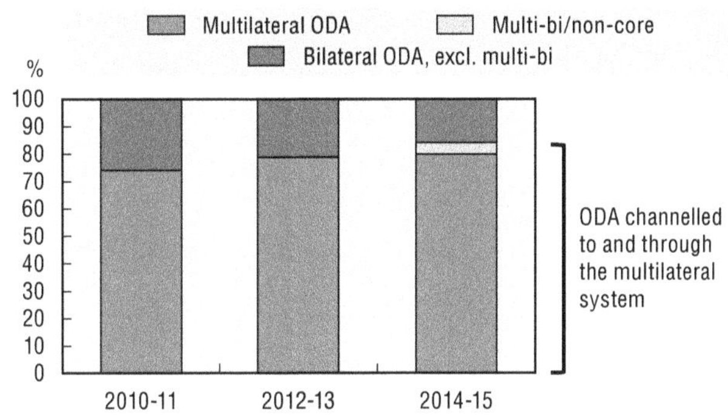

StatLink http://dx.doi.org/10.1787/888933482166

In 2015, 47.7% of bilateral ODA was programmed with partner countries. The Slovak Republic's share of country programmable aid was close to the DAC country average (48.8%) in 2015 and project-type interventions made up 47.9% of this aid. Fifteen per cent of bilateral ODA was classified as "other and unallocated".

Figure 31.3. **Composition of bilateral ODA, 2015, gross disbursements, Slovak Republic**

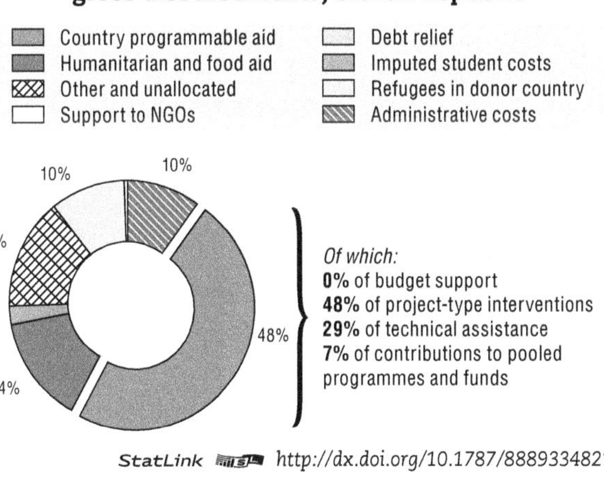

StatLink http://dx.doi.org/10.1787/888933482175

In 2015, USD 3.7 million of bilateral ODA was channelled to and through civil society organisations (CSOs). Slovak ODA to and through CSOs increased between 2014 and 2015, both in volume (+54%) and as a share of bilateral aid (from 17.6% to 21.6%). The DAC average was 16.9% in 2015.

Figure 31.4. **Bilateral ODA to and through CSOs, two year averages, gross disbursements, Slovak Republic**

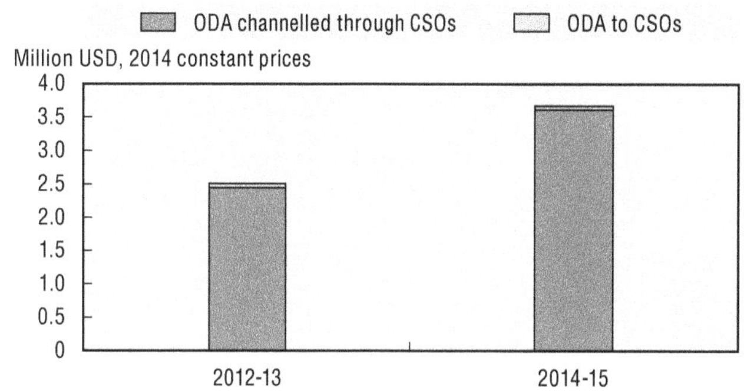

StatLink http://dx.doi.org/10.1787/888933482180

Bilateral ODA was primarily focused on Eastern Europe. In 2015, USD 7 million was allocated to Eastern Europe, USD 1.6 million to sub-Saharan Africa, and USD 0.9 million to south and central Asia.

Figure 31.5. **Share of bilateral ODA by region, 2014-15 average, gross disbursements, Slovak Republic**

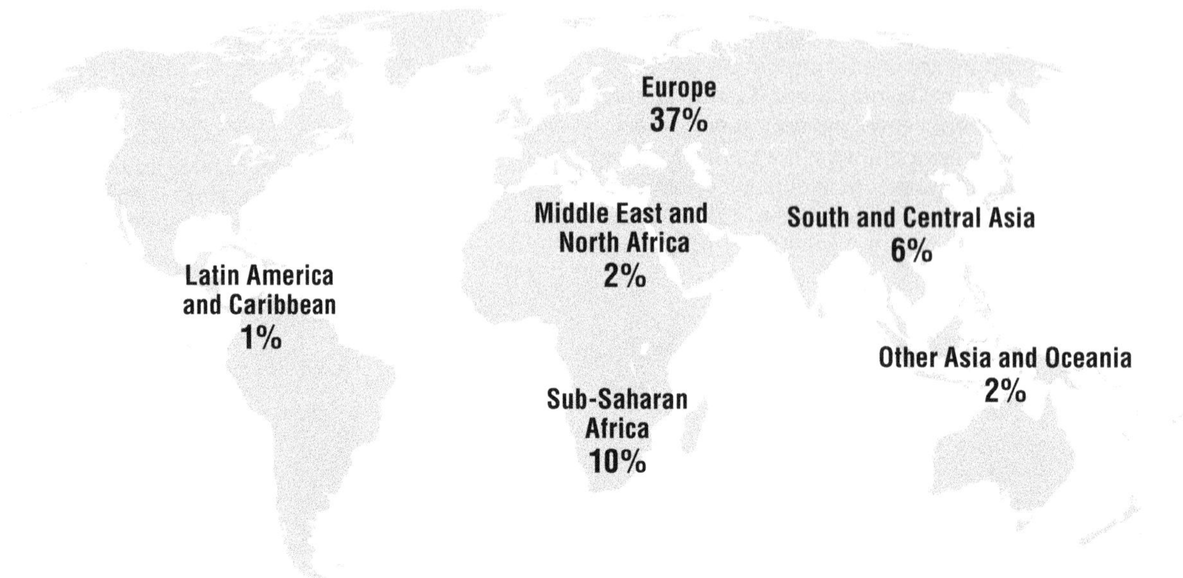

Note: 42% of bilateral ODA allocated was unspecified by region in 2014-15. This share is not represented on the map.

StatLink http://dx.doi.org/10.1787/888933482199

In 2015, 46.1% of bilateral ODA went to the Slovak Republic's top 10 recipients. It focuses on ten priority partners, of which there are three programme countries (Afghanistan, Kenya, Moldova), six project countries (Albania, Belarus, Bosnia and Herzegovina, Georgia, Kosovo, Ukraine) and South Sudan. Nine priority countries are among its top 10 recipients. In 2015, its support to fragile contexts reached USD 2.5 million (14.3% of gross bilateral ODA).

Figure 31.6. **Bilateral ODA to top recipients, 2014-15 average, gross disbursements, Slovak Republic**

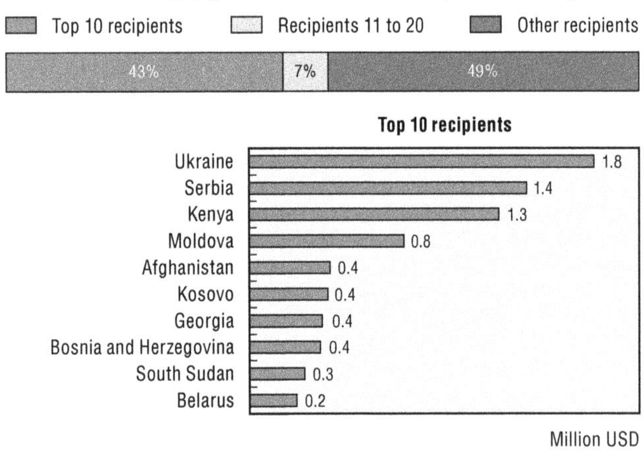

StatLink http://dx.doi.org/10.1787/888933482200

In 2015, 5.4% of bilateral ODA was allocated to least developed countries (LDCs), amounting to USD 0.9 million. This is a decrease from 20.6% in 2013 and 7.1% in 2014 and is lower than the 2015 DAC average of 24.3%. Lower middle-income countries received the highest share of bilateral ODA in 2015 (26%), noting that 45.3% of bilateral aid is unallocated by income group.

At 0.02% of GNI in 2015, total ODA to LDCs was below the UN target of 0.15% of GNI.

Figure 31.7. **Bilateral ODA by income group, two year averages, gross disbursements, Slovak Republic**

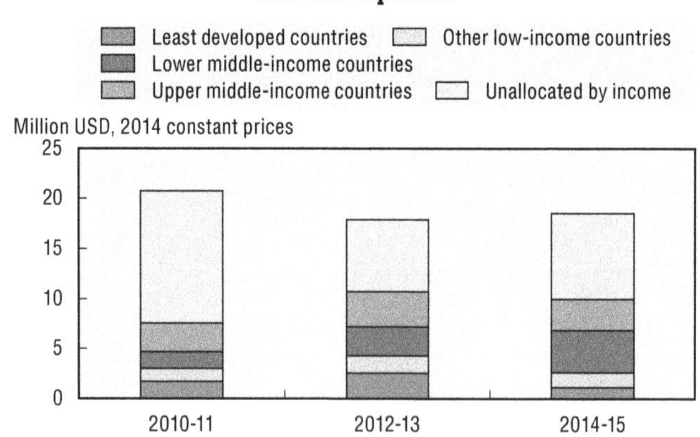

StatLink http://dx.doi.org/10.1787/888933482210

In 2015, 55.5% of bilateral ODA (USD 10.5 million) was allocated to social infrastructure and services, with a strong focus on education (USD 4.1 million) and support to government and civil society (USD 5 million). Humanitarian aid amounted to USD 2.5 million. The Slovak Republic's bilateral co-operation focuses on seven areas: education, healthcare, good governance and building of civil society, agriculture and forestry, water and sanitation, energy, and support to economic development. Priority sectors of engagement are identified in the country strategy papers for programme countries. The Slovak Republic will support sectors in its "project" countries on the basis of the diverse needs of the countries undergoing transformation and on the Slovak Republic's own experience.

Figure 31.8. **Share of bilateral ODA by sector, 2014-15 average, commitments, Slovak Republic**

StatLink http://dx.doi.org/10.1787/888933482221

USD 0.1 million of bilateral ODA supported gender equality in 2015. The Slovak Republic recognises that gender equality and women's empowerment are crucial for eradicating poverty and promoting economic growth and social development. It plans to mainstream gender equality into its development co-operation programme. In 2015, 0.6% of Slovak bilateral allocable aid had gender equality and women's empowerment as a principal or significant objective, compared with 2.4% in 2014 and the DAC country average of 36.3%.

USD 2.1 million supported the environment in 2015. The Slovak Republic is increasingly integrating the environment and climate change into its development co-operation, in accordance with its commitments to mitigation, adaptation and protection of biodiversity. In 2015, 14.5% of its bilateral allocable aid supported the environment and 2% (USD 0.3 million) focused specifically on climate change, compared with the respective DAC country averages of 33.2% and 26.2%.

Figure 31.9. **Bilateral allocable ODA in support of global and local environment objectives, 2014-15 average, commitments, Slovak Republic**

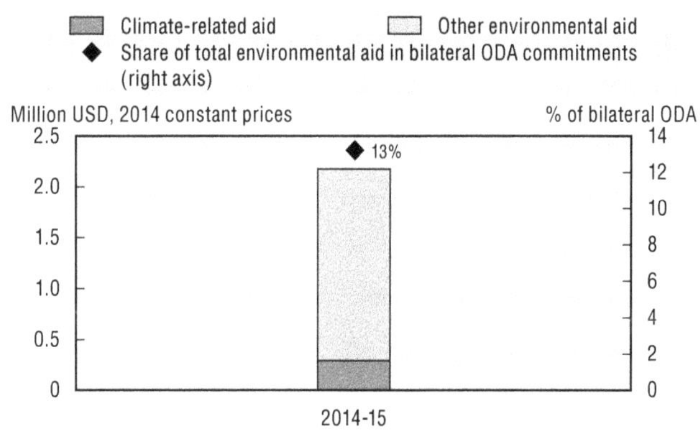

StatLink http://dx.doi.org/10.1787/888933482237

Note to reader: Annex B provides "Methodological notes on the profiles of Development Assistance Committee members".

SLOVENIA

Slovenia's contribution to data for development

Slovenia engages in statistical capacity building in developing countries through its national statistical office. Support for statistical capacity building, which focuses on national statistical systems, is provided mainly through technical assistance with the objective to improve statistical production and strengthen data dissemination.

The Statistical Office of Slovenia engages in technical assistance within the context of bilateral government to government projects – for instance by hosting study visits and providing consultancies to Bosnia and Herzegovina in several sectors including agriculture, energy, forestry, business, and general methodology and statistical standards – or within the context of twinning projects financed by the EU – for instance the Instrument for Pre-accession Assistance (IPA) twinning projects in Bosnia and Herzegovina and the Former Yugoslav Republic of Macedonia.

According to the 2017 Partner Report on Support to Statistics (PRESS) dataset, Slovenia committed on average USD 0.02 million per year to finance national statistical capacities and systems in developing countries in 2013-15.

Financial flows from Slovenia to developing countries

In 2016, Slovenia provided USD 80 million in net ODA (preliminary data), which represented 0.18% of gross national income (GNI) and a rise of 25.3% in real terms from 2015 due to increased contributions to international organisations. It shall strive to increase its ODA/GNI to 0.33% by 2030 as agreed at the EU level. Slovenia's share of untied ODA (excluding administrative costs and in-donor refugee costs) was 12.4% in 2015, while the DAC average was 78.1%. The grant element of total ODA was 100% in 2015. At present, data on other official flows and private grants (funds raised by non-governmental organisations and foundations) from Slovenia to developing countries are not available. Data on private flows at market terms are available for 2015 (amounting to USD 111.1 million).

In 2016, in-donor refugee costs were USD 8 million, an increase of 7.1% in real terms over 2015, and represented 9.6% of Slovenia's total net ODA.

Figure 32.1. **Net ODA: Trends in volume and as a share of GNI, 2005-16, Slovenia**

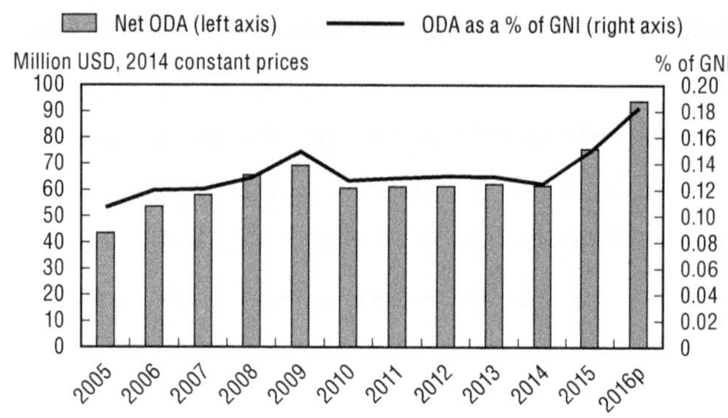

p: Preliminary data.

StatLink http://dx.doi.org/10.1787/888933482240

Slovenia's use of ODA to mobilise other resources for sustainable development

- **USD 0.1 million** of ODA (-69.6% in real terms from 2014) was committed to promote aid for trade and improve developing countries' trade performance and integration into the world economy in 2015.

Slovenia's performance against commitments for effective development co-operation

Table 32.1. **Results of the 2016 Global Partnership monitoring round, Slovenia**

	Alignment and ownership by partner country (%)				Predictability (%)		Transparency		
	Use of country-led results frameworks	Funding recorded in countries' national budgets	Funding through countries' systems	Untied ODA	Annual predictability	Medium-term predictability	Retrospective statistics (OECD CRS)	Information for forecasting (OECD FSS)	Publishing to IATI
2016	33.3	0.0	0.0	12.4	0.0	33.3	Good	Good	-

Note: Please refer to Annex B for details on the indicators.

StatLink http://dx.doi.org/10.1787/888933483208

Slovenia's official development assistance

In 2015, 39.7% of ODA was provided bilaterally. In 2015, 60.3% of Slovenia's ODA was channelled to multilateral organisations, compared with the DAC country average of 26.2%. Slovenia principally allocated its multilateral contributions to the European Union (EU general budget and European Development Fund) to meet its mandatory contributions. The remainder of Slovenia's multilateral ODA consisted of contributions to the World Bank Group, as well as small contributions to the Global Environment Facility and United Nations agencies. In addition, it channelled 11.2% of its bilateral ODA for specific projects implemented by multilateral organisations (multi-bi/non-core contributions).

Figure 32.2. **Share of ODA channelled to and through the multilateral system, two year averages, gross disbursements, Slovenia**

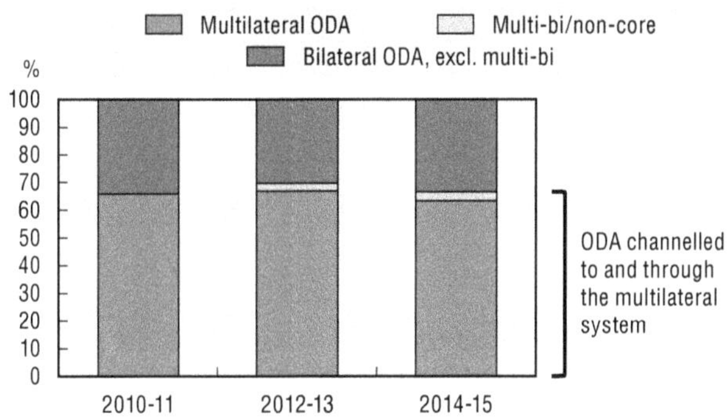

StatLink http://dx.doi.org/10.1787/888933482254

In 2015, 25.6% of bilateral ODA was programmed with partner countries. Slovenia's share of country programmable aid was lower than the DAC country average of 48.8% in 2015 and project-type interventions made up 49% of this aid. Imputed student costs and refugees in donor country costs accounted for nearly half of bilateral aid.

Figure 32.3. **Composition of bilateral ODA, 2015, gross disbursements, Slovenia**

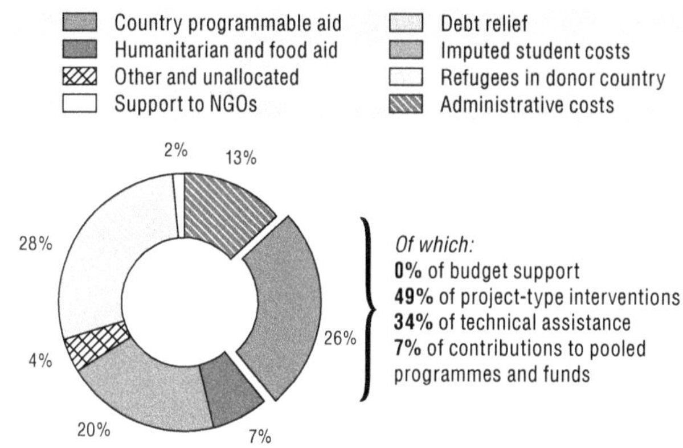

StatLink http://dx.doi.org/10.1787/888933482264

In 2015, USD 2 million of bilateral ODA was channelled to and through civil society organisations (CSOs). This was equivalent to 7.8% of bilateral ODA, compared with the DAC country average of 16.9%. Aid to and through CSOs decreased between 2014 and 2015, both in volume (-32.1%) and as a share of bilateral ODA (from 17.1% in 2014).

Figure 32.4. **Bilateral ODA to and through CSOs, two year averages, gross disbursements, Slovenia**

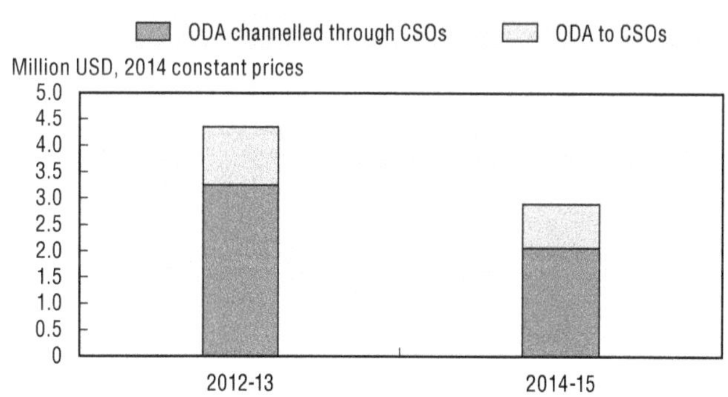

StatLink http://dx.doi.org/10.1787/888933482272

Bilateral ODA heavily focused on Eastern Europe (with a strong emphasis on South East Europe). In 2015, USD 12 million was allocated to Eastern Europe and USD 0.27 million to sub-Saharan Africa.

Figure 32.5. **Share of bilateral ODA by region, 2014-15 average, gross disbursements, Slovenia**

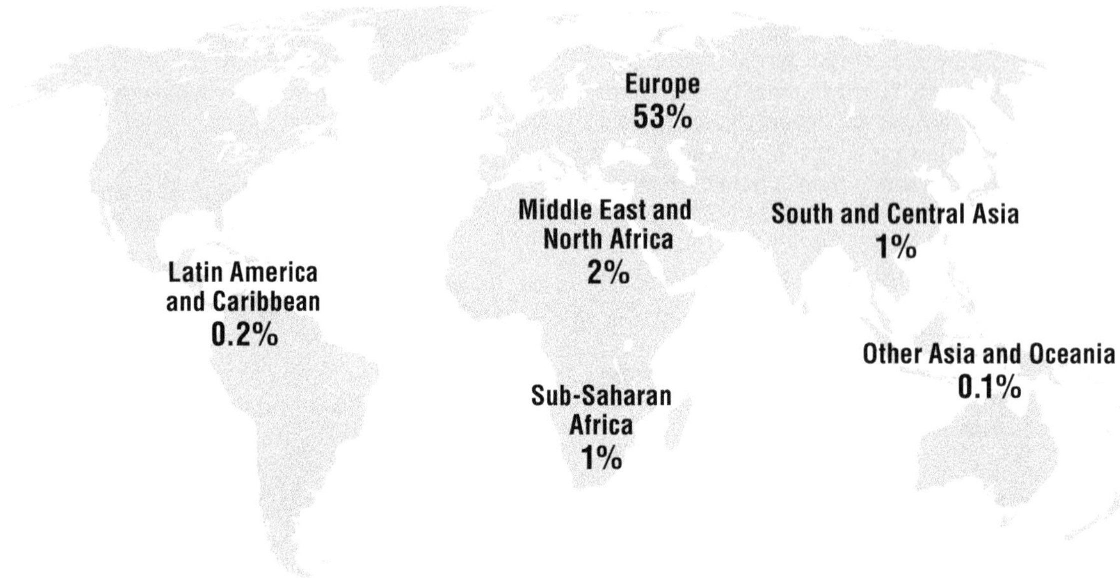

Note: 42% of bilateral ODA allocated was unspecified by region in 2014-15. This share is not represented on the map.

StatLink http://dx.doi.org/10.1787/888933482282

In 2015, 48.4% of bilateral ODA went to Slovenia's top 10 recipients. Slovenia has eight priority partner countries, all of which are among its top 10 recipients. In 2015, its support to fragile contexts reached USD 0.9 million (3.6% of gross bilateral ODA).

Figure 32.6. **Bilateral ODA to top recipients, 2014-15 average, gross disbursements, Slovenia**

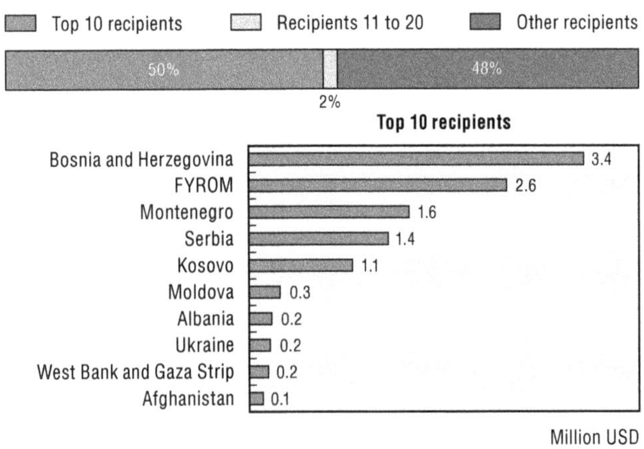

StatLink http://dx.doi.org/10.1787/888933482293

In 2015, 1.6% of bilateral ODA was allocated to least developed countries (LDCs), amounting to USD 0.4 million. This is a decrease from 7.9% in 2011, and is far below the 2015 DAC average of 24.3%. Upper middle-income countries received the highest share of bilateral ODA in 2015 (39.1%), while 51% was unallocated by income group.

At 0.02% of GNI in 2015, total ODA to LDCs was below the UN target of 0.15% of GNI.

Figure 32.7. **Bilateral ODA by income group, two year averages, gross disbursements, Slovenia**

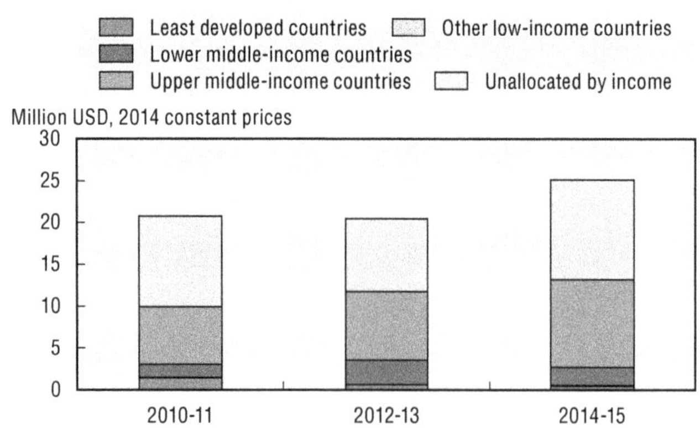

StatLink http://dx.doi.org/10.1787/888933482307

In 2015, 44.7% of Slovenia's bilateral ODA was allocated to social infrastructure and services (USD 10.8 million), with a strong focus on education (USD 6.4 million) and support to government and civil society (USD 3.5 million). Humanitarian aid amounted to USD 2.1 million. Slovenia's bilateral co-operation also focused on social services, economic services and infrastructure, and multisectoral priorities (including climate change adaptation and good governance).

Figure 32.8. **Share of bilateral ODA by sector, 2014-15 average, commitments, Slovenia**

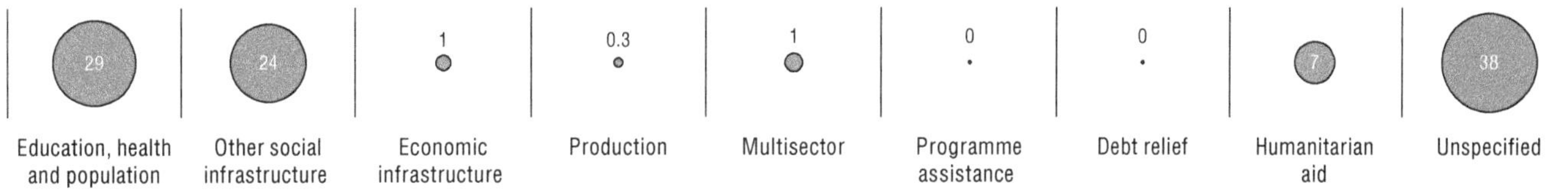

StatLink http://dx.doi.org/10.1787/888933482318

USD 1.2 million of bilateral ODA supported gender equality in 2015. Gender equality and women's empowerment is one of the cross-cutting themes of Slovenia's development co-operation. The Ministry for Foreign Affairs has developed guidelines on gender equality and women's empowerment in development co-operation. In 2015, 16.3% of Slovenian bilateral allocable aid had gender equality and women's empowerment as a principal or significant objective, compared with the DAC country average of 36.3%. Slovenia has a gender focus in the population and reproductive health sector.

Figure 32.9. **Share of bilateral allocable ODA in support of gender equality by sector, 2015, commitments, Slovenia**

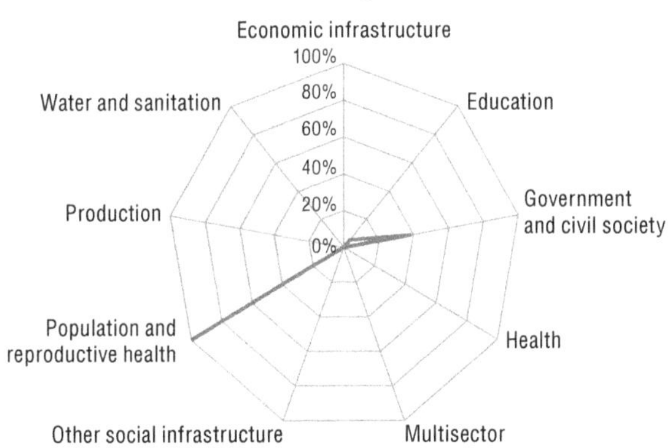

StatLink http://dx.doi.org/10.1787/888933482326

USD 2.2 million supported the environment in 2015. Environmental protection, with a focus on sustainable water management, is one of the priority themes for Slovenia's development co-operation. In 2015, 24.6% of Slovenian bilateral allocable aid focused on the environment and 17.7% (or USD 1.5 million) focused specifically on climate change, compared with the respective DAC country averages of 33.2% and 26.2%.

Figure 32.10. **Bilateral allocable ODA in support of global and local environment objectives, two year averages, commitments, Slovenia**

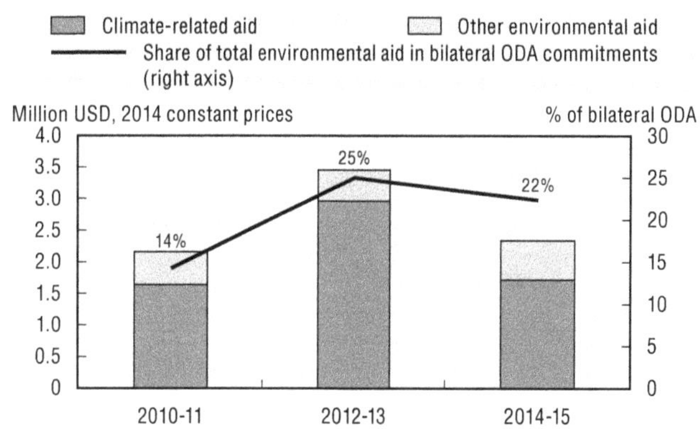

StatLink http://dx.doi.org/10.1787/888933482337

Note to reader: Annex B provides "Methodological notes on the profiles of Development Assistance Committee members".

Reference

OECD (2017), *OECD Development Co-operation Peer Reviews: Slovenia 2017*, OECD Publishing, Paris, forthcoming.

SPAIN

Spain's contribution to data for development

According to the 2017 Partner Report on Support to Statistics (PRESS) dataset, Spain committed on average USD 0.48 million per year to finance national statistical capacities and systems in developing countries in 2013-15.

Financial flows from Spain to developing countries

Figure 33.1. **Net resource flows to developing countries, 2005-15, Spain**

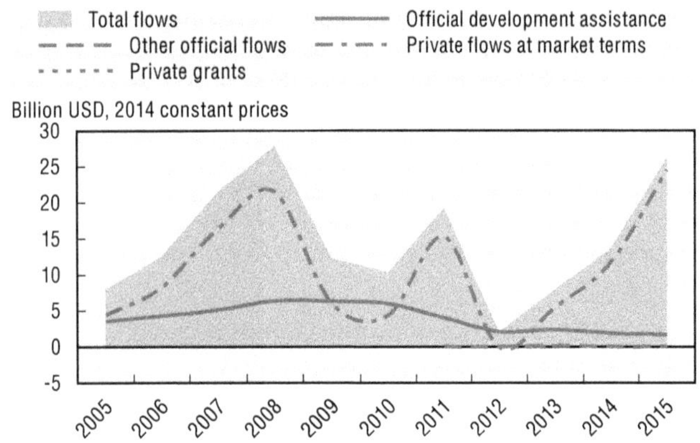

Note: Data on other official flows are not available for 2006, 2008 or 2010. Data on private grants are only available for 2012 and 2013.

StatLink http://dx.doi.org/10.1787/888933482343

Spain's use of ODA to mobilise other resources for sustainable development

- **USD 55 500** of official development assistance (ODA) was committed to the mobilisation of domestic resources in developing countries, e.g. to support the development of their tax systems, in 2015.
- **USD 50.4 million** of ODA (-52.9% in real terms from 2014) was committed to promote aid for trade and improve developing countries' trade performance and integration into the world economy in 2015.

Spain's performance against commitments for effective development co-operation

Table 33.1. **Results of the 2016 Global Partnership monitoring round, Spain**

	Alignment and ownership by partner country (%)				Predictability (%)		Transparency		
	Use of country-led results frameworks	Funding recorded in countries' national budgets	Funding through countries' systems	Untied ODA	Annual predictability	Medium-term predictability	Retrospective statistics (OECD CRS)	Information for forecasting (OECD FSS)	Publishing to IATI
2016	89.6	88.7	34.8	80.8	87.0	39.4	Good	Needs improvement	Needs improvement
Baseline	-	76.8	69.1	64.4	87.5	39.3	Good	Needs improvement	-
Trend	-	⇑	⇓	⇑	⇓	⇑	=	=	-

Note: Please refer to Annex B for details on the indicators.

StatLink http://dx.doi.org/10.1787/888933483219

Spain's official development assistance

In 2016, Spain provided USD 4.1 billion in net ODA (preliminary data), which represented 0.33% of gross national income (GNI) and a 192.3% increase in real terms from 2015, due to exceptional debt relief for Cuba. Spain is committed, at EU level, to collectively achieve a 0.7% ODA/GNI ratio by 2030. Spain's share of untied ODA (excluding administrative costs and in-donor refugee costs) decreased from 83.6% in 2014 to 80.8% in 2015, compared with the DAC average of 78.1% in 2015. The grant element of total ODA was 100% in 2015.

In 2016, in-donor refugee costs were USD 32 million, a decrease of 1% in real terms over 2015, and represented 0.8% of Spain's total net ODA.

Figure 33.2. **Net ODA: Trends in volume and as a share of GNI, 2000-16, Spain**

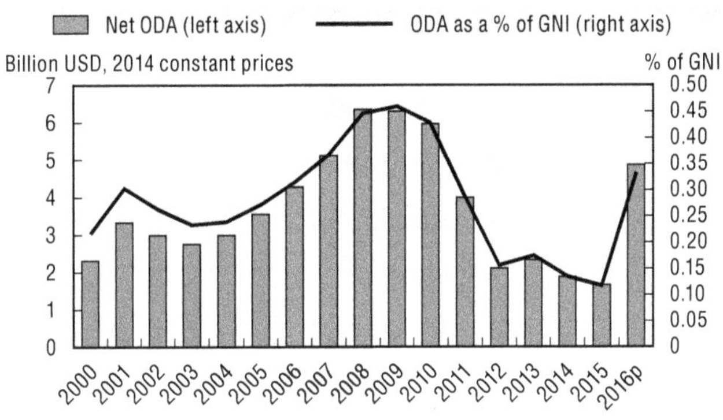

p: Preliminary data.

StatLink http://dx.doi.org/10.1787/888933482358

In 2015, 42.1% of Spain's ODA was provided bilaterally. It allocated 57.9% of total ODA as core contributions to multilateral organisations, compared to the DAC country average of 26.2%. In addition, it channelled 10.5% of its bilateral ODA to specific projects implemented by multilateral organisations (multi-bi/non-core contributions).

Figure 33.3. **Share of ODA channelled to and through the multilateral system, two year averages, gross disbursements, Spain**

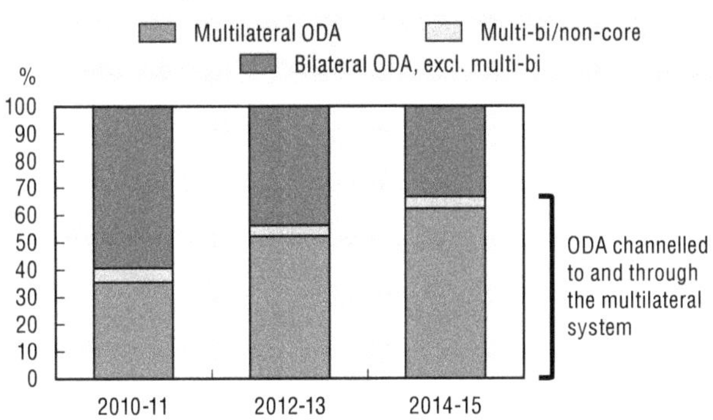

StatLink http://dx.doi.org/10.1787/888933482368

In 2015, 25.8% of bilateral ODA was programmed with partner countries. Spain's share of country programmable aid was lower than the DAC country average (48.8%) and project-type interventions accounted for 64% of this aid. Thirty-two per cent of bilateral aid was reported as "other and unallocated".

Figure 33.4. **Composition of bilateral ODA, 2015, gross disbursements, Spain**

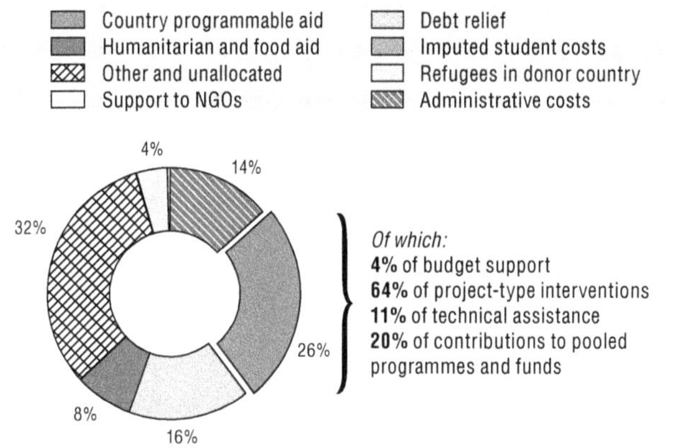

StatLink http://dx.doi.org/10.1787/888933482371

In 2015, USD 217.3 million of bilateral ODA was channelled to and through civil society organisations (CSOs). Between 2014 and 2015, ODA channelled to and through CSOs fell both in volume (-10.3%) and as a share of bilateral aid (from 40.8% in 2014 to 28.7% in 2015). The share provided in 2015 is above the DAC country average of 16.9%.

Figure 33.5. **Bilateral ODA to and through CSOs, two year averages, gross disbursements, Spain**

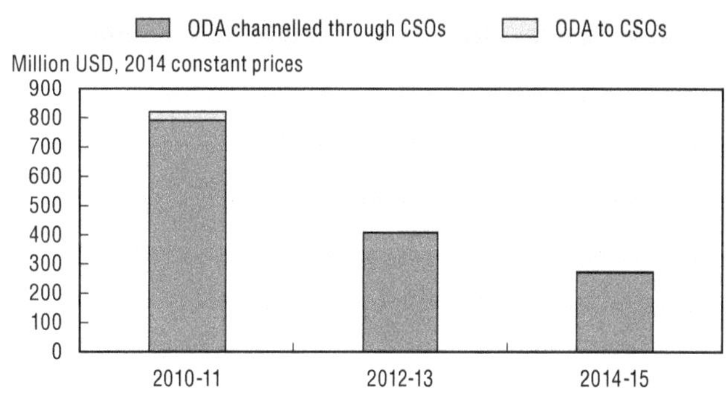

StatLink http://dx.doi.org/10.1787/888933482383

Bilateral ODA was primarily focused on Latin America and the Caribbean and sub-Saharan Africa. In 2015, USD 298.6 million was allocated to Latin America and the Caribbean and USD 98.7 million was allocated to sub-Saharan Africa.

Figure 33.6. **Share of bilateral ODA by region, 2014-15 average, gross disbursements, Spain**

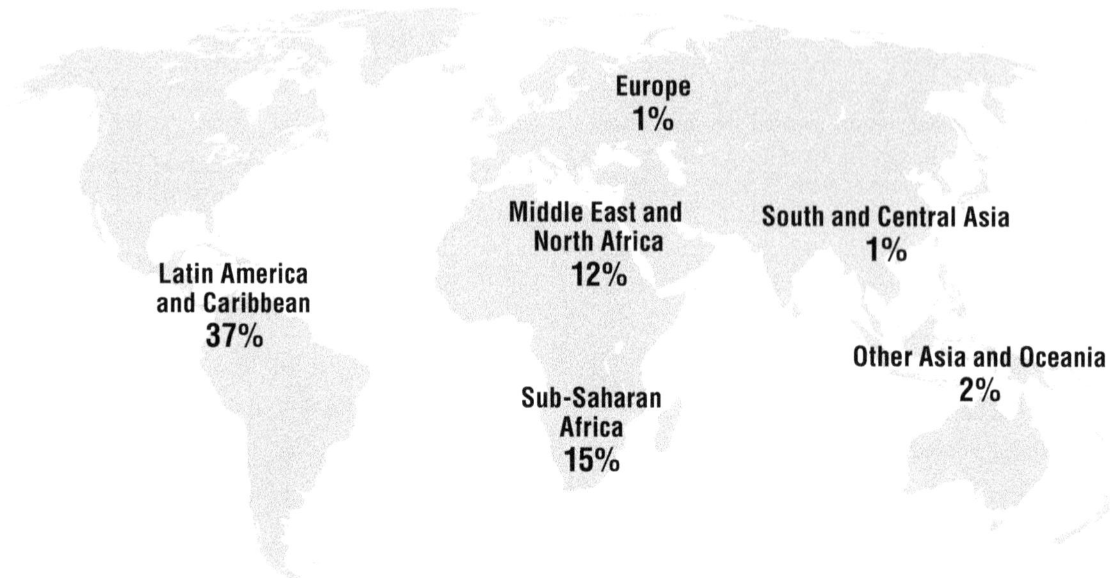

Note: 32% of ODA allocated was unspecified by region in 2014-15. This share is not represented on the map.

StatLink http://dx.doi.org/10.1787/888933482399

In 2015, 36.3% of bilateral ODA went to Spain's top 10 recipients. Spain reduced the number of its priority partner countries from 50 in 2012 to 23 in 2015. Nine of its top 10 recipients are priority partner countries. In 2015, its support to fragile contexts reached USD 136.3 million (18% of gross bilateral ODA).

Figure 33.7. **Bilateral ODA to top recipients, 2014-15 average, gross disbursements, Spain**

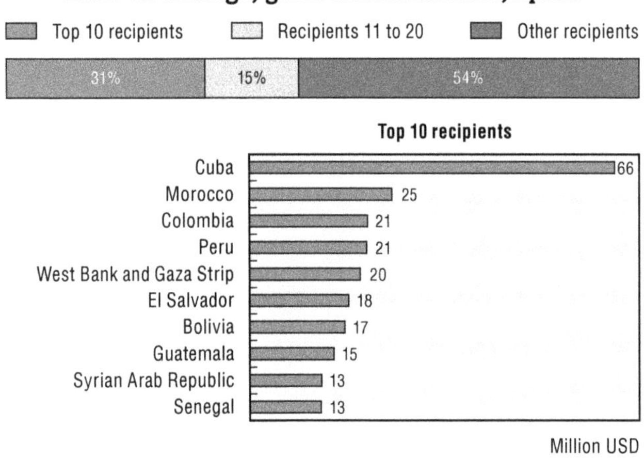

StatLink http://dx.doi.org/10.1787/888933482402

In 2015, 12% of bilateral ODA was allocated to least developed countries (LDCs), amounting to USD 90.7 million. This is a decrease from 17.8% in 2014 and is lower than the 24.6% share of 2012 and the 2015 DAC average of 24.3%. Upper middle-income countries received the highest share of bilateral ODA in 2015 (29.3%), noting that 39.3% was unallocated by income.

At 0.03% of GNI in 2015, total ODA to LDCs was below the UN target of 0.15% of GNI.

Figure 33.8. **Bilateral ODA by income group, two year averages, gross disbursements, Spain**

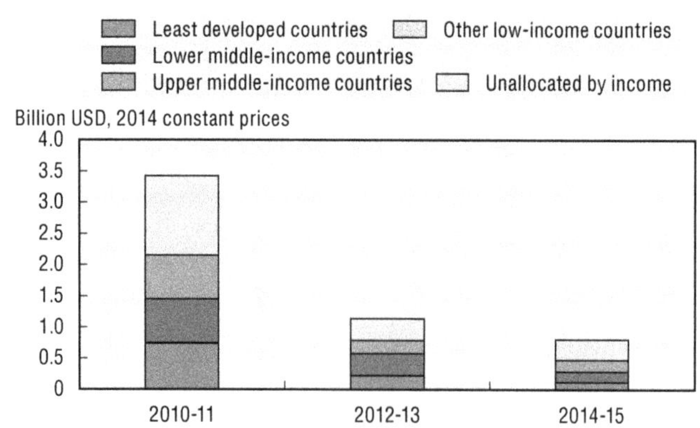

StatLink http://dx.doi.org/10.1787/888933482411

In 2015, 28.9% of bilateral ODA (USD 199.6 million) was allocated to social infrastructure and services, with a strong focus on support to government and civil society (USD 90.7 million), education (USD 32.2 million), and health (USD 25.1 million). USD 28.2 million was allocated to agriculture (accounted as ODA to production sectors) and USD 121.7 million was allocated to debt relief. Humanitarian aid amounted to USD 47.6 million.

Figure 33.9. **Share of bilateral ODA by sector, 2014-15 average, commitments, Spain**

StatLink http://dx.doi.org/10.1787/888933482424

USD 151.9 million of bilateral ODA supported gender equality in 2015. Gender equality is an emblem of Spain's development co-operation and is prioritised in its latest strategy. The 2016 DAC Peer Review, however, found that there is room for improvement if gender equality is to be effectively mainstreamed into operations on the ground (OECD, 2016). In 2015, 35.8% of Spanish bilateral allocable aid had gender equality and women's empowerment as a principal or significant objective, below the DAC country average of 36.3%. This is down from 69.8% in 2014. Spain's aid to population and reproductive health, production, and education focuses on gender.

Figure 33.10. **Share of bilateral allocable ODA in support of gender equality by sector, 2015, commitments, Spain**

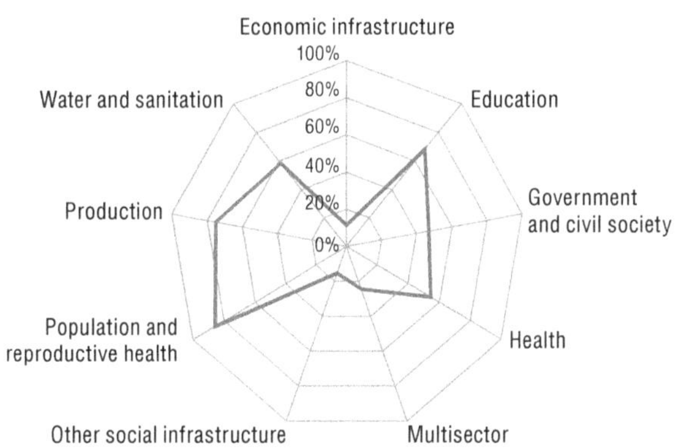

StatLink http://dx.doi.org/10.1787/888933482430

USD 91.3 million of Spain's bilateral ODA supported the environment in 2015. Spain is committed to ensuring the environment is mainstreamed into its projects and programmes, but implementation challenges remain. In 2015, 21.5% (down from 33.8% in 2014) of Spanish bilateral allocable aid supported the environment and 13.8% (USD 58.7 million) focused particularly on climate change, compared with the respective DAC country averages of 33.2% and 26.2%.

Figure 33.11. **Bilateral allocable ODA in support of global and local environment objectives, two year averages, commitments, Spain**

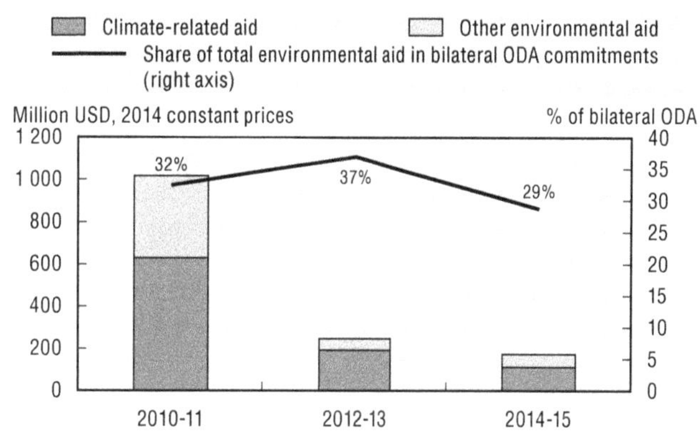

StatLink http://dx.doi.org/10.1787/888933482442

Note to reader: Annex B provides "Methodological notes on the profiles of Development Assistance Committee members".

Reference

OECD (2016), *OECD Development Co-operation Peer Reviews: Spain 2016*, OECD Publishing, Paris, *http://dx.doi.org/10.1787/9789264251175-en.*

SWEDEN

Sweden's contribution to data for development

Strengthening statistical capacities and systems in developing countries is an important part of Sweden's development co-operation which has been included in the Budget Bill for 2017 and the recently adopted Aid Policy Framework. Sweden engages in statistical capacity building in developing countries to support the improvement of their statistical production, strengthen data dissemination and improve statistical literacy of data users. Support is offered to national statistical systems mainly in the form of technical assistance – with financial support and funding for equipment being offered for some projects – and focuses mainly on gender and trade statistics.

Sweden considers its co-operation between the Swedish Statistical Authority and national counterparts in Burkina Faso and Mali to implement "continuous household surveys" to have been successful in enabling national authorities to build up long-term analytical capacity. Sweden gives financial contributions to the UN Global Pulse, which harnesses big data for development and humanitarian action.

According to the 2017 Partner Report on Support to Statistics (PRESS) dataset, Sweden committed on average USD 20.89 million per year to finance national statistical capacities and systems in developing countries in 2013-15.

Financial flows from Sweden to developing countries

Figure 34.1. **Net resource flows to developing countries, 2005-15, Sweden**

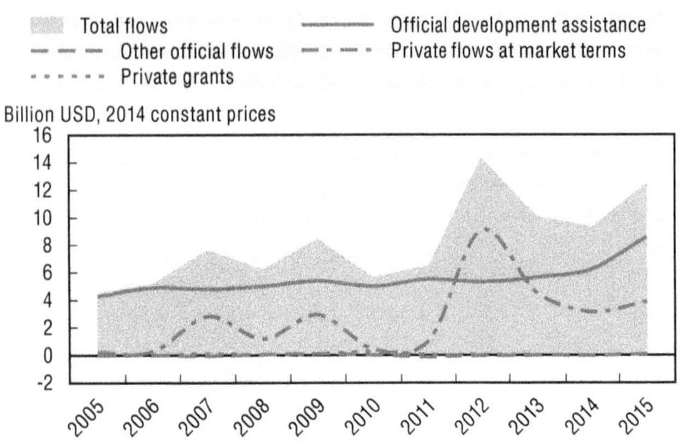

Note: Data on private grants are not available for 2014 or 2015.

StatLink http://dx.doi.org/10.1787/888933482452

Sweden's use of ODA to mobilise other resources for sustainable development

- **USD 3.7 million** of official development assistance (ODA) was committed to the mobilisation of domestic resources in developing countries, e.g. to support the development of their tax systems, in 2015.
- **USD 285 million** of ODA (-23.2% in real terms from 2014) was committed to promote aid for trade and improve developing countries' trade performance and integration into the world economy in 2015.

Sweden's performance against commitments for effective development co-operation

Table 34.1. **Results of the 2016 Global Partnership monitoring round, Sweden**

	Alignment and ownership by partner country (%)				Predictability (%)		Transparency		
	Use of country-led results frameworks	Funding recorded in countries' national budgets	Funding through countries' systems	Untied ODA	Annual predictability	Medium-term predictability	Retrospective statistics (OECD CRS)	Information for forecasting (OECD FSS)	Publishing to IATI
2016	54.4	59.6	62.6	86.8	75.7	69.2	Good	Excellent	Excellent
Baseline	-	73.8	65.9	93.6	78.7	78.0	Good	Excellent	-
Trend	-	⇓	⇓	⇓	⇓	⇓	=	=	-

Note: Please refer to Annex B for details on the indicators.

StatLink http://dx.doi.org/10.1787/888933483223

Sweden's official development assistance

In 2016, Sweden provided USD 4.9 billion in net ODA (preliminary data), which represented 0.94% of gross national income (GNI) and a 31.1% decrease in real terms from 2015, mostly due to lower costs for in-donor refugees compared to 2015, as well as lower contributions to multilateral organisations due to advance payments paid in 2015. Sweden is one of only six DAC members to have met the UN target of 0.7% and the government is committed by law to continue delivering 1% of its GNI to ODA, which is backed by a broad bipartisan support in parliament. Sweden's share of untied ODA (excluding administrative costs and in-donor refugee costs) slightly increased from 85.8% in 2014 to 86.8% in 2015, and remains above the DAC average of 78.1% in 2015. The grant element of total ODA was 100% in 2015.

In 2016, in-donor refugee costs were USD 821 million, a decrease of 65.6% in real terms over 2015, and represented 16.9% of Sweden's total net ODA.

Figure 34.2. **Net ODA: Trends in volume and as a share of GNI, 2000-16, Sweden**

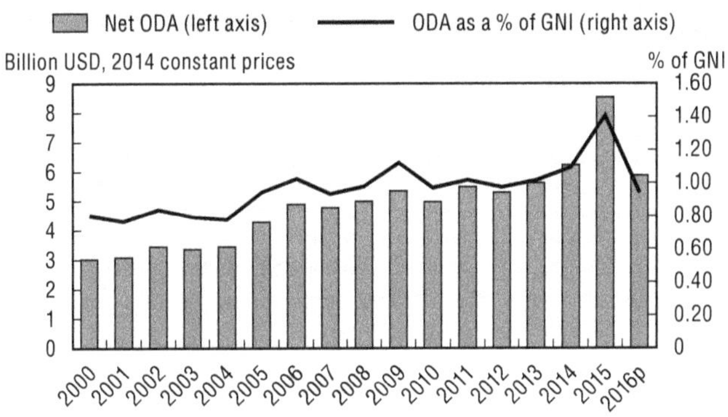

p: Preliminary data.

StatLink http://dx.doi.org/10.1787/888933482467

In 2015, 68.5% of ODA was provided bilaterally. Sweden allocated 31.6% of total ODA as core contributions to multilateral organisations, compared with the DAC country average of 26.2%. In addition, it channelled 15.6% of its bilateral ODA to specific projects implemented by multilateral organisations (multi-bi/non-core contributions).

Figure 34.3. **Share of ODA channelled to and through the multilateral system, two year averages, gross disbursements, Sweden**

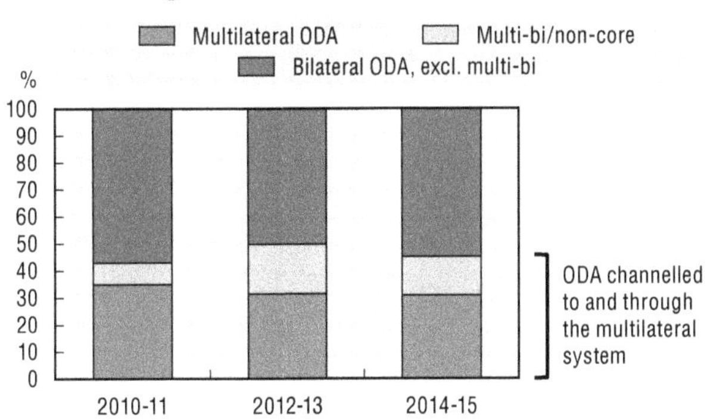

StatLink http://dx.doi.org/10.1787/888933482476

In 2015, 22% of bilateral ODA was programmed with partner countries, making Sweden's share of country programmable aid lower than the DAC country average (48.8%). Project-type interventions accounted for 48.8% of this aid. Forty-nine per cent of bilateral ODA was allocated to refugees in donor country.

Figure 34.4. **Composition of bilateral ODA, 2015, gross disbursements, Sweden**

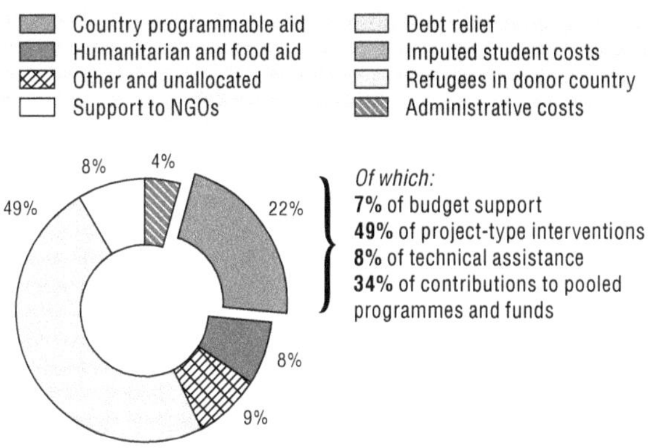

StatLink http://dx.doi.org/10.1787/888933482480

In 2015, USD 964.9 million of bilateral ODA was channelled to and through civil society organisations (CSOs). Between 2014 and 2015, ODA channelled to and through CSOs remained quite stable in terms of volume (+0.7% between 2014 and 2015), but decreased as a share of bilateral aid (from 26.1% to 19.7%). This share was higher than the 2015 DAC country average of 16.9%.

Figure 34.5. **Bilateral ODA to and through CSOs, two year averages, gross disbursements, Sweden**

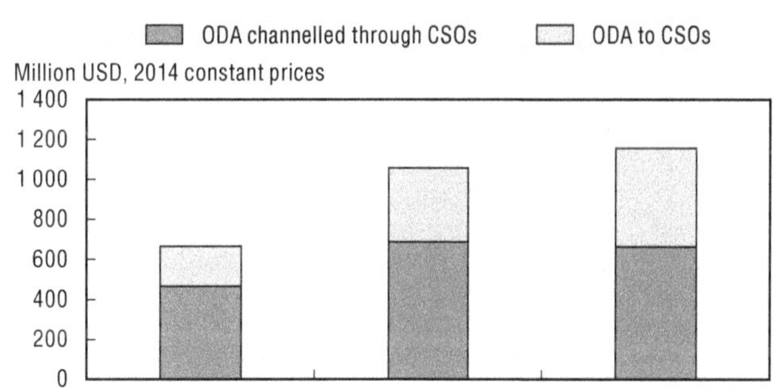

StatLink http://dx.doi.org/10.1787/888933482496

Bilateral ODA was primarily focused on sub-Saharan Africa. In 2015, USD 838 million was allocated to sub-Saharan Africa, USD 220.3 million to south and central Asia, and USD 187.7 million to the Middle East.

Figure 34.6. **Share of bilateral ODA by region, 2014-15 average, gross disbursements, Sweden**

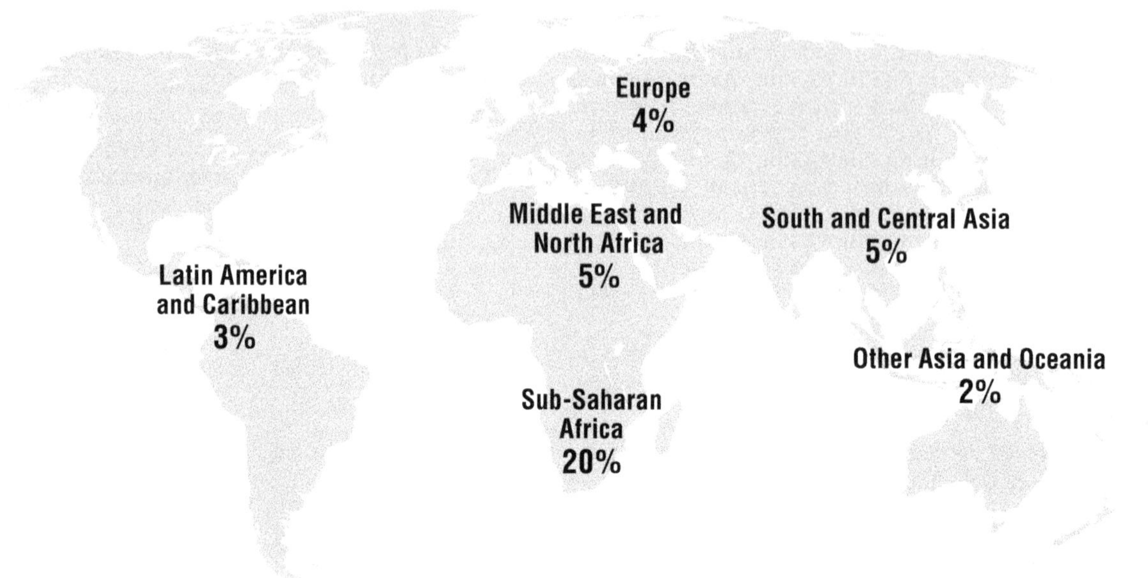

Note: 61% of bilateral ODA allocated was unspecified by region in 2014-15. This share is not represented on the map.

StatLink http://dx.doi.org/10.1787/888933482504

In 2015, 13.7% of bilateral ODA went to Sweden's top 10 recipients. All of its top 10 recipients are priority partners for Sweden. In 2015, its support to fragile contexts reached USD 1.1 billion (23.1% of gross bilateral ODA).

Figure 34.7. **Bilateral ODA to top recipients, 2014-15, gross disbursements, Sweden**

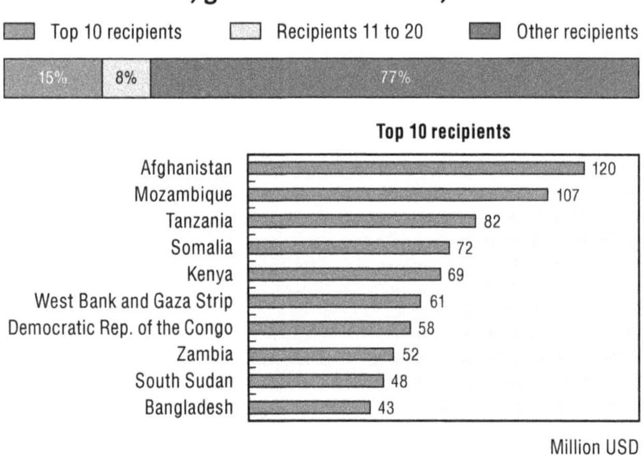

StatLink http://dx.doi.org/10.1787/888933482511

In 2015, 17.8% of bilateral ODA (USD 875.6 million) was allocated to least developed countries (LDCs). This is a decrease from 22.5% allocated to LDCs in 2015, and is lower than the DAC average of 24.3%. LDCs received the highest share of bilateral ODA in 2015, noting that 71.5% was unallocated by income group.

At 0.29% of GNI in 2015, total ODA to LDCs exceeds the UN target of 0.15% GNI.

Figure 34.8. **Bilateral ODA by income group, two year averages, gross disbursements, Sweden**

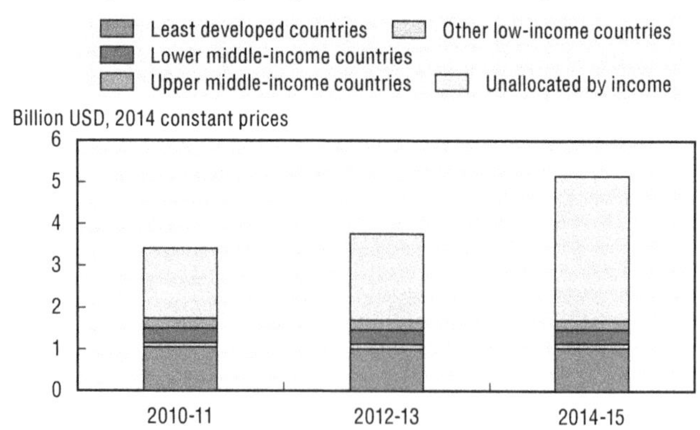

StatLink http://dx.doi.org/10.1787/888933482529

In 2015, 22.2% of bilateral ODA was allocated to social infrastructure and services, for a total of USD 958.5 million, with a strong focus on support to government and civil society (USD 673.2 million). Humanitarian aid amounted to USD 128.1 million.

Figure 34.9. **Share of bilateral ODA by sector, 2014-15 average, commitments, Sweden**

StatLink http://dx.doi.org/10.1787/888933482534

USD 1.5 billion of bilateral ODA supported gender equality in 2015. Gender equality has been solidly integrated into Sweden's projects and programmes (OECD, 2014) as a cross-cutting thematic priority. In 2015, 88.8% of Swedish bilateral sector-allocable aid had gender equality and women's empowerment as a principal or significant objective (up from 83.9% in 2014), compared with the DAC country average of 36.3%. Sweden's aid has an important gender focus in all sectors. Sweden has also been striving to promote gender mainstreaming in its multilateral partners' activities and in global fora. In addition, the Swedish government has adopted a new Feminist Foreign Policy approach, for which development co-operation is a key channel of delivery.

Figure 34.10. **Share of bilateral allocable ODA in support of gender equality by sector, 2015, commitments, Sweden**

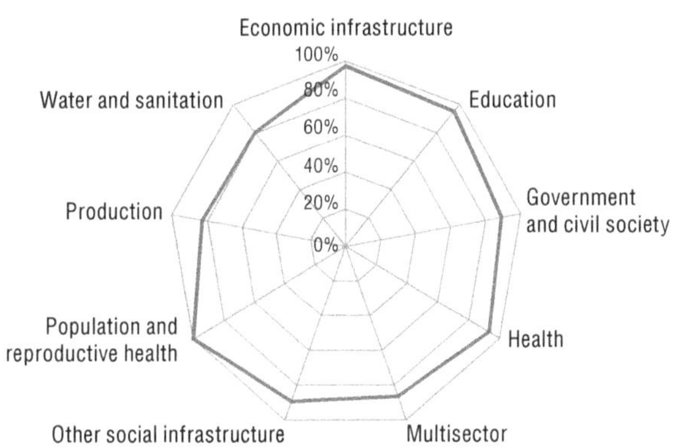

StatLink http://dx.doi.org/10.1787/888933482548

USD 678.2 million of bilateral ODA supported the environment in 2015. Sweden's new aid policy* places a greater emphasis on addressing climate change and environmental challenges, in line with its commitment to the 2030 Agenda and the COP 21 Paris Agreement. For example, Sweden is the largest per capita donor to the Green Climate Fund and the Global Environment Facility and also contributes to climate financing in developing countries via the Swedish International Development Co-operation Agency. In 2015, 39.6% of its bilateral allocable aid supported the environment and 27.7% (USD 474.9 million) focused on climate change, compared with the respective DAC country averages of 33.2% and 26.2%.

Figure 34.11. **Bilateral allocable ODA in support of global and local environment objectives, two year averages, commitments, Sweden**

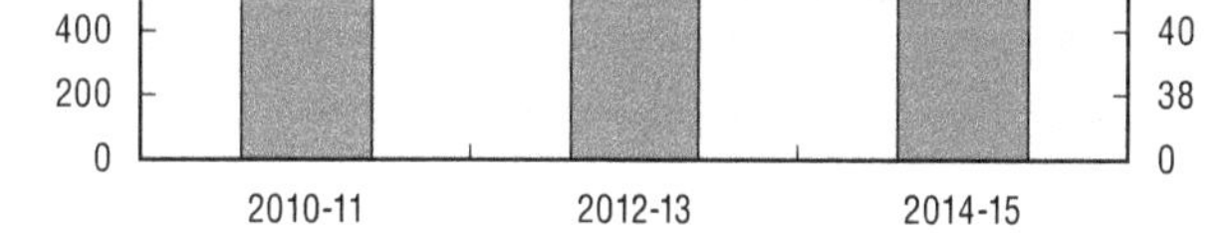

StatLink http://dx.doi.org/10.1787/888933482552

Note to reader: Annex B provides "Methodological notes on the profiles of Development Assistance Committee members".

Reference

OECD (2014), *OECD Development Co-operation Peer Reviews: Sweden 2013*, OECD Publishing, Paris, *http://dx.doi.org/10.1787/9789264196254-en*.

* Available in Swedish at: *www.regeringen.se/rattsdokument/skrivelse/2016/12/skr-20161760*.

SWITZERLAND

Switzerland's contribution to data for development

Switzerland recognises the crucial importance of reliable statistics for transparency and accountability. It is an active advocate for closer collaboration and better co-ordination between policy makers and data specialists, especially in the context of Agenda 2030 and the Sustainable Development Goals. It played such a role at the first UN World Data Forum which took place in Cape Town in January 2017.

Switzerland supports statistical capacity building through its bilateral and multilateral co-operation. The aim for its capacity-building support is to add value to projects in priority countries and regions and on priority themes. It also emphasises the importance of quality assurance and quality improvement of data. The Swiss Agency for Development and Cooperation (SDC) has been supporting the Palestinian Central Bureau of Statistics to produce timely and reliable statistics since 1995. The SDC also partners with the Swiss Federal Statistical Office on censuses and other data projects.

According to the 2017 Partner Report on Support to Statistics (PRESS) dataset, Switzerland committed on average USD 4.82 million per year to finance national statistical capacities and systems in developing countries in 2013-15.

Financial flows from Switzerland to developing countries

Figure 35.1. **Net resource flows to developing countries, 2005-15, Switzerland**

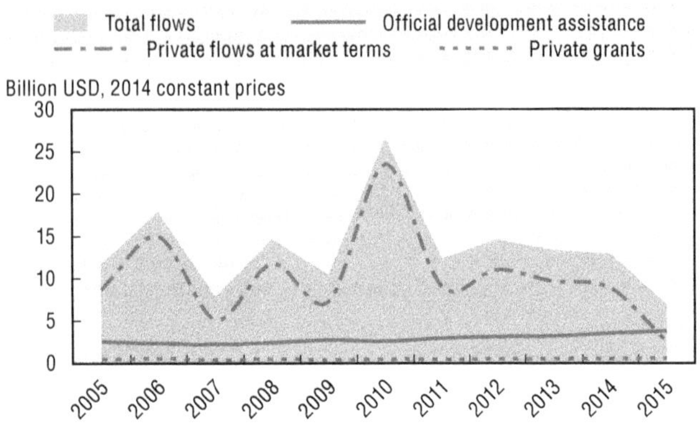

Note: Data on other official flows are only available for 2006 and 2014-15.

StatLink http://dx.doi.org/10.1787/888933482566

Switzerland's use of ODA to mobilise other resources for sustainable development

- **USD 7.8 million** of official development assistance (ODA) was committed to the mobilisation of domestic resources in developing countries, e.g. to support the development of their tax systems, in 2015.
- **USD 295.7 million** of ODA (-26.8% in real terms from 2014) was committed to promote aid for trade and improve developing countries' trade performance and integration into the world economy in 2015.

Switzerland's performance against commitments for effective development co-operation

Table 35.1. **Results of the 2016 Global Partnership monitoring round, Switzerland**

	Alignment and ownership by partner country (%)				Predictability (%)		Transparency		
	Use of country-led results frameworks	Funding recorded in countries' national budgets	Funding through countries' systems	Untied ODA	Annual predictability	Medium-term predictability	Retrospective statistics (OECD CRS)	Information for forecasting (OECD FSS)	Publishing to IATI
2016	51.3	44.6	37.4	94.6	77.3	65.4	Fair	Excellent	Fair
Baseline	-	35.6	27.1	84.8	75.7	76.9	Fair	Excellent	-
Trend	-	⇑	⇑	⇑	⇑	⇓	=	=	-

Note: Please refer to Annex B for details on the indicators.

StatLink http://dx.doi.org/10.1787/888933483233

Switzerland's official development assistance

In 2016, Switzerland provided USD 3.6 billion in net ODA (preliminary data), which represented 0.54% of gross national income (GNI) and a 4.2% increase in real terms from 2015, due to increased in-donor refugee costs, even though the aid budget was cut. The tightening of the Swiss federal budget has decreased the target of ODA to GNI from 0.5% to 0.48%, as approved by parliament. The government announced it might cut the budget further, further decreasing the aid to national income ratio by 2020. Switzerland's share of untied ODA (excluding administrative costs and in-donor refugee costs) was 94.6% in 2015 (up from 93.9% in 2014), above the DAC average of 78.1%. The grant element of total ODA was 100% in 2015.

In 2016, in-donor refugee costs were USD 691 million, an increase of 43.5% in real terms over 2015, and represented 19.4% of Switzerland's total net ODA.

Figure 35.2. **Net ODA: Trends in volume and as a share of GNI, 2000-16, Switzerland**

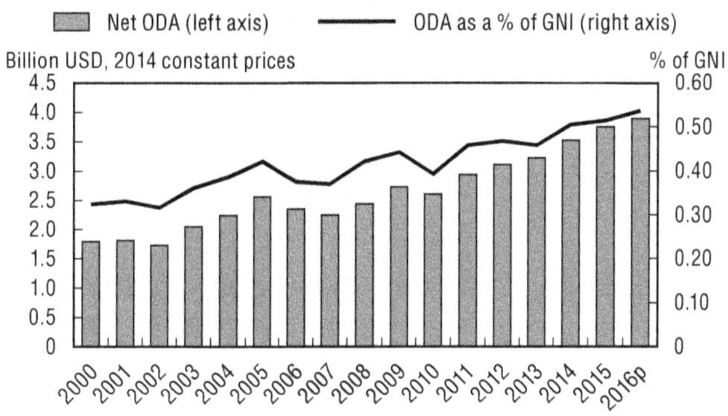

p: Preliminary data.

StatLink http://dx.doi.org/10.1787/888933482577

In 2015, 77.7% of ODA was provided bilaterally. Switzerland allocated 22.3% of total ODA as core contributions to multilateral organisations, compared with the DAC country average of 26.2%. In addition, it channelled 22.6% of its bilateral ODA to specific projects implemented by multilateral organisations (multi-bi/non-core contributions).

Figure 35.3. **Share of ODA channelled to and through the multilateral system, two year averages, gross disbursements, Switzerland**

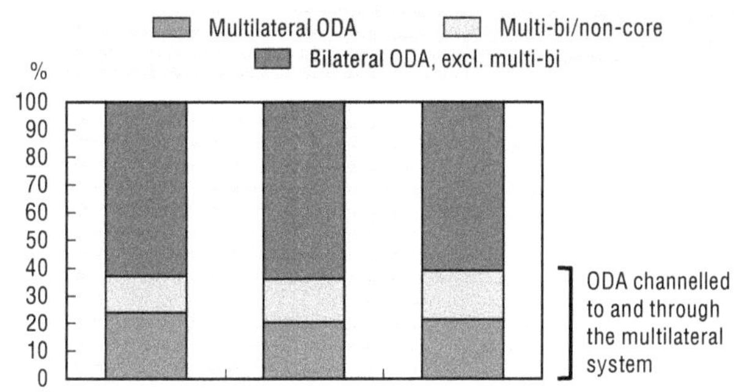

StatLink http://dx.doi.org/10.1787/888933482580

In 2015, 42.7% of bilateral ODA was programmed with partner countries. The share of country programmable aid was lower than the DAC country average (48.8%) and project-type interventions made up 87.3% of this aid.

Figure 35.4. **Composition of bilateral ODA, 2015, gross disbursements, Switzerland**

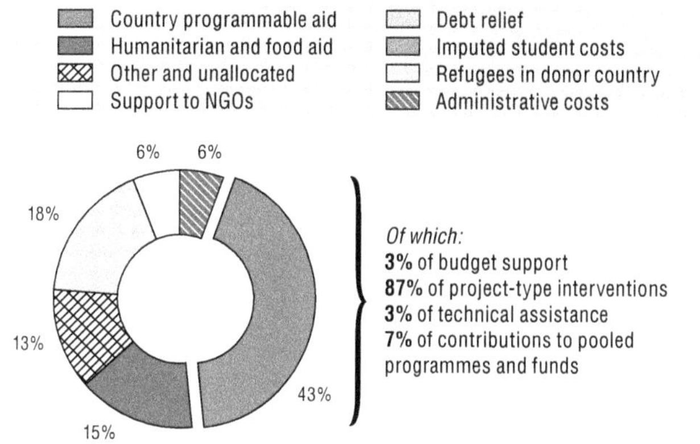

StatLink http://dx.doi.org/10.1787/888933482592

In 2015, USD 856.9 million of bilateral ODA was channelled to and through civil society organisations (CSOs). Between 2014 and 2015, ODA channelled to and through CSOs increased both in terms of volume (+11.4%) and as a share of bilateral aid (from 28.6% to 30.6%). The share in 2015 was higher than the DAC country average of 16.9%.

Figure 35.5. **Bilateral ODA to and through CSOs, two year averages, gross disbursements, Switzerland**

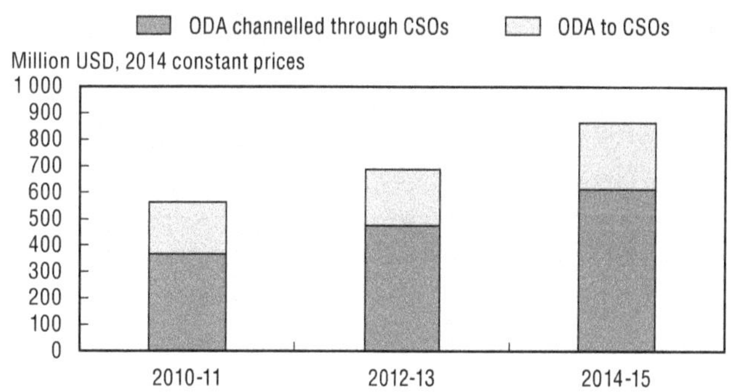

StatLink http://dx.doi.org/10.1787/888933482602

Bilateral ODA primarily focused on sub-Saharan Africa. In 2015, USD 538.9 million was allocated to sub-Saharan Africa, USD 311.8 million to south and central Asia, and USD 188.8 million to Eastern Europe.

Figure 35.6. **Share of bilateral ODA by region, 2014-15 average, gross disbursements, Switzerland**

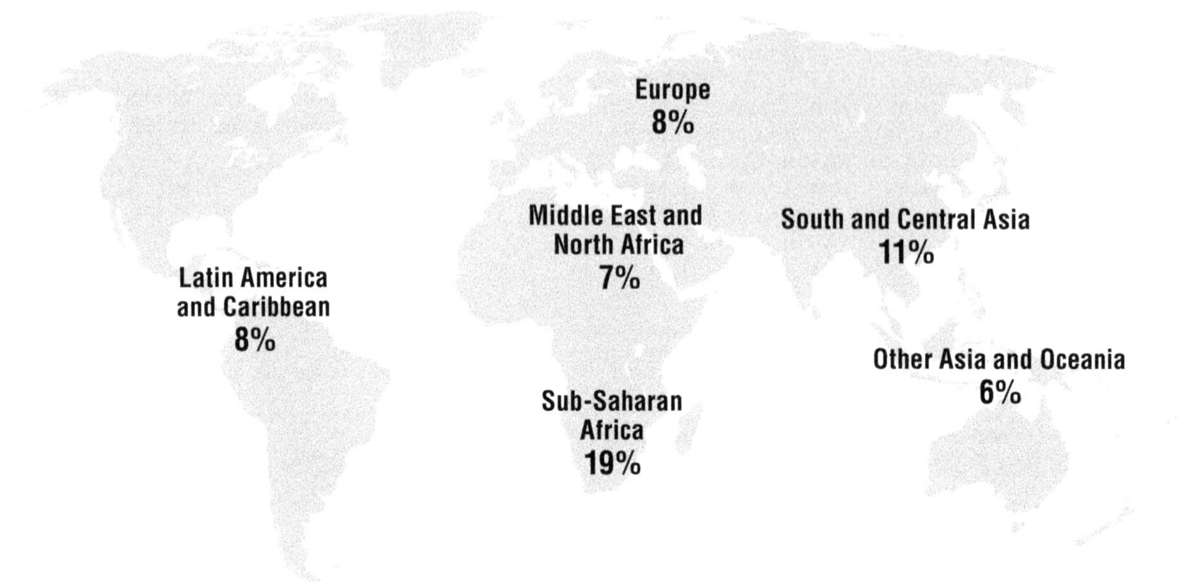

Note: 41% of bilateral ODA allocated was unspecified by region in 2014-15. This share is not represented on the map.

StatLink http://dx.doi.org/10.1787/888933482617

In 2015, 14.3% of bilateral ODA went to Switzerland's top 10 recipients. Nine countries on the list of top 10 recipients were priority partners for Switzerland. According the new Dispatch 2017-20, Switzerland will remain active in the same number of regions, countries and territories, with a total of 43 priority partners. Swiss support to fragile contexts reached USD 780.5 million in 2015 (27.6% of gross bilateral ODA).

In 2015, 22.4% of bilateral ODA was allocated to LDCs, amounting to USD 632.1 million. This share has remained relatively stable in recent years, but at a lower level compared to the DAC average (24.3% in 2015). LDCs received the highest share of bilateral ODA in 2015, noting that 48.8% was unallocated by income group.

At 0.14% of its GNI in 2015, total ODA to LDCs was lower than the UN target of 0.15% of GNI.

Figure 35.7. **Bilateral ODA to top recipients, 2014-15 average, gross disbursements, Switzerland**

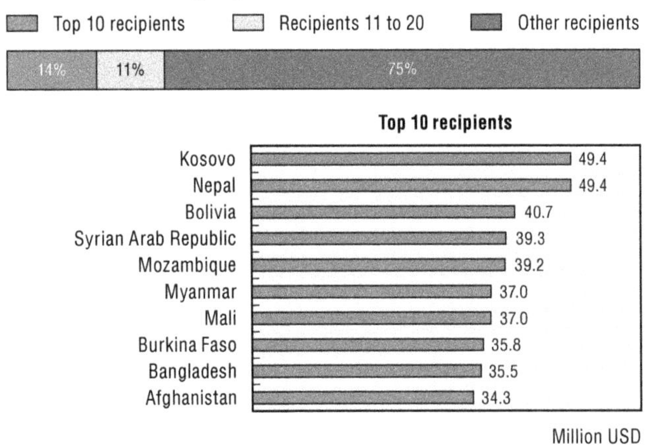

StatLink http://dx.doi.org/10.1787/888933482628

Figure 35.8. **Bilateral ODA by income group, two year averages, gross disbursements, Switzerland**

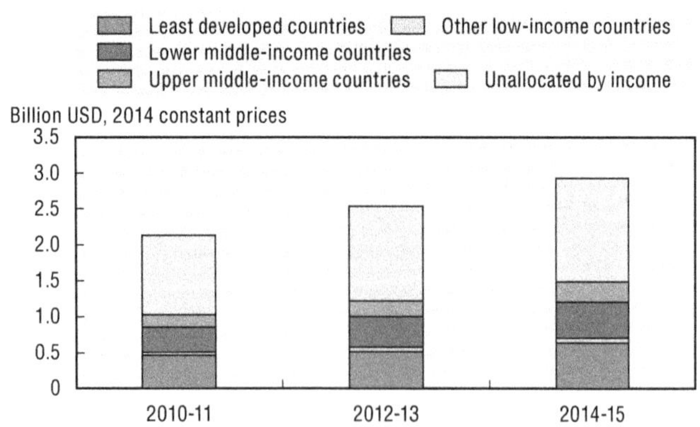

StatLink http://dx.doi.org/10.1787/888933482632

In 2015, 31.6% of bilateral ODA (USD 824.1 million) was allocated to social infrastructure and services, with a strong focus on support to government and civil society (USD 425.4 million) and water and sanitation (USD 147.3 million). Humanitarian aid amounted to USD 425.6 million.

Figure 35.9. **Share of bilateral ODA by sector, 2014-15 average, commitments, Switzerland**

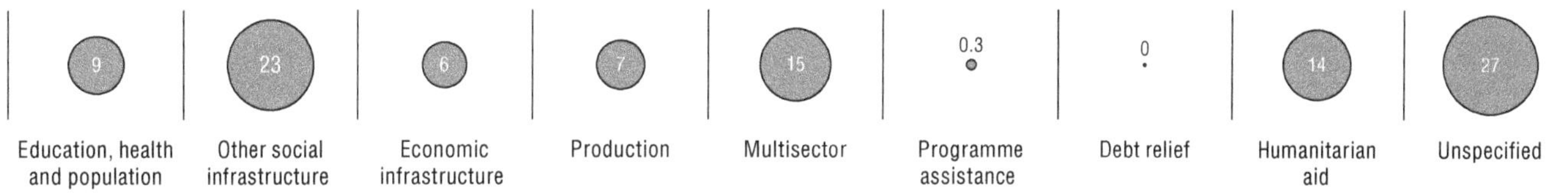

StatLink http://dx.doi.org/10.1787/888933482648

USD 283.3 million of bilateral ODA supported gender equality in 2015. Switzerland has improved integration of gender equality into its projects, programmes and policy dialogue through clear guidance (OECD, 2014), with priority areas including conflict and fragile contexts, rural economies and local governance. In 2015, 14.7% of Swiss aid had gender equality and women's empowerment as a principal or significant objective, compared with the DAC country average of 36.3%. This is slightly up from 2014 (13%). Switzerland's aid to population and reproductive health focuses on gender.

Figure 35.10. **Share of bilateral allocable ODA in support of gender equality by sector, 2015, commitments, Switzerland**

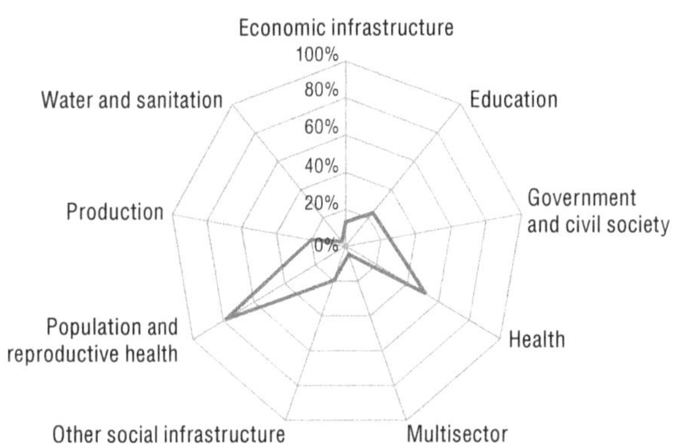

StatLink http://dx.doi.org/10.1787/888933482653

USD 332.1 million of bilateral ODA supported the environment in 2015. Switzerland is committed to integrating the environment into its programming and projects. In 2015, 17.2% of its bilateral allocable aid supported the environment, compared with the DAC country average of 33.2%. This share has slightly decreased since 2014 (21%). In 2015, 11.9% (USD 229 million) of Swiss bilateral allocable aid focused specifically on climate change, compared with the DAC country average of 26.2%.

Figure 35.11. **Bilateral allocable ODA in support of global and local environment objectives, two year averages, commitments, Switzerland**

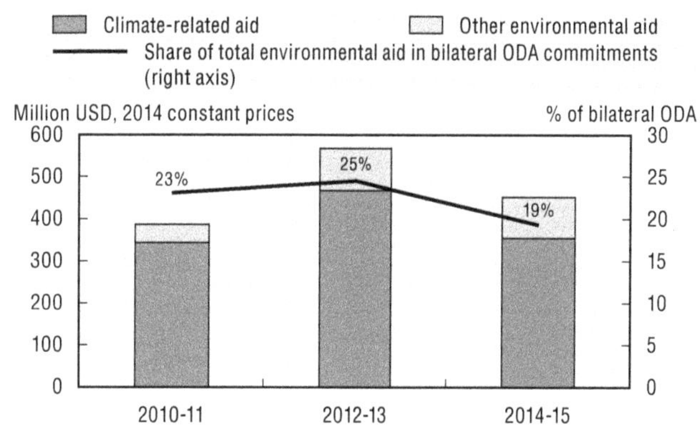

StatLink http://dx.doi.org/10.1787/888933482666

Note to reader: Annex B provides "Methodological notes on the profiles of Development Assistance Committee members".

Reference

OECD (2014), *OECD Development Co-operation Peer Reviews: Switzerland 2013*, OECD Publishing, Paris, *http://dx.doi.org/10.1787/9789264196322-en*.

UNITED KINGDOM

The United Kingdom's contribution to data for development

The United Kingdom invests in improving institutional and technical capacity and aims to stimulate and satisfy national demand for data by supporting comprehensive national strategies for the development of statistics. Its support ranges from technical assistance and financial support to national statistical offices to funding for equipment and improving donor co-ordination.

Through DFID, the United Kingdom supports an innovative project of the UN Statistics Division to develop an on line international data and visualisation platform for the Sustainable Development Goals indicators. The project will help developing countries to build their capacity in collecting, analysing and disseminating disaggregated data; modernise national statistical systems with up-to-date technology and skills; engage with key users of data; and enable multiple actors to use statistics for evidence-based decisions.

The United Kingdom is looking into the potential of big data for development co-operation and its Office for National Statistics is a member of the Global Working Group on Big Data for Official Statistics. DFID is exploring ways in which big data can improve understanding, delivery and monitoring of development challenges.

According to the 2017 Partner Report on Support to Statistics (PRESS) dataset, the United Kingdom committed on average USD 30.29 million per year to finance national statistical capacities and systems in developing countries in 2013-15.

Financial flows from the United Kingdom to developing countries

Figure 36.1. **Net resource flows to developing countries, 2005-15, United Kingdom**

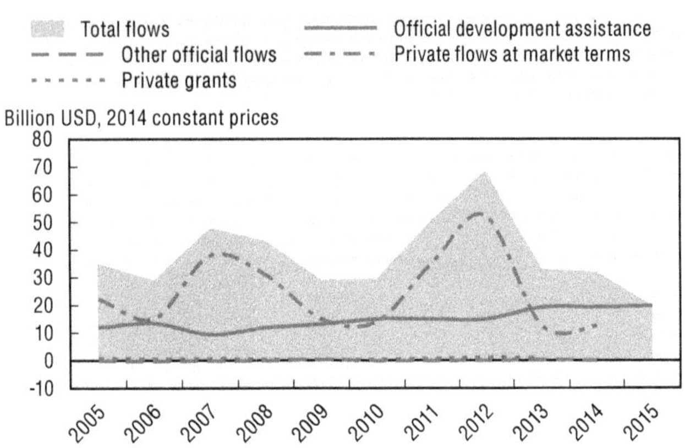

Note: Data on other official flows and on private flows at market terms are not available for 2015. Data on private grants are not available for 2014 or 2015.

StatLink http://dx.doi.org/10.1787/888933482670

The United Kingdom's use of ODA to mobilise other resources for sustainable development

- **USD 61 million** of official development assistance (ODA) was committed to the mobilisation of domestic resources in developing countries, e.g. to support the development of their tax systems, in 2015.
- **USD 1.7 billion** of ODA (+71.2% in real terms from 2014) was committed to promote aid for trade and improve developing countries' trade performance and integration into the world economy in 2015.

The United Kingdom's performance against commitments for effective development co-operation

Table 36.1. **Results of the 2016 Global Partnership monitoring round, United Kingdom**

	Alignment and ownership by partner country (%)				Predictability (%)		Transparency		
	Use of country-led results frameworks	Funding recorded in countries' national budgets	Funding through countries' systems	Untied ODA	Annual predictability	Medium-term predictability	Retrospective statistics (OECD CRS)	Information for forecasting (OECD FSS)	Publishing to IATI
2016	43.3	77.6	64.6	100.0	65.3	57.9	Needs improvement	Good	Good
Baseline	-	70.5	66.7	99.9	79.2	84.7	Needs improvement	Fair	-
Trend	-	⇑	⇓	⇑	⇓	⇓	=	⇑	-

Note: Please refer to Annex B for details on the indicators.

StatLink http://dx.doi.org/10.1787/888933483241

The United Kingdom's official development assistance

In 2016, the United Kingdom provided USD 18 billion in net ODA (preliminary data), which represented 0.7% of gross national income (GNI) and an 8.4% increase in real terms from 2015, mainly due to the scaling up of its aid. The United Kingdom is one of only six DAC members to have met the UN target of 0.7% of ODA/GNI in 2016. It is committed to keeping this ratio stable. All of the United Kingdom's ODA (excluding administrative costs and in-donor refugee costs) was untied in 2015, while the DAC average was 78.1%. The grant element of total ODA was 100% in 2015.

In 2016, in-donor refugee costs were USD 549 million, an increase of 59.2% in real terms over 2015, and represented 3.0% of the United Kingdom's total net ODA.

Figure 36.2. **Net ODA: Trends in volume and as a share of GNI, 2000-16, United Kingdom**

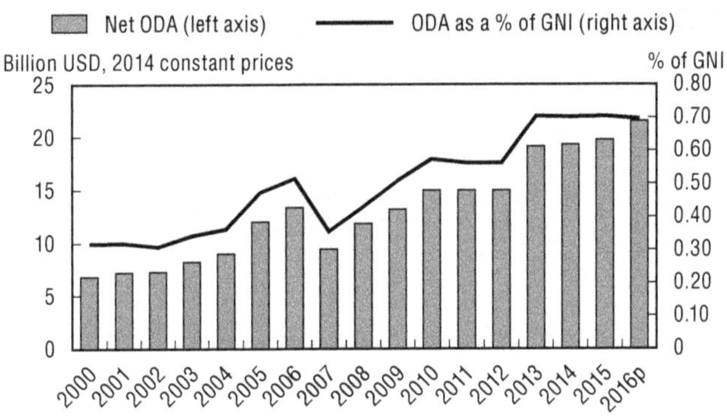

p: Preliminary data.

StatLink http://dx.doi.org/10.1787/888933482685

In 2015, 63.4% of ODA was provided bilaterally. The United Kingdom allocated 36.6% of total ODA as core contributions to multilateral organisations, compared with the DAC country average of 26.2%. In addition, it channelled 28.1% of its bilateral ODA for specific projects implemented by multilateral organisations (multi-bi/non-core contributions).

Figure 36.3. **Share of ODA channelled to and through the multilateral system, two year averages, gross disbursements, United Kingdom**

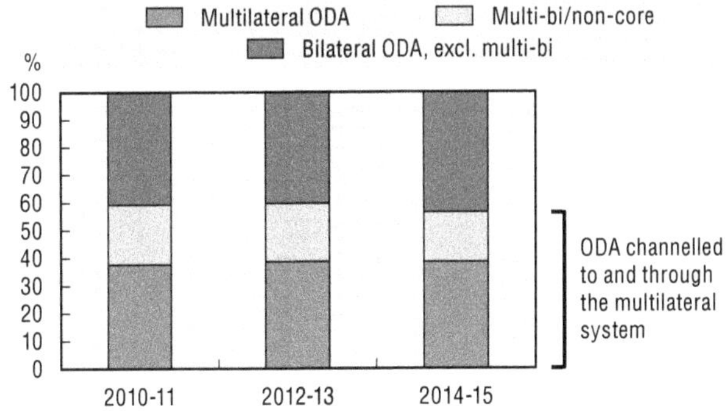

StatLink http://dx.doi.org/10.1787/888933482697

In 2015, 47.5% of bilateral ODA was programmed with partner countries. The United Kingdom's share of country programmable aid was lower than the DAC country average (48.8%) and project-type interventions accounted for 64.8% of this aid. Twenty-one per cent of bilateral ODA was categorised as "other and unallocated" aid, and 16.7% as "humanitarian and food aid".

Figure 36.4. **Composition of bilateral ODA, 2015, gross disbursements, United Kingdom**

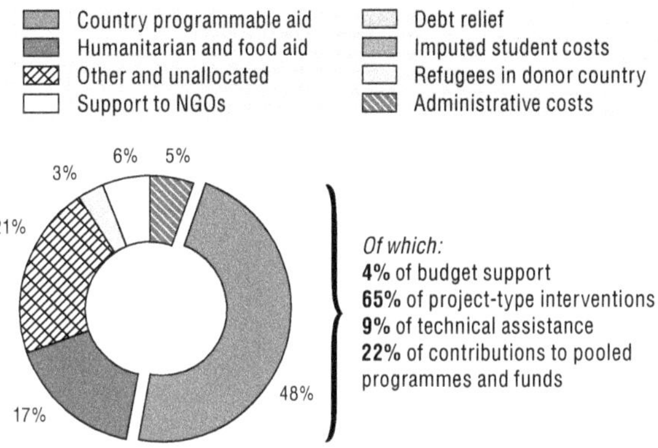

StatLink http://dx.doi.org/10.1787/888933482700

In 2015, USD 2.5 billion of bilateral ODA was channelled to and through civil society organisations (CSOs). ODA channelled to and through CSOs has increased in recent years in volume (+4% between 2014 and 2015), and remained stable as a share of bilateral ODA (21.5% in 2015). The DAC country average was 16.9% in 2015.

Figure 36.5. **Bilateral ODA to and through CSOs, two year averages, gross disbursements, United Kingdom**

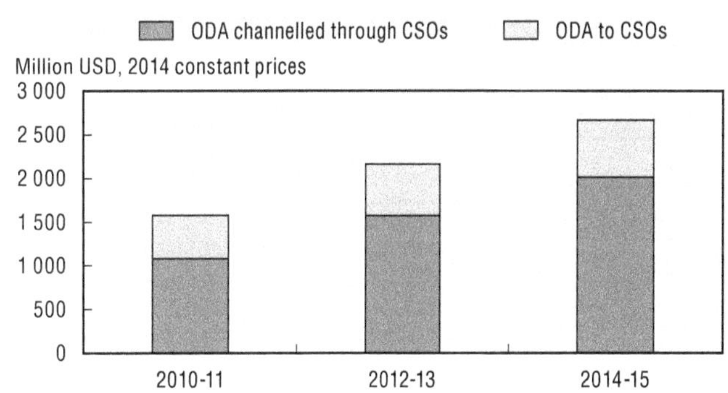

StatLink http://dx.doi.org/10.1787/888933482715

Bilateral ODA was primarily focused on sub-Saharan Africa. In 2015, USD 3.9 billion was allocated to sub-Saharan Africa and USD 2 billion to south and central Asia.

Figure 36.6. **Share of bilateral ODA by region, 2014-15 average, gross disbursements, United Kingdom**

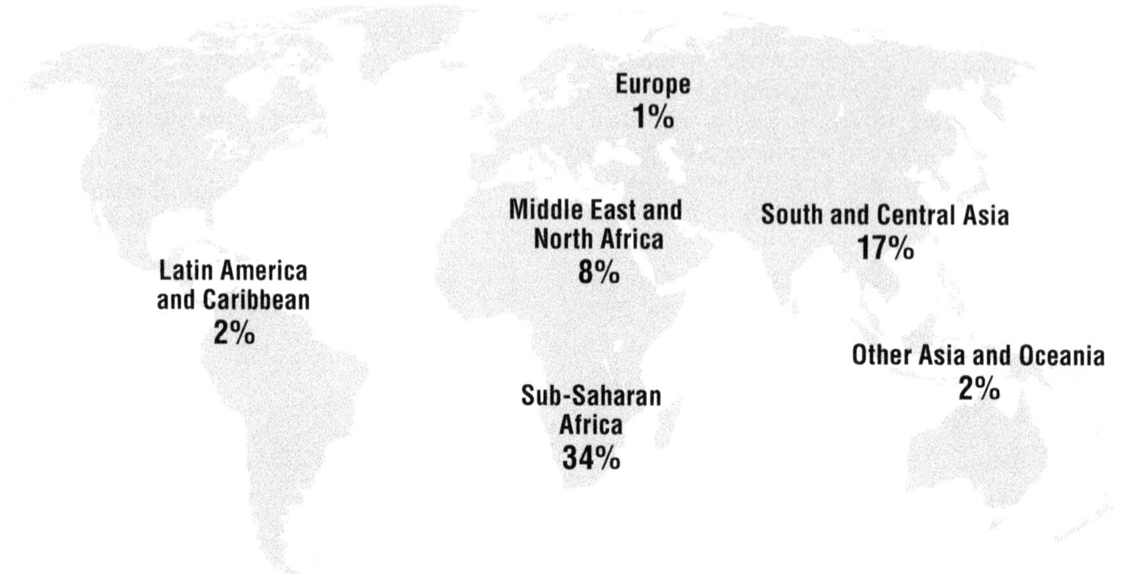

Note: 36% of bilateral ODA allocated was unspecified by region in 2014-15. This share is not represented on the map.

StatLink http://dx.doi.org/10.1787/888933482722

In 2015, 32.6% of bilateral ODA went to the United Kingdom's top 10 recipients. The United Kingdom works in countries across Africa, Asia and the Middle East, where it also has regional programmes, including in the Caribbean. All of its top 10 recipients in 2014-15 are among its priority partner countries. DFID has increased its focus on the poorest and most fragile states: in 2015, its support to fragile contexts reached USD 5.7 billion (48.1% of gross bilateral ODA).

Figure 36.7. **Bilateral ODA to top recipients, 2014-15 average, gross disbursements, United Kingdom**

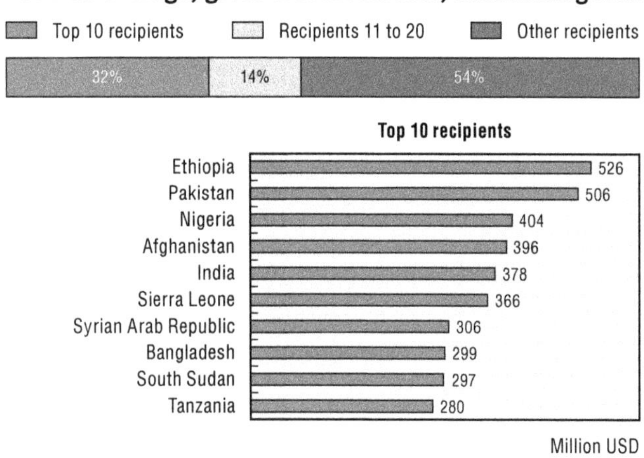

StatLink http://dx.doi.org/10.1787/888933482735

In 2015, 32.5% of bilateral ODA was allocated to least developed countries (LDCs), amounting to USD 3.9 billion. This share has remained relatively stable in recent years, and is higher than the 2015 DAC average of 24.3%. LDCs received the highest share of bilateral ODA in 2015 compared with other income groups.

At 0.23% of GNI in 2015, total ODA to LDCs was above the UN target of 0.15% of GNI.

Figure 36.8. **Bilateral ODA by income group, two year averages, gross disbursements, United Kingdom**

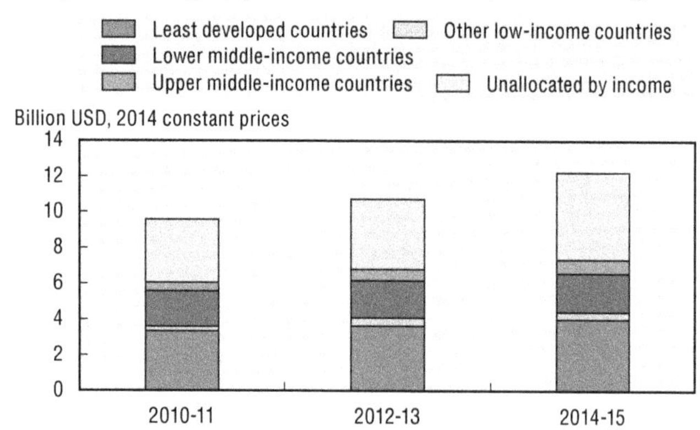

StatLink http://dx.doi.org/10.1787/888933482746

In 2015, 33.4% of bilateral ODA was allocated to social infrastructure and services, at a total of USD 3 billion, with a strong focus on government and civil society (USD 998.7 million), health (USD 632.8 million), and education (USD 600.3 million). USD 1.1 billion was allocated to economic infrastructure and services, particularly to banking and financial services (USD 719.4 million). Humanitarian aid amounted to USD 1.5 billion.

Figure 36.9. **Share of bilateral ODA by sector, 2014-15 average, commitments, United Kingdom**

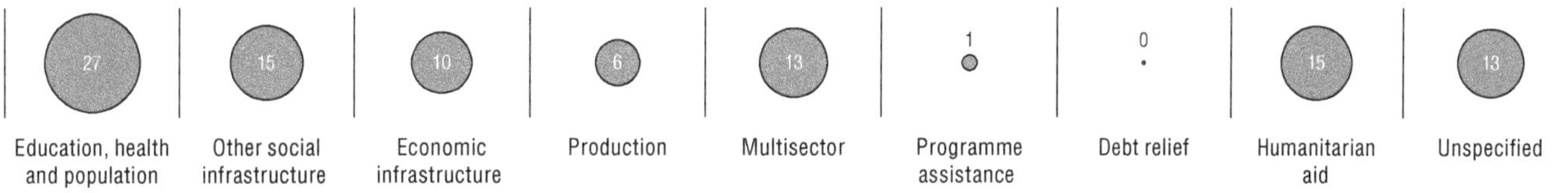

StatLink http://dx.doi.org/10.1787/888933482750

USD 2.1 billion of bilateral ODA supported gender equality in 2015. The United Kingdom's focus on women and girls was reinforced by the 2014 Development Act on Gender Equality. Gender equality is embedded in the bilateral programme, and issues affecting women and girls are also raised on the global stage. In 2015, 40.5% of the United Kingdom's bilateral allocable aid had gender equality and women's empowerment as a principal or significant objective, compared with the DAC country average of 36.3%. This represents a decrease from 60.7% in 2014. The United Kingdom's aid to water and sanitation, population and reproductive health, other social infrastructure, and education focuses on gender.

Figure 36.10. **Share of bilateral allocable ODA in support of gender equality by sector, 2015, commitments, United Kingdom**

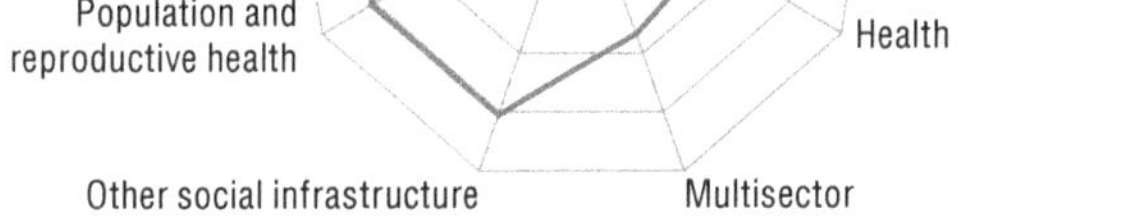

StatLink http://dx.doi.org/10.1787/888933482763

USD 2.5 billion of bilateral ODA supported the environment in 2015. The United Kingdom has set combating climate change as one of the six strategic priorities of its business plan. DFID has a comprehensive policy framework to support its engagement in the areas of environment and climate change. In particular, it has introduced a new climate and environment assessment requirement that looks at the impact of all programmes on the vulnerability of poor communities to environmental disasters and it has created an initiative called Future Fit, designed to integrate climate issues into DFID's core business (OECD, 2014). In 2015, 33.1% of its bilateral allocable aid supported the environment and 30.6% (USD 2.3 billion) focused on climate change, compared with the respective DAC country averages of 33.2% and 26.2%.

Figure 36.11. **Bilateral allocable ODA in support of global and local environment objectives, two year averages, commitments, United Kingdom**

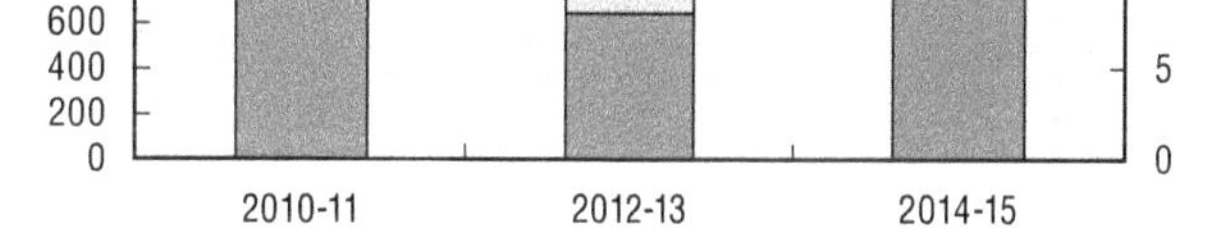

StatLink http://dx.doi.org/10.1787/888933482773

Note to reader: Annex B provides "Methodological notes on the profiles of Development Assistance Committee members".

Reference

OECD (2014), *OECD Development Co-operation Peer Reviews: United Kingdom 2014*, OECD Publishing, Paris, *http://dx.doi.org/10.1787/9789264226579-en.*

UNITED STATES

The United States' contribution to data for development

The United States engages in statistical capacity building in developing countries to improve statistical production; strengthen data dissemination; and promote the use of data by policy makers, civil society and citizens. It does this mainly through technical assistance and funding for equipment.

The United States seeks to harness the data revolution for sustainable development by: 1) supporting governments' efforts to generate, strengthen and use official statistics for monitoring, evaluation and decision making; and 2) promoting innovation to generate, triangulate and use real-time, disaggregated data from multiple sources (e.g. big, geospatial and citizen-generated data). It supports two key initiatives: the Global Partnership for Sustainable Development Data, which aims to fill data gaps and invest in national and local capacity building for a more effective and efficient use of data; and the Data Collaboratives for Local Impact Program in sub-Saharan Africa, a joint initiative of the President's Emergency Plan for AIDS Relief and the Millennium Challenge Corporation to build national and local capacity to use data to drive decision making, maximise impact, and increase transparency and mutual accountability.

According to the 2017 Partner Report on Support to Statistics (PRESS) dataset, the United States committed on average USD 9.08 million per year to finance national statistical capacities and systems in developing countries in 2013-15.

Financial flows from the United States to developing countries

Figure 37.1. **Net resource flows to developing countries, 2005-15, United States**

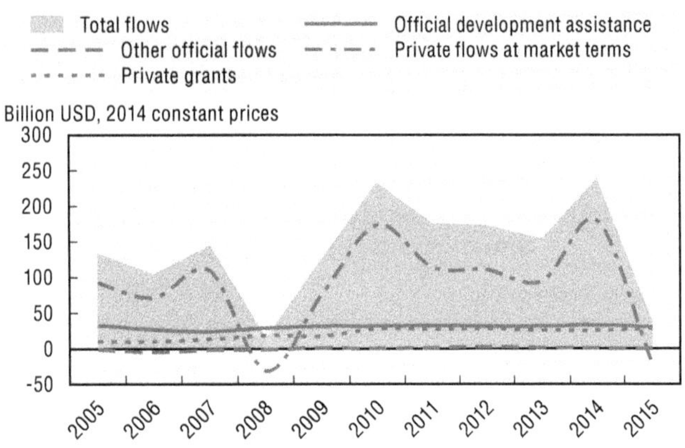

StatLink http://dx.doi.org/10.1787/888933482782

The United States' use of ODA to mobilise other resources for sustainable development

- **USD 26.9 million** of official development assistance (ODA) was committed to the mobilisation of domestic resources in developing countries, e.g. to support the development of their tax systems, in 2015.
- **USD 3.4 billion** of ODA (+14.7% in real terms from 2014) was committed to promote aid for trade and improve developing countries' trade performance and integration into the world economy in 2015.

The United States' performance against commitments for effective development co-operation

Table 37.1. **Results of the 2016 Global Partnership monitoring round, United States**

	Alignment and ownership by partner country (%)				Predictability (%)		Transparency		
	Use of country-led results frameworks	Funding recorded in countries' national budgets	Funding through countries' systems	Untied ODA	Annual predictability	Medium-term predictability	Retrospective statistics (OECD CRS)	Information for forecasting (OECD FSS)	Publishing to IATI
2016	49.2	36.6	20.5	55.5	91.7	73.7	Fair	Needs improvement	Fair
Baseline	-	32.5	11.1	56.7	81.7	62.9	Fair	Needs improvement	-
Trend	-	⇑	⇑	⇓	⇑	⇑	=	=	-

Note: Please refer to Annex B for details on the indicators.

StatLink http://dx.doi.org/10.1787/888933483250

The United States' official development assistance

In 2016, the United States provided USD 33.6 billion in net ODA (preliminary data), which represented 0.18% of gross national income (GNI) and a 7% increase in real terms from 2015. The United States' share of untied ODA (excluding administrative costs and in-donor refugee costs) was 55.5% in 2015 (down from 62.5% in 2014), while the DAC average was 78.1%. The grant element of total ODA was 100% in 2015.

In 2016, in-donor refugee costs were USD 1.7 billion, an increase of 38.5% in real terms over 2015, and represented 5.0% of the United States' total net ODA.

Figure 37.2. **Net ODA: Trends in volume and as a share of GNI, 2000-16, United States**

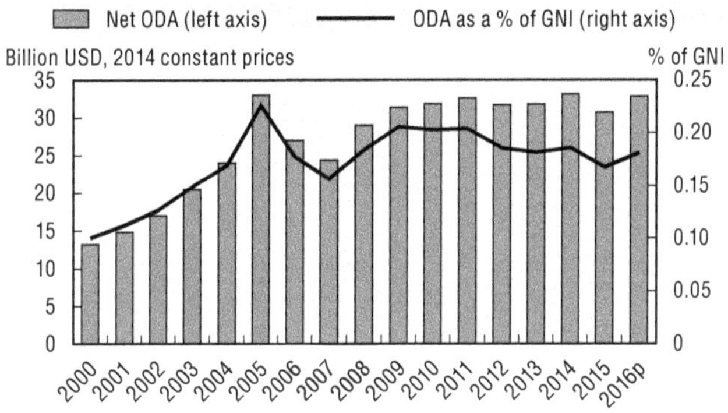

p: Preliminary data.

StatLink http://dx.doi.org/10.1787/888933482796

In 2015, 86.4% of ODA was provided bilaterally. The United States allocated 13.7% of total ODA as core contributions to multilateral organisations, compared with the DAC country average of 26.2%. In addition, it channelled 20.8% of its bilateral ODA to specific projects implemented by multilateral organisations (multi-bi/ non-core contributions).

Figure 37.3. **Share of ODA channelled to and through the multilateral system, two year averages, gross disbursements, United States**

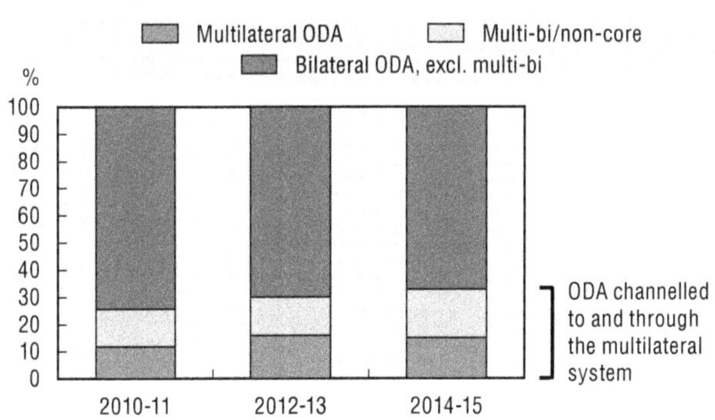

StatLink http://dx.doi.org/10.1787/888933482807

In 2015, 49.4% of bilateral ODA was programmed with partner countries. The share of country programmable aid was above the DAC country average (48.8%); project-type interventions amounted to 85% of this aid. Twenty-five per cent of bilateral ODA was allocated to humanitarian and food aid.

Figure 37.4. **Composition of bilateral ODA, 2015, gross disbursements, United States**

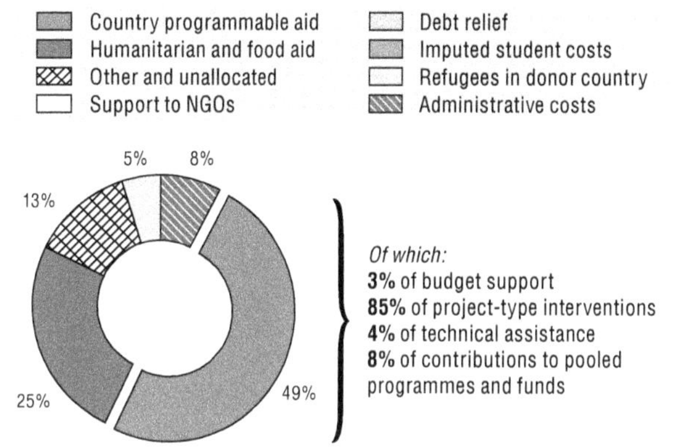

StatLink http://dx.doi.org/10.1787/888933482811

In 2015, USD 7.2 billion of bilateral ODA was channelled to and through civil society organisations (CSOs). ODA channelled to and through CSOs has increased in recent years in volume (with a 6.6% increase between 2014 and 2015), and as a share of bilateral aid (from 23.6% to 26.2%). This share was higher than the 2015 DAC average of 16.9%.

Figure 37.5. **Bilateral ODA to and through CSOs, two year averages, gross disbursements, United States**

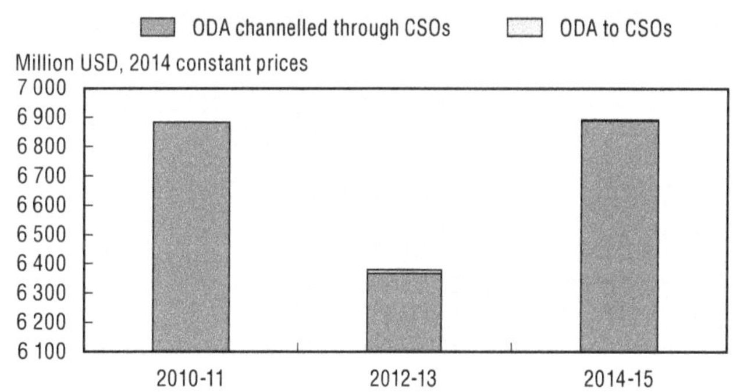

Note: Data on ODA to CSOs are only available for 2012.

StatLink http://dx.doi.org/10.1787/888933482826

The largest share of bilateral ODA was directed to sub-Saharan Africa. In 2015, USD 9.5 billion was allocated to sub-Saharan Africa, USD 3.4 billion to south and central Asia, and USD 2.6 billion to the Middle East.

Figure 37.6. **Share of bilateral ODA by region, 2014-15 average, gross disbursements, United States**

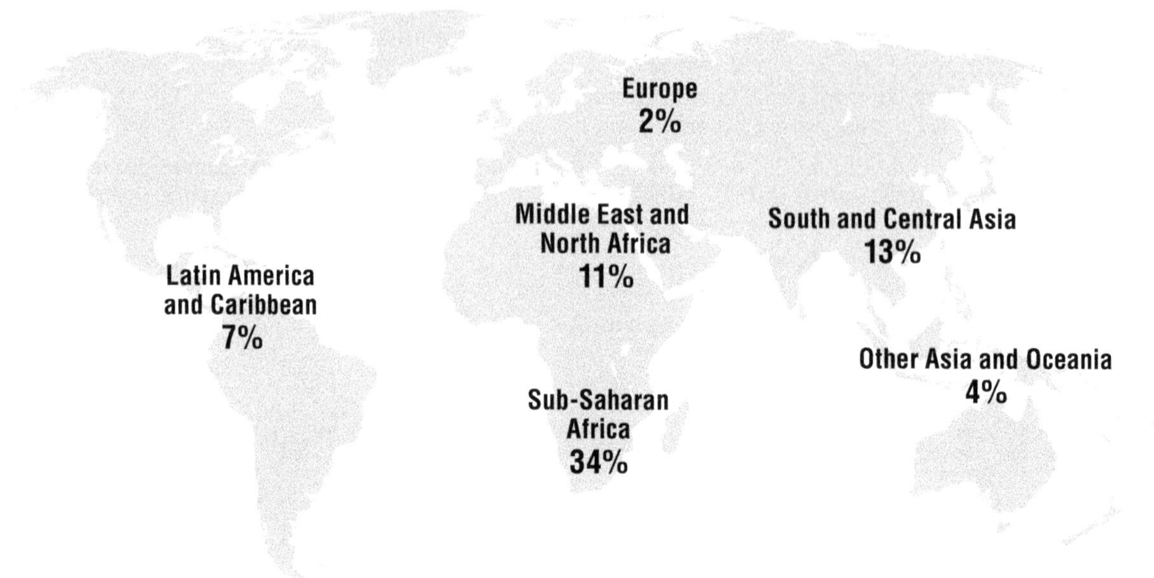

Note: 29% of bilateral ODA allocated was unspecified by region in 2014-15. This share is not represented on the map.

StatLink http://dx.doi.org/10.1787/888933482839

In 2015, 28.4% of bilateral ODA went to the United States' top 10 recipients. The United States provides development assistance to 137 countries, and the share of ODA to its top recipients is declining. Its support to fragile contexts reached USD 12.7 billion in 2015 (46.5% of gross bilateral ODA).

Figure 37.7. **Bilateral ODA to top recipients, 2014-15 average, gross disbursements, United States**

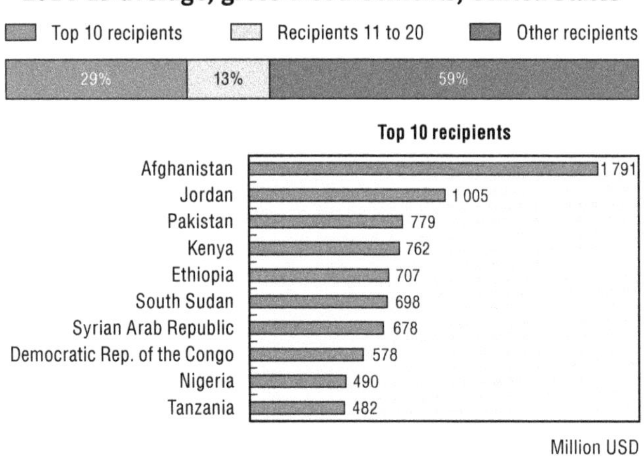

StatLink http://dx.doi.org/10.1787/888933482847

In 2015, 33.5% of bilateral ODA was allocated to LDCs, amounting to USD 9.2 billion. This share has increased since 2014 (30.9%), and is higher than the 2015 DAC average of 24.3%. LDCs received the highest share of bilateral ODA in 2015, compared with other income groups.

At 0.06% of GNI in 2015, total ODA to LDCs was lower than the UN target of 0.15% of GNI.

Figure 37.8. **Bilateral ODA by income group, two year averages, gross disbursements, United States**

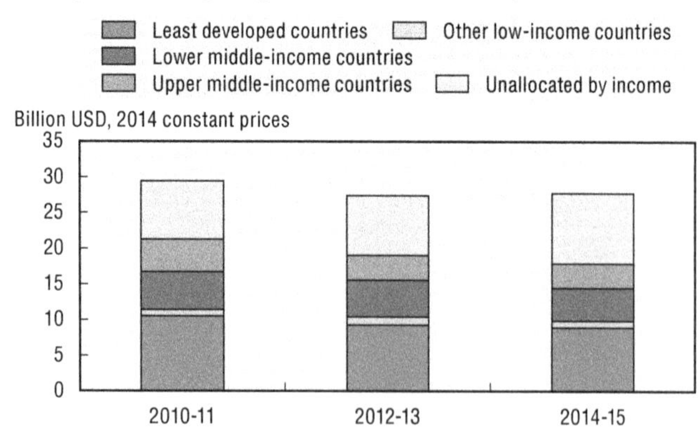

StatLink http://dx.doi.org/10.1787/888933482856

In 2015, 48.4% of bilateral ODA was allocated to social infrastructure and services, totalling USD 14.6 billion, with a strong focus on population policies and programmes (USD 6.6 billion) and support to government and civil society (USD 3.7 billion). Humanitarian aid amounted to USD 6.6 billion.

Figure 37.9. **Share of bilateral ODA by sector, 2014-15 average, commitments, United States**

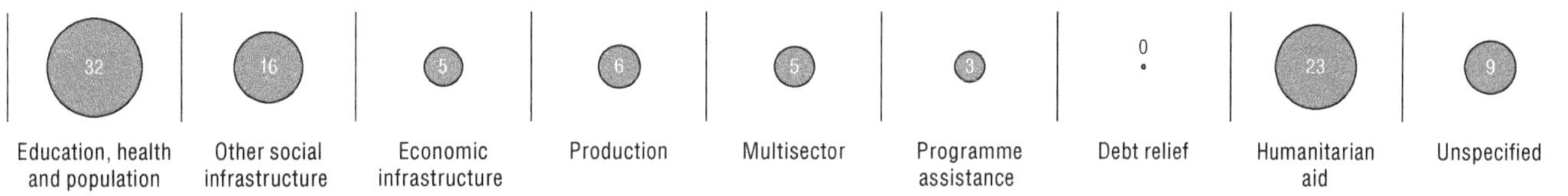

StatLink http://dx.doi.org/10.1787/888933482869

USD 5.2 billion of bilateral ODA supported gender equality. In 2015, 19.3% of the United States' bilateral allocable aid had gender equality and women's empowerment as a principal or significant objective, compared with the DAC country average of 36.3%. This is down from 22.6% in 2014. Nevertheless, strong political leadership has led to the adoption of an array of gender equality policies at the State Department and USAID. The adoption of additional policy guidance on Promoting Gender Equality and Advancing the Status of Women and Girls in 2014 has made gender equality a top strategic priority in US foreign policy (OECD, 2016).

Figure 37.10. **Share of bilateral allocable ODA in support of gender equality by sector, 2015, commitments, United States**

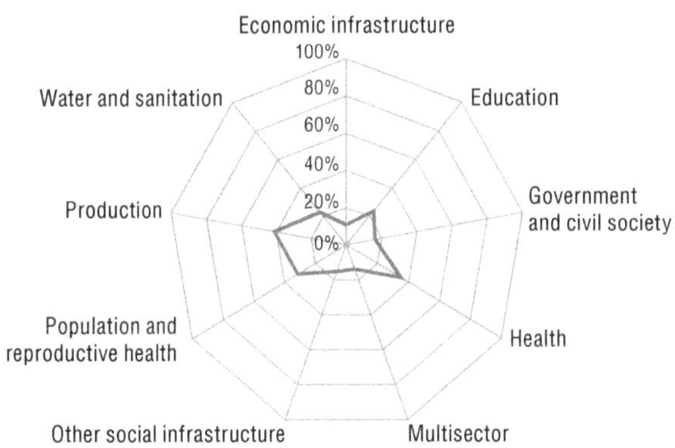

StatLink http://dx.doi.org/10.1787/888933482871

USD 2.8 billion of bilateral ODA supported the environment in 2015. The government has increasingly mainstreamed environmental issues in recent years. Particularly, USAID's Global Climate Change and Development Strategy 2012-16 led to the incorporation of climate change in all agency programming (OECD, 2016). In 2015, 10.4% of its bilateral allocable aid supported the environment and 3.5% (USD 938 million) focused specifically on climate change, compared with the respective DAC country averages of 33.2% and 26.2%. The United States has developed a new data-screening process to significantly improve reporting on environment and Rio markers.

Figure 37.11. **Bilateral allocable ODA in support of global and local environment objectives, two year averages, commitments, United States**

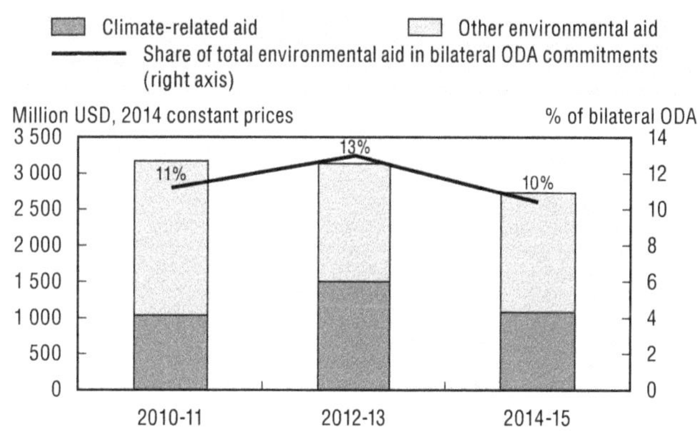

StatLink http://dx.doi.org/10.1787/888933482883

Note to reader: Annex B provides "Methodological notes on the profiles of Development Assistance Committee members".

Reference

OECD (2016), *OECD Development Co-operation Peer Reviews: United States 2016*, OECD Publishing, Paris, *http://dx.doi.org/10.1787/9789264266971-en*.

Development Co-operation Report 2017
Data for Development

Profiles of other development co-operation providers

This chapter presents information on the volume and key features of the development co-operation provided by countries that are not members of the Development Assistance Committee (DAC). Estimated development co-operation flows by 30 providers beyond the DAC reached USD 24.6 billion in 2015, compared to USD 32.0 billion in 2014. The chapter includes the 20 providers who reported to the OECD on their development co-operation programmes, as well as 10 other providers that are priority partners for the DAC. For the priority partners, the OECD estimates the volume of their programme based on official government reports, complemented by web-based research (mainly on contributions to multilateral organisations). The Bill & Melinda Gates Foundation, the only private funding entity that reported to the OECD, is also included in this chapter.

The statistical data for Israel are supplied by and under the responsibility of the relevant Israeli authorities. The use of such data by the OECD is without prejudice to the status of the Golan Heights, East Jerusalem and Israeli settlements in the West Bank under the terms of international law.

This chapter was prepared by Marisa Berbegal Ibañez, Juan Casado Asensio, Michael Laird, Nadine Piefer and Ann Zimmerman of the Development Co-operation Directorate, OECD.

One of the main changes in the international development co-operation landscape in recent years has been the substantial attention given to providers of development co-operation that are not members of the Development Assistance Committee (DAC).[1] Although often referred to as a single group, these providers are, in fact, quite heterogeneous and include the "BRICS" (Brazil, the Russian Federation, India, China and South Africa), as well as some Latin American, African and Southeast Asian countries that are mostly middle-income countries and both provide and receive development co-operation. Their development co-operation is often rooted in the tradition of South-South co-operation. Arab countries – many of which have a long tradition of providing development co-operation – are also included in this group (although Qatar and the United Arab Emirates are deepening their engagement with the DAC), along with several middle and high-income countries in Central and South East Europe as well as some countries in south Caucasus and Central Asia.

As their development co-operation programmes grow, there is an increasing demand for information on these countries' programmes. For partner countries in particular, it is important to know more about the financial flows that are reaching them. Policy makers from these partner countries need this information to make informed decisions and to co-ordinate their activities. Publishing these data also allows researchers to study these countries' programmes, and the general public to see how public funds are being used.

Twenty bilateral providers beyond the DAC currently report to the OECD – in varying degrees of comprehensiveness and detail – on their development co-operation programmes. The OECD DAC engages with several other countries to exchange ideas and share experiences on how to measure development co-operation. Some countries do not report to the OECD, but do publish data on their programmes. However, this information is often incomplete and not comparable with DAC statistics. For these reasons, the OECD estimates the size of the development co-operation programmes of ten other bilateral providers that do not report to the OECD but with whom the DAC collaborates in various ways (Brazil, Chile, the People's Republic of China [hereafter "China"], Colombia, Costa Rica, India, Indonesia, Mexico, Qatar and South Africa), taking account of the development co-operation concepts used in DAC statistics.

One important instrument for engagement highlighted in the DAC Global Relations Strategy is "monitoring the concessional and non-concessional development finance flows from public and private actors, particularly the official development co-operation flows of major non-member economies, and supporting [their] efforts [...] to establish and improve their statistical collection and reporting systems" (OECD, 2016a). Therefore, the OECD DAC welcomes additional or improved (i.e. more detailed and more comprehensive) reporting by countries providing development co-operation. Data submitted and OECD estimates are continuously updated and made available on the "Development finance reporting of countries beyond the DAC" webpage.[2]

The subsequent sections of this chapter provide further information on the following development co-operation programmes:

- The first section covers the bilateral providers that report to the OECD, with a particular focus on: 1) OECD members that are not members of the DAC (Estonia, Israel, Latvia and Turkey); 2) OECD accession countries (Lithuania and the Russian Federation); and 3) other major providers of development co-operation that reported detailed and comprehensive data to the OECD (the United Arab Emirates [UAE], a DAC Participant;[3] Azerbaijan; Kazakhstan; Kuwait; and Romania).
- The second section covers several providers of development co-operation that do not report to the OECD, focusing on: OECD member countries that are not members of the DAC (Chile and Mexico); OECD accession countries (Colombia and Costa Rica); the OECD Key Partners (Brazil, China, India, Indonesia and South Africa); and Qatar, a DAC Participant[4] and a significant provider of development co-operation that publishes reports on its development co-operation programme which enables the OECD to make estimates.
- The final section provides information on the Bill & Melinda Gates Foundation, the only private foundation that reports on its activities to the OECD.

Providers of development co-operation that report to the OECD

Net concessional development co-operation by the 20 providers that report to the OECD fell from USD 25.2 billion in 2014 to USD 17.7 billion in 2015. This is mainly due to a significant decline in development co-operation from Saudi Arabia. Net official development assistance (ODA) from the UAE also fell, as did the programmes of many other reporting countries. The programmes of the Russian Federation and Turkey increased most substantially between 2014 and 2015. More figures and information on these trends can be found in the following sub-sections.

Azerbaijan

In 2015, Azerbaijan's net ODA amounted to USD 13 million, compared to USD 16 million in 2014. The ratio of ODA as a share of GNI remained unchanged at 0.02%.

Azerbaijan's Ministry of Foreign Affairs is responsible for setting the overall development co-operation guidelines of the country. Project implementation is the responsibility of the Azerbaijan International Development Agency (AIDA), which was established in 2011 within the Ministry of Foreign Affairs. The AIDA's annual budget allocation is provided from the state budget. The AIDA co-ordinates the activities of all relevant government bodies in the field of development, ensuring that their activities are consistent with Azerbaijan's foreign policy objectives.

In 2015, Azerbaijan provided its bilateral co-operation mostly to Kyrgyzstan and Tajikistan. The main sectors for Azerbaijan's bilateral development co-operation were humanitarian aid, governance and civil society, and other social infrastructure.

Multilateral ODA accounted for 45% of Azerbaijan's net disbursements in 2015, provided primarily through the regional development banks (accounting for 58% of multilateral ODA in 2015).

Azerbaijan is a DAC invitee since 2017. In 2016, the country reported for the first time to the OECD figures on its development co-operation programme (on its 2014 and 2015 flows). The OECD hosted a visit by officials from the Azerbaijan International Development Agency in 2016.

Figure 38.1. **ODA key statistics: Azerbaijan**

AZERBAIJAN

Gross bilateral ODA, 2015 (disbursements), unless otherwise shown

Net ODA	2014	2015	Change 2014/15
Current (million USD)	16	13	-18%
Constant (2015 million USD)	14	13	-9%
In Azerbaijani manat (million)	12	13	7%
ODA/GNI	0.02%	0.02%	
Bilateral share	64%	55%	

Top recipients of gross ODA (million USD)	
1 Kyrgyzstan	1.0
2 Tajikistan	0.5
3 Nepal	0.1
4 Pakistan	0.1
5 Jordan	0.1
6 Turkey	0.0
7 Gabon	0.0
8 Togo	0.0
Memo: Share of gross bilateral ODA	
Top 20 recipients	24%
Top 10 recipients	24%
Top 5 recipients	24%

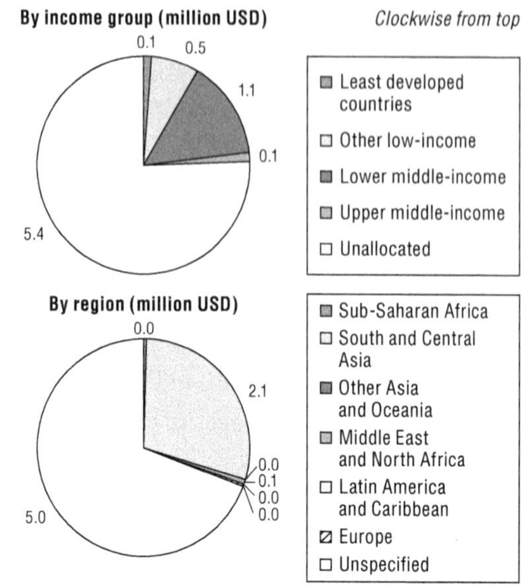

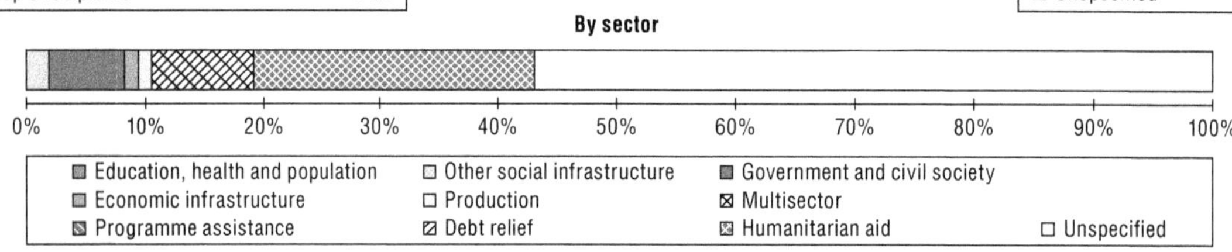

Source: OECD (2016c), "Azerbaijan's official development assistance (ODA)", webpage, OECD, Paris, *www.oecd.org/dac/dac-global-relations/azerbaijan-official-development-assistance.htm.*

StatLink http://dx.doi.org/10.1787/888933482895

Estonia

In 2016, preliminary data show that ODA reached USD 44 million (0.19% of GNI). In 2015, Estonia's net ODA amounted to USD 34 million, representing an increase of 7% in real terms over 2014. The ratio of ODA as a share of GNI also rose, from 0.14% to 0.15%. Estonia's development co-operation is provided in line with its Strategy for Development Co-operation and Humanitarian Aid for the period 2016-20. This strategy sets out the goals and objectives of Estonia's development co-operation, its sectoral and geographical priorities, as well as its estimated financial allocations for ODA. The Ministry of Foreign Affairs is the key institution responsible for managing and co-ordinating Estonia's development co-operation.

In 2015, Estonia provided its bilateral development co-operation mostly to Ukraine, Afghanistan, Georgia and Moldova, often in the form of small-scale technical co-operation projects. The main sectors of Estonia's bilateral development co-operation were governance and civil society, humanitarian aid, and education. Cross-cutting themes for Estonia's development co-operation were information and communication technologies, transparency and democratic participation, and the rights of women and children.

Multilateral ODA accounted for 56% of Estonia's total ODA in 2015, provided primarily through the European Union (accounting for 72% of its multilateral ODA in 2015), as well as through the World Bank and the United Nations.

Figure 38.2. **ODA key statistics: Estonia**

ESTONIA

Gross bilateral ODA, 2015 (disbursements), unless otherwise shown

Net ODA	2014	2015	Change 2014/15
Current (million USD)	38	34	-10%
Constant (2015 million USD)	32	34	7%
In euro (million)	28	31	8%
ODA/GNI	0.14%	0.15%	
Bilateral share	40%	44%	

Top ten recipients of gross ODA (million USD)	
1 Ukraine	2.8
2 Afghanistan	1.7
3 Georgia	1.1
4 Moldova	1.0
5 Kyrgyzstan	0.5
6 West Bank and Gaza Strip	0.3
7 Syrian Arab Republic	0.3
8 Jordan	0.3
9 Belarus	0.3
10 Turkey	0.2
Memo: Share of gross bilateral ODA	
Top 20 recipients	62%
Top 10 recipients	56%
Top 5 recipients	47%

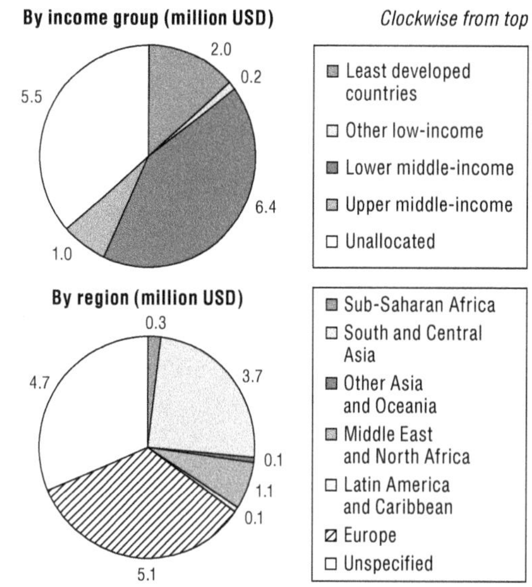

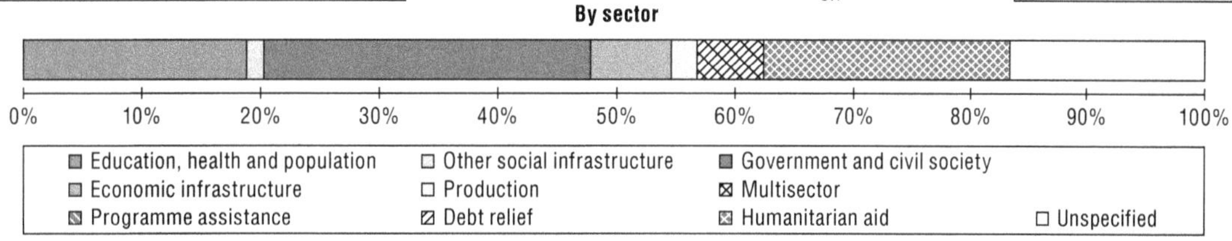

Source: OECD (2016d), "Estonia's official development assistance (ODA)", webpage, OECD, Paris, *www.oecd.org/dac/dac-global-relations/estonias-official-development-assistance.htm.*

StatLink http://dx.doi.org/10.1787/888933482905

Estonia, which joined the OECD in 2010, is an observer to the DAC. In 2016, Estonia participated in the meetings of the DAC, including its high-level and senior-level meetings, as well as the meeting of the Working Party on Development Finance Statistics.

Israel

In 2016, preliminary data show that ODA reached USD 220 million (0.07% of GNI). In 2015, Israel's net ODA amounted to USD 198 million, representing an increase of 5% in real terms over 2014. The ratio of ODA as a share of GNI remained stable at 0.07%.

Israel's Agency for International Development Co-operation – MASHAV, a division of the Ministry of Foreign Affairs – is in charge of planning, implementing and co-ordinating Israel's development co-operation.

In 2015, Israel provided its bilateral development co-operation mostly to Jordan, the Syrian Arab Republic, and the West Bank and Gaza Strip. The priority sectors for Israel's bilateral development co-operation were water resources management, desert agriculture and combating desertification, early childhood education, rural and community development, emergency and disaster medicine, public health, and women's empowerment. Israel provides its bilateral development co-operation mostly in the form of technical co-operation projects and capacity building, provided both in Israel and in developing countries.

Israel is also engaged in triangular co-operation, sharing its experience with other countries. It partners with several international organisations (e.g. the United Nations Development Programme, the Food and Agriculture Organization of the United Nations, and the World Food Programme) and DAC members (e.g. Canada, France, Germany, Italy and the United States) to support developing countries in areas in which it has a comparative advantage.

Multilateral ODA accounted for USD 20 million in 2015, representing 10% of Israel's total ODA. It was provided primarily through the United Nations (accounting for 46% of its multilateral ODA in 2015), as well as through the World Bank Group (43%), regional development banks (3%) and other multilateral organisations.

Israel, which joined the OECD in 2010, is an observer to the DAC. In 2016, Israel participated in the meetings of the DAC, including its high-level and senior-level meetings, as well as the meetings of several DAC subsidiary bodies: the Network on Environment and Development Co-operation, the Network on Gender Equality, and the Advisory Group on Investment and Development.

Kazakhstan

In 2015, Kazakhstan's net ODA amounted to USD 43 million, compared to USD 33 million in 2014, an increase of 43% in real terms. The ratio of ODA as a share of GNI was 0.02% in 2015.

The Foreign Policy Concept of Kazakhstan 2014-2020 guides Kazakhstan's contribution to the international community's development co-operation efforts. The ODA Concept of Kazakhstan (April 2013) sets out a roadmap for becoming a provider of development co-operation. Law No. 263-V

Figure 38.3. **ODA key statistics: Kazakhstan**

KAZAKHSTAN

Gross bilateral ODA, 2015 (disbursements), unless otherwise shown

Net ODA	2014	2015	Change 2014/15
Current (million USD)	33	43	29%
Constant (2015 million USD)	30	43	43%
In Kazakhstani tenge (million)	5 980	9 525	59%
ODA/GNI	0.02%	0.02%	
Bilateral share	81%	79%	

Top recipients of gross ODA (million USD)	
1 Afghanistan	8.2
2 Tajikistan	6.4
3 Ukraine	1.1
4 Syrian Arab Republic	0.3
5 Kyrgyzstan	0.3
6 Serbia	0.2
7 Nepal	0.2
8 Pakistan	0.1

Memo: Share of gross bilateral ODA	
Top 20 recipients	50%
Top 10 recipients	50%
Top 5 recipients	48%

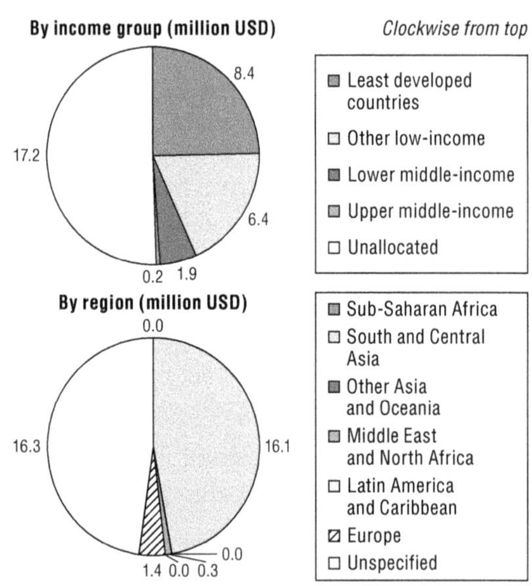

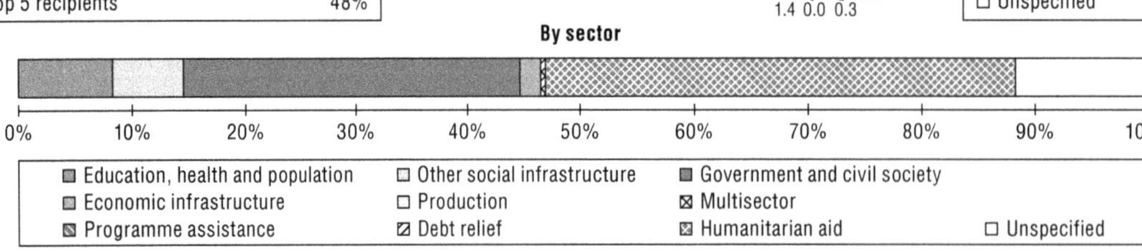

Source: OECD (2016e), "Kazakhstan's official development assistance (ODA)", webpage, OECD, Paris, *www.oecd.org/dac/dac-global-relations/kazakhstan-official-development-assistance.htm*.

StatLink http://dx.doi.org/10.1787/888933482918

on Official Development Assistance (December 2014) describes the main objectives, principles, competences and sectoral priorities of Kazakhstan's ODA.

The ODA Law provides the legal basis for establishing an agency under the Ministry of Foreign Affairs, provisionally known as the Kazakhstan Agency for International Development Assistance, to implement development co-operation activities. For the moment, the Ministry of Foreign Affairs is the designated authority to implement the main lines of Kazakhstan's ODA policy, including ODA activities.

In 2015, Kazakhstan provided its bilateral development co-operation mostly to Afghanistan, Tajikistan and Ukraine. The main sectors for Kazakhstan's bilateral development co-operation were humanitarian aid, governance and civil society, and education, Multilateral ODA accounted for 21% of Kazakhstan's net disbursements in 2015, provided primarily through the United Nations (accounting for 80% of its multilateral ODA in 2015), as well as through the other multilateral organisations.

In 2016, Kazakhstan, a DAC Invitee,[5] participated in the meeting of the DAC Working Party on Development Finance Statistics.

Kuwait

In 2015, net ODA reported by the Kuwait Fund for Arab Economic Development (KFAED) amounted to USD 304 million, representing an increase of 22% in real terms over 2014. Kuwait's total involvement in development co-operation exceeds this amount but the volume of the activities of other institutions is not known.

Figure 38.4. **ODA key statistics: Kuwait Fund for Arab Economic Development**

KUWAIT (KFAED)

Gross bilateral ODA, 2015 (disbursements), unless otherwise shown

Net ODA	2014	2015	Change 2014/15
Current (million USD)	277	304	10%
Constant (2015 million USD)	249	304	22%
In Kuwaiti dinar (million)	79	92	16%
Bilateral share	83%	100%	

Top ten recipients of gross ODA (million USD)	
1 Morocco	106.4
2 Jordan	86.5
3 Sudan	82.8
4 Egypt	69.3
5 Pakistan	44.4
6 Lebanon	27.4
7 Serbia	22.1
8 Djibouti	15.2
9 Senegal	11.9
10 Mali	11.9
Memo: Share of gross bilateral ODA	
Top 20 recipients	90%
Top 10 recipients	76%
Top 5 recipients	62%

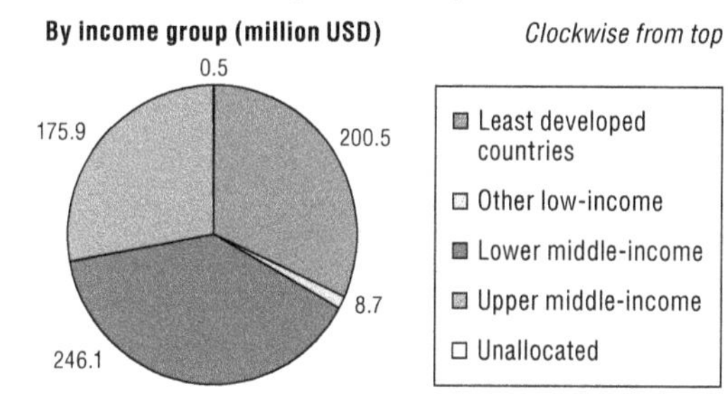

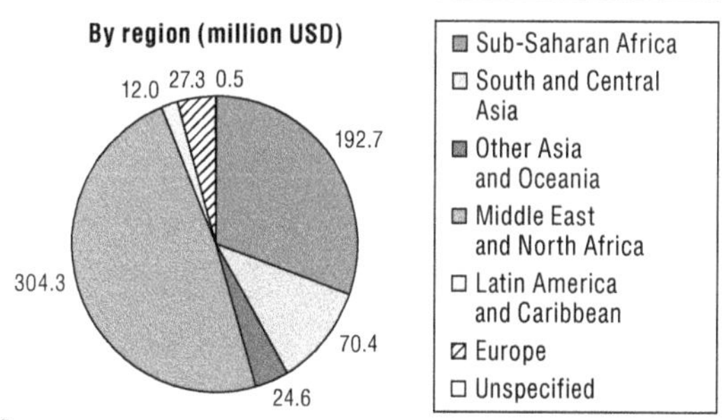

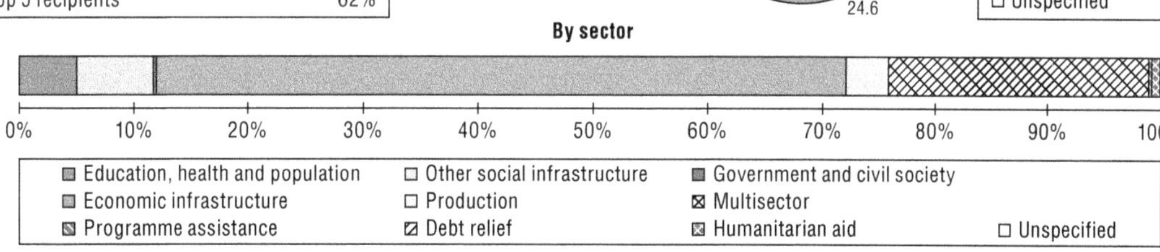

Source: OECD (2016f), "Kuwait's official development assistance (ODA)", webpage, OECD, Paris, *www.oecd.org/dac/dac-global-relations/kuwaits-official-development-assistance.htm.*

StatLink http://dx.doi.org/10.1787/888933482924

Kuwait's Law No. 35 of 1961 created the legal basis for the KFAED to act as an implementing agency in all developing countries on behalf of the Kuwaiti government. The KFAED acts under the overall supervision of the Prime Minister, who in practice delegates this mandate to the Minister of Finance. Other ministries, public authorities and non-governmental organisations (NGOs) also contribute to promoting development internationally, notably the Ministry of Foreign Affairs which can also provide humanitarian assistance.

The Kuwait Fund primarily provides concessional loans and loans to co-finance projects with other international, regional or national development partners. In addition, the fund provides guarantees. It also administers Kuwaiti government grants (outside its budget) and provides some grants for technical, economic and financial studies and assistance.

In 2015, the Kuwait Fund provided its bilateral development co-operation mostly to Morocco, Jordan, Sudan, Egypt and Pakistan. The main sectors for the KFAED's bilateral development co-operation were economic infrastructure (energy), multisector aid for basic social services, and education and health.

The Kuwait Fund is a member of the Arab Coordination Group. In 2016, it participated in the Arab-DAC Dialogue on Development held at the OPEC Fund for International Development.

Latvia

In 2016, preliminary data show that ODA reached USD 28 million (0.10% of GNI). In 2015, Latvia's net ODA amounted to USD 23 million, representing an increase of 9% in real terms over 2014. The ODA/GNI ratio rose from 0.08% to 0.09%. Latvia's development co-operation is provided in line with the Latvian Development Co-operation Policy Strategy 2016-20, which defines the goals, principles and directions of Latvia's development co-operation. The Ministry of Foreign Affairs is responsible for formulating development co-operation policy and for co-ordinating activities.

In 2015, Latvia provided its bilateral development co-operation mostly to Ukraine, Georgia, Syria and Moldova. The priority sectors for Latvia's bilateral development co-operation were: 1) public governance and capacity building, particularly in justice and internal affairs, fighting corruption, administrative policy development and support to decentralisation, and strengthening local and regional authorities; 2) fostering entrepreneurship, particularly strengthening small and medium enterprises and export capacity; 3) conflict prevention, peace and security; 4) fostering democratic engagement in decision making and gender equality; and 5) education. Latvia provides its bilateral development co-operation mostly in the form of small-scale technical co-operation projects.

Multilateral ODA accounted for 90% of Latvia's total ODA in 2015, provided primarily through the European Union (accounting for 84% of its multilateral ODA in 2015), as well as through the World Bank Group (9%) and the United Nations (4%).

Latvia, which joined the OECD in 2016, is an observer to the DAC. In 2016, Latvia participated in the meetings of the DAC, including its high-level and senior-level meetings, as well as the meeting of the DAC Working Party on Development Finance Statistics. The OECD hosted a visit from officials from the Ministry of Foreign Affairs and OECD staff participated in a seminar in Riga on "Latvian Bilateral Development Cooperation in 2016: Towards Effectiveness, Results and Partnerships".

Lithuania

In 2016, preliminary data show that ODA reached USD 58 million (0.14% of GNI). In 2015, Lithuania's net ODA amounted to USD 48 million, representing an increase of 26% in real terms over 2014. The ODA/GNI ratio rose from 0.10% to 0.12%.

The Law on Development Co-operation and Humanitarian Aid, adopted in 2013 and updated in 2016, provides the framework for Lithuania's development co-operation policy and outlines its mission, goals, principles, priorities, responsibilities and financing. The main principles of Lithuania's development co-operation are: partnership with partner countries, partner country's ownership, solidarity, efficiency, transparency and responsibility, co-ordination and complementarity, and policy coherence. In 2016, Lithuania adopted a new inter-governmental Development Cooperation Action Plan for the period 2017-19, which aims to support effective development policies in line with achieving the Sustainable Development Goals by 2030 and in accordance with the needs of partner countries. The Ministry of Foreign Affairs is responsible for implementing and co-ordinating Lithuania's development co-operation.

In 2015, Lithuania provided its bilateral development co-operation mostly to Ukraine and Belarus. The main sectors for Lithuania's bilateral development co-operation were education, humanitarian aid, and governance and civil society. Lithuania provides its bilateral development co-operation mostly in the form of small-scale technical co-operation projects.

Multilateral ODA accounted for 80% of Lithuania's total ODA in 2015, provided primarily through the European Union (accounting for 84% of its multilateral ODA in 2015), as well as through the World Bank Group (10%) and the United Nations (4%).

In 2016, Lithuania, an OECD accession country, participated in the DAC senior-level and high-level meetings, as well as in several meetings of DAC subsidiary bodies: the Network on Development Evaluation, the Network on Gender Equality, the Network on Governance and the Working Party on Development Finance Statistics.

Figure 38.5. **ODA key statistics: Lithuania**

LITHUANIA

Gross bilateral ODA, 2015 (disbursements), unless otherwise shown

Net ODA	2014	2015	Change 2014/15
Current (million USD)	46	48	6%
Constant (2015 million USD)	38	48	26%
In euro (million)	34	43	26%
ODA/GNI	0.10%	0.12%	
Bilateral share	14%	20%	

Top ten recipients of gross ODA (million USD)	
1 Ukraine	1.7
2 Belarus	1.2
3 Georgia	0.2
4 Syrian Arab Republic	0.1
5 Moldova	0.1
6 Malaysia	0.0
7 Kosovo	0.0
8 China (People's Republic of)	0.0
9 Kazakhstan	0.0
10 Brazil	0.0
Memo: Share of gross bilateral ODA	
Top 20 recipients	36%
Top 10 recipients	34%
Top 5 recipients	33%

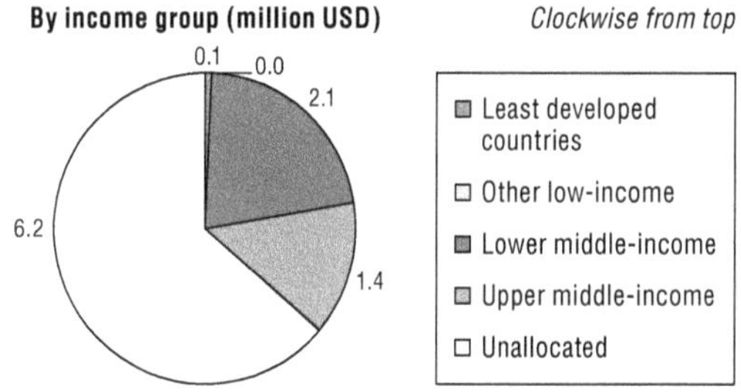

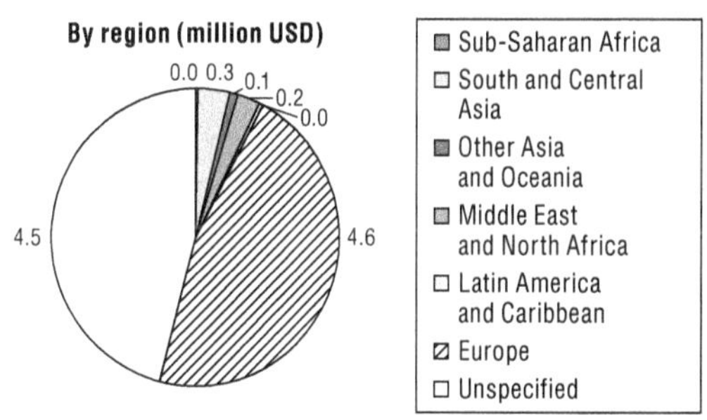

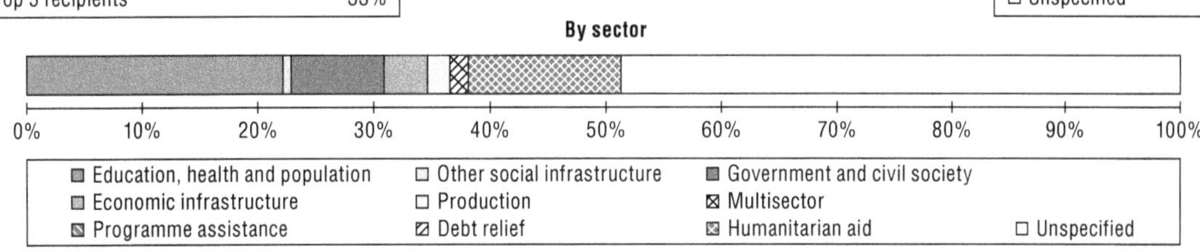

Source: OECD (2016g), "Lithuania's official development assistance (ODA)", webpage, OECD, Paris, *www.oecd.org/dac/dac-global-relations/lithuania-official-development-assistance.htm*.

StatLink http://dx.doi.org/10.1787/888933482932

Romania

In 2016, preliminary data show that ODA reached USD 198 million (0.11% of GNI). In 2015, Romania's net ODA amounted to USD 158 million, representing a decrease of 18% in real terms over 2014. The ODA/GNI ratio fell from 0.11% to 0.09%.

Law No. 213/2016 provides the legal basis for the development co-operation and humanitarian aid activities financed from Romanian public funds. The Ministry of Foreign Affairs is the national co-ordinator of Romania's development co-operation and humanitarian aid policy. It monitors progress made in achieving the objectives and commitments assumed by Romania, reports annually to the government on activities implemented, and signs funding agreements. An Advisory Committee, composed of representatives from line ministries, public institutions, civil society, academia and the private sector, is responsible for ensuring the co-ordination and unity of strategic planning and priorities in the field of development co-operation. Law No. 213/2016 also created an Agency for International Development Cooperation, RoAid, which is responsible for implementing development co-operation and humanitarian aid-related activities.

In 2015, Romania provided its bilateral development co-operation mostly to Moldova, Serbia and Tunisia. The main sectors of Romania's bilateral development co-operation were education, governance and civil society, and humanitarian aid. Romania provides its bilateral development co-operation mostly in the form of grants for financial and technical support.

Multilateral ODA accounted for 79% of Romania's total ODA in 2015, provided primarily through the European Union (accounting for 83% of its multilateral ODA in 2015), as well as through the World Bank Group (10%) and the United Nations (4%).

Figure 38.6. **ODA key statistics: Romania**

ROMANIA

Gross bilateral ODA, 2015 (disbursements), unless otherwise shown

Net ODA	2014	2015	Change 2014/15
Current (million USD)	214	158	-26%
Constant (2015 million USD)	192	158	-18%
In Romanian new leu (million)	726	633	-13%
ODA/GNI	0.11%	0.09%	
Bilateral share	33%	21%	

Top ten recipients of gross ODA (million USD)	
1 Moldova	18.4
2 Serbia	1.7
3 Tunisia	1.5
4 Syrian Arab Republic	1.0
5 Morocco	0.9
6 Jordan	0.8
7 Albania	0.7
8 Turkey	0.6
9 Iraq	0.6
10 Ukraine	0.6
Memo: Share of gross bilateral ODA	
Top 20 recipients	90%
Top 10 recipients	81%
Top 5 recipients	71%

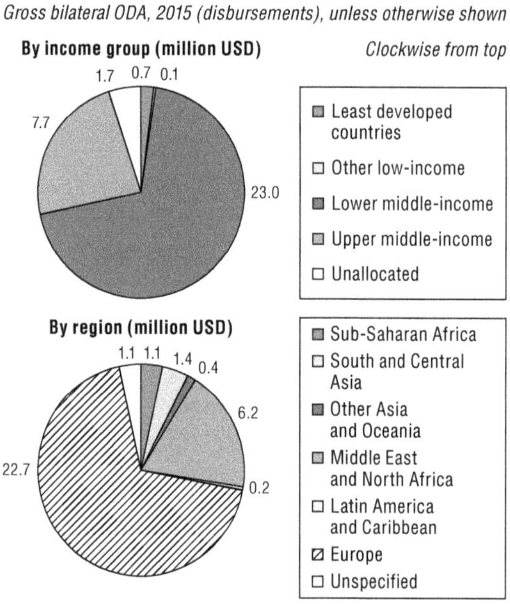

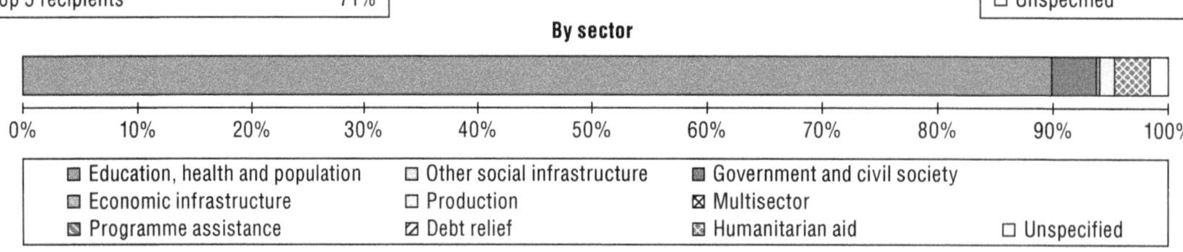

Source: OECD (2016h), "Romania's official development assistance (ODA)", webpage, OECD, Paris, *www.oecd.org/dac/dac-global-relations/romania-official-development-assistance.htm.*

StatLink http://dx.doi.org/10.1787/888933482947

In 2016, Romania, a DAC Invitee, participated in a meeting of the DAC Working Party on Development Finance Statistics.

Russian Federation

In 2016, preliminary data show that ODA reached USD 1.0 billion (0.08% of GNI). In 2015, the Russian Federation's net ODA amounted to USD 1.2 billion compared to USD 876 million in 2014, an increase of 95% in real terms. The ratio of ODA as a share of GNI rose from 0.05% to 0.09%.

The Russian Federation's development co-operation is provided in line with the Concept of Russia's State Policy in the Field of International Development Assistance, approved by the President of the Russian Federation in 2014. The concept sets out the objectives, principles and priorities of the Russian Federation's development co-operation, as well as the criteria for providing assistance to partner countries. The Ministry of Foreign Affairs and the Ministry of Finance, in co-operation with other government agencies, play a leading role in formulating the Russian Federation's development co-operation policy and supervise its implementation.

In 2015, the Russian Federation provided its bilateral development assistance mainly to the members of the Commonwealth of Independent States,[6] as well as Syria, Serbia and Guinea. The priority sectors of the Russian Federation's bilateral development co-operation were health, public finance, food security, nutrition and education. The Russian Federation provides its bilateral development co-operation in the form of technical assistance projects, capacity building and scholarships, as well as budget support and debt relief.

The Russian Federation's multilateral ODA accounted for 22% its total ODA, provided through the World Bank Group (accounting for 53% of its multilateral ODA in 2015), as well as through the United Nations (36%), regional development banks (1%) and other multilateral organisations.

In 2016, the Russian Federation, an OECD accession country, participated in the DAC senior-level meeting and the meeting of the DAC Working Party on Development Finance Statistics.

Turkey

In 2016, preliminary data show that ODA reached USD 6.2 billion (0.79% of GNI). In 2015, Turkey's net ODA amounted to USD 3.9 billion, representing an increase of 26% in real terms over 2014. The ratio of ODA as a share of GNI rose from 0.45% in 2014 to 0.50% in 2015. As in 2013 and 2014, the increase in Turkey's ODA mostly related to its response to the refugee crisis in its neighbouring country, Syria. The share of Turkey's total ODA allocated to Syria increased to 70% in 2015, compared to 65% in 2014 and 52% in 2013. Turkey's development co-operation is provided in line with the Statutory Decree on the Organization and Duties of the Turkish Co-operation and Co-ordination Agency (TIKA), adopted in 2011. The agency designs and co-ordinates Turkey's bilateral development co-operation activities and implements projects in collaboration with other ministries, NGOs and the private sector. TIKA is an autonomous institution attached to the Prime Minister's Office. Other public institutions, NGOs and the private sector also implement projects and programmes funded through Turkey's ODA.

In 2015, Turkey provided the largest share of its bilateral development co-operation to Syria, Somalia, Kyrgyzstan, Albania and Afghanistan. The main sectors for Turkey's bilateral development co-operation were humanitarian aid and refugee support, governance and civil society, and education, health and population.

Multilateral ODA accounted for 2% of Turkey's total ODA in 2015, provided through the United Nations (accounting for 25% of its multilateral ODA), as well as through regional development banks (33%), the International Development Association (8%) and other multilateral organisations.

Turkey, a founding member of the OECD, is an observer to the DAC. In 2016, Turkey participated in the meetings of the DAC, including its high-level and senior-level meetings, as well as meetings of the DAC International Network on Conflict and Fragility and the Working Party on Development Finance Statistics.

Figure 38.7. **ODA key statistics: Turkey**

TURKEY

Gross bilateral ODA, 2015 (disbursements), unless otherwise shown

Net ODA	2014	2015	Change 2014/15
Current (million USD)	3 591	3 919	9%
Constant (2015 million USD)	3 101	3 919	26%
In Turkish new lira (million)	7 861	10 672	36%
ODA/GNI	0.45%	0.50%	
Bilateral share	98%	98%	

Top ten recipients of gross ODA (million USD)	
1 Syrian Arab Republic	2 694.0
2 Somalia	314.8
3 Kyrgyzstan	98.4
4 Albania	85.7
5 Afghanistan	56.8
6 West Bank and Gaza Strip	29.8
7 Bosnia and Herzegovina	26.0
8 FYROM	25.6
9 Kazakhstan	24.4
10 Sudan	22.0
Memo: Share of gross bilateral ODA	
Top 20 recipients	85%
Top 10 recipients	82%
Top 5 recipients	79%

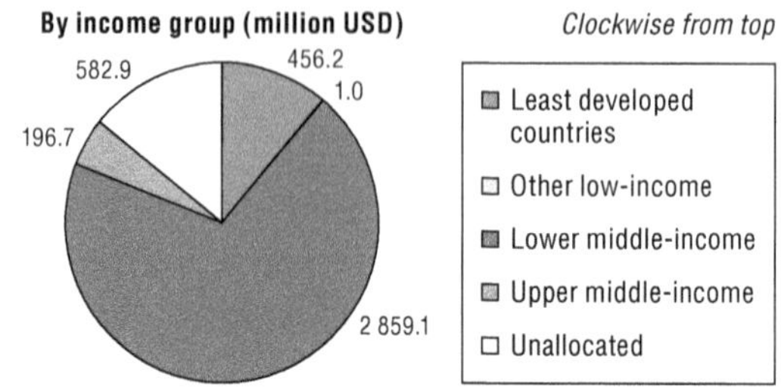

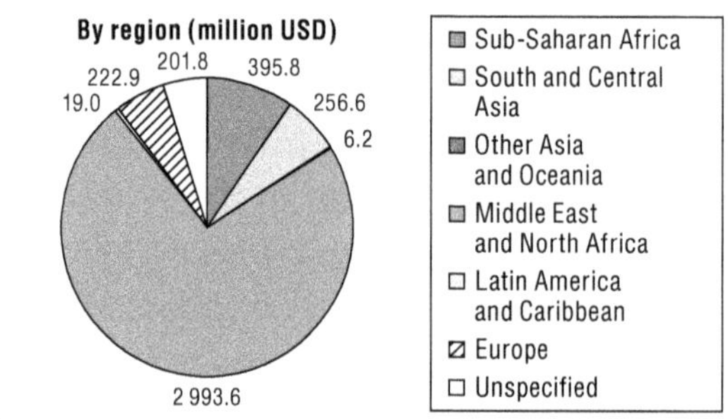

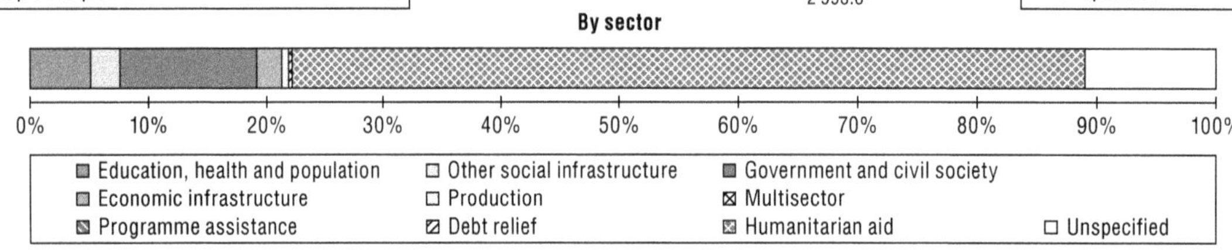

Source: OECD (2016i), "Turkey's official development assistance (ODA)", webpage, OECD, Paris, *www.oecd.org/dac/dac-global-relations/turkeys-official-development-assistanceoda.htm.*

StatLink http://dx.doi.org/10.1787/888933482950

United Arab Emirates

In 2015, the United Arab Emirates' (UAE) total net ODA reached USD 4.4 billion, representing a decrease in real terms of 4% over 2014. The ratio of ODA as a share of GNI also fell in 2015 to 1.18%, down from 1.26% in 2014. Preliminary data show that ODA reached USD 4.1 billion in 2016 (1.12% of GNI). The decrease is mostly explained by a USD 56 million drop in ODA to North Africa, mostly to Egypt but also to Morocco. The UAE nevertheless remained well above the United Nations' ODA/GNI target for economically advanced countries of 0.7%.[7]

Up until its merger with the Ministry of Foreign Affairs in February 2016, the former Ministry of International Co-operation and Development, created in 2013, maintained overall responsibility for setting policy, geographical and sectoral priorities; identifying modalities and mechanisms for foreign aid distribution and implementation; and documenting aid flows. In December 2016 the Ministry of Foreign Affairs and International Cooperation launched the UAE's new development co-operation strategy for 2017-21 (Government of the United Arab Emirates, 2016).

In 2015, the UAE provided its bilateral co-operation mostly to Egypt, Yemen, Jordan, Iraq, Morocco, Sudan and Pakistan. The main sectors of the UAE's bilateral disbursements were programme assistance, economic infrastructure (energy and transport) and humanitarian aid. The UAE provides its bilateral programme mostly in the form of grants.

Multilateral ODA accounted for 1% of the country's total ODA in 2015, provided primarily through the United Nations (75%) The UAE is a Participant in the DAC. In 2016, it participated in the DAC senior-level and high-level meetings, as well as the meetings of the DAC Network on Gender Equality and the DAC Working Party on Development Finance Statistics. The UAE also participated in the 2016 Arab-DAC Dialogue on Development held at the OPEC Fund for International Development.

Figure 38.8. **ODA key statistics: United Arab Emirates**

UNITED ARAB EMIRATES

Gross bilateral ODA, 2015 (disbursements), unless otherwise shown

Net ODA	2014	2015	Change 2014/15
Current (million USD)	5 080	4 381	-14%
Constant (2015 million USD)	4 577	4 381	-4%
In UAE dirham (million)	18 658	16 091	-14%
ODA/GNI	1.26%	1.18%	
Bilateral share	97%	99%	

Top ten recipients of gross ODA (million USD)		
1	Egypt	2 460.3
2	Yemen	889.6
3	Jordan	215.7
4	Iraq	99.9
5	Morocco	99.4
6	Sudan	93.9
7	Pakistan	82.8
8	Libya	62.7
9	Afghanistan	56.8
10	Mauritania	43.2
Memo: Share of gross bilateral ODA		
Top 20 recipients		96%
Top 10 recipients		92%
Top 5 recipients		84%

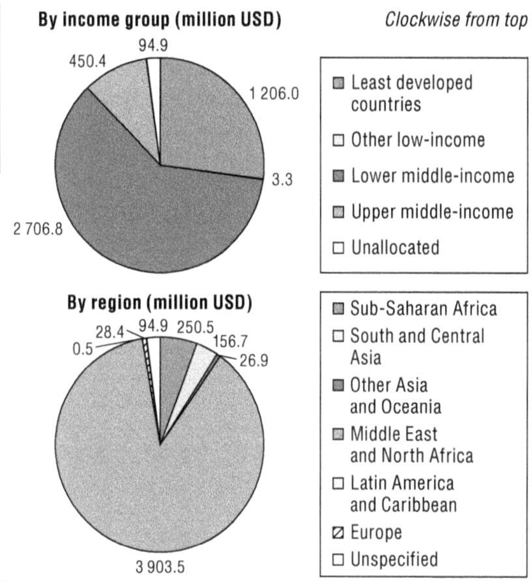

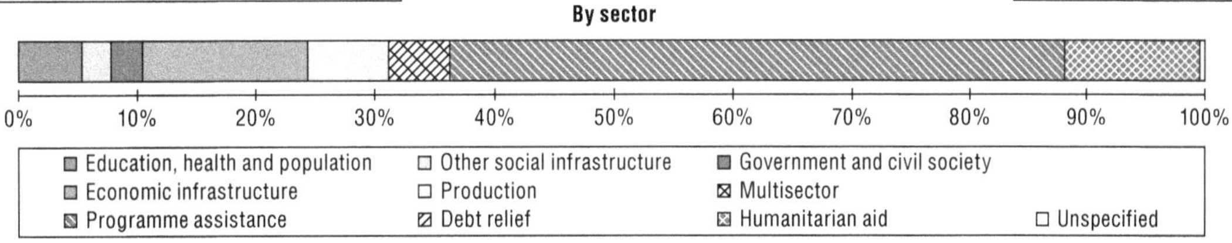

Source: OECD (2016j), "United Arab Emirates' official development assistance (ODA)", webpage, OECD, Paris, *www.oecd.org/dac/dac-global-relations/uae-official-development-assistance.htm.*

StatLink http://dx.doi.org/10.1787/888933482968

Overview of other providers that report to the OECD

In 2015, **Saudi Arabia**'s[8] development co-operation fell to USD 6.8 billion, representing a decrease in real terms of 45% since 2014.

Among the eight European Union member states that are not members of the DAC, Estonia and Latvia (OECD members), Lithuania (OECD accession country), and Romania (which reports at activity level) were discussed above. Four other European Union member states also report to the OECD: in 2015, **Bulgaria**'s ODA decreased by 7% in real terms over 2014, to reach USD 41 million, while **Malta**'s development co-operation fell to USD 17 million, a decrease of 10% in real terms. **Croatia**'s ODA reached USD 51 million in 2015, a decrease in real terms of 21% over 2014. The ODA of **Cyprus**[9, 10] reached USD 18 million in 2015, an increase of 9% in real terms over 2014. **Timor-Leste**'s development co-operation rose to USD 4.0 million, compared to USD 3.4 million in 2014. **Thailand** reported that its development co-operation decreased from USD 69 million in 2014 to USD 62 million in 2015. In 2015, **Chinese Taipei**'s development co-operation increased by 3% in real terms compared to 2014, reaching USD 255 million. **Liechtenstein**'s development co-operation decreased slightly, from USD 27 million in 2014 to USD 24 million in 2015. In 2014 – the latest year for which a GNI figure for Liechtenstein is available – its ODA/GNI ratio reached 0.50%, compared to 0.64% in 2013.

Non-reporting countries

A number of significant providers of development co-operation do not report their development finance flows to the OECD, although they are welcome to do so. A conservative estimate by the OECD indicates that total gross concessional development finance by these ten non-reporting countries amounted to USD 6.9 billion in 2015. Their development co-operation programmes are discussed below, and include two OECD member countries (Chile and Mexico), two OECD accession countries (Colombia and Costa Rica) and the OECD Key Partners (Brazil, China, India, Indonesia and South Africa). Like Azerbaijan, Kazakhstan, Thailand and Turkey, presented in the previous section, these countries have a dual role since they both receive and provide development co-operation. Estimates for Qatar, a DAC Participant, are also included.

Table 38.1. **Estimates of gross concessional flows for development co-operation, 2010-15**

Million USD

	2011	2012	2013	2014	2015	Source
Brazil[1]	469	411	316	..	..	Institute of Applied Economic Research (IPEA) and Brazilian Cooperation Agency (ABC)
Chile	24	38	44	49	33	Ministry of Finance
China (People's Republic of)	2 785	3 123	2 997	3 401	3 113	*Fiscal Yearbook*, Ministry of Finance
Colombia	22	27	42	45	42	Strategic institutional plans, Presidential Agency of International Cooperation
Costa Rica	..	..	21	24	10	Annual budget laws, Ministry of Finance
India[2]	794	1 077	1 223	1 398	1 772	Annual budget figures, Ministry of Finance
Indonesia	16	26	49	56	..	Ministry of National Development Planning
Mexico	99	203	526	169		Mexican Agency for International Development Cooperation (AMEXCID)
Qatar	733	543	1 344	..	..	Foreign aid reports, Ministry of Foreign Affairs
South Africa[2]	229	191	191	148	100	Estimates of public expenditures, National Treasury

Notes: These data are OECD estimates of concessional flows for development from countries that do not report to DAC statistical systems. Unlike the figures of reporting countries, these estimates are on a gross basis because information on repayments is not available.

Estimates are based on publically available information and are therefore not necessarily complete or comparable. For some countries, estimates on funds channelled through multilateral organisations are based on data from the UN Department of Economic and Social Affairs, *www.aidflows.org*; and websites of other multilateral organisations.

Data include only development-related contributions. This means local resources – financing from a country through multilateral organisations earmarked to programmes within that same country – are excluded. Moreover, as for reporting countries, coefficients are applied to core contributions to multilateral organisations that do not exclusively work in countries eligible for receiving ODA. These coefficients reflect the developmental part of the multilateral organisations' activities.

1. See note 11 at end of this chapter.
2. Figures for India and South Africa are based on their fiscal years. For example, 2012 data correspond to fiscal year 2012/13.

StatLink http://dx.doi.org/10.1787/888933483269

Brazil

Brazil is a South-South co-operation provider. The most recent available figures on Brazil's development co-operation programme are for 2013 (IPEA and ABC, 2016) and were published in 2016. The 2013 figure – a total of USD 397 million – includes activities that are not, or not entirely, included as development co-operation in DAC statistics (and may also exclude some development activities that would be included in DAC statistics).[11] The OECD estimates that Brazil's development co-operation amounted to USD 316 million in 2013 (Table 38.2), down from USD 411 million in 2012. Of these USD 316 million, 66%, or USD 208 million, were channelled through multilateral organisations. More recent estimates by the OECD suggest that Brazil channelled USD 96 million through multilateral organisations in 2015 (derived from the multilateral organisations' websites).

Table 38.2. **Estimated development-oriented contributions to and through multilateral organisations, 2015**

Current USD million

	Brazil	Chile	China (People's Republic of)	Colombia	Costa Rica	India	Indonesia	Mexico	Qatar	South Africa
Total United Nations	**54.3**	**11.4**	**206.6**	**13.2**	**2.1**	**59.3**	**14.2**	**50.0**	**64.3**	**18.7**
United Nations Organization (18%)	14.3	1.6	25.1	1.3	0.2	3.3	1.7	9.0	1.0	1.8
Food and Agriculture Organization (51%)	8.7	1.1	18.8	5.4	0.1	2.0	1.1	13.7	0.6	2.5
UN Educational, Scientific and Cultural Organization (60%)	6.0	3.3	18.5	0.0	0.2	5.0	1.0	5.9	1.8	1.1
World Health Organization (76%)	1.9	0.6	24.9	0.1	0.2	9.1	2.2	6.5	0.9	1.9
UN Department of Peacekeeping Operations (7%)	0.7	0.1	38.8	0.1	0.0	0.2	0.1	0.4	1.0	0.1
World Food Programme (100%)	7.2	0.3	10.5	1.4		1.4			1.3	
International Fund for Agricultural Development (100%)			7.0	0.2		13.0	3.6	1.7		
International Labour Organization (60%)	8.0	1.3	15.2	0.0	0.3	2.0	1.0	0.2	0.6	2.3
UN Industrial Development Organization (100%)		0.5	13.9	0.3		6.7	0.5	0.3	0.3	0.5
International Atomic Energy Agency (33%)		0.7	10.5	0.1	0.2	1.5	0.8	3.5	0.3	1.1
UN Development Programme (100%)	0.5	1.1	8.1	3.8	0.7	9.7	0.8	2.0	0.5	2.6
Other United Nations	6.9	0.7	15.4	0.5	0.1	5.5	1.4	6.7	56.0	4.6
Total regional development banks	**41.6**	**11.4**	**21.3**	**17.7**	**4.1**	**41.8**		**36.0**	**8.3**	**26.9**
Inter-American Development Bank (100%)	41.6	11.4		11.4	1.6			26.8		
African Development Bank (100%)			9.6			34.4				26.9
Islamic Development Bank (100%)			10.0						8.3	
Central American Bank for Economic Integration (100%)				5.4	2.5					
Asian Development Bank (100%)						7.5				
Caribbean Development Bank (100%)			1.8	0.9				9.2		
World Bank Group (total)					**3.0**	**65.5**				**12.3**
Other multilateral organisations			**5.0**		**0.7**	**21.7**				**22.9**
African Union (100%)										15.6
Global Environment Facility (100%)						2.9				
The Global Fund (100%)			5.0			4.3				
Southern African Development Community (100%)										4.0
Other organisations					0.7	14.6				3.4
Overall total	**95.9**	**22.8**	**232.9**	**30.9**	**9.9**	**188.3**	**14.2**	**86.0**	**72.7**	**80.8**

Notes: Data include only development-related contributions. DAC coefficients – the percentage of an organisation's core budget allocated to developmental purposes in developing countries (see first column in parenthesis) – are applied to core contributions. Lastly, local resources, financing from a country through multilateral organisations destined to programmes within that same country, are excluded.
The information in this table is mainly based on data from the UN Department of Economic and Social Affairs (DESA), *www.aidflows.org*; and websites of other multilateral organisations and national publications of the countries involved. Not all data on contributions to multilateral organisations are made publicly available, so the presented information may not be complete.

StatLink http://dx.doi.org/10.1787/888933483271

The Ministry of External Relations oversees Brazil's development co-operation, while the Brazilian Cooperation Agency provides technical co-operation. Apart from technical co-operation, Brazil's bilateral co-operation includes humanitarian assistance, scientific and technological co-operation, scholarships and imputed student costs, and refugee costs.

Brazil is also engaged in triangular co-operation, partnering with several international organisations (e.g. the United Nations Development Programme; the Food and Agriculture Organization of the United Nations; the World Food Programme; the International Labour Organization; the United Nations Office on Drugs and Crime; and the United Nations Educational, Scientific and Cultural Organization and DAC members (e.g. Germany, Japan, Spain and the United States). These programmes support developing countries (e.g. South American countries, Lusophone African countries, Haiti and Timor-Leste) in areas such as agriculture, food security, health and public administration.

Brazil's development co-operation to multilateral organisations was primarily channelled through the United Nations (57%) in 2015 and the Inter-American Development Bank (43%).

Brazil is a Key Partner of the OECD. In 2016, Brazil participated in the DAC senior-level and high-level meetings as well as meetings of the DAC subsidiary bodies: the Advisory Group on Investment and Development and the Working Party on Development Finance Statistics.

Chile

Chile's total concessional finance for development reached USD 33 million in 2015 compared to USD 49 million in 2014 (OECD estimates based on Government of Chile, 2015, 2014; and websites of multilateral organisations). In 2015, Chile channelled USD 22.8 million through multilateral organisations.

In 2015, the Chilean Agency for International Co-operation was renamed the Chilean Agency for International Co-operation and Development (AGCID) to emphasise its developmental focus. Chile released a policy in 2015 that sets out its vision to 2030 based on the following principles: 1) promoting people's dignity; 2) strengthening democracy; 3) promoting peace; 4) strengthening the role of Latin America and the Caribbean in global governance; and 5) supporting regional integration and convergence in Latin America and the Caribbean. This vision is being implemented through a strategy for 2015-18 that emphasises promoting inclusive and sustainable development, the need for strong partnerships, and the importance of consolidating Chile's national system for international co-operation, including a stronger role for AGCID. The agency manages and co-ordinates incoming and outgoing bilateral, triangular and regional development co-operation.

Chile's priority partner countries are primarily in Latin America and the Caribbean. Its co-operation programme is spread across a range of sectors, including governance and institutional strengthening; poverty reduction and social development; and support to industry, innovation and competitiveness. Chile's bilateral co-operation is mostly provided in the form of technical assistance and scholarships.

Chile is also engaged in triangular co-operation, partnering with several international organisations (e.g. the Inter-American Development Bank and the World Food Programme), Mexico and DAC members (e.g. Australia, Canada, France, Germany, Korea, Japan, New Zealand, Spain, Switzerland and the United States) to support development in other developing countries (e.g. Bolivia, Colombia, the Dominican Republic, Ecuador, El Salvador, Guatemala and Paraguay).

Chile's development co-operation through multilateral organisations was primarily channelled through the United Nations (50%) and the Inter-American Development Bank (50%) in 2015.

Chile, which joined the OECD in 2010, is an observer to the DAC. In 2016, Chile participated in the meetings of the DAC, including its high-level and senior-level meetings, as well as a meeting of the DAC Working Party on Development Finance Statistics. Chile hosted the first LAC-DAC Dialogue on Development Co-operation in Santiago in June 2016 which it co-chaired with Mexico.

China (People's Republic of)

China's total concessional finance for development reached USD 3.1 billion in 2015, compared to USD 3.4 billion in 2014 (OECD estimates based on Government of China, 2015; and websites of multilateral organisations). In 2015, China channelled USD 233 million through multilateral organisations. The second *White Paper on China's Foreign Aid* includes information on the overall geographical and sectoral distribution of the Chinese programme between 2010 and 2012 (Government of China, 2014).

China's Eight Principles for Economic Aid and Technical Assistance to Other Countries, announced by Premier Zhou Enlai in 1964, set out the core principles of China's foreign development co-operation (Government of China, 1964). The Ministry of Commerce's Department of Foreign Assistance is at the centre of the Chinese system and manages over 90% of its bilateral funding. It is responsible for drafting the development co-operation budget and regulations, managing foreign development co-operation joint ventures, programming zero-interest loans and grants, and co-ordinating concessional loans with the China Exim Bank (the latter are not included in OECD estimates because little information is available on their objectives or financial terms).

China does not have specific priority countries (aside from the Democratic People's Republic of Korea). Its grant aid is distributed more or less equally to some 120 partner countries. The main sectors are public facilities, industry and economic infrastructure. China offers eight different forms of co-operation with complete projects (turn-key projects) being the major modality. China also provides humanitarian assistance.

China engages in triangular co-operation, partnering with several international organisations (e.g. the United Nations Development Programme, the United Nations Industrial Development Organization and the World Bank) and DAC members (e.g. the Netherlands, New Zealand, the United Kingdom and the United States).

China's development co-operation through multilateral organisations was primarily channelled through the United Nations (89%) and the regional development banks (9%). China is also a founding member of the new Asian Infrastructure Investment Bank, a multilateral development bank with its headquarters in China.

China is a Key Partner of the OECD. In 2016, China participated in the DAC high-level and senior-level meeting and a meeting of the DAC Working Party on Development Finance Statistics (WP-STAT).

Colombia

Colombia's total concessional finance for development reached USD 42 million in 2015, compared to USD 45 million in 2014 (OECD estimates based on Government of Colombia, 2014, 2015; and websites of multilateral organisations). In 2015, Colombia channelled USD 30.9 million in development-orientated contributions through multilateral organisations and USD 10.8 million through South-South co-operation programmes and initiatives.

The Colombian Presidential Agency of International Co-operation (APC-Colombia), created in 2011, sets priorities and ensures alignment of Colombia's development co-operation with its National Development Plan and foreign policy. The agency manages and co-ordinates Colombia's incoming and outgoing development co-operation and, through the Roadmap for International Co-operation, sets out Colombia's strengths and good practices that can be shared with other countries. It has also introduced a national co-ordination scheme as well as monitoring systems.

Through its South-South co-operation, Colombia shares its knowledge and experience in areas such as entrepreneurship, security, food security, culture, agricultural innovation, social development, climate change and disaster risk management, tourism, statistics, and employment. Seventy-four countries in Latin America and the Caribbean, Africa, Asia, and the Middle East benefited from Colombian programmes and policies in support of their own development efforts in 2015. In addition, Colombia is an active partner in developing projects in regional mechanisms such as the Pacific Alliance, the Ibero-American General Secretariat and the Forum for East Asia-Latin America Cooperation.

Colombia is also engaged in triangular co-operation, partnering with several international organisations (e.g. the United Nations Population Fund and the Organization of American States) and DAC members (e.g. Australia, Canada, Germany, Japan, Korea and the United States) to support other developing countries – mainly in Central America and the Caribbean – in a wide range of areas.

In 2015, Colombia's development-oriented contributions through multilateral organisations were channelled through the United Nations (43%), the Inter-American Development Bank (37%) and the Central American Bank for Economic Integration (17%).

In 2016, Colombia, an OECD accession country, participated in the DAC senior-level and high-level meetings as well as meetings of several DAC subsidiary bodies: the Advisory Group on Investment and Development and the Working Party on Development Finance Statistics.

Costa Rica

Costa Rica's total concessional finance for development reached USD 10 million in 2015, compared to USD 24 million in 2014 (OECD estimates based on Government of Costa Rica, 2014, 2015; and websites of multilateral organisations). In 2014, Costa Rica channelled USD 10 million through multilateral organisations.[12]

The Directorate General for International Co-operation of the Ministry of Foreign Affairs manages Costa Rica's incoming and outgoing development co-operation. Fundecooperación para el Desarrollo Sostenible is a non-governmental organisation that is in charge of monitoring and administering the Programme of South-South Cooperation on Sustainable Development with Benin, Bhutan and Costa Rica as well as some triangular co-operation projects. It also acts as a platform for alliances among the government, civil society, academia and private stakeholders.

Costa Rica mainly provides development co-operation in the form of technical co-operation through bilateral and regional initiatives. Spain has a triangular co-operation fund to support Costa Rica in its triangular co-operation projects with other Central American and Caribbean countries (e.g. El Salvador, Guatemala and Honduras) in areas such as social cohesion, competitiveness and production, and participative democracy. Costa Rica also participates in projects of the German regional fund for the promotion of triangular co-operation in Latin America and the Caribbean.

In 2015, Costa Rica's multilateral development co-operation was primarily channelled through the International Development Association (30%) and the Central American Bank for Economic Integration (25%).

India

India's total concessional development finance reached USD 1.8 billion in 2015, compared to USD 1.4 billion in 2014 (OECD estimates based on Government of India, 2015a, 2015b). India channelled USD 106 million (6% of its concessional development finance) through multilateral organisations in 2015, compared to USD 141 million in 2014.

The Development Partnership Administration within the Ministry of External Affairs co-ordinates India's bilateral development co-operation. It manages grants and the Indian Technical & Economic Cooperation Programme. The Ministry of Finance manages multilateral assistance and exercises administrative oversight over the concessional loans and lines of credit provided by the Exim Bank.

India's priority partner countries are its neighbours in South Asia. Between 2009 and 2015, Bhutan received 61% of India's bilateral development co-operation, followed by Afghanistan (9%), Sri Lanka (7%), Nepal (5%), Bangladesh (3%), Myanmar (2%) and the Maldives (2%). Recently, co-operation with Africa has increased. The main sectors of India's development co-operation are health, education, energy (hydropower) and information technology.

In 2015, India's multilateral flows were primarily channelled through the International Development Association (35%), as well as through the United Nations (31%).

India is a Key Partner of the OECD. The DAC Chair visited India in March 2016 to speak at the "Conference on South-South Co-operation: Issues and Emerging Challenges", organised by the Research and Information System for Developing Countries with the support of the Indian Ministry of External Affairs.

Indonesia

Indonesia's total development co-operation reached USD 56 million in 2014, compared to USD 49 million in 2013 (OECD estimates).[13]

Several government regulations, national plans and presidential instructions guide Indonesia's development co-operation. The National Development Planning Agency (BAPPENAS) is responsible for developing and co-ordinating Indonesia's national strategy for development co-operation. Together with the Ministry of Foreign Affairs, the Ministry of Finance and the State Secretariat, BAPPENAS constitutes the National Coordination Team on South-South and Triangular Cooperation.

Indonesia co-operates bilaterally with around 40 partner countries, most of them in Asia, in a variety of sectors. Bilateral co-operation consists mainly of scholarships and technical co-operation projects.

Indonesia is also engaged in triangular co-operation, partnering with several international organisations and DAC members such as Germany, Japan, Norway, the United States and others.

According to OECD estimates, in 2015 Indonesia channelled all of its multilateral development co-operation through the United Nations.

Indonesia is a Key Partner of the OECD; in 2016 it participated in the DAC high-level and senior-level meetings.

Mexico

In 2016, Mexico published figures on its development co-operation programme for 2014 (Government of Mexico, 2016); these are the most recent consolidated figures available on Mexico's development co-operation.[14] According to these figures, Mexico's international development co-operation reached USD 288 million in 2014, down from USD 396 million in 2013 (Government of Mexico, 2016). Out of the total disbursed in 2014, the OECD estimates that at least USD 169 million would count as development co-operation in DAC statistics. Mexico channelled 63% of the USD 168 million through multilateral organisations in 2014 (OECD estimates based on Government of Mexico, 2016; and websites of multilateral organisations). More recent estimates by the OECD suggest that Mexico channelled USD 86 million through multilateral organisations in 2015.

The Law on International Co-operation for Development (2011) mandated the government to set up the International Development Co-operation Program and the Mexican Agency of International Development Cooperation (AMEXCID), as well as the tools necessary to programme, co-ordinate, implement, monitor, report and evaluate development co-operation. The Ministry of Foreign Affairs has overall responsibility for Mexico's development co-operation, which is co-ordinated by AMEXCID and implemented through public institutions.

Mexico's priority partner countries are those in Latin America and the Caribbean, with a special focus on Central America. The priority sectors for its bilateral development co-operation are public administration, agriculture, environmental protection, statistics, education, science and technology, and health. Mexico's bilateral development co-operation is provided mainly through technical and scientific co-operation provided by civil servants who are experts in the topic. The main mechanism for regional co-operation is the Mesoamerican Integration and Development Project that covers initiatives in public health, environmental sustainability, risk management, food security, trade facilitation, transport, energy and telecommunications. Based on the experience in Mesoamerica, Mexico has also launched other regional initiatives in the Caribbean and the Northern Triangle, for example in immigration. Mexico also financed infrastructure development in the region through the "Yucatán Fund".

Mexico is engaged in triangular co-operation, partnering with DAC members (e.g. Germany, Japan and Spain), Chile and several international organisations (e.g. the Inter-American Institute for Cooperation on Agriculture, the United Nations Children's Fund [UNICEF], the United Nations Development Programme and the World Trade Organization) to support other developing countries, mainly in Latin America and the Caribbean. Mexico is also developing co-operation mechanisms with other partners, such as civil society, the private sector and foundations.

Mexico's development co-operation through multilateral organisations in 2015 was primarily channelled through the United Nations (60%) and the Inter-American Development Bank (30%).

Mexico, which joined the OECD in 1994, is an observer to the DAC. In 2016, Mexico participated in the meetings of the DAC, including its high-level and senior-level meetings, as well as meetings of some DAC subsidiary bodies: the Advisory Group on Investment and Development, the Network on Gender Equality, the Network on Development Evaluation (EvalNet) and the Working Party on Development Finance Statistics. Together with Chile, Mexico co-chaired the first LAC-DAC Dialogue on Development Co-operation that took place in Santiago in 2016. Mexico also reported statistics on its triangular co-operation activities to the OECD in 2016.

Qatar

The latest foreign aid report published by Qatar covers 2013 (Government of Qatar, 2014). Based on that report, the OECD estimates that Qatar's development co-operation amounted to USD 1.3 billion in 2013, up from USD 543 million in 2012. More recent estimates by the OECD suggest that Qatar channelled USD 72.7 million through multilateral organisations in 2015, mainly through the United Nations (90%) and the Islamic Development Bank (10%) (websites of multilateral organisations).

Qatar views development co-operation as an integral part of its foreign policy. The Office of the Minister's Assistant for International Cooperation Affairs in the Ministry of Foreign Affairs is responsible for development co-operation and humanitarian assistance, although most other ministries and governmental agencies can also work on development co-operation. The Qatar Development Fund is a public organisation established through Law 19 of 2002 mandated to co-ordinate and implement foreign development assistance on behalf of the state of Qatar.

In 2013, the main recipients of Qatari development co-operation were Syria, Morocco, West Bank and Gaza Strip, Egypt, and Yemen. The main sectors were humanitarian aid, construction, and multi sectoral and budget support.

In 2016, Qatar became a Participant of the DAC and since then has participated in the DAC senior-level meeting and meetings of the Working Party on Development Finance Statistics. The OECD hosted a visit from officials from the Qatari Authority for Charitable Activities.

South Africa

South Africa's total concessional finance for development reached USD 100 million in 2015, compared to USD 148 million in 2014 (OECD estimates based on Government of South Africa, 2016; and websites of multilateral organisations). In 2015, South Africa channelled USD 80.4 million through multilateral organisations. Beyond development co-operation, South Africa uses several other development finance instruments, including loan and equity investments provided by the Development Bank of Southern Africa and the Industrial Development Corporation, as well as payments to the Southern African Customs Union and expenditure in the area of peace and security.

The Strategic Plan 2015-20 (Government of South Africa, 2015) of South Africa's Department of International Relations and Cooperation (DIRCO) emphasises co-operation with "the African continent" and "strengthening South-South relations". DIRCO is responsible for strategy and foreign policy formulation, and other line ministries are involved in the implementation of development co-operation projects. The National Treasury has a co-ordinating function in terms of managing incoming ODA and funds for outgoing development co-operation. DIRCO and the National Treasury are on the advisory committee of the African Renaissance and International Cooperation Fund (ARF). All South African departments are eligible to apply for ARF funding for development co-operation projects. South Africa's development co-operation structures may change when the South African Development Partnership Agency becomes operational under the Department of International Relations and Cooperation.

South Africa prioritises co-operation with the African continent, with a strong focus on member countries of the Southern African Development Community. The priority sectors of its bilateral development co-operation are peace, security, post-conflict reconstruction, regional integration, governance and humanitarian assistance. South Africa provides its bilateral development co-operation mostly in the form of technical co-operation.

South Africa is also engaged in triangular co-operation, partnering with several DAC members (e.g. Canada, Germany, Norway, Spain, Sweden and the United States) to support other African countries in areas such as governance, public security and post-conflict reconstruction.

In 2015, South Africa's development co-operation through multilateral organisations was primarily channelled through regional organisations such as the African Development Bank (33%) and the United Nations (23%).

South Africa is a Key Partner of the OECD and in 2016 participated in the DAC senior-level and high-level meetings and the meeting of the DAC Working Party on Development Finance Statistics.

Private development flows

Private philanthropy is contributing substantially to the reshaping of the development landscape. This is particularly relevant in the context of the 2030 Agenda, which emphasises private philanthropy's role in advancing the Sustainable Development Goals (SDGs), as pointed out in the Addis Ababa Action Agenda on Financing for Development. At present, the Bill & Melinda Gates Foundation is the only private entity reporting to the OECD on its development-related grants and programme-related investments. Disbursements by the Gates Foundation in 2015 were higher than in 2014, at USD 3.2 billion. Two-thirds of its geographically allocated grants target African countries, directly or indirectly.

In 2015, 78% of the Gates Foundation's sector-allocable disbursements were extended to the health sector (including reproductive health). These exclude core contributions of USD 245 million to multilateral organisations working in the health sector. The Gates Foundation was the fourth-largest international source of funds for health after the United States; the Global Fund for Fighting AIDS, Tuberculosis and Malaria; and the United Kingdom. The Gates Foundation channelled a significant part of its expenditures through NGOs from both partner and provider countries, international NGOs, multilateral agencies, universities and other teaching or research institutes. The World Health Organization, UNICEF and the Gavi Alliance are the main institutions with which the foundation collaborated.

During 2016-17, the OECD carried out a large-scale Survey on Global Private Philanthropy for Development, with the objective of collecting activity-level data and detailed information from major philanthropic foundations active in development co-operation. Data collected at the time of publishing show that private philanthropy provided between 2013 and 2015 reached USD 21.3 billion for development, mainly for health and reproductive health (55%), agriculture (9%), and education (8%). Of the funds that are geographically allocable, the activities mainly benefited Africa (54%), Asia (29%) and America (14%). The results of this exercise (foreseen to be published in 2018) will update and expand on private development flows.

Notes

1. The DAC encourages bilateral providers of development co-operation that fulfil the DAC accession criteria to apply to join the Committee as a member (in the case of OECD countries) or as an associate (in the case of other countries), independent of whether they receive official development assistance. The DAC is open to countries that: 1) have appropriate strategies, policies and institutional frameworks for development co-operation; 2) have an accepted measure of effort in providing development co-operation; and 3) have a system of performance monitoring and evaluation.
2. See: *www.oecd.org/dac/dac-global-relations/non-dac-reporting.htm*.
3. As a Participant, the UAE can attend DAC meetings, contribute to DAC activities and adhere to DAC recommendations on a voluntary basis, without being a full member of the committee.
4. As a Participant, Qatar can attend DAC meetings, contribute to DAC activities and adhere to DAC recommendations on a voluntary basis, without being a full member of the committee.
5. An Invitee may be invited, on a case-by-case basis, to participate in formal meetings of the DAC or its subsidiary bodies. An Invitee may take part in discussions but does not take part in decision-making processes, nor is it bound by the DAC's conclusions, proposals or decisions.
6. The members of the Commonwealth of Independent States are Armenia, Azerbaijan, Belarus, Kazakhstan, Kyrgyzstan, Moldova, the Russian Federation, Tajikistan and Uzbekistan.
7. For more information on this target, see: *www.oecd.org/dac/stats/ODA-history-of-the-0-7-target.pdf*.
8. Saudi Arabia's reporting to the OECD on its development co-operation programme consists of aggregate figures on humanitarian and development assistance by region, multilateral aid, and loan disbursements and repayments by the Saudi Fund for Development.
9. Footnote by Turkey: The information in this document with reference to "Cyprus" relates to the southern part of the Island. There is no single authority representing both Turkish and Greek Cypriot people on the Island. Turkey recognises the Turkish Republic of Northern Cyprus (TRNC). Until a lasting and equitable solution is found within the context of the United Nations, Turkey shall preserve its position concerning the "Cyprus issue".
10. Footnote by all the European Union Member States of the OECD and the European Union: The Republic of Cyprus is recognised by all members of the United Nations with the exception of Turkey. The information in this document relates to the area under the effective control of the Government of the Republic of Cyprus.
11. Brazil's development co-operation is significantly higher according to the official figures published by the Brazilian government. The OECD uses these data but, for the purposes of this analysis, only includes in its estimates: 1) activities in low and middle-income countries; and 2) contributions to multilateral agencies whose main aim is promoting the economic development and welfare of developing countries (or a percentage of these contributions when a multilateral agency does not work exclusively on developmental activities in

developing countries). The OECD also excludes bilateral peacekeeping activities. Brazil's official data may exclude some activities that would be included as development co-operation in DAC statistics, and so are also excluded from the OECD estimates that are based on Brazil's own data.

12. The difference between the estimations for 2014 and 2015 is due to an adjustment in the OECD's estimations of Costa Rica's contributions to multilateral organisations. Estimations for 2015 are based on additional information received from the Treasury of the government of Costa Rica.
13. Aggregate figures reported by the government of Indonesia to the OECD indicate that Indonesia's development co-operation reached USD 49 million in 2013 and USD 56 million in 2014, although no detailed information was provided.
14. Since the approval of the Mexican Law on International Development Cooperation in 2011, Mexico has started collecting data on an annual basis on development co-operation activities by federal institutions. In 2014, the Mexican Agency for International Development Cooperation launched the National Registry of International Development Cooperation and improved the methodological work to define its own directives for quantifying its development co-operation.

References

Government of Chile (2015), *Informe de ejecución trimestral periodo 2015* (in Spanish), Ministry of Finance, Santiago, *www.dipres.gob.cl/595/articles-141941_doc_pdf.pdf* (accessed 11 April 2017).

Government of Chile (2014), *Informe de ejecución trimestral periodo 2014* (in Spanish), Ministry of Finance, Santiago, *www.dipres.gob.cl/595/articles-128121_doc_pdf.pdf* (accessed 7 March 2016).

Government of China (2015), "The central level expenditure budget table 2015" (in Chinese), Ministry of Finance of the People's Republic of China website, Beijing, *http://yss.mof.gov.cn/2016czys/201603/t20160325_1924491.html* (accessed 14 April 2017).

Government of China (2014), *China's Foreign Aid*, White Paper, Information Office of the State Council of the People's Republic of China, Beijing, *http://news.xinhuanet.com/english/china/2014-07/10/c_133474011.htm* (accessed 6 March 2015).

Government of China (1964), *China's Eight Principles for Economic Aid and Technical Assistance to Other Countries*, Government of China, Beijing, *http://english1.english.gov.cn/official/2011-04/21/content_1849913_10.htm*.

Government of Colombia (2015), *Informe de gestión 2015* (in Spanish), Presidential Agency of International Cooperation, Bogota, *www.apccolombia.gov.co/sites/default/files/archivos_usuario/2016/07/informe-de-gestion-apc-colombia-2015_0.pdf* (accessed 28 March 2017).

Government of Colombia (2014), *Plan estratégico institucional y plan de acción annual* (in Spanish), Presidential Agency of International Cooperation, Bogota.

Government of Costa Rica (2015), *Budget Law 2015* (in Spanish), Ministry of Finance, San José, *www.hacienda.go.cr/docs/55255f1966c39_LeyActMarzo_204.pdf* (accessed 7 March 2016).

Government of Costa Rica (2014), *Budget Law 2014* (in Spanish), Ministry of Finance, San José, *www.hacienda.go.cr/docs/529f42a24b3e0_Ley2014_Tit204.pdf* (accessed 7 March 2016).

Government of India (2015a), "Grants and loans to foreign governments 2015-2016", *Expenditure Budget Vol. 1*, Ministry of External Affairs, New Delhi, *http://indiabudget.nic.in/ub2015-16/eb/stat11.pdf* (accessed 7 March 2016).

Government of India (2015b), "Contributions to international bodies 2015-2016", *Expenditure Budget Vol. 1*, Ministry of External Affairs, New Delhi, *http://indiabudget.nic.in/ub2015-16/eb/cont.pdf* (accessed 7 March 2016).

Government of Mexico (2016), "Cooperación internacional para el desarrollo otorgada por México en 2014" (in Spanish), website, Mexican Agency for International Development Cooperation, *www.gob.mx/amexcid/acciones-y-programas/cuantificacion-de-la-cooperacion-mexicana* (accessed 5 December 2016).

Government of Qatar (2014), *Foreign Aid Report 2013*, Ministry of Foreign Affairs, Doha.

Government of South Africa (2016), *Annual Report 2015/16 Financial Year. Vote 6: Department of International Relations and Cooperation*, *www.dirco.gov.za/department/report_2015_2016/annual_report%202015_2016.pdf* (accessed 2 May 2017).

Government of South Africa (2015), *Strategic Plan 2015-2020*, Department of International Relations and Cooperation, Pretoria, *www.dfa.gov.za/department/strategic_plan_2015_2018/strategic_plan2015_2020.pdf* (accessed 7 March 2016).

Government of the United Arab Emirates (2016), "Promoting global prosperity and peace: UAE policy for foreign assistance 2021-17", Ministry of Foreign Affairs and International Cooperation, Abu Dhabi.

IPEA and ABC (2016), *Cooperação Brasileira para o Desenvolvimento Internacional 2011-2013* (in Portuguese), Instituto de Pesquisa Econômica Aplicada and Agência Brasileira de Cooperação, Brasilia, *www.ipea.gov.br/portal/images/stories/PDFs/livros/livros/161017_livro_cobradi_2011_2013.pdf* (accessed 2 December 2016).

OECD (2016a), "The DAC global relations strategy", OECD, Paris, *www.oecd.org/dac/dac-global-relations/DCD-DAC(2016)28_FINAL_DAC_Global_Relations_Strategy%20(3).pdf* (accessed 25 April 2017).

OECD (2016b), "DAC Survey on Global Private Philanthropy for Development", OECD, Paris, *www.oecd.org/dac/stats/beyond-oda-foundations.htm* (accessed 16 April 2017).

OECD (2016c), "Azerbaijan's official development assistance (ODA)", webpage, OECD, Paris, *www.oecd.org/dac/dac-global-relations/azerbaijan-official-development-assistance.htm* (accessed 10 May 2017).

OECD (2016d), "Estonia's official development assistance (ODA)", webpage, OECD, Paris, *www.oecd.org/dac/dac-global-relations/estonias-official-development-assistance.htm* (accessed 16 April 2017).

OECD (2016e), "Kazakhstan's official development assistance (ODA)", webpage, OECD, Paris, *www.oecd.org/dac/dac-global-relations/kazakhstan-official-development-assistance.htm* (accessed 16 April 2017).

OECD (2016f), "Kuwait's official development assistance (ODA)",webpage, OECD, Paris, *www.oecd.org/dac/dac-global-relations/kuwaits-official-development-assistance.htm* (accessed 16 April 2017).

OECD (2016g), "Lithuania's official development assistance (ODA)", webpage, OECD, Paris, *www.oecd.org/dac/dac-global-relations/lithuania-official-development-assistance.htm* (accessed 16 April 2017).

OECD (2016h), "Romania's official development assistance (ODA)", webpage, OECD, Paris, *www.oecd.org/dac/dac-global-relations/romania-official-development-assistance.htm* (accessed 16 April 2017).

OECD (2016i), "Turkey's official development assistance (ODA)", webpage, OECD, Paris, *www.oecd.org/dac/dac-global-relations/turkeys-official-development-assistanceoda.htm* (accessed 16 April 2017).

OECD (2016j), "United Arab Emirates' official development assistance (ODA)", webpage, OECD, Paris, *www.oecd.org/dac/dac-global-relations/uae-official-development-assistance.htm* (accessed 16 April 2017).

Further reading

Benn, J. and W. Luijkx (2017), "Emerging providers' international co-operation for development", *OECD Development Co-operation Working Papers*, No. 33, OECD Publishing, Paris, *http://dx.doi.org/10.1787/15d6a3c7-en.*

Government of Mexico (2015), "Cooperación internacional para el desarrollo otorgada por México en 2013" (in Spanish), website, Mexican Agency for International Development Cooperation, *https://infoamexcid.sre.gob.mx/amexcid/ccid2013/index.html* (accessed 5 February 2016).

OECD (2015), "Development co-operation by countries beyond the DAC", OECD, Paris, *www.oecd.org/dac/dac-global-relations/Development%20Co-operation%20by%20Countries%20beyond%20the%20DAC.pdf.*

OECD (2014), "Non-DAC countries and the debate on measuring post-2015 development finance", OECD, Paris, *www.oecd.org/dac/financing-sustainable-development/DCD-DAC(2014)6-ENG.pdf.*

ANNEX A

Technical notes on definitions and measurement

The coverage of the data presented in the *Development Co-operation Report* has changed in recent years. The main points are as follows.

Changes in the concept of official development assistance and the coverage of gross national income

While the definition of official development assistance (ODA) has not changed since 1972, some changes in interpretation have tended to broaden the scope of the concept. The main changes are: the recording of administrative costs as ODA (from 1979), the imputation as ODA of the share of subsidies to educational systems representing the cost of educating students from aid recipient countries (first specifically identified in 1984), and the inclusion of assistance provided by donor countries in the first year after the arrival of a refugee from an aid recipient country (eligible to be reported as of the early 1980s but only widely used since 1991).

Precise quantification of the effects of these changes is difficult because changes in data collection methodology and coverage are often not directly apparent from members' statistical returns. The amounts involved can, however, be substantial. For example, reporting by Canada in 1993 included for the first time a figure for in-Canada refugee support. The amount involved (USD 184 million) represented almost 8% of total Canadian ODA. Aid flows reported by Australia in the late 1980s have been estimated to be approximately 12% higher than had they been calculated according to the rules and procedures that applied 15 years earlier (Scott, 1989).

The coverage of national income has also been expanding through the inclusion of new areas of economic activity and the improvement of collection methods. The 1993 System of National Accounts (SNA) broadened the coverage of gross national product, renaming it gross national income (GNI). The new SNA 2008,[1] which is gradually being implemented by members, tends to increase GNI, which, in turn, will lower ODA/GNI ratios for some countries.

Recipient country coverage

Since 1990, the following entities were added to the DAC List of ODA Recipients at the dates shown: the Black Communities of South Africa (1991; now listed as South Africa); Kazakhstan, Kyrgyzstan, Tajikistan, Turkmenistan and Uzbekistan (1992); Armenia, Azerbaijan and Georgia (1993); Palestinian Administered Areas (1994; now listed as West Bank and Gaza Strip); Moldova (1997); Belarus, Libya and Ukraine (2005); Kosovo (2009); South Sudan (2011).

Over the same period, the following countries and territories were removed from the DAC List of ODA Recipients at the dates shown: Portugal (1991); French Guyana, Guadeloupe, Martinique, Réunion, and St. Pierre and Miquelon (1992); Greece (1994); Bahamas, Brunei, Kuwait, Qatar, Singapore and the United Arab Emirates (1996); Bermuda, Cayman Islands, Cyprus, Falkland Islands, Hong Kong (China), Israel and Chinese Taipei (1997); Aruba, the British Virgin Islands, French Polynesia, Gibraltar, Korea, Libya, Macao, the Netherlands Antilles, New Caledonia and the Northern Marianas (2000); Malta and Slovenia (2003); Bahrain (2005); Saudi Arabia, and Turks and Caicos Islands (2008); Barbados, Croatia, Mayotte, Oman, and Trinidad and Tobago (2011); Anguilla, and Saint Kitts and Nevis (2014).

From 1993 to 2004, several Central and Eastern European Countries (CEEC)/New Independent States (NIS) countries in transition and more advanced developing countries were included on a separate list of recipients of official aid. This list has now been abolished.

Donor country coverage

Portugal, one of the founding members of the Development Assistance Committee (DAC) in 1961, withdrew from the DAC in 1974 and re-joined in 1991. Spain joined the DAC in 1991; Luxembourg in 1992; Greece in 1999; Korea in 2010; and the Czech Republic, Iceland, Poland, the Slovak Republic and Slovenia joined in 2013.[2] Their assistance is now counted within the DAC total. ODA flows from these countries before they joined the DAC have been added to earlier years' data where available. The accession of new members has added to total DAC ODA, but has usually reduced the overall ODA/GNI ratio, since their programmes are often smaller in relation to GNI than those of the longer established donors.

Treatment of debt forgiveness

The treatment of the forgiveness of loans not originally reported as ODA varied in earlier years. Up to and including 1992, where forgiveness of non-ODA debt met the tests of ODA, it was reportable as ODA. From 1990 to 1992 inclusive, it remained reportable as part of a country's ODA but was excluded from the DAC total. The amounts treated as such are shown in Table A.2. From 1993, forgiveness of debt originally intended for military purposes has been reportable as other official flows, whereas forgiveness of other non-ODA loans (mainly export credits) recorded as ODA is included both in country data and in total DAC ODA in the same way as it was until 1989.

The forgiveness of outstanding loan principal originally reported as ODA does not give rise to a new net disbursement of ODA. Statistically, the benefit is reflected in the fact that because the cancelled repayments will not take place, net ODA disbursements will not be reduced.

Reporting year

All data in this publication refer to calendar years, unless otherwise stated.

Table A.1. **DAC List of ODA Recipients**

Effective for reporting on 2014, 2015 and 2016 flows

Least developed countries	Other low-income countries (per capita GNI ≤ USD 1 045 in 2013)	Lower middle-income countries and territories (per capita GNI USD 1 046-USD 4 125 in 2013)	Upper middle-income countries and territories (per capita GNI USD 4 126-USD 12 745 in 2013)
Afghanistan	Democratic People's Republic of Korea	Armenia	Albania
Angola	Kenya	Bolivia	Algeria
Bangladesh	Tajikistan	Cabo Verde	Antigua and Barbuda
Benin	Zimbabwe	Cameroon	Argentina
Bhutan		Congo	Azerbaijan
Burkina Faso		Côte d'Ivoire	Belarus
Burundi		Egypt	Belize
Cambodia		El Salvador	Bosnia and Herzegovina
Central African Republic		Georgia	Botswana
Chad		Ghana	Brazil
Comoros		Guatemala	Chile
Democratic Republic of the Congo		Guyana	China (People's Republic of)
Djibouti		Honduras	Colombia
Equatorial Guinea		India	Cook Islands
Eritrea		Indonesia	Costa Rica
Ethiopia		Kosovo	Cuba
Gambia		Kyrgyzstan	Dominica
Guinea		Micronesia	Dominican Republic
Guinea-Bissau		Moldova	Ecuador
Haiti		Mongolia	Fiji
Kiribati		Morocco	Former Yugoslav Republic of Macedonia
Lao People's Democratic Republic		Nicaragua	Gabon
Lesotho		Nigeria	Grenada
Liberia		Pakistan	Iran
Madagascar		Papua New Guinea	Iraq
Malawi		Paraguay	Jamaica
Mali		Philippines	Jordan
Mauritania		Samoa	Kazakhstan
Mozambique		Sri Lanka	Lebanon
Myanmar		Swaziland	Libya
Nepal		Syrian Arab Republic	Malaysia
Niger		Tokelau	Maldives
Rwanda		Ukraine	Marshall Islands
Sao Tome and Principe		Uzbekistan	Mauritius
Senegal		Viet Nam	Mexico
Sierra Leone		West Bank and Gaza Strip	Montenegro
Solomon Islands			Montserrat
Somalia			Namibia
South Sudan			Nauru
Sudan			Niue
Tanzania			Palau
Timor-Leste			Panama
Togo			Peru
Tuvalu			Saint Helena
Uganda			Saint Lucia
Vanuatu			Saint Vincent and the Grenadines
Yemen			Serbia
Zambia			Seychelles
			South Africa
			Suriname
			Thailand
			Tonga
			Tunisia
			Turkey
			Turkmenistan
			Uruguay
			Venezuela
			Wallis and Futuna

Table A.2. **Debt forgiveness of non-ODA claims**[1]

Million USD

	1990	1991	1992
Australia	..	..	4.2
Austria	..	4.2	25.3
Belgium	..	..	30.2
France	294.0	..	108.5
Germany	..	..	620.4
Japan	15.0	6.8	32.0
Netherlands	12.0	..	11.4
Norway	..	..	46.8
Sweden	5.0	..	7.1
United Kingdom	8.0	17.0	90.4
United States	1 200.0	1 855.0	894.0
Total DAC	**1 534.0**	**1 882.9**	**1 870.2**

1. These data are included in the ODA figures of individual countries but are excluded from DAC total ODA in all tables showing performance by donor.

StatLink http://dx.doi.org/10.1787/888933133989

Notes

1. *www.oecd.org/std/na/sna-2008-main-changes.htm.*
2. Hungary joined the DAC on 6 December 2016. Data for Hungary are included under "reporting countries beyond the DAC" in this report.

Reference

Scott, S. (1989), "Some aspects of the 1988-89 aid budget", in *Quarterly Aid Round-Up*, No. 6, Australian International Development Assistance Bureau, Canberra, pp. 11-18.

ANNEX B

Methodological notes on the profiles of Development Assistance Committee members

General point: unless otherwise stated, and with the exception of data on official development assistance (ODA) allocation by sector, and ODA supporting gender equality and environment objectives (whose figures refer to commitments), all figures in the profiles refer to gross bilateral disbursements. The term DAC country average refers to weighted averages of Development Assistance Committee (DAC) countries for the specific allocation. Allocations by the European Union institutions and Hungary are excluded from this calculation. All of the data presented in the profiles are publicly available at: *www.oecd.org/dac/stats*, *http://effectivecooperation.org* and *www.paris21.org*.

The remainder of this annex describes the methodology and sources for: ODA committed to finance national statistical capacities and systems in developing countries, domestic resource mobilisation, aid for trade, countries' performance against commitments for effective development co-operation, in-donor refugee costs, country programmable aid, ODA to least developed countries, support to fragile contexts, the Gender Equality Policy Marker, the Environment markers, and bilateral allocable aid.

ODA committed to finance national statistical capacities and systems in developing countries

The data used in the profiles come from the forthcoming PARIS21's 2017 Partner Report on Support to Statistics (PRESS) dataset.

To provide a full picture of international support to statistics, the PRESS report draws on three distinct data sources. The first source of data is the OECD Creditor Reporting System (CRS), which records data from OECD-DAC members and some non-DAC donors, and provides a comprehensive accounting of ODA. Donors report specific codes for the sector targeted by their aid activity. Statistical capacity building is designated by the CRS purpose Code 16062.

Second, when statistical capacity building is a component of a larger project, it is not identified by this code, causing the CRS figures to underestimate actual levels of support. PARIS21 seeks to reduce this downward bias by searching project descriptions in the CRS for terms indicating a component of statistical capacity building. The methodology is presented in Box 3 of the 2016 PRESS at: *www.paris21.org/PRESS2016*.

Third, and finally, the PARIS21 Secretariat supplements this data with an on line questionnaire completed by a global network of reporters. The questionnaire covers a subset of the variables collected in the CRS and some additional variables specific to statistical capacity building. Reporting to the questionnaire is voluntary, offering an opportunity for actors to share information on their statistical activities. Reporters to this questionnaire are countries that do not report to the CRS, as well as multilateral institutions with large portfolios of statistical projects that have requested to report to the PARIS21 Secretariat directly.

Sources: OECD (2017), "Creditor Reporting System: Aid activities", *OECD International Development Statistics* (database), *http://dx.doi.org/10.1787/data-00061-en* and *www.paris21.org*.

Domestic resource mobilisation

The figures on the amount of ODA that supports the mobilisation of domestic resources in developing countries come from the DAC's CRS database. This database contains detailed information on individual aid activities, including the purpose of aid. In order to identify domestic resource mobilisation-related activities, a purpose code (CRS Code 15114) is used. This code had previously been voluntary but was established as an official purpose code in 2016, and as a result the previous approach of complementing reporting under the voluntary code with a key-word search for tax-related activities has been abandoned.

Source: OECD (2017), "Creditor Reporting System: Aid activities", *OECD International Development Statistics* (database), *http://dx.doi.org/10.1787/data-00061-en.*

Aid for trade

According to the World Trade Organization (WTO) Task Force on Aid for Trade, projects and programmes are part of aid for trade if these activities have been identified as trade-related development priorities in the partner country's national development strategies. Furthermore, the WTO Task Force concluded that to measure aid-for-trade flows, the following categories should be included: technical assistance for trade policy and regulations, trade-related infrastructure, productive capacity building (including trade development), trade-related adjustment, other trade-related needs.

The DAC's CRS database was recognised as the best available data source for tracking global aid-for-trade flows. It should be kept in mind that the CRS does not provide data that match exactly all of the above aid-for-trade categories. In fact, the CRS provides proxies under four headings: trade policy and regulations, economic infrastructure, building productive capacity, and trade-related adjustment. The CRS covers all ODA, but only those activities reported under the above four categories can be identified as aid for trade. It is not possible to distinguish activities in the context of "other trade-related needs". To estimate the volume of such "other" activities, donors would need to examine aid projects in sectors other than those considered so far – for example in health and education – and indicate what share, if any, of these activities has an important trade component. A health programme, for instance, might permit increased trade from localities where the disease burden was previously a constraint on trade. Consequently, accurately monitoring aid for trade would require comparison of the CRS data with donor and partner countries' self-assessments of their aid for trade.

Source: OECD (2017), "Creditor Reporting System: Aid activities", *OECD International Development Statistics* (database), *http://dx.doi.org/10.1787/data-00061-en.*

Countries' performance against commitments for effective development co-operation (Table 1. Results of the 2016 Global Partnership monitoring round)

In the table for each profile, the "baseline" row refers to 2010 data, with the exception of data on medium-term predictability and the two measurements of transparency (OECD CRS and Forward Spending Survey), which refer to 2013 data. The "2016" row refers to data from the latest monitoring round, except for untied ODA, which refers to the latest data released by OECD for the year 2015.

The source and methodology for data on funding recorded in countries' national budgets, funding channelled through partner countries' systems, annual predictability and medium-term predictability, and the three transparency assessments can be consulted at OECD/UNDP (2016),

"Annex B. Monitoring data: Development partners" in: *Making Development Co-operation More Effective: 2016 Progress Report*. Data for these indicators were reported in 2016, reflecting the behaviour of development co-operation flows during the previous fiscal year. Note that for the transparency assessment labelled as publishing to IATI, the 2016 value represents the baseline for the indicator.

The source for data on untied ODA is OECD (2017), "Creditor Reporting System: Aid activities", *OECD International Development Statistics* (database), *http://dx.doi.org/10.1787/data-00061-en*.

The methodology for the indicator on the extent of use of country-led results frameworks can be found at: *https://unstats.un.org/sdgs/metadata/files/Metadata-17-15-01.pdf* (cf. metadata for SDG 17.15). The 2016 value represents the baseline for this indicator. The underlying data is sourced from OECD/UNDP (2016), "Annex B. Monitoring data: Development partners" in: *Making Development Co-operation More Effective: 2016 Progress Report*, OECD Publishing, Paris.

In-donor refugee costs

Specific instructions on the reporting of in-donor refugee costs were first introduced in the DAC Statistical Reporting Directives in 1988 and have changed little since then.

In-donor refugee costs: extract from DAC Statistical Reporting Directives (*www.oecd.org/dac/financing-sustainable-development/development-finance-standards/DCDDAC(2016)3FINAL.pdf*): a refugee is a person who is outside his/her home country because of a well-founded fear of persecution on account of race, religion, nationality, social group or political opinion. Assistance to persons who have fled from their homes because of civil war or severe unrest may also be counted under this item. Official sector expenditures for the sustenance of refugees in donor countries can be counted as ODA during the first 12 months of their stay.* This includes payments for refugees' transport to the host country and temporary sustenance (food, shelter and training); these expenditures should not be allocated geographically. However, this item also includes expenditures for voluntary resettlement of refugees in a developing country; these are allocated geographically according to the country of resettlement. Expenditures on deportation or other forcible measures to repatriate refugees should not be counted as ODA. Amounts spent to promote the integration of refugees into the economy of the donor country, or resettle them elsewhere than in a developing country, are also excluded.

Because in-donor refugee costs are not allocated geographically, the reporting of these costs can increase the share of bilateral ODA that is not specified by country.

Country programmable aid

Country programmable aid (CPA) is a subset of gross bilateral ODA. The CPA tracks the proportion of ODA over which recipient countries have, or could have, a significant say. The CPA reflects the amount of aid that involves a cross-border flow and is subject to multi-year planning at country/regional level.

The CPA is defined through exclusions, by subtracting from total gross bilateral ODA activities that: 1) are inherently unpredictable (humanitarian aid and debt relief); 2) entail no cross-border flows (administrative costs, imputed student costs, promotion of development awareness, and costs related to research and refugees in donor countries); and 3) do not form part of co-operation agreements between governments (food aid, aid from local governments, core funding to non-governmental organisations, ODA equity investments, aid through secondary agencies, and aid which is not allocable by country or region).

* Contributions by one donor to another donor to cover such expenditures should be recorded as ODA by the contributing country. The receiving country should reduce the expenditure reported under this item by the same amount.

The CPA is measured in disbursement terms and does not net out loan repayments since these are not usually factored into country aid decisions. The CPA is derived from the standard DAC and CRS databases.

Source: OECD (2017), "Country programmable aid (CPA)", *OECD International Development Statistics* (database), *http://stats.oecd.org/Index.aspx?DataSetCode=CPA*.

For further information, see: *www.oecd.org/development/effectiveness/countryprogrammableaidcpa frequentlyaskedquestions.htm*.

ODA to least developed countries

ODA to least developed countries (LDCs) is presented in different manners. Bilateral flows reflect the funds that are provided directly by a donor country to an aid-recipient country.

However, when calculating a donor's total ODA effort with regards to the UN target for LDCs, an estimate needs to be made to impute aid by multilateral organisations back to the funders of those bodies. For more information on imputed multilateral flows, see: *www.oecd.org/dac/stats/oecdmethodologyforcalculatingimputedmultilateraloda.htm*.

Support to fragile contexts

Support to fragile contexts corresponds to gross bilateral ODA to the list of fragile contexts as identified in the OECD fragility framework diagram which appeared on page 23 of the OECD's report *States of Fragility 2016: Understanding Violence*, OECD Publishing, Paris, *http://dx.doi.org/10.1787/9789264267213-en*.

For information on the *States of Fragility* report, see: *www.oecd.org/dac/governance-peace/conflictandfragility/rf.htm*.

Gender Equality Policy Marker

The DAC Gender Equality Policy Marker is a statistical instrument to measure aid that is focused on achieving gender equality and women's empowerment. Activities are classified as "principal" when gender equality is a primary objective, "significant" when gender equality is an important but secondary objective, or "not targeted". In the profiles of DAC members, the basis of calculation is bilateral allocable, screened aid.

Source: OECD (2017), "Aid projects targeting gender equality and women's empowerment (CRS)", *OECD International Development Statistics* (database), *http://stats.oecd.org/Index.aspx?DataSetCode=GENDER*.

Environment markers

The figure "Bilateral ODA in support of global and local environment objectives, two year averages, commitments" presented in each DAC member profile nets out the overlaps between Rio and environment markers: it shows climate-related aid as a sub-category of total environmental aid; biodiversity and desertification are also included (either overlapping with climate-related aid or as additional – other – environmental aid) but not separately identified for the sake of readability of the figure. One activity can address several policy objectives at the same time. This reflects the fact that the three Rio conventions (targeting global environmental objectives) and local environmental objectives are mutually reinforcing. The same activity can, for example, be marked for climate change mitigation and biodiversity, or for biodiversity and desertification.

"Climate-related aid" covers both aid to climate mitigation and to adaptation from 2010 onwards, but only mitigation aid pre-2010. Reported figures for 2006-09 may appear lower than in practice, and may reflect a break in the series, given that pre-2010 adaptation spend is not marked. In the profiles of DAC members, the basis of calculation is bilateral allocable ODA. More details are available at: *www.oecd.org/dac/stats/rioconventions.htm*.

Source: OECD (2017), "Aid activities targeting global environmental objectives", *OECD International Development Statistics* (database), *http://stats.oecd.org/Index.aspx?DataSetCode=RIOMARKERS*.

Bilateral allocable aid

Bilateral allocable aid is the basis of calculation used for all markers (gender equality and environmental markers). It covers bilateral ODA with types of aid A02 (sector budget support), B01 (core support to NGOs), B03 (specific fund managed by international organisation), B04 (pooled funding), C01 (projects), D01 (donor country personnel), D02 (other technical assistance) and E01 (scholarships).

ORGANISATION FOR ECONOMIC CO-OPERATION AND DEVELOPMENT

The OECD is a unique forum where governments work together to address the economic, social and environmental challenges of globalisation. The OECD is also at the forefront of efforts to understand and to help governments respond to new developments and concerns, such as corporate governance, the information economy and the challenges of an ageing population. The Organisation provides a setting where governments can compare policy experiences, seek answers to common problems, identify good practice and work to co-ordinate domestic and international policies.

The OECD member countries are: Australia, Austria, Belgium, Canada, Chile, the Czech Republic, Denmark, Estonia, Finland, France, Germany, Greece, Hungary, Iceland, Ireland, Israel, Italy, Japan, Korea, Latvia, Luxembourg, Mexico, the Netherlands, New Zealand, Norway, Poland, Portugal, the Slovak Republic, Slovenia, Spain, Sweden, Switzerland, Turkey, the United Kingdom and the United States. The European Union takes part in the work of the OECD.

OECD Publishing disseminates widely the results of the Organisation's statistics gathering and research on economic, social and environmental issues, as well as the conventions, guidelines and standards agreed by its members.

DEVELOPMENT ASSISTANCE COMMITTEE

To achieve its aims, the OECD has set up a number of specialised committees. One of these is the Development Assistance Committee (DAC), whose mandate is to promote development co-operation and other policies so as to contribute to sustainable development – including pro-poor economic growth, poverty reduction and the improvement of living standards in developing countries – and to a future in which no country will depend on aid. To this end, the DAC has grouped the world's main donors, defining and monitoring global standards in key areas of development.

The members of the DAC are Australia, Austria, Belgium, Canada, the Czech Republic, Denmark, the European Union, Finland, France, Germany, Greece, Hungary, Iceland, Ireland, Italy, Japan, Korea, Luxembourg, the Netherlands, New Zealand, Norway, Poland, Portugal, the Slovak Republic, Slovenia, Spain, Sweden, Switzerland, the United Kingdom and the United States.

The DAC issues guidelines and reference documents in the DAC Guidelines and Reference Series to inform and assist members in the conduct of their development co-operation programmes.

OECD PUBLISHING, 2, rue André-Pascal, 75775 PARIS CEDEX 16
(43 2017 04 1 P) ISBN 978-92-64-27446-4 – 2017

www.ingramcontent.com/pod-product-compliance
Ingram Content Group UK Ltd.
Pitfield, Milton Keynes, MK11 3LW, UK
UKHW051457290926
15471UKWH00008B/1256

9 789264 274464